YOUNG OFFENDERS:
LAW, POLICY AND PRACTICE

AUSTRALIA
LBC Information Services—Sydney

CANADA AND USA
Carswell—Toronto

NEW ZEALAND
Brooker's—Auckland

SINGAPORE AND MALAYSIA
Sweet & Maxwell (Asia)—Singapore and Kuala Lumpur

YOUNG OFFENDERS:
LAW, POLICY AND PRACTICE

SECOND EDITION

By

Caroline Ball

LL.B, Ph.D, Barrister, Senior Lecturer in Law, University of East Anglia

Kevin McCormac

MA, Barrister, formerly Justices' Chief Executive for West Sussex

&

Nigel Stone

LL.B, MA, LL.M, Senior Lecturer in Criminology, University of East Anglia and Member of the Parole Board

LONDON
SWEET & MAXWELL
2001

Published in 2001 by
Sweet & Maxwell Limited of
100 Avenue Road
Swiss Cottage
London NW3 3PF
(*http://www.sweetandmaxwell.co.uk*)

Typeset by LBJ Typesetting Ltd of Kingsclere
Printed and bound in Great Britain by MPG Books Ltd, Bodmin, Cornwall

No natural forests were destroyed
to make this product,
only farmed timber was used and replanted

ISBN 0 421 657 103

A catalogue record for this book
is available from the British Library

TABLE OF CONTENTS

PREFACE

"Behind almost every adult persistent offender lies an earlier experience as a juvenile offender." This quotation from *Criminal Justice: The Way Forward* (2001) captures the present Government's commitment since it took office in May 1997 to place the reform of the youth justice system at the centre of its criminal justice policy programme. Reforms are grounded in the belief that the blight inflicted by adult crime can be best reduced if youthful offending can be "nipped in the bud" through effective, early, up-stream intervention. In consequence, though youth justice has long served as a restless laboratory for penal experiment, the landscape of youth justice has undergone particularly profound change since the first edition of this book. The Crime and Disorder Act 1998 was intended to give strategic direction and organisational coherence, counteracting what was castigated as a rudderless culture of complacency and excuse, allegedly failing either to deal with young offenders efficiently or to make them properly accountable for their behaviour and its consequences. This statute, together with Part I of the Youth Justice and Criminal Evidence Act 1999, has fostered themes in criminal justice, such as offender rather than offence-centredness, restorative justice, crime prevention and greater continuity between custodial sentencing and post-custody supervision, which are now poised for development in the adult sphere. As the legislative circus seems set to move on to a new encampment, allowing the new youth justice measures and structures opportunity to find their feet in practice, and given, too, the welcome consolidation provided by the Powers of Criminal Courts (Sentencing) Act 2000, it seems timely to offer a guide to the changed legal framework.

Our second take on the subject has clearly required very substantial re-writing, not a light tweaking and modest up-dating. This is thus a very different and, we hope, enhanced production. But our aim has remained to provide a coherent account of the law and its underpinning policy in an accessible way that will serve the needs of all with a practical or academic stake in the youth justice system: practitioners in the multi-disciplinary business of representing, working with or making decisions about young offenders; advocates, court advisers, judges, magistrates and youth offending team members as they seek to apply expeditiously what remains a complex labyrinth of provisions; and students.

Once again we remain well aware that our end product may seem a bloodless, somewhat dry text that is heavy on law, light on the other two ingredients of policy and practice. We freely acknowledged in the first edition that we could not hope to do justice to the rich literature detailing the lives, offending and victimisation patterns of young people, and the background factors of adversity, parental indifference, school exclusion, growing up in care and substance dependency that research demonstrates to be associated with youth crime (see, for example, Flood-Page *et al.*, 2000). Our shortcomings reflect not our ignorance or indifference but the impossibility of including an adequate criminological and social policy perspective within the practical limits of the text. We have however sought to identify the authoritative official guidance directed at practitioners and by which their performance is increasingly measured and also the empirical findings that are emerging about the realities of the law in practice.

One obvious problem we have faced is the extent of coverage we should give to criminal justice issues and provisions that are not exclusive to youth justice. While we understandably resisted the opportunity to be ultra-comprehensive and we recognise that readers will also need to refer to texts of a more generic nature, we have tried to bear in mind that some practitioners such as YOT members will not necessarily be familiar with the wider landscape of the criminal process and thus have attempted to increase the text's usefulness as a one-stop shop.

Whilst we take collective responsibility for the whole of the book, the writing task was again divided: Ball wrote Chapters 1–5, McCormac wrote Chapters 6–10 and Stone Chapters 11–30. The typescript was delivered in October 2000 but we have sought to incorporate developments up to March 31, 2001.

References

Criminal Justice: The Way Forward Cm 5074 (HMSO, London, 2001). Flood-Page C., Campbell S., Harrington V. and Miller J., *Youth Crime: Findings from the 1998/99 Youth Lifestyles Survey*, Research Study 209 (Home Office, London 2001).

TABLE OF CASES

TABLE OF STATUTES

TABLE OF STATUTORY INSTRUMENTS

GLOSSARY

ABH	Actual bodily harm
ACPO	Association of Chief Police Officers
ACR 1995	Attendance Centre Rules 1995
ACR	Automatic Conditional Release
C.J.	Chief Justice
C.F.L.Q.	Child and Family Law Quarterly
CA 1989	Children Act 1989
CYPA 1933	Children and Young Persons Act 1933
CYPA 1969	Children and Young Persons Act 1969
CI	Circular Instruction
CPO	Community Punishment Order
CPRO	Community Punishment and Rehabilitation Order
CSO	Community Service Order
CS	Community Service
CCSOR 1992	Community Service Supervision Order Regulations 1992
CDA 1998	Crime and Disorder Act 1998
C(S)A 1997	Crime (Sentences) Act 1997
Cr.App.R.	Criminal Appeal Reports
Cr.App.R.(S.)	Criminal Appeal Reports (Sentencing)
CE(A)A 1997	Criminal Evidence (Amendment) Act 1997
CJA 1967	Criminal Justice Act 1967
CJA 1991	Criminal Justice Act 1991
CJCSA 2000	Criminal Justice and Court Services Act 2000
CJPOA 1994	Criminal Justice and Public Order Act 1994
Crim.L.R.	Criminal Law Review
CPS	Crown Prosecution Service
DTO	Detention and Training Order
DPP	Director of Public Prosecutions
DTTO	Drug Treatment and Testing Order
ECHR	European Court of Human Rights
EHRR	European Human Rights Reports
H.M.P.	Her Majesty's Pleasure
HOC	Home Office Circular
HRA 1998	Human Rights Act 1998
LEA	Local Education Authority
L.J.	Lord Justice
MCA 1980	Magistrates' Courts Act 1980
MC(CYP)R 1992	Magistrates' Courts (Children and Young Persons) Rules 1992
MNTI	Magistrates' New Training Initiative
MHA 1983	Mental Health Act 1983
NAPO	National Association of Probation Officers
OPA 1861	Offences Against the Person Act 1861

PLO	Panel Liaison Officer
PSA	Petty Sessions Area
PACE 1984	Police and Criminal Evidence Act 1984
PNC	Police National Computer
PCC(S)A 2000	Powers of Criminal Courts (Sentencing) Act 2000
PDH	Preliminary Directions Hearings
PSR	Pre-sentence Report
ROA 1974	Rehabilitation of Offenders Act 1974
RSC	Rules of the Supreme Court
SOA 1956	Sexual Offences Act 1956
SOA 1997	Sex Offenders Act 1997
SMD	Special Measures Directions
TA 1968	Theft Act 1968
UN	United Nations
UNCRC	United Nations Convention on the Rights of the Child
W.L.R.	Weekly Law Reports
YOI	Young Offender Institution
YJB	Youth Justice Board
YJCEA 1999	Youth Justice and Criminal Evidence Act 1999
YOT	Youth Offending Team
YTC	Youth Treatment Centre

PART 1

YOUTH JUSTICE AT THE BEGINNING OF THE TWENTY-FIRST CENTURY

CHAPTER 1

The Twentieth Century Legacy

1.00 The term youth justice encompasses all aspects of the complex system involving the treatment of children and young people who commit offences. The parallel strands of the law relating to police investigations, diversion from prosecution, the pre-trial process, bail, remands and the use of secure accommodation, the youth court, youth offending teams, trials, sentence and post-sentence supervision all come under the youth justice umbrella and form the substance of this substantially revised edition.

1.01 By way of introduction, the legacy of the last century will be briefly reviewed, together with the endemic themes of complexity, disparity, deprivation, discrimination, and persistence, in order to set youth justice at the beginning of the twenty-first century in context. The development throughout the century of separate courts, new sentencing powers, diversion from court, and the influence of international treaty obligations, are mapped rather than being addressed in detail. They, and the recurrent impact of conflicting ideologies, are thoroughly and expertly addressed elsewhere.[1] An analytical overview of recent developments in the sentencing of young offenders can be found in Chapter 11, below. Finally, the authors question the extent, if any, to which the swings in youth justice policy and the confused objectives of legislation formulated and enacted during the 1990s may have unintended consequences.

SEPARATE COURTS

1.02 The origins of a separate youth court, located at the interface of adult criminal justice and child welfare, are bound up with the public health, education and child protection reforms introduced throughout the nineteenth century. These reforms sought to address, both as a matter of philanthropy and social control, the threat posed to an ordered society by the extremes of poverty, ill health, and poor housing caused by the rapid growth of towns and cities during the industrial revolution.[2] In living conditions graphically described in a report by Lord Ashley to the House of Commons in 1948,[3] and brought to the attention of their contemporaries by Dickens and other writers, crime was rife and revolution, endemic in the middle of the century in much of Europe, was only just below the surface. As Parsloe suggests—

---

[1] L. Gelsthorpe and A. Morris "Juvenile Justice 1945–1992" in *Oxford Handbook of Criminal Justice* (M. Maguire, R. Morgan and R. Reiner ed., Oxford University Press, Oxford, 1994); T. Newburn, "Youth, Crime, and Justice", in *Oxford Handbook of Criminal Justice*, (2nd ed., Oxford University Press, Oxford, 1997); J. Muncie, *Youth and Crime* (Sage, London, 1999).
[2] See P. Parsloe, *Juvenile Justice in Britain and the United States* (Routledge, Kegan Paul, London, 1978); R. Harris and D. Webb, *Welfare, Power and Juvenile Justice* (Tavistock, 1987); A. Morris and H. Giller, *Understanding Juvenile Justice* (Croom Helm, London, 1987).
[3] Parsloe, *op.cit.*, at p. 106.

"Like their contemporaries in the United States, middle class Britons were moved by pity and fear, by evangelical urges and those of self interest, to improve the lot of the masses. The impetus underlying innovations in the treatment of criminal and destitute children came from these ambivalent motives, so that genuine concern for the welfare of children mingled with a wish to control them and prevent their developing into adult criminals or paupers." [4]

1.03 The introduction of separate courts for young offenders and institutions to avoid the imprisonment of children with adults were innovations founded on this ambivalence. Not only founded on it, but demonstrating it in a variety of guises from its development to the present day.[5] Throughout the last century whilst generally the history of former juvenile court has been one of a developing special jurisdiction separated and different from the adult court, it has also demonstrated a marked diversity of interpretation of procedural rules, sentencing practice and general ethos.[6] In many juvenile courts it was an ethos which reflected the statutory duty of the juvenile court when reaching its decisions "to have regard to the welfare of the child".[7] In contrast, in others, practices and procedures which "can appear to operate against both the best interests of the child and the principles of natural and criminal justice simultaneously" were commonplace.[8] By the end of the twentieth century a sequence of events and a more punitive approach to children who commit criminal offences had to a large extent eroded the separate welfare ethos of the former juvenile court.[9]

EARLY DEVELOPMENTS

1.04 By the end of the nineteenth century, initially tentative attempts to increase the use of magistrates' summary jurisdiction for juvenile offenders had culminated in the provisions of the Summary Jurisdiction Act 1879 (SJA 1879) under which juveniles under the age of 16 could be tried summarily for nearly all indictable offences, thus keeping them away from the more serious adult criminals at quarter sessions and the assize courts. A number of separate courts for juveniles had also been set up in Birmingham and other cities through the initiative of local magistrates.[10] Concurrent with these reforms were two other important developments: the introduction of some rudimentary child protection legislation, and the setting up of reformatories and industrial schools. These institutions accommodated large numbers of children, from what a leading reformer, Mary Carpenter, described as the "dangerous and perishing classes"[11], thus substantially reducing the

---

[4] Parsloe, *Juvenile Justice in Britain and the United States* (Routledge, Kegan Paul, London, 1978) at p. 107
[5] See R. Anderson, *Representation in the Juvenile Court* (Routledge, London, 1978); L. Hilgendorf, "*Social Workers and Solicitors in Child Care Cases* (HMSO, London, 1981); H.Parker, M. Casburn and D. Turnbull, *Receiving Juvenile Justice* (Blackwell, Oxford, 1981); V. Bailey, *Delinquency and Citizenship* (Clarendon Press, Oxford, 1987); S. Brown, *Magistrates at Work* (Open University Press, Milton Keynes, 1991).
[6] See R. Anderson, *op. cit.;* P. Priestley, *et al., Justice for Juveniles* (Kegan Paul, 1977); H. Parker, *et al.,* 1981, *op. cit.;* H. Parker, M. Sumner and G. Jarvis, *Unmasking the Magistrates* (Open University Press, Milton Keynes, 1989); C. Ball, "Secret Justice: the Use Made of School Reports in the Juvenile Court" (1983) 13 British Journal of Social Work 197.
[7] s.44 of the CYPA 1933.
[8] H. Parker, *op.cit.,* at p. 243.
[9] C. Ball, "Youth justice and the youth court—the end of a separate system?" (1995) 7 C.F.L.Q., 196.
[10] P. Parsloe, *op. cit.*
[11] M. Carpenter, *Reformatory Schools for the Children of the Perishing and Dangerous Classes and for Juvenile Offenders* (C. Gilpin, London, 1851).

incidence of child imprisonment. Whether the creation of a separate jurisdiction to deal with young offenders, and the creation of forms of residential containment separate from the prison system, were reforms motivated by philanthropy or an essentially authoritarian and coercive response to a period of rapid, possibly unprecedented, social change, or a mixture of the two, is an issue which has long occupied and continues to fascinate commentators.[12]

1.05 The Children Act 1908 (CA 1908), one of the cluster of criminal justice related reforms introduced by the Liberal government in the first decade of the century, provides the first example of what can be identified as a recurrent phenomenon: piecemeal juvenile justice reforms, begun on local initiatives, which then require legislation to achieve their implementation on a national basis. Partly consolidating and partly reforming, the 1908 Act built on earlier statutes which had extended summary jurisdiction over juveniles, and local initiatives which had sought to separate juveniles from adults in the summary courts. By making separate courts for the hearing of most criminal proceedings against juveniles—as well as all child protection and vagrancy cases—mandatory throughout England and Wales, the CA 1908 provided a foundation for future reforms. It also, by uniting in the new court the twin jurisdictional strands—one relating to young offenders and the other to children in need of protection—either, according to the commentators perspective, institutionalised ambivalence or provided an underpinning legitimacy for a welfare approach to young offenders.[13]

TOWARDS A SPECIALIST COURT

1.06 The 1908 Act established separate courts for juveniles, but it was not for another quarter century that there was statutory recognition of the need for specially qualified magistrates to adjudicate in the new courts. The distinctive feature of the juvenile or children's courts introduced by the 1908 Act was the fact that hearings had to be held in a separate building or at a different time from adult courts, and that public access was restricted. Apart from this they were criminal courts of due process, indistinguishable from other magistrates' courts. The development of a court for dealing with children that was not only separate but also presided over by magistrates of both sexes, theoretically selected on the basis of their interest in and experience of children, proved to be a slow process.[14]

1.07 The first substantial reform came, appropriately enough, in the year of the appointment of the first women magistrates, when the Juvenile Courts (Metropolis) Act 1920 (JC(M)A 1920) provided for police (stipendiary) magistrates to be nominated by the Secretary of State to sit as presidents of juvenile courts on the basis of their previous experience and special qualifications. The Act stipulated that the stipendiaries should sit with two justices, one of whom should be a woman, chosen from a panel nominated for the purpose by the Secretary of State. Outside London, official guidance[15] recommending the trial of juveniles by specialist magistrates sitting in separate courts met with varied response.[16]

---

[12] See A. Platt, *The Child Savers: the Invention of Delinquency* (Chicago University Press, Chicago, 1968); M. Foucault, *Discipline and Punish* (Harmondsworth, London, 1977); Morris and Giller, *op. cit.*
[13] See R. Anderson, *op. cit.;* P. Parsloe, *op. cit.,* A. Morris and H. Giller, *op. cit.,* J. Pitts, *The Politics of Juvenile Crime* (Sage, London, 1990).
[14] V. Bailey, *op. cit.*
[15] Home Office Circular, dated April 21, 1923.
[16] Evidence from the Children's Department to the Committee on the Treatment of Young Offenders, 1927.

1.08 In 1925 the Committee on the Treatment of Young Offenders, chaired by Sir Thomas Molony, was set up to "inquire into the treatment of young offenders and young people who, owing to bad associations or surroundings, require protection and training, and to report what changes, if any, are desirable in the present law or its administration". The Committee was urged by many witnesses to abandon the magistrates' jurisdiction and adopt a radical shift towards the social welfare orientation of the American juvenile courts. Had this happened the embryonic juvenile courts in England and Wales would at this stage have ceased, like those in the United States of America, to be courts of due process, instead adopting an entirely welfare approach. Despite the sympathy of several members with the arguments presented, the Committee were not prepared to go as far as recommending that juveniles should be dealt with outside the criminal jurisdiction. They reasoned that there was—

> "some danger in adopting any principle which might lead to ignoring the offence on which the action of the juvenile court in dealing with delinquents must be based. It is true that in many instances the offence may be trivial and the circumstances point to neglect rather than delinquency; but there remain cases where serious offences are committed, and neither in the public interest nor for the welfare of the young offender is it right they should be minimised. Two considerations presented themselves strongly to our minds. In the first place it is very important that a young person should have the fullest opportunity of meeting a charge made against him . . . Secondly, when the offence is really serious and has been proved it is right that its gravity should be brought home to the offender".[17]

1.09 The passage reflects what might be regarded as the traditional lawyer's view of the criminal court as providing protection of the individual defendant through due process as well as dispensing punishment. Despite this essentially traditional view, the extent to which the philosophical approach to offenders was changing to one of rehabilitation—a change that would have a profound impact on criminal justice policy and legislation for the next 50 years—is apparent in another passage—

> "It may be said that the reformation of the offender has become in recent years the keynote of the administration of justice. If this is true of the adult, the same principle must be applied with even greater force to the young offender whose character is still plastic and the more readily moulded by wise and sympathetic treatment."[18]

1.10 In achieving the hoped for rehabilitation, the juvenile court was seen as the agent of reform—

> "The juvenile court performs very important functions which are not generally realised by the public and not always appreciated to their full by the Magistrates themselves. Before it appear boys and girls under 16 who are often wayward or mischievous and in some cases serious offenders; who are sometimes dull of mind or undeveloped, but more often full of vitality and

---

[17] *Report of the Committee on the Treatment of Young Offenders*, Cmd. 2831, 1927, at p. 19
[18] *ibid.*, at p. 5.

intelligence, though misdirected; who are all by youthfulness hopeful subjects for care and training. The decision of the Magistrates with regard to the immediate future of these boys and girls must to a large extent influence their whole lives".[19]

1.11 Nor was the Committee in much doubt as to the qualifications needed by those who would adjudicate—

"The qualities which are needed in every magistrate who sits in the juvenile court are a love of young people, sympathy with their interests, and an imaginative insight into their difficulties. The rest is largely common sense".[20]

1.12 Following the Molony Committee's recommendations, the main constitutional reform introduced by the Children and Young Persons Act 1933 Act (CYPA 1933) was intended to remedy the identified deficit in interest and expertise amongst those adjudicating in criminal and child protection proceedings in juvenile courts. Under the new legislation only magistrates elected to the new juvenile court panel, for each petty sessional division, supposedly for their special expertise and interest in young people, could adjudicate. For the first time they also had to reach their decisions in criminal as well as care proceedings having "regard to the welfare of the child".[21] Contemporary accounts suggest that, whatever the intentions, the quality and suitability of the juvenile panel, magistrates continued to be very variable.[22] In 1936, for instance, it was estimated that 13 per cent of panel members were over 70 years old, and some were in their nineties.[23] In that year compulsory retirement from the juvenile panel at 70 was introduced.[24]

POST-WAR DEVELOPMENTS

1.13 The age of criminal responsibility was raised from eight to 10 years by the Children and Young Persons Act 1963. Apart from that and some changes in sentencing powers, despite the sweeping post-war welfare reforms and the radical nature of juvenile justice policy proposals in the 1960s, little changed in relation to the trial of young offenders. The fact that lay magistrates still retain, albeit now in separate courts, jurisdiction over both young offenders and children in need of care and protection reflects the resilience demonstrated at the time, by those with a vested interest in the juvenile court.[25] Determined attempts were made by reformers to bring the jurisdiction to an end, and to replace it with a more welfare oriented family council with wider and possibly more expert membership.[26] Magistrates, lawyers and the probation service united in opposition to these proposals which mirrored those which resulted in the introduction of children's hearings in Scotland.[27]

---

[19] Report of the Committee on the Treatment of Young Offenders, Cmd. 2831, 1927, at p. 15.
[20] *ibid.*, at p. 25.
[21] s.44(1).
[22] See Bailey, *op. cit.*; W. Elkin, *English Juvenile Courts* (Kegan Paul, London, 1938).
[23] W. Elkin, *op.cit.*
[24] A general retirement age for lay magistrates of 70 was introduced in 1954. From that year until 1991, the upper age limit for membership of the juvenile panel was reduced to 65. In 1991 it reverted to 70.
[25] J. Harwin, "The Battle for the Delinquent" in *Yearbook of Social Policy in Britain 1980–1981* (C. Jones and J. Stevenson ed., Routledge and Kegan Paul, London, 1981).
[26] Lord Longford, *Crime—a challenge to us all* (Labour Party, London, 1964); J. Harwin, *op. cit.*; L. Gelsthorpe and A. Morris, "Juvenile Justice 1945–1992" in *Oxford Handbook of Criminology* (M. Maguire, R. Morgan and R. Reiner ed., Oxford University Press, Oxford, 1997) p. 949.
[27] A. Lockyer and F. Stone, *Juvenile Justice in Scotland: Twenty-five years of the Welfare Approach* (T & T Clark, Edinburgh, 1998).

1.14   Although efforts to abolish the juvenile court failed, they were followed by legislation, the Children and Young Persons Act 1969 (CYPA 1969) which, had it ever been fully implemented, would effectively have decriminalised the court.[28] Full implementation would have resulted in the raising the age of criminal responsibility to 14, substantial restrictions on the circumstances in which young people aged 14 to 16 could be prosecuted, and the replacement of magistrates' powers to make custodial sentences with care and supervision orders administered by the new local authority social services departments. It was legislation with which few magistrates had sympathy. When, following the election of a Conservative government, partial implementation left them with a confused mix of welfare structures and punitive powers, the consequence was an unprecedented rise in the use of custodial sentences for young offenders (Table 1), and a corresponding decline in the use of non residential welfare disposals.[29] Deep discontent with the Act was expressed across the political and ideological spectrum, resulting in some unlikely alliances and a departure from the political consensus on crime control policies which had existed for most of the century.[30]

Table 1:— Males aged 14–16 years sentenced to custody for indictable offences

1971	3,200
1975	5,900
1981	7,700

1.15   In the 1970s monitoring by researchers at Lancaster University of social services departments' pre-trial procedures and subsequent juvenile court sentences, led to identification of the extent to which early intervention in the lives of young offenders had adverse consequences.[31] Clear evidence was produced by the Lancaster researchers and others of the causal link between the provision of information about adverse social circumstances in reports for courts, early social work intervention, and a swift rise up the tariff ladder in to care and custody.[32] Effective dissemination of these research findings and a general disillusionment with the rehabilitative ideal which had underpinned criminal justice since the 1920s, led to a search for a replacement.[33] Critics of the welfare model largely supported what was loosely and possibly seductively termed the "justice" model. A model based on justice is a concept with which few would argue, but was also one to which incompatible groups could adhere.[34] For those with libertarian concern for the welfare of young offenders, the justice model required diversion from the criminal process for as long as possible, sentencing based on desert, the avoidance of custody, the protection of due process, and determinate sentences. For the political

[28] A. Bottoms, "On the Decriminalisation of the English Juvenile Court" in *Crime, Criminology and Public Policy*, (R. Hood ed., Heinemann, London, 1974).
[29] L. Gelsthorpe and A. Morris, *op. cit.*
[30] See D. Downes and R. Morgan, "Dumping the 'Hostages to Fortune'? The Politics of Law and Order in Post-War Britain" in *Oxford Handbook of Criminology, op. cit.* p. 87; T. Newburn, "Youth, Crime and Justice", *ibid.*, p. 613.
[31] D. Thorpe, C. Green and D. Smith, *Punishment and Welfare* (Lancaster University, 1979).
[32] P. Cawson, *Young Offenders in Care* (D.H.S.S., London, 1981).
[33] See A. Morris and H. Giller, *What Justice for Juveniles?* (Justice for Children, London, 1979); D. Thorpe, D. Smith, C. Green and J. Paley, *Out of Care* (Allen and Unwin, London, 1980); A. Morris, H. Giller, E. Schwed, and H. Geach, *Justice for Children* (Macmillan, London, 1980).
[34] R. H. Preston, "Social theology and penal theory and practice: the collapse of the rehabilitative ideal and the search for an alternative", in *The Coming Penal Crisis* (A. E. Bottoms and R. H. Preston ed., Scottish Academic Press, Edinburgh, 1980).

right a justice model is one unambiguously founded on due process and punishment. The 1980s saw the former approach having some impact, but losing to the latter in the early 1990s.

1.16 From the early 1980s, and accelerating through the decade, there was a substantial decrease in the use of custody for the whole known juvenile offender (those cautioned and found guilty) population. Several interlocking factors appear causal. Gelsthorpe and Morris[35] following Farringdon[36] suggest it was in the main the impact of diversion practices rather than the specific sentencing initiatives introduced at that time[37] that made the greatest impact on custody rates. In some areas, however, the sharply focussed use of court ordered programmes of activities as alternatives to custodial sentences, appeared to raise the tariff level of supervision orders with specified activities thereby producing substantial local reductions in custodial sentencing.[38] Overall during the decade custodial sentences on 14–16 year old males dropped from 7,700 in 1981 to 1,400 in 1991.[39] Newburn provides a satisfyingly detailed analysis of the contradictions apparent during this period when Thatcherism was well established, and yet the response to youth offending appeared to reveal a "successful revolution"[40] in terms of an apparent drop in youth crime, the diversion of young offenders from criminal proceedings, and a substantial reduction in the use of custodial sentences.

THE END OF THE CONCURRENT CARE AND CRIMINAL JURISDICTION

1.17 Amongst the many faults apparent in the state of child care law, identified in evidence to the House of Commons select committee chaired by Rene Short in 1982–83, was the unsatisfactory nature of the magistrates' juvenile court as a forum for care and related proceedings.[41] Although falling short of the unified family court proposed by the committee, the concentration of magistrates' jurisdiction in domestic and all proceedings under the Children Act 1989 (CA 1989) in the new family proceedings court, for which magistrates were specially selected and trained, was widely welcomed. Implementation of the 1989 Act in 1991 left the juvenile court with a solely criminal jurisdiction, and without many welfare minded magistrates who had moved to the family proceedings court.[42] A year later, implementation of the Criminal Justice Act 1991(CJA 1991) changed the name of the court to the youth court, and included 17-year-olds within its jurisdiction. It has been argued elsewhere that these changes, combined with increasingly punitive attitudes to young offenders, substantially eroded the separate system for dealing with children and young people who commit offences.[43] It also "forcefully symbolises the separation of the 'deprived' and the 'delinquent'".[44]

---

[35] L. Gelsthorpe and A. Morris, *op. cit.* at pp. 976–977.

[36] D. P. Farrington and P. A. Langan, "Changes in Crime and Punishment in England and America in the 1980s" (1992) 9 Justice Quarterly 5.

[37] Under the Criminal Justice Acts 1982 and 1988; see also E. Burney, *Sentencing Young People* (Gower, Aldershot, 1985).

[38] R. Allen, "Out of Jail: the reduction in the use of penal custody for male juveniles 1981–1988" (1991) 30 Howard Journal 30.

[39] Home Office, *Criminal Statistics* (HMSO, London, 1992).

[40] Newburn, *op. cit.* at 643.

[41] *Children in Care*, Second Report from the Social Services Committee, House of Commons 360 —I (HMSO, London, 1984).

[42] C. Ball, "Young Offenders and the Youth Court" [1992] Crim. L.R. 277.

[43] C. Ball, "Youth Justice and the Youth Court—the end of a separate system?" (1995) 7, C.F.L.Q. 417.

[44] L. Gelsthorpe and A. Morris, *op. cit.* at p. 981.

DIVERSION FROM COURT

1.18   The diversion of offenders of all ages from the criminal process, through informal or formal cautions, has its roots in the discretion in the hands of the police, since the first forces were formed, to decide to take no action or to administer a caution instead of proceeding to prosecution. Official policy on the use of cautions was set out in a series of Home Office circulars, from the early 1970s to 1994. Those up to 1990 reflect a policy aimed at encouraging, at first for juveniles but more recently also for adults, the diversion of offenders from the criminal process. Despite official guidance favouring the use of cautioning, the fact that cautioning was never put on a statutory footing made the practice particularly vulnerable to discrepant interpretation both between one police force and another, and even within a single force.[45] Home Office statistics and research studies consistently showed wide discrepancies between cautioning policies and practices in different police authorities.[46] In 1981 the variation for males under 17 cautioned for indictable offences covered 32 percentage points; by 1985 use of cautioning had increased, but so had the range—from a high of 84 per cent in Northamptonshire to 48 per cent in Humberside. As Giller and Tutt suggested, the statistics demonstrated that "Justice by geography continues despite attempts to reduce diversity by exhortation in the form of central government circulars".[47]

1.19   New Home Office guidance in 1985[48] encouraged police forces both to increase their use of cautioning and to follow consistent policies based on general principles spelt out in the guidelines attached to the circular. The policy thrust in regard to juveniles was unambiguously set out in the introduction to the guidelines—

> "It is recognised both in theory and in practice that delay in the entry of a young person into the formal criminal justice system may help to prevent his entry into that system altogether. The Secretary of State commends to chief officers the policy that the prosecution of a juvenile is not a step to be taken without the fullest consideration of whether the public interest (and the interest of the juvenile concerned) may be better served by a course of action which falls short of prosecution. Thus chief officers will wish to ensure that their arrangements for dealing with juveniles are such that prosecution will not occur unless it is absolutely necessary . . ."

A particular warning was issued in paragraph 7 of the Circular regarding the dangers of 'net widening'.

1.20   The following years saw a further dramatic increase in the use of cautioning. By 1990, 75 per cent of males under 17 were being cautioned for indictable offences nationally and the variation between police forces rates had dropped to 24 per cent.[49] National standards for cautioning were introduced in further guidance.[50] Based on

[45] See J. A. Ditchfield, *Police Cautioning in England and Wales*, Home Office Research Study, No. 37 (HMSO, London, 1976); N. Tutt and H. Giller, "Police Cautioning of Juveniles: the Practice of Diversity" [1983] Crim. L.R. 587; H. Giller and N. Tutt, "Police Cautioning of Juveniles: the Continuing Practice of Diversity" [1987] Crim. L.R. 367; R. Evans and C. Wilkinson, "Variations in Police Cautioning Policy and Practice in England and Wales" (1990) 29 Howard Journal 155.
[46] R. Evans, "Comparing Young Adult and Juvenile Cautioning Rates in the Metropolitan Police District" [1993] Crim. L.R. 572.
[47] *op. cit.*, at 374.
[48] Home Office Circular 14/1985.
[49] *Criminal Statistics* (HMSO, 1991).
[50] HOC 59/1990.

research, which identified that 16-year-olds were four times more likely than 17-year-olds to be cautioned rather than prosecuted, the guidance encouraged greater use of cautions for young adults as well as juvenile offenders.

1.21 In 1994, reflecting what Bottoms terms "populist punitiveness",[51] and in contravention of treaty obligations under the UN Convention on the Rights of the Child (UNCRC),[52] the well-established policy of encouraging the diversion of children and young people from court by means of a caution was sharply reversed. Juveniles were removed from the category of vulnerable people in the national standards for cautioning and the use of more than one caution, except in exceptional circumstances, was discouraged. Predictions made at the time that the policy shift would see an inevitable rise in youth court appearances were realised in some areas, although in others police policies on cautioning did not appear to be substantially altered.[53]

INTERNATIONAL TREATY OBLIGATIONS

1.22 Recognition of the rights of children to special protection in international law began with the League of Nations Declaration of the Rights of the Child (the Declaration of Geneva) in 1924, which set out a robust statement of basic principles relating to succour, development and protection. During the second half of the twentieth century, successive U.K. governments have ratified international instruments emanating from the United Nations and the Council of Europe, of which the UN Convention on the Rights of the Child and the European Convention on Human Rights have had the greatest impact on domestic law.

1.23 The UNCRC, a "long and ambitious list of children's rights",[54] is not a part of domestic law but its influence on many provisions in the Children Act 1989 is clear. Although the Convention predates recognition of children's rights at a level beyond the basic principles set out in the Geneva Declaration, and the Convention cannot be said to be child oriented,[55] decisions against the United Kingdom in the European Court of Human Rights (ECHR) have importantly enhanced children's rights. Recent examples can be found in regard to a child's right not to suffer inhuman or degrading treatment under Article 3,[56] and the right to a fair trial (Article 6).[57] The Human Rights Act 1998 now makes the rights contained in the Convention directly enforceable at all levels of the U.K. courts. When considering challenges under the Convention, domestic courts have to take ECHR jurisprudence into account.

1.24 The Convention is essentially adult oriented, and the UNCRC addresses all aspects of children's rights. There is one international instrument that is solely concerned with children who commit criminal offences. The United Nations Standard Minimum Rules for the Administration of Juvenile Justice, the Beijing rules adopted by the UN in 1985, provide a detailed and comprehensive framework

---

[51] A. Bottoms, "The Philosophy and Politics of Punishment and Sentencing", in *The Politics of Sentencing Reform* (C. Clarkson and R. Morgan, ed., Oxford University Press, Oxford, 1995).
[52] Article 40(3)(b).
[53] Audit Commission, *Misspent Youth: Young People and Crime* (Audit Commission, London, 1996) at p. 22.
[54] J. Fortin, *Children's Rights and the Developing Law* (Butterworths, London, 1998) p. 33).
[55] G. Van Beuren, "Child-Orientated Justice: An International Challenge for Europe" (1992) 6 Int.J. of Law and the Family 381.
[56] *A v. U.K.* (27 E.H.R.R.) 611.
[57] *T v. U.K. and V v. U.K.* (ECHR) [2000] Crim. L.R. 187.

for the standards to be met by a national youth justice system at each stage of the process for dealing with children who commit criminal offences. The Rules are not binding on national governments, but they provide, through the breadth of their understanding of juvenile crime and humane response to it, a yardstick against which national provision can be measured.

1.25   During the last decade, as the youth justice system in England and Wales has become more punitive, the extent to which the law relating to young offenders breaches basic international instruments has attracted much criticism. This criticism was robustly formalised in the report of the UN Committee on the Rights of the Child in 1995.[58] In her detailed survey of the developing law of children's rights, Fortin identifies and elaborates on the aspects of the system which attract most international criticism.[59] They include the low age of criminal responsibility, issues related to diversion from court, the erosion of the difference between youth courts and adult courts, and, the lack of a welfare approach to young offenders. The latter is unambiguously required by Article 3 of the UNCRC—

> "In all actions concerning children, whether undertaken by public or private social welfare institutions, courts of law, administrative authorities or legislative bodies, the best interests of the child shall be a primary consideration."

1.26   The U.K. government has been able with impunity to be contemptuous of criticism from the UN Committee monitoring the UNCRC. In contrast, the less child oriented but judicially enforceable Convention has forced amendment of domestic law in regard to young offenders, most recently in regard to indeterminate sentences for those found guilty of homicide, and to procedure to ensure the right to a fair trial for very young offenders charged with grave crimes.[60]

RECURRENT THEMES

Complexity

1.27   Incremental amendments to primary legislation throughout the last 30 years of the twentieth century left the law relating to the sentencing of children and young persons in a state which was in some respects impenetrable. The authors of the 1996 Labour party consultation paper *Tackling Youth Crime: Reforming Youth Justice* recognised this, quoting with approval an editorial from *The Magistrate* in which it was suggested that "the law relating to young offenders is in a state of complexity which makes it inaccessible to lawyers, pre-sentence report writers and magistrates, and incomprehensible to most defendants and families".

1.28   The range of new, and in many respects overlapping orders introduced by the Crime and Disorder Act 1988 (CDA 1998) and the Youth Justice and Criminal Evidence Act 1999 (YJCEA 1999) added further to the complexity. The welcome codification of all sentencing powers under the Powers of Criminal Courts (Sentencing) Act 2000 (PCC(S)A 2000) at least means that all sentences can be found within a single statute. What is not yet clear is whether courts will be confused by the volume of powers, particularly at the interface of those which are

---

[58] *Concluding Observations of the Committee on the Rights of the Child: United Kingdom of Great Britain and Northern Ireland*, CRC/C/15/Add34 (Centre for Human Rights, Geneva, January 1995).
[59] J. Fortin, *op. cit.* Chap. 19.
[60] *T v. U.K. and V v. U.K., op. cit.*

or are not community sentences.[61] There is also considerable potential for confusion in relation to those new orders such as the action plan order and child safety order which substantially overlap with existing orders in criminal and care proceedings.

1.29 Whatever the problems with the complexity of sentencing law, they pale into insignificance when compared with the provisions relating to the keeping of children in secure accommodation (See paras 9.26–9.35). The secure accommodation provisions under section 25 of the CA 1989 and section 23 of the CYPA 1969 (as amended by the CJA 1991, the Criminal Justice and Public Order Act 1994 (CJPO 1994), and the CDA 1998) are, and have been since their hasty introduction in 1982, labyrinthine in nature and in urgent need of radical reform. They remain untouched by the PCC(S)A 2000 which is only concerned with sentencing. Reform has to come, since it seems almost inevitable that there will be successful challenges to the provisions under the Human Rights Act 1998 (HRA 1998).

Disparity

1.30

"The symbiotic relationship of local courts, local prosecution services and local probation and social services departments is the core factor which transmutes any statutory change in the criminal justice system into a variegated pattern taking its colour scheme from local systems."[62]

Since the time that details of each petty sessional division's sentencing were first available, the disparities between courts with similar catchment areas and offenders from similar socio-economic backgrounds committing similar offences have been manifest.[63] But it is not only the courts. The whole route through which the young offender must travel between suspicion and eventual sentence is vulnerable to discrepant, possibly even idiosyncratic, discretionary interpretation of policy, guidance and legislation, which may profoundly alter the outcome of proceedings at the end of the day.[64]

Social deprivation

1.31 The consistency of research findings regarding the association of clusters of factors such as low family income, poor housing, unemployment, low educational attainment, harsh and erratic discipline within the home, drugs, and early experience of violence or abuse with juvenile crime cannot be ignored. The evidence spans the century, although post-war studies probably have more relevance in that some extremes of disadvantage were removed by the welfare state. From original large cohort research starting in the 1950s[65] and detailed studies of young offenders in institutions undertaken in the 1960s and '70s,[66] through a

---

[61] See Chapter 16.

[62] E. Burney, *Sentencing Young People* (Gower, Aldershot, 1985) p. 90.

[63] R. Hood, *Sentencing the Motoring Offender* (Heinemann, London, 1972); E. Burney, *JP. Magistrate, Court and Community* (Hutchinson, London, 1979); R. Tarling and M. Wetherett, *Sentencing Practice in Magistrates' Courts*, Home Office Research Study No. 56 (HMSO, London,1980).

[64] R. Anderson, *Representation in the Juvenile Court* (Routledge, London, 1978); P. Priestley, D. Fears and R. Fuller, *Justice for Juveniles* (Routledge, Kegan Paul, London, 1977; E. Burney (1979) *op. cit*; L. Hilgendorf, *Social Workers and Solicitors in Child Care Cases* (HMSO, London, 1981); H. Parker, M. Casburn and D. Turnbull, *Receiving Juvenile Justice* (Blackwell, Oxford, 1981); H. Parker, M. Sumner and G. Jarvis, *Unmasking the Magistrates* (Open University Press, Milton Keynes, 1989); C. Ball, "Secret Justice: the Use Made of School Reports in the Juvenile Court" (1983) 13 *British Journal of Social Work*, 197; S. Brown, *Magistrates at Work* (Open University Press, Milton Keynes,1991).

[65] D. West and D. Farrington, *Who Becomes Delinquent?* (Heinemann, London, 1973).

[66] S. Millham, R. Bullock and K. Hosie, *Locking up Children* (Saxon House, London, 1978); P. Cawson, *Young Offenders in Care* (D.H.S.S., London, 1981).

recent immensely detailed review of research findings across a quarter century,[67] to a reworking of a vast wealth of data from a 1950s study in the United States[68] and, closer to home, studies of persistent young offenders[69] and of factors which protect young people from criminal careers,[70] the message is identical. Economic, family, educational and employment disadvantage and deprivation do not *cause* delinquency but the strengths of the association are overwhelming.

Ethnic minorities and discrimination

1.32   The issue of racial bias within the criminal justice system is a difficult and contentious one that applies equally to young offenders. There is no doubt that, as with adults, black (Afro-Caribbean and other African origins) juveniles are over represented throughout the system. This despite the fact that a major self report study found that levels of offending admitted by white and black young people were very similar, although there was a substantial difference in the types of offences committed.[71] Offending levels by young people in the South Asian ethnic minority groups were much lower. Even if levels of offending by white and black youths are very similar, black young people are over represented throughout the system, whereas other ethnic minority groups who suffer equally as victims of racial abuse are not. Young black people are more often stopped by the police, prosecuted rather than cautioned, charged with offences only triable in the Crown Court, committed for trial in the Crown Court, remanded in and sentenced to custody.[72] They were also less likely than white youths to receive cautions rather than being prosecuted, though, as with sentencing discrepancies, a higher incidence of refusal to admit guilt amongst black youths may affect cautioning rates in the same way that not guilty pleas lose sentencing discount.

1.33   Despite the over representation and the many claims that have been made, there is very little research evidence of racial discrimination at each stage of the criminal justice process. Indeed there is regrettably little reliable large scale research into racial bias in relation to adult or young offenders at any stage of the process, even sentencing. A review of the main empirical research was summarised for the Royal Commission on Criminal Justice in 1993.[73] The most substantial and methodologically sophisticated study in the last decade is limited in its relevance to young offenders in that it studied sentencing in Crown Courts and not by magistrates.[74] When the Audit Commission surveyed police forces in England and Wales in January 1996, a third of forces reported making no use of the ethnic monitoring data that they are required to produce for the Home Office under section 95 of the CJA 1991.

1.34   Smith, in a thoughtful analysis, suggests that endemic, low level, discrimination against black minorities throughout the criminal justice system interacts with high rates of offending amongst the same groups.[75] He suggests that crime arises

---

[67] D. Farrington, "Human Development and Criminal Careers" in *Oxford Handbook of Criminology*, *op. cit.*

[68] R. Sampson and J. Laub, *Crime in the Making* (Harvard University Press, Cambridge, Massachusetts, USA, 1993).

[69] A. Hagell and T. Newburn, *Persistent Young Offenders* (Policy Studies Institute, London, 1994).

[70] J. Graham and B. Bowling, Young people and crime (Home Office, London, 1996).

[71] *ibid.*

[72] Audit Commission, *Misspent Youth: Young People and Crime* (Audit Commission, London, 1996) p. 44 .

[73] M. Fitzgerald, *Ethnic Minorities and the Criminal Justice System*, Royal Commission on Criminal Justice (HMSO, London, 1993).

[74] R. Hood, *Race and Sentencing* (Clarendon Press, Oxford, 1992).

[75] D. J. Smith, "Ethnic Origins, Crime and Criminal Justice" in *Oxford Handbook of Criminology, op. cit.*, p. 703.

from a sequence of interactions and "It seems likely that in certain sequences racial hostility on one side and antagonism to authority on the other become mutually reinforcing". This leads in turn to a spiral of increased rates of offending, generating an increase in racial hostility and discrimination, producing a "cycle of deviance amplification".

Persistence

1.35 Notions of a hard core of persistent young offenders responsible for most serious crime committed by juveniles recur throughout the post-war period. Political responses, in terms of a bifurcated approach encouraging courts to impose harsh penalties for the most serious offenders, whilst either diverting from court or sentencing the less serious more leniently, have similarly reappeared in varying guises. In the same way the development of strategies designed to identify very young offenders, likely to grow into persistent offenders, and to divert them from criminal careers appear enduringly appealing. As researchers and commentators have identified, the essence of the problem of achieving these aims lies in identification and prediction.[76]

1.36 The fact that, although at least one third of males will have been convicted of at least one criminal offence by the time they reach the age of 30, a small number of juveniles may be responsible for a substantial proportion of youth offending at any one time is not challenged. What is problematic is the appropriate response. Evidence from studies in the 1990s suggest that most repeat offending is property related and transient in nature. The data also reveal the extent to which repeat young offenders live chaotic lives in dysfunctional families, and suffer across the range of educational and poverty related disadvantage.[77]

1.37 The targeting of "persistent" young offenders was a feature of the penal policy of successive governments in the 1990s. The secure training orders introduced by the Conservatives in the Criminal Justice and Public Order Act 1994, but not implemented, could only be imposed if offenders aged 12–14 years satisfied statutory criteria for persistence.[78] Detention and training orders under the CDA 1998 can be imposed on young offenders under the age of 15 if the court is "of the opinion that he is a persistent offender."[79] Persistence is not statutorily defined, in the 1998 Act, leaving the courts at liberty to determine its existence on the facts of each case.[80] Although the orders can only be imposed if the criteria set out in section 79 of the PCC(S)A 2000 for imposing custodial sentences are satisfied, problems with the interpretation of "so serious" by the courts, makes it likely that the new custodial orders will be readily imposed.[81] Given the uniformity of high rates of re-offending amongst juveniles leaving the whole range of residential establishments, the widespread use of custody for very young offenders regarded as "persistent" is unlikely to achieve the government's aim of a reduction in youth offending.[82]

---

[76] A. Hagell and T. Newburn, *op.cit.*; R. Tarling, *Analysing Offending: Data, Models and Interpretation* (HMSO, London, 1993).
[77] Hagell and Newburn, *op. cit.*; A. Crowley, *A Criminal Waste: A Study of Child Offenders Eligible for Secure Training Centres* (Children's Society, London, 1998).
[78] CDA 1998, s.1(5).
[79] Powers of the Criminal Courts (Sentencing) Act 2000, s.100(2)(a).
[80] *R v. C (Young Person: Persistent Offender)*, *The Times,* October 11, 2000.
[81] A. Ashworth and A. Von Hirsch, "Recognising Elephants: the Problem of the Custody Threshold" [1997] Crim. L.R. 187.
[82] J. Muncie, *op. cit.*

YOUTH JUSTICE IN THE 1990S—A "RECIPE FOR UNINTENDED CONSEQUENCES?"[83]

1.38 In contrast to the previous decade, an extraordinary explosion of public anguish concerning children and young people accompanied by punitive political response took place during the 1990s. Running parallel to the substantial reduction in youth court appearances and custodial sentences described above, and the lengthy gestation in the Home Office of new sentencing policies, the 1980s had seen the long, carefully considered, thoroughly debated radical reform of private and public child law and the courts in which it is administered.[84] The 1990s, having started quietly, demonstrated how quickly public perceptions and opportunistic political responses can bring about change. The decade was characterised in the early years by media-encouraged hysterical reaction, firstly to disturbances in which crowds of young people were in violent confrontations with the police. This was followed by the police and press identification of "persistent" young offenders responsible for mini crime waves, and finally by the horrific murder of a two-year-old by two 10-year-old boys.[85] The cumulative effect allowed "long-standing concerns about young or very young offenders to be dusted down, distorted, sometimes exaggerated, and then served up in symbolic form via the mass media".[86]

1.39 The demonisation of young people and retributive responses to the perceived threat they posed to the fabric of society gathered pace.[87] Ministers, sensing the public mood, responded opportunistically with a sequence of punitive measures. In March 1993, the Home Secretary, Kenneth Clark, announced the introduction of a new custodial sentence aimed at persistent young offenders. Secure training orders, under which 12–15-year-old children would receive education and training in "secure training units", were to be introduced. On release the offenders would be subject to an indefinite period of rigorous supervision. The next Home Secretary, Michael Howard, actively encouraged the use of more and longer custodial sentences for juveniles as well as adults. The CDA 1998 increased the maximum sentence of detention in a young offender institution for 15–17-year-old boys from one year to two and introduced secure training orders for 12–14-year-olds. In the event, implementation of the secure training order provisions was delayed by the refusal of local councils to give planning permission. Youth justice workers and organisations, mindful of the potential for the abuse of vulnerable and damaged children and the abject failure of residential institutions to reduce offending, were deeply opposed to implementation. This was in contrast to the Labour opposition, which after an initial critical reaction chose instead to seek to outbid the government on punitive law and order soundbites. "Tough on crime, tough on the causes of crime" is not evenly reflected in policies either immediately before or since the change of government in 1997. What is apparent is that since the mid 1990s the political consensus on crime control policies, missing since the 1950s, returned, this time in punitive form.

---

[83] C. Ball, "Youth Justice and Criminal Evidence Act 1999: a significant move towards restorative justice or a recipe for unintended consequences?" [2000] Crim. L.R. 211.
[84] C. Ball, " Children Act 1989: origins, aims and current concerns" in *Social Work and Social Welfare Year Book No. 2* (P. Carter, T.Jeffs and M. Smith ed., Open University Press, Milton Keynes, 1991).
[85] A. Hagell and T. Newburn, *Persistent Young Offenders* (Policy Studies Institute, London, 1994)
[86] T. Newburn, *op. cit.*, at p. 646.
[87] A. Ashworth, "Abolishing the Presumption of Incapacity: C v. DPP" (1994) 6 Journal of Child Law 174.

POLICY DEVELOPMENT

1.40 Reform of the youth justice system was a clear policy priority of the Labour Party in opposition.[88] The policies generated and their realisation in the CDA 1998 and the Youth Justice and Criminal Evidence Act 1999 (YJCEA 1999) reflect several strands which bear a striking resemblance to the confusing elision of welfare and justice which dominated juvenile justice throughout most of the last century. This continuing confusion is possibly most symbolically manifested by the fact that whilst the new statutory aim of the youth justice system is to "prevent offending by children and young persons",[89] courts still have a statutory duty, when reaching decisions, "to have regard to the welfare of the child or young person".[90] A duty that it would be hard for the government to abolish, since, as we have seen,[91] to do so would be in breach of treaty obligations under Article 3 of the UN Convention on the Rights of the Child.

1.41 The welfare strands in new policies and legislation include recognition of, though some would say insufficient response to, the sort of interventions in early life which research indicates hold out the best chance of reducing criminality; the importation of elements of welfare oriented strategies which have been identified as successful in reducing youth offending in other jurisdictions, and adherence to the rhetoric of "restorative justice". On the "justice"—more properly described as "punitive"—side the reforms are permeated by overt managerialism and very substantial elements of the "populist punitivism" of the previous administration. Each strand requires some further exploration.

The welfare elements

Interventions in early life

1.42 Every youth justice related policy document published since 1996 has made reference to Graham and Bowling's large sample self report survey of offending by young people.[92] The aim of the study was to estimate the extent, nature, and frequency of offending amongst 14–25 year olds and to identify the reasons why some young people start to offend and what influences others not to enter, or once entered not to continue in, criminal careers. The research confirmed earlier studies in regard to the key factors associated with youth offending. Low parental supervision, truancy and exclusion from school, having friends and/or siblings who were in trouble with the police, and poor family attachment were identified as the variables most strongly correlated with offending. In discussion the authors clearly identify the need for a response "to universally target the onset of offending via a variety of social policies", and for most minor offenders "to avoid the costly intervention of the criminal justice system".[93]

1.43 The extent to which new policies and provisions make such a response is debatable. The government would claim that they do so through rehabililtation (change) programmes under the final warning scheme,[94] anti-social behaviour

[88] See J. Straw and A. Michael *Tackling Youth Crime: Reforming Youth Justice* (Labour Party, London, 1996).
[89] CDA 1998, s.37(1).
[90] CYPA 1933, s.44(1).
[91] Above, at 1.25.
[92] *op. cit.*
[93] *ibid.*, at pp. 83–84.
[94] CDA 1998, ss.65 and 66.

orders,[95] parenting orders,[96] child safety orders,[97] action plan orders,[98] and the involvement of parents in the negotiation of contracts of behaviour with youth offending panels.[99] Commentators observe that the long-term nature of many of the social factors associated with offending behaviour can only be effectively addressed by long-term preventative strategies which engage with and support families. They express doubt as to the efficacy of the whole complex range of new over-lapping measures.[1]

Welfare oriented strategies from other jurisdictions

1.44   As Ball has identified elsewhere,[2] referral of young offenders to panels draws elements from family group conferences and children's hearings panels in Scotland without recognising that such strategies can only work effectively within the context of a policy spectrum of which they form an integral part. Family group conferences which originated in New Zealand, were developed in a rather different way in Australia, and then imported in adapted form as part of a diversionary programme by Thames Valley Police.[3] The children's hearings system which has resulted in almost all offenders under the age of 16 being diverted from the criminal justice system, to be dealt with in the same way as children in need of compulsory measures of care of protection, were introduced in Scotland under the Social Work (Scotland) Act 1968.[4] The differences between the New Zealand and Scottish systems and the mandatory sentence for most first time offenders of referral to youth offending panels by youth courts are only too apparent. Children's hearings and family group conferences operate instead of a court appearance rather than a sentence, thus inviting rather than coercing the co-operation of families.[5] Youth offending panels, in contrast will be seeking to engage with young offenders sentenced to a referral order by the court, compulsorily accompanied by a parent, and with the threat of return to court if the required "programme of behaviour" is not successfully completed. On a practical level, hearings and family group conferences require the involvement of well trained, dedicated members of local communities with an interest in the welfare of children. They also require time for a meaningful dialogue between the panel, the offender, the family, and possibly, when willing, the victim. In both Scotland and New Zealand 70–80 per cent of offenders are dealt with informally outside the children's hearing panels and family group conferences, thus only allowing a manageable number of cases to reach a

---

[95] *ibid.*, s.1.
[96] *ibid.*, s.8.
[97] *ibid.*, s.11.
[98] PCC(S)A 2000, Part III.
[99] PCC(S)A 2000, s. 69.
[1] See J. Fionda, "New Labour, Old Hat: Youth Justice and the Crime and Disorder Act 1998" [1999] Crim. L.R. 36; C. Wonnacott, "The counterfeit contract—reform, pretence and muddled principles in the new referral order" (1999) C.F.L.Q. 11, 3, 271–287; J. Dignan, "The Crime and Disorder Act and the Prospects for Restorative Justice" [1999] Crim. L.R. 48–60; L. Gelsthorpe and A. Morris "Much ado about nothing—a critical comment on key provisions relating to children in the Crime and Disorder Act 1998" (1999) 11 Child and Family Law Quarterly 209; and C. Ball, "The Youth Justice and Criminal Evidence Act 1999, Part I: a significant move towards restorative justice, or a recipe for unintended consequences?" [2000] Crim. L.R. 211.
[2] C. Ball (2000), *op.cit.*
[3] See, for instance, R. Allen (1996) *Children and Crime*, Institute for Public Policy Research, Chaps 8 and 9.
[4] The provisions relating to children's hearings have been largely re-enacted in Part II of the Children (Scotland) Act 1995.
[5] R. Allen, *op. cit.* and J. Dignan, "The Crime and Disorder Act and the Prospects for Restorative Justice" [1999] Crim. L.R. 48–60.

panel or hearing and a meaningful dialogue to take place. The sheer volume of likely referrals to youth offending panels makes it probable that responses may become mechanistic and as a consequence panel membership may not prove attractive voluntary work for people of the calibre needed.

Restorative justice

1.45 The rhetoric of restorative justice entered the policy making process leading to the reforms of the late 1990s at quite a late stage. The term does not appear in the 1996 pre-manifesto consultation paper *Tackling Youth Crime: Reforming Youth Justice*,[6] although the concept of offenders making reparation to victims does. By the following year, in the white paper *No More Excuses—a new approach to tackling youth crime in England and Wales*,[7] the government was suggesting that the proposals for the reform of the youth court "build on the principles underlying the concept of restorative justice".[8] Picking up on an earlier policy document from the NACRO Young Offenders Committee,[9] these principles are spelt out as restoration, reintegration, and responsibility. Thereafter the term appears frequently in the notes of guidance which accompany both the CDA 1998 and the YJCEA 1999. The principles of restorative justice are particularly claimed to underpin rehabilitation (change) programmes under the final warning scheme,[10] the whole referral order process,[11] reparation orders,[12] action plan orders,[13] and parenting orders.[14]

1.46 The extent to which the new provisions truly reflect adherence to the principles of restorative justice has been the subject of considerable critical comment.[15] The thrust of the critique is at two levels, both of equal siginficance. At what might be categorised as the micro level, there is for instance concern that the government has paid lip service to an important body of research on the prevention of delinquency through the improvement of child rearing, whilst ignoring the essentially voluntary nature of the supportive parenting programmes described.[16] At the macro level, there is concern that the ideological confusion apparent in the twin track focus on punishment and welfare, in the guise of restorative justice, make claims of adherence to the principles of restorative justice more apparent than real.

The "justice" strands

Managerialism

1.47 By the late 1980s, commentators were identifying the extent to which the welfare versus justice debate which had dominated juvenile justice since the

---

[6] *op. cit.*

[7] *op. cit.*

[8] *ibid.*, para. 9.21.

[9] *A New Three Rs for Young Offenders* (NACRO, London, January, 1997).

[10] CDA 1998, ss.65 and 66.

[11] PCC(S)A 2000, Part III.

[12] *ibid.*, s.73.

[13] *ibid.*, s.69.

[14] CDA 1998, s.8.

[15] See J. Fionda, *op. cit.*; C. Wonnacott, "The counterfeit contract—reform, pretence and muddled principles in the new referral order" (1999) C.F.L.Q. 11, 3, 271–287; J. Dignan, "The Crime and Disorder Act and the Prospects for Restorative Justice" [1999] Crim. L.R. 48–60; L. Gelsthorpe and A. Morris "Much ado about nothing—a critical comment on key provisions relating to children in the Crime and Disorder Act 1998" (1999) 11 C.F.L.Q. 209; and C. Ball, "The Youth Justice and Criminal Evidence Act 1999, Part I: a significant move towards restorative justice, or a recipe for unintended consequences? [2000] Crim. L.R. 211.

[16] D. Utting, J. Bright and C. Henricson, *Crime and the Family—Improving child rearing and preventing delinquency,* (Family Policy Studies Centre, London, 1993).

mid-1970s was no longer relevant. New strategies for diversion and new sentencing initiatives were instead characterised by inter-agency co-operation, the cost-effective and efficient management of the delinquent population, and the achievement of measurable outcomes.[17] The continuing and burgeoning influence of the managerialist approach is apparent, albeit in a rather simplistic form, throughout New Labour's restructuring of the youth justice system.[18] The 1996 Audit Commission report *Misspent Youth* spelt out with considerable clarity the extent to which its researches identified expense, inefficiency, delay and inconsistency throughout a system which was ultimately ineffective in reducing offending behaviour. The Commission's recommendations favoured central policy direction of local multi-agency teams co-ordinated by local authorities, answerable to the Board for local performance. These policies are enacted in the CDA 1998, Part III, with the creation of the Youth Justice Board for England and Wales and local multi-agency youth offending teams working within a framework of national standards.

1.48   The extent to which the national board and local YOTs are successful in achieving the main aim of the system—to reduce offending by children and young people—"will be largely dependent on their autonomy and independence to develop good practice and effective policy in youth justice."[19] As yet, there is little published on the outcomes of local initiatives funded by the Board, and it is to be hoped that where outcomes are successful they will be developed more widely. Until that time, the heavily managerialist style of new national standards and of the guidance issued by the Board on a range of issues does not inspire confidence that they will allow the development of the sort of imaginative, demanding, community based programmes which appeared able to address offending behaviour in the 1980s.[20]

Continuing punitiveness

1.49   **The abolition of the presumption of doli incapax.**   The age of criminal responsibility in the United Kingdom as a whole[21] is significantly lower than that in the rest of Europe. Despite this, the well established legal principle that a child under the age of 14 was *doli incapax*—incapable of forming criminal intent—unless the court could be satisfied that he knew what he was doing was "seriously wrong", was abolished in 1999.[22] The previous government had signaled their intention to legislate to this effect as soon as the House of Lords, reversing a Divisional Court decision, refused to do so on the basis that such a serious step should only be taken by Parliament.[23] The Labour government justified the abolition on the basis that the child's welfare is promoted by preventing offending, ignoring the fact that there is no evidence to support the view that early court appearances have any beneficial effect in terms of discouraging re-offending. Although it did not appear that report writers, legal representatives, or the courts, were assiduous in applying the principle

---

[17] See J. Pratt "Corporatism: the third model of juvenile justice" (1989) 29 Brit. J. Criminol. 236; H. Parker *et al.* (1989) *op. cit.* and D. Smith, "Corporatism and the New Youth Justice" in *The New Youth Justice* (B. Goldson ed., Russell House Publishing, Lyme Regis, 2000).

[18] A. Morris and L. Gelsthorpe, "Something Old, Something Borrowed, Something Blue, but Something New? A comment on the prospects for restorative justice under the Crime and Disorder Act 1998" [2000] Crim. L.R. 18.

[19] J. Fionda, *op. cit.* at p. 40.

[20] R. Allen, *op. cit.*; A. Rutherford, *Growing Out of Crime: the New Era* (Waterside Press, Basingstoke, 1992).

[21] It is 10 in England and Wales, and eight in Scotland and Northern Ireland.

[22] CDA 1998, s.34.

[23] *C. v. DPP* [1995] 2 W.L.R. 383.

prior to abolition, its existence at least provided symbolic recognition of the vulnerability of children.[24] As Fionda suggests in her critique of the 1998 Act, outright abolition, rather than a reversal of the presumption which would have allowed children to raise the defence of *doli incapax* "indicates a dangerous blindness to the incapacities of childhood."[25]

1.50 Custodial sentences. Detention and training orders were introduced in the 1998 Act to replace with a single order the "chaotic and dysfunctional range of custodial facilities for young offenders"[26] which preceded them. The single order replacing detention in a young offender institution for those aged 15 years and over and the secure training orders for 12–14-year-olds introduced by the previous government. The truly punitive feature of the detention and training order lies in the fact that there is the potential to apply the provisions to 10 and 11-year-olds. It is very difficult to find a rational rather than a populist punitive policy behind this extension of custodial sentences for young children. These already appear more than adequate in both the criminal and civil courts. The power to commit children of this age for trial for grave crimes in the Crown Court under section 91 of the PCC(S)A 2000 remains in place. In addition, where very young children are persistently committing such grave crimes that the public is in need of protection from them, it is likely that the threshold conditions for the making of a care order would be satisfied.[27] Instead of being prosecuted in criminal proceedings such children would be better dealt with by means of a care order made in the family proceedings court, where necessary accompanied by a secure accommodation order.[28] Children of any age can be dealt with in care proceedings and then placed in secure accommodation.

UNINTENDED CONSEQUENCES

1.51 The history of the criminal justice system is riddled with examples of the extent to which legislative initiatives founded on conflicting ideologies have consequences which diverge widely from the intention of the legislators.[29] From community service orders, through suspended sentences of imprisonment, to youth custody, examples abound throughout the criminal justice system of the use by magistrates and judges of new sentences for offenders committing less serious offences than those for which the penalty was intended. In relation to young offenders, the most glaring example of an outcome which was the direct opposite of what had been intended, was the rise in the use of custody following partial implementation of the CYPA 1969.

1.52 Wherever criminal justice legislation is based on conflicting ideologies, past experience shows that the potential for unanticipated consequences is increased. It seems unlikely that the reforms introduced by the CDA 1998 and the YJCEA 1999, with their confused mix of disparate ideological underpinnings, will break this pattern.

---

[24] See for instance: J. Muncie, *op. cit.*, at 255; C. Ball and J. Connolly, "Educationally Disaffected Young Offenders: Youth Court and Agency Responses to Truancy and School Exclusion" (2000) 40 Brit. J. Criminol. 594 at 610.
[25] J. Fionda, *op. cit.* at 39.
[26] J. Straw and A. Michael, *op. cit.*, at p. 15.
[27] Children Act 1989, s.31(2).
[28] See, 9.26, below.
[29] R. Harris and D. Webb, *op. cit.*

CHAPTER 2

The New Structure of Youth Justice

BACKGROUND

2.01 In opposition, the Labour party made reform of the youth justice system a clear policy priority.[1] As we have seen, in formulating policy, shadow ministers were substantially influenced by the Audit Commission's damning report on the ineffectiveness and expense of the current system,[2] the Home Office review of delay in the criminal justice system,[3] and by Graham and Bowling's seminal large scale self-report study *Young People and Crime*.[4] Once in power, the Home Secretary immediately established a Youth Justice Task Force to advise him on proposals for reform. Within the first six months of the new government, the Home Office published three discussion papers covering a wide range of issues including diversion, restorative justice, new orders and management of the system. At the end of 1997, the white paper *No More Excuses: A New Approach to Tackling Youth Crime in England and Wales* set out proposals for youth justice reform later enacted in the Crime and Disorder Act 1998.[5]

AIM OF THE SYSTEM

2.02 Under the 1998 Act, the principal aim of the youth justice system, and the duty of all persons carrying out functions in relation to the system, is "to prevent offending by children and young persons."[6] This aim is elaborated in an inter-departmental circular—

> "The principal aim of the youth justice system established by section 37 of the Crime and Disorder Act is to prevent offending by children and young people. As set out in the framework document on the principal aim published in September 1998, the Government intends that this should be achieved through the following objectives:
>
>   • the swift administration of justice so that every young person accused of breaking the law has the matter resolved without delay;
>   • confronting young offenders with the consequences of their offending, for themselves and their family, their victims and their community, and helping them to develop a sense of personal responsibility;

---

[1] J. Straw and A. Michael, *Tackling Youth Crime, Reforming Youth Justice* (Labour Party, London, 1996).
[2] *Misspent Youth: Young People and Crime* (Audit Commission, London, 1996).
[3] *Review of Delay in the Criminal Justice System: a Report* (Home Office, London, 1997).
[4] J. Graham and B. Bowling, Home Office Research Study, No. 145 (Home Office, London, 1995).
[5] Cmnd. 3809.
[6] s.37(1).

- intervention which tackles the particular factors (personal, family, social, educational or health) that put the young person at risk of offending and which strengthens "protective factors";
- punishment proportionate to the seriousness and persistence of offending;
- encouraging reparation to victims by young offenders; and
- reinforcing the responsibilities of parents."[7]

2.03 These aims are restated in the National Standards for Youth Justice published by the Youth Justice Board in April 2000.

The primary responsibility for the provision of youth justice services to achieve these aims rests with local authorities, working within the policy imperatives set by the national Youth Justice Board. The responsibilities require some elaboration.

Local Youth Justice Services

2.04 Under section 38:

"(1) It shall be the duty of each local authority acting in co-operation with the persons and bodies mentioned in subsection (2) below, to secure that, to such an extent as is appropriate for their area, all youth justice services are available there.

(2) It shall be the duty of—

(a) every chief officer of police or police authority any part of whose police area lies within the local authority's area; and

(b) every probation committee or health authority any part of whose area lies within that area,

to co-operate in the discharge by the local authority of their duty under subsection (1) above."

2.05 The comprehensive range of "youth justice services" is set out in subsection (4)—

(a) the provision of persons to act as appropriate adults to safeguard the interests of children and young persons detained or questioned by police officers;

(b) the assessment of children and young persons, and the provision for them of rehabilitation programmes, for the purposes of section 66(2) below;

(c) the provision of support for children and young persons remanded or committed on bail while awaiting trial or sentence;

(d) the placement in local authority accommodation of children and young persons remanded or committed to such accommodation under section 23 of the Children and Young Persons Act 1969 ("the 1969 Act");

(e) the provision of reports or other information required by courts in criminal proceedings against children and young persons;

(f) the provision of persons to act as responsible officers in relation to parenting orders, child safety orders, reparation orders and action plan orders;

---

[7] *Inter-Departmental Circular on Establishing Youth Offending Teams,* December 22, 1998, issued by the Home Office, Department of Health, Welsh Office and Department for Education and Employment.

(g) the supervision of young persons sentenced to a probation order, a community service order or a combination order;

(h) the supervision of children and young persons sentenced to a detention and training order or a supervision order;

(i) the post-release supervision of children and young persons under section 37(4A) or 65 of the 1991 Act or section 31 of the Crime (Sentences) Act 1997 ("the 1997 Act");

(j) the performance of functions under subsection (1) of section 75 below by such persons as may be authorised by the Secretary of State under that subsection.

(5) The Secretary of State may by order amend subsection (4) above so as to extend, restrict or otherwise alter the definition of "youth justice services" for the time being specified in that subsection.

2.06   Subsection (4) was amended by the Youth Justice and Criminal Evidence Act 1999 to add the implementation of referral orders within the meaning of Part I of that Act.[8]

In order to carry out their duty to provide the range of youth justice services, every local authority, either acting on its own or with others has to establish one or more Youth Offending Teams (YOT) for their areas.[9] The work of the YOT is considered in more detail below.[10]

The Youth Justice Board

2.07   The 1997 discussion paper *New National and Local Focus on Youth Crime* outlined measures designed to deliver youth justice services through central control of local delivery. The Youth Justice Board, set up under the 1998 Act,[11] sets policy through guidelines and national standards for implementation by YOTs.[12] Membership of the Board is limited to 10–12 persons, appointed by the Home Secretary, some at least of whom should have had "extensive recent experience of the youth justice system".[13] Detailed provisions regarding terms of appointment, length of tenure and removal from office are set out in Schedule 2 of the Act.

2.08   The wide-ranging advisory, monitoring, research commissioning, information dissemination and good practice promotion functions of the Board are prescribed in great detail in section 41(5). The Board has wide advisory powers in regard to the operation of the youth justice system and the provision of youth justice services, and also has to comply with directions given by the Secretary of State and act in accordance with any guidance given by him.[14]

Youth Offending Teams

2.09   The circular which elaborated on the objectives of the youth justice system, envisaged that the new youth offending teams would be "one of the main vehicles by which the principal aim, and the supporting objectives, would be

---

[8] CDA, s.38(4)(k).
[9] *ibid.*, s.39.
[10] See 2.09.
[11] s.41.
[12] See below, para. 2.14.
[13] CDA, s.41(4).
[14] *ibid.*, ss.(7).

delivered."[15] In addition to placing a statutory duty on local authorities to establish YOTs, section 39 requires local chief officers of police, probation committees and health authorities to co-operate with the local authority in fulfilling the duty, and empowers them to make financial contribution for this purpose, either directly or through a fund.[16] The duties of the YOT are to co-ordinate youth justice services and to carry out any functions entrusted to them under the youth justice plan, made under section 40.[17]

2.10 Prior to the setting up of YOTs, an inter-departmental circular proposed "the formation of a **steering group** for the youth offending team(s) for the area, comprising the local authority chief executive and the chief officers for social services, education, police, probation and health, plus any others (*e.g.* justices' clerk and/or justices' chief executive) invited onto the steering group."[18] The circular emphasised the need for those asked to serve on the steering group to have "the authority and skills to negotiate with the other services on matters concerning the youth offending team (including resource allocation) without having to refer back continually to their chief officer, though they will need to account properly to their own agency for their decisions". [19]

2.11 YOTs were set up in pilot areas at the end of September 1998, and nationally in April 2000. The initial experience of the pilot teams, which used some or all of the new CDA provisions, were evaluated over the first few months of operation by a team from the Universities of Sheffield and Hull. An interim report, focusing on the process of establishing YOTs was published in April 1999.[20]

2.12 The YOT manager is clearly identified in guidance[21] and in the interim report on the evaluation of pilot teams as a key appointment with primary responsibility for strategic planning rather than day to day management. The manager's independence from the agency from which they may have been appointed is also identified as being important. Throughout the *Interim Report on Youth Offending Teams*, there is a strong emphasis on the need for YOT managers and workers to recognise the "new context of work with young offenders the CDA 1998 has created."[22]

2.13 Membership of the YOT is prescribed, to the extent that—

"A youth offending team shall include at least one of each of the following, namely—

(a) a probation officer;
(b) a social worker or a local authority social services department;
(c) a police officer;
(d) a person nominated by a health authority any part of whose area lies within the local authority's area;
(e) a person nominated by the chief education officer appointed by the local authority under section 532 of the Education Act 1996."[23]

---

[15] *Inter-Departmental Circular On Establishing Youth Offending Teams*, December 22, 1998, issued by the Home Office, Department Of Health, Welsh Office and Department for Education and Employment, para. 10.
[16] CDA, s.39(3) and (4).
[17] *ibid.*, s.(7)
[18] *ibid.*, para. 34.
[19] *ibid.*, para. 35.
[20] *Interim Report on Youth Offending Teams* (Home Office, London, 1999)
[21] *ibid.*, paras 75–79.
[22] *op. cit.*, p. 15.
[23] CDA, s.39(5).

2.14   The National Standards for Youth Justice are issued jointly by the Youth Justice Board (YJB), Home Office, Department for Education and Employment, Department of Health, Lord Chancellor's Department, and National Assembly for Wales. They prescribe the role of YOTs and other agencies within the youth justice system in all their key areas of work, and "provide a benchmark against which the quality and effectiveness of work can be inspected".[24] In particular they—

> "● Set clear requirements for supervision which includes quality of work, frequency of contact , and response to non-compliance;
>
> ● help to speed up the court process so that sanctions against offending will be experienced more immediately;
>
> ● improve the effectiveness of information sharing and exchange;
>
> ● ensure the needs of victims of crime are respected and prioritised;
>
> ● encourage reparation by young offenders to victims who want it;
>
> ● prioritise the protection of the public from re-offending, harm and fear of crime;
>
> ● protect the rights of children, many of whom may also be victims of crime themselves, and promote good practice in working with them;
>
> ● ensure Youth Offending Teams take a lead role in the planning and provision of services designed to prevent offending by children and young people which the CDA requires to be in place locally; and
>
> ● require that all intervention is delivered fairly, consistently and without improper discrimination, in a way which values and respects the cultural and racial diversity of the whole community."[25]

2.15   The standards are laid out in a way which reflects the above content, indicating the individual responsible for ensuring compliance, and the source of the responsibility, whether statutory or set out in guidance. As an example, National Standards for Work with Young People Following Arrest, begins—

> "2.1 YOT managers must ensure that appropriate adults can be provided to police stations in their area, whether or not the arrested child or young person lives in their area. They must ensure that staff or YOT accredited volunteers who act as appropriate adults are trained and supported in this role, and that they are provided with a copy of the Police and Criminal Evidence Act 1984 (PACE) Codes of Practice."

The YOT manager is designated as having responsibility and the sources are identified as PACE 1984, s.60(1)(a) and s.66, and the Codes of Practice.

Youth Courts

2.16   When compared with innovative reforms which have resulted in the establishment of the Youth Justice Board (YJB) and local YOTs, the constitution and jurisdiction of the youth court, set out in Part III, remain relatively unchanged.

---

[24] *National Standards for Youth Justice, op.cit.,* para. 2.
[25] *op. cit.,* para. 4.

The main reform, leaving aside the tranch of new orders to be administered by the court,[26] is that youth courts are now subject to the targets set by the YJB for completion of each stage of a young offenders progress through the criminal justice system, and to national standards. These require the setting up of an effective user group involving all agencies with a central role in the local youth court. The group is to be concerned with—

"1. Improving the effective and timely exchange of information concerning young offenders;
2. Ensuring the quality of the local Youth Justice Services Agreement by making arrangements for monitoring;
3. Providing a forum where the YOT manager reports on the outcomes of the YOT's work;
4. Developing the efficiency and effectiveness of court work."[27]

Responsibility for inter-agency liaison is allocated to the Justices' Clerk and YOT Manager, who are required to agree who organises and records the meetings and invites the attendance of the local Victim Support and Witness Service.

Looking ahead

2.17 Measures under the 1998 Act were fully implemented in 2000, and referral orders under the 1999 Act, currently the subject of pilot trials will be implemented in 2002.[28] Although it is inevitable that it will be some time before a clear picture emerges, the promised routine monitoring of all aspects of the system should, together with the annual youth justice plans required of every YOT, ensure that there is greater managerial clarity regarding the working of the system than in the past. Real understanding of the use of the provisions and the way they impact on young offenders and their families will depend on funding and access for high quality independent research.

---

[26] See Chap. 5 and Part VI, below.
[27] *op. cit.*, para. 6.1.
[28] Now PCC(S)A 2000, Part III.

Part II

Children in Trouble:
Young Offenders and the Police

CHAPTER 3

Young Offenders and the Police

THE INVESTIGATION OF CRIME

3.01 To the police officer investigating a crime, the age of the offender, unless it becomes apparent that he or she is under the age of ten and therefore below the age of criminal responsibility, only becomes an issue when the officer wishes to search or question the suspect. If the suspected offender is under ten the investigation will be concluded without the possibility of charge.[1]

Juveniles suspected by the police of involvement in the commission of offences are subject to the same provisions regarding police investigations and interrogation as adults, with additional safeguards. The Police and Criminal Evidence Act 1984 (PACE), with its accompanying Codes of Practice,[2] provides a comprehensive statutory framework regulating police powers of arrest and interrogation. The tension between the police seeking extension of their powers to investigate offences and apprehend and interrogate offenders, and the protection of suspects from the perceived excesses of police powers is a continuing one.[3] Amendments to PACE introduced by the Criminal Justice and Public Order Act 1994 (CJPOA 1994), together with substantial changes to the Codes of Guidance under the Act (see below), tilted the balance towards the police at the cost of the protection of more vulnerable defendants including those vulnerable through youth.

3.02 Prior to the 1990 revision of the codes, there were no special provisions relating to young offenders in regard to the investigation of crime. Juveniles were treated as adults at the earlier stage of the process, despite the fact that young people, and especially black young people, are likely in many areas to be subject to rather more intensive attention from the police than adults.[4] The first Home Office Circular on PACE[5] issued to the police and the courts gave the following guidance:—

> "In any situation where a constable exercises a power of search under this Act, the co-operation of the citizen should not be taken as implying consent, and the exercise of the power should be noted in the appropriate record. Whilst it is legitimate to invite co-operation from the public in circumstances where there is no power to require it, the subject of a voluntary search must properly understand the position and not be left with the impression that a power is being exercised."

3.03 However, as Zander commented, "there are too many situations where the concept of consensual search has been used as a way of avoiding the main thrust

---

[1] s.16 of the CYPA, 1933.
[2] Code A, revised 1999 and Codes B–E, revised 1995.
[3] A. Sanders, "From Suspect to Trial" in *The Oxford Handbook of Criminology* (M. Maguire, R. Morgan and R. Reiner ed., 2nd ed., Oxford University Press, Oxford, 1997).
[4] *Race and the Criminal Justice System* (Home Office, London, 1994)
[5] HOC 88/1985.

of the safeguards."[6] As a result of early concerns that police officers were able to avoid the restrictions in Code A regarding searches by classifying too many as "voluntary", the 1991 revision provided additional guidance as regards all suspects. The most recent version states that in circumstances in which he is searching a person on a voluntary basis, "an officer should always make it clear that he is seeking the consent of the person concerned to the search being carried out by telling the person that he need not consent and that without his consent he will not be searched".[7] Improper action in this respect will invalidate a voluntary search. The Code goes on to make it clear that "Juveniles, persons suffering from a mental handicap and others who appear not to be capable of giving an informed consent should not be subject to a voluntary search".[8]

3.04   The provisions of sections 76 to 78 of PACE 1984 reflect the extent to which the questioning of suspects and the making of admissions are of such importance in the detection of crime and the conviction of offenders that detailed rules are needed to ensure that questioning is fairly conducted and recorded. Where a police officer conducts an interview with a person suspected of an offence he must administer the caution, the original wording of which was substantially amended in 1995 to reflect the end to the right to silence—

> "You do not have to say anything. But it may harm your defence if you do not mention when questioned something which you later rely on in court. Anything you do say may be given in evidence."[9]

3.05   If a juvenile is cautioned in the absence of the appropriate adult, the caution must be repeated in the adult's presence.[10] Although the rules appear clear, as Bevan and Lidstone suggest, in many circumstances the recognised stages of police investigation—suspicion, caution, questioning and arrest—do not necessarily follow that sequence.[11] More importantly the borderline between questioning that follows suspicion which requires a caution, and questioning directed at preliminary matters such as discovering identity or whereabouts, is frequently blurred. In their study a decade ago, Evans and Ferguson observed that information obtained from informal questioning of juveniles, for instance in the car travelling to the police station, may subsequently be used as the basis for formal interrogations.[12]

Interviews at school

3.06   Juveniles may only be interviewed at school "in exceptional circumstances" and then only where the principal or his nominee agrees,[13] and in the presence of his parent or guardian or an appropriate adult.[14] Every effort should be made to notify the juvenile's parents or an appropriate adult. Failing that, the head teacher or a nominee may act as appropriate adult provided the juvenile is not suspected of an offence against the educational establishment.

---

[6] M. Zander, *Police and Criminal Evidence Act 1984* (3rd ed., Sweet and Maxwell, London, 1995), p. 8.
[7] PACE Notes of Guidance, Code A 1D(b).
[8] *ibid.*, 1E.
[9] *ibid.*, Code C, 10.4.
[10] *ibid.*, 10.6.
[11] V. Bevan and K. Lidstone, *The Investigation of Crime: A Guide to Police Powers* (2nd ed., Butterworths, London, 1996).
[12] R. Evans, and T. Ferguson, *Comparing Different Juvenile Cautioning Systems in One Police Force Area* (1991) Report to the Home Office Research and Planning Unit.
[13] PACE Code C, 11.15.
[14] See para. 3.26 below.

Arrest

3.07 Police powers of arrest are set out in Part III of PACE. Young people are only treated differently from adults to the extent that Code C provides that they should preferably not be arrested at school unless this is unavoidable, in which case the head teacher or the head teacher's nominee must be informed.[15]

Children under ten years

3.08 A child under the age of ten years is below the age of criminal responsibility and should not be arrested.[16] Where an arrest of a child who later turns out to be below that age takes place, the child should be released as soon as it becomes apparent that they are under ten years.[17]

JUVENILES AT THE POLICE STATION

General

3.09 The provisions of Part IV of PACE, which is concerned with detention at a police station following arrest, and of Part V on the questioning and treatment of persons by the police, apply to juveniles in the same way as to adults, with additional safeguards. The need for a range of additional safeguards for juveniles and other vulnerable groups is set out with great clarity in the Code of Practice for the Detention, Treatment and Questioning of Persons by Police Officers issued under PACE—

> "It is important to bear in mind that, although juveniles or persons who are mentally ill or handicapped are often capable of providing reliable evidence, they may, without knowing or wishing to do so, be particularly prone in certain circumstances to provide information which is unreliable, misleading or incriminating. Special care should therefore always be exercised in questioning such a person and the appropriate adult should be involved if there is any doubt about a person's age, mental state or capacity. Because of the risk of unreliable evidence it is also important to obtain corroboration of any facts admitted whenever possible."[18]

The consequences of failure to exercise such care in an interview, which under the Code of Practice is not limited to questioning in a police station, were confirmed in the case of *Delroy Fogah*[18a], in which a 16-year-old boy suspected of robbery was asked a series of questions in the street by police officers during which he confessed to involvement in the robbery. At the Crown Court the judge, following the decision in *Absolam*,[18b] held that the questions amounted to an interview and, as the interview took place in the absence of an appropriate adult, the confession could not be admitted.

Arrested juveniles

3.10 For the purposes of Part IV of PACE which provides the statutory framework for detention by the police, both as regards condition and duration, an

[15] PACE Code C, Notes for Guidance, 11C.
[16] s.16 of the CYPA, 1963.
[17] PACE, s.34(2), and see para. 3.12 below.
[18] PACE, Code C, Notes for Guidance, 11B.
[18a] [1989] Crim. L.R. 141.
[18b] [1988] 88 Cr.App.R. 332.

"arrested juvenile" means "a person arrested with or without a warrant who appears to be under the age of 17".[19] In this chapter all references to juveniles will be to 10 to 16-year-olds except where reference is made to the separation of 17-year-olds from adult defendants.

A person is in police detention for the purposes of the Police and Criminal Evidence Act (s.118(2)) if—

"(a) he has been taken to a police station after being arrested for an offence . . . or

(b) he is arrested at a police station after attending voluntarily at the station or accompanying a constable to it . . ."

The custody officer

3.11   The Act requires that detention of arrested persons must be at a police station designated by a chief officer to be used for the purpose of detaining arrested persons (s.35) and that each designated station must have a custody officer, preferably of the rank of sergeant or above, whose role is clearly separated from that of the investigating officer (s.36(5)). The duties of the custody officer are to ensure that all persons in detention at police stations are treated in accordance with the Act and the Codes of Practice issued under the Act, and that all matters required to be recorded are recorded in the custody record which must be opened when the arrested person appears before the custody officer. It is the custody officer therefore who has responsibility for ensuring that juveniles detained at police stations are treated in accordance with the provisions of the Act and the Codes of Practice, which apply to all detained persons and that the additional safeguards in that and other legislation which apply only to juveniles are met.

Police protection under the Children Act 1989

3.12   When the person arrested is a child the custody officer has to determine whether the child is aged ten years and therefore capable of criminal responsibility.[20] If a child under ten is mistakenly arrested and brought to a police station the custody officer must normally arrange for the child's immediate release.[21] If, however, the circumstances are such that "a constable has reasonable cause to believe that the child would otherwise be likely to suffer significant harm" the child who for the purposes of the Children Act 1989 (CA 1989) is a person under the age of 18[22] may be taken into police protection.[23]

The child may only be kept in police protection for a maximum of 72 hours, and as soon as is possible the constable concerned must ensure that the case is inquired into by the officer designated by the chief officer of the police area. Once that officer has completed his or her inquiry the child must be released from police protection unless there is still reasonable cause to believe that he or she would be likely to suffer significant harm if released.[24]

3.13   As well as arranging for the designated officer to make inquiries, the constable who has taken a child into police protection must inform the parents and

---

[19] s.37(15).
[20] s.16 of the CYPA, 1963.
[21] PACE, s.34(2).
[22] s.105 of the CA 1989.
[23] *ibid.*, s.46(1).
[24] *ibid.*, s.46(3) and (5).

other people specified in section 46(4), the local authority in whose area the child was found, and that in which the child normally resides, and the child, of the steps that have been and are proposed to be taken. In the case of the child an explanation must also be given of the reasons for the police actions and such efforts as are reasonably practicable must be taken to discover the child's wishes and feelings. The constable must also ensure that, if not released, the child is moved to accommodation provided by the local authority.[25]

The designated officer, as well as inquiring into the case, has a number of other responsibilities. In appropriate cases, where protection is needed for longer than the 72 hours of police protection, this could include applying, on behalf of the local authority for the area in which the child is normally resident, for an emergency protection order under section 44, although this will more usually by done by the local authority.

Guidance under the CA 1989 emphasises the need for interagency liaison between the police and local authorities in order to ensure "that no child taken into police protection need be accommodated in a police station, and that his reception into local authority accommodation is achieved with the minimum of trauma".[26]

Release or detention

3.14   Apart from the need to discharge a child who is below the age of criminal responsibility or possibly to take him or her into police protection under the CA 1989, the custody officer has to decide whether any person detained at a designated police station should be charged or released, or detained, with or without charge. Under PACE, if the person is charged he must be released with or without bail, unless.

   (i) "his name or address cannot be ascertained or the custody officer has reasonable grounds for doubting whether a name or address furnished by him as his name or address is his real name and address;

  (ii) the custody officer has reasonable grounds for believing that the detection of the person arrested is necessary for his own protection or to prevent him from causing physical injury to any other person or from causing loss of or damage to property, or

 (iii) the custody officer has reasonable grounds for believing that the person arrested will fail to appear in court to answer to bail or that his detention is necessary to prevent him from interfering with the administration of justice or with the investigation of offences or of a particular offence;"[27]

or, in addition, in the case of a juvenile only:

"the custody officer has reasonable grounds for believing that he ought to be detained in his own interests."[28]

3.15   The most often quoted illustration of the sort of circumstances in which it was envisaged that a juvenile might need to be detained in his own interests is that given in the Committee stage debate on PACE.[29] It was suggested that where a

---

[25] s.43(3)(f) of the CA 1989.
[26] Children Act 1989, Guidance and Regulations (Department of Health, 1990) Vol. 1, para. 4.77.
[27] PACE, s.38(1)(a).
[28] *ibid.*, 38(1)(b)(ii).
[29] Hansard, Committee E, February 14, 1984, col. 1127.

runaway juvenile boarding a train in the North of England without paying his fare was arrested and charged in London, and his parents could not collect him until the next day, it would not be in his interests to release him on to the streets overnight.

A person, adult or juvenile in police detention must be immediately released if at any time the custody officer becomes aware that the grounds for detention of the person have ceased to apply and there are no other grounds justifying continued detention.[29a]

If the custody officer decides that he has sufficient evidence to charge a person with the offence for which he was arrested, the person must be charged, either on bail or without bail (s.37(7)). If at the time of release no decision has been taken as to whether the person is to be prosecuted or not, the custody officer must inform him (s.37(8)). This will be the case with most juveniles, since the decision as to whether the offender will be charged or issued with a reprimand or warning may not be made immediately.[30]

Juveniles arrested on a warrant

3.16   Juveniles arrested on a warrant must not be released

". . . unless the juvenile or a parent or guardian (with or without sureties) enters into a recognisance for such amount as the custody officer at the police station where he is detained considers will secure his attendance at the hearing of the charge, and the recognisance entered into in pursuance of this section may, if the custody officer thinks fit, be conditioned for the attendance of the parent or guardian at the hearing in addition to the child or young person." (C YPA 1969, s.29, substituted by PACE 1984, Sched. 6, para. 19(b)).

Detention in custody before charge

3.17   Under section 37 of PACE 1984 the custody officer who does not have sufficient evidence to charge the person before him may only authorise the detention of the arrested person if he has reasonable grounds to believe that detention without charge is necessary "to secure or preserve evidence relating to an offence for which he is under arrest or to obtain such evidence by questioning him".[31] Where a custody officer authorises such detention he must make a written record of the grounds for the detention, and, unless one of the exceptions set out in section 37(6) apply, inform the arrested person of the grounds for his detention and of his rights. These rights are—

(1)   to have someone informed of his detention;

(2)   to consult a solicitor; and

(3)   to consult the Code of Practice governing detention or any other Code of Practice.[32]

3.18   In addition to oral information the detained person, whether adult or juvenile, must be given a written statement of these three rights and sign an acknowledgement on the custody record.

[29a] PACE, s.34(2).
[30] s.65. of the CDA 1998. Also see Chap. 4.
[31] *ibid.*, s.37(2).
[32] PACE Code C, paras 3.1–3.4.

1. The right of an arrested person to have someone informed

3.19 It is the right of anyone to have a friend or relative or other person who is known to him or who is likely to take an interest in his welfare told that he has been arrested and is being detained at a police station.[33] Children and young people up to the age of 16 who have been arrested or detained under the prevention of terrorism provisions have additional rights under section 57 of PACE 1984 which amended section 34(2) of the CYPA 1933. The 1933 Act provided that where a child or young person has been arrested reasonable steps must be taken to inform his parent or guardian. Section 57, and the accompanying Codes and notes of Guidance, re-affirm and extend the provision in relation to the detention and interrogation of children and young people by requiring that—

"(2) Where a child or young person is in police detention, such steps as are practicable shall be taken to ascertain the identity of a person responsible for his welfare.

(3) If it is practicable to ascertain the identity of a person responsible for the welfare of the child or young person, that person shall be informed, unless it is not practicable to do so—

(a) that the child or young person has been arrested;
(b) why he has been arrested; and
(c) where he is being detained."

Subsection (4) requires such information to be given "as soon as it is practicable to do so."

3.20 The person to be informed is widely defined to include the child's parent or guardian or "any other person who has for the time being assumed responsibility for his welfare". This definition is further elaborated in Code C, 3.7—

"If the person is a juvenile, the custody officer must, if it is practicable, ascertain the identity of a person responsible for his welfare. That person may be his parent or guardian (or if he is in care, the care authority or voluntary organisation) or any other person who has for the time being, assumed responsibility for his welfare. That person must be informed as soon as practicable that the juvenile has been arrested, why he has been arrested and where he is detained. This right is in addition to the juvenile's right in section 5 of the code not to be held incommunicado."

The person informed of the juvenile's arrest will generally also act as an "appropriate adult" for the purposes of Code C (see paras 3.25–3.37 below) although this will not always be the case.

Children in care or under supervision

3.21 Note 3C of the Code further provides—

"If the juvenile is in the care of a local authority or voluntary organisation but is living with his parents or other adults responsible for his welfare then, although there is no legal obligation on the police to inform them, they as well

---

[33] PACE, s.56(1).

as the local authority or organisation should normally be contacted unless suspected of involvement in the offence concerned. Even if a juvenile in care is not living with his parents, consideration should be given to informing them as well."

Compliance with these requirements, apart from representing good practice, might be seen as more important now than at the time the note of guidance was drafted since, following implementation of the Children Act 1989, a care order gives parental responsibility to a local authority together with, rather than instead of, the parents.[34]

Where a juvenile is known to be the subject of a supervision order reasonable steps must be taken to notify the person supervising him.[35]

2. The right to legal advice

3.22   As Cape suggests, although the traditional view has been that the trial "is the crowning glory of the adversarial criminal justice system", most cases are in fact won or lost at the police station, and it is here, where "Confessions, sometimes false confessions, are obtained from suspects, evidence is gathered, deals are done, which will inevitably influence the course of subsequent events" that the advice of a skilled lawyer is essential.[36] Under section 58 PACE 1984 a person who is in police detention is entitled, if he so requests, to consult a solicitor privately at any time, and as soon as is practicable unless any of the exceptions set out in section 58(8) apply, and in any event within 36 hours of being detained. The duty solicitor scheme originally established under section 59 PACE 1984 which now comes under the Legal Aid Board Duty Solicitor Arrangements 1994 is intended to provide free legal advice round the clock on request to anyone held at a police station.[37]

Research undertaken prior to the revision of the PACE codes of practice in 1995 suggested that all suspects, but particularly juveniles, were disadvantaged by police practices in regard to the provision of legal advice.[38] Substantial revision of the codes followed recommendations in the 1993 report of the Royal Commission on Criminal Justice[39] and the removal of the so-called "right to silence" under the CJPOA 1994.[40] Further research was undertaken by the Home Office Research Unit after implementation of the revised codes. The researchers found that the provision of legal advice to both adults and juveniles had risen significantly, although 60 per cent of all suspects did not request legal advice and there were continuing widespread variations between police stations[41]. It was also observed that very few custody officers complied with the requirement in the revised code that they should ask for reasons for a refusal of legal advice and record the answer.[42]

3.23   Where the appropriate adult is not present when the custody officer informs a juvenile of the reasons for his detention and of his right to legal advice,

---

[34] s.33.
[35] Code C, 3.8.
[36] E. Cape, *Defending Suspects at Police Stations* (Legal Action Group, London, 1993) at p. 1.
[37] Legal Advice and Assistance at Police Stations (Remuneration) Regulations 1989 (as amended).
[38] D. Brown, T. Ellis and K. Larcombe, *Changing the Code: Police detention under the revised codes of practice*, Home Office Research Study No. 129 (HMSO, London, 1992); D. Dixon "Juvenile Suspects and the Police and Criminal Evidence Act" in *Children and the Law: Essays in Honour of Professor H.K. Bevan* (D. Freestone ed., Hull University Press, Hull, 1990).
[39] HMSO, London.
[40] ss.34–37.
[41] T. Bucke and D. Brown, *In police custody: police powers and suspects' rights under the revised PACE codes of practice*, Home Office Research Study No. 174 (Home Office, London, 1997).
[42] Code C, para. 6.5.

that information should be repeated in the presence of the detained person when the person acting as appropriate adult arrives.[43] However it is clearly intended that the right of the appropriate adult to request a solicitor is an additional one that exists to protect the rights of juveniles or others at risk, who may not understand details of their right to legal advice when it is initially given to them by the custody officer, rather than the adult being the arbiter of whether or not the juvenile gets legal advice.

3. The right to consult the codes

3.24 Research evidence suggests that very few detainees ask to see the Codes, and that those who do are put off by their length and complexity.[43a]

THE "APPROPRIATE ADULT"

3.25 The Royal Commission on Criminal Procedure which reported in 1981 felt it essential that a juvenile being interviewed should have an adult, other than the police present, and that—

> "the adult should be someone in whom the juvenile has confidence, his parents or guardian, or someone else he knows, a social worker or school teacher. Juveniles may not as readily understand the significance of questions or of what they themselves say and are likely to be more suggestible than adults. They may need the support of an adult presence; of someone to befriend, advise and assist them to make their decisions."[44]

The requirements

3.26 The requirement that when the police wish to interview an arrested juvenile, whether at a police station or not, they may only do so in the presence of an appropriate adult, was introduced as a result of this recommendation.[45] An exception may only be made if the circumstances are such as to pose an immediate danger to persons or serious harm to property.[46] The courts have interpreted the requirement strictly and have excluded admissions made in the absence of an appropriate adult as being unreliable under section 76 of the Act.[47] Research evidence suggests that urgent interviews without an appropriate adult are rarely undertaken with juveniles; in 1992 Brown and his colleagues only reported two cases in a sample of 1000.[48]

Appropriate adults

3.27 The "appropriate adult" is defined in the first part of Code C—

> "1.7 In this Code "the appropriate adult" means—

---

[43] Code C, para. 3.11.
[43a] Brown *et al.* (1992), *op. cit.*, n.38.
[44] Cmnd. 8092, HMSO, at para. 4.103.
[45] PACE, Code C, 3.9 and notes for guidance 3C.
[46] *ibid.*, Code C, 11.14 and Annex C.
[47] Absolam (1988) 88 Cr.App.R. 332; *Delroy Fogah* [1989] Crim.L.R. 141.
[48] *op. cit.*

(a) in the case of a juvenile:

> (i) his parent or guardian (or if he is in care, the care authority or voluntary organisation). The term "in care" is used in this code to cover all cases in which a juvenile is "looked after" by a local authority under the terms of the Children Act 1989;
> (ii) a social worker; or
> (iii) failing either of the above, another responsible adult aged 18 or over who is not a police officer or employed by the police."

3.28 Although the child's parent or guardian should normally be the "appropriate adult" the Notes for Guidance to section 1 of Code C detail circumstances in which someone else should take on the role—

> "A person, including a parent or guardian, should not be an appropriate adult if he is suspected of involvement in the offence in question, is the victim, is a witness, is involved in the investigation or has received admissions prior to attending to act as the appropriate adult. If the parent of a juvenile is estranged from the juvenile, he should not be asked to act as the appropriate adult if the juvenile expressly and specifically objects to his presence." (Note 1C)

3.29 Similarly if a child in care admits an offence to a social worker, it is suggested that—

> "If a juvenile admits an offence to or in the presence of a social worker other than during the time that the social worker is acting as the appropriate adult for that juvenile, another social worker should be the appropriate adult in the interests of fairness." (Note 1D)

Problems arise for police custody officers when parents refuse to attend or juveniles express extreme reluctance to have their parents or guardians notified. In such circumstances formerly a local authority social worker, if one was available, or another adult nominated by the juvenile would have been sought. The Code specifically provides that a solicitor or lay visitor who is present in a professional capacity may not act as appropriate adult (Note 1F), though there is some doubt as to whether the prohibition extends to unqualified employees of law firms.

Under the CDA 1998, the provision of appropriate adults is listed as one of the statutory tasks of local authority youth justice services to be carried out by YOTs.[49] The recruitment and training of volunteers to replace social workers as appropriate adults was a recommendation of the Audit Commission based on the perception of some local authority youth justice workers spending as much as 10 per cent of their time on appropriate adult duties.[50]

The role of the appropriate adult

3.30 The appropriate adult has an important role to play—

> "He should be informed that he is not expected to act simply as an observer; and also that the purposes of his presence are, first, to advise the person being

---

[49] s.38(4)(a).
[50] *Misspent Youth* (Audit Commission, London, 1996).

questioned and to observe whether or not the interview is being conducted properly and fairly, and, secondly, to facilitate communication with the person being interviewed."[51]

The custody officer must explain the role of the appropriate adult to the juvenile and inform him that he has the right to consult privately with the adult at any time.[52]

The role of appropriate adult is, therefore, the potentially difficult one of providing support whilst not interfering with the proper conduct of the interrogation. It is very much in the juvenile's interests that the adult should be both sympathetic to, and understanding of, the young person's predicament and fulfil the role positively. In practice both these conditions, that of suitability to act, and competence in performing the role of appropriate adult, proved problematic in the past. The responsibility of YOTs for the provision of suitably trained people to act as appropriate adults, if taken seriously could lead to young offenders being better served than in the past, though there will still be a preference for a parent fulfilling the role.

Competence to act

3.31 There is a presumption that a parent will be competent to act, but this presumption does not extend to parents who are estranged from their children.[53] Following the decision in *D.P.P. v. Blake*[53a] the PACE Code was altered to endorse this point. Nor can a parent who has not the mental capacity to appreciate the gravity of the situation or the role he or she is expected to fulfil be properly regarded as an "appropriate adult" regardless of whether the police were aware of this at the time. In *Morse*[54] it was held that empathy with the interviewee was not enough. Medical evidence, given on appeal subsequent to conviction based on evidence of several admissions made by a 16-year-old at an interview at which the defendant's father acted as "appropriate adult", showed that the father had an IQ of between 60 and 70, was virtually illiterate and probably incapable of understanding the gravity of his son's situation. There was no question of any impropriety on the part of the police.

3.32 The test, it is suggested in commentary on the case, "being whether the evidence would have such an adverse effect on the fairness of the proceedings that it ought not to be admitted". This test was applied in *W. and Another*[55] when the Court of Appeal held that a mentally ill mother who would, had she been suspected of an offence, have herself been entitled to the assistance of an appropriate person, could nonetheless act as appropriate adult for her 13-year-old daughter. The trial judge formed the view that, since he was satisfied that the interview had been conducted fairly and was not overly long, the mother was capable of giving her daughter appropriate support despite her illness.

Effectiveness in the role of "appropriate adult"

3.33 Even if they are competent to act, experience would suggest that in the past, in the role of appropriate adult, both parents and social workers very often,

[51] PACE, Code C, 11.16
[52] *ibid.*, 3.12.
[53] *ibid.*, Notes for Guidance 1C.
[53a] [1989] 1 W.L.R. 432
[54] [1991] Crim. L.R. 195.
[55] [1994] Crim. L.R. 130.

for a variety of reasons, fail to provide effective support. Evans[56] in research into police interviews with juveniles, funded by the Royal Commission on Criminal Justice, found that approximately three quarters of all parents and other appropriate adults who attended interviews made "no contribution whatsoever" and that when they did contribute parents "were as likely to be unsupportive . . . as supportive of their children".[57] As Dixon suggests—

> "Like suspects some parents can be disorientated, scared and compliant to police requests. It should not be forgotten that, in the Confait investigation, the inaccurate confessions were countersigned by some of the suspects' parents (although they were not present at the original interrogations)."[58]

3.34 The tape recording of interviews should militate against overtly "hectoring" questioning, but there is reason to believe that many parents will not act in a supportive way, either because they are overwhelmed by the experience, or because the see their role as being "to assist the police in extracting 'the truth' from their children, often by means which police officers could not use in their presence".[59] If parents go too far in putting pressure on their children the evidence could be excluded as having been obtained "by oppression" under PACE 1984, s.76(2), or as being "unfair" under section 78. However, admonitions by parents to their children to "tell the truth", even forcefully expressed, do not provide grounds for excluding admissions, providing that the police questioning was fair.[60] Nothing appeared to have changed when Bucke and Brown undertook their study in 1995. They observed more than 30 per cent of family members to be distressed or hostile towards suspects, and a further 30 per cent to be neutral, a term that covers instances of profound indifference.[61]

3.35 Juveniles may not in the past have got a much better deal from having a social worker to act as their appropriate adult.[62] Social workers got little training for the role and many felt threatened by the police culture which they perceived as hostile. They were observed by researchers to be often as unfamiliar as parents with the boundaries of what is acceptable in regard to the police questioning of suspects.[63] As Evans suggested, the fact that professionals acting as appropriate adults—

> "are either not aware of, ignore or are unable or unwilling to assert themselves in order to ensure that the PACE code of practice which emphasise the potential vulnerability of juveniles is implemented",

may have allowed the police to "exploit the interrogative susceptibility of suspects".[64]

3.36 In her review of practical problems identified in implementing the appropriate adult scheme in practice, Hodgson,[65] drawing on a wide spectrum of

[56] R. Evans, *The Conduct of Police Interviews with Juveniles*, Research Study No. 8, Royal Commission on Criminal Justice (HMSO, London, 1993).
[57] *ibid.*, at 39.
[58] D. Dixon "Juvenile Suspects and the Police and Criminal evidence Act" in *Children and the Law: essays in Honour of Professor H. K. Bevan* (D. Freestone ed., Hull University Press, Hull, 1990 at 119.
[59] *ibid.*, at 118; Evans (1993) *op. cit.*
[60] *Jefferson, Skerritt, Readman and Keogh* (1993) 99 Cr.App.R. 13.
[61] *op. cit.*, Chap. 2.
[62] T. Thomas, *The Police and Social Workers* (2nd ed., Arena, Aldershot, 1994).
[63] Sanders, *et al.* 1989, *op. cit.*
[64] Evans, (1993) *ibid.*
[65] J. Hodgson "Vulnerable Suspects and the Appropriate Adult" [1997] Crim. L. R. 785.

studies, concluded that although the scheme provides a potentially important safeguard for vulnerable suspects, its value has not yet been realised.

In contrast, by 1995, Bucke and Brown observed considerably more effective practice by social workers acting as appropriate adults, with the majority being calm and supportive towards the suspect and the police in a way that contrasted strongly with the behaviour of family members.[66]

It would be encouraging to think that it was the negative evidence regarding social worker's abilities to provide proper support for young people when being interviewed by the police that led to, the provision of "appropriate adult" services being identified in the white paper *No More Excuses* as one of the responsibilities of the new statutory Youth Offending Teams.[67] It seems more likely that the very substantial savings that the Audit Commission identified as achievable through the recruiting and training of volunteers to undertake the role instead of social workers may have driven the new policy. There is no reason why, with a proper understanding of their role and adequate training and support, volunteers should not provide the necessary protection.

The appropriate adult as a "youth justice service"

3.37 National standards require YOT managers to—

"ensure that appropriate adults can be provided to police stations in their area, whether or not the arrested child or young person lives in their area. They must ensure that staff or YOT accredited volunteers who act as appropriate adults are trained and supported in this role and that they are provided with a copy of the PACE codes of practice".[68]

It is the joint responsibility of the police and YOT managers to ensure that when an appropriate adult is requested they attend the police station at an agreed time.[69]

3.38 National standards place additional responsibilities on appropriate adults which go considerably further than the traditional role in the police station.

"When a young person has been charged, if his or her parents, primary carer or other adult relative were not present at the interview with the police, the appropriate adult must try to contact them within 24 hours or prior to court, whichever is sooner to inform them and offer information about the court appearance. They must remind them that the young person's failure to attend court would be an offence."[70]

YOT managers appear to have made a variety of arrangements for recruiting and training volunteers to take on the role of appropriate adults.

ACCOMMODATION OF DETAINED JUVENILES

3.39 The Code provides that juveniles should not be detained in police cells

"unless no other secure accommodation is available and the custody officer considers that it is not practicable to supervise him if he is not placed in a cell

---

[66] Bucke and Brown (1997), *op. cit.*, Chap. 2.
[67] *op. cit.*, para 8.10.
[68] *National Standards for Youth Justice, op. cit.*, para. 2.1.
[69] *ibid.*, para. 2.3.
[70] *ibid.*, para. 2.4.

or the custody officer considers that a cell provides more comfortable accommodation than other secure accommodation in the police station",

and that a juvenile may not be placed in a cell with a detained adult (Code C, 8.8). If he is placed in a cell, the reasons must be recorded (8.12). Guidance provides that whenever possible "juveniles and other people at risk should be visited more frequently" than other people.[71]

Time limits on detention without charge

3.40 The rules regarding time limits on detention without charge and reviews of detention under Part IV of PACE 1984 apply to juveniles in the same way as to adult detainees, except that when an arrested juvenile is transferred to local authority accommodation the custody officer ceases to be subject to the duty to ensure that all the provisions of the Act and the codes set out in section 39(1) are complied with in regard to him (s.39(4)).

The maximum period for which an arrested person can ordinarily be detained at a police station without charge is 24 hours; detention beyond 24 hours is only permissible in respect of "serious arrestable offences" (PACE, s.41). A superintendent or more senior police officer may authorise continued detention for up to 12 hours beyond the 24 hours if there are reasonable grounds for believing that such detention is necessary to secure or preserve evidence, or obtain it by questioning, and if certain other conditions are satisfied. A magistrates' court may issue a warrant for up to a further 36 hours on the same criteria, and that may be extended for a further 36 hours up to an absolute maximum of 96 hours. A detainee must appear before the magistrates on the applications for warrants for further detention and may be legally represented (s.43).

IDENTIFICATION

3.41 The provisions of PACE 1984, Part V apply to juveniles in the same way as to adults with additional protection in the form of consents by parents or guardians.

Fingerprints

3.42 The taking of fingerprints requires consent to be given by the appropriate person, that is to say the person themselves if they are aged 17 years or over, the young person and parent or guardian for 14–16-year-olds and only the parent and guardian for a child aged 10–13 (Code D, 1.11). Where a juvenile is in the care of the local authority or a voluntary agency a representative of the authority or agency may consent as parent or guardian (Note of Guidance, 1E). The police must give reasons for taking the prints and inform the suspect that they will be destroyed in certain circumstances (see below). Where fingerprints are taken at a police station, consent must be given in writing (3.1) and the reason for taking the fingerprints must be entered on the custody record.

Fingerprints may be taken without the appropriate person's consent either after charge for a recordable offence, or if a police officer of at least the rank of superintendent authorises the taking of fingerprints on the grounds there are

---

[71] PACE Code C, Notes for Guidance, 8A.

reasonable grounds for suspecting the involvement of the person whose fingerprints are to be taken in a criminal offence, and for believing that his fingerprints will tend to confirm or disprove the persons involvement (para. 3.2). Where fingerprints are taken without consent, the person must be told the reason why they are being taken and this must be recorded in the custody book under PACE, s.63. The circumstances in which such authorisation can be given were very considerably widened firstly by CJPOA 1994 and most recently by the Criminal Evidence (Amendment) Act 1997 (CEAA 1997). The revised PACE sections 63 and 63A can be found in Schedule 2 of that Act.

3.43 Section 27(1) of PACE provides that a convicted person whose fingerprints were not taken in the course of investigations or since the conviction may be ordered to attend at a police station in order that prints may be taken. Under CDA 1998,[72] this provision was extended to include young offenders given a reprimand or warning under section 65 of that Act.[73]

Section 63A of PACE as amended by CEAA 1997, extends the use that can be made of fingerprints or other samples taken for another purpose.

Body samples

3.44 The Act, amended by Part IV of the CJPOA 1994, distinguishes between two kinds of body samples. Intimate samples, which are dealt with in section 62, include blood, semen or other tissue fluid, urine, saliva, pubic hair, a swab taken from a person's body orifice other than the mouth, and, following the recommendation of the 1993 Royal Commission on Criminal Justice, dental impressions. Non-intimate samples include samples, other than intimate samples, or a foot print or print of any other part of the body except a hand, and "a swab taken from any part of a person's body including the mouth but not any other body orifice" (s.65(3)c).

Intimate samples

3.45 The taking of intimate samples, which apart from urine and saliva can only be performed by a doctor or dentist, requires the permission of an officer of or above the rank of superintendent. That authority can only be given if the offence in question is a recordable offence, and there are reasonable grounds for believing that the sample will tend to confirm or disprove the suspect's involvement in the offence (s.62).

The taking of an intimate samples requires the written consent of the suspect. The same consent rules as for the taking of fingerprints apply to the taking of intimate samples from juveniles; consent must be given by a parent or guardian for a child aged 10 to 13 years and by both the young person and a parent or guardian for those aged 14 to 16. When consent is being invited an officer must tell the suspect that the required authorisation has been given, and the nature of the offence in which it is suspected that he or she is involved.

3.46 Although the taking of an intimate sample requires consent and a reminder to the person to be searched of his entitlement to legal advice, there is no requirement to advise the suspect that he may refuse consent, nor that the sample cannot be taken without consent. Refusing consent is not neutral, in that under the PACE 1984 s.62(10) the court may "draw such inferences from refusal as appear

---

[72] Schedule 8, para. 61.
[73] PACE, s.27(4A).

proper; and the refusal may, on the basis of such inferences, be treated as, or as capable of amounting to, corroboration of any evidence against the person in relation to which the refusal is material".

The provisions of the subsection clearly diminish the protection of the requirement for consent, however Code D, para. 5.2 provides some protection with the requirement that before consent to the taking of an intimate sample is sought the person must be warned that a refusal may be treated as corroborating relevant prosecution evidence.

The PACE provisions on intimate samples do not apply to samples taken under sections 5 to 12 of the Road Traffic Act 1972 (drink/driving provisions).

Non-intimate samples

3.47   These normally require consent, with the same provisos for juveniles as with intimate samples. However, an officer of the rank of superintendent or above can authorise the compulsory taking of non intimate samples under PACE, s.63. The circumstances in which such authorisation can be given were very considerably widened firstly by CJPOA 1994 and most recently by the CE(A)A 1997. The revised sections 63 and 63A can be found in Schedule 2 to that Act.

Identification by witnesses

3.48   The Code of Practice on Identification (Code D) provides four alternative methods that can be used in disputed identification cases: an identification parade, a group identification, a video film, and a confrontation. The participation of a juvenile in any of these requires the presence of an appropriate adult (Code D, 1.14) and requirements regarding the suspect's consent are as set out above. A full account of the procedures police have to follow in regard to disputed identification are described and discussed elsewhere.[74]

Charging of Detained Juveniles

3.49   Under paragraph 16 of Code C when it is decided that there is sufficient evidence to charge a juvenile, and that there is sufficient evidence for a prosecution to succeed, and that person has said all that he wishes to say about the offence, he should be brought without delay before the custody officer in the presence of the appropriate adult. The custody officer must administer the caution before either charging the juvenile or informing him that he may be prosecuted. The mandatory notice with the particulars of any offence with which the juvenile is charged must be given to the appropriate adult as well as to the juvenile.

After a person has been charged or informed that he or she may be prosecuted for an offence, no further questions may be put unless they are necessary—

> "for the purpose of preventing or minimising harm or loss to some other person or to the public or for clearing up any ambiguity in a previous answer or statement, or where it is in the interests of justice that the person should have put to him and have an opportunity to comment on information concerning the offence which has come to light since he was charged or informed that he might be prosecuted. Before any such questions are put to

---

[74] Bevan and Lidstone, *op. cit.*, 1996 at 379–390.

him, he shall be warned that he does not have to say anything but anything he does say may be given in evidence and reminded of his right to legal advice . . ." (Code C, 16.5).

Detention of juveniles after charge

3.50 When a juvenile is charged he must be released unless the conditions for refusing to release an adult with or without bail are met (PACE, s.38(1)(a)). If a juvenile is detained he must be brought before a magistrates' court in accordance with the provisions of section 46(1), as soon as is practicable and in any event, in almost all circumstances, not later than the day following charge.

Section 38 presumes that all detained juveniles will be accommodated by the local authority—

"(6) Where a custody officer authorises an arrested juvenile to be kept in police detention under subsection (1) above, the custody officer shall, unless he certifies—

(a) that, by reason of such circumstances as are specified in the certificate, it is impracticable for him to do so, or
(b) in the case of an arrested juvenile who has attained the age of 12 years, that no secure accommodation is available and that keeping him in other local authority accommodation would not be adequate to protect the public from serious harm from him,

secure that the arrested juvenile is moved to local authority' accommodation".

3.51 Section 38(6) as amended by the CJA 1991, s.59 and the CJPOA 1994, s.24, provides the only circumstances in which the police can keep a 12–16-year-old in police custody. The revised Code provides—

"Where a juvenile is charged with an offence and the custody officer authorises his continued detention he must try to make arrangements for the juvenile to be taken into care of a local authority to be detained pending appearance in court unless he certifies that it is impracticable to do so, or, in the case of a juvenile of at least 12 years of age, no secure accommodation is available and there is a risk to the public of serious harm from that juvenile . . ." (16.6)

To reinforce this the Notes for Guidance (16B) state—

"Except as provided in 16.6 above, neither a juvenile's behaviour nor the nature of the offence with which he is charged provides grounds for the custody officer to decide that it is impracticable to seek to arrange for his transfer to the care of the local authority. Similarly, the lack of secure local authority accommodation shall not make it impracticable for the custody officer to transfer him. The availability of secure accommodation is only a factor in relation to a juvenile aged 12 or over when the local authority accommodation would not be adequate to protect the public from serious harm from the juvenile. The obligation to transfer a juvenile to local authority accommodation applies as much to a juvenile charged during the daytime as it does to a juvenile to be held overnight, subject to a requirement to bring the juvenile before a court under s.46 of the Police and Criminal Evidence Act 1984."

The guidance suggests that the effect of the revised subsection is to require that all juveniles who are not released on bail should be transferred to local authority accommodation with two exceptions.

i) Any juvenile aged 10–16 years

   Any juvenile may be held by the police themselves if the custody officer certifies that it is impracticable to make the transfer to local authority accommodation.

ii) 12–16-year-olds

   Under PACE, s.38.

   (6) "(b) in the case of an arrested juvenile who has attained the age of 12 years, that no secure accommodation is available and that keeping him in any other local authority accommodation would not be adequate to protect the public from serious harm from him, secure that the arrested juvenile is moved to local authority accommodation.

   (6A) In this section—
   'local authority accommodation' means accommodation provided by or on behalf of a local authority (within the meaning of the Children Act 1989); 'secure accommodation' means accommodation provided for the purposes of restricting liberty; 'sexual offence' and 'violent offence' have the same meaning as in Part I of the Criminal Justice Act 1991; and any reference, in relation to an arrested juvenile charged with a violent or sexual offence, to protecting the public from serious harm from him shall be construed as reference to protecting members of the public from death or serious personal injury, whether physical or psychological, occasioned by such further offences committed by him.
   (6B) Where an arrested juvenile is moved to local authority accommodation under subsection (6) above it shall be lawful for any person acting on behalf of the authority to detain him."

Detention of seventeen-year-olds

Under the CJA 1991 17-year-olds come within the provisions of section 31 of the CYPA 1933 under which children and young persons detained in a police station, being conveyed to or from, or waiting to attend or return from a criminal court must be separated from adults who have been charged with criminal offences. The only exceptions being if the adults are relatives or adults with whom the juvenile is jointly charged.

For all other pre-trial purposes seventeen-year-olds are regarded as adults.

CHAPTER 4

Reprimands and Final Warnings

4.01 Police reprimands and final warnings, introduced under the Crime and Disorder Act 1998[1] (CDA 1998) to replace the existing non-statutory scheme of police cautions, came into force in 2000. The rationale for the change was signalled in a pre-manifesto paper[2] by the Labour party when in opposition. Quoting police evidence to the 1993 Home Affairs Select Committee about the use of repeat cautioning, and identifying the extremes of variation between cautioning rates in different police forces, the authors concluded—

> "Cautioning is being applied inconsistently across the country and too often is not associated with effective intervention to make young offenders and their parents confront offending behaviour."[3]

4.02 In the white paper *No More Excuses—a New Approach to Tackling Youth Crime in England and Wales*,[4] earlier talk of leaving discretion to the police to use informal methods of talking to young people about offending behaviour prior to the issue of a formal warning was left behind. Instead, the proposal was for a formal scheme of a single police reprimand for non-serious offences. The reprimand to be followed, if another offence was committed, with a final warning accompanied by intervention similar to "cautioning-plus" schemes on the model of those already operating in Aylesbury and Northamptonshire.[5] Any subsequent offence would automatically result in prosecution, unless two years had elapsed since the earlier final warning, and the offence was a minor one. Neither the reprimand nor the final warning would be required should the police decide that the offence was sufficiently serious for immediate prosecution.

4.03 The white paper proposals were enacted in sections 65 and 66 of the 1998 Act. Pilot schemes began in September 1998 and the provisions came into force nationally in June 2000. Although the statute refers only to "warnings" rather than "final warnings", it is noticeable that Home Office notes of guidance are entitled "The Final Warning Scheme". The fact that the guidance issued in draft for the pilot schemes was substantially rewritten prior to national implementation is a reflection of the complexity of the task, and the minutely prescriptive nature of the scheme. It seems more than likely that unanticipated outcomes and practical problems will result in further amendments within the foreseeable future.

4.04 Guidance to both the police and YOTs makes it clear that the final warning scheme is intended to contribute towards delivery of the principal aim of the youth justice system—"to prevent offending by children and young persons"[6] by:

---

[1] Sections 65 and 66.
[2] Jack Straw and Alun Michael, *Tackling Youth Crime: Reforming Youth Justice* (Labour Party, London, 1996).
[3] *op. cit.*, at 4.
[4] Cmnd 3809, Home Office.
[5] Northamptonshire Diversion Unit, *Diverting People from Crime* (NACRO, London, 1998).
[6] s.37(1) of the CDA, 1998.

- ending repeat cautions and providing "a progressive and meaningful response to offending behaviour;"

- ensuring "appropriate and effective action to help prevent re-offending;" and

- ensuring that "juveniles who do re-offend after a warning are dealt with quickly and effectively through the courts." [7]

The centrality of the statutory scheme is endorsed in guidance which makes it clear that there is little latitude for police officers to exercise any discretion to take informal action.

"There will remain only strictly limited discretion for the police officer to take informal action, by giving firm advice to a young person and his or her parents in exceptional circumstances where this is considered to be an effective deterrent to future offending—normally only in cases of minor non-recordable offences or anti-social behaviour falling short of inherently criminal activity. To ensure that the final warning scheme has a real impact on offending behaviour any informal action should be confined to such circumstances." [8]

On the other hand, the issuing of a warning where one is not otherwise considered appropriate, in order to trigger involvement in a rehabilitation programme, is discouraged. Where a first offence is deemed insufficiently serious for a warning, but the police officer considers that the offender requires professional help, there is provision for reference to the YOT or 'an appropriate local agency' for advice and help. [9]

STATUTORY REQUIREMENTS

4.05 Under section 65(1) of the Crime and Disorder Act, a reprimand or warning can only be given where—

"(a) a constable has evidence that a child or young person ("the offender") has committed the offence;
(b) the constable considers that the evidence is such that, if the offender were prosecuted for the offence, there would be a realistic prospect of his being convicted;
(c) the offender admits to the constable that he committed the offence;
(d) the offender has not previously been convicted of an offence; and
(e) the constable is satisfied that it would not be in the public interest for the offender to be prosecuted."

The police have responsibility for issuing reprimands and warnings and for referring young people who have been given a "final warning" to the YOT. The police may, and indeed are encouraged in guidance to ask the local YOT to undertake a prior assessment in order to "explore the young person's attitude to intervention and assess the likelihood of him or her engaging with a rehabilitation

---

[7] *The Final Warning Scheme: Guidance for Youth Offending Teams* (Home Office, London, 2000) para. 1.
[8] *The Final Warning Scheme: Guidance for Police* (Home Office, London, 2000) para. 12.
[9] *ibid.*, para. 24.

(change) programme."[10] The assessment, based on the Youth Justice Board's ASSET tool,[11] and involving a visit to the young person, his or her family and, where relevant, the victim, has to be undertaken by the YOT within 10 working days. Despite the encouragement in the guidance, early indications are that involvement of YOTs prior to the issuing of a warning is very unusual, and that in most areas the police do not contact YOTs until after a warning has been administered.

4.06 Aspects of the law relating to reprimands and early warnings has already been the subject of statutory clarification. Doubts were expressed[12] as to the legality, given the wording of s.34(5) of PACE, of guidance to the police[13] suggesting that offenders could be bailed under s.34(5) whilst a YOT assessment was taking place. The issue has been clarified by an amendment to s.34(5)(b) introduced by the Criminal Justice and Courts Services Act 2000 (CJCSA 2000),[14] which explicity allows the offender to be bailed if he may be reprimanded or warned as an alternative to proceedings being taken against him.

The guidance for the police elaborates on the statutory requirements, and has the Association of Chief Police Officers' (ACPO) Gravity Factors[15] annexed to aid determination in regard to the "public interest" in prosecution.[16] It should be noted that the Youth Justice Board ASSET tool uses a different eight rather than four point gravity scale.[17]

4.07 Where the requirements set out in section 65(1) are satisfied, and the officer in the case is assessing whether a reprimand, or prosecution final warning will be appropriate, the decision should take the key factors set out in the guidance into account. These are: the young persons offending history; the seriousness of the offence, having regard to its nature and surrounding circumstances (both of which are addressed in the ACPO gravity factors); and, where assessment suggests that either a warning or a charge is appropriate, whether a warning is sufficient to prevent re-offending.[18]

With regard to offending history, the guidance leaves officers with only very limited discretion.

> "In considering this factor, officers should have regard to the following—[19]
>
> - **first time** offenders should normally receive a reprimand for a less serious offence;
> - **second time** offenders who have been reprimanded previously cannot be given a further reprimand—they should either be warned or, if the circumstances warrant it, charged. Second time offenders who have already received a warning cannot be given a reprimand and should not receive a further warning. They should be charged. The only exception is where the new offence has been committed more than two years since the previous warning and the offence and its circumstances are not so serious as to require a charge;
> - **third time** offenders who have already received a reprimand and a warning cannot be given a further reprimand and should not usually receive a

---

[10] *The Final Warning Scheme—Guidance for Police* (Home Office, London, 2000) para. 26.
[11] See 4.20, below.
[12] NACRO Youth Crime Section Briefing *Final Warnings—Implementation Issues,* June 2000.
[13] *Guidance for Police, op. cit.,* para. 63.
[14] s.56(2)
[15] Annex C.
[16] s.65(1)(e) of the CDA, 1998.
[17] *Young Offender Assessment Profile—Explanatory Notes* (Youth Justice Board ASSET), Annex B.
[18] *Guidance for Police, op. cit.,* at para. 15.
[19] Reference is to offending occasions rather than individual offences.

further warning. They should be charged unless the new offence has been committed more than two years since the previous warning and the offence and its circumstances are not so serious as to require a charge;

- those offending for the **fourth time**, or more, who have previously received a reprimand or warning, cannot receive a reprimand or warning in any circumstances. They must be charged."[20]

4.08   Where a young person has cautions imposed before section 67(8) of the CDA 1998 was implemented, these will continue to be taken into account. An offender with one previous caution will be treated as having a previous reprimand and an offender with two previous cautions as having received a final warning.[21]

Once the decision to charge has been reached, the Crown Prosecution Service (CPS) will consider, in line with its Code and guidance devised to take account of the final warning scheme,[22] whether to proceed with the prosecution.

Seriousness of the offence

4.09   Offences which can only be dealt with on indictment, will only in exceptional circumstances be dealt with by reprimand or warning, and for the most serious—such as murder or rape—diversion from prosecution will never be an option. The seriousness of the offence is clearly crucial to the exercise of discretion in cases in which a choice between a reprimand or warning, or a warning or charge can be made. As the guidance indicates, where there is any freedom for the exercise of discretion, each case has to be considered on its individual facts "taking into account the circumstances of the offender, including any aggravating or mitigating factors relating to the offence."[23] The age and maturity of the offender is recognised as being of relevance in most cases. Details of the factors to be taken into account are provided in the list of ACPO gravity factors specific to each type of offence.[24]

The impact of the offence on the victim is regarded as being a key factor in determining the seriousness of the offence.

> "Therefore wherever possible the police should contact the victim to establish his or her view about the offence; the nature and extent of any harm or loss; and its significance relative to the victim's circumstances. This could be done through the preparation of a victim statement. Contact with the victim must be carried out with sensitivity and only by a police officer trained in victim awareness. The victim's view about the offence may influence the view taken on its seriousness but cannot be conclusive."

The final gravity score attributed to the offence should be clearly marked on the form which is passed to the YOT.

The administration of reprimands and warnings

4.10   Reprimands and warnings must be given orally by a police officer.[25] In the case of an offender under the age of 17, this must be in the presence of an

---

[20] *Guidance for Police, op. cit.*, para. 16.
[21] Schedule 9 of the CDA 1998.
[22] *Code for Crown Prosecutors*, 2000.
[23] *Guidance for Police, op. cit.*, para. 21.
[24] *ibid.*, Annex C.
[25] CDA 1998, s.65(5)(a).

appropriate adult. Section 65(5) of the 1998 Act originally required reprimands and warnings to be given at a police station. The section has been amended to the extent that the Secretary of State may specify other places where reprimands and warnings may be given.[26]

Reprimands

4.11 In giving a reprimand, the officer should specify the offence(s) which led to it and

"make it clear that—

- the reprimand is a serious matter
- any further offending behaviour will result in a warning or prosecution in all but the most exceptional circumstances
- a record of the reprimand will be kept by the police at least until the offender is 18
- the young person's reprimand may be cited in any future criminal proceedings
- if the offence is one covered by the Sex Offenders Act 1997, the young person is required to register with the police for inclusion on the sex offenders register. . ."[27]

Guidance to YOTs makes it clear that although there is nothing to prevent the provision of intervention aimed at preventing re-offending after the issue of a reprimand, "the statutory requirement to provide assessment and, as appropriate, rehabilitation (change) programmes for all those who receive a final warning must take priority over any additional work undertaken by youth offending teams in support of reprimands".[28]

Warnings

4.12 Whilst the administration of a reprimand is relatively straightforward, a three tier structure of warnings is apparent from the guidance: restorative conferences, restorative warnings and standard warnings.

4.13 *Restorative conferences*—The maximum opportunity for reparation to the victim is envisaged as being provided when the warning is administered as part of a restorative conference designed to face the young offender directly with the impact of the offence on the victim and to decide on appropriate reparation. Restorative conferences can only take place if the offence is deemed suitable, and victim and the young offender and his/her parents are willing to participate. Guidance specifies that "No pressure should be applied to participate and no victim should be made to feel embarrassed or unhelpful by his or her reluctance to participate."[29] If the police have requested an assessment before deciding whether to issue a warning, the YOT will already have discussed with the young offender and his or her parent(s) their willingness to participate in a restorative conference and/or a restorative warning. Where, as in the vast majority of cases, there has been no prior YOT assessment the police should themselves visit the family to elicit this information.[30]

---

[26] CJCA 2000, s.56(1).
[27] *Guidance for Police, op. cit.*, para. 72.
[28] *The Crime and Disorder Act: The Establishment and Operation of Rehabilitation (Change) Programmes under the Final Warning Scheme* (Home Office, London, 2000) at para. 44.
[29] *ibid.*, para. 50.
[30] *Guidance to the Police, op. cit.*, para. 44.

Restorative conferences and warnings are the subject of detailed guidance.[31] They
have to be conducted by a trained facilitator, and ideally conferences will result in a
voluntary reparation agreement which should be passed on to the YOT for
inclusion in any rehabilitation programme following the warning. Exceptionally a
restorative conference resulting in an apology and reparation may obviate the need
for a rehabilitative programme.[32]

4.14 *Restorative warnings*—Where the offence is suitable, and the victim—
although not prepared to attend a restorative conference—is willing to have their
views represented, the young offender can still be made aware of the personal
impact of the offence. In these circumstances a police officer or YOT member
should agree with the victim a written form of what will be said, and the same
person should be responsible for conveying the victim's views when the restorative
warning is administered.

4.15 *Standard warnings*—Where the offence is so-called 'victimless', or otherwise unsuitable for a restorative approach, but otherwise a warning is considered to
be the appropriate response, a standard warning without a restorative element can
be administered.

Explaining the effect of warnings

4.16 When giving a warning "the officer should specify the offence(s) which
has led to it and make it clear that—

- the warning is a serious matter

- any further offences will result in charges being brought in all but the most
  exceptional circumstance

- a record of the warning will be kept by the police until the offender is 18
  or the warning is more than two years old, whichever is the later

- the warning may be cited in any future criminal proceedings

- if the young person is convicted of a further offence within two years of
  getting the warning, the option of conditional discharge will only be open
  to the courts in exceptional circumstances. The young person can in most
  cases expect a more serious sentence.

- if the offence is one covered by the Sex Offenders Act 1997, the young
  person is required to register with the police for inclusion on the sex
  offenders register

- the warning will trigger referral to a local youth offending team
  the youth offending team will assess the young person and, unless they
  consider it inappropriate, prepare a rehabilitation (change) programme
  designed to tackle the reasons for the young person's offending behaviour,
  prevent any future offending and to help repair some of the harm done

- unreasonable non-compliance with the rehabilitation (change) programme
  would be recorded and could be cited in any future criminal proceedings

- referral to the youth offending team will be immediate and the young
  person can expect to be contacted within five working days

[31] *ibid.*, Annex E.
[32] *Guidance for YOTs, op. cit.*, para. 66.

- any questions about what will happen next should be put to the youth offending team (the officer should also give contact details for the team)."

4.17 Young offenders and their parents or carers should receive a copy of the *Standard leaflet on warnings for young offenders.*[33] If the offence is one which comes within the definition in the Sex Offenders Act 1997 (SOA 1997), the police officer must explain to the young person and the appropriate adult that on receiving a reprimand or warning for such an offence they will be required to register with the police for inclusion on the sex offenders register. It should be noted that unless there is a change in the law, the CYPA 1933, which allows local authorities to hold a list of offenders *convicted* of an offence under Schedule One of that Act does not allow the names of those who receive reprimands or warnings to be added to that list.

Once a reprimand or warning has been administered, national standards require that the local YOT is notified within one working day.

Recording and citation of reprimands and warnings

4.18 Where a warning is given for recordable offences, proof of the warning will come from fingerprints. If the warning was given for a non-recordable offence, the proof will be provided by a form signed by the young person, the police officer and the parent, carer or other appropriate adult at the time the warning was given.

The Police National Computer (PNC) system is being amended to record reprimands and early warnings. The effective implementation of the system is clearly dependent on speedy and accurate recording of recordable and non-recordable offences. Whilst the former can be dealt with on the PNC, each police force will need to develop a system for the recording of reprimands, warnings and convictions for non-recordable offences which mirrors the information kept on the PNC. Where a young person has recently moved into an area, forces will also need to check in regard to non-recordable offences with the previous home force.

Reprimands, warnings and reports of failure to participate in a rehabilitation programme may be cited in court in the same circumstances as convictions.[34] On the other hand, reprimands and warnings are not criminal convictions and do not technically constitute a criminal record. They can, however, be kept by the police for up to ten years, and if proposed changes to the Rehabilitation of Offenders Act 1974 are enacted, they would come within the scope of the Act and exceptions to it.

YOT responsibilities

4.19 Guidance recommends that protocols are developed to cover the circumstances in which a member of the YOT is present to assist in explaining to a young person the implications of a warning, the nature of the programme designed to achieve rehabilitation, and the arrangements for their involvement in the programme. Whether or not a member of the YOT is present when the warning is given, guidance indicates that the police should inform YOTs on a daily basis of the names, addresses and telephone numbers of young people who have received a warning, together with details of the offence and the name of, and contact details for, the victim. It is also suggested that the police officer in the case should pass on

---

[33] *ibid.*, Annex G.
[34] s.66(5) of the CDA, 1998.

to the YOT "any additional information obtained during the course of the investigation which may be relevant to the process of assessment."[35]

When a young offender has been referred to the YOT following a warning, the team has a statutory duty to assess him or her, and unless it is not considered appropriate to arrange for the young person to participate in a rehabilitation (change) programme. For instance where a restorative conference has already resulted in an apology and reparation and further intervention is not considered necessary to prevent re-offending.[36]

The ASSET assessment tool

4.20 ASSET is an assessment tool developed by the University of Oxford Centre for Criminological Research for the Youth Justice Board for use by YOTs for all young offenders. There is a core form and a number of ancillary forms for special purposes such as bail assessment or the assessment of risk of serious harm from the young person. It is envisaged that the core ASSET form accompanies a young offender wherever he or she goes in the youth justice system, and that it will be constantly updated. The forms are accompanied by a very detailed set of explanatory notes intended to:—

> "define, explain and illustrate the *content* of the ASSET forms. To that end they consist of clarification of some of the terms and concepts used in ASSET; background information about why particular topics have been included; examples of how the different sections link together and guidance on how the assessment should relate to practical decisions about intervention and supervision."[37]

4.21   The Youth Justice Board has published national standards[38] which specify when ASSET should be used. These require the YOT to contact "all offenders who have received a final warning within five working days of the warning" and within 10 days to have undertaken an ASSET assessment.[39] If the ASSET assessment indicates the need for a rehabilitation (change) programme, the YOT must:—

> "produce a programme that addresses factors that contributed to the offending and opportunities for reparation to victims. It must be consistent with any programme of reparation agreed in a restorative conference and take account of school, work or religious commitments."[40]

The rehabilitation (change) programme

4.22   Guidance to YOTs recognises that the activities to be included in each programme are to some extent bound to depend on local resources. An audit of available youth justice services formed part of the planning for implementation of the YOTs in 1999. In addition, the drawing up of annual youth justice plans in consultation with the police, probation service and health authority should set out how assessment work and rehabilitation (change) programmes in support of

---

[35] *op. cit.*, para. 32.
[36] *Guidance for YOTs, op. cit.*, para. 66.
[37] *Young Offender Assessment Profile — Explanatory Notes* (Youth Justice Board ASSET) at p. 3.
[38] *National Standards for Youth Justice* (Youth Justice Board and Home Office, 2000).
[39] *ibid.*, para. 5.3.
[40] *ibid.*, para. 5.4.

warnings, are to be delivered by the YOTs. The plan should include details of the extent to which individuals and services outside the teams will be involved in the delivery of programmes.

Involvement of the victim

4.23 Where the victim has been involved in a reparation conference at which voluntary reparation agreement has been reached, this should be incorporated into the rehabilitation programme. The terms of the agreement will determine whether reparation is direct in terms of an apology, voluntary financial compensation, compensation in kind through voluntary work, the making good of damage, or indirect through a donation to charity or some community activity. Guidance indicates that the victim should always be consulted about the form of any reparation, and his or her views taken into account before any decision is taken.

CHAPTER 5

Civil Orders

5.01 Criminal proceedings against young offenders and local authorities' child care responsibilities for children beyond the control of their parents co-existed from the beginning of the twentieth century,[1] and still do so. Recent legislation has introduced a third strand of civil orders targeted at troublesome children under the age of criminal responsibility as well as those aged 10 to 17 years, and their parents. This chapter examines the range of civil and quasi-civil orders currently available under the CA 1989 and the CDA 1998.

CHILDREN ACT 1989

5.02 Despite the fact that most local authority social services departments, under increasing resource pressures, appear to have abrogated their child care responsibilities for young offenders,[2] the statutory duties remain. Under Part III of the 1989 Act, a child who is committing offences is likely to come within the definition of a "child in need" under section 17, in that "he is unlikely to achieve or maintain, or to have the opportunity of achieving or maintaining, a reasonable standard of health or development without the provision for him or services by a local authority. . .".[3] In regard to such children, local authorities are required to take reasonable steps to reduce the need to bring criminal proceedings,[4] and to encourage children within their area not to commit criminal offences.[5] The duty now co-exists with the duty on all bodies carrying out functions under the 1998 Act, to have regard to the principal aim of the youth justice system—to prevent offending by children and young persons.[6]

Care proceedings as an alternative to criminal proceedings

5.03 The strict criteria set out in the so-called "threshold conditions" which have to be satisfied before a court can make a care or supervision order under the 1989 Act, preclude the use of care proceedings as an alternative to criminal proceedings in all but the most extreme cases. There is no doubt, however, that some of the most disturbed children committing very serious crimes would satisfy the threshold conditions in section 31.[7]

> "(2) A court may only make a care order or a supervision order if it is satisfied—

---

[1] Children Act 1908.
[2] B. Anderson, 'The Criminal Justice Acts: "Justice" by Geography' in *The Handbook of Children's Rights: Comparative Policy and Practice*, (B. Franklin, ed., Routledge, London, 1995).
[3] s.17(10)(a).
[4] Sched. 2, Part I, para. 7(a)(ii) of the CA 1989.
[5] *ibid.*, para. 7(b).
[6] s.37.
[7] C.Ball and J. Connolly, "Educationally Disaffected Young Offenders: Youth Court and Agency Responses to Truancy and School Exclusion" (2000) Brit. J. Criminol., 40, 4 594.

(a) that the child concerned is suffering, or is likely to suffer, significant harm; and

(b) that the harm, or likelihood of harm, is attributable to—

    (i) the care given to the child, or likely to be given to him if the order were not made, not being what it would be reasonable to expect a parent to give him; or

    (ii) the child's being beyond parental control."

Care and supervision orders can be made on children under the age of 17 who are not married.[8]

5.04 Local authorities appear understandably reluctant to make applications for care orders on young offenders who satisfy the threshold conditions, since by doing so, they would subsequently be very likely to have to incur the expense of placement in secure accommodation.[9] Where custodial orders are made in criminal proceedings, the Home Office resources the sentence, even if the child is placed in local authority secure accommodation. The lack of a mechanism by which in suitable cases a youth court could require a local authority to undertake an investigation similar to that under section 37 in the Children Act, and, if the child's welfare required it, make an application for a care order in the family proceedings court, was identified as a lacuna in the Criminal Justice Act 1991.[10]

Supervision orders in a variety of guises are available as sentences for all youth court defendants, except, once the referral order provisions are available nationally,[11] for offenders appearing for the first time in the youth court.[12-13] This makes the likelihood of a local authority using care proceedings in order to secure a supervision order on a child above the age of criminal responsibility appear remote in the extreme. Children under the age of 10 may be placed under the supervision of the local authority in civil proceedings if made the subject of a child safety order under section 12 of the 1998 Act.

NON-CRIMINAL ORDERS AND POLICE POWERS UNDER THE CRIME AND DISORDER ACT 1998

5.05 The rationale for the range of civil and quasi civil orders, and police powers, some targeted at children below the age of criminal responsibility, can be found throughout the Home Office consultation paper *Tackling Youth Crime*[14] and the 1997 white paper *No More Excuses*.[15] The orders and powers in the 1998 Act are predicated on the aim of protecting the public and creating safer communities by "nipping criminal and anti-social behaviour in the bud".[16] As Fionda notes in her critique of the youth justice provisions in the Act, some of the orders bear a strong resemblance to proposals set out in the last consultation paper published by

---

[8] s.32(3) of the CA 1989.

[9] See below at paras 9.26–9.36.

[10] *A False Sense of Security: the case against locking up more children* (The Children's Society, London, 1993) at p. 31; C. Ball, "*R v. B (Young Offender: Sentencing Powers)* Paying due regard to the welfare of the child in criminal proceedings" (1998) 10 C.F.L.Q. 4, 417 at 423.

[11] Probably early in 2002.

[12-13] s.1 of the YJCEA, 1999.

[14] 1997

[15] *op. cit.*

[16] J. Fionda "New Labour, Old Hat: Youth Justice and the Crime and Disorder Act 1998" [1999] Crim. L.R. 36, at 45.

the Conservative government.[17] She also suggests that anti-social behaviour orders made on juveniles in adult magistrates' courts may contravene the Government's treaty obligations under article 40 of the United Nations Convention on the Rights of the Child.

Anti-social behaviour orders

5.06   Anti-social behaviour orders may be made by an adult magistrates' court on persons over the age of 10 years on the application of a council for the local government area or a chief officer of police any part of whose police area lies within the area (the "relevant authority"[18]). The conditions that have to be fulfilled before an order can be made are set out in section 1(1)—

> "(a)   that the person has acted, since the commencement date, in an anti-social manner, that is to say, in a manner that caused or was likely to cause harassment, alarm or distress to one or more persons not of the same household as himself; and
>
> (b)   that such an order is necessary to protect persons in the local government area in which the harassment, alarm or distress was caused or was likely to be caused from further anti-social acts by him."

If the conditions are proved, the magistrates' court may make an anti-social behaviour order which prohibits the offender from doing anything described in the order. The standard of proof is the civil standard of the balance of probabilities. The order can be made for a fixed period over the minimum of two years, or indefinitely until a further order.[19] When an anti-social behaviour order is made on a juvenile, national standards for youth justice require that the police inform the YOT within one working day.[20]

If the order is breached by an adult, the person in breach is liable on summary conviction for a term of imprisonment of up to six months or a fine not exceeding the statutory maximum or both. The maximum penalty in the Crown Court on indictment is five years. Breaches by juveniles will be dealt with in the youth court by use of fines or detention and training orders.[21]

Child Safety Orders

5.07

> "The child safety order is a designed to protect children under ten who are at risk of being involved in crime or who have already started to behave in am anti-social or criminal manner. It will be available to local authorities in the family proceedings court. Under a child safety order, a court will be able to require a child, for example, to be at home at specified times or to stay away from certain people and places. The court could also prohibit certain conduct such as truanting from school. A child safety order could be linked with a parenting order if the court felt that to be appropriate. If the requirements in the order are not complied with, it will be open to the local authority to commence care proceedings under Section 31(1) of the Children Act 1989".[22]

---

[17] *ibid.*
[18] s.1(1) of the CDA 1998.
[19] *ibid.*, s.1(7).
[20] National Standards for Youth Justice, para. 7.10.1.
[21] *Crime and Disorder Act, Anti-Social Behaviour Order: Guidance*, (Home Office, London, 2000).
[22] *No More Excuses, op. cit.*, para 5.5.

Giving an illustration of how the child safety order might work, the white paper[23] sketches the following scenario.

> "[A]n eight year old girl found shoplifting with a group of older girls in the local shopping centre might be referred by the police to social services. The local authority could apply to the court for a child safety order. The order might require her to stay away from the shopping centre, not mix with the older girls and (with the agreement of the organisers) attend a local youth programme to make use of her leisure time."

5.08   The child safety order proposed in the white paper is enacted in the ss.11–13 of the CDA 1998. On the application of the local authority, a family proceedings court may make a child safety order on a child under the age of ten years. The order places the child under the supervision of the "responsible officer" (a local authority social worker or a member of a YOT) for a maximum period of three months or in exceptional circumstances for up to 12 months.[24]

National Standards for Youth Justice,[25] require that the YOT and social services managers must produce an agreement which specifies the circumstances in which child safety orders may be applied for, and who shall be named as the responsible officer. This standard refers to detailed guidance which seeks to set the order in the wider context of other child protection measures, acknowledging that "the child safety order needs to be seen in the context of other work to safeguard and promote the welfare of children and take into account the contribution which a number of agencies can make to preventing offending."[26]

5.09   Before it can make a child safety order, the court has to be satisfied that arrangements for implementing the orders are available in the area in which the child resides and, on the basis of the civil evidential test of the balance of probabilities,[27] that one or more of the statutory conditions for making the order are satisfied. The conditions set out in section 11(3) are—

"(a)   that the child has committed an act which, if he had been aged 10 or over, would have constituted an offence;

(b)   that a child safety order is necessary for the purpose of preventing the commission by a child of such an act as is mentioned in paragraph (a) above;

(c)   that the child has contravened a ban imposed by a curfew notice; and

(d)   that the child has acted in a manner likely to cause harassment, alarm or distress to one or more persons not of the same household as himself."

Before making an order the court has to obtain and consider information about "the child's family circumstances and the likely effect of the order on those circumstances".[28] When making the order the court has to explain to the child's parent or guardian in ordinary language: the effect of the order it proposes to make and of any requirements it includes; the consequences if the child fails to comply; and, the power of the court to review the order on the application of the parent or

---

[23] *ibid.*
[24] s.11(4) of the CDA, 1998.
[25] See para. 2.14, above.
[26] CDA 1998, *Guidance Document: Child Safety Order* (Home Office: London, 1999) at para. 3.1.
[27] *ibid.*, s.11(6).
[28] *ibid.*, s.12(1).

guardian or the responsible officer.[29] Requirements in an order should where possible avoid any conflict with the parent's religious beliefs or "interference with the times, if any, at which the child normally attends school".[30] There is no requirement for either the child or the parent or guardian to consent to the making of a child safety order.

5.10   When a child safety order is in force and a court is considering an application by the parent or the responsible officer for discharge or variation of the terms of the order, it may discharge the order or vary its terms. If an application to discharge is refused, no further application may be made without leave of the court.[31]

Where a court is satisfied on the application of the responsible officer that a child who is subject to a parental responsibility order has failed to comply with any requirement, it may discharge the order and make a care order under section 31(1) of the CA 1989 or may vary the child safety order.[32] Subsection (7) of Section 12 provides that the care order may be made whether or not the conditions set out in section 31(2) of the 1989 Act are satisfied. It appears likely that courts taking this action are likely to be challenged on the basis that they are acting in breach of Article 8 (the right to family life) or Article 6 (the right to a fair trial) of the ECHR.

Appeals against the making of a child safety order by a family proceedings court lie to the Family Division of the High Court. The appellate court has wide powers to make orders necessary to determination of the appeal and "such incidental or consequential orders as appear to be just". Orders made on appeal are treated as orders of the magistrates rather than of the High Court.[33]

Local child curfew schemes

5.11   "[F]or their own good, and to prevent neighbourhood crime or disorder, young children should not be out, unsupervised late at night".[34] The purpose envisaged for curfew schemes under the 1998 Act is to provide, as part of the area's wider community safety strategy, "an effective and immediate method of dealing with clearly identified problems of anti-social and disorderly children who are too young to be left out unsupervised late at night".[35] Provisions in section 14 of the Act give local authorities powers, after consultation with the police and other persons it considers appropriate, to make a local child curfew scheme for the purpose of maintaining order. Such a scheme will last for not more than 90 days, and requires confirmation by the Secretary of State. The scheme will ban children of specified ages under the age of ten from being present in the public place to which the ban applies within specified hours between 9pm and 6am, unless under the control of a parent or other responsible adult. The area to which the scheme applies must be identified by notice and otherwise publicised.

If, when a scheme is in operation, a constable finds a child in a public place in contravention of a ban imposed by a curfew notice, he must inform the local authority and remove the child to his place of residence.[36] Where the constable has reasonable cause to believe that the child would suffer significant harm if removed

---

[29] *ibid.*, s.12(2).
[30] *ibid.*, s.12(3).
[31] *ibid.*, s.12(4) and (5).
[32] *ibid.*, s.12(6).
[33] *ibid.*, s.13.
[34] *No More Excuses, op. cit.*, para. 5.6.
[35] *ibid.*, para 5.8.
[36] s.15 of the CDA, 1998.

to that place, he can remove the child to suitable accommodation by taking the child into police protection.[37] If a child is found to have contravened a ban imposed by a child curfew notice, the local authority comes under a duty to investigate the child's case under the Children Act 1989, s.47.[38]

Removal of truants to designated premises

5.12   Under Section 16 of the 1998 Act, a local authority may notify the chief officer of police that it has designated premises as "premises to which children and young persons of compulsory school age may be removed".[39] Following such notification, a police officer of the rank of superintendent or above may direct the exercise of powers to remove children of compulsory school age found to be absent from school without lawful excuse, in a public place "in a specified area during a specified period"[40] to the school from which he is absent or the designated premises.

Comment

5.13   Whatever the intention, it is hard to escape the conclusion that these new orders not only extend liability to children under the age of criminal responsibility, but they also effectively criminalise non-criminal behaviour.[41] As Fionda points out, by extending "the concept of 'delinquency' to behaviour which falls short of criminal offending", the criminal justice agencies may well "widen the youth justice net in exactly the way that many commentators predicted in their critiques of a welfare approach to youth justice."[42]

---

[37] s.46 of the CA, 1989.
[38] s.15(4) of the CDA, 1998.
[39] *ibid.*, s.16(1)(a).
[40] *ibid.*, s.16(3).
[41] A. Morris and L. Gelsthorpe, "Something Old, Something Borrowed, Something Blue, but Something New? A comment on the prospects for restorative justice under the Crime and Disorder Act 1998." [2000] Crim. L.R. 18.
[42] J. Fionda, "New Labour, Old Hat: Youth Justice and the Crime and Disorder Act 1998" *op. cit.,* at 45.

PART III

THE YOUTH COURT

CHAPTER 6

Constitution

THE YOUTH COURT PANEL

6.01 A youth court is a magistrates' court especially established for the purpose of dealing with criminal proceedings against those under the age of 18.[1] Almost every case against a person of that age will start and finish in the youth court. The exceptions to this are set out in Chapter 7 (see para. 7.02). The only magistrates who may sit in a youth court are those who are members of a youth court panel.[2]

For the area comprising Inner London[3] and the City of London (together called the Metropolitan area) there is a single panel.[4] Outside that area each petty sessional division must form a youth court panel, although this may be a combined panel with another or other petty sessional divisions (for rules regarding combined panels, see below, para. 6.06 *et seq.*).

6.02 A Youth Court panel will consist of a District Judge (Magistrates' Courts) and any justice appointed to the panel by the Lord Chancellor (for the Inner London panel) or by the Bench of which they are a member (outside Inner London). Within Inner London, the panel is appointed by the Lord Chancellor in accordance with the Youth Courts (London) Order 1994.[5] The formation of the Greater London Magistrates' Courts Authority[6] (creating a single Magistrates' Courts Committee for Greater London) may lead to changes in the arrangements for panels in Inner and Outer London.

A youth court will consist of either a District Judge (Magistrates' Courts) sitting alone or a chairman and other panel members. The chairman will be either a District Judge (Magistrates' Courts) (Inner London only) or a lay justice specially selected for that purpose. Where the court consists of three members, there should be at least one man and one woman but, outside Inner London, this can be disregarded if it is not possible and an adjournment of the case is not expedient.[7] The differently phrased provisions for Inner London[8] appear to provide that the absence of either a man or a woman can only be remedied by a District Judge (Magistrates' Courts) sitting alone or a qualified chairman sitting with one other member.[9] Presumably, this curiosity is unintended. Prior to disregarding the provision of sitting with a bench of mixed gender, the Court must invite the representations of all parties in open court and make the decision bearing in mind the importance of the requirement.[10] Whilst acknowledging the logic of this

---

[1] Children and Young Persons Act, ss.45 and 107.
[2] Sched. 2, para. 2 of the CYPA 1933.
[3] As defined in Justices' of the Peace Act 1997, s.2.
[4] Sched. 2, of the CYPA 1993 subject to amendment by s.77 of the Access to Justice Act 1999 when in force.
[5] S.I. 1994 No. 1695.
[6] Access to Justice Act 1999.
[7] Youth Court (Constitution) Rules 1954, S.I. 1954 No. 1711 (as amended) rule 12.
[8] Sched. 2, paras 14–18 of the CYPA 1933.
[9] *ibid.*, paras 15 and 17.
[10] *R. v. Birmingham Justices* 2000 (164) J.P. 523.

decision in the light of the law as it stands, it seems curious that a District Judge (Magistrates' Courts) can adjudicate alone but two male or two female lay justices cannot normally expect to adjudicate.

6.03 Outside the Metropolitan area, the justices for each petty sessional division elect a panel every three years. The election takes place at the October meeting of the justices and the panel members are appointed for three years from the following January 1.[11] Elections were held in October 2000 and will be held every three years thereafter. Any vacancy that arises within the life of the panel may be filled by the justices for the petty sessional division at any time and the person appointed will serve until the end of the tenure of the panel.[12] In selecting a panel, justices must appoint those "especially qualified" for dealing with juvenile cases.[13]

No further guidance is given; youth panel justices are elected triennially by all the members of the bench without any scrutiny of the extent to which they are "especially qualified" for the work of the youth court. This is in marked contrast to the position in Scotland, where applicants to join the Children's Panel undergo a rigorous selection process to determine their suitability for making decisions in the interests of the welfare of the children and young people appearing before the hearing (Ravenscroft, 1987). However, work has commenced to develop the competences provided for the youth court within the context of the Magistrates' New Training Initiative (MNTI) and to set standards of performance against which those competences will be measured. Similarly, in February 2001, the Justices' Clerks' Society published detailed competences for all legal advisers who support magistrates in youth courts. These set a clear standard for the conduct of this important role.[13a]

6.04 From 1954 until 1991 the age of retirement from the juvenile panel was set at 65, rather than the general retirement age from the bench of 70 years. There is now some concern regarding the extent to which the age of the majority of youth panel justices distances them from the problems and lifestyles of defendants. Recent evidence suggests that with nearly 70 per cent of justices appointed to the youth panel for the first time within the five years before the study being over 45, and 13 per cent over 55 years, the age profile of newly appointed youth panel justices may be such as to at least question whether due attention is being paid to the requirement for members of the panel to be "especially qualified" in this respect (Ball, 1995).

The size of the panel

6.05 In deciding on the number to be appointed to a youth court panel the justices for an area are directed to ensure that there are sufficient members to provide for enough courts to deal expeditiously with the business of the court. This is particularly important with the need to ensure that young offenders come quickly before the court once a decision has been made to prosecute. The appearance should be within three days if the defendant is not in custody. The number should also be sufficient to allow for tribunals to consist of at least one man and one woman.[14] Outside Inner London—where special arrangements exist for the alloca-tion of justices to the youth court panel—it is considered important that justices do

---

[11] Youth Courts (Constitution) Rules 1954, rr. 1 & 4.
[12] 1954 Rules, rr. 6 & 7.
[13] 1954 Rules, r.1.
[13a] Justices' Clerks' Society—The Legal Adviser Competence Framework, January 2001.
[14] *R. v. Birmingham Justices* 2000 (164) J.P. 523.

enough youth court work to maintain and develop expertise, but without such sittings becoming so predominant that individual justices cannot maintain and develop their experience of other work. The Lord Chancellor has indicated that it is desirable that each panel member should complete at least 13 sittings a year in the youth court in order that they may obtain, retain, and develop a proper understanding of the special work, powers and responsibilities of the panel.[15] In practice, wide fluctuations exist in the number of sittings undertaken. Data from a survey of over 450 justices on 20 panels of various sizes from throughout England and Wales demonstrates the extent of these variations. At one extreme, on one panel 18 per cent of magistrates sit for more than 35 half days in a year, whilst in another almost a quarter of all panel members managed fewer than the required 13 sittings. Even on those panels where the average sittings exceed 12, there are often individual members who sit significantly less often than the approved minimum. At the other extreme individual justices recorded more than 60 half days (Ball, 1995). The Lord Chancellor has indicated that he expects that a magistrate will not be a member of both youth court and family panels unless there are insufficient justices on a bench to form an appropriately sized panel without such duplication (Mackay, 1994). In practice the survey suggests that nearly a third of all youth court panel justices were also members of the family proceedings panel (Ball, 1995).

Combined panels

6.06 No panel can operate effectively with fewer than six members. This is because of the risk of a justice being disqualified in an individual case through having heard convictions during a remand application, and therefore being unable to deal with the determination of guilt if a not guilty plea is entered (Magistrates' Courts Act 1980, s.42). In practice, any panel of fewer than eight members will prove very difficult to work. If there is insufficient work for eight panel members to complete at least 13 sittings, then the panel may find it necessary to combine with another. In the past, despite Home Office guidance[16] urging panels to combine in order that justices "obtain sufficient experience of this important and specialized work", there was considerable resistance to amalgamation from small panels reluctant to lose their identity. For instance a survey undertaken in 1981 showed large numbers of juvenile courts serving rural areas were held only monthly and staffed by such large panels that individual justices often only sat once or twice a year (Ball, 1983b). However, the following 20 years has shown substantial amalgamation of Benches and a growing awareness of the need for Youth Panels to combine even where Benches remain separate.

6.07 If justices cannot appoint sufficient panel members from their own number, they may seek combination with an adjoining panel or they may appoint a justice assigned to another petty sessions area in the same commission area who is especially qualified for dealing with juvenile cases.[17]

Outside Inner London, a member of a youth panel can be transferred temporarily to another panel where necessary to deal with youth court cases. During the transfer, the justice can still sit on youth cases as a member of the originating panel. The request for transfer is made between the relevant Justices' Clerks and must be granted where the Justices' Clerk for the transferring Bench considers the better administration of justice will be served and where the justice concerned agrees.

---

[15] LCD Circular AC (92)5.
[16] HOC 138/79.
[17] Youth Court (Constitution) Rules 1954, r.1(4).

Where the panels operate in different commission areas, the transfer can only take place if the Lord Chancellor appoints the transferring justice to the commission for the new area.[18] A person elected as a chairman by the originating panel may chair a youth court in the new area.[19] The rules appear to envisage transfer for a particular case (perhaps where a fair hearing cannot be given by local justices) since the request for transfer must specify the youth court proceedings to be heard. Nonetheless, the provision is sufficiently broad to allow transfer to be sought to cover a shortfall in membership of a panel caused by a lack of suitable candidates or a sudden surge in workload.

6.08　　The procedure for combination of a panel allows a magistrates' courts committee to make a recommendation to the Lord Chancellor that he make an order forming a combined panel to cover two or more petty sessions areas within the same magistrates' courts committee and Commission Areas 8 and 9.[20] Before submitting a recommendation to the Lord Chancellor, a magistrates' courts committee must consult—

(a)　the justices for any petty sessions area involved in the proposed combination which is in the area covered by the magistrates' courts committee;

(b)　any other magistrates' courts committee covering a petty sessions area to be involved in the combined area.[21]

6.09　　When the recommendation is submitted, the magistrates' courts committee must give notice to those described in (a) and (b) above.[22] If the Lord Chancellor proposes to make an order different from that recommended to him, notice must be given to any magistrates' courts committee concerned and to the justices for any petty sessions area involved who have a maximum of one month to respond.[23] The Lord Chancellor may also direct a magistrates' courts committee to review the function of youth courts in its area and make a report containing recommendations for combination orders or justifying the lack of such a recommendation.[24] This elaborate procedure should be compared with the simpler, speedier process for combination of family panels.[25] There appears to be no benefit to be gained by involving the Lord Chancellor in the process of combination and the procedure could, with advantage, be allied to that applicable to family panels.

The conduct of panel business

6.10　　Each youth court panel must meet at least twice a year to discuss and consider matters of relevance to its business[26] which should involve contact with others involved in juvenile justice.

Youth courts carry out functions in relation to the Youth Justice system (as defined in section 42(1) of the CDA 1998) and they must have regard to the principal aim of the system which is to prevent offending by children and young persons.[27] In relation to any case brought before a court, the court must also have

---

[18] 1954 Rules, r.1(5).
[19] r. 13(3).
[20] Sched. 2, para. 4 of the CYPA 1933.
[21] *ibid.*, para. 10.
[22] *ibid.*, para. 10.
[23] *ibid.*, paras 11 and 12.
[24] *ibid.*, para. 5.
[25] Family Courts (Constitution) Rules 1991, para. 11.
[26] Youth Courts (Constitution) Rules 1954 (as amended), r.10.
[27] s.37 of the CDA 1998.

regard to the welfare of the child or young person.[28] In order to fulfil both responsibilities, panels must ensure that they fully understand the approaches of others involved in dealing with children and young persons who have committed offences and that they are fully aware of the resources available to assist the court in achieving its legitimate sentencing aim of reducing the risk of re-offending. It is quite appropriate for a panel to take a lead in ensuring a proper exchange of information amongst all relevant parties as part of its responsibility to set the timetable for proceedings but it must always be mindful of the responsibility under the European Convention on Human Rights to provide an independent tribunal for the hearing of cases.[29] Guidance from the Youth Justice Board suggests that there should be a court user group specifically for those involved in youth court proceedings. There is even greater importance for young offenders in bringing cases quickly to a conclusion but also in ensuring that proper consideration is given to the best way to deal with offences to reflect the needs of the offender, any victim and society in general. A well run panel will both meet the needs of its members for training, information and review of practice and also take necessary initiatives to ensure that justice is given its proper priority whilst stimulating, encouraging and challenging all involved to assure the timely progress of cases.

THE YOUTH COURT

6.11 A youth court should be made up of a District Judge (Magistrates' Courts), a District Judge (Magistrates' Court) and two panel members or, where three justices are due to sit, three justices from the panel, including a man and a woman. There is no exception to the maximum of three justices, but if, due to circumstances unforeseen when the rota was drawn up, no man or no woman is available and the other panel members present consider it inexpedient in the interests of justice to adjourn (Youth Court (Constitution) Rules 1954, r. 12), a bench may be properly constituted without a gender mix. See also 6.02 above for the procedure to be followed in deciding whether or not to adjourn.

Tasks which a single justice may perform in the adult court—for example remands and committals for trial—may be undertaken by a single justice within a youth court even though the court will not consist of a man and a woman.[30] As with adult courts, many of the powers of a single justice may be exercised by a Justices' Clerk or by a person authorised by the Clerk.[31]

Chairmanship

6.12 The youth court must sit under the chairmanship of a chairman or deputy chairman elected by the panel members. This election should take place as soon as practicable after the election of the panel; nominations are not excluded but any voting must be by secret ballot. Additional or replacement chairman or deputy chairmen may be elected at any time.[32] If no elected chairman or deputy chairman is available at the time of the court, the other panel members present may choose one of their number to preside.[33] If a chairman or deputy chairman is present but

---

[28] s.44 of the CYPA 1933.
[29] Article 6.
[30] r.12(4).
[31] Justices' Clerks' Rules 1999, S.I. 1999 No. 2784.
[32] r.9.
[33] r.13(2).

considers it appropriate for another member of the court to act as chairman, he or she may nominate that member to act as chairman providing that the elected chairman or deputy chairman continues to sit throughout the court.[34] Unless elected as a chairman or deputy chairman, a District Judge (Magistrates' Courts) cannot sit chairing a youth court with two lay justices.[35]

Although many panels have adopted a practice whereby the chairman does not seek to continue after a certain time in office, generally not exceeding six years, at the present time this is a voluntary arrangement.

Appointment of presiding justices in inner london

6.13   In contrast to the potentially haphazard election of chairmen in the rest of England and Wales (though more Benches are approaching the task with the same sophistication as is applied to chairmanship in the adult court), within the Inner London Magistrates' Courts (now part of the Greater London Magistrates' Courts Authority area), a statutory procedure (the Inner London Juvenile Courts (Selection of Chairmen) Order 1990) is applied to lay justices by the Inner London Youth Panel's Bench Training and Development Committee. A District Judge (Magistrates' Courts) appointed to the Panel is entitled to chair a youth court when sitting with lay justices.

The Bench Training and Development Committee consists of nine members elected at the Annual General Meeting of the Panel. Five members will be drawn from approved Presiding Justices (that is, those authorised to chair courts), three members will be drawn from those members of the Panel who are not Presiding Justices and one will be a District Judge (Magistrates' Courts) nominated by the Senior District Judge (Chief Magistrate).

Among its tasks, the committee will compile each year a list of Presiding Justices. The criteria for determining the length of the list are the numbers necessary to enable each court to sit under the chairmanship of an approved Presiding Justice and the need to ensure that each Presiding Justice is able to sit in the chair often enough to maintain the required level of competence.

The committee also provides for the mentoring of justices newly appointed to the Panel and the appraisal of all Panel members including Presiding Justices.

6.14   In order to be approved as a Presiding Justice, a member of the Panel must be selected by the Bench Training and Development Committee to attend a chairmanship course. The selection process balances the qualities of the individual with the needs of the Panel and the training available. To qualify for consideration, a justice must—

- have been a magistrate for at least six years
- have been a youth court magistrate for at least five years
- have achieved the four basic competencies for adult court magistrates[36]
- have achieved the youth court winger competencies
- have demonstrated the competencies in a wide range of youth court contexts
- have indicated that they wish to act as chairman

[34] r.13(1A).
[35] r.13(1) and r.9.
[36] See Magistrates' New Training Initiative (MNTI), Judicial Studies Board.

- be able to make sufficient time available
- be willing to undertake the training required
- have demonstrated a commitment to the work of the Youth Panel.

A justice who has completed the course may be appointed as a Presiding Justice if they wish providing there is a need for an appointment and they have demonstrated the required competencies. An appeal procedure exists, ultimately, in limited circumstances, to the Lord Chancellor.

Training

6.15   When a justice is appointed to a youth court panel there is an obligation to undertake training, the content of which is currently determined by Justices' Clerks in consultation with training officers. It typically consists of an introduction to the powers and practice of youth courts supported by an observation of such courts in operation and visits to establishments responsible for the accommodation of children where the court removes them from their home surroundings.

The courtroom and care of young people

6.16   A youth court will normally sit in courtrooms that are located in a place that makes it as easy as possible to segregate young offenders from adult offenders and which are constructed in a way that assists easy communication between those conducting the hearing and the parties. Court chairmen are encouraged to speak directly to young people before the court (trials have taken place in six areas to explore better ways of achieving this—see below at 6.17) and seating arrangements should be designed with this in mind. As a result, young people are often in the centre of the courtroom with advocates and other professionals at the side or behind them. Care must be taken to ensure that young people (or the adults with them) are not actually more intimidated by this openness.

As a result of consideration by the ECHR of the appropriateness of the arrangements in a Crown Court where children were charged with very serious offences,[37] the Lord Chief Justice issued a practice direction on February 17, 2000 setting out the procedures to be followed. This direction emphasises that the process of the trial should not expose a young defendant to avoidable intimidation, humiliation or distress and that all possible steps should be taken to help the young defendant to understand the proceedings and to participate in them. This is a factor in determining whether a case is heard in the Crown Court or in a Youth Court.[37a]

6.17   Where there is a joint indictment of an adult and a young defendant, the presumption is in favour of a separate trial for the young defendant. A joint trial will only follow if that is in the interests of justice and would not be unduly prejudicial to the welfare of the young defendant.[38] Court procedures should be modified as necessary.

The main part of the Practice Direction refers to the trial itself.[39] The following are the key points—

- All participants to be on the same level

---

[37] *V. v. United Kingdom; T. v. United Kingdom*, [2000] Crim. L.R. 187, *The Times*, December 17, 1999.
[37a] *R. v. B., The Times*, February 27, 2001.
[38] Practice Direction, para. 4; [2000] 2 All E.R. 285.
[39] Paras 9–16.

- Young defendant to be free to sit with his family or similar
- Young defendant to be sat where easy informal communication can take place with legal representatives and others
- Timetable to take full account of the inability to concentrate for long periods
- Neither robes nor wigs to be worn
- Normally police and security officers should not be in uniform
- Attendance at the trial to be restricted with consideration being given to relaying the proceedings to another room in the court complex for the benefit of the media

In order to explore ways of conducting youth courts more openly and in a way which commands the confidence of victims and the public and yet engages young offenders and their parent(s), a project took place in six courts during 1998 and 1999 with follow up work in 2000.[39a] It is clear from this project that change needs careful planning and training and that benefits are only likely in the medium term. However, it is possible to improve contact between the court and the young offender by changes to the physical layout of the courtroom and by the use of a different communication approach.[39b] The project has demonstrated that direct communication between magistrates and young offenders was a welcome and viable development and that, on the whole, the young offenders responded well to it. Initial concerns about the wide disparity between offenders (both in age and in criminal sophistication) did not in fact lead to any particular problems in practice. Good training and clear guidelines helped to overcome initial nervousness on behalf of magistrates and was seen as essential as was the importance of parental attendance with the young offender at the sentencing stage.

Arrangements must be made to prevent a person under 17 years from associating with an adult who is not a relative but who is charged with any offence (unless jointly charged with the person under 17) whilst being conveyed to or from a criminal court by the police or whilst waiting before or after attending such a court. If the person under 17 is a girl, then arrangements must be made for her to be in the care of a woman whilst being conveyed to court or waiting before or after attendance in court.[40]

Presence in the Courtroom

6.18   There are severe restrictions on those who may be in a youth court while the court is sitting.

The court may not allow to remain,

- members of the public with no connection with the case; or (as in the adult court) anyone under 14 years (except an infant in arms) unless they are the defendant or a witness or their presence is otherwise needed for the purposes of justice.[41]

[39a] Youth Court Demonstration Project, Leicestershire and Rotherham Magistrates' Courts.
[39b] Evaluation of the Youth Court Demonstration Project, Home Office Research Study 214, Home Office, 2000.
[40] s.31 of the CYPA 1933.
[41] s.3 of the CYPA 1933.

The court may allow to remain,

- members and officers of the court;
- parties to the case before the court;
- solicitors and counsel acting for the parties to the case before the court (note that solicitors and counsel in other cases have no right to be present in the courtroom);
- witnesses and other persons directly concerned with the case—this will include social workers, probation officers or members of other similar agencies with an interest or potential interest in the case;[42]
- bona fide representatives of newspapers and news agencies;
- such other persons as the court may specifically authorise to be present— this will allow justices under training, trainee social workers and others with a bona fide interest to be allowed to attend.[43]

6.19 Although not a party to the case in criminal proceedings, the victim may wish to attend court proceedings. In most circumstances, this will be appropriate and sometimes it will be of value to the victim in dealing with the consequences of the crime. Responsibility remains with the prosecutor to ensure that the court is given relevant information about the impact of the crime on any victim.

One aspect of the Youth Court Demonstration Project (see above at para. 6.17)[43a] was to explore greater opportunities for victims to attend the court hearing. During the project, only a few victims actually attended—information about the outcome appeared more important. The attendance of the victim may inhibit the freedom with which other participants conduct the case.

The small amount of research that has been published regarding the perceptions of juveniles and their families involved in court proceedings, suggests that even when the numbers of people in the courtroom are kept to a minimum, and considerable care is taken to explain the roles of those present, there is confusion as to who people are and their role in the proceedings.[44] Good practice would suggest, and magistrates' training encourages, the chairman to greet the defendant and those accompanying him by name, and to explain to them in very simple terms the identity and role of the various people in court. See also the Youth Court Demonstration Project at para. 6.17 above.[44a]

6.20 As with an adult, a young offender may wish to be supported by a "McKenzie friend" rather than a solicitor or barrister. Such an individual can assist the defendant in presenting his case without acting as an advocate on his behalf. The approach of the court will vary depending on whether the hearing is in public or in private. Youth court proceedings are public but with restrictions on who of the public may be present. In exercising their discretion, the court should normally allow someone to act as a "McKenzie friend" unless satisfied that fairness and the interests of justice do not require some assistance to be given. Reasons should be given for refusal.[45]

---

[42] *Southwark Juvenile Court* [1973] 3 All E.R. 383.
[43] s.47(2) of the CYPA 1933.
[43a] Evaluation of the Youth Court Demonstration Project, Home Office Research Study 214, Home Office, 2000.
[44] Morris and Giller, 1977; Parker *et al.*, 1981; Ball, 1981.
[44a] Evaluation of the Youth Court Demonstration Project, Home Office Research Study 214 (Home Office, 2000).
[45] *R. v. Bow County Court ex parte Pelling*, July 28, 1999, CA (unreported) 1999/0478.

4–018 The courtroom layout

6.21 Courtroom fittings very often leave little choice about where people will sit, but in a youth court there are important considerations regarding communications which need to guide the use of any flexibility that can be introduced into even the most formal courtroom. It is suggested that these include:

- the defendant being seated both so that he or she is the centre of attention, but also near to a parent or other supportive adult and an advocate (if there is one);

- the defendant being so positioned so as to allow eye contact with the bench without being so close as to allow intimidation in either direction;

- care being exercised to ensure that witnesses can be seen and spoken to by all in the court, without being sufficiently close to the defendant or his supporters to allow intimidation.

- sufficient flexibility in the layout to allow for sole or multiple defendants.

The layout of a courtroom was considered by the European Court of Human Rights and in the subsequent Practice Direction issued by the Lord Chief Justice. The key issues are set out at para. 6.17 above.

Recording of Decisions

6.22 By Magistrates' Courts Rules 1981, r. 66, every magistrates' court must keep a register recording matters prescribed by that rule. By Magistrates' Courts (Children and Young Persons) Rules 1992, r. 25, that part of the register that relates to proceedings in a youth court must be kept in a separate book. This register has to record the adjudications of the court.[46]

Whilst there is no obligation to record reasons given by a court for a decision, increasingly, magistrates are required to give reasons for specific decisions or parts of decisions and those reasons are to be recorded in the register.

However, it is likely that the requirements of a fair trial developed through the European Courts will lead to reasons being given more often in magistrates' courts. Such reasons should be recorded on the court papers and may need to be made available to the parties to the proceedings in the same way as reasons for magistrates' family proceedings courts.[47] When the Crown Court is sitting as an appellate court, it should give reasons for its decision in other than the most straightforward cases. Failure to do so will vitiate the decision.[48]

The register is open to inspection at any reasonable hour by any justice of the peace or by anyone authorised to inspect the register by a justice or by the Lord Chancellor.[49] The Home Secretary, by letter of February 9, 1893, requested that police officers be allowed access to the registers.[50] It was at that time that the Home Secretary decided that responsibility for collecting information to create criminal statistics should be with the police rather than with the courts.

[46] Magistrates Courts Rules, 1981, r. 66.
[47] See Family Proceedings Courts (Children Act 1989) Rules 1991, rule 21.
[48] *R. v. Kingston Crown Court ex p. Bell* (2000) 164 J.P. 633.
[49] Magistrates' Court Rules 1981, r. 66.
[50] 57 J.P. at 105.

CHAPTER 7

Procedure

7.01 The basic rule is that all those under 18 prosecuted for criminal offences are dealt with by a youth court.[1] The age of the juvenile is that which appears to the court to be his age after considering any available evidence.[2] Age changes at the commencement of the anniversary of the date of birth.[3] The procedure to be adopted where a juvenile becomes 18 after committing the offence but before the proceedings are concluded is described below at para. 7.32

7.02 There are five exceptions to this basic rule—

(a) **The juvenile is charged with homicide.**[4] Although there is no definition of homicide, it is likely to include any offence in which it is alleged that the juvenile caused death, for example, murder, manslaughter and including, commentators suggest, causing death by dangerous driving (Draycott and Carr, 2000).

(b) **Remand.** An adult or youth court has equal power to remand a juvenile whether bail is granted or refused.[5] An adult court remanding to the care of a local authority may also grant a secure accommodation order at the same time. (See Chapter 9, para. 9.26[6] *et seq.* for the criteria for making secure accommodation orders, and jurisdiction to renew them.)

(c) **Connection with an adult.** If a juvenile—

(i) is **jointly charged with an adult;**[7]
(ii) **has an adult charged as an aider and abettor** to the offence committed by the juvenile;[8]
(iii) **is charged as an aider and abettor to an adult;**[9]
(iv) **is charged with an offence arising out of the same circumstances as those giving rise to proceedings against an adult;**[10]

7.03 then the adult court may also deal with the juvenile. There are restrictions on the sentences that can be imposed on the juvenile by the adult court (see Chapter 13 below). Where an adult court is dealing with a juvenile because he is jointly charged with an adult, and the adult pleads guilty and the juvenile pleads not guilty, the adult court may remit the juvenile to a

[1] s.46(1) of the CYPA 1933.
[2] s.150(4) of the Magistrates' Court Act 1980 (MCA 1980).
[3] s.9 of the Family Law Reform Act 1969 (FLRA 1969).
[4] s.24 of the MCA 1980.
[5] s.46(2) of the CYPA 1933.
[6] s.60(3) of the CJA 1991.
[7] s.46(1)(a) of the CYPA 1933.
[8] s.46(1)(b) of the CYPA 1933.
[9] s.18(1)(a) of the CYPA 1963.
[10] s.18(1)(b) of the CYPA 1963.

youth court for trial.[11] Similarly, where the justices decide to commit the adult for trial (or to discharge him) but to proceed to summary trial of the information against the juvenile. There is no appeal available to the juvenile against the order of remittal.[12] The court may remit the juvenile to a youth court that acts either for the same place as the remitting court or for the place where the young person habitually resides. The remitting court may make any necessary directions regarding custody or bail until the juvenile can be brought before the youth court.[13]

(d) **Crown Court.** This court has power to deal with a juvenile committed for trial. For consideration of committal for trial, see below (para. 7–33).

(e) **Where a court other than a youth court has started to deal with a person believing them to be an adult but then discovers they are under 18,** the court may continue to deal fully with the offender, if it thinks fit.[14] For restrictions on sentence, see Chapter 13 below. There is also the reverse power for a youth court to continue to deal with a person discovered to be 18 or over.[15]

REPORTING OF YOUTH COURT PROCEEDINGS

7.04 There are restrictions on what may be reported of proceedings:

(a) before youth courts;

(b) before magistrates' courts that are not youth courts when they are dealing with an application to vary or discharge a supervision order in accordance with the CYPA 1969, s.15 or 16, or;

(c) on appeal (including case stated) from those courts.

7.05 The relevant provisions are contained in the CYPAs 1933 and 1963 as amended and in the YJCEA 1999. They will all be subject to scrutiny against the rights contained in the ECHR and UNCRC.

The 1933 and 1963 Acts and (when in force) section 45 of the YJCEA 1999 deal with the situation once a case gets as far as being court proceedings; when in force, section 44 of the 1999 Act will deal with the identification of a person under 18 during the stage of a criminal investigation prior to a decision whether to institute proceedings. Relevant principles in the UNCRC are contained in Article 3.1 and Article 40(2)(b)(vii) and in the ECHR in Article 6.1. The UN Convention provides at Article 3.1 that "In all actions concerning children, whether undertaken by public or private social welfare institutions, in courts of law . . . the best . . . interests of the child shall be a primary consideration" and at Article 40(2)(b) (vii) that "Any child alleged as or accused of having infringed the penal law has at least the following guarantees: "to have his or her privacy fully respected at all stages of the proceedings".

The European Convention provides at Article 6.1 that "the press and public may be excluded from all or part of a trial . . . where the interests of juveniles or the

---

[11] s.29 of the MCA 1980.
[12] s.29(4) of the MCA 1980.
[13] s.29 of the MCA 1980.
[14] s.46(1)(c) and s.46(1A) of the CYPA 1933.
[15] s.48(1) of the CYPA 1933.

protection of the private lives of the parties so require". The interaction of these provisions and the existing statutory powers was considered in a thorough judgment of the Divisional Court in *R. v. Central Criminal Court, ex p. S and P.*[16]

The consequences of prejudicial pre-trial publicity on the right to a fair trial[16a] were considered by the Privy Council in *Montgomery v. HM Advocate and Another, Coulter v. HM Advocate and Another*[16b] The test to be applied is an objective one. In the context of a jury trial, it will take account of the length of time since publication, the focussing effect of listening to evidence over a prolonged period and the likely effect of the directions of the trial judge. It would seem that it would have to be an extreme case in order to justify a finding that the right to a fair trial was prejudiced in this way.

Youth Court Proceedings

7.06 Section 49 of the CYPA 1933 has been much amended, most recently by the (yet to be implemented) YJCEA 1999. When in force, Chapter IV of the 1999 Act will provide more extensive protections which are referred to in the text below. The 1933 Act, in its amended form, provides that nothing is to be included in any publication which is likely to lead members of the public to identify a person under 18 as someone concerned in the proceedings.[17] This is a broad definition designed to protect any person under 18 from identification. The prohibition:

- applies to any publication;
- applies to specified proceedings;
- controls identification by members of the public;
- protects person only whilst under 18; and
- extends to anyone "concerned in the proceedings".

"Publication" is not to be restrictively defined. It includes any speech, any writing, any relevant programme[18] or other communication, in whatever form, that is addressed to the public either at large or any section of it. It does not include a document prepared for use in particular legal proceedings. The exception for legal proceedings would, presumably, allow a court list to be displayed in a public area of the court but would not allow the name of a person protected to be called over a tannoy system within a courthouse or, it is suggested, called out loud in a public waiting area in a courthouse.

7.07 The "proceedings specified" are proceedings in a youth court, on appeal from a youth court (including by case stated), to vary or revoke a supervision order[19] including an appeal from a magistrates' court's decision on such a matter[20].

Identification has to be to "members of the public". This protects transmission within and between, for example, the offices of legal representatives for the prosecution or defence and the court and, presumably with, for example, researchers and others with a legitimate interest in the proceedings who are not a section of the public.

---

[16] (1999) 163 J.P. 776
[16a] Article 6, European Convention on Human Rights.
[16b] *The Times,* December 6, 2000.
[17] Section 49(1).
[18] Section 49(11).
[19] Under sections 15 or 16 CYPA 1969.
[20] s.49(2) of the CYPA 1933.

7.08   How does it apply to victims of crime or the witnesses to the crime? Is a letter notifying six witnesses of the date of a trial which includes the name of the defendant in breach of the prohibition? Clearly, it would not breach the spirit of the legislation, which is designed to prevent undesirable publication of the details of young people for their own welfare and to enhance the prospects of rehabilitation, but the document is arguably not "prepared for use in particular proceedings".[21] Therefore, the issue will be whether the witnesses are a "section of the public". It should be possible to exclude from such a definition a group with a specific interest in the case which it is essential to fulfil in order to allow the case to proceed. Witnesses may need to be warned not to divulge the name of the defendant or others under 18 covered by the legislation. Disclosure to friends in small numbers is unlikely to be covered by the provisions but loud talk in a crowded public house might be.

A person under 18 is "concerned in proceedings" if he is—

- the person against whom the proceedings are taken;

- a person in respect of whom the proceedings are taken;

- a person proposed to be called as a witness.[22]

7.09   Defendants, victims and witnesses are well protected if under the age of 18. The broad prohibition on what may be published will often lead to it being impossible to name an adult where the connection between the adult and the person under 18 is such that identifying the older would identify the younger.

The prohibition can be lifted[23] (in whole or in part) by a court or by a single justice.[24] After conviction, it can be lifted in certain respects if the court/justice is satisfied that it is in the public interest to do so.[25] In relation to any stage of the case, the restriction may be lifted where a court or justice is satisfied that that is necessary to avoid injustice to the person under 18 or where it is necessary to assist in tracing such a person who is unlawfully at large.[26]

Public interest

7.10   There was a time when the Government perceived great public concern that people under 18 could commit very serious crimes but not face the glare of adverse publicity. The previous restrictions were relaxed to allow a court or a justice of the peace to permit certain information to be given. This power extends to—

- proceedings in a youth court or on appeal from a youth court; and

- proceedings relating:

  - to prosecution for an offence;
  - to the way in which the defendant (or his parent/guardian) should be dealt with;
  - to changing an order made in respect of an offence; and

---

[21] s.49(3) of the CYPA 1933.
[22] s.49(4) of the CYPA 1933.
[23] *ibid.*, s.49(5).
[24] *ibid.*, s.49(8).
[25] *ibid.*, s.49(4A).
[26] *ibid.*, s.49(5).

- to enforcement of an order made in respect of an offence or rules or requirements relating to an Attendance Centre Order or secure training order.

7.11 All the parties to the proceedings are entitled to make representations to the court before such an order is made.[27] There is no reason why the press should not be permitted to make representations also.[28] Reasons for a decision should be given[29] but these need not be elaborately stated[30] nor minutely dissected.[31]

Since this provision was inserted into the Act, much has changed in relation to the best way of dealing with young people who come into contact with the criminal law. The position in the youth court is different from that in the adult court[32] and it is rare that the criteria for removal of anonymity would be met in the youth court.[33] The principal aim of the criminal justice system regarding young offenders is the prevention of offending by children and young people.[34] There is a link with rights to privacy, particularly those in the UNCRC, and the longer term interests of the person under 18 need to be considered. Even the most serious young offender will need to be rehabilitated into society at some time and continuing adverse publicity is likely to make that very difficult.

"Necessary to avoid injustice" to a person under 18.

7.12 This provision[35] allows a court to allow such publicity as is necessary where the restriction is causing avoidable injustice to the person under 18 concerned. It is difficult to envisage any situation where that will be appropriate though it may apply where a defendant has been acquitted or, perhaps, convicted of a lesser charge than popularly believed to be the case or where there is serious speculation that a person under 18, who is in fact a witness, is the defendant.

Unlawfully at large

7.13 There will be times when a person under 18 has disappeared during the time they are before the court for an offence. Providing the offence is one of violence,[36] or is a sexual offence,[37] or is an offence punishable with imprisonment for 14 years or more[38] and providing application is made by the Director of Public Prosecutions, having given notice to any legal representative of the person under 18,[39] the court may relax the restrictions on publicity if that is necessary to apprehend him.[40] A person is unlawfully at large whether away from a place of custody or whether, having been released on bail, he is liable to arrest with or without a warrant.[41]

---

[27] *ibid.*, s.49(4B).
[28] *McKerry v. Teesdale and Wear Valley Justices*, (2000) 164 J.P. 355.
[29] *R. v. Central Criminal Court ex. p. S and P* (1999) 163 J.P. 776.
[30] *McKerry v. Teesdale and Wear Valley Justices, op. cit.*
[31] *R. v. Central Criminal Court ex parte S and P, op. cit.*
[32] *R. v. CCC ex p. S and P, op. cit.*
[33] per Lord Bingham, C.J., *McKerry v. Teesdale and Wear Valley Justices*, 355 at 361 E.
[34] s.37 of the CDA 1998.
[35] s.49(5) of the CYPA 1933.
[36] Defined in s.31(1) of the CJA 1991.
[37] *ibid.*
[38] s.49(6) of the CYPA 1933.
[39] *ibid.*, s.49(7).
[40] *ibid.*, s.49(5)(b).
[41] *ibid.*, s.49(11).

Variation and revocation of supervision orders

7.14 Where this takes place in a youth court (or on appeal from a youth court), the provisions of section 49 of the CYPA 1933 automatically apply. Where the proceedings take place in a magistrates' court other than a youth court (or on appeal from such a court) the provisions only apply if the court announces during the course of the proceedings that they apply. A duty is placed on the court to make that announcement.[42] The consequence of failing to fulfil that duty is that the restrictions do not apply.[43]

Other criminal proceedings

7.15 Section 49 applies to youth court proceedings and appeals from youth courts and should be applied in magistrates' courts dealing with proceedings to vary or revoke a supervision order. In other criminal proceedings (for example, in a Crown Court or a magistrates' court other than a youth court), the court has the power to impose restrictions on publicity.[44] See also the provisions in the *Practice Direction (Crown Court: Trial of Children and Young Persons)*[45] proposing restricted presence of the media in the courtroom but the provision of relay facilities to another room in the court complex.[46] For the procedure in respect of other non-criminal proceedings once the 1999 Act amendments are brought into force, see section 39 of the 1933 Act below.

Such a court may direct that no matter relating to any person concerned in the proceedings shall, while that person is under 18, be included in any publication if it is likely to lead members of the public to identify him as a person concerned in the proceedings.[47] This follows closely the wording of section 49(1) of the 1933 Act as amended by the YJCEA 1999. See above for discussion on "members of the public".[48]

7.16 The definition of a person "concerned in proceedings"[49] is narrower than that contained in section 49(4) of the CYPA 1933. In relation to witnesses, section 45 applies only to a "witness in the proceedings" whereas section 49 of the 1933 Act applies to "a person called or proposed to be called to give evidence in the proceedings". The reason for this difference in terminology is unclear but the section 45 definition appears to exclude a person who is not actually called to give evidence. In respect of both provisions, the protection ceases once the person concerned becomes 18 whatever the state of the proceedings.

If a direction is made under section 45(3) of the 1999 Act (when in force), its effect may be limited by a further excepting direction. This may be because dispensing with the restriction is necessary in the interests of justice[50] or because it is in the public interest to remove a restriction that is imposing a substantial and unreasonable restriction on the reporting of the proceedings.[51] No criteria are given for the making of a direction under section 45(3) of the 1999 Act but the two grounds for giving excepting directions are on the grounds of the interests of justice

---

[42] *ibid.*, s.49(10).
[43] *ibid.*
[44] s.45 of the YJCEA 1999 when in force [2000] 2 All E.R. 285.
[45] Issued February 17, 2000.
[46] Paras 14 & 15.
[47] s.45(3) of the YJCEA 1999.
[48] 7.08 above.
[49] s.45(7) of the YJCEA 1999.
[50] s.45(4) of the YJCEA 1999.
[51] *ibid.*, s.45(5).

and on the grounds of the public interest, the latter being more tightly defined than the former. There has been substantial case law in respect of the previous provision[52] the key elements of which are noted below at 7.24 and encompass both the procedure for seeking an order and the criteria for when a direction or a removal of a restriction was being considered.

7.17 In making a direction, the court should allow representations to be made by all the parties to the proceedings and should also allow representations from those with an interest in publishing the material.[53] The welfare of the person under 18 is *a* primary consideration[54] and the court must have regard to it.[55] However, the discretion of the court is not to be unnecessarily constrained.[56] Reasons should be given for the decision but they do not need to be elaborate[57] nor should they be subjected to detailed textual analysis.[58] The fact of conviction may well be relevant in deciding whether to lift an order made prior to trial. The court must balance the desirability of protecting young people from adverse publicity with the public interest in the reporting of cases. For a thorough review of the approach to this delicate balancing exercise, see *R. v. Central Criminal Court ex. p. S and P.*[59]

Interests of justice

7.18 The court has a wide discretion to limit the restriction on publicity where that is in the "interests of justice". This is a different criterion from that in section 49(4A) of the CYPA 1933 which allows removal of the restrictions that automatically apply in the youth court, etc, where that is in the "public interest".[60] In order to be faced with this issue, the court must have decided that a restriction on reporting was appropriate and normally this will be the case for any person under 18. In what circumstances might the interests of justice make partial publicity necessary? One example might be where further witnesses are known to exist but have not yet come forward.

Public interest

7.19 The second ground on which the restriction imposed by section 45(3) of the 1999 Act (when in force) can be relaxed is where the effect of those restrictions is to impose a substantial and unreasonable restriction on the reporting of the proceedings which it is in the public interest to relax.[61] This criterion has three elements—the restriction must be substantial, it must be unreasonable and it must be in the public interest to relax it. There will be cases where it is quite possible to report all that needs to be reported without including anything likely to lead members of the public to identify a person under 18 as concerned in the proceedings. However, there will be other cases where that is not possible and this provision will allow a court to govern the extent of disclosure that is appropriate. The conclusion of the proceedings is not sufficient reason in itself for use of this power but it may be a factor.[62]

---

[52] s.39 of the CYPA 1933.
[53] *McKerry v. Teesdale and Wear Valley Justices* (2000) 164 J.P. 355.
[54] UNCRC.
[55] s.45(6) of the YJCEA 1999.
[56] *R. v. Central Criminal Court ex. p. S and P* (1999) 163 J.P. 776.
[57] *McKerry v. Teesdale and Wear Valley Justices, op. cit.*
[58] (1999) 163 J.P. 776.
[59] *op. cit.*
[60] See 7.10 above
[61] s.45(5) of the YCEA 1999.
[62] *R. v. Central Criminal Court ex. p. S and P* (1999) 163 J.P. 776.

Non-criminal proceedings

7.20   The previous provision allowing courts other than a Youth Court to restrict publication was section 39 of the CYPA 1933. As a result of the bringing into force of the YJCEA 1999 at some future date, section 39 will be restricted to proceedings that are not criminal proceedings. This widely drawn power will remain available, therefore, for courts dealing with non-criminal proceedings which do not have their own restrictions on publicity where a person under 18 is a person by or against or in respect of whom the proceedings are taken or who is a witness in the proceedings.[63]

Protection prior to commencement of proceedings

7.21   A restriction similar to that imposed automatically to certain proceedings by section 49 of the 1933 Act will be applied to the stage between the commencement of a criminal investigation and the commencement of court proceedings by section 44 of the 1999 Act when in force. A "criminal investigation" is an investigation by a person charged with the duty of investigating offences (including a police officer) in order to ascertain whether a person should be charged with an offence.[64] Nothing can be published that is likely to lead members of the public to identify a person under 18 as a person involved in the offence. A person is "involved in an offence" where he is the person by whom the offence is alleged to have been committed[65] or against or in respect of whom the offence is committed, or a person alleged to be a witness to the commission of the offence.[66] The latter class will only be protected once a specific order bringing this provision into force is made by the Secretary of State.[67] The anonymity given to victims of certain sexual offences by section 1 of the Sexual Offences (Amendment) Act 1992 takes precedence over this power.[68] The protection of section 44 can be dispensed with, either entirely or to a limited extent, where it is in the interests of justice to do so.[69] The power to dispense with the protection can be exercised by any court with a criminal jurisdiction.[70] If an application is made to a magistrates' court, the power can be exercised by a single justice.[71] If application is made to a magistrates' court, appeal lies to the Crown Court against grant or refusal.[72] Any party to the proceedings before the magistrates' court may appeal as of right; anyone else may appeal with the leave of the Crown Court.[73] The welfare of the person under 18 must be considered in deciding whether to dispense with the protection.[74]

7.22   At this stage, the protection can be waived by anyone who would otherwise be protected except for the alleged offender or a potential witness (aged under 16) to the commission of the offence to whom section 1 of the Sexual Offences (Amendment) Act 1992 applies.[75] There must be written consent specific

---

[63] s.39(1)(a) of the CYPA 1933.
[64] s.44(13) of the YJCEA 1999.
[65] *ibid.*, s.44(4)(a).
[66] *ibid.*, s.44(4)(b).
[67] *ibid.*, s.44(5).
[68] *ibid.*, s.44(4).
[69] *ibid.*, s.44(7).
[70] *ibid.*, s.44(9).
[71] *ibid.*, s.44(10).
[72] *ibid.*, s.44(11).
[73] *ibid.*
[74] *ibid.*, s.44(8).
[75] *ibid.*, s.50(4), (5), and (6).

to the publication.[76] This consent can be withdrawn.[77] If the protected person is under 16, the consent will need to be given by an "appropriate person".[78] The written consent is invalidated where it is proved that any person interfered with the peace and comfort of the person giving the consent or the protected person (if different) with the intent of obtaining that consent.[79] It is also a defence to a publisher that, at the time of the offence arising from the publication, he was not aware, nor suspected, nor had reason to suspect, that the criminal investigation had begun.[80]

Adult Courts

7.23   There has been a tendency for an adult court to make an order restricting publicity automatically whenever a defendant is under 18. Whilst it will usually be right to make the order, on each occasion the court should consider the situation before it and balance the need to protect juveniles against the legitimate interest of the public in knowing the identity of those who commit criminal offences. In *Crown Court at Leicester, ex p. S (a minor)*[81] a twelve year old boy was charged with arson, having set fire to an ambulance station causing damage to both the station and ambulances estimated at £2.5m. The Divisional Court decided to overturn a decision of the trial Judge to allow the identity of the child to be disclosed. In the judgment, Watkins L.J. described the way to consider such decisions:

> "the correct approach to the exercise of the power given by section 39 is that reports of proceedings should not be restricted unless there are reasons to do so which outweigh the legitimate interest of the public in receiving fair and accurate reports of criminal proceedings and knowing the identity of those in the community who have been guilty of criminal conduct and who may, therefore, present a danger or threat to the community in which they live. The mere fact that the person before the court is a child or young person will normally be a good reason for restricting reports . . . and it will, in our opinion, only be in rare and exceptional cases that directions under section 39 will not be given . . ."

7.24   In reaching a conclusion that this case was not rare and exceptional, the Divisional Court took into account:

(a) The effect on the child of the reactions of others who lived in the same community home if they were to discover the nature of the allegations against him;

(b) The effect on the family of the child;

---

[76] *ibid.*, s.44(5).
[77] *ibid.*, s.50(6).
[78] See ss.50(9)–(12) of the YJCEA 1999.
[79] *ibid.*, s.50(8).
[80] *ibid.*, s.50(2).
[81] [1992] 2 All E.R. 659.

(c) The passing of 18 months from the date of offence to the date of appearance in the Crown Court;

(d) The fact that the child would not be released into the community for some time.

No application for an order is needed but one will often be made by the magistrates' legal adviser, although it may be made by any person involved in the proceedings. Indeed, it has been suggested that the prosecutor should be expected to remind a court of the need to consider making an order where it appears that the need may be overlooked.[82] If a representative of the press wishes to object to the order being made, that representative should be allowed to be heard. Indeed, a court has complete discretion to hear representations from parties that the court considers to have a legitimate interest in whether or not an order should be made.[83] If the order is made, it can only be in the terms of the section but it must be in terms that are clear and readily ascertainable by those affected by it. Ideally, the order will be reduced to writing especially where there was any possibility of doubt as to the extent of the order[84]. It will then be for a publisher to decide whether the information intending to be published would be likely to lead to a breach of the section. One consequence of making an order may be that it will effectively prevent the identifying of the defendants who are adults since identifying the defendants may inevitably identify the child. In such circumstances there is no power under section 39 to specifically prohibit the publication of the details of an adult. Any publisher will need to make his own decision knowing that prosecution may follow if that decision is wrong. In *Crown Court at Southwark ex p. Godwin*, two (adult) defendants appeared at the Crown Court charged with acts of indecency on two young children who belonged to the same close knit community. At the time of the offences one of the defendants lived next door to the children and used to act as child minder for them. Defence counsel successfully argued that the close knit nature of the community to which both children and defendants belonged meant that naming the defendants was likely to have the effect of naming the children and the trial Judge added to the section 39 order a prohibition against the revealing of the names and addresses of the defendants. The Court of Appeal confirmed that this order was outside the scope of the section and could not be imposed. The issue of naming defendants was part of the practical application of the order and was for potential publishers to consider. Additional controls are contained in Contempt of Court Act 1981, s.4 (power to postpone reporting of proceedings) and s.11 (prohibiting publication of matters withheld from the public during the course of proceedings).

Location and Time Limits

7.25 Territorially, the court has the same jurisdiction as with an adult. Similarly, with the time during which proceedings can be started. Thus—

---

[82] *Crown Court at Southwark, ex p. Godwin* [1991] 3 All E.R. 818 at 820c, per Glidewell L.J.
[83] *Central Criminal Court, ex p. Crook and Godwin*, 159 J.P. 295; [1995] F.C.R. 153.
[84] *ex p. Crook and Godwin*.

Nature of offence	Proceedings to be Commenced Within	Territorial Limits
1. Summary	six months unless offence extension or restriction	Commission Area (but see MCA 1980, s.2(6) allowing court dealing with a person for an offence committed within a Commission Area to deal also with any other summary offence for which he could be tried by a magistrates'court for any other area).
or		
2. Indictable (including those triable either way)	No Limit	No Limit

7.26 Proceedings commence by way of information, that is a document describing the specific offence in ordinary language avoiding as far as possible the use of technical terms and giving such particulars as necessary to give reasonable information of the nature of the charge.[85] A written information is laid when it is received at the office of the Justices' Chief Executive for the area.[86] This is so even where the information is a letter from the Crown Prosecution Service informing of an intention to charge and providing enough detail to satisfy 1981 Rules, r. 100, even though neither the prosecutor nor the recipient regarded the letter as an information.[87]

7.27 The time limits given are the maximum periods and are subject to the line of authorities regarding abuse of the process of the court. These give to the court power to dismiss proceedings where there has been inordinate delay and prejudice to the defence.[88] Delay due merely to the complexity of the case or contributed to by the actions of the defendant will not found relief.[89] The defendant must show on the balance of probabilities that, owing to the delay, he would suffer serious prejudice to the extent that no fair trial could be held.

In addition, the principles in the ECHR enforceable in English and Welsh courts through the Human Rights Act 1998, require fairness and "equality of arms" in the trial process. Parties need proper time to prepare their case but justice also requires that issues are brought to a conclusion as rapidly as possible. This is particularly so with young offenders. The principal aim of the youth justice system is to prevent offending by children and young people.[90] Presenting an offender quickly with the consequences of their behaviour is an important step in that process.

7.28 The first edition of this work commented that excessive and unproductive delay in the conclusion of cases was harmful, particularly for those under 18. This

---

[85] Magistrates' Courts Rules 1981, r. 100.
[86] *Manchester Stiperdiary Magistrate, ex p. Hill* (1982) 2 All E.R. 963.
[87] *Kennett Justices, ex p. Humphrey and Wyatt* (1993) Crim. L.R. 787.
[88] *Gateshead Justices, ex p. Smith* [1984] J.P. 609.
[89] *AG Reference (No. 1 of 1990)* [1992] 3 All E.R. 169.
[90] s.37 of the CDA 1998.

theme was taken up by the Labour party and a pledge included in its manifesto that the average time between arrest and sentence for persistent young offenders[91] should be halved by 2002. Interim targets were set and are generally being achieved, not least because of the impact of the procedures in the CDA 1998. The creation of the Youth Justice Board is also an indication of the priority attached to dealing properly with young people at risk of offending. Whilst initial emphasis is on persistent young offenders, the principle holds good for all young offenders and applies equally to the magistrates' court and the Crown Court. Because of the nature of the offences, and the inevitable preliminaries to committal, it is particularly important that the Crown Court pays special attention to those cases involving young offenders, many of whom will be jointly charged with adult offenders.

In its publication *Speeding up Youth Justice*,[92] the Youth Justice Board created a template showing the various events, actions, decisions and consultations involved in taking a case involving a young offender through the criminal justice system. Priorities for improved performance are identified and detailed recommendations made. The Government has set target times for each of the key stages—arrest to charge (2 days), charge to first appearance (7 days), first appearance to start of trial or committal (28 days) and verdict to sentence (14 days). In the Crown Court, there are also targets for committal to preliminary directions hearing (PDH) (14 days) and PDH to start of trial (28 days).[93]

7.29   All involved should be seeking to achieve these targets unless there are compelling reasons in an individual case as to why they should be exceeded. However, care must be taken to ensure that the proper emphasis on speed does not override the other elements of justice and welfare that exist. The whole process needs to be streamlined so that, for instance, the defence advocate who is to deal with the case in the Crown Court can be brought into the matter early enough to allow proper briefing and identification of issues. Inappropriate haste at an early stage can lead to waste at a later stage.

Some evidence on what needs to be done can be found in the report "How long youth cases take" published by the Inspectorates of the Crown Prosecution Service, Magistrates' Courts and Police.[94] Implementation of the CDA 1998 followed the publication of the report.

In addition to the target times published by the Government,[95] statutory time limits apply where a defendant is in custody and, at the time of publication, are undergoing trial in a number of magistrates' courts whether or not the defendant is in custody.[96]

Custody time limits

7.30   The Prosecution of Offences Act 1985 permits the Secretary of State to set time limits both for the prosecution to complete any specified stage in the proceedings and for the time to be spent in custody.[97] Limits for time in custody have been set.[98] In relation to a magistrates' court, the period in custody during the

---

[91] 142 days in 1996.
[92] Youth Justice Board, May 1999.
[93] *Speeding up Youth Justice*, p. 15.
[94] Published in March 1999 and based on research in October and November 1998.
[95] *Measuring Performance to Reduce Delays in the Youth Justice System*, HO/LCD, 1998.
[96] s.22A of the Prosecution of Offences Act 1985.
[97] Section 22(1).
[98] Prosecution of Offences (Custody Time Limits) Regulations 1987, S.I. 1987 No. 299 as amended.

preliminary stage of proceedings must not exceed 70 days for an indictable only offence. For an indictable offence triable either way, the maximum period is 70 days between first appearance and start of summary trial or committal for trial unless a decision to proceed to summary trial was taken within 56 days of first appearance. If so, the maximum period in custody between the first appearance and the start of the summary trial must not exceed 56 days. In relation to young offenders, all indictable offences other than homicide are to be tried summarily unless they come within the provisions of section 24 MCA of the 1980.[99] How does this affect the custody time limit? The Divisional Court has ruled that the limit is 56 days[1] since, other than homicide, all indictable offences against young offenders were triable either way for these purposes. Presumably, since such offences have to be tried summarily unless the court determines for committal, the normal maximum period will be 56 days unless within those 56 days the court determines for trial on indictment in which case the 70 day period will apply. This conclusion is reached by consideration of the wording of regulation 4(3) of the 1987 Regulations[2] and section 24 of the 1980 Act. Where the young person appears with an adult in the adult court, the same reasoning follows because of section 24(1)(b) of the 1980 Act.

Other time limits

7.31   A new section 22A was inserted into the Prosecution of Offences Act 1985 by section 44 of the CDA 1998 and is currently operating in a number of pilot areas. Time limits are set for all offences dealt with in a youth court[3] for the period from first appearance to commencement of trial (99 days),[4] from arrest to first appearance (36 days)[5] and from conviction to sentence (29 days).[6] If the prosecution wish to apply for an extension of the time limit imposed by regulation 4 or regulation 5, the application must be made before the limit has expired and on giving at least two days notice to the defendant or his legal representative and the court.[7] The defendant may waive the notice to him and the court may authorise non-service of the notice or the giving of less than two days notice. If the pilots are successful, the limits will apply to all courts and it is likely that the length of time (which is presently erring on the side of generosity) will steadily be reduced. The dangers of leaving the commencement of a trial to the end of the permitted period were illustrated in *R. v. Kingston Crown Court, ex p. Bell*.[8] The prosecution had failed to comply with various timetables set by the court with the result that the trial was scheduled to start on the last but one permissible day. New information came to light justifying the granting of a defence application to adjourn but the Youth Court refused to extend the time limit on the grounds that there was a strong causal connection between the earlier lack of diligence by the prosecution and the inability to start the trial within the 99 days. That decision was upheld by the Divisional Court. In the words of Jackson J.[9]—

> "The 1999 Regulations serve an important social purpose. That is to speed up the process of dealing with youth crime. There is a . . . clear obligation on all

---

[99] See para. 7.33 below.
[1] *R. v. Stratford Justices, ex. p. S.* [1999] Crim. L.R. 146.
[2] See n. 74.
[3] Prosecution of Offences (Youth Court Time Limits) Regulations 1999, S.I. 1999 No. 2743.
[4] *ibid.*, reg. 4.
[5] *ibid.*, reg. 5.
[6] *ibid.*, reg. 6.
[7] *ibid.*, reg. 7.
[8] (2000) 164 J.P. 633
[9] (2000) 164 J.P. 633

agencies in the criminal justice system to perform their functions reasonably promptly. It is not acceptable for the prosecution to breach court orders and to delay, so that the trial is pushed right back to the last day or two of the permitted 99 day period."

The importance of the time limit as a factor in assessing competing priorities where there is insufficient court time for all cases to proceed was considered in *Re C*.[10] Although not oveturning an extension to the time limit granted by justices, the Divisional Court expressed considerable sympathy for the defendant who was seeking to rely on the statutory time limits which "should be firmly observed".[11] The fact that a case is subject to a time limit which is about to expire should be an important factor in listing decisions.

Where a custody time limit expires and is not extended, a defendant is released on bail. Where a general time limit expires and is not extended, the case is brought to an end subject to the prosecutor instituting fresh proceedings.[12] An unsuccessful challenge to the prosecutor was made in *R (on the application of the Director of Public Prosecutions) v. Croydon Youth Court*.[13] Justices had upheld a defence application to stay the new information on the ground of abuse of process but the Divisional Court disagreed. The Court acknowledged that the Crown Prosecution Service had the power to re-institute proceedings, a decision which has to be taken by a senior officer. Where the decision is made to re-institute proceedings, it will only be rarely that they should be stayed for abuse of process. The Court appeared to agree that an application to stay re-instituted proceedings on the grounds of abuse of process would be better made to the Divisional Court than to a magistrates' court or youth court.

Attainment of age 18

7.32 A young person who becomes 18 between the date of the offence and the first court appearance will be dealt with by an adult court.[14] A young person who becomes 18 after the first hearing may continue to be dealt with in the youth court.[15] If the offence is triable either way, the court will have to determine the mode of trial if a decision for summary trial is not taken before the 18th birthday and in those circumstances the young person will have the right to refuse to consent to summary trial. The point at which the decision for summary trial is deemed to have been taken has been considered on a number of occasions. The current position is that it will be when the plea is taken. If that is before the young person becomes 18 then, unless the crime is homicide or is a grave one within the meaning of section 91, Powers of Criminal Courts (Sentencing) Act 2000, it may only be dealt with summarily and the entry of the plea settled that issue. If a not guilty plea is entered but the court cannot start taking evidence straightaway, it is preferable for the papers to be marked "remanded for summary trial"[16] but failure to do so is

[10] (2000) 164 J.P. 693.
[11] per Rafferty J. at 698.
[12] Prosecution of Offences Act 1985, s.22B.
[13] (2001) 165 J.P.
[14] *R. v. Amersham Juvenile Court, ex. p. Wilson* [1981] Q.B. 974, followed in *R. v. Uxbridge Youth Court, ex p. H, The Times*, April 7, 1998.
[15] s.29 of the 1963 Act.
[16] *R. v. Lewes Juvenile Court, ex p. Turner* (1984) 149 J.P. 186.

not fatal. No submissions will be expected to be made since there is no alternative to summary trial at that point.[17] If a young person appearing before a youth court has further offences preferred against him after he becomes 18 these new cases can only be dealt with in the adult court even if they were committed whilst the offender was under 18. In *Chelsea JJ., ex p. DPP*[18] a juvenile was charged with wounding with intent and appeared before the juvenile court. After he became 17 (then the age at which juveniles became adult) a further charge of attempted murder was preferred against him on the same facts as the wounding charge. The Divisional Court held that the juvenile court had no power to deal with the later charge. Alternatively, at any time before the start of the trial,[19] or after conviction and before sentence, a youth court may remit an 18 year old to an adult magistrates' court acting for the same area as the youth court.[20] That court may deal with the case as if the whole case had been dealt with before it.[21] There is no appeal against the remittal.[22] The case will be adjourned by the remitting court and the usual provisions apply regarding bail or custody.[23]

Committal for Trial and Transfer General

7.33 Where a person under 18 is charged with homicide, the case must be committed to the Crown Court for trial. Where a person under 18 is charged with any other indictable offence, whether or not it is capable of being tried either at the Crown Court or in the magistrates' court, a magistrates' court may commit the young person to the Crown Court for trial in two circumstances:

1. If the young person is aged 10 to 17 inclusive and the offence is punishable in the case of an adult with 14 years imprisonment or more, or is an offence of indecent assault on a woman or a man, of causing death by dangerous driving or by careless driving under the influence of drink or drugs the magistrates' court may commit the young person to the Crown Court for trial if it believes that it is likely that it will wish to use the power of long term detention available under s.91(3) of the Powers of Criminal Courts (Sentencing) Act 2000.[24] For circumstances in which long term detention is appropriate see Chapter 29. The power to use long term detention is only available where the young person is *committed for trial*; committal for sentence is not sufficient.[25] [The removal of the power to commit for sentence under section 37 of the MCA 1980 makes this distinction less significant.] Section 91(1) provides "where a person aged under 18 is *convicted on indictment . . .*").

2 If a person under 18 is charged jointly with a person aged 18 or more and the court considers it necessary in the interests of justice to commit then both for trial.[26] This discretion must be exercised when both the juvenile

---

[17] For an analysis of the authorities and the law, see *R. v. West London J.J., ex p. S–W*, (2001) 165 J.P., [2000] Crim. L.R. 926.
[18] [1963] 3 All E.R. 657.
[19] Defined in section 22(11B) Prosecution of Offences Act 1985.
[20] s.47(1) of the CDA 1998.
[21] *ibid.*, s.47(4).
[22] *ibid.*, s.47(2)(a).
[23] *ibid.*, s.47(2)&(3).
[24] s.24(1)(a) of the MCA 1980.
[25] 91(1) of the 2000 Act.
[26] s.24(1)(b) of the 1980 Act.

and the adult are before the court; if a decision is to commit for trial, the actual committal may take place on different occasions for the juvenile and the adult (*Crown Court at Doncaster, ex p. CPS.*[27]

Alternatively, in respect of certain offences where a child[28] who is alleged to be a victim of the offence or a witness to its commission and who is to be called as a witness at the trial, the Director of Public Prosecutions may serve notice of transfer to the Crown Court where of the opinion that there is sufficient evidence for the defendant to be committed for trial and the welfare of the child dictates that the case should be taken over by the Crown Court without delay.[29] The majority of such cases will involve adult defendants and may well be subject to the transfer of indictable only provisions to the Crown Court provisions.[30] However, where the defendant is a youth, the Director of Public Prosecutions should exercise this option only where satisfied that the youth court would consider that it was a grave crime within the meaning of s.91 to the PCC(S)A 2000.[31]

7.34   A number of practical problems may follow—

(a)   Can a court change its mind over whether or not to commit for trial?

(b)   What is the significance of new charges?

(c)   What should the court do with cases that cannot be committed for trial?

(d)   What should be done where all jointly charged adults are discharged or plead guilty?

(a) Varying mode of trial decision

7.35   Where a court has begun to try an information summarily or has started to inquire into an offence as examining justices, a change in the mode of trial decision can be made in accordance with section 25(5) of the MCA 1980. Where summary trial is concerned, that decision must be made before the conclusion of the evidence for the prosecution.[32] Where an inquiry has begun, the decision can be made at any time during the inquiry.[33] There is no power to change a determination except in accordance with these provisions.[34] If summary trial is accepted and a guilty plea entered, there is no power to change the decision. If summary trial is accepted and a not guilty plea entered, a change can be made under section 25(6) only where the court has begun to try the information; if, a not guilty plea having been entered, all that happens is that the case is put over to another day for trial, the process of determining guilt or innocence has not "begun".[35] The Director of Public Prosecutions may not use his powers to transfer a case to the Crown Court[36] to override acceptance by the justices of summary trial although it can precede the mode of

---

[27] [1987] Crim. L.R. 395.
[28] As defined in s.53(6) to the Criminal Justice Act 1991.
[29] s.53 to the Criminal Justice Act 1991 and s.32 to the Criminal Justice Act 1988.
[30] s.51 to the Crime and Disorder Act 1998.
[31] *R. v. T., R. v. K., The Times,* January 11, 2001.
[32] s.25(6) of the MCA 1980.
[33] *ibid.,* s.25(7).
[34] *R. v. Fareham Youth Court and Morey ex. p. CPS* (1999) 163 J.P. 812.
[35] *R. v. Horseferry Road Magistrates ex p. K* [1997] Q.B. 23.
[36] s.53 of the CJA 1991.

trial decision[37] as well as following a determination for trial on indictment. The court is entitled to keep the decision under review and to change its decision where, for instance, new material relevant to seriousness was adduced.

(b) New charges

7.36 The Crown Prosecution Service must only use the power to transfer for very grave offences as it is highly undesirable that cases involving young defendants and young witnesses end up being tried in the Crown Court.[38] If new charges are brought, which the court determines should be dealt with on indictment, this cannot affect an earlier decision to accept summary trial on other charges except in the circumstances prescribed by section 25(6) MCA 1980, that is, where the summary trial has commenced. It may, however, be possible for the prosecution to withdraw the earlier charges and then add them to the indictment in the Crown Court in some circumstances. In *R. v. S*,[39] a youth court had been faced with a defendant charged with offences of indecent assault and offences of assault occasioning actual bodily harm (ABH). The court determined to decline jurisdiction on the indecent assaults but to accept jurisdiction on the actual bodily harm matters. Subsequently, the prosecutor determined that the actual bodily harm matters were so closely linked to the indecent assaults that they should be tried together. Although guilty pleas had been indicated to the ABH matters, no convictions had been recorded. The prosecutor withdrew the ABH charges with a view to joining them on the indictment as part of the process following from the use of the transfer provisions.[40] Emphasising the lack of impropriety, abuse or attempt to avoid the sentencing limitations existing in the magistrates' courts (at that time), the Court of Appeal concluded that this course of action was not in breach of section 24 of the MCA 1980.

(c) Other cases

7.37 When committing a young person for trial under section 24(1) of the 1980 Act, the court may also commit any other indictable offences with which the young person is also charged if these charges could also be joined in the same indictment.[41] It may also commit for any summary offences punishable with imprisonment or disqualification from driving which arises out of circumstances the same as (or connected to) those giving rise to the indictable offence being committed.[42] In some ways, this power is more widely available for young offenders than for adults; it only applies where the principal offence is an indictable offence triable either way. For a young offender, all indictable offences except homicide are triable either way.[43] However, there will still be circumstances where there are cases that cannot be committed for trial. Whilst it is generally desirable that all outstanding matters are dealt with on one sentencing occasion,[44] it is also important that cases against young offenders are dealt with as quickly as possible as an aid to preventing further offending. By section 10 (3A) of the MCA 1980, a youth court is not to be required to adjourn any proceedings only because it has committed the

---

[37] *R. v. D.P.P. ex. p. Brewer* [1995] Crim. L.R. 168.
[38] *R. v. T., R. v. K, The Times,* January 11, 2001.
[39] *The Times,* March 18, 1998, CA.
[40] s.53 of the CJA 1991.
[41] s.24(1A) & (2) of the MCA 1980.
[42] s.41 of the CJA 1988.
[43] *R. v. Stratford Justices ex. p. S* [1999] Crim. L.R. 146.
[44] See, for example, *R. v. S, op. cit.*

young person for trial on another offence or the young person is charged with another offence. Joint guidance issued by the Magistrates' Association and the Justices' Clerks' Society also encourages courts to deal rapidly with outstanding cases. This approach assists in dealing with situations where a young offender can delay the day of reckoning simply by continuing to commit offences.

If the committal proceedings are taking place in the adult magistrates' court, any cases that cannot be committed must be remitted to the Youth Court unless they fall within the categories of case capable of being dealt with in the adult court.[45] In such circumstances, the adult court should follow the principle of section 10(3A) of the MCA 1980 and proceed to sentence as rapidly as possible.

(d) Adult not committed for trial

7.38 If a young person is charged jointly with an adult and the case against the adult is deemed suitable for the Crown Court, it does not necessarily follow that the case against the young person will also need to go to the Crown Court. The criterion is that it is "necessary in the interests of justice to commit both for trial".[46] The complexity of this decision has been increased by the Direction that the Crown Court would ordinarily separate the trials of jointly charged young and adult offenders unless a joint trial was in the interests of justice and would not be unduly prejudicial to the welfare of the young person.[47] If the case against the young person is deemed suitable for summary trial and the young person pleads not guilty, the adult court may remit the young person for trial to a youth court for the same area or for the area where the young person habitually resides.[48] This remittal must take place before evidence is called in relation to the determination of guilt or innocence. The adult court must, however, make the determination of mode of trial.[49] Similarly, where the young person pleads guilty, the court may proceed to sentence (within its limited powers) or remit to the youth court for sentence. Where an adult court discharges the adult offenders but finds sufficient evidence to commit a young offender, it cannot proceed to committal under section 24(1)(b) of the MCA 1980 but must consider whether the offence falls within section 24(1)(a)—grave offences. If it does, the adult court should proceed to commit. If it does not, it should proceed to summary trial with the same options as identified above regarding remittal to a youth court. In such circumstances, the mode of trial decision cannot be remitted to the youth court.[50]

7.39 If the adult offender indicates a plea of guilty which is accepted, the young offender cannot be committed for trial under section 24(1)(b) which requires it to be necessary to commit both young and adult defendants for trial. Moreover, a young person cannot be committed for sentence and must, therefore, either be committed for trial under section 24(1)(a)—grave offences—or the court must proceed to summary trial.

If both the adult and the young person plead not guilty, the trial will be dealt with in the adult court. If the adult pleads guilty and the young person pleads not guilty, the adult court may either deal with the trial or remit the young defendant to a youth court for trial.[51] If both the adult and the young person plead guilty or

---

[45] See 7.02 above.
[46] s.24(1)(b) of the MCA 1980.
[47] *Practice Direction (Crown Court: Trial of children and young persons)*, February 17, 2000.
[48] s.29(2) of the MCA 1980.
[49] *R. v. Haringey J.J. ex. p. Fawzy* [1998] 1 Cr.App.Rep. 41; *sub nom. R. v. Tottenham Youth Court ex p. Fawzy* (1998) 162 J.P. 241.
[50] *ibid.*
[51] s.29(2) of the MCA 1980 and *ibid.*

are found guilty, the adult court can proceed to sentence both (with limited powers for the young defendant) or remit the young defendant to the youth court for sentence.[52]

Determining what is a grave crime

7.40 This is an area of the law that has become unnecessarily complex. For many years, the approach was that custody other than detention under what was section 53(2) Children and Young Persons Act 1933 (now section 91 of the Powers of Criminal Courts (Sentencing) Act 2000) was appropriate up to the prescribed maximum and then detention under section 53(2) started at one year above that maximum. The introduction of detention and training orders,[53] which can be made by a youth court or the Crown Court for up to two years, the removal of the power of committal for sentence of young offenders, and judicial consideration, have sought to bring improvements though not with total success.

Fresh judicial guidance was given in *R. v. A.M. and related appeals*[54] which pre-dated the introduction of detention and training orders. The Court of Appeal reminded sentencing courts of the statement in *R. v. Fairhurst*[55] on the balance between the objective of keeping young offenders out of long terms of custody and the need to impose sufficiently substantial sentences on those who had committed serious crime both as punishment and deterrence and to protect the public.[56] It had also formed the view that the gap between the maximum of detention in a young offender institution (as it then was) and detention under section 53(2) Children and Young Persons Act 1933 (as it then was) was no longer helpful or appropriate. A court should not exceed the 24 month limit without much careful thought, but if it concluded that a longer sentence (even though not much longer) was called for, then it should impose whatever was appropriate. For a youth court, this decision has to be taken at the mode of trial by assessing whether the power to order more than 24 months ought to be available to the sentencing court. Such a sentence may be appropriate even for younger offenders with no previous convictions if the offences are very serious.[57] There is also the possibility that the prescriptive provision on the length of a detention and training order[58] may add to the complication.[59] There is no reason why the court cannot take account of the defendant's previous convictions in deciding whether it is necessary to commit for trial. The existence of previous convictions may be a relevant factor in determining the length of sentence that should be available to the sentencing court.[60] Indeed, that consideration may be essential in determining what sentencing options should be available. For offenders aged 12–14 a detetention and training order is only available in respect of a persistent offender.[61] If custody is an option needed to be available to the sentencing court and if the offender is not a persistent offender, then the case will need to be committed to the Crown Court. Assistance in determining whether an offender is a persistent offender can be found in *R. v. Andrew Benjamin Smith*[62] (no pre convictions, series of offences over two days

---

[52] s.56 of the CYPA Act 1933.
[53] ss. 73–79 of the Crime and Disorder Act 1998 now ss. 100–107 PCC(S)A 2000.
[54] [1998] 2 Cr.App.R. R. 57 *The Times*, December 11, 1997, CA.
[55] [1986] 1 W.L.R. 1374.
[56] *ibid.*, at p. 1376/7
[57] *R. v. J–R and G*, (2001) 165 J.P. 140 [2000] Crim. L.R. 1022.
[58] s.101(1) of the PCC(S)A 2000.
[59] See commentary to *R. v. McKay and others* [1999] Crim. L.R. 755.
[60] See also Chap. 29, below.
[61] Powers of Criminal Courts (Sentencing) Act 2000, s.100(2)(a).
[62] (2000) 164 J.P. 681.

justified finding that offender a persistent offender) and in *R. v. J.D.*[63] (offence of different character from previous offences did not justify finding that offender a persistent offender).

The court may also take account of the offence in question and any other associated offence in determing seriousness. Thus, where a defendant was convicted on indictment of burglary (which was capable of being a grave crime) and aggravated vehicle taking (which was not), a sentence of detention under what was then Children and Young Persons Act 1933, s.53(2)[64] was justified by the combination of the offences even though the burglary of itself would not have justified such a sentence.[65]

7.41   A defendant who pleads guilty will normally be entitled to credit for that with a reduced sentence. That credit can be by way of not using the power to order detention under section 91 of the PCC(S)A 2000 (where available to the sentencing court) allowing the imposition of the maximum 24 months.[66]

There will be circumstances in which detention under section 91 of the PCC(S)A 2000 is the only custodial sentence available. This was the situation in *R. v. Devizes Youth Court ex parte M.*[67] A 12-year-old boy had committed an offence of arson. The youth court took the view that a custodial sentence should be an option available to the sentencing court and, therefore, committed the young defendant for trial. It was argued that that was inappropriate both because no reasonable youth court could have concluded that detention under what was then section 53(2) Children and Young Persons Act 1933 needed to be available and because exposure to a trial in the Crown Court would have deprived the defendant of a fair trial as required by article 6 of the ECHR. Both arguments were rejected by the Divisional Court. The justices approach to the primary decision was correct and it would be for the judge in the Crown Court to consider how to conduct the trial.

7.42   The issue of how to conduct cases in the Crown Court involving young defendants was the subject of a Practice Direction of the Lord Chief Justice on February 17, 2000[68] following the decision of the European Court of Human Rights in *V. v. United Kingdom; T. v. United Kingdom.*[69] The principles apply equally to magistrates' courts and, in many ways, reflect normal practice in youth courts. The Practice Direction emphasises the need to take account of the welfare of the young defendant,[70] to ensure that the trial process does not expose the young defendant to avoidable intimidation, humiliation or distress and to enable the young defendant to understand and participate in the proceedings. Key elements are—

- proper planning at the plea and directions hearing
- presumption in favour of separate trials for jointly charged adult and young defendants
- courtroom to have all participants on a similar level
- young defendant to be able to sit with family etc. and to have easy access to legal representatives

---

[63] (2001) 165 J.P. 1.
[64] Now Powers of Criminal Courts (Sentencing) Act 2000, s.91.
[65] *R. v. P.* [2000] All E.R. (D) 1938.
[66] cf. *R. v. Pinkney* [1998] Cr.App.R. (S.) 57. See also *R. v. F. and W.* (2001) 165 J.P. 77 and *R. v. D.* (2001) 165 J.P. 1.
[67] (2000) 164 J.P. 330
[68] [2000] 1 Cr.App.R. 483.
[69] [2000] Crim. L.R. 187.
[70] s.44 of the CYPA 1933.

- trial timetable to take account of a young defendants ability to concentrate for long periods

The choice of the Crown Court centre at the time of committal will be in accordance with a further Practice Direction.[71] The Crown Court may move the location of a trial where appropriate.[72]

Targets have been set for the time to be taken at the various stages of criminal proceedings.[73] Between committal and the plea and directions hearing, the target time is 14 days, between the PDH and the start of trial, 28 days and between verdict and sentence, 14 days.[74]

7.43 The leading case of *R. v. Fairhurst*[75] has been adapted to changing circumstances, most notably by *R. v. Wainfur*[76] and *R. v. A.M. and related appeals*.[77] *Fairhurst* emphasised that, in order to invoke what was then section 53(2) Children and Young Persons Act 1933 (now s.91 of the PCC(S)A 2000) it is not necessary that the crime should be one of exceptional gravity; it simply requires an offence that might call for detention for longer than the period otherwise available. For some offenders, particularly in the younger age range, this may be the only custodial option available.[78] The need for magistrates to ensure that they took advice from their legal adviser was emphasised in *R. v. Inner London Youth Court ex p. D.P.P.*[79] Issues such as the age of the witnesses and the desirability for a speedy disposal should not affect the decision; once it is appropriate that the sentencing court should have the option of detention under s.91 of the PCC(S)A 2000, committal for trial must follow.[80]

7.44 There have been a number of guidelines from the Court of Appeal and from the Divisional Court on the circumstances where magistrates should not accept jurisdiction—

Billam[81]

> "A charge of rape should always be committed for trial. The judgment of the Court of Appeal given by Lord Lane C.J. states 'In the case of a juvenile the court will in most cases exercise the power to order detention under CYPA 1933 s.53(2) . . . It is important that a magistrates' court dealing with a juvenile charged with rape should *never* accept jurisdiction to deal with the case itself . . .'"

Corcoran[82]

> "The defendant should have been committed for trial. He was charged with two charges of robbery, 13 of burglary, two of taking a vehicle, one of going equipped and two of failing to surrender. He asked for 52 other offences to be taken into consideration (including four attempted robberies)."

---

[71] *Practice Direction (Crown Court: Allocation of business)(No.3) issued by the Lord Chief Justice* on January 18, 2000.
[72] s.76 of the Supreme Court Act 1981.
[73] See 7.38 above.
[74] *Measuring Performance to Reduce Delays in the Youth Justice System*, HO/LCD, September 1998.
[75] [1986] 1 W.L.R. 1374.
[76] [1997] Cr.App.R.(S.) 43.
[77] *The Times*, December 11, 1997, CA.
[78] See First and Fifth propositions in *Fairhurst* [1986] 1 W.L.R. 1374.
[79] [1996] Crim. L.R. 834
[80] *R. v. Devizes Youth Court and others ex. p. A*, (2000) 164 J.P. 330.
[81] [1986] 1 All E.R. 985.
[82] [1986] Crim. L.R. 568.

Metcalfe[83]

"The defendant received a three year term of detention for attempted robbery. He had broken into the home of a man aged 69 wearing a hood and carrying an axe. He also pleaded guilty to two offences of burglary and had several previous convictions for burglary."

Learmonth[84]

"Committal appropriate where the charge was assault with intent to rob and there were four other offences of burglary. In this case the defendant crept up behind a woman in the dark, put a dog chain around her neck, pulled it tight and robbed her. He had also committed four offences of burglary. It was agreed that three years detention was richly deserved."

Saunders[85]

"Those indulging in racial violence must expect a further term of up to two years for racial aggravation to be added to their sentence, even if that resulted in a non-custodial sentence becoming a custodial one."

North Hampshire Youth Court ex parte D.P.P.[86]

"Unlawful wounding with intent to do grievous bodily harm was a very serious offence, particularly where a weapon or shod foot was used. A sentencing court may choose not to impose a custodial sentence or not to impose such a sentence of more than two years length, but it should have the option open to it."

7.45 Note should be taken of the anomalies created or perpetuated by the Criminal Justice Acts 1991 and 1993 highlighted by the decision in *Nagar*[87] and in the illustrative commentary that follows that report at pp. 136 and 137. Since burglary of commercial premises now carries a maximum of only ten years imprisonment for an adult, a juvenile may not be committed to the Crown Court for trial. As the commentary points out, he may be committed for handling stolen goods (maximum 14 years) but not unlawful wounding (maximum five years). He may be committed for causing death by dangerous driving or by careless driving whilst under the influence of drink or drugs but not for causing death by aggravated vehicle taking.

Procedure

7.46 The procedure to be followed by a magistrates' court during and after committal for trial is much the same as for an adult. These procedures are set out in the 1980 Act, ss.4–8 and 1981 Rules, rr. 5–11. The differences are—

    (a) The restrictions on reports of proceedings contained in the 1980 Act, s.8 apply, as do the provisions of section 44 of the Youth Justice and Criminal Evidence Act 1999 when in force (see above para. 7.05).

---

[83] [1986] Crim. L.R. 569.
[84] (1988) 153 J.P. 18.
[85] *The Times*, January 28, 2000.
[86] (2000) 164 J.P. 377.
[87] [1994] Crim. L.R. 136.

(b) After the committal, the justices' chief executive must display a public notice giving details of the defendant and the charge.[88] If the defendant is under *17*, his name and address must not be in the notice unless the justices have directed that it should be in order to avoid injustice to him, the defendant. Additional restrictions will apply as a result of chapter IV of the Youth Justice and Criminal Evidence Act 1999 when in force (see 7.05).

(d) The Justices' Chief Executive must send to the Crown Court a statement indicating whether an order has been made under CYPA 1933, s.39(1), 1981 Rules, r. 11(2)(m).

Consideration is sensibly being given to reducing delay in dealing with serious offences involving juveniles by removing the need for committal. If implemented, the procedure would provide that, once a youth court has determined that a case had to be dealt with in the Crown Court, the youth court will immediately send it to the Crown Court where a timetable will be set and other case management decisions made.

---

[88] s.6(5) of the MCA 1980.

CHAPTER 8

Commencing Proceedings

8.01 There are no limitations restricting the institution of proceedings against a person under 18. However, national standards for working with young people were introduced by the Youth Justice Board in April 2000 and cover preventative work, work following arrest and pre-court work amongst other issues. Statutory provisions still remain in force and require that anyone who decides to lay an information against a person they have reason to believe to be under 18 must notify—

(a) The local authority for the area in which the person under 18 resides (if the prospective defendant does not appear to reside in the area of any local authority, notice must be given to the local authority in whose area it is alleged that the offence (or one of the offences) was committed, CYPA 1969, s. 5(8)). Residence is defined as the usual home of the prospective defendant—where he lives and has his meals.[1]

(b) If the prospective defendant is under 18, an officer of a local probation board for the area covered by the court.[2]

In practice, notification to the (multi-agency) YOT discharges these responsibilities.

8.02 National Standards for Youth Justice were introduced by the Youth Justice Board for work commenced on or after April 1, 2000. They are being reviewed in the light of the first year's experience. As indicated above, various parts of these standards affect the activities around the commencement of proceedings—

- Standard 2: provision by YOT of appropriate adults to support young persons under arrest; obligation on Police to notify YOT within 1 day where a young person has been charged or has received a reprimand or final warning.

- Standard 3: formal assessment using specified process before any intervention made with the young person by the YOT.

- Standard 5: contact to be made by YOT with young person receiving final warning and assessment undertaken.

- Standard 6: defining obligation to state commitments between the court and the YOT regarding the exchange of information and time and quality standards; providing for bail support and court duty.

8.03 The standards do not have the force of law but will be adopted as the normal course of conduct by YOTs, subject to local variations caused by geography,

---

[1] *Stoke-on-Trent Corporation v. Cheshire County Council* (1915) 3 K.B. 699; *South Shields Corporation v. Liverpool Corporation* (1943) 1 All E.R. 338.
[2] s.34(2) of the 1969 Act.

volume of work, and resources. However, the pre-existing legal provisions remain largely in force, in particular, the requirement that if a local authority (including the local education authority) institutes the proceedings or is notified of the bringing of the proceedings, it is under a duty, unless the local authority considers it unnecessary, to investigate and provide to the court information about the home surroundings, school record, health and character of the defendant that, in the opinion of the local authority, is likely to assist the court.[3] However, in practice a local authority will only provide such information at this stage where the child is already being looked after by them. In other circumstances, the information will not be provided until after the juvenile has been found guilty.[4] Where the defendant is 13 or over but under 18, the local authority need not investigate or provide information to the court about the defendant's home surroundings if arrangements exist for that information to be supplied by an officer of the local probation board. The arrangements can be made as a result of the direction of the justices or of the Probation Board for the area.[5] It appears that the local authority is still obliged to provide information that it *already possesses* about the home surroundings, school record, health and character, since s.34(3) of the 1969 Act applies only to exempt local authorities from making investigations or from providing information which it does not already possess. Information in the possession of the local authority which appears to a local authority likely to assist the court, must be provided to the court, unless the local authority considers it unnecessary to do so.[6] Research evidence suggests these provisions have been subject to immensely diverse interpretation, and that in many instances whether or not courts receive such information will vary infinitely from one local authority to another.[7] However, one of the consequences of the introduction of YOTs working to national standards is intended to bring all areas up to the standard of the best.

8.04 If the court does not receive sufficient information it may request the local authority (in practice, the YOT) to provide information, or further information, regarding home surroundings, school record, health and character. It is the duty of the local authority to comply with that request.[8] The court may also require that information from an officer of a local probation board. In reality, the emphasis on speed and the options open to a court will almost always mean the information is sought after conviction and from the multi-agency youth offending team. National standards provide for the style and content of both pre-sentence reports and specific sentence reports (see Chapter 12 below).

THE CONDUCT OF PROCEEDINGS

8.05 The Director of Public Prosecutions is the head of the Crown Prosecution Service and it is through that service that prosecutions are conducted. Any person or body, except a police force, instituting proceedings (see definition below), may continue to conduct those proceedings subject to the right of the Director of Public Prosecutions to take over the conduct at any stage.[9] The Director is obliged to take over all criminal proceedings instituted on behalf of a police force other than

---

[3] s.9(1) of the 1969 Act.
[4] Chapter 12.
[5] s.34(3) of the 1969 Act.
[6] s.9(1) and s.34(3) of the 1969 Act.
[7] Parer *et al*, 1983 and 1989; Brown, 1991; Ball, 1983 and 1995.
[8] s.9(2) of the 1969 Act.
[9] s.6 of the Prosecution of Offences Act 1985.

specified proceedings. This obligation extends to all binding over proceedings instituted on behalf of a police force and all proceedings begun by way of a summons for the forfeiture of obscene articles issued under Obscene Publications Act 1959, s. 3.[10]

8.06 The emphasis is on speed. Whilst there must be proper time for the defence to prepare its case,[11] it is in the best interests of a young person for a case to be brought quickly to court. The provisions in the CDA 1998[12] enable that to happen with the court having the responsibility to set the timetable and to balance the needs of all parties. For a young offender, the first appearance before the court should almost always take place within three days of charge and the court will expect the parties to be ready to move the case forward very quickly. A joint circular issued by the Home Office and the Lord Chancellor's Department[13] sets out a timescale for various stages in the proceedings where they involve a persistent young offender—arrest to charge (2 days), charge to first appearance (7 days), first appearance to start of trial or committal (28 days) and verdict to sentence (14 days). In the Crown Court, there are also targets for committal to PDH (14 days) and PDH to start of trial (28 days).

8.07 For all young offenders, guidance from the Youth Justice Board[14] emphasises the importance of:

"bringing charged youths to an effective first court appearance, normally at the next sitting of the youth court after the person is charged with the offence

- ensuring that all first hearings make substantive progress and processing straightforward guilty pleas on the day of their first appearance wherever possible
- reducing to a minimum the incidence and duration of adjournments when contested cases come to trial, including adjournments before sentencing."

The paper then describes what has to be done to achieve these goals. The key to success will be the ability of the youth court (and, in particular, Justices' Clerks and those to whom they delegate powers to conduct directions hearings) to set rigorous timetables that are fair but demanding and which are kept to. This in turn requires commitments from prosecution bodies and from the regulations governing the financing of publicly funded defence advocates to ensure that all the incentives in their systems are geared towards proper and speedy preparation of cases.

8.08 Proceedings are Instituted—

(a) Where the proceedings are begun by way of summons, at the time when the information for the offence is laid before the person who issues the summons.

---

[10] s.3(2) of the Prosecution of Offences Act 1985.
[11] Article 6 ECHR.
[12] See, for instance, section 44 inserting a new section 22A into the Prosecution of Offences Act 1985.
[13] *Measuring Performance to Reduce Delays in the Youth Justice System*, September 1998.
[14] *Speeding Up Youth Justice*, May 1999.

(b) Where proceedings are begun with the issue of a warrant on an information being laid, at the time that the information for the offence is laid before the person issuing the warrant.

(c) Where a person is charged with an offence after having been taken into custody without a warrant, at the time when the offender is informed of the particulars of the charge.

(d) Where a bill of indictment is preferred under Administration of Justice (Miscellaneous Provisions) Act 1933, s. 2(2)(b), at the time when the bill of indictment is preferred before the court.

Where as a result of these provisions there is the potential for there being more than one time for the institution of the proceedings, the time to be used is the earliest possible.[15]

Specified Proceedings

8.09 Proceedings are specified when they come within the Prosecution of Offences Act 1985 (Specified Proceedings) Order 1985. Even if included within that order, proceedings are only specified if the defendant is given the opportunity to plead guilty by letter and they will cease to be specified if that opportunity is not taken up. Common offences coming within this definition likely to be committed by persons under 18 are fixed penalty offences within the meaning of Road Traffic Offenders Act 1988, s.51, and other relatively minor road traffic offences. Since implementation of the CJA 1991 16-and 17-year-old defendants have been able to plead guilty by post under MCA 1980, s.12. Where the opportunity to plead guilty without attending court is accepted by the defendant, it is the responsibility of the clerk of the court to read out the statement of the facts of the offence and any written mitigation submitted.[16] The definition of a police force includes not only the normal constabulary—a police force maintained by a Police Authority—but also other specified forces including the Metropolitan Police, the City of London Police, the British Transport Police, various Docks Police, the Mersey Tunnel Law Enforcement Officers, the Ministry of Defence Police, the Royal Parks Constabulary (England) and the Atomic Energy Authority Constabulary.[17]

The role of the Crown Prosecutor in Instituting Proceedings

8.10 The Crown Prosecutor decides—

(a) Whether proceedings should be instituted,

(b) Whether, having been instituted, they should be discontinued,

(c) What charges should be preferred.

Their powers are delegated from the Director of Public Prosecutions and are guided by a code, the most recent version of which was published in October, 2000.
8.11 The code provides for two main criteria: evidential sufficiency and public interest. Additional provisions are included relating to juveniles which confirm the

---

[15] s.15(2) of the 1985 Act.
[16] s.12(7) of the MCA 1980.
[17] s.3(3) of the 1985 Act and S.I. 1985/1956.

requirement for the crown prosecutor that in deciding whether or not the public interest requires a prosecution, the interests of the youth should be fully considered.[18] The code affirms that a youth will only be referred to the Crown Prosecution Service after a reprimand or final warning unless the offence is so serious that neither is appropriate. Since reprimands and final warnings are designed to prevent re-offending and since a further offence is alleged thereby indicating that attempts to divert the youth from the court system have not been effective, it is likley the public interest will require prosecution.[19] In *R. v. Director of Public Prosecutions, ex p. C*[20] an attempt was made to challenge a decision to prosecute rather than caution. The Divisional Court affirmed that such decisions are susceptible to judicial review but only where it can be shown that the decision was made regardless of (or contrary to) a settled policy of the Director of Public Prosecutions evolved in the public interest. It would be only rarely that a defendant would succeed. The code draws attention to the serious harm that the stigma of a conviction can cause to the prospects of a young offender (whether a youth or a young adult) but requires that to be balanced against the seriousness of the offence and the past behaviour of the young person.[21]

---

[18] See para. 6.8.
[19] Code for Crown Prosecutors, para. 6.10.
[20] (2001) 165 J.P. 102.
[21] *ibid.*

CHAPTER 9

Remands and Secure Accommodation

9.01 Whenever a case is adjourned, a youth court will consider whether or not to remand the defendant. There is no obligation to remand as there is for certain offences for which a person over 18 appears before a court,[1] however note the requirement not to grant bail in certain circumstances[2]. If a young person who has not been bailed to attend does not appear but is represented by a legal representative, then he is deemed not to be absent.[3] Generally, the powers of adjournment and the restrictions on the lengths of remands on bail are the same as in an adult magistrates' court. However, the power to adjourn after conviction for the purpose of obtaining information about the offender is affected by the section 48(3) of the Children and Young Persons Act 1933. After conviction, a court may adjourn for no more than four weeks to enable inquiries to be made or to determine the most suitable way of dealing with the case.[4] If the court remands the accused in custody, the limit becomes three weeks (*ibid.*). By section 48(3), a youth court remanding a juvenile for information to be obtained about him, must ensure that the juvenile appears before a court at least once in every twenty one days. No distinction is drawn between remands before or after conviction. As mentioned, there is no obligation to remand a person under 18 when a case is adjourned. Simple adjournment may, therefore, avoid the potential difficulty where a four week adjournment is required. Section 10(3) of the 1980 Act refers to adjournment time limits, section 48(3) of the 1933 Act refers to remand time limits. If there is a conflict, it is resolved in favour of the 1933 Act by section 152 of the 1980 Act, s.152.

GRANT OF BAIL

9.02 The provisions relating to the granting of bail are similar to those that apply to an adult and therefore appear only in summary. For a detailed exposition see *Archbold*.[5] In addition to those powers, the court may require a parent or guardian who appears with a person under 18 to attend (see Chapter 10). Each Youth Offending Team must ensure that there is local bail support and supervisory provision and that all young offenders detained in police custody are referred to it.[6]

Unless charged with treason, any person charged with an offence shall be granted bail unless one of the exceptions to this right applies[7] or the charge is one of

---

[1] s.18(4) of the 1980 Act.
[2] s.25 of the CJPOA Act.
[3] s.122 of the 1980 Act.
[4] s.10(3) of the 1980 Act.
[5] 2000, section 1, chap. 3.
[6] *National Standards for Youth Justice*, para. 6.3.2.
[7] s.41 of the 1980 Act; s.4 of the Bail Act 1976.

murder, attempted murder, manslaughter, rape or attempted rape and the person charged has previously been convicted of any of these offences or of culpable homicide. If the previous conviction was for manslaughter or culpable homicide the sentence must have been imprisonment or long term detention.[8]

9.03   If the defendant is charged only with offences that are *not* imprisonable bail may only be refused—

- if the defendant has previously failed to surrender to bail and, in view of that failure, the court believes that the defendant would fail to surrender if released on bail on this occasion;[9] or
- if the court is satisfied that the defendant should be kept in custody for his own protection, or, if he is a child or young person, for his own welfare;[10] or
- if the defendent is in custody in pursuance of a sentence of a court or of any authority acting under any of the Service Acts;[11] or
- if, having been released on bail in or in connection with proceedings for an offence, the defendant has been arrested under 1976 Act, s.7 for failing to surrender to the custody of the court or as being in breach of conditions of bail or likely to be in breach of such conditions.[12]

9.04   If the defendant is being proceeded against for at least one offence punishable with imprisonment in the case of an adult, bail may be refused—

- if the court is satisfied that there are substantial grounds for believing that the defendant would—
  - fail to surrender to custody; or
  - commit an offence while on bail; or
  - interfere with witnesses or otherwise obstruct the course of justice, whether in relation to himself or any other person.[13]
- if the defendant is charged with or convicted of an indictable offence (whether or not triable either way) committed whilst on bail in criminal proceedings;[14] or
- if the court is satisfied that the defendant should be kept in custody for his own protection, or if he is a child or young person, for his own welfare;[15] or
- if the defendant is in custody in pursuance of a sentence of a court or of any authority acting under any of the Service Acts;[16] or
- where the court is satisfied that it has not been practicable to obtain sufficient information for the purpose of taking the decisions required regarding bail because of lack of time since the proceedings started;[17] or
- if, having been released on bail in or in connection with proceedings for an offence, the defendant has been arrested under 1976 Act, s.7 for failing

---

[8] s.25 of the CJPOA 1994.
[9] Sched. 1, Part II, para. 2 of the 1976 Act.
[10] Sched. 1, Part II, para. 3 of the 1976 Act.
[11] Sched. 1, Part II, para. 4 of the 1976 Act.
[12] *ibid.*, para. 5 of the 1976 Act.
[13] Sched. 1, Part I, para. 2 of the 1976 Act.
[14] *ibid.*, para. 2A of the 1976 Act.
[15] *ibid.*, para. 3 of the 1976 Act.
[16] *ibid.*, para. 4 of the 1976 Act.
[17] Sched. 1, Part 1, para. 5 of the 1976 Act.

to surrender to the custody of the court or as being in breach of conditions of bail or likely to be in breach of such conditions;[18] or

- where the case is adjourned for enquiries or for a report to be prepared, if it appears to the court impracticable to complete the enquiries or make the report unless the defendant is kept in custody.[19]

The only variant in these restrictions between a person under the age of 18 and a person over that age is the additional ground that bail may be refused if it is necessary to keep the defendant in custody for his own welfare.[20]

Bail granted in respect of an indictable offence (whether or not triable either way) may be reconsidered by the court on application by the prosecutor. This application can only be made if based on information not available to whoever granted bail.[21]

Requirements of Bail

9.05 A grant of bail will require the defendant to attend court on the date, at the time and at the place set. Failure to do so without reasonable cause is an offence punishable by fining up to level 5 (currently £5,000 for an adult, £1,000 for a young person aged 14–17 and £250 for a child aged 10–13) and/or up to three months custody in a magistrates' court or up to 12 months custody and/or a fine in the Crown Court if committed to that court either because the defendant is committed for trial or because the magistrates' court feels the defendant requires greater punishment than it has the power to impose.[22] A person who fails to surrender at the right time and place and also fails to surrender to the court as soon as reasonably practicable after that time, also commits an offence punishable as above.[23] In addition, a person likely to breach a condition of bail or in breach of such condition is liable to arrest.[24]

9.06 A defendant prosecuted for failing to surrender without reasonable cause has the burden upon him to prove that reasonable cause on the balance of probabilities. In *Laidlaw v. Atkinson*,[25] a defendant, having handed his charge sheet to his solicitor without making a note of the date of hearing, mistakenly formed the opinion that he was to surrender to custody on a later date than the due date. This was not capable of being a reasonable cause for failing to surrender even though his solicitor had given him a date for formal consultation after the hearing date and the defendant had other matters before the same court on different days. It was accepted that the failure to surrender was not deliberate. In the judgment, it was said

> "the learned magistrate was of the opinion that this was not a matter of mere confusion on the part of the defendant but that those extraneous factors caused the confusion to arise . . . No doubt the reasons outlined played a part in the defendants confusion and could be said to amount to mitigation but there was no question of anything having arisen to prevent the defendants

[18] Sched. 1, Part 1, para. 6 of the 1976 Act.
[19] Sched. 1, Part 1, para. 7 of the 1976 Act.
[20] Sched. 1, Part II, para. 3 of the 1976 Act.
[21] s.5B of the 1976 Act.
[22] s.6(1) of the 1976 Act.
[23] s.6(2) of the 1976 Act.
[24] s.7 of the 1976 Act.
[25] [1986] *The Times*, August 2, 1986.

attendance. He had been told when bailed of the date on which he was to surrender to custody and been given a signed copy of the bail form. If he was going to part with it he should have made a note of the date. The error was his responsibility and it could not be said that those reasons could amount to a reasonable cause."

Bail granted must be without conditions unless the court believes those conditions to be necessary to prevent a failure to surrender to custody, the commission of an offence whilst on bail or the interference with witnesses or other obstruction of the course of justice. Further conditions may be imposed if they are necessary for the purpose of enabling enquiries to be made or a report to be made to assist the court in dealing with the offence.[26] No condition may be imposed on anyone other than the defendant and each condition must be necessary for the purposes provided, thus it will rarely be lawful to impose a condition of reporting to a police station on a person where the court is satisfied only that a condition is necessary to prevent the commission of further offences whilst on bail. A surety may be taken where necessary to avoid the non-attendance of the defendant.

9.07   A young person granted bail may be required to reside where the local authority directs, if that condition is considered necessary in accordance with 1976 Act, Sched. 1. In those circumstances, the young person is being looked after by the local authority which may, therefore, apply for a secure accommodation order.[27] However as a remand to local authority accommodation does not confer parental responsibility on the local authority no compensation order can be made against the authority even though the offence was committed whilst the young person was on remand to the local authority accommodation.[28]

Breach (or anticipated breach) of conditions may lead to immediate arrest[29] whereupon the person arrested must be brought before a justice for the Petty Sessions area in which he was arrested, unless arrested within 24 hours of the time at which he was due to surrender to the court, and may be remanded otherwise than on bail (see below).

9.08   A person arrested for being in breach of the conditions of bail more than 24 hours before the time at which he was due to surrender to the court must be brought before a justice within 24 hours (not counting Good Friday, Christmas Day or Sundays). The arrested person must be brought before the justice within that time not just into the precincts of the court.[30] There is no power to adjourn the proceedings and the court must proceed to determine whether to release the defendant or remand him in some other way. It can be argued that the provisions of section 7(4) of the Bail Act 1976 require the personal attendance of the accused, the phraseology used imposing a specific requirement which eliminates the possibility of applying section 122(3) MCA 1980 and allowing a legally represented absent defendant to be deemed to be present. However, this presents a number of practical problems, both where a defendant is too ill to attend and where more time is needed for preparation. The strict interpretation applied in *ex parte G* would allow a defendant who is too unwell to appear in court (whether self induced or not) to avoid the consequence of breaching the bail conditions. The principle behind the legislation is that the issue must be brought very quickly to the

---

[26] Sched. 1, para. 8 of the 1976 Act.
[27] *Re C (a Minor) (Secure accommodation order: Jurisdiction)* [1994] 2 F.C.R. 1153.
[28] *North Yorkshire County Council v. Selby Youth Court* [1994] 1 All E.R. 991.
[29] s.7(3) of the 1976 Act. 33 s.6 of the 1976 Act.
[30] *R. v. Governor of Glen Parva Y.O.I. ex p. G (A Minor)* [1998] Q.B. 877.

tribunal that has power to review the status of the remand. Bail conditions are imposed because they are necessary to prevent offending, disappearance or interference with witnesses. It is not in the interests of justice for a person breaching such a condition to evade responsibility unjustifiably and there would appear to be every reason, therefore, to interpret the requirement of section 7(4) of the Bail Act 1976 as not precluding an absent but represented defendant from being deemed to be present. If a defendant is able to attend (or is not able to attend but is represented), there must be proper time for preparation.[31] Once a defendant has appeared within the 24 hours, it would appear compatible with the Convention right for time to be allowed for preparation and the conclusion of the case postponed for consideration later that day. A decision will have to be made during the day.[31a]

Where an arrested juvenile is in police custody, section 38(6) of PACE obliges the police to consider transferring the juvenile to local authority accommodation. A juvenile arrested as in breach of bail conditions is not, however, an "arrested juvenile" within the terms of the Act which defines the phrase as a person under 17 kept in custody after arrest for an offence.[32] Failure to comply with a condition of bail is not an offence and the juvenile, therefore, can quite legitimately be kept in police detention pending appearance before a justice.

Appeal Against Refusal of Bail

9.09 A right of appeal against the refusal of bail exists allowing a defendant to seek bail in the High Court or the Crown Court. The right to apply to the High Court is in every case. The procedure is contained in R.S.C. 1965, Ord. 79, r. 9. The right to apply to the Crown Court exists where the defendant is committed for trial to the Crown Court or where the magistrates' court has issued a Certificate of Full Argument.[33] The procedure is contained in Crown Court Rules 1982, rr. 19 and 20.

Appeal against the granting of bail

9.10 Where bail is granted by a magistrates' court for certain offences despite objections by the prosecutor, an appeal by the prosecutor may be made to a Judge of a Crown Court (Bail (Amendment) Act 1993). The conditions to be satisfied apply to those under 18 years in the same way as to adults, except that if oral notice of appeal is given, the court must remand a person under 17 to local authority accommodation unless the appeal is disposed of.

Remands when bail is refused

9.11 Two different sets of provisions apply to persons under 18. One set applies to those aged 17, another to those under that age. Within the latter category there are further variants depending on age and gender. YOTs are expected to provide bail information to the Crown Prosecution Service to assist in reaching the decision whether to seek a remand to secure facilities. Courts are expected to seek a YOT assessment before making such a remand.[34]

---

[31] Article 6 ECHR.
[31a] *R. (on the application of the DPP) v. Havering Magistrates' Court*, CO 39721 2000, December 15, 2000, DC.
[32] s.37(15) of the PACE Act 1984.
[33] s.6 of the Bail Act 1976.
[34] *National Standards for Youth Justice*, paras 6.4 and 6.5.

Defendants aged 17 years

A person of this age who is refused bail will be remanded to prison custody in the same way as a person over that age, since the 1969 Act, s.23 which deals with alternative places of remand is restricted to those under 17 years: see definition of young person in 1969 Act, s.23(12). The normal maximum period of remand is eight clear days, that is with eight days elapsing between the date of remand and the date of next appearance excluding both those days.[35] This period may, however, be extended to up to 28 clear days in accordance with the 1980 Act, s. 128A if the following conditions are met:

1. The defendant has previously been remanded in custody for this offence (*i.e.* this is at least the second appearance)

2. The defendant is before the court.

3. The court can set a date on which the next stage of the proceedings can take place after hearing any representations that the parties to the proceedings wish to make.

A further hearing simply for a remand in custody or on bail is not a further stage of the proceedings—it would be expected to be, for instance, mode of trial, entry of plea, committal for trial or hearing of a contested case. A defendant remanded under this provision may apply for bail during the period of remand.[36]

9.12 If a court wishes to extend the period of remand beyond eight clear days but cannot use the provisions of section 128A—either because it is the first remand or it is not able to fulfill one of the other conditions—it may seek the consent of the defendant to up to three remands taking place in the absence of the defendant.[37] For a defendant aged 17, the court also has the power, as with an adult, to transfer the remand hearings to a court nearer to the remand prison.[38]

As an alternative to remand to prison, a defendant aged 17 may be remanded to police custody for a maximum of three clear days.[39] Such a remand may only be for the purpose of enabling enquiries to be made into other offences. Once that need ceases the defendant must be brought back before the court even if that is before the end of the remand period.[40]

Defendants aged under 17 years

9.13 These complex and much amended provisions appear to have reached a state where a reasonable degree of stability can be not only hoped for but expected! The primary provision is section 23 of the CYPA1969 which has most recently been amended by sections 97 and 98 of the CDA 1998 and by Schedule 7 para. 39 to the Criminal Justice and Court Services Act 2000, when in force. The implementation of these provisions from June 1, 1999 was accompanied by a helpful guide[41] which includes a useful flow chart which is reproduced at p. 128. Unfortunately, we still have two versions of section 23 depending on whether or not the defendant is a 15-

---

[35] s.128(6) of the 1980 Act.
[36] s.128A(3) of the 1980 Act.
[37] *ibid.*
[38] s.130 of the 1980 Act.
[39] s.128(7) of the 1980 Act.
[40] s.128(8) of the 1980 Act.
[41] *Court-ordered Secure Remands Implementation Guidance*, Home Office 1999. The document, with updates, can be found at http://www.homeoffice.gov.uk/cdact/index.htm.

or 16-year-old boy. It seems inconceivable that we need two variations of the same section current at the same time.

Defendants aged 10 or 11 years.

9.14 If bail is refused, the court will remand to local authority accommodation either with or without conditions.[42] If authority is required to keep the defendant in secure accommodation, the local authority will need to apply for that authority in accordance with section 25 of the Children Act 1989. This application can be made in the normal way to the family proceedings court or can be made to a youth court or other magistrates' court.[43] A child under 13 can only be placed in secure accommodation with the approval of the Secretary of State for Health.[44]

Defendants aged 12, 13 or 14 years and also girls aged 15 or 16

If bail is refused, the court will remand to local authority accommodation either with or without conditions.[45] If authority is required to keep the defendant in secure accommodation, the local authority may apply for authority under section 25 of the CA 1989 or the court may require the local authority to comply with a security requirement. A security requirement is a requirement that the defendant be placed and kept in secure accommodation.[46] Secure accommodation is accommodation provided in a community home, a voluntary home or a registered children's home for the purpose of restricting liberty and approved for that purpose by the Secretary of State.[47] The importance of each of the elements of this definition became apparent in *R. v. Secretary of State for the Home Department ex p. A*,[48] where a defendant sought the benefit of reduction in the length of a custodial sentence as a result of time spent in a registered children's home (not approved by the Secretary of State for the purpose of restricting liberty) whilst subject to a court imposed curfew. The court held that that was not secure accommodation within the terms of the Act.

9.15 The court may only make a security requirement after consulting the designated local authority, that is the local authority who is already "looking after" the defendant or, if the defendant is not being looked after by a local authority, the authority in whose area it appears that he resides or in which one of the offences was committed.[49] The extent of consultation is that which is reasonably practicable in all the circumstances of the case.[50] A security requirement may not be imposed if the defendant is not legally represented unless, having had proper opportunity, the defendant has failed to apply for legal aid (or equivalent right to representation at public expense after the implementation in April 2001 of the amendments in the Access to Justice Act 1999, schedule 4).[51]

9.16 Two criteria need to be met, one relating to the nature of the offending and the other to the necessity for such a remand. Regarding the offending, the defendant must either be charged with or convicted of a violent or sexual offence[52]

---

[42] s.23(1) of the CYPA 1969.
[43] s.60(3) of the CJA 1991.
[44] Regulation 4 of the Children (Secure Accommodation) Regulations 1991
[45] s.23(1) CYPA 1969.
[46] s.23(4) CYPA 1969.
[47] s.23(12) CYPA 1969.
[48] (2000) 164 J.P. 141.
[49] s.23(2) of the CYPA 1969.
[50] *ibid.*, s.23(13)(b).
[51] *ibid.*, s.23(5A).
[52] Defined in Part I of the CJA 1991.

or of an offence punishable in the case of an adult with 14 years imprisonment or more or must have a recent history of absconding while remanded to local authority accommodation and be charged with or convicted of an imprisonable offence said to have been committed while on remand to local authority accommodation.[53] Where reliance is placed on the first limb (charged with/convicted of certain offences), does the conviction have to be in the proceedings in which the remand is being considered? This point was argued in *Re C.*[54] The court decided that there was no reason to limit the provision in that way. Therefore, once a young person is convicted of a violent or sexual offence or of an offence punishable in the case of an adult with 14 years imprisonment or more, that young person will always satisfy this part of the test. The Divisional Court could see no reason to follow "convicted" by "in these proceedings" where Parliament had not chosen to insert that extra phrase.

9.17   In determining whether there is a history of absconding, it may be helpful to refer to *R. v. Southwark Crown Court ex p. Ager*[55] which accepted one previous instance as sufficient to prove a history of failing to comply under now superseded sentencing provisions.

Regarding the necessity for such a remand, the court must be satisfied that only such a remand is adequate to protect the public from serious harm from the defendant.[56] Where the offence criterion met is in relation to a violent or sexual offence, the serious harm is death or serious personal injury, whether physical or psychological, caused by a violent or sexual offence committed by the defendant.[57]

9.18   On imposing a security requirement, the court must state in open court that it is of the opinion that only such a requirement is adequate to protect the public from serious harm from the defendant and also explain to the defendant why it is of that opinion.[58] That explanation is to be in ordinary language, presumably straightforward non-technical language that the defendant is likely to understand. Magistrates are not expected to give formal judgments[59] nor should pronouncements given to people who had been present in the hearing be subject to detailed scrutiny.[60] The need for the reason to be shortly stated is emphasised by the obligation for a magistrates' court to record it both in the warrant of commitment and in the court register.[61]

Defendants who are boys aged 15 or 16

As with other young people, boys aged 15 or 16 can be remanded to local authority accommodation and the local authority may apply for a secure accommodation order by way of section 25 of the CA 1989 (see above). If the court considers it may wish to impose a security requirement then it has to consider some varied criteria.[62] It may also have the option of a remand to Prison Service accommodation.[63] Where a court is considering a remand to a secure facility, it will

---

[53] s.23(5) of the CYPA 1969.
[54] Divisional Court, unreported, October 22, 1993, CO-2974–93.
[55] [1990] Crim. L.R. 531.
[56] s.23(5) of the CYPA 1969.
[57] *ibid*, s.23(13)(c).
[58] *ibid.*, s.23(6).
[59] *McKerry v. Teesdale and Wear Valley Justices*, (2000) 164 J.P. 355.
[60] *R. v. Central Criminal Court ex parte S and P* (1999) 163 J.P. 776.
[61] s.23(6) of the CYPA 1969.
[62] s.23 of the CYPA 1969 as amended by s.98 of the CDA 1998 and sched. 7, para. 39 to the Criminal Justice and Court Services Act 2000 when in force.
[63] *ibid.*, s.23(4) as amended by s.98 of the CDA 1998.

normally ask the YOT to make an assessment.[64] YOT managers must provide a bail information service at each court to provide factual verified information to assist the Crown Prosecution Service to decide whether there is information that would enable them to ask the court to remand on bail rather than to secure facilities.[65] YOT managers must also ensure that a vulnerability assessment is undertaken by a properly trained YOT member where the court is considering a remand to secure facilities.[66] The responsibility for making the arrangements to place the defendant in the correct establishment lies with the YOT.[67] Responsibility for the physical transfer of defendants to local authority accommodation is an area of uncertainty. The government view is that the responsibility lies with the local authority and not with the prisoner escort and custody services.[68] However, this appears to depend on a dubious interpretation of the status of a person remanded to local authority accommodation. The key phrase is the definition of a prisoner as a person detained in legal custody as a result of a requirement imposed by a court.[69] Is a remand into local authority accommodation a detention in custody? If not, is a requirement by the court that the defendant remain in the custody of the court until delivered to the local authority accommodation sufficient to make the defendant a prisoner for this purpose?

9.19 A boy aged 15 or 16 who meets the criteria in section 23(5) of the CYPA 1969 (see above) will normally be remanded to a prison (pending implementation of para. 39 of the sched. 7 to the CJCSA 2000, a remand centre may be available instead of a prison). However, the court may instead remand to local authority accommodation with a security requirement where—

- after such consultation as is reasonably practicable[70] with a probation officer, social worker or member of a Youth Offending Team,[71] the court declares the defendant to be a person who it would be undesirable to remand to a prison (or, for the time being, a remand centre) because of his physical or emotional immaturity or propensity to harm himself[72] *and*
- secure accommodation is available for him.[73]

9.20 The Youth Offending Team manager is responsible for carrying out an assessment of vulnerability.[74] With the pressure on accommodation, it is inevitable that a court will be faced with a situation where a boy aged 15 or 16 meets the section 23(5) criteria (nature of offence and need for public protection) and meets the section 23(4)(a)(i) criterion (comes within the modified section 23(5A) "undesirability on account of vulnerability") yet there is no local authority accommodation available. In those circumstances, statute provides for a remand to a remand centre or prison.[75] However, does this meet the obligations placed on both the court and the local authority as public authorities by the ECHR and other

---

[64] *National Standards for Youth Justice*, standard 6.4.
[65] *ibid.*, standard 6.4.2.
[66] *ibid.*, standard 6.5.1.
[67] *ibid.*, standard 6.5.2.
[68] *Court-ordered Secure Remands, Implementation Guidance*, para. 4.4, Home Office, 1999.
[69] s.92(1) of the CJA 1991.
[70] s.23(13) of the CYPA 1969.
[71] *ibid.*, s.23(4). as modified by s.98 of the CDA 1998.
[72] s.23(5A) of the CYPA 1969 as modified by s.98 of the CDA 1998.
[73] s.23(4) of the CYPA 1969 as modified by s.98 of the CDA 1998.
[74] *National Standards for Youth Justice*, standard 6.5.1.
[75] s.23(4)(b) and (c) of the CYPA 1969 as modified by s.98 of the CDA 1998.

international commitments and standards? Certainly, the Court must have regard to the welfare of the young person[76] and should at the very least remand to a remand centre or prison for a very short period in order to allow a local authority to obtain the necessary secure accommodation. The lack of suitable secure accommodation will be a powerful reason for giving the particular case a very high priority by all involved so that the court can proceed to its determination of guilt or innocence (and sentence, if necessary) at the earliest possible opportunity. In response to a question in the House of Lords,[77] the words of H.M. Chief Inspector of Prisons were quoted with approval

> "The vast majority of young people in custody need individual attention given to the problems which produced their criminal behaviour. If all they get is akin to being stored in a warehouse, then the chances of their reoffending, creating yet more victims, are very great indeed."

9.21 It may also be argued that the differential provisions for boys and girls contravenes the provisions of article 14 of ECHR prohibiting discrimination on any ground. Can it be said that boys are being unfairly discriminated against? Probably not—the remand provisions are essentially the same for boys and girls, it is the place of remand that is different and this could be justified on objective and reasonable grounds because of the volume of boys requiring such accommodation and the protections built in for those who are most vulnerable.

Where the remand to a secure facility is in respect of an indictable offence (whether or not triable either way in the case of an adult) other than homicide, the maximum period of remand is governed by the 56 day custody time limit.[78]

Remands to local authority accommodation

9.22 A young person age 10 to 16 who is remanded to local authority accommodation will be remanded to be looked after by a local authority designated by the court.[79] If the young person is already being looked after by a local authority, then it will be that local authority that is to be designated. If not, it will be the local authority for the area where the court believes the young person to reside or for the area where the offence was committed. Where a security requirement is not imposed, the court may impose conditions on the young person and may impose requirements on the local authority.

9.23

    (a) *Young Person*: Having first consulted the local authority—and this consultation means such as is reasonably practicable in the case[80]—a court may impose on the person remanded to local authority accommodation such conditions that could have been imposed if bail had been granted which appear to the court to be necessary to secure the surrender to custody of the defendant, to prevent the commission of further offences, to prevent the obstruction of the course of justice or to ensure availability

---

[76] s.44 of the CYPA 1933.

[77] December 15, 1997, Parliamentary Under-Secretary of State, Lord Williams of Mostyn.

[78] Provided by s.22 of the Prosecution of Offences Act 1985 and the Prosecution of Offences (Custody Time Limits) Regulations S.I. 1987 No. 299 as applied in *R. v. Stratford Youth Court ex p. S* (1998) 162 J.P. 552.

[79] s.23(2) of the CYPA 1969.

[80] s.23(13)(b) of the 1969 Act.

to assist in the preparation of a report for the court.[81] The court may not require a defendant remanded to local authority accommodation to reside in a specific place.[82] There is no power to impose obligations on the parent or guardian of the defendant.

(b) *Local authority* After consultation with the local authority, the court may impose requirements on the authority to secure compliance with the bail type conditions by the defendant.[83] These conditions may be imposed at the time of the remand, or between remands, on application of the local authority.[84] A court may also stipulate that the local authority shall not place the defendant with a person named in the order.[85] Subject to this, the local authority has discretion as to the accommodation it provides for the defendant. The court may not require the local authority to accommodate the defendant in specific accommodation.[86]

9.24 Any of these conditions may be varied or revoked by the court at any time on application of either the local authority or the defendant.[87] In this context "court" includes a single justice.[88] If the court utilises this power to impose conditions on a defendant it must give its reasons in ordinary language in open court and those reasons must be included both in the warrant of commitment and in the court register.[89]

9.25 Section 23A to the 1969 Act gives the police powers to arrest a child or young person who breaches a condition of remand to local authority accommodation and the court will have the same powers and responsibilities as if the defendant had been arrested for breach of a condition of bail (see para. 9.08 above).

SECURE ACCOMMODATION

General Considerations

9.26

"Restricting the liberty of children is a serious step which must be taken only where there is no appropriate alternative".[90]

The Children Act 1989 defines secure accommodation as "accommodation provided for the purpose of restricting liberty".[91] Such accommodation must be registered with the Department of Health. At the present time most secure places are provided by local authorities, however, in order to encourage greater provision, the law was amended in 1994 to allow private sector secure places, subject to Department of Health regulation.[92] On March 31, 2000 there were 441 approved

---

[81] s.23(7) of the 1969 Act.
[82] *Cleveland C.C. v. D.P.P.*, L.S. Gaz. 92/06, February 8, 1995.
[83] s.23(9)(a) of the 1969 Act.
[84] s.23(10) of the 1969 Act.
[85] s.23(9)(b) of the 1969 Act.
[86] *Cleveland C.C. v. D.P.P., ibid.*
[87] s.23(11) of the 1969 Act.
[88] s.23(12) of the 1969 Act.
[89] s.23(8) of the 1969 Act.
[90] Department of Health, *Children Act 1989, Guidance and Regulations*, Vol. 1, (DOH, London, 1991).
[91] s.25(1) of the CA 1989.
[92] s.19 of the Crime and Disorder Act 1994.

places in secure accommodation. The Secure Accommodation Development Programme funded by the Department of Health and the Home Office resulted in an
increase of 32 per cent in the number of secure places available between 1997 and
1999, and a rise of 16 per cent in the number of children accommodated.

The labyrinthine provisions which have developed since 1982 to curtail local
authorities' powers to restrict the liberty of children in the public care are at the
interface of child care and youth justice. They also provide possibly the most
extreme example of the current complexity of much of the law relating to young
offenders.[93] It seems likely that the Human Rights Act 1998 will result in further
amendments or possibly, and desirably, in root and branch reform. There is a
widespread view that aspects of the secure accommodation provisions will continue
to attract challenges in the courts for being in breach of Articles 5 (the right to
liberty), 6 (the right to a fair trial), and 8 (the right to family life) of the ECHR[94]
see *W. Borough Council v. A.K.*[94a] for a thorough analysis of the impact of Article 5
and a conclusion that an order did not breach the Convention. Also see *In Re M (a
child: secure accommodation order)*[94b] for consideration of the impact of Article 6
confirming that the minimum rights in Article 6(3) applied even though such
applications were not criminal proceedings.

Placement in Secure Accommodation

9.27   Children looked after by local authorities[95] may only be placed in secure
accommodation if statutory criteria are satisfied. The general principles are set out
in section 25(1) of the Children Act 1989.

> "A child who is being looked after by a local authority may not be placed, and,
> if placed may not be kept in accommodation provided for the purpose of
> restricting liberty ("secure accommodation") unless it appears:
>
> (a) that—
>
>   (i) he has a history of absconding and is likely to abscond from any other
>   description of accommodation; and
>   (ii) if he absconds he is likely to suffer significant harm; or
>
> (b) that if he is kept in any other description of accommodation he is likely to
>   injure himself or other persons."

The section further provides that a local authority may only detain a child meeting
the criteria in secure accommodation for 72 hours (or an aggregate of 72 hours in
28 days). Only a court on an application for a secure accommodation order[96] may
authorise detention in secure accommodation for more than 72 hours. If satisfied
that the criteria are met, the court may authorise detention for up to three months
in the first instance and subsequently for periods of up to six months.[97]

---

[93] See for instance N. Timms and R. Harris "Juvenile Courts and Secure accommodation" (1993)
Journal of Social Welfare and Family Law, 40; C.R. Smith and P.R Gardner, "Secure accommodation
under the Children Act 1989: legislative confusion and social ambivalence" (1996) *Journal of Social
Welfare and Family Law* 173–187; C. Ball "*R v. B (Young Offender: Sentencing Powers)* Paying due
regard to the welfare of the child in criminal proceedings", *op. cit.*
[94] See, for example, H. Swindells *et al.*, *Family Law and the Human Rights Act 1998* (Family Law,
Bristol, 1999), Chap. 6.
[94a] (2001) 165 J.P.
[94b] *The Times*, April 5, 2001.
[95] s.22(1) of the CA 1989.
[96] *ibid.*, s.25(2) and Children (Secure Accommodation) Regulations 1991 (S.I. 1991 No.1505), reg. 10.
[97] *ibid.*, regs. 11 and 12.

9.28 No child under the age of 13 may be placed in secure accommodation without the prior approval of the Secretary of State.[98] Sixteen- and 17-year-olds accommodated under section 20(5) of the Children Act 1989, which allows local authorities to provide accommodation for any person aged 16 to 20 years "if they consider that doing so will safeguard or promote his welfare", may not be placed in secure accommodation.[99] It should also be noted that section 25 does not apply to children detained under any provision of the Mental Health Act 1983. Nor does it apply to children convicted of homicide or other grave offences in respect of whom an order has been made under section 91 of the PCC(S)A 2000, and who may serve all or part of their sentence in local authority secure accommodation.

9.29 In addition to children in care under care orders, local authorities have to provide accommodation for children accommodated under section 20, children who are removed or kept away from their homes for their protection under Part V of the 1989 Act, and also—

- those whom they are requested by the police to receive under s38(6) of PACE;

- children and young persons remanded directly to secure accommodation by the courts under section 23(4) of the CYPA 1969;

- children remanded to local authority accommodation under section 21 of the CA 1989, and are then placed in secure accommodation; or

- who are the subject of a supervision order imposing a residence require-ment under section 12AA of the CYPA 1969.[1]

On March 31, 2000, 34 per cent of all children in secure accommodation were on remand under section 23(4) of the 1969 Act; 21 per cent were detained for grave crimes, 18 per cent were accommodated on remand under CA 1989, s.21, and 11 per cent were accommodated under CA 1989, s.20.[2]

The criteria for placing and keeping children who are detained or remanded in secure accommodation are modified in respect of

- children and young persons charged with or convicted of a violent or sexual offence, or of an offence punishable in the case of an adult with imprisonment for a term of 14 years or more, or

- who have "a recent history of absconding while remanded to local authority accommodation, and are charged with or has been convicted of an imprisonable offence alleged or found to have been committed while he was so remanded."[3]

The modified criteria replace the words from "unless it appears" in section 25(1) above until the end of subsection (1) with—

"unless it appears that any accommodation other than that provided for the purpose of restricting liberty is inappropriate because—

---

[98] *ibid.*, reg. 4.
[99] *ibid.*, reg. 5(2)(a).
[1] s.21(2)(c) of the CA 1989.
[2] Department of Health, *Statistical Bulletin*, 2000/15.
[3] Children (Secure Accommodation) Regulations 1991, *op.cit.*, reg. 6(1)(b)(ii).

(a) the child is likely to abscond from such other accommodation, or

(b) the child is likely to injure himself or other people if he is kept in any such other accommodation."[4]

The use of Secure Accommodation for Young Offenders

Children detained by the police under section 38(6) of the Police and Criminal Evidence Act

9.30 Where a juvenile is being detained by the police prior to a court appearance, it is for the local authority to determine whether the criteria for placing the child in secure accommodation are met. The police may only detain a child or young person in police custody rather than local authority accommodation if they certify that it is impracticable to effect a transfer.[5] In the case of an offender aged 12–16 years, where there is no secure accommodation available and there is a risk to the public of serious harm from the juvenile, the police may keep them in detention.[6] Except in those circumstances, "neither a juvenile's behaviour nor the nature of the offence with which he is charged provide grounds for the custody officer to decide that it is impracticable to seek to arrange for his transfer to the care of the local authority".[7]

Children and young persons remanded into local authority accommodation

9.31 The maximum period for which a court may authorise that a child who has been remanded to local authority accommodation under section 23 of the Children and Young Persons Act 1969 may be kept in secure accommodation is the period of the remand, up to a maximum of 28 days. This applies for both the initial remand period and any subsequent remands.[8]

9.32 The local authority is governed by section 25 of the 1989 Act in its use of secure accommodation. Although authority for use of such accommodation for more than 72 hours is normally sought from a family procedings court, power is given to a youth court or a magistrates' court remanding or committing a person under 17 to local authority accommodation also to grant this authority.[9] It need not necessarily be the court that ordered the remand that considers the application for a secure accommodation order. In *Liverpool City Council v. B.*[10] a juvenile had been remanded into the care of Liverpool City Council by a court sitting outside its boundary. The council could apply under section 25 to the Liverpool Youth Court since the wording of section 60(3) ("In the case of a . . . young person remanded . . . to local authority accommodation by a youth court . . ., any application under section 25 . . . shall . . . be made to *that* court") was used in a generic sense meaning a youth court rather than a family court. The application should be made to the appropriate youth court and it was said to be clearly appropriate for the Liverpool City Council to apply to the Liverpool Youth Court. The Crown Court does not have power to grant such an order and application must be made to any family proceedings court[11] and Children (Allocation of Proceedings) Order 1991,

---

[4] *ibid.*, reg. 6(2).
[5] "Impracticable" does not relate to the juvenile, but for instance to weather conditions making roads impassable.
[6] PACE, Code C para. 16.6 and *Notes for Guidance*, para. 16B.
[7] *ibid.*
[8] Children (Secure Accommodation) Regulations, *op cit.*, reg. 13.
[9] s.60(3) of the CJA 1991.
[10] [1995] 1 W.L.R. 505.
[11] s.60(3) of the CJA 1991.

art. 3(1)(a)) once the Crown Court itself remands to local authority accommodation. Until that time, the committal from the magistrates' court or youth court subsists and application will need to be made to a court of the same type as the committing court. The application, however, must be made by the local authority.[12] The following important provisions relate to an application for such an order:

9.33
1. A local authority that can prove the grounds for an order is entitled to receive an order.[13]

2. An order may not be made if the defendant is not legally represented unless he has been given the opportunity to apply for representation at public expense and has not done so.[14]

3. The criteria vary depending on the nature of the offence or the offender—

   (a) If there is a charge of a violent or sexual offence, or
   (b) If there is a charge for an offence punishable with 14 years imprisonment or more in the case of an adult, or
   (c) If the offender has a recent history of absconding whilst remanded to local authority accommodation and is charged with an offence said to have been committed whilst on remand to local authority accommodation,

then the local authority may not use secure accommodation unless it appears that any accommodation other than that provided to restrict liberty is inappropriate because either the defendant is likely to abscond from any other type of accommodation or is likely to injure himself or other people if kept in any other type of accommodation.[15]

9.34 If the defendant does not meet (a) to (c) above, secure accommodation may only be used or authorised if it appears that the defendant has a history of absconding, is likely to abscond from any other type of accommodation and, if he does so, is likely to suffer significant harm or if it appears that if he is kept elsewhere he is likely to injure himself or other people.[16]

The interaction of section 25 of the 1989 Act with the welfare principle contained in section 1 of that Act was considered in *Re M* (see above). This was a civil case. It was held that the welfare of the child was a relevant but not the paramount consideration and the criteria in section 1 were not applicable. As was pointed out, the power to make an order under section 25 could arise on the ground that the child was likely to injure others rather than himself. Use of the power in such circumstances might be inconsistent with the child's welfare being paramount. The same approach was adopted in relation to an application in criminal proceedings in *AE v. Staffordshire County Council*.[17]

Applications for orders are governed by provisions contained in Magistrates' Courts (Children and Young Persons) Rules 1992, Part III which provide for a simpler, speedier procedure than that contained in the equivalent rules governing

[12] Children (Secure Accommodation) Regulations 1991, reg. 8.
[13] s.25(4) of the 1989 Act and *Re M (A minor: Secure Accommodation Order)* [1995] 3 All E.R. 407.
[14] There must be a proper opportunity for instructions to be given: *Re AS (Secure Accommodation Order)* [1999] 1 F.L.R. 103.
[15] s.25(1) of the CA 1989, as modified by the 1991 Regulations, reg.6.
[16] *ibid.*
[17] [1995] 2 F.C.R. 84.

applications made to family proceedings courts. Thus there is no statutory requirement to give reasons (since that is contained in the Family Proceedings Courts (Children Act 1989) Rules 1991 which do not apply) but there is the obligation to invite representations and to explain the nature and effect of the order contained in Magistrates' Courts (Children and Young Persons) Rules 1992, r.22. It is very important that there is a clear recording of the facts found and that sworn evidence is received.[18] The ECHR will also cause reasons to be given sufficient to enable the parties to understand the basis of the decision. The rules as to notice must be strictly complied with and require the applicant to send a notice to the court giving the grounds for the proceedings and the names and addresses of the persons to whom a copy of the notice is sent. The categories of person are described in rule 14(2) and rule 14(3), as the defendant, unless that is inappropriate because of his age and understanding, and the defendants' parent or guardian if their whereabouts are known to the applicant or can readily be ascertained by him.

9.35 Parent or guardian includes a person who is the father of the child although not married to the mother at the time of birth but who has applied under the 1989 Act for acquisition of parental responsibility but whose application has not yet been determined.[19] There is no power to appoint an officer of CAFCASS in these proceedings and the rules provide for the defendant to have the case conducted on his behalf by his parent or guardian in the absence of any request from him to the contrary unless he is legally represented. The court is also entitled to allow some other person to represent the defendant and present his case in certain circumstances.[20] There is an obligation on the court to arrange for copies of any written report to be made available before the hearing as far as practicable to the applicant, the defendant's legal representative, the parent or guardian of the defendant and the defendant except where it is impracticable to disclose the report or undesirable in the case of the defendant.[21] Any written report can be received and considered by the court without being read aloud.[22]

9.36 Since provisions controlling the previously unrestricted powers of local authorities to keep children for whom they were responsible, whether under a court order or not, in accommodation intended to restrict liberty were first introduced by the Criminal Justice Act 1982 the law in this area has become increasingly complex. Many of those who have wrestled with the labyrinthine twists of the law and procedure in regard to secure accommodation, whether as judges, magistrates, their clerks, or legal or social work practitioners, will sympathise with Hollis J.'s comment in *Re C. (Secure Accommodation Order: Bail*[23] that it was a pity that Parliament had not taken the opportunity to spell out local authorities' powers over bailed children in the Children Act 1989. Most would probably go further and suggest that a careful review and revision of the whole of primary and delegated legislation relating to the use of secure accommodation, both for offenders on remand and children looked after by local authorities under other responsibilities, is long overdue.

---

[18] Re AS (Secure Accommodation Order) [1999] 1 F.L.R. 103.
[19] (rule 14(3)(c)).
[20] 1992 Rules, r.18(2).
[21] 1992 Rules, r.21(1).
[22] 1992 Rules, r.21(3).
[23] [1994] 2 F.L.R. 922.

CHAPTER 10

The Trial Process

10.01 In the youth court the normal procedure of a criminal trial is followed, with the prosecution having to satisfy the court of the defendant's guilt beyond reasonable doubt. Procedures in the youth court are governed by the Magistrates' Courts (Children and Young Persons) Rules 1992.

CAPACITY

10.02 Children under the age of 10 years are below the age of criminal responsibility. This is an irrebutable presumption. Children under the age of 10 years who commit offences may in certain circumstances be the subject of care proceedings under the Children Act 1989, s.31, but can never be the subject of criminal proceedings. The principle, recognised in common law for at least 200 years, that a child under the age of 14 was presumed to be *doli incapax*, or incapable of forming criminal intent, was abolished by section 34 of the Crime and Disorder Act 1998. However, the procedures do come within both the ECHR and the UNCRC. The way in which proceedings are conducted in the Crown Court are subject to a practice direction of the Lord Chief Justice.[1] Whilst the age of criminal responsibility is lower in England and Wales than in many other European jurisdictions, that is not something which the European Court would say is incompatible with the Convention rights. The Court is, however, concerned to ensure that the rights of the young person are properly safeguarded—rights to take a proper part in the proceedings and rights to privacy in particular—and that proper regard is had to the welfare of the young person.

THE TRIAL PROCESS

10.03 Parents are generally expected to attend hearings where the defendant is under the age of 16, and may be required to do so if they are aged 16 or 17, the court having the power to compel that attendance where necessary (Children and Young Persons Act 1933, s.34A and Magistrates' Courts (Children and Young Persons) Rules 1992, r. 26). The increase in the emphasis on assisting parents to enable their child to avoid re-offending makes the effective use of this power even more important. Courts are often faced with difficult decisions where there is a conflict between the desire for speed in concluding a case and the desirability of ensuring that a parent is present. Youth panels generally have a policy regarding the extent to which they will expect one or both parents (where both have a significant role in the life of the child) to attend a hearing. The wording of section 34A is mandatory as far as a child or young person under 16 is concerned but can be read

---

[1] *Practice Direction (Crown Court: Trial of children and young persons)* [2000] 1 Cr.App.R. 483, *The Times*, February 17, 2000. See 6.16 above.

as either requiring attendance of any person who is a parent or guardian or simply requiring the attendance of one such person. It is submitted that the latter interpretation is preferable—the provision is designed for the benefit of the child or young person in ensuring that there is a responsible family member present. If the court intends to make an order requiring the co-operation of a particular person, then that person can be brought before the court. Where a child or young person is in the care of a local authority, then it is the local authority which will be required to attend (if necessary, in addition to the parent or guardian if the child or young person is in fact living with the parent or guardian).[2] It is important that courts use the presence of the parent or guardian as effectively as possible in order to enhance the likelihood of the court appearance assisting in the reduction of re-offending. Part of the purpose of the Youth Court Demonstration Project[2a] was to explore better ways of communicating with youg people and their parents. This was generally welcomed by parents but requires considerable skill by the court to overcome the understandable fear of the parent that they may make things worse by saying the "wrong" thing.[2b] Evidence given in the youth court on oath, or by a person under 18 in another court, will require the form of oath prescribed by Children and Young Persons Act 1963, s.28(1): "I promise before Almighty God to tell the truth, the whole truth, and nothing but the truth". If the wrong form of oath is used the evidence is not invalidated.[3]

10.04   Before taking a plea the court must explain to the defendant in simple language suitable to his age and understanding the charge and the nature of the proceedings.[4] The rule does not impose a duty on the court to give a detailed or elaborate explanation of charge, but the court should ensure that the essential legal elements are explained, in order that the defendant can make an informed plea.[5] This explanation is an important part of the obligation placed on the Court by the ECHR to ensure that the defendant fully understands the allegation so that there can be proper preparation of the defence.[6] This obligation should have been fulfilled at the time of charge or when the summons was issued and so the use of this rule should normally be a check that the Convention obligation has been discharged. The defendant is entitled to have sufficient information to understand the nature of the offence alleged and the reasons for the allegation. There is a requirement for advance information to be made available in indictable offences (whether or not triable either way) but not in relation to summary offences. However, the expectation that the European Convention on Human Rights requires such information to be given when requested was anticipated in *R. v. Stratford Justices, ex p. Imbert*.[7] The emphasis is on a fair trial—the defendant must know what information is put before the Court and must have adequate time to prepare his response to that information. Whilst it is for the Court dealing with the matter to decide whether the procedure is fair, nonetheless the Divisional Court expressed the view that it was desirable that prosecution witness statements be made available to defendants in all but the most exceptional cases where a not guilty plea was entered.

---

[2] s.34A(2) of the CYPA 1933.
[2a] For evaluation of the project, see Home Office Research Study 214, Home Office, 2000.
[2b] Home Office Research Study 214, pages 19–24 and Appendix F.
[3] s.28(2) of the 1963 Act.
[4] 1992 Rules, r.6.
[5] *Blandford Justices, ex p. G. (an infant)* [1967] 1 Q.B. 82.
[6] Article 6(3)(a).
[7] (1999) 163 J.P. 693.

10.05 If the child is not legally represented, the court must allow his parent or guardian to assist in conducting the case.[8] If the parent or guardian cannot be found or cannot reasonably be required to attend, the court may allow any relative or responsible person to take the parent's role.[9] If the defendant is not supported as allowed by Rule 5, and in seeking to question a witness, makes assertions, the court may convert those assertions into questions as necessary and, in order to do so, may question the defendant to clarify or develop the assertions.[10]

When all the prosecution evidence is heard, the court must decide if a *prima facie* case is made out. If so, the defence will have the right to give and call evidence. If the defendant is not legally represented it must be explained to him that he may give evidence or address the court and any other witnesses must be heard.[11]

The powers to deal with a juvenile found to be in contempt of court are limited. The power of magistrates' courts is contained in Contempt of Court Act 1981, s.12 which gives power to commit the offender to custody for up to one month or impose a fine. However, the power to commit to custody is subject to the statutory restrictions prohibiting committal of a person under 17 to custody: see section 89 of the PCC(S)A 2000, and *Selby Justices, ex p. Frame*.[12] Nor is there power to make a probation order.[13] The same result obtains in use of the powers of the Crown Court.[14] The only available sanction is a fine.

A Child or Young Person as a Witness

10.06 A justice system can only operate effectively if it can receive cogent evidence from witnesses who have relevant information to give. It has become increasingly clear that witnesses' experience of the criminal justice system has generally been so poor that many, having given evidence once, will say that they would be unwilling to do so again. Children and young people are particularly vulnerable yet it is very important for public safety, for the welfare of children generally and for the interests of justice that children and young people are able to give evidence in a way that enables the court to be confident that it is reliable.

10.07 The very limited protection in statute was substantially extended by the Criminal Justice Acts 1988 and 1991 which built upon recommendations contained in the report of the advisory group on video evidence chaired by Judge Pigot.[15] The Pigot report identified as major concerns:

(a) The need to provide the court with the most reliable evidence available;

(b) The need to bring to justice those who commit offences against very young children;

(c) The stress suffered by children giving evidence in the traditional setting;

(d) The effect of stress in reducing ability to recall and describe;

(e) The possibility that the way in which that stress manifests itself may create the wrong impression.

---

[8] 1992 Rules, r.5(1).
[9] 1992 Rules, r.5(2).
[10] 1992 Rules, r.8.
[11] 1992 Rules, r.9.
[12] [1991] 2 All E.R. 344.
[13] *Palmer* [1992] All E.R. 289.
[14] *Byas* [1995] Crim L.R. 439.
[15] Home Office, 1989.

10.08   The recommendations of Pigot were not implemented in full but in part in this jurisdiction—so-called "half-Pigot". The deficiencies in this approach and the developing awareness of the importance of improving the prospects of reliable evidence being obtained led to the establishment of an interdepartmental review of the treatment of vulnerable and intimidated witnesses in the criminal justice system. This resulted in a report—"Speaking Up for Justice".[16] Proposals in that report were enacted in the YJCEA 1999 which, when in force, will provide for substantial changes in the competence of witnesses,[17] in the use of sworn and unsworn evidence,[18] in the provision of special measures for vulnerable and intimidated witnesses[19] and in protecting witnesses from cross-examination by defendants in person in certain circumstances.[20] Implementation of the Act is to be phased. Sections 53–57 were due to be implemented by the end of 2000 but have been delayed. It is anticipated that they will be brought into force during 2001 and this book is written on that basis. Sections 16–33 are due to be phased in between the end of 2000 and the Spring of 2003[21] and reference is made to both existing and new provisions. Sections 34, 35 and 38–40 were implemented from September 4, 2000 and sections 41–43 from December 4, 2000. Some of these provisions are subject to legal challenge the outcome of which is awaited at the time of going to print. This book is written on the assumption that section 36 and 37 will be brought into force during 2001.

10.09   When fully in force, the Act will improve the facilities capable of being made available to witnesses, make more certain the decisions to be made, particularly for child witnesses, and improve some of the procedural complexities. Inevitably, where such a sensitive balancing exercise has to be conducted between the right to a fair trial[22] and the rights of witnesses[23] and also between the importance of encouraging witnesses to crime to speak and enabling defendants to challenge evidence robustly, unsatisfactory solutions will remain. Academic commentators have sympathetically described the expected impacts of the new legislation and identified those areas where problems are likely to arise.[24]

10.10   The establishment of the interdepartmental working group followed from a manifesto commitment of the Labour Party prior to its election as the party of government. The group referred extensively to research amongst which was the result of a study conducted at Bristol University[25] which also sounded warning notes which the Act has not addressed fully. Concerns continue to exist, for example, that evidence by video link or by recorded testimony appears to be less persuasive to a jury than live evidence although decidedly advantageous to the witness. If the provisions are to achieve their goal, there will need to be cultural changes as well as procedural ones.[26] These cultural changes will be encouraged by revised guidance issued by the Home Office *Achieving Best Evidence in Criminal*

---

[16] Home Office, June 1998.
[17] ss.53 and 54.
[18] ss.55–57.
[19] ss.16–33.
[20] ss.34–40.
[21] See timetable in Action for Justice, Home Office Justice and Victims Unit, 1999.
[22] Article 6 of the European Convention on Human Rights.
[23] For example, Article 8 of the European Convention on Human Rights.
[24] See D. Birch, "A Better Deal for Vulnerable Witnesses", [2000] Crim. L.R. 223 and L. Hoyano, "Variations on a Theme by Pigot: Special Measures Directions for Child Witnesses" [2000] Crim. L.R. 250.
[25] G. Davis *et al.*, *An Assessment of the Admissibility and Sufficiency of Evidence in Child Abuse Prosecution* (Home Office, London, 1999).
[26] See also *Support for Child Witnesses in Hampshire* (NSPCC, February 1999)

Proceedings: Guidance for vulnerable and intimidated witnesses including children.[27] This guidance is part of the Action for Justice programme designed to implement the *Speaking Up for Justice* report. Revising and updating the Memorandum of Good Practice on video recorded interviews,[28] the guidance also covers pre-trial witness support and preparation at the court stage. This extensive guidance is essential for anyone involved in any part of the process of obtaining evidence from a child or young person. Guidance is given on the planning and conduct of interviews with a view to obtaining good quality evidence whilst safeguarding the welfare of the child or young person and also on the proper preparation of witnesses for the court hearing, including guidance for the court and for advocates.

In relation to the ability to give evidence, there will now be two issues to be resolved. Firstly, is the witness competent to give evidence? Secondly, if so, will that evidence be given sworn or unsworn?[29]

Competence

10.11 The starting point is that everyone is competent to give evidence regardless of age.[30] A defendant cannot give evidence for the prosecution in the proceedings in which he is a defendant[31] whilst still at risk of conviction.[32] A defendant who has pleaded guilty could give evidence for the prosecution though there is the inevitable risk that the evidence may be slanted to minimise the defendant's criminality. A person ceases to be competent if they are not able to understand questions put to them as a witness and to give answers which can be understood.[33] Considerable assistance can now be offered to assist witnesses in understanding questions and to assist courts to receive intelligible answers[34] but there are dangers. Not every means of conveying information can be sufficiently reliable. In *Re D (a Child)(Evidence: Facilitated Communication), The Times*, July 26, 2000, the President of the Family Division rejected for the purpose of evidence a means of communication designed to assist a communicatively impaired person while using a keyboard or similar. This particular means was viewed with considerable scepticism in the medical community and although the defendant (aged 17) had motor skills of about a two year old, his linguistic and social skills were considerably lower. Those factors had to be taken into account when assessing the validity of the responses received.

10.12 Although offering considerable improvements on the previous provisions, there are still a number of practical questions left unanswered such as the nature of interpretation – should it be simply verbatim or should it convey what is believed to be meant both to and from the witness – and the nature of the questions that a witness should be able to understand – should they be just those directly relevant to the main issue or may it be any issue that might properly be raised?[35]

A wider range of special measure directions are available in certain circumstances where the Court is satisfied that the quality of the evidence would otherwise be diminished by virtue of a number of specified circumstances.[36] Those relating

---

[27] In advanced draft stage as a consultation paper at the time of going to print.
[28] Home Office, 1992.
[29] ss.53–57 of the YJCEA 1999.
[30] *ibid.*, s.53(1).
[31] *ibid.*, s.53(4).
[32] *ibid.*, s.53(5).
[33] *ibid.*, s.53(3).
[34] For example, *ibid.*, ss.29 and 30.
[35] See D. Birch, *op. cit.* [2000] Crim. L.R. 223 at pp. 227–231.
[36] ss.16–33 of the YJCEA 1999.

particularly to children as witnesses are discussed below at para. 10.17. The
potential breadth of this power was illustrated in *R. v Richards*.[36a] A witness refused
to give evidence unless the public gallery was cleared. She had no particular reason
other than that she did not feel comfortable. It was clear she would not give
evidence (and she was the prosecution's main witness in a case of murder) unless
the gallery was cleared. The judge ordered the gallery to be cleared, the evidence
was given and the defendant convicted. The defendant appealed arguing that the
decision was contrary to the requirement of Article 6 of the ECHR that proceedings should be in public. The Court of Appeal upheld the decision of the trial
Judge. Although there is a broad principle that a criminal trial should be held
without excluding a member of the public who wished to be present, if justice
would not be achieved by sticking to that principle then the more fundamental
principle, that justice had to be done, had to prevail.

Sworn or unsworn?

10.13   A witness who is at least 14 years old will be required to give evidence
on oath if the Court is satisfied that he or she sufficiently appreciates the solemnity
of the occasion and the particular responsibility to tell the truth which is involved
in taking the oath.[37] A person who is able to give intelligible testimony is presumed
to have that "sufficient appreciation" unless evidence tending to show the contrary
is adduced.[38] A person is able to give intelligible testimony if able to understand
questions put to him as a witness and give answers which can be understood.[39] It is
the responsibility of the Court to determine the issue of whether a witness can be
sworn[40] and the issue can be raised by the Court or by a party. Where the witness
needs to be questioned for this purpose, that questioning is to be undertaken by the
Court in the presence of the parties.[41] Where evidence is adduced, the party
wishing to call the witness must satisfy the Court of the matters in section 55(2) on
the balance of probabilities.[42] Expert evidence may be received[43] though the
decision in *G. v. Director of Public Prosecutions*[43a] emphasises that, generally, the
test of whether a person can give intelligible testimony is a simple test well within
the capacity of a judge or magistrate. There will, however, be instances where
appreciating the extent of understanding is a complex matter and there the Court
will be assisted by the evidence of an expert.

10.14   A person will give unsworn evidence if they are able to give intelligible
testimony but are not entitled to be sworn either because they are under 14 years or
because the court is not satisfied that they have sufficient appreciation of the
solemnity of the occasion or the particular responsibility to tell the truth which is
involved in taking the oath.[44] A deposition may be taken as if the evidence had been
given on oath.[45] No appeal is to be allowed solely on the basis that a conviction is
unsafe because a witness who gave evidence unsworn ought to have been sworn.[46]
Giving false evidence unsworn is an offence punishable on summary conviction.[47]

[36a] [1999] Crim. L.R. 764.
[37] *ibid.*, s.55(2).
[38] *ibid.*, s.55(3).
[39] *ibid.*, s.55(8).
[40] *ibid.*, s.55(1).
[41] *ibid.*, s.55(7).
[42] *ibid.*, s.55(4).
[43] *ibid.*, s.55(6).
[43a] [1998] Q.B. 919.
[44] *ibid.*, s.56(2).
[45] *ibid.*, s.56(3).
[46] *ibid.*, s.56(5).
[47] *ibid.*, s.57.

It is clear that a person able to give intelligible testimony may be inhibited from doing so for a wide variety of reasons. The 1999 Act substantially increases the discretion of the court in making it as likely as possible that that testimony will be received. The next paragraphs describe the effect of those provisions and are followed by a description of those provisions which preceded the Act with a note as to what will happen to them as the 1999 Act is implemented.

Special measures

10.15 When in force, the YJCEA 1999 will provide courts with a range of measures to assist in enabling a competent witness to give their evidence as well as possible. The special measures apply to a witness in criminal proceedings (but not to the person accused of the offence) who is eligible because of age, because of incapacity or because of fear or distress in connection with giving evidence in the proceedings.[48] All apply equally in any Court though it is likely that some of the necessary facilities may be made available more quickly in some Courts than in others. This may influence the courthouse to which the hearing of a case is allocated.

A witness under 17 at the time of the hearing (that is, the time when the Court determines whether the witness is eligible for assistance and, if so, what assistance is to be given[49]) is automatically eligible for assistance. If assistance is given solely on the grounds of eligibility by age, that assistance will generally end on the witness attaining 17 unless the witness has already started to give evidence.[50] The exception is for video recorded examination in chief and cross examination which is authorised and completed before the witness becomes 17.[51] The very prescriptive approach to protecting child witnesses is set out in section 21(3–7).

Any other witness who falls within the categories described above will only be eligible for assistance if the Court considers that the quality of the witness's evidence is likely to be diminished because of the incapacity or the fear or distress.[53] Quality of evidence is defined in terms of completeness, coherence and accuracy. Coherence is the ability to answer the questions that are put in a way which can be understood both individually and collectively.[54]

10.16 A complainant in a sexual offence[55] who is a witness in proceedings relating to that offence is automatically eligible for assistance whatever their age though that entitlement can be waived.[56]

The type of special measures available vary with the criterion by which the witness qualifies for assistance. If entitlement is based on age or incapacity,[57] the full range of special measures is available to the court. If entitlement is based on fear and distress, all special measures are available except those contained in section 29 (witness to be examined through an intermediary) and section 30 (witness to have specified aids to communication). A special measures direction may only be made where the facilities exist in the area—this will be made known by notification from the Secretary of State.[58]

[48] *ibid.*, ss.16 and 17.
[49] *ibid.*, ss.16(3) and 19(2).
[50] *ibid.*, s.21(8).
[51-52] *ibid.*, s.21(9).
[53] s.16(1) of the YJCEA 1999.
[54] *ibid.*, s.16(5).
[55] Defined in s.62 of the YJCEA 1999.
[56] *ibid.*, s.17(4).
[57] *ibid.*, s.16.
[58] *ibid.*, s.18(2).

Gateways to and Procedures for the Special Measures Directions [SMD]

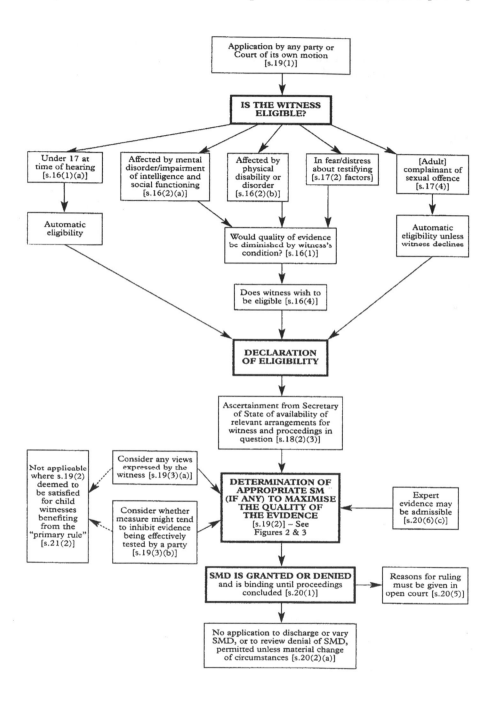

Special Measures Directions [SMD] for Young Witnesses

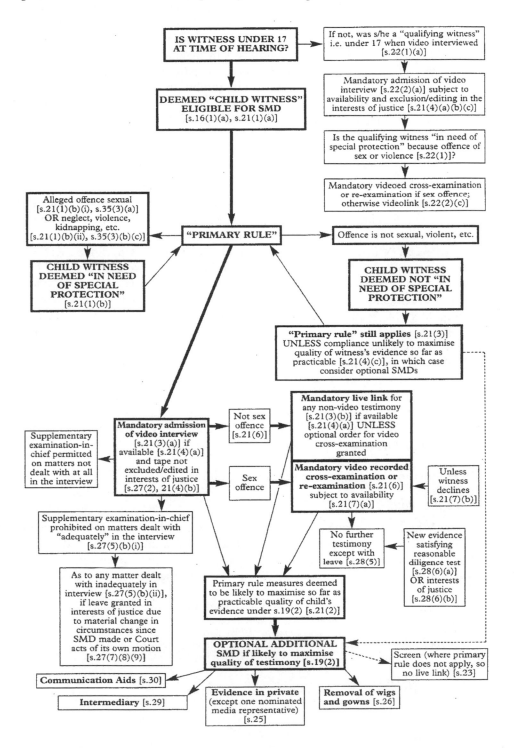

IS WITNESS UNDER 17 AT TIME OF HEARING?

If not, was s/he a "qualifying witness" i.e. under 17 when video interviewed [s.22(1)(a)]

DEEMED "CHILD WITNESS" ELIGIBLE FOR SMD [s.16(1)(a), s.21(1)(a)]

Mandatory admission of video interview [s.22(2)(a)] subject to availability and exclusion/editing in the interests of justice [s.21(4)(a)(b)(c)]

Is the qualifying witness "in need of special protection" because offence of sex or violence [s.22(1)]?

Mandatory videoed cross-examination or re-examination if sex offence; otherwise videolink [s.22(2)(c)]

Alleged offence sexual [s.21(1)(b)(i), s.35(3)(a)] OR neglect, violence, kidnapping, etc. [s.21(1)(b)(ii), s.35(3)(b)(c)]

"PRIMARY RULE"

Offence is not sexual, violent, etc.

CHILD WITNESS DEEMED "IN NEED OF SPECIAL PROTECTION" [s.21(1)(b)]

CHILD WITNESS DEEMED NOT "IN NEED OF SPECIAL PROTECTION"

"Primary rule" still applies [s.21(3)] UNLESS compliance unlikely to maximise quality of witness's evidence so far as practicable [s.21(4)(c)], in which case consider optional SMDs

Mandatory admission of video interview [s.21(3)(a)] if available [s.21(4)(a)] and tape not excluded/edited in interests of justice [s.27(2), 21(4)(b)]

Not sex offence [s.21(6)]

Sex offence

Mandatory live link for any non-video testimony [s.21(3)(b)] if available [s.21(4)(a)] UNLESS optional order for video cross-examination granted

Mandatory video recorded cross-examination or re-examination [s.21(6)] subject to availability [s.21(7)(a)]

Unless witness declines [s.21(7)(b)]

Supplementary examination-in-chief permitted on matters not dealt with at all in the interview

Supplementary examination-in-chief prohibited on matters dealt with "adequately" in the interview [s.27(5)(b)(i)]

No further testimony except with leave [s.28(5)]

New evidence satisfying reasonable diligence test [s.28(6)(a)] OR interests of justice [s.28(6)(b)]

As to any matter dealt with inadequately in interview [s.27(5)(b)(ii)], if leave granted in interests of justice due to material change in circumstances since SMD made or Court acts of its own motion [s.27(7)(8)(9)]

Primary rule measures deemed to be likely to maximise so far as practicable quality of child's evidence under s.19(2) [s.21(2)]

OPTIONAL ADDITIONAL SMD if likely to maximise quality of testimony [s.19(2)]

Screen (where primary rule does not apply, so no live link) [s.23]

Communication Aids [s.30]

Intermediary [s.29]

Evidence in private (except one nominated media representative) [s.25]

Removal of wigs and gowns [s.26]

The process for considering a special measures direction is set out in the preceeding flow charts.[59] The issue of whether or not a special measures direction is needed may be raised by a party or by the Court.[60] The Court will decide on the basis of whether any of the special measures available is likely to improve the quality of the evidence given by the witness.[61] In making that decision, the Court will consider all the circumstances of the case but particularly any views given by the witness and whether the measure might inhibit the effective testing of the evidence by a party to the proceedings. Once made, an order will last until the proceedings are completed,[62] or the order discharged or varied[63] unless the order is made on the basis of the witness being under 17, in which case see para. 10.15 above.

In need of special protection

10.17   There is a special category of child witnesses deemed to be in need of special protection. These are witnesses under the age of 17 to offences set out in section 35 of the 1999 Act—certain sexual offences, kidnapping, assaults and other serious offences. Where a witness in criminal proceedings is a child, there is a potentially complex hierarchy of decisions to follow—see flowchart on page 129.[64]

Such children have the benefit of an additional set of provisions giving added protection which extend the video recording of evidence in chief[65] to include video recording of cross examination (other than by the accused in person) and re-examination[66] insofar as the facilities are available and the witness has not indicated that they do not wish that facility to be made available to them.[67]

The child witness who is not in need of special protection will have access to a range of protective measures, subject to the necessary facilities being available. The order of consideration of the issues by the Court is set out in section 21(2) of the 1999 Act. There is a presumption in favour of video recording of evidence in chief and other evidence by live link.[68] This does not apply to the extent that the court is satisfied that compliance would not be likely to maximise the quality of the evidence.[69]

These provisions develop those previously in force.

Current procedures

10.18   Where the attendance at court of a person under 18 to give evidence in respect of an offence under the 1933 Act, Sched. 1 would involve serious danger to his life or health, a justice of the peace may take a deposition from that person if satisfied on the evidence of a duly qualified medical practitioner that such danger

---

[59] This flowchart was compiled by Laura Hoyano, Fellow and Tutor in Law at Wadham College, Oxford and is reproduced with permission and with grateful appreciation. It was first published in *Variations on a Theme by Pigot: Special Measures Directions for Child Witnesses* [2000] Crim. L.R. 250 (Sweet & Maxwell). For a further development of issues concerning child witnesses see L. Hoyano and C. Keenan, *Innocents Betrayed? Evaluating Legal Responses to Allegations of Child Abuse* (Oxford Univesity Press, forthcoming).
[60] s.19(1) of the YJCEA 1999.
[61] *ibid.*, s.19(2)(a).
[62] *ibid.*, s.20(1).
[63] *ibid.*, s.20(2).
[64] See n.59 above.
[65] *ibid.*, s.21(3)(a).
[66] *ibid.*, s.21(6).
[67] *ibid.*, s.21(4)(c).
[68] *ibid.*, s.21(3).
[69] *ibid.*, s.21(4)(c).

would be involved.[70] Such a deposition is not admissible *against* the defendant unless it is proved that reasonable notice of the intention to take the deposition had been served on the defendant and that he (or his legal representative) would have had an opportunity to cross examine the witness making the deposition. The provision will not be affected by the YJCEA 1999.[71]

10.19 Consideration of the extent of the definition of an offence involving "assault on, or injury or a threat of injury, to a person" was given *in R. v. McAndrew-Bingham*.[72] The offence in question was one of attempted abduction contrary to section 2 of the Child Abduction Act 1984. Although no force or threat of force was used on this occasion, the nature of the offence was such that it might involve the use or threat of force and, therefore, the offence came within the definition (thus triggering the provisions of the 1988 Act) even though the particular circumstances that lead to the charge may not themselves have involved the use or threat of force. This broader approach is very much in keeping with the principle of the 1999 Act which should make such mental gymnastics unnecessary.

10.20 In proceedings before a youth court, or on appeal to the Crown Court from such proceeding, or on indictment—or on appeal from such hearings—for any of the types of offences listed in 1 to 9 below, if the witness is a child, with the leave of the court, evidence may be given by live television link, that is with the witness outside the courtroom but able to be seen and heard by those in the courtroom by means of a television link. Note that this power does not apply to a magistrates' court other than a youth court.[73] This provision is repealed by schedule 6 of the 1999 Act when in force.

These qualifying offences are—

1. one involving assault on or injury or threat of injury to a person;

2. an offence of cruelty to a person under 16 under Children and Young Persons Act 1933, s.1;

3. an offence under the Sexual Offences Act 1956;

4. an offence under the Indecency with Children Act 1960;

5. an offence under the Sexual Offences Act 1967;

6. an offence under Criminal Law Act 1977, s.54 (incitement to incestuous sexual intercourse);

7. an offence under the Protection of Children Act 1978;

8. an offence of attempting or conspiring to commit any of the above;

9. an offence of aiding, abetting, counselling, procuring or inciting the commission of the above.

10.21 Any party may seek the leave of the court by giving notice to the clerk of the court with a copy to every other party to the proceedings.[74] The notice must be in the prescribed form[75] or in a form to the like effect[76] and must be given within

---

[70] 1933 Act, s.42.
[71] 1933 Act, s.43.
[72] [1999] Crim L.R. 830.
[73] 1988 Act, 32(1A).
[74] 1992 Rules, r.23(2) and (4).
[75] Form 51 in 1992 Rules, Sched. 2.
[76] 1992 Rules, r.2.

28 days of the first time a defendant appears before the court.[77] This period may be
extended (whether or not it has already expired) by written application to be dealt
with in the same way as an application for leave.[78] Any party who receives such a
notice has fourteen days in which to object. Written notice of objection must be
given to the clerk of the court and the applicant, and must give the reasons for the
opposition.[79]

10.22   If an application is made, a single justice will decide whether to grant it.
That decision can be made without a hearing unless the justice directs otherwise, in
which case the court will notify the parties of the time and date of the hearing.[80] A
decision whether or not to grant leave must be communicated to all parties and to
the person who will accompany the witness if that person is known. If leave is
granted, the notification must include the court location and, where the witness is
to be called by the prosecution, the name of the witness, and if known, the name,
occupation and relationship to the witness of the person who is to accompany the
witness. The person to accompany the witness must be acceptable to a justice of the
peace and no other person may accompany the witness except with the leave of
that justice.[81] For these purposes a child is a person under 14 years of age for
offences falling within categories 1 and 2 above or a person under 17 years of age
for offences falling within 3 to 7 above. Offences under 8 or 9 above are defined by
reference to the principal offence, *i.e.* the definition of a child is a person under 14
if the offence is aiding and abetting an assault.[82] If a youth court does not have
access to the facilities to allow this to be done, it may sit to hear the proceedings at
another place which does have those facilities providing the place is formally
appointed for this purpose by the justices for the petty sessions area for which the
youth court acts.[83] This may include places outside the normal jurisdictional limits
of the youth court.[84] When in force, schedule 6 to the YJCEA 1999 will repeal the
provisions of the CJA 1988 referred to above.

10.23   The phrasing of this formal appointment requirement seems to indicate
that the decision be made by the whole bench for the area of the youth court,
presumably at one of its normal business meetings. Such a procedure appears
unnecessarily cumbersome; it is imperative that cases involving young people are
dealt with very quickly—this is likely to be even more necessary if the sensitivity of
the witness requires the use of a television link. It would appear perfectly adequate
for the court which is to hear the case to designate the place of hearing taking into
account all the needs of the participants which would allow the maximum
flexibility in selecting the most readily available convenient location at the time
needed. Similar criteria already have statutory precedent in guiding magistrates'
courts as to the Crown Court to which to commit a defendant for trial.[85]

A youth court dealing with an offender will be sitting in a "petty sessional
courthouse".[86] Such a courthouse is defined as,

    (a)   a courthouse or place at which justices are accustomed to assemble for
        holding special or petty sessions or for the time being appointed as a

---

[77] 1992 Rules, r.3.
[78] 1992 Rules, rr.8 and 9.
[79] 1992 Rules, r.23(5).
[80] 1992 Rules, r.23(6).
[81] 1992 Rules, r.10.
[82] s.32A(7) of the 1988 Act.
[83] s.32(3A) of the 1988 Act.
[84] s.32(3B) of the 1988 Act.
[85] s.7 of the Magistrates' Courts Act.
[86] s.121(3) of the 1980 Act.

substitute for such a courthouse or place, including, where justices are accustomed to assemble for either special petty sessions at more than one courthouse or place in a petty sessional division, any such courthouse or place;

(b) a courthouse or place at which a District Judge (Magistrates' Courts) is authorised by law to do alone any act authorised to be done by more than one justice of the peace.[87]

10.24 No procedure is established to govern the appointment of petty sessional courthouse and it would not seem inappropriate for the youth court to exercise this power where necessary. This is particularly attractive since a justice for any area may act as a justice for that area in any commission area which adjoins his own.[88]

Extra statutory developments

10.25 Much attention has rightly been paid to problems encountered by witnesses waiting to go into court. It is unacceptable—

(a) For a prosecution witness (particularly the alleged victim) to be put in an area where they come into contact with the defendant;

(b) For a witness not to be properly prepared for what will happen in the courtroom with an understanding of what is expected, who will be present and what they will be expecting from the witness;

(c) For those conducting the questioning to be untrained in the best ways of handling a child witness;

(d) For judges, magistrates and their legal advisors to be unaware of the needs of child witnesses and possible reactions to the stress of a court experience.

10.26 As a result of an initiative of the Trials Issues Group, there is a service level agreement in each area that defines the various responsibilities in relation to witnesses. It is important that these responsibilities are reviewed regularly in the light of changes in practice and that all who come into contact with witnesses are fully aware of what is expected of them.

---

[87] s.150 of the MCA 1980.
[88] s.68(1) of the Justices of the Peace Act 1997.

CHAPTER 11

Sentencing Juveniles: General Considerations

11.01   Young offenders or children in trouble? This familiar question poses the overarching dilemma for sentencing in youth justice. Is the juvenile law breaker to be regarded essentially as a criminal to be held responsible for his or her actions and punished accordingly, albeit with some concessions to youth, or in a fundamentally different way, giving wide consideration to the young person's problems, personality and potential? Is the youth court simply a junior criminal court or a special welfare tribunal which happens to be triggered by an offending event? As Walgrave[1] points out, all systems of juvenile justice struggle to "construct a kind of synthesis or compromise between two basic principles that are very hard to reconcile": on the one hand a penal response emphasising legality, proportionality and responsibility; on the other, a developmental response which doubts how functional penality can be for minors. Walgrave suggests that systems commonly resort to "*mystifications du langage*" to camouflage the irreconcilability of these rationales. The murder in Merseyside in November 1993 of a two-year-old by two boys aged ten served to galvanise concern about the capabilities of very young children for the most serious criminal behaviour, yet also to point up the shortcomings of holding children to account under adult procedures, systems and principles. This case uniquely highlighted our confusion about offending children: we are increasingly fearful for their safety and well-being in an ever more hazardous social world yet frightened of their potential to inflict wanton harm because of their apparent lack of obvious stake in the social order.

11.02   This chapter seeks to explore the evolving attempt at synthesis in this sentencing jurisdiction. Since the welfarist vision of the White Paper *Children in Trouble*,[2] the direction in the tide towards desert-based penalty has been clear, causing commentators[3] to identify the erosion of difference between the treatment of children and adults, leaving limited conceptual basis for a distinctive and separate approach to child offenders. Yet, as Zedner[4] has observed, "the sentencing of juveniles has powerfully resisted being subsumed into the general body of sentencing theory for adults". Because youth offending continues to be experienced as the pre-eminent crime problem—

> "the sentencing of young offenders continues to enjoy (or perhaps better, to endure) a rapidity of change and innovation not found in the rest of the

---

[1] L. Walgrave (1996) "Restorative Juvenile Justice", in *Children and Young People in Conflict with the Law* (Research Highlights in Social Work No. 30, S. Asquith ed., Jessica Kingsley Publishers, London, 1996).

[2] Home Office (1968) Cmnd. 3601, London: HMSO.

[3] *e.g.* C Ball (1995) "Youth Justice and the Youth Court: The End of a Separate System" *Child and Family Law Quarterly*, 7, 196–208.

[4] L. Zedner (1998) "Sentencing Young Offenders", in *Fundamentals of Sentencing Theory* (A. Ashworth and M. Wasik ed., Clarendon Press, Oxford, 1998) at p. 165.

system. It is as if the sentencing of young offenders represents an experimental laboratory where new ideas (to say nothing of ministerial whims) flourish with little regard to research findings, still less to any theoretical or conceptual framework".[5]

11.03 Among ideas undergoing laboratory testing as a result of the CDA 1998, a kind of "restorative justice" is being pursued through reparation orders and allied initiatives, which may take root in due course in equivalent adult measures. More recently, the new principal aim for youth justice under CDA 1998, s.37 of "preventing offending"—appearing to place retributive purposes in a subsidiary position to correctional intervention—has helped to pave the way for referral orders introduced by the YJCEA 1999, and an enthusiasm for earlier custodial sentencing is likely to be stimulated by the detention and training order, promising a coherent experience of joined-up sentence intervention spanning institution and community. Such initiatives appear to provide the impetus for the current review of sentencing across the adult board, prompted by concern that our present approach achieves too little of consequentialist worth, has little regard to outcomes, pays insufficient weight to the needs of victims and "focuses too much on the offence and not sufficiently on offenders and their future behaviour".[6] Though the 1998 Act has been criticised as "old hat", a "melting pot of principles and ideologies" that fails to resolve confusion over "punishment and welfare,"[7] it may also be read as trying to break from that old dialectic in ways that may point to change in the adult system.

THE CHANGING STRUCTURE OF THE 1991 ACT

11.04 The Criminal Justice Act 1991 introduced what in effect were four sentencing bands: discharge, fine, community penalties and custodial sentences. The initial coherence has since changed so that there are in effect five bands with less distinctive identity. In summary and with particular reference to youth, these are as follows.

Discharge

11.05 Appropriately used where it is unnecessary to impose any sanction on the offender, a discharge, when used conditionally, leaves open the possibility of later punishment if the offender commits a further offence during the specified period. It may be hoped that the experience of prosecution and a court appearance will serve to express public disapproval, teaching and deterring the offender. This disposal no longer carries much support under the Government's approach of "no more excuses". The argument runs that if a young person has failed to heed reprimand and warning they are unlikely to take notice of a measure that is likely to appear toothless and inconsequential. The drama and tension of the courtroom is believed to be lost on most young defendants, the Home Secretary[8] criticising the youth court as an arena where—

> "the young offender is, at best, a spectator in a theatre where other people are the actors. At worst the young offender is wholly detached and contemptuous

---

[5] See footnote 4, p. 166.
[6] *A Review of the Sentencing Framework*, (Home Office, London, 2000).
[7] J. Fionda, *op.cit.*, at 41.
[8] *Hansard* (1999) H.C. vol. 334, col. 1224.

of what is going on . . . never asked to engage his brain as to what he has done, or why he hurt the victim."

The decline of the conditional discharge as a consequence of the final warning provisions of CDA 1998 is addressed further in Chapter 15, though the introduction of referral orders (Chapter 16) may possibly see more resort to absolute discharging.

Financial penalties

11.06 Though the 1990 White Paper[9] was enthusiastic about the advantages of financial penalties as a means of requiring offenders to pay back something to the community and punishing without affecting employment and family responsibilities, such measures are now considered to lack impact upon youthful defendants, being insufficiently demanding of a personal response and commitment in face of anti-social behaviour, placing the burden more on the parents than on the young wrongdoer, failing to address prevention of future crime, and perhaps even increasing the risk of property crime. The days of expecting young defendants to suffer the effect of conviction by having to surrender their pocket money or to get a part-time job appear to be over in favour of more active reparation and initiatives to combat re-offending.

Non-custodial, non-community orders

11.07 Whereas the 1991 Act sought to bring together a stable of measures that restrict the offender's liberty in response to offending of sufficient seriousness to warrant such interventive demands, the measures introduced by three Acts in 1997–1999 broke from that principle by empowering courts to order restrictive intervention for any offending, irrespective of offence seriousness. This threshold was first breached for offenders who have shown poor response to financial penalties but such measures are seen as particularly suited to the minds and hearts of juvenile offenders. The reparation order and referral order, clearly seeking to "engage the brains" of their recipients, are detailed in Chapter 16.

Community sentences

11.08 The orthodoxy of the 1991 Act was that when an offence is too serious to be properly punished by financial penalties alone, the punishment should be partial restriction on liberty and freedom of movement. This band of sentencing brought together a number of different restrictive orders, to be selected on the basis of the offence's degree of seriousness and the offender's circumstances— commensurability and suitability in tandem. The stable of measures continues to expand. Juvenile defendants are eligible for a greater number of community orders than any other age group before the courts, as explored in Chapter 17 *et seq.*.

Custody

11.09 The 1990 White Paper viewed the most severe penalty available to the courts somewhat sceptically, as "likely to diminish an offender's sense of responsibility and self-reliance", to teach new criminal skills and to impact negatively on family lives and identities. Young offenders were felt to be at particular risk of

---

[9] *Crime, Justice and Protecting the Public* Cm. 965, para. 1.6.

being confirmed in a criminal career. The 1991 Act introduced a common custody threshold for all offenders, the primary criterion being that the offence is "so serious" that only a custodial sentence can be justified. A second criterion, aimed at more worrying violent or sexual offenders permits custody to be imposed where only such a sentence will be adequate to protect the public from serious harm. The provisions and problems faced in sending juveniles to custody are considered further in this Chapter and in Chapter 27 *et seq.* It will be seen that much hope is now invested in a new form of custodial sentence aimed at minors, bridging custody and community, in overcoming the enduring dilemmas posed by incarcerating juveniles.

ASSESSING SERIOUSNESS

11.10   Offence seriousness is thus the key conceptual building block of sentencing and, though ultimately this rests on a subjective judgement, the 2000 Act succeeding the 1991 Act, provides a degree of assistance in making that assessment.

(i) The circumstances of the offence

An unsurprising starting point is for the court to—

"take into account all such information about the circumstances of the offence or (as the case may be) of the offence and the offence or offences associated with it including any aggravating or mitigating factors."

This is the common wording of both PCC(S)A 2000, s.36(1) and s.81(4)(a) in regard to forming an opinion:

(a) whether a custodial sentence is justified and, if so, for what term, or

(b) whether a community sentence is warranted and, if so, what restriction on liberty would be commensurate with the seriousness of the offence.

Under PCC(S)A 2000, s.128(2) the amount of any fine fixed by a court should reflect the seriousness of the offence.

Associated offence

11.11   By PCC(S)A 2000, s.161(1) an offence is associated with another on quite straightforward grounds, if—

(a) the offender is convicted of it in the proceedings in which he is convicted of the other offence or (although convicted of it in earlier proceedings) is sentenced for it at the same time as he is sentenced for that offence; or

(b) the offender admits the commission of it in the proceedings in which he is sentenced for the other offence and requests the court to take it into consideration in sentencing him for that offence.

Thus if a sentencer dealing with an offence committed during the operational period of a conditional discharge also opts to impose a sentence for the offence in respect of which the discharge was granted, that earlier offence is an associated offence. If, however, no penalty is imposed for that earlier offence it does not rank as an associated offence.[10] Similarly, if a community rehabilitation order, community punishment order or community punishment and rehabilitation order is revoked and a fresh sentence is passed for the offence for which the order was made, that offence is "associated" with any fresh offence for which the court is also passing sentence.

11.12 Whereas the pre-CJA 1991 restriction on use of custody for young offenders based on offence seriousness, under CJA 1982, s.1(4A)(c), required the sentencing court to weigh each offence separately, the 1991 Act introduced the "two offence" rule, enabling the court to assess the combined seriousness of the offence and one associated offence, the intention being to give the court some latitude without the prospect of offenders receiving custodial sentences on the strength of the aggregate of a number of offences, all of a relatively minor nature. This compromise proved short-lived and the present ambit of consideration was first enacted by CJA 1993, allowing courts to take account of all associated offences. In consequence, young offenders facing sentence for a number of offences are in effect dealt with statutorily in a manner that pre-dates 1982 legislation.

Statutory aggravating factors

11.13 PCC(S)A 2000 does not specify how aspects of an offence and its surrounding circumstances shall be weighed, with two important exceptions.

(i) Section 151(2), requires a court to treat the fact that the offence was committed while the offender was on bail as an aggravating factor. This provision does not distinguish between bail imposed by a court and bail imposed by the police under PACE 1984, Part IV, nor between bail imposed prior to conviction and bail following conviction. The subsection applies even if the defendant was acquitted of the alleged offence in respect of which he was bailed or proceedings were discontinued in respect of a suspected offence. These are nevertheless matters that a sentencing court might wish to take into account.

(ii) Where a court is considering the seriousness of an offence other than one that by its nature is racially aggravated (*e.g.* a racially aggravated assault under CDA 1998 s.29) s.153(2) requires a court to treat the fact that the offence was "racially aggravated" as an aggravating factor, and shall state in open court that the offence was so aggravated. "Racially aggravated" is as defined by CDA 1998, s.28.

Crime and Disorder Act 1998, s.28

(1) An offence is racially aggravated for the purposes of sections 29 to 32 below if—

(a) at the time of committing the offence, or immediately before or after doing so, the offender demonstrates towards the victim of the offence hostility based on the victim's membership (or presumed membership) of a racial group; or

(b) the offence is motivated (wholly or partly) by hostility towards members of a racial group based on their membership of that group.

---

[10] *Godfrey* (1993) 14 Cr.App.R.(S.) 804.

(2) In subsection (1)(a) above—

"membership", in relation to a racial group, includes association with members of that group; "presumed" means presumed by the offender.

(3) It is immaterial for the purposes of paragraph (a) or (b) of subsection (1) above whether or not the offender's hostility is also based, to any extent, on—

(a) the fact or presumption that any person or group of persons belongs to any religious group; or

(b) any other factor not mentioned in that paragraph.

(4) In this section "racial group" means a group of persons defined by reference to race, colour, nationality (including citizenship) or ethnic or national origins.

11.14 In *Saunders*,[11] the Court of Appeal indicated that it will often be appropriate if the sentencer first considers (though need not express it) what would be the proper sentence in the absence of racial aggravation, before adding a further term for the racial element. The Court indicated that even if the basic offence does not cross the "so serious" threshold, the aggravating element may well result in that criterion being satisfied. When passing sentence, the court should have regard to the circumstances of the individual case, including: the nature of hostility demonstrated, whether by language, gestures or weapons; the location of the offence, the same behaviour being likely to attract a heavier penalty if it occurs in a crowded church, mosque or synagogue than in an empty public house. *Saunders* involved racially aggravated assault occasioning actual bodily harm, which is now a distinct offence carrying a maximum sentence two years higher than that pertaining to that offence in its unaggravated form. The Appeal Court in *Morrison*,[12] a case of racially aggravated burglary under the generic provisions of s.153(2), clarified that *Saunders* should not be regarded as authority for the proposition that the maximum additional term intended to reflect racial aggravation, applicable in any instance, is limited to two years. Each case will depend on its own circumstances. In assessing the extent of racial aggravation, sentencers should distinguish between a racially motivated offence and an offence where racist language is used in the course of commission of the offence.[13]

In all other respects, a court must fall back on conventional considerations that inform the assessment of culpability, having regard to Court of Appeal guidance, the *Mode of Trial Guidelines*, and the Magistrates' Association *Sentencing Guidelines* (updated 2000).

(ii) Criminal record

11.15 One of the most controversial aspects of the 1991 Act as originally enacted was the provision of section 29(1) that—

"an offence shall not be regarded as more serious for the purposes of any provision of this Part (of the Act) by reason of any previous convictions of the offender or any failure of his to respond to previous sentences."

---

[11] [2000] 2 Cr.App.R.(S) 71.
[12] [2000] Crim.L.R. 605.
[13] *Foster* [2000] Crim.L.R. 1030.

Many sentencers felt that this provision prevented the taking into account of proper and natural considerations in passing sentence. However, the White Paper[14] had sought to emphasise that offenders could properly be dealt with by repeated financial or community penalties and should not receive custodial sentences purely on the basis of some incremental upward drift. The Court of Appeal's comments in *Queen*[15] were cited with approval—

> ". . . an offender should not be sentenced for the offences which he has committed in the past and for which he has already been punished. The proper way to look at the matter is to decide a sentence which is appropriate for the offence . . . before the court."

Though some critics of the original subsection suggested that the effect was to treat the recidivist and the first time offender on an equal footing, it was clear that having few or no previous convictions could be taken into account and be the basis for mitigation under CJA 1991, s.28(1)-now PCC(S)A 2000, s.158(1).[16] The Court of Appeal has often indicated that a first time offender is entitled to significant "discount" or reduction in sentence and that there is a progressive loss of such credit in the event of further offending. The principle was well illustrated in *Reynolds*[17] in which two co-offenders convicted of domestic burglary were differentiated on the basis (inter alia) that one had previous convictions for that kind of offence. He received a custodial sentence while his co-offender received a community service order.

The wording of section 29(1) was amended by CJA 1993, s.66(6) and this provision now is contained in PCC(S)A 2000, s.151(1)—

11.16

> (1) In considering the seriousness of any offence, the court may take into account any previous convictions of the offender or any failure of his to respond to previous sentences.

It remains unclear whether this change restores the pre-1991 Act position or makes it more easy for persistent minor offenders to receive sentences out of proportion to their present offence.

The real question posed to the sentencer is the extent to which previous offences or "failure to respond" can heighten the seriousness of the present offence. Seriousness remains the crucial consideration. The existence of previous offences may well throw doubt on present claims by the offender that the current offence was an isolated lapse or was committed on a spur of the moment impulse or that they are genuinely remorseful for their behaviour. Previous convictions may point to an element of planning, deliberation or targeting or otherwise disclose aggravating features of the present offence. Failure to learn from the experience of earlier prosecutions is not inherently aggravating and may, on the contrary, point to the existence of greater difficulties in coping with life in a conventional way, the absence of legitimate life opportunities and the decreased likelihood of a rational response to deterrent sentencing.

11.17 As regards "failure to respond", this clearly affects "suitability" for a particular community sentence but the relationship with "seriousness" is less

---

[14] Home Office, 1990, para. 2.18.
[15] (1981) 3 Cr.App.R. (S.) 245.
[16] See para. 11.18
[17] [1983] Crim.L.R. 467.

apparent. It is unclear whether "failure" means non-compliance (*e.g.* with the requirements of a community order) or re-offending during the course of a previous order or re-offending after the completion of a previous order or sentence. In regard to the latter, what passage of time should elapse after which re-offending should not be regarded as a "failure"? In other words, what do we count as "success"? Presumably re-offending on a lesser scale of seriousness is success of a kind. Should past sentences be regarded differently in terms of the success or failure that should be expected of them? How should we weigh "response" to an earlier custodial sentence, given the official pessimism voiced in the 1990 White Paper about the prospects of rehabilitative success and the recognition of the disadvantages faced by those seeking to resettle on release? For an argument that section 29(1) does not confer wide discretion or permit "cumulative" sentencing, see Wasik and von Hirsch[18] who contend that the subsection is best understood as giving continued statutory force to the principle of progressive loss of mitigation, permitting aggravation of sentence on account of record only in narrowly construed instances. The authors suggest, for instance, that "a sentence shall not be seen as a directive to behave well, valid indefinitely". "The principal relevance of an offender's failure to comply with the requirements of a community sentence should lie elsewhere, in assisting the court to determine, under section 6 of the 1991 Act, the offender's "suitability" for a particular form of community sentence on a future occasion", and should not bear upon the severity of the sentence.

(iii) General scope for mitigation

11.18   By PCC(S)A 2000, s.158(1) "nothing . . . shall prevent a court from mitigating an offender's sentence by taking into account such matters as, in the opinion of the court, are relevant in mitigation of sentence". This provision gives wide discretionary scope to take account of any factor which the court views as material and relevant. This clearly enables the sentencer to go beyond the circumstances of the offence to encompass other matters in the offender's circumstances and background, arising both before and after the offence itself, and including the merits and attractions of any proposals for dealing with the offender in a constructive way as put forward, for example in a pre-sentence report. The Act does not offer any pointers as to what should be considered relevant. The following factors are conventionally considered—

11.19
  (a) early admission of offence and co-operation with the police;

  (b) age (see para. 11.31);

  (c) state of health/exceptional strain or adversity prior to offence;

  (d) meritorious conduct in another sphere of life;

  (e) educational/employment/sporting record and prospects;

  (f) adverse effects of prosecution and prospective sentence on third parties, particularly the family of the offender;

  (g) "natural" punishment suffered by the offender as a result of the offence or prosecution;

---

[18] Wasik M. and von Hirsch A., *Section 29 Revised: Previous Convictions in Sentencing* (1994) Crim.L.R. 555.

(h) extent of remorse and any attempt to make good the harm or loss caused;

(i) attempts by the offender to change their lifestyle and habits since the offence;

(j) the likely adverse effects upon the offender of a custodial sentence;

(k) previous good character.

11.20 As made clear in *Cox*:[19]

"Although an offender may qualify for a custodial sentence by virtue of PCC(S)A 2000, s.79(2), the court is still required to consider whether such a sentence is appropriate having regard to the mitigating factors available and relevant to the offender, as opposed to such factors as are relevant to the offence."[20]

(iv) Totality of sentence

11.21 PCC(S)A 2000, s.158(2) seeks to embody in statute the principle that the court should consider any penalty it proposes in the light of the overall sentence it intends to pass.

"Without prejudice to the generality of s.158(1) nothing . . . shall prevent a court

(a) from mitigating any penalty included in an offender's sentence by taking into account any other penalty included in that sentence; or

(b) in a case of an offender who is convicted of one or more other offences, from mitigating his sentence by applying any rule of law as to the totality of sentences."

This is a discretionary invitation rather than a requirement. The effect is to enable the sentencer to consider the overall effect of different penalties within a single sentence or of different sentences for offences dealt with on the same occasion, lest otherwise the combined impact proves disproportionate to the overall gravity of the offender's behaviour.

(v) Guilty plea

11.22 It has long been a principle of sentencing that a plea of guilty is a mitigating factor, normally entitling the defendant to a "discount" in sentence of between one-quarter and one-third, depending on the strength of the evidence against the defendant and the promptness of plea. This has been in recognition of the defendant's remorse or at least a preparedness to accept responsibility, and also the time and expense saved. This principle was given explicit recognition by CJPOA 1994, s.48 and now by PCC(S)A 2000, s.152—

(1) In determining what sentence to pass on an offender who has pleaded guilty to an offence in proceedings before that or another court a court shall take into account—

---

[19] [1993] 1 W.L.R. 188.
[20] As illustration of this principle, see *C.B.* [2000] 1 Cr.App.R.(S.) 177, outlined at 27.10.

(a) the stage in the proceedings for the offence at which the offender indicated his intention to plead guilty, and

(b) the circumstances in which this indication was given.

(2) If, as a result of taking into account any matter referred to in subsection (1) above, the court imposes a punishment on the offender which is less severe than the punishment it would otherwise have imposed, it shall state in open court that it has done so.

Note that subsection (1) turns upon an indication of intention, not upon the moment of plea..

SPECIAL CONSIDERATIONS FOR YOUTH

11.23 Though youthful offenders broadly stand to be sentenced according to the same principles and ground-rules that govern adult sentencing, a number of special factors apply:

(i) the welfare principles

(ii) the prevention of offending

(iii) youth as mitigation

(iv) parental responsibility

(v) youth and custody.

(i) The welfare principles

Section 44(1) of the CYPA 1933 enshrines a two-pronged statement of guiding purpose, though the first element tends to be the more often quoted—

"Every court in dealing with a child or young person who is brought before it, either as an offender or otherwise, shall have regard to the welfare of the child or young person, and shall in a proper case take steps for removing him from undesirable surroundings and for securing that proper provision is made for his education and training."

11.24 Both elements have the confident ring of child-saving entrepreneurship[21] reflecting the spirit of the times in which the 1933 Act was passed, when the juvenile court exercised a dual jurisdiction dealing with delinquency and child protection and had at its disposal measures such as approved school and fit person orders. Though these principles of "protection and welfare"[22] have survived unscathed for nearly 60 years, what continuing relevance do they have for the present, very different era of youth justice, or are they merely a residual totem of little or no practical bite or significance? Substantial evidence[23] indicates that young

---

[21] A. Platt *The Child Savers: The Invention of Delinquency* (Chicago University Press, Chicago, 1968).
[22] As s.44(1) was characterised by Lord Hope of Craighead in *ex. p. Venables and Thompson* [1998] A.C. 407.
[23] A. Hagell & T. Newburn, *Persistent Young Offenders* (Policy Studies, Institute, London, 1994); J. Stewart, D. Smith & G. Stewart, *Understanding Offending Behaviour* (Longman, Harlow, 1994; A. Bottoms *Intensive Community Supervision for Young Offenders: Outcomes, Processes, Cost* University of Cambridge Institute of Criminology (Cambridge, 1995); A. Crowley *A Criminal Waste* (The Children's Society, London, 1998).

people, particularly those prosecuted more frequently, have significant welfare needs and experience an "intensifying cycle of disadvantage"[24] but the predominant trend of the past 25 years has been to seek solutions through enhanced support systems, multi-agency initiatives and correctional programmes within their home communities rather than by residential or custodial segregation.

The principle should not be confused or considered on a par with the Children Act 1989, s.1 which makes the child's welfare the paramount consideration when a court determines any question with respect to the upbringing of a child or the administration of a child's property or income. In the criminal jurisdiction, the welfare of the juvenile is an obligatory consideration but not the sole or paramount consideration. If that were so, it would be hard to imagine circumstances in which the court could validly impose prison custody upon a juvenile.

11.25 The framework of CJA 1991 was introduced without any explicit reference to or attempt to reconcile the welfare principles. In seeking some degree of integration, it seems correct to assert that the principle of proportionality or commensurability promoted by the 1991 Act and now the 2000 Act cannot be set aside in favour of welfare-based arguments for more substantial intervention aimed at achieving the longer-term good of the young defendant. Though the "criminal care order" previously available under CYPA 1969, s.7(7) was repealed by the Children Act 1989, there is scope for a court determined to remove a juvenile from "undesirable surroundings" to make inappropriately disproportionate use of power to include residential requirements in a supervision order or community rehabilitation order, or to invest hope in the rehabilitative potential of a detention and training order without reference to the "so serious" threshold test for a custodial sentence.[25] The alternate criterion permitting custody on grounds public protection can only be exercised as an incapacitation sentence, not on welfare grounds.

It may also be asserted that the principle permits the court to depart from commensurability in favour of a less onerous sentence by giving greater weight to mitigating or tempering factors, such as the negative consequences of a custodial sentence or the more positive potential of alternative sentences in meeting the young defendant's developmental needs. Courts may thus nod to s.44 without detailed consideration in achieving an adjustment of sentence to reflect the offender's youthfulness, such as in *Baldwin*[26] where the Court of Appeal spoke of "bearing in mind our s.44 duties". This interpretation of the welfare principles as requiring or permitting "restraint" in sentencing will be considered further in the context of youth as mitigation.[27]

11.26 Meantime, it is possible to note what little active and specific consideration has been given to s.44(1) by appeal courts in the past decade. The sub-section has been applied primarily to issues posed by young offenders facing indeterminate detention. Thus the House of Lords invoked s.44(1) in *ex p. Venables and Thompson*,[28] Lord Hope[29] stating that the principles should apply "to keep the protection and welfare of the child under review throughout the period while he is in custody" in respect of a mandatory sentence of detention at Her Majesty's pleasure. Similarly, in *ex p. Furber*[29a] it was felt right that s.44(1) should be applied

---

[24] K. Haines & M. Drakeford, *Young People and Youth Justice* (Macmillan, Basingstoke, 1998).
[25] See para. 27.03.
[26] [1997] 2 Cr.App.R.(S.) 260.
[27] See para. 11.31.
[28] [1998] A.C. 407.
[29] At p. 507.
[29a] [1998] 1 Cr. App.R.(S.) 208.

in setting a less severe penal element or "tariff" period to be served before consideration of release on licence from a discretionary life term. The Appeal Court also referred to s.44(1) in *Brown*[30] when determining that a s.53(3) sentence was more appropriate than a YOI sentence of the same length to afford a vulnerable defendant a regime more suited to her problems.

However, in *Attorney-General's References 59, 60 and 63*,[31] the Court of Appeal pointed out that "sentencers must bear in mind that the welfare of young offenders is never the only consideration to be taken into account" and placed greater emphasis in dealing with instances of deliberate infliction of serious violence on meeting the public's "legitimate expectation that such an offender will be severely punished". Subsequently, in *O'Grady*,[32] the Appeal Court upheld a sentence of six months detention on a 14-year-old, despite a defence argument that a supervision order proposed in pre-sentence reports was entirely suitable and more appropriate for his welfare problems—a background of "total neglect" and school exclusion, so that he was in local authority care, being "out of his depth academically and socially". The Court noted that he was now reported to be making "rapid progress" at the secure centre where he had been placed under sentence and commented that "there are cases, and this appears to be one, where promoting the welfare of a child may involve imposing a custodial sentence".

11.27 Section 44(1) apart, it has been suggested[33] that since the repeal of power to make a care order in criminal proceedings the youth court has suffered a sentencing lacuna and that there should be a procedural bridge between its criminal jurisdiction and the civil responsibilities of the family proceedings court. Such a bridge could be provided by giving the youth court (or the Crown Court) a power similar to that provided to family courts by the Children Act 1989, s.37 requiring a local authority to undertake an investigation of the juvenile's circumstances and to consider whether it would be appropriate to make application for a care or supervision order in the civil court, or to provide services or assistance for the child or his family, or to take any other appropriate action with respect to the child. Alternatively, in exceptional cases where prosecution brings to light previously unknown but clearly dysfunctional family circumstances and it appears that the matter would be better dealt with in care proceedings, in the best interests of the child, then a criminal court could have power to stay prosecution and exercise power of transfer to the family proceedings court.

11.28 Section 44(1) can be contrasted with principles adopted by the United Nations in developing international law on the administration of juvenile justice, principally in the Convention on the Rights of the Child, adopted in November 1989 and entering into force in September 1990. The Convention defines a child as anyone under the age of 18 (unless majority is attained earlier under national legislation). The Convention (article 40) establishes as the aim of child penal justice the entitlement of children to be treated in a manner consistent with—

> "the child's age and the desirability of promoting the child's reintegration and the child's assuming a constructive role in society."

"Reintegration" is identified as a preferable concept to "rehabilitation" which can be the basis for the removal of children as a heavy-handed form of institutional

---

[30] [1999] 1 Cr. App.R.(S.) 132.
[31] [1999] 2 Cr.App.R.(S.) 128.
[32] [2000] 1 Cr.App.R.(S.) 112 (See para. 27.33).
[33] Children's Society, *A False Sense of Security: The Case Against Locking Up More Children* (The Children's Society, London, 1993); C. Ball (1998) "*R. v. B.*: Paying Due Regard to the Welfare of the Child in Criminal Proceedings", *Child and Family Law Quarterly*, 10(4), 417–424.

quarantine. As yet, the Convention does not incorporate any system for individual children to challenge national legislation before the UN Committee on the Rights of the Child.[34]

(ii) The prevention of offending

11.29 In parallel with the "welfare principles", CDA 1998, s.37 introduced an overarching aim for youth justice, with a corresponding duty upon those carrying out functions in the youth justice system including, implicitly, sentencers.

CDA 1998, s.37

(1) It shall be the principal aim of the youth justice system to prevent offending by children and young persons.

(2) In addition to any other duty to which they are subject, it shall be the duty of all persons and bodies carrying out functions in relation to the youth justice system to have regard to that aim.

Explaining the purpose of this new mission statement, aimed, it would seem, primarily at YOT practitioners, the Minister of State told the Committee dealing with the Bill—

"Many debates have taken place about the balance between considering the welfare of a child before the court, determining the appropriate punishment and preventing re-offending. That long-standing debate has sometimes contributed to muddled decisions by practitioners in the youth justice system . . . The clause is intended to end both the uncertainty about what is expected of those who work for youth justice agencies, and the confusion about balancing the interests of the offender, the victim and the community."

11.30 How can the aim of s.37(1) be reconciled with the principles of s.44(1)? Of course, there need be no conflict, in the sense that promoting the welfare of the child may be the most effective or promising means of reducing and preventing the child's further offending. Alternatively, the welfare of the child may best be met by measures that are crime-reductive, preventive or reformative for that child, thus sparing him the disadvantages, disruption, stigma, etc. of further prosecution. However, to the extent that the two sets of considerations are not readily reconcilable, it would appear that s.37 takes precedence. It will be noted that, unlike s.44, s.37 is not centred on the individual offender. It may thus be that the prevention of youthful offending can be promoted at the cost of the welfare of the individual young offender. The most obvious instance would be where a sentence is passed which is intended to deter others, making an example of the defendant in a way that may undermine rather than promote his developmental needs. It could also be considered that the detention of a young offender considered to be a malign influence on other young persons in their circle would assist in preventing crime in a local neighbourhood—in other words by imposing a kind of incapacitative sentence. The courts have long felt able to balance such considerations and to give priority to crime-reductive intentions, without obvious "confusion" or need of a mission statement of guide them, so it is likely that s.37 will not make any

---

[34] See G. van Buerer, "Child-Orientated Justice: An International Challenge for Europe" (1992) *International Journal of Law and the Family* 6, 381.

significant difference to sentencing practice. However, a defence advocate or PSR writer may seek to fulfill the spirit of s.37 by arguing that a particular course of action, such as a custodial sentence, could make the young person in question more rather than less likely to re-offend, perhaps because of the contamination effect of custody or the undermining of current community opportunities.

(iii) Youth as mitigation

11.31   To what extent should youth be treated as an intrinsic mitigating factor? Children and young persons have some degree of built-in protection from the full severity of adult sentencing by being subject to a distinctive spectrum of penalties, either peculiar to their age such as the attendance centre or modified versions of adult penalties. But there is a broad expectation that the courts should also deal less severely with the young. As Walker and Padfield[35] have remarked, the underlying reasoning is hardly ever made clear. The rationale appears to draw upon the following considerations, some of which relate to moral culpability and some to the impact of penalty.[36]

Reduced culpability

11.32

- The young are not so culpable because they have not had the experience and have not acquired the capacity to realise as fully as adults the consequences of their actions for themselves or others. Their ability to appreciate the pain and distress they are causing to others lacks adult capacity for empathy and sensitivity.

- Young people have less capacity to resist temptation and peer group pressure.

- The young should be accorded a greater degree of tolerance and latitude to allow for a greater degree of self-expression and experimentation in adolescence. They should be given more scope to learn from their mistakes without undue penalisation or stigma.

- By reason of their youth, adolescents are more likely to be able to claim credit for previous good character or the absence of serious offending in their records.

- Young people tend to have less stake in society with reduced benefits and recognition and thus their communal liabilities and sense of responsibility or obligation should be correspondingly reduced. In this respect it is worth noting the growing research on the extent of youthful victimisation. Though we are accustomed to think of youth as perpetrators of crime, Anderson *et al.*[37] demonstrated that 11–15-year-olds had to cope with startling levels of property, violent and sexual crime that adults would find intolerable, with little recourse to police or other adults who were perceived to be indifferent or hostile to their problems. In Brown's research,[38] young people reported that their encounters with authority

---

[35] N. Walker and N. Padfield, *Sentencing: Theory, Law and Practice* (Butterworths, London, 1996).
[36] Since this issue was discussed in the First edition, the argument had been further explored by Zedner (footnote 4).
[37] S. Anderson, G. Kinsey, I. Loader, and C. Smith *Cautionary Tales: Young People, Crime and Policy in Edinburgh* (Aldershot, Avebury, 1994).
[38] S. Brown (1995) "Crime and Safety in Whose Community? Age, Everyday Life and Problems for Youth Policy", *Youth and Policy*, 48, 27–48.

inclined them to keep the adult world at bay, thus amplifying perceptions that they "share a deliberately exclusive world in which they reject adult values".

- Young people appearing before the courts have often been subject to poor, disadvantaged or disrupted upbringing, featuring abuse, loss, lack of parental care and example, a negative experience of schooling or ineffective state care, and have not yet had time to distance themselves from such experiences.[39] For a discussion of the general scope for mitigation on the basis of deprivation, abuse and disadvantage in life, compatibly with desert theory, see Ashworth.[40] In practice, the Court of Appeal gives mixed messages. In *Hart*,[41] the Court commented—

"There are gaps in the social services through which these men have fallen or have thrust themselves. But it is not the task of the courts to remedy those deficiencies. The court must take the offenders . . . as they find them."

11.33 However, in *Mills*[42] the Court was moved by "compelling mitigation" relating to a 13-year-old defendant located in his very adverse and disrupted upbringing to substitute a supervision order for a custodial sentence, albeit in circumstances that suggested that his life was beginning to show new hope based on a fresh beginning with a concerned relative.[43] But in *Attorney-General's Ref. No. 69 of 1999*,[44] where a 16-year-old had an adverse lack of decent upbringing without parental interest, the Court criticised the judge for being "over-persuaded by personal circumstances" and replaced a community order with a substantial custodial term.

- With certain crimes, for example more complex regulatory offences, the young person's ability to understand the wrongness of that behaviour is still undeveloped.

11.34 It is not suggested that the juvenile's cognitive abilities, life experience and capacity for discernment should be evaluated by case-by-case individual assessment but that the notion of reduced culpability can be adopted as a broad normative principle that it is appropriate to make less societal demands of youth. This can be viewed as a sliding scale so that, as the young person approaches adulthood, a greater degree of responsibility can be expected of them, possibly analogous with the capacity to take greater personal responsibility for decisions regarding medical treatment.[45]

Reduced penalty

11.35
- Young people's offending is frequently a "passing phase" and reactions to their transient misbehaviour should thus be kept in check in order to avoid counter-productively alienating them from society.

---

[39] See n. 23.
[40] A. Ashworth, "Justifying the Grounds of Mitigation" (1994) *Criminal Justice Ethics, 13(1)*, 5–10.
[41] (1983) 5 Cr.App.R.(S.) 385.
[42] [2000] 2 Cr. App.R.(S.) 128 (see para. 27.37).
[43] See also *Bool and White* [1998] 1 Cr.App.R(S.) 32, noted at para. 27.17.
[44] [2000] 2 Cr. App. R.(S.) 53 (see para. 27.105).
[45] *Gillick v. West Norfolk and Wisbech Area Health Authority and the D.H.S.S.* [1986] A.C. 112.

- Punishment which may damage young people's prospects and opportunities should be kept to a minimum and should seek as far as possible to integrate young people and promote their future citizenship.

- Punishment impacts more heavily upon young people, for example two years loss of liberty in the life of an adolescent is of greater significance than the same penalty for an adult. The principle of equal impact[46] would thus require us to take into account differing sensibilities.

- Young people may be more receptive to learning the error of their ways and thus more open to rehabilitative or constructive sentencing options. Thus in *Seymour*,[47] May L.J. commented—

"A sentence other than a custodial one is perhaps justified, particularly in the case of a young offender, if there is any indication that he is beginning to realise the extent of his past criminality and the situation to which offences of a similar nature will take him if they are persisted in."

- Young people are more likely to be vulnerable to contaminating influences if exposed to incarcerating or segregating penalties and are thus likely to become more entrenched in offending ways. We must on no account persuade ourselves that custodial sentences are justified to meet a need for "training in a contained environment".[48]

11.36 However, the Court of Appeal sometimes appears influenced in its decision to uphold a custodial sentence by information that the young offender is responding well to and benefiting from the "structured environment" in which they have been placed.[49] In *Branston*[50] the Court reduced sentence in the light of the hostility that a youth from a good background had experienced from other trainees.

Though these principles may operate widely but usually implicitly, there are clearly instances of serious crime where the court has had to balance "on the one hand the need for punishment, expiation and deterrence and, on the other hand, the interests of the offender, his educational prospects and his future in general".[51] In *Stewart*[52] Lord Lane C.J., stated—

"There are occasions when the duty of the judge to pass a sentence as short as possible upon a young man must give way to the corresponding duty to see that the public is protected so far as the court can from the activities of a person who has displayed himself to be as merciless and as unrepentant as this appellant had."

11.37 Sentence of 12 years youth custody was upheld on a 19 year old who had pleaded guilty to grievous bodily harm with intent (blinding an elderly woman in one eye with a pair of scissors), robbery and malicious wounding, having been previously convicted of stabbing a person in the course of a robbery. As Walker and

---

[46] A. Ashworth, *Sentencing and Criminal Justice* (Butterworths, London, 1995) p. 79.
[47] (1983) 5 Cr.App.R.(S.) 85.
[48] *Hart and Hart* [1984] Crim L.R. 189.
[49] See *O'Grady* [2000] 1 Cr. App. R.(S.) 112 (noted at para. 27.33).
[50] [1997] 2 Cr. App. R.(S.) 184 (see para. 27.42).
[51] *Forshaw* (1984) 6 Cr.App.R.(S.) 413.
[52] (1985) 7 Cr.App.R.(S.) 33.

Padfield[53] note, "if violence of a kind regarded as pathological and dangerous is manifested early, this is regarded as especially alarming, and the person may be detained for a very long period."

The case of *Powell*[54] where a 16 year old with a previous conviction for indecent assault received six years section 53(2) detention for rape of a 15-year-old girl, nicely illustrates the courts' attempts to balance the various considerations posed by the very serious youthful offender. Stating that age was not so much a mitigating factor in such instances and upholding sentence, Macpherson J. commented that the offender—

> "must be able to see light at the end of the tunnel but in those circumstances the tunnel should be a long one so that as much attention can be given to this man as is possible during the ensuing years during his teens".

(iv) Parental responsibility

11.38   The parental context of young offenders' lives cannot be excluded from any informed sentencing assessment but how much responsibility should be placed on parents and how does this dovetail with the personal responsibility of the juvenile? If much of children's offending has its origins in family experience, communication, discipline and example, in parental criminality, depth of attachment between parent and child, extent of maternal supervision or of paternal sharing of interests, as criminologists have established, should the court's focus be as much on the parent as on the young defendant? Policy pronouncements tend either to demand that parents exercise effective authority over their children's activities or alternatively to lament parental weakness and incompetence. As Zedner[55] suggests:

> "Parents cannot easily escape responsibility: either they are 'good' disciplinary parents who must be held to account for the failure of that discipline or they are 'bad' reckless parents whose lack of authority and poor example is the cause of their offspring's misdeeds."

11.39   Is the aim of youth justice policy to stimulate greater levels of informal social control within the family as the prime arena of socialisation by making parents more accountable for the exercise of their duties or to afford the State greater powers of intervention and policing by subjecting parents to compulsory correctional measures, backed by sanctions for non-co-operation? Should the juvenile/youth court have a distinctive ethos which encourages parents to share their views, problems and ideas rather than feel defensively on trial alongside their child? And when does childhood end, freeing parents of their formal responsibilities and liabilities? These dilemmas have exercised policy makers for decades—in 1847 a Select Committee of the House of Lords recommended that a proportion of the cost of conviction and punishment of young offenders should be paid by their parents.[56] Within the present vision of youth justice, how does the attribution of parental responsibility and the message that parents are to blame fit within a new

---

[53] n. 35, p. 55.
[54] (1994) 15 Cr.App.R. (S.) 611.
[55] n. 4, at p. 177.
[56] Cited in Zedner (n. 4) at p. 176.

approach of *No More Excuses*, demanding that the young offender take responsibility for their criminal conduct?

One obvious starting point is to try to locate parental responsibility on a sliding scale from age 10 when it may be assumed that parents retain a substantial grip on their child's actions to an age when young people are increasingly making their own decisions under the powerful influence of factors outside the family fold. Though this may be somewhat simplistic developmental psychology, this approach was favoured by the 1990 White Paper[57] which asserted that by the age of 16 and 17 young people "are at an indeterminate stage between childhood and adulthood" when they "should begin to take more responsibility for the consequences of their own decisions and actions".

11.40 Use of a young person's 16th birthday as a convenient dividing line was adopted in the somewhat modest measures pursued by the Criminal Justice Act 1991 in the quest for increased parental responsibility—

(a) parents' liability for their children's financial penalties (see para. 15.29);

(b) a requirement that courts should bind over the parents or guardian of offenders aged under 16 to exercise care and control of their children (see para. 14.02).

The parental bind over was the single big idea of practical substance in respect of parents in the 1990 White Paper and has not found wide support among youth court sentencers, though binding over was later extended to ensuring compliance with a community sentence (see para. 14.08). In a survey of magistrates and other criminal justice practitioners following implementation of the 1991 Act, the Home Office found that only 40 per cent of magistrates thought that the Act's provisions regarding parental responsibility were working well, compared with 39 per cent who considered that they were working either badly or not at all and five per cent who felt that they had achieved no change. Among other practitioners there was a clear tendency to think that the Act's provisions in this respect were working badly/not at all.[58]

11.41 It has remained open to youth justice workers to engage with parents in the course of supervision to encourage them to take greater interest in their children's activities and to communicate more effectively within the home. Initiatives have been made to engage with parents of young offenders in self-help support groups so that ideas can be pooled and efforts made to counteract the sense of baffled isolation that parents can experience. However, this potential source of change has not been espoused widely by practitioners who have tended to use scarce supervision time in engaging the young offender in offending behaviour programmes without engaging significantly with parents. In a study of supervision order practice undertaken with boys, Bottoms[59] found that the extent of parental involvement was slight but nearly half of parents of children attending intensive programmes said that they would have valued greater involvement. Such participation could serve to extend the usefulness of the experience of supervisory programmes so that they had greater potential to act as a bridge to continuing advantages rather than a pocket of opportunity isolated from the young person's life in general.

---

[57] n. 9 at Chapter 8.
[58] G. Mair and C. May, *Practitioners' Views of the Criminal Justice Act: A Survey of Criminal Justice Agencies*, Research and Planning Unit Paper No. 91 (Home Office, London, 1995).
[59] See n. 23.

11.42   In a bid to breath life into parental responsibility, the 1997 White Paper proposed a more active set of demands—

> (c) a requirement that courts should make parents of children aged under 16 subject to a parenting order combining specific requirements with counselling and guidance, where satisfied that this measure would help to prevent re-offending (see para. 14.11).

Though this measure has greater appeal than the rather negative sanction of the parental bind over which it will almost certainly eclipse, it remains a controversial weapon which has been criticised as a naive gesture that may yield counter-productive consequences. If parents are keen to co-operate and to improve their performance, a stigmatising and sanction-backed intervention may be considered unnecessary. If parents are facing considerable personal difficulties, perhaps still resonating from their own poor experience of socialisation in childhood, the limited scope of the parenting order will make little impression on entrenched problems and may raise hopes that cannot be fulfilled, thus fuelling resentment and aggravating already fraught relationships within the home. Such policing initiatives may "drive a further wedge into a family structure already cracking under various stresses and strains".[60] It has been hypothesised that parents who wish to free themselves of children who have brought troubles to their door and who have found more attraction in the influence and attitudes of their immediate peer group will be prompted to give up their responsibilities, expecting the local authority to provide accommodation or leaving the young person to make their own arrangements in premature independence. It should not be overlooked how tenuous family relationships can become in adolescence and the extent of homelessness among the under-16s.

11.43   In addition to these measures aimed directly at parents, there is potential in new sentencing measures, particularly the referral order and the action plan order, to stimulate parental concern and involvement, as the *National Standards for Youth Justice*[61] recognise. However, it has proved very difficult to utilise sentencing powers to promote parental responsibility. Difficult conceptual questions remain as to how to weight the culpability of the child in the light of weak parental performance and the extent, if any, to which poor parenting should regarded as a mitigating factor under PCC(S)A 2000, s.158(1). Additionally, there are unresolved procedural issues as to how best to incorporate parents effectively into court hearings. How should parents be represented, both in being heard on whether measures against them should be imposed and in subsequent enforcement proceedings? Given these difficulties, there is arguably more promise not in sentencing reforms but in the fulfillment of the duty placed on local authorities by the Children Act 1989, Sched. 2 to take reasonable steps to reduce the need to bring criminal proceedings against children, to encourage children not to commit criminal offences[62] and to provide advice, guidance and counselling for children and their families.[63]

11.44   Effective exercise of parental responsibility can be marked in mitigation of sentence upon the juvenile. If a parent, out of consideration for their child, believes that it is in the public interest to report the child to the police, this

---

[60] R. Noon "Binding Over Parents under s.58 CJA 1991" (1992) J.P. 156, 803–04 at p. 804.
[61] Youth Justice Board (2000).
[62] para. 7(a)(ii) and (b).
[63] para. 9.

responsible action should be taken into account and credit given in passing sentence, said the Court of Appeal in *Catterall*[64] where a father had told the police that his son had been abusing drugs, leading to his arrest for possessing and supplying Class A and B drugs, principally ecstasy.

> "The appellant's father cares so much about his future that he was prepared to disclose the offences to the police. He and the appellant's mother are likely to support the appellant's attempts to give up his habit and it was to this end that they brought the position to the notice of the police."

(v) Youth custody and containment: retreat or advance?

11.45 Dealing with the problem of young offending by incarceration has been a constant controversy. A decade ago a widespread retreat from inappropriate use of custodial sentencing was clearly articulated in the White Paper *Crime, Justice and Protecting the Public*[65] which reported that, in the wake of efforts during the 1980s to maximise use of community sentencing,[66] "there is no evidence that the reduction in the use of custodial sentences has resulted in increases in juvenile crime". Going on to question whether it was necessary to retain a sentence of detention in YOIs for girls under 18, the White Paper commented—

> "in all parts of the country there are good, demanding and constructive community programmes for juvenile offenders who need intensive supervision. These programmes are capable of dealing with all but the most serious offenders."

11.46 Following the raising of the minimum age for YOI detention to 15,[67] the united voice of the penal reform lobby[68] argued that this minimum should be raised further to age 16, asserting—

> "Holding juveniles in the prison system has no place in a civilised society. It is a recipe for intimidation, criminal contamination and suicide attempts. As a way of reducing crime it is spectacularly ineffective, as over 70 per cent of juveniles are reconvicted within two years of release. The small number of juveniles for whom detention in a secure establishment is necessary should be held in local authority secure accommodation."

Apart from the concern about the custodial experience of bullying, self-harm, and the cultivation of criminal techniques, attention was also drawn to the likelihood of young people becoming isolated, often serving sentence far from home, creating real difficulties for visits from families and the social workers or probation officers who have to plan and supervise their resettlement.

11.47 Within a fortnight of the implementation of the 1991 Act, however, the Home Secretary was signalling an intention "to lock up, educate and train" young offenders who were said to be responsible for a disproportionate share of

---

[64] (1993) 14 Cr.App.R.(S.) 724, affirmed in *Ferrett* [1998] 2 Cr.App.R.(S.) 384 (see para. 27.53).
[65] n. 8, para. 8.24 *et seq.*
[66] Some court areas and youth justice teams celebrated being "custody-free zones".
[67] Criminal Justice Act 1991, amending CJA 1982.
[68] Penal Affairs Consortium, *The Case Against Sentencing 15-year-olds to Prison Service Custody* (Penal Affairs Consortium, London, 1992).

offending. In consequence, the Criminal Justice and Public Order Act 1994 enacted a triple boost to custodial sentencing powers—

- the secure training order (the forerunner of the detention and training order) for 12–14-year-olds who satisfied a double-pronged criterion (conviction of three or more imprisonable offences and non-compliance or re-offending while subject to a supervision order), to be served in a new form of custodial institution, secure training centres;

- raising the maximum period of YOI detention for defendants aged under 18 from 12 to 24 months;

- reducing the minimum age for detention for grave crimes from 14 to ten.

11.48   The rationale and arrangements for secure training orders came under severe criticism on the following grounds—

(a) The qualifying criterion did not serve to identify those presenting most significant problems as persistent offenders and, in any case, the evidence to support the belief that a small core of convicted young offenders account for a very large proportion of known offending was not established.[69]

(b) Existing sentencing powers, such as supervision orders with an additional residence requirement, were adequate to address the problems of such young offenders but were not used to advantage.[70]

(c) Rather than resorting to expensive new centres serving large geographical areas, often at long distance from children's homes and families, a modest expansion of local authority secure accommodation would provide a more constructive resource at far less cost.

(d) Research into the effectiveness of previous experiments in institutional training, such as approved schools, community homes with education, secure units or the Northern Ireland training school at Lisneven, said to be the blueprint for the new centres, indicated that these increased rather than reduced the likelihood of re-offending.[71]

The reality of secure training centres

11.49   Critics predicted that the new centres would struggle to maintain educational standards, prevent bullying and assure residents' safety, the Director of the Howard League for Penal Reform[72] suggesting that the draft rules designed to regulate the centres were "a recipe for child abuse and concealed horrors". In face of such dire forecasts, perhaps the reality was not quite so disastrous but the Social Services Inspectorate's report on the Medway Secure Training Centre in September/October 1998,[73] the first of five planned centres, opening for business for up to 40

---

[69] A. Hagell and T. Newburn *Persistent Young Offenders* (Policy Studies Institute, London, 1944); A. Crowley, *A Criminal Waste* (The Children's Society, London 1998).
[70] Save the Children, *Children aged 12–14 and the Criminal Justice System* Save the Children Fund, London, 1994).
[71] Summarised in New Approaches to Juvenile Crime, *Creating More Criminals: The case against the new "secure training order" for juvenile offenders* (NACRO, London, 1994).
[72] F. Crook, "A Recipe for child Abuse," *The Guardian*, July 20, 1994.
[73] Social Services Inspectorate, *Inspection of Medway Secure Training Centre, September/October 1998* (Department of Health, London, 1999).

children at a time in April 1998, was certainly not very encouraging. A total of 56 children had been admitted, 37 being aged 14 and ten aged 12 or 13. Medway had clearly experienced a turbulent opening period and had struggled in the absence of an experienced, skilled staff group who had not been up to the task of dealing with challenging and disruptive behaviour. Good order was a very fragile feature and had frequently broken down so that the staff overrelied on restraint and single separation as the means of control. This caused trainees to feel aggrieved and powerless, and confirmed them in a victim role which in turn "enabled them to justify their own aggressive and destructive behaviour and strengthened their criminogenic attitudes".[74] "Major failings" were noted in the management of complex situations such as self-harm, suicide avoidance, bullying and de-toxification (in a tobacco and substance-free environment). Educational provision was beginning to improve but was still unsatisfactory. The Inspectors concluded that the Medway Centre was "facing a crisis", surpassing the kind of difficulties many secure units face in their early months. The policies were sound but the delivery was found significantly wanting.

11.50 Medway's first year has since been evaluated for the Home Office,[75] offering little ground for comfort. Of 102 children who completed their custodial stay in the period April 1998–April 1999, the average age on arrival was 14½, all except three being boys. 94 percent spending less than six months at the Centre, with 49 per cent spending less than three months, taking account of the length of their order and the time already spent on remand. Their backgrounds reflected what is familiar about the lives of persistent young offenders, 69 per cent having been looked after by a local authority at some point in their lives and 46 per cent having experienced school exclusion. They had extensive offending histories with an average of 22 convictions each. Though the Centre had experienced initial confusion about the theoretical model on which its intervention was based, causing staff to be ill-prepared to deal with trainees, "a significant proportion of trainees left Medway in a positive frame of mind, keen to change their behaviour". However, they found this hard to put into practice. Frequent breakdowns in inter-agency co-operation and communication left them disillusioned, one flaw being delays in re-engaging them in education during their community supervision phase of sentence. Sessions with their supervising officers could be brief and superficial. Some 85 per cent failed to comply with supervision requirements, more than two-thirds within four weeks of discharge from Medway and a quarter within their first week. Three-quarters who failed to comply went on to do this more than once. Some 36 per cent of those who acted in a breachable way were recalled to secure training centre. Two-thirds of trainees committed criminal offences leading to arrest before expiry of their order, half within four weeks after release. The most common offences committed during supervision were: possession of drugs; driving without a licence; criminal damage; shop theft; taking without owner's consent. A fifth of trainees were given a new custodial sentence before the end of their order for offending since release. The researchers concluded that Medway was able to demonstrate "little success in providing an intervention that successfully prevented re-offending".

Criticism of young offender institutions

11.51 Meantime, critics were expressing concern about the mainstream penal system's ability to make safe, positive provision for young offenders. The challenge

---

[74] n. 9, para. 8.8.
[75] A. Hagell, N. Hazel and C. Shaw, *Evaluation of Medway Secure Training Centre*, Occasional Paper (Home Office, London, 2000).

presented to custodial staff was well expressed by the Prison Governors Association[76] who attempted to convey the reality of life in a typical YOI as the equivalent of managing "a room full of about 50 naughty spaniel pups, with a few Rottweilers, a Pekinese or two and a timber wolf thrown in."

A Commission of Inquiry, established by the Howard League[77] concluded that "the prison system is unable to protect young people or address the problems of damaged and troubled teenagers", identifying the dangers of bullying, assault, "taxing", area or racial rivalry and self-harm which are prominent features of young offender establishments, sucking in the more assertive and blighting the lives of more vulnerable detainees. In similar vein, a survey of 79 young offenders in two YOIs,[78] Onley and Glen Parva, reported that all respondents admitted being involved in bullying in some way, 85 per cent as bullies or bystanders. In terms of outcomes, Bottoms' study[79] of boys receiving custodial sentences and intensive community supervision found no statistically significant evidence that community supervision was better at preventing re-offending, as measured by further convictions, though if self-reported re-offending was incorporated in the follow-up assessment, there was some basis for claiming a modest advantage for intensive supervision. However, when a personal problem checklist was used to investigate the effect of different interventions, the subsample who had served a custodial sentence perceived themselves as having relatively more problems one year after the termination of intervention. Custody thus appeared to lead over time to more social problems, which could result indirectly in increased criminal conduct, though the study did not extend to further follow-up to test this hypothesis.

11.52   Perhaps the most thorough and authoritative recent overview of young prisoners has been provided by the Chief Inspector of Prisons.[80] His report notes that "there is no such thing as a neutral experience for children in custody. They are either helped or damaged." Placing his finger on the core dilemma at the core of custody for young offenders, he argues—

> "Because incarceration can be such a corrupting influence for young people the very difficult problem which faces the authorities is how to provide conditions in which the punishment of the court, 'deprivation of liberty', can be served in such a way as to provide the public with a reasonable prospect that young prisoners on discharge will not re-offend."[81]

Identifying the absence of overall vision and leadership in the development of regimes for young people, he identifies that—

> "In recent years the massively increased numbers of children sent to custody have been dumped on Prison Service establishments, in a prison system that has not, traditionally, recognised that it has a role in caring for children in need of care, development and control. Within this system children are, quite frankly, lost."[82]

---

[76] Written evidence to House of Commons Home Affairs Committee, *Juvenile Offenders (6th Report)* (HMSO, London, 1993).
[77] Howard League for Penal Reform, *Banged Up, Beaten Up, Cutting Up* (Howard League, London, 1995).
[78] Kidscape, *Bullying Pays! A Survey of Young Offenders* (Kidscape, London, 1994).
[79] A. Bottoms, Intensive Community Supervision for Young Offenders: Outcomes, Process and Cost (University of Cambridge, Cambridge, 1995).
[80] H.M. Chief Inspector of Prisons, *Young Prisoners: A Thematic Review* H.M. (Inspectorate of Prisons, Home Office, London, 1997).
[81] n. 80, para. 1.09.
[82] n. 80, para. 8.04.

11.53 Given their population size and the absence of a nurturing ethos or sense of individual attention, he asserts that establishments, with a few honourable exceptions, "are forced into doing little more than warehouse adolescents,"[83] having insufficient staff or instructors or facilities to provide a purposeful regime. The treatment of young prisoners has become "something of a lottery", the minority of winners benefiting from the few very good establishments. Institutions with the poorest regimes unsurprisingly appeared to have the highest incidence of the use of control and restraint. Further, once in custody, "more often than not no one outside takes responsibility for (children) any more: there is little communication with other agencies and families are rarely involved in their children's care". The report compares Prison Service resources unfavourably with parallel provision, in many instances falling—

"far below the minimum conditions in Social Services Department secure units required by the Children Act 1989 and the UN Convention on the Rights of the Child. Indeed, I can find no evidence that the Prison Service has acknowledged the Children Act as having any relevance to children held in Prison Service establishments. More damage is done to immature adolescents than to any other type of prisoner, by current conditions."[84]

Seeking to discover the application of the 1989 Act to children aged under 18 held in Prison Service custody, the Chief Inspector obtained counsel's opinion that the Act does not apply to juveniles detained under powers conferred by the Prison Act 1952, either on remand in custody or following conviction and sentence. Noting too that the Prison Service asserts that, unlike directors of local authority secure accommodation, Governors of establishments holding juveniles are neither *in loco parentis* nor are they guardians, he queries "who then is *in loco parentis*, and if it is not the Governor, who is it?"[85]

11.54 This report offers a wealth of detail and shrewd summary of the state of our prisons for children at the end of the 20th century but the Chief Inspector concludes that "the chaos which surrounds the treatment of children in custody" convinces him that children should no longer be the responsibility of the Prison Service because it is "essentially an organisation for adults". As further demonstration of the challenge prison establishments face in delivering regimes suitable for children, reference may be made to recent inspections by the Chief Inspector since the Thematic Review of young offender institutions which were anticipating contractual responsibility for detention and training orders. In their most recent inspections the Inspectorate apply the following tests of whether an establishment is "healthy"[86]—

(i) the weakest young prisoners feel safe;

---

[83] n. 80, para. 8.02.
[84] n. 80, preface. N. Colthup "Child Protection in Prison" (1996) *Criminal Justice, 14,* 16–17, describes an initiative at HMP Hull to apply child protection procedures in respect of boys aged 16–17 enabling the local authority to undertake Children Act 1989, s.47 inquiries.
[85] n. 80, para. 2.24. The Chief Inspector has since reported (see n. 93, at p.9): "the provisions of the Children Act are held only to apply to the Prison Service 'in principle'. As the provisions of the Act are binding on the probation and social services, there is therefore an invidious position that a child can cease to be subject to the exactness of the law when serving a sentence in Prison Service Custody, which is reversed when he or she returns to the community. The Prison Service claims it is 'morally bound' by the provisions of the Act."
[86] First devised in H.M. Chief Inspector of Prisons, *Suicide is Everyone's Concern: Thematic Review* (H.M. Inspectorate of Prisons, Home Office, London, 1999) Chap. 7.

(ii)   young prisoners are treated with respect;

(iii) all young prisoners are engaged in constructive purposeful activity and are expected to improve themselves;

(iv)   young prisoners are enabled to strengthen links with their family and prepare for release to a life free from re-offending.

HMYOI Feltham

11.55   This huge establishment has had to serve the remand needs of London and surrounding counties, thus swamping its capacity to make adequate provision for sentenced young prisoners. The 1998 inspection[87] demonstrated starkly that Feltham was a very unhealthy location for young people. The demands made on Feltham "to meet the daily needs of the courts have destroyed any chance of providing a safe environment within which they can be encouraged to put offending behaviour behind them." Though some good offending behaviour programmes were available, these were limited in number. Overall, the institution was failing to provide a basic level of care or of positive human interaction. Juveniles were "in the charge of staff who were not suitably trained"—"The impression was that it was all too much trouble and we were not sure that staff themselves knew their role." "There was little to suggest that staff cared what happened to the young prisoners in their charge . . . on many units staff were preoccupied with surviving the day." On re-inspection in September 1999 the Inspectorate[88] found the foundations laid for change, though "real and visible improvements in the treatment of and conditions for young prisoners" had not yet been achieved. Plans were in place to house juveniles in a separate part of the establishment but child sex offenders were not being identified adequately and child protection procedures were not in place to ensure the safety of juveniles. Purposeful activity was taking place for only 15 hours per week. Frequent cancellation of evening association meant that young persons could not rely on time out of cell in which to telephone their families. The lack of sentence planning and offending behaviour programmes meant that little constructive work was being carried out to prepare young offenders for release. (Feltham has since attracted continuing adverse publicity. In August 2000 the deputy governor resigned in protest at what he described as "dangerous and anti-social" conditions.)

HMYOI Onley

11.56   Though providing a good atmosphere and a safe environment, with many good, caring staff who treated their charges well, the establishment was "running on automatic pilot"—"the under-resourcing and shortage of investment had resulted in impoverished regimes", particularly for juveniles. For example, those under school-leaving age were not receiving their statutory entitlement to 15 hours educational provision per week. Purposeful activity was restricted to 15/17 hours per week which was viewed as clearly unacceptable. Young prisoners were

---

[87] H.M. Chief Inspector of Prisons, *HMYOI Feltham: Report of an Unannounced Full Inspection 30 November 4 December 1998* (H.M. Inspectorate of Prisons, Home Office, London, 1999).
[88] H.M. Chief Inspector of Prisons, *HMYOI Feltham: Report on a Short Unannounced Inspection 28–30 September 1999* (H.M. Inspectorate of Prisons, Home Office, London, 2000).

spending long periods in their cells, with inadequate opportunity for outdoor exercise and frequently cancelled association time. Plans for the new Children's Units did not at that stage did not provide for any new workshops suitable for craft and vocational training, and staff felt unprepared for their new responsibilities. The Inspectorate were "astonished at several punitive adjudications which had resulted in young people spending extra time in custody following relatively minor misdemeanours".[89]

HMYOI Hollesley Bay

11.57 Though suffering the disadvantages of a rather remote rural location and holding a pocket of multi-racial Britain served by an almost entirely white staff group, the establishment had made good progress in preparing for its juvenile responsibilities and showed clear potential in delivering a "rich regime" for children, in line with Youth Justice Board expectations. Concern was expressed for the needs of more vulnerable young people—a more proactive and effective approach was required to deal with bullying; the needs of young people who were depressed and withdrawn were not being adequately recognised; staff were insufficiently briefed on child protection procedures to ensure an appropriate response to children who had been exposed to sexual abuse. Training plans were well constructed but often completed too late to benefit those serving shorter sentences.[90]

HMYOI Werrington

11.58 The establishment was commended as a "centre of excellence" in its work with juveniles, in line with the changes necessary for a detention and training order regime. It was found to have the most comprehensive child protection procedures found in any Prison Service establishment accommodating children. The local Social Services Department guaranteed seven day emergency cover. Policy and procedures to deal with potential self-harm were comprehensive and familiar to staff. However, the location of sex offenders was insufficiently known to staff to ensure vigilance.[91]

HMYOI Portland

11.59 This establishment is housed in forbidding buildings originally intended for convicts in the early 19th Century and much remained to be done to bring it up to date in ethos and attitude, and to break from traditional practices and expectations that this YOI should operate an essentially disciplinary regime as the "Wandsworth" for the under-21s. Young offenders were expected "to demonstrate total compliance with petty rules and . . . too many staff wanted to be seen as austere authority figures" rather than as role models of good adult behaviour showing concern for young prisoners' welfare and well-being. The establishment had a worrying level of assaults and bullying among trainees. While different

---

[89] H.M. Chief Inspector of Prisons, *HMYOI Onley: Report of a Full Announced Inspection 6–10 September 1999* (H.M. Inspectorate of Prisons, Home Office, London, 1999).
[90] H.M. Chief Inspector of Prisons, *HMYOI Hollesley Bay: Report of an Unannounced Full Inspection 30 November–4 December 1999*, H.M. Inspectorate of Prisons, Home Office, London, 1999).
[91] H.M. Chief Inspector of Prisons, *HMYOI Werrington: Report of an Unannounced Short Inspection 9– 11 November 1999* (H.M. Inspectorate of Prisons, Home Office, London, 2000).

departments such as education, chaplaincy and vocational training staff were achieving promising work, they were struggling with inadequate resources and an overall lack of integration in achieving a coherent programme of purposeful activity, particularly for those serving shorter sentences. Very little was being done to prepare young persons for release, given that 50 per cent were leaving without a fixed address to return to. Anticipating the difficulties that Portland would face in meeting the standards of the Youth Justice Board, the Inspectorate expressed themselves—[91a]

> "at a total loss to understand why management had failed to provide sufficient classrooms, sporting facilities, skill training areas and administration offices to serve the juvenile population. We could not see how the demanding regime for juveniles as required by the Youth Justice Board could be delivered when separated from the young adult offender population."

In sum, the report "discloses some wholly unacceptable treatment of and conditions for young offenders, including children, which are far removed from published intentions". (Since this report, it has been announced that HMYOI Portland will cease to receive juveniles.)

HMYOI Brinsford

Though located near HMYOI Werrington, the Inspectorate were dismayed to find that none of the qualities found there had been applied here. The Brinsford regime "with all the indicators we found of self-harm, fear for safety and bullying, puts most of its juvenile population at risk"[91b]. There had been five deaths in an eight month period, 35 incidents of self-harm by attempted hanging or mutilation in a 12 month period and 369 occasions where ill-designed isolation rooms had been occupied by vulnerable trainees. The institution had inadequate arrangements for dealing with the often adverse impact of the first night in custody and no use was made of local Area Child Protection Committee procedures. Assessment of vulnerability and educational needs were poor and an educational ethos failed to permeate the Brinsford regime, classes being mainly limited to tackling basic literacy skills. Visits facilities were not conducive to good experience of contact with families and links with YOTs and social services departments were notably inadequate. The report notes that "unless there is rapid and purposeful improvement, Brinsford would be a continuously failing establishment".

Recent trends in custodial sentencing of juveniles

11.60 The Chief Inspector of Prisons has commented on the increasing numbers of young people in prison service custody. The following Table shows the use of custodial sentences for males aged 15–17, indicating that the decline in numbers of custodial sentences occurring in the first year of operation of the 1991 Act has been reversed.

[91a] H.M. Chief Inspector of Prisons, *HMYOI Portland: Report of a Full Announced Full Inspection 24 October–3 November 1999* (H.M. Inspectorate of Prisons, Home Office, London, 2000).
[91b] H.M. Chief Inspector of Prisons, *HYMOI Brinsford: Report of an Announced Inspection 19–23 June 2000* (H.M. Inspectorate of Prisons, Home Office, London, 2001).

	Total number (indictable offences: all court)	as % of all sentenced for indictable offences: magistrates' courts	as % of all sentenced for indictable offences: Crown Court	Average sentence length (months)
1988	7,200	9.3	51.4	
1993	3,600	10.5	52.2	7.3
1994	4,000	10.7	58.0	7.3
1995	4,500	10.8	60.0	8.2
1996	5,300	10.8	66.2	10.5
1997	5,700	10.3	65.4	11.1
1998	5,600	10.1	62.2	10.2

Source: *Criminal Statistics for England & Wales, 1998*

11.61 A further 1,000 males aged 15–17 were sentenced to immediate custody in 1998 for summary offences, 700 for non-motoring matters. For girls aged 15–17, involving far fewer numbers (some 300 in 1998 compared with around 200 in 1988 and 100 in 1993), the percentage use of custody for indictable offences has risen from 2.2 per cent in 1993 to 3.9 per cent in 1998 in magistrates' courts and from 30.9 per cent to 38.1 per cent in the Crown Court. A total of 5,900 sentenced offenders aged 17 or under were received in 1999. On July 31, 2000, 1,897 young offenders (72 being girls) were being held under sentence, an increase from 1,710 in mid-1999.[92]

Local Variations in Use of Custody

In order to understand better the substantial variations in rates of magisterial custodial sentencing of young offenders (the average being 7.7 per cent but the rate rising to in excess of 28 per cent in some areas), the Youth Justice Board commissioned a survey of 20 petty sessions areas for 1995–98.[92a] The research showed that while some high custody areas suffer from above average levels of serious crime, local custodial rates could not be explained by variations in levels of offending. Indeed, in some cases a reverse association appears to exist. A significant number of custodial disposals seemed far from inevitable and there was scope for reduction in use of detention for less serious offences. Low custody areas achieved higher scores in an audit of PSR quality, albeit that sentencers in those areas did not regard reports prepared in their area any more highly than sentencers elsewhere. Magistrates were not well informed as to how their local custody rate compared with the national pattern. Sentencers in higher custody rate areas attributed this to local offending patterns. Sentencers did not consider that improvements in PSRs, better youth justice services or closer links with YOTs would reduce their rate of detention, though those services are more highly regarded in low custody areas. No

---

[92] Research & Development Statistics (Home Office, London, 2000).
[92a] NACRO *Factors Associated with Differential Rates of Youth Custodial Sentencing* (Youth Justice Board, London, 2000).

single factor emerged that could satisfactorily explain custody variations but it was clear that a local sentencing culture prevails in court areas, reflected in and reinforced by local training provisions.

Though detailed statistics capturing the use made of detention and training orders since inception of this sentence have not yet been published, the Chief Inspector of Prisons has observed that magistrates have increased their use of detention in this format, particularly for four to six month terms. He believes that they see the sentence as "an opportunity for YOTs to secure the re-engagement of children with mainstream services who, in many cases have abandoned them".[92b] He comments that such terms in reality present a very short timespan in which to assess the needs of a juvenile, treat and prepare him or her for release, given the "growing evidence" that many of those being sentenced to DTOs bring with them a "frightening degree of social neglect—they have been described as the detritus of long-standing social exclusion." He identifies that nearly 50 per cent of children in YOIs have been or are still in local authority care, though many have lost contact with their social workers and their corresponding entitlements. "Most children in YOIs have a very fractured educational experience and very significant learning deficits . . . many have immense family difficulties." Given his powerful critique of Prison Service establishments servicing DTO sentences, summarised above, the hopes and expectations of sentencers are likely to remain unmet, at least in the short-term. It remains to be seen whether the advent of intensive supervision and surveillance programmes in the community (see 11.65), though available also in the post-custodial phase of a DTO, will attract significant confidence among sentencers to prompt greater use of community sentencing and thus divert multi-need repeat offenders from custody.

Recent incidence of self-harm

11.62 Much concern has been expressed about the vulnerability of young offenders in custody. The number of recorded incidents of attempted suicide and deliberate self-harm in prison service detention for the age group 15–17 was 31 in 1996 and 51 in 1997. Though no cause for complacency, the rate of self-harm among this age group was not higher than for other age groups in the custodial population. In the five years 1994–98, a total of eight self-inflicted deaths were recorded for this age group, all boys.[93] As regards more recent episodes of self-harm in YOIs, involving both juveniles and young adult offenders[94]—

> *self-inflicted deaths:* 1997 (5); 1998 (5); 1999 (8); 2000 (to July 5) (1)
> *self-harm incidents:* 1996–7 (793); 1997–98 (879); 1998–99 (944).

The way forward

11.63 In his preface to his 1998 Inspection of HMYOI Feltham[95] the Chief Inspector of Prisons asked staff whether "they would be happy for their sons, or the sons of any of their friends, to be on the receiving end of the treatment and conditions described in the report which are unacceptable in a civilised country". The vision of the new youth justice system anticipates that the mistakes of the past

---

[92b] n. 91b, at p. 6.
[93] n. 86.
[94] *Hansard*, H.L. Written Answer, July 11, 2000, cols. 13–14.
[95] n. 87.

in the incarceration of children can be avoided as we head into a new era of child-focused provision, able to provide safe, healthy, positive regimes for this vulnerable, impressionable and volatile age group. The reports of individual institutions summarised above show that real change can be achieved but also that there is a long way yet to go. The lessons from the Medway Secure Training Centre (see para. 11.50), intended as a new dawn in the custodial care of children, demonstrate the scope for unintended consequences and the difficulty of translating vision into reality.

The Youth Justice Board now has the task of carrying forward the hope that the "juvenile secure estate", including prison service establishments which have been repeatedly condemned as "no place for children,"[96] can serve the developmental, educational, emotional, health and training needs of children. It is worth noting the "essential components of good practice in new custodial institutions" identified by Hagell et al.[97]: a clear theoretical model from the outset; a child-centred focus; an incremental and strategic plan for implementation of elements of the intervention; a positive ethos; a supported staff group; knowledge of the client group. The Prison Service is seeking to drive forward a fresh approach through Prison Service Order 4950 (outlined in Chapter 28 at para. 28.30. The Board's National Standards for Youth Justice[98] show a positive commitment to seeking to ensure a coherent, seamless approach to sentence, so that the custodial and community elements are matched, backed by good inter-agency co-operation, clear information flow and collective planning for community reintegration, so that intervention spans both components. However, the detention and training order has the potential for children to be incarcerated "in greater numbers, at younger ages and for longer periods".[99] There is no little risk that a governmental policy approach to youth justice that "treats children and young people as offenders first and as children second"[1] may combine with revived sentencer enthusiasm for custody as a potentially effective correctional experience, coupled with tensions between the Youth Justice Board and the Prison Service over service delivery issues, to place the new custodial system under pressure of numbers which will undermine the best efforts of the practitioners charged with realising the fragile new vision.

Protection under international law

11.64 It seems worthwhile to identify the protection intended to be afforded to young people in detention under international conventions[2]—

- Detention should be used as a measure of last resort and for the shortest appropriate time.[3]

- A child should not be subjected to cruel, inhuman or degrading punishment.[4]

---

[96] Department of Health People Like Us: The Report of the Review of the Safeguards for Children Living Away from Home (The Stationery Office, London, 1997) at para. 5.10.
[97] n. 75, p. xi.
[98] Youth Justice Board (2000).
[99] G. Monaghan "The Courts and the New Youth Justice" (2000) at p.5, in B. Goldson The New Youth Justice Russell House Publishing, Lyme Regis, 2000).
[1] S. Moore "Child Incarceration and the New Youth Justice" at p. 125 in B. Goldson. The New Youth Justice (Russell House Publishing, Lyme Regis, 2000).
[2] Summarised in Chief Inspector of Prisons (footnote 80), Appendix 2.
[3] United Nations, Convention on the Rights of the Child (1989) Article 37(b).
[4] n. 3, Article 37(a).

- Every young person in detention has the right to maintain contact with his or her family.[5]

- While in custody, juveniles should receive care, protection and all necessary individual assistance—social, educational, vocational, psychological, medical and physical—that they may require in view of their age, sex and personality.[6]

- All personnel dealing with young people should be specially trained.[7]

- Detention of young people should be decentralised and near their home.[8]

Intensive Supervision and Surveillance Programmes

11.65 Commencing in 2001, the Youth Justice Board[9] is awarding grants to YOTs to establish intensive supervision and surveillance programmes (ISSPs) targeted on those young offenders who commit a disproportionately high number of offences, in light of evidence that three per cent of young offenders commit approximately 25 per cent of all offences.[10] Though access to ISSPs will be dependent on whether YOTs bid for and are successful in securing funding, in principle ISSPs will be available for those who (a) have been charged or warned for an imprisonable offence on four or more separate occasions within the preceding 12 months and (b) have previously received at least one community or custodial penalty. The programme is not restricted to a particular kind of sentencing disposal but is generic and can form part of a bail supervision package, or a supervision or community rehabilitation order (as a requirement of their order), or the community element of a detention and training order (as a condition of licence). For those serving a community sentence, the programme should last at least six months; for those completing detention and training orders, the ISSP period will be determined by the length of their DTO.

11.66 Intensive supervision must contain core modules combining: (i) a strong focus on education and training, particularly addressing numeracy and literacy; (ii) restorative reparation; (iii) intensive courses designed to change offending behaviour; (iv) training in inter-personal skills; (v) family support. Provision of suitable accommodation, whether through remand fostering, hostel accommodation, staff-supported flats or foyer provisions, will be integral to programme resources. Surveillance will be provided through at least one of a range of options: intelligence-led policing; 'tracking' by support staff; electronic monitoring; voice verification (currently being piloted). YOTs must ensure that the whereabouts of young offenders subject to ISSP are checked at least twice daily but there must be facility for surveillance for 24 hours a day, seven days a week. The key objectives of ISSPs are: "to reduce the rate of re-offending in the target group by five per cent and the seriousness of that re-offending by 2003–4; to tackle the underlying problems of the target group, with particular emphasis on their educational needs; to "provide reassurance to the community that the behaviour of repeat young offenders is being closely monitored and that any relapse will be effectively and

---

[5] n. 3, article 37.
[6] United Nations, *Standard Minimum Rules for the Administration of Juvenile Justice* (1985) Rule 13.5.
[7] n. 6, Rule 22.2.
[8] n. 6.
[9] Youth Justice Board (2000) *Intensive Supervision and Surveillance Programmes.*
[10] J. Graham and B. Bowling *Young People and Crime* Research Study 145 (Home Office, London, 1995).

swiftly dealt with". Though the ISSP initiative is not stated to have a diversionary purpose, it remains to be seen whether this new resource will promote greater use of community programmes for offenders who might otherwise receive detention and training orders. Given the duration and intensity specified for ISSPs by the Youth Justice Board, namely at least five hours structured supervision daily Monday to Friday during the first three months, with daily contact for at least one hour thereafter, the demands of this kind of programme appear to exceed the scope under PCC(S)A 2000 Sched. 6 to include additional requirements in supervision orders (see Chapter 20).

CHAPTER 12

Prior to Sentence

12.01 This chapter brings together the miscellany of considerations and procedural channels that inform the court in approaching the sentencing of juveniles.

INFORMATION TO ASSIST THE COURT

Statements by the Offender and Parent(s)

12.02 Where a juvenile offender has been found guilty of an offence in the youth court, whether on a plea of guilty or after trial, the Magistrates' Court (Children and Young Persons) Rules 1992, r. 10(2)(a) require that the juvenile and their parent or guardian, if present, "shall be given the opportunity of making a statement". This should be given irrespective of whether the offender is legally represented.

The scope for direct communication between sentencer and defendant or their parent may well be inhibited by the formality of the occasion but it has been suggested that magistrates find it valuable to gain impressions by this means. Based on her research and observations in juvenile courts, Brown[1] reported, that magistrates sought clues from the appearance and presentation of parents and defendants in the following respects—

12.03
(a) moral character and "decency" of the parent;

(b) evidence of an affective bond between parent and offender;

(c) ability of the parent to control their offspring, *e.g.* whether the parent is over-protective or indulgent, whether care is backed with structure and discipline, whether the parent is able to be assertive towards the child or is "at the end of their tether";

(d) signs of the juvenile's malleability and deference as opposed to a lack of respect for authority.

12.04 Though this research is somewhat dated the obvious risks are that misleading impressions may be gained based on stereotypical assumptions and limited perceptions. Brown suggested that the defendant and their parent were disadvantaged by their lack of familiarity with court routines and conventions and are likely to confine themselves to "compliant utterances appropriate to the vocabulary of integration and control", avoiding challenge to "the logic of the magistrate or the smooth running of court business", delay in proceedings and embarrassment to the Bench. The potential for good effective dialogue within the

---

[1] S. Brown, *Magistrates at Work* (Open University Press, Milton Keynes, 1991).

conventions and timetable of the court was very difficult to achieve and requires skill, sensitivity and clarity of expression by the Chair. Though detailed research on the contemporary culture of the youth court is still awaited, some sense of the scope for sentencers to engage in effective dialogue with offenders and their families is provided by Allen *et al.* in an evaluation of the Youth Court Demonstration Project, conducted in Rotherham and Leicestershire, 1998–2000.[1a] Three out of 10 magistrates said that they had changed their minds about what sentence to give as a result of changes initiated by the Project, usually because as a result of engaging more with defendants and parents they had become aware of matters that previously they would not have found out about. There appears scope for sentencers to gain information by this route beyond what they may learn from PSRs or advocates' submissions. Objective evidence of changed sentencing practice was more tentative but the researchers identified statistically significant indication of increased use of discharges and probation orders and decreased use of fines, supervision orders and detention in the Rotherham court.

Previous Cautions

12.05 Among the available information to be taken into consideration by youth court about the juvenile's "general conduct", in furtherance MC (C & YP) Rules 1992, r. 10(2)(b) cautions previously administered by the police may be cited. The National Standards for Cautioning[2] stated—

> "Formal cautions should be cited in court if they are relevant to the offence under consideration. In presenting antecedents, care should be taken to distinguish between cautions and convictions, which should usually be listed on separate sheets of paper."

12.06 Now that cautions for young offenders are becoming a matter only of historical interest, the more pertinent provision is CDA 1998, s.66(5) governing reprimands and warnings, as detailed in Chapter 4, which specifies that any reprimand or warning under CDA 1998, s.65, and "any report of a failure . . . to participate in a rehabilitation programme arranged for" the defendant under s.66(2) "may be cited in criminal proceedings in the same circumstances as a conviction . . . may be cited". Home Office guidance[3] has clarified that "in practice, this means that they should be made available to the court".

Pre-Sentence Reports

12.07 A "pre-sentence report" means a report in writing containing information "with a view to assisting the court to determine the most suitable method of dealing with an offender", made or submitted by "an appropriate officer": PCC(S)A 2000, s.162(1). For this purpose, where an offender is aged under 18, "an appropriate officer" means: (i) a member of a youth offending team; (ii) a probation officer; or (iii) a social worker of a local authority social services department: s.162(2). In tandem with this provision, CYPA 1969, s.9(1) continues to apply, placing the local authority under a duty, where a young offender is facing prosecution—

[1a] C. Allen, I. Crow and M. Cavadino, *Evaluation of the Youth Court Demonstration Project* Research Study 214 (Home Office, London, 2000).
[2] Home Office Circular, 18/1994, Note 6A.
[3] Home Office (1998) *Final Warning Scheme*, para. 40.

"to make such investigations and provide the court before which the proceedings are heard with such information relating to the home surroundings, school record" health and character of the young person[4] in respect of whom the proceedings are brought as appear to the authority likely to assist the court."

12.08 This duty is qualified by the rider "unless of the opinion that it is unnecessary to do so". However, section 9(2) specifies that if the court requests the authority to make investigations and provide information, then the authority has a duty to comply with that request. CYPA 1969, s.34(3) provides that if the juvenile has reached the age specified by the Secretary of State[5] and the authority does not already have information about the juvenile's home surroundings, then the authority need not make section 9(1) investigations if there are local arrangements for this information to be provided by a probation officer. These provisions, long pre-dating youth offending teams, should now be viewed in the context of the duty to obtain and consider pre-sentence reports as required by PCC(S)A 2000.

It should be noted that those preparing pre-sentence reports are responsible only to the court, and solicitors representing defendants should not make direct requests to those agencies for reports upon their clients. Any such requests should be made to the court.[6]

12.09 Within the definition of pre-sentence reports provided by section 162(1), it should be noted "it is for the trial judge (or the magistrates) to decide whether the report actually available to the court is adequate for sentencing purposes and constitutes proper compliance with the statute".[6a] It is not necessary for the report to have addressed the particular order that the court may have in mind. The Act does not prevent oral information or opinion being offered to supplement a written report.

Though the Home Secretary is empowered by section 162 to make rules regulating the content of powers, no rules have yet been made. Instead the National Standards for the Supervision of Offenders in the Community (revised 2000) and the National Standards for Youth Justice (2000) cover the preparation and content of pre-sentence reports.

Duty to consider reports

12.10 The Magistrates' Courts (Children and Young Persons) Rules 1992, r. 10(2)(b) places a broad requirement upon youth courts, following a finding of guilt, to take into consideration:

"all available information as to the general conduct, home surroundings, school record and medical history of the child or young person, as may be necessary to enable it to deal with the care in his interests and, in particular, shall take into consideration such information as aforesaid which is provided in pursuance of CYPA 1969, s.9."

If such information is not fully available, the court shall consider the desirability of adjourning the proceedings for such enquiry as may be necessary.[7] Note that the

[4] Amended by S.I. 1970 No. 1882 to include children aged 10–13.
[5] designated as 13 by S.I. 1970, No. 1882.
[6] *Adams* [1970] Crim. L.R. 693.
[6a] *per* Lord Taylor C.J. in *Okinikan* [1993] 1 W.L.R. 173.
[7] r. 10(2)(c).

court is not placed under a duty to obtain this background information but must heed it if it is available, either because the local authority or the Probation Service has supplied it, or because the court has opted to seek such information. These provisions are thus secondary to the mandatory requirements of PCC(S)A 2000.

Within the sentencing framework introduced by CJA 1991 and continued by the 2000 Act, a court must obtain and consider a pre-sentence report before reaching a sentencing decision in four important respects, three in regard to custodial sentences and one in respect of community sentences.

12.11 (i) Custodial Sentences. A pre-sentence report is required (PCC(S)A 2000, s.81(1))—

(a) Before forming the opinion that an offence is so serious that only a custodial sentence can be justified for it.

(b) Before forming the opinion in regard to a violent or sexual offence that only a custodial sentence would be adequate to protect the public from serious harm from the offender.

(c) In regard to offences where the court has formed either opinion (a) or (b), before determining the length of sentence commensurate with the seriousness of the offence or, in regard to a violent or sexual offence, before determining whether a longer sentence than is commensurate with the seriousness of the offence is necessary to protect the public from serious harm from the offender and, if so, for how long.

A custodial sentence imposed under PCC(S)A 2000, s.79(3) on grounds of the offender's refusal to give consent to a requirement in a community sentence proposed by the court requiring that consent may be imposed without the necessity of a pre-sentence report,[8] though a report is very likely to have been obtained in enabling the court to propose the community sentence to which consent is declined.

12.12 Sentencing without a Report or with a Previous Report. PCC(S)A 2000, s.81(2) empowers a court dealing with a defendant aged 18 or more to pass a custodial sentence without a pre-sentence report if of the opinion that it is unnecessary to obtain one. For younger defendants a special compromise applies.[9]

PCC(S)A 2000, s.81

(3) In a case where the offender is aged under 18 and the offence is not triable only on indictment and there is no other offence associated with it that is triable only on indictment, the court shall not form such an opinion as is mentioned in subsection (2) above unless—

(a) there exists a previous pre-sentence report obtained in respect of the offender; and

(b) the court has had regard to the information contained in that report, or, if there is more than one such report, the most recent report.

12.13 The court may thus proceed to sentence without a report where the offence or any other associated offence is triable only on indictment, if the court is

---

[8] *Meredith* (1994) 15 Cr.App.R.(S.) 528.
[9] s. 81(3).

of the opinion that it is unnecessary to obtain a report. This is intended to give the Crown Court the discretion to proceed without a report in very serious cases where a custodial sentence is inevitable, but it appears also to apply where a youth court is dealing with more serious offences, either one to which PCC(S)A 2000, s.91 does not apply (*e.g.* threat to kill, riot, attempted sexual intercourse with a girl under 13, causing death by dangerous driving, perjury), or with a section 91 offence which it has opted to deal with summarily. It seems highly unlikely that a youth court dealing with such matters would decide that a report is unnecessary.

12.14 When a court is dealing with a child or young person for an either way or summary offence, the implication of s.81(3) is that any report can serve the purpose of informing the sentencing decision, irrespective of its out-datedness or its relevance to the offence for which the juvenile has now been convicted. It is difficult to see how a past report prepared specifically for a different sentencing occasion can be reliable in understanding the young offender's current offence, their current circumstances, their response to the sentence which was passed on the earlier occasion or the current options available to the court. Changes can occur rapidly in the lives and attitudes of adolescents and also within the range of non-custodial options available under local inter-agency provisions for young offenders. Courts may thus prefer to seek up-to-date reports as a matter of good practice even if this is no longer a formal requirement.

12.15 In *Massheder*,[10] the Crown Court judge had imposed a sentence of 18 months detention under CYPA 1933, s.53, on a boy aged 15 for arson, without the benefit of a report, on the grounds that the offence was very serious and beyond anything in the nature of probation and because the Social Services Department requested to provide a report had not done so because of an industrial dispute. The Court of Appeal stated that a report was necessary in a case of this nature, "to give help and balance to the consideration of all available courses open to the court . . . Without a report it is impossible to say categorically that this was not a case for a supervision order". A supervision order for two years was substituted. The fact that the judge had originally sought a report unsuccessfully implied that a report was considered "necessary". If a court gives indication that it would ideally have liked more information about the offender before passing sentence, this could well be incompatible with a conclusion that a report is "unnecessary".

12.16 Reports on Appeal. PCC(S)A 2000, s.81(5) governs procedure on appeal. Though a custodial sentence, imposed on grounds of the seriousness of the offence or the protection of the public from serious harm without the benefit of a pre-sentence report is not invalidated by that omission, a court hearing an appeal against such a sentence should ordinarily obtain and consider such a report. Section 81(6) provides that the appeal court need not obtain and consider such a report if of the opinion either that the court below was justified in its opinion that a report was unnecessary or, even if the court below was not so justified, that a report is nevertheless unnecessary. However, in respect of an appellant aged under 18, the compromise that applies under s.81(3) at initial point of sentence applies also on appeal under identical provisions contained in s.81(7). Thus if a youth court dealing with an either way offence imposes a desertion and training order without considering a pre-sentence report, it would be open to the Crown Court to deal with an appeal against sentence with the benefit only of a report prepared for an earlier sentencing occasion.

---

[10] (1983) 5 Cr. App. R.(S.) 442.

12.17 (ii) Community Sentences. A pre-sentence report is required before forming an opinion as to the suitability for the offender of one or more of the following orders whether for an offence triable only on indictment or otherwise—[11]

(a) a community rehabilitation order which includes additional requirements under PCC(S)A 2000, Sched. 2;

(b) a community punishment order;

(c) a community punishment and rehabilitation order;

(d) a drug treatment and testing order;

(e) a supervision order which includes additional requirements under PCC(S)A 2000, Sched. 6.

A court must obtain and consider written reports that are not pre-sentence reports or information not necessarily given in writing before imposing various other community or non-custodial orders, as outlined at para. 12.33.

12.18 Sentencing without a Report or with a Previous Report. Provisions similar to those relating to custodial sentencing apply to community sentences so that a court dealing with a defendant aged 18 or over can dispense with a pre-sentence report if of the opinion that it is unnecessary to obtain one.[12] A special compromise applies to younger defendants in regard to either way and summary offences.[13]

PCC(S)A 2000, s.36

(6) In a case where the offender is aged under 18 and the offence is not triable only on indictment and there is no other offence associated with it that is triable only on indictment, the court shall not form such an opinion as is mentioned in subsection (5) above unless—

(a) there exists a previous pre-sentence report obtained in respect of the offender; and

(b) the court has had regard to the information contained in that report, or, if there is more than one such report, the most recent report.

The comments above relating to sentencing of young offenders to custody without the benefit of a pre-sentence report apply equally in the context of community sentences.

12.19 Reports on Appeal. PCC(S)A 2000, s.36(7) governs procedure on appeal. Though a specified community sentence passed without the benefit of a pre-sentence report is not invalidated by that omission, a court hearing an appeal against such a sentence should ordinarily obtain and consider such a report. Section 36(8) provides that the appeal court need not obtain and consider a report if of the opinion either that the court below was justified in its opinion that a report was unnecessary or, even if the court below was not so justified, that a report is

---

[11] s. 36(3).
[12] PCC(S)A 2000, s.36(5).
[13] s. 36(6).

nevertheless unnecessary. However, in respect of an appellant aged under 18, the compromise that applies under s.36(6) at initial point of sentence applies also on appeal under identical provisions contained in s.36(9).

Mentally Disordered Offenders

12.20   PCC(S)A 2000, s.82(3)(a) mentions consideration of a pre-sentence report as one source which the court may use in fulfilling the requirement to consider information relating to the mental condition of an offender who is or appears to be mentally disordered, before passing a custodial sentence on such an offender, whether for an offence triable only on indictment or otherwise. There is no general requirement that a pre-sentence report shall be obtained before passing sentence on a mentally disordered offender but s.82(1) requires consideration of a medical report before passing a custodial sentence upon an offender who is or appears to be mentally disordered.[14]

Adjournment for Reports

Magistrates Courts Act 1980, s.10

(3)   A magistrates' court may, for the purpose of enabling inquiries to be made or of determining the most suitable method of dealing with the case, exercise its power to adjourn after convicting the accused and before sentencing him or otherwise dealing with him; but, if it does so, the adjournment shall not be for more than four weeks at a time unless the court remands the accused in custody and, where it so remands him, the adjournment shall not be for more than three weeks at a time.

12.21   This provision must be read subject to CYPA 1933 s.48(3) which specifies—

(3) When a youth court has remanded a child or young person for information to be obtained with respect to him, any youth court acting for the same petty sessional division or place—(a) may in his absence extend the period for which he is remanded, so however, that he appears before a court or a justice of the peace at least once in every twentyone days; (b) when the required information has been obtained, may deal with him finally.

If the young person is remanded to local authority accommodation following a finding of guilt, the magistrates' power of remand is limited to a maximum of three weeks. A court is not obliged to sentence at the end of the first such adjournment and may further adjourn, for example if the reports required are not ready. Power of adjournment must be exercised for the purposes specified in section 10(3). It would be in excess of jurisdiction to purport to remand the defendant to local authority accommodation or custody ostensibly to obtain a report or other information but in reality for the purpose of punishment or correction. Thus in *Toynbee Hall Juvenile Court Justices, ex p. Joseph*[15] the Divisional Court quashed the remand of a boy aged 16 convicted of travelling by railway without payment of fare where the court had indicated as the reason for remanding him that it was for his own good as he was a liar who had to learn not to defraud the railway.

---

[14] see para. 12.48.
[15] [1939] 3 All E.R. 16.

Timescale for Preparation of Pre-Sentence Reports

12.22 Distinct from the statutory provisions governing remand for reports (see above), the *National Standards for Youth Justice*[16] specify a timescale for completion, according to the category of young offender. Ordinarily, pre-sentence reports must be produced within 15 working days of request. However, pre-sentence reports concerning "persistent young offenders" (those who have been dealt with by the courts on three or more occasions and who commit another offence within three years of last appearing before a court) who are subject to greater priority and minimisation of delay must be produced within ten working days of request (see para. 12.5). In achieving these targets, the following timetable applies—

- PSRs should be allocated on the day the request is made.

- Defendants who are bailed should be given an interview appointment before leaving court. A YOT member "must see all young offenders who have been bailed for a PSR before they leave court to explain the purpose of the report . . . and to give written information about when and where the appointment will take place" (para.6.6.3).

- Where it is not possible to complete a PSR, for whatever reason, the PSR writer must give the court written information explaining the reason.

- To reduce delay, the PSR writer must inform the court and defence solicitor in advance if a future adjournment is to be proposed.

Contents of pre-sentence reports

12.23 The *National Standards for Youth Justice*[17] specify that PSRs must adopt the following standard headings:

- *sources of information*;

- *offence analysis*, including what is known about the impact of the offence on any victim, and assessment of the offender's awareness of the consequences to self, family and any victims;

- *assessment of risk to the community*, including risk of re-offending and risk of harm;

- *conclusion*.

Implied promises

12.24 A series of cases have illustrated the principle, first enunciated in *Gillam*[18] that if the court adjourns for reports in circumstances which justifiably lead the offender to expect that the sentence, will be non-custodial, provided that the report proves to be favourable, then the court is bound by the implied promise it has given.

"When a judge . . . purposely postpones sentence so that an alternative to prison can be examined and that alternative is found to be a satisfactory one in

---

[16] Youth Justice Board (2000), para. 6.8.2.
[17] Youth Justice Board (2000), para. 6.8.1.
[18] (1980) 2 Cr.App.R.(S.) 267.

all respects, the court ought to adopt the alternative. A feeling of injustice is otherwise aroused."[19]

In *Gillam* the judge asked that the offender's suitability for community service should be assessed. In the parallel case of *Ward*[20] the adjournment was to allow a period of bail assessment at a hostel with a view to a requirement of residence. In *McMurray*[21] the adjournment was to allow assessment of suitability for attendance at a probation centre. The fact that the subsequent judge or bench considers a non-custodial sentence to be unacceptably lenient for the offence does not negate the implied promise at the earlier hearing. The *Gillam* principle has been held to bind the Crown Court in dealing with an appeal from a magistrates' court *Gutteridge v. DPP*.[22]

12.25   The *Gillam* principle depends upon "there having been something in the nature of a promise, express or implied, that if a particular proposal is recommended, it will be adopted".[23] Thus courts became accustomed to using a formula of words designed to avoid tying the hands of the sentencers at the subsequent hearing.

It is clear from a number of decision since CJA 1991 that the principle still applies where the court on adjourning for a pre-sentence report gives a positive indication or uses words which create a justifiable expectation that a favourable report would lead to a non-custodial sentence. However, where a court adjourns for a report, there is no obligation to give a specific warning that a custodial sentence remains a possibility. While it may be desirable practice to give such a warning, mere failure to warn, even if granting bail in the interim, does not in itself justify an expectation of a non-custodial sentence. The Court of Appeal in *Renan*[24] made clear that "Silence by the judge . . . should never be taken as an indication that a non-custodial sentence will be considered appropriate" and also indicated that the defence advocate has a duty to ensure that the defendant understands the position.

PSRs and bail

12.26   In cases where the court requires a pre-sentence report before deciding the appropriate sentence, the normal practice should be to grant bail unless there are exceptional reasons for denying bail. The Bail Act 1976, Sched. 1, Part I, para. 7 provides that an offender convicted of an imprisonable offence need not be granted bail where his or her case is adjourned for inquiries or a report "if it appears to the court that it would be impracticable to complete the inquiries or make the report without keeping the defendant in custody". For a child or young person under the age of 17, remand will be to local authority accommodation under the provisions of CYPA 1969, s.23(1), unless the offender is a boy aged 15 or 16 and falls within the provisions of CJA 1991, s.23(5).[25]

If it is considered that the offender will not voluntarily attend appointments with a report writer, the court may consider imposing a condition of bail under the Bail Act 1976, s.3(6)(d) to comply with such requirements as appear to the court to be necessary to secure that:

---

[19] *per* Watkins L.J. in *Gillam*, p.269.
[20] (1982) 4 Cr.App.R.(S.) 103.
[21] (1987) 9 Cr.App.R.(S.) 101.
[22] (1987) 9 Cr.App.R.(S.) 279.
[23] *per* Croom-Johnson J. in *Moss* (1983) 5 Cr.App.R.(S.) 209.
[24] [1994] Crim. L.R. 379.
[25] see para. 9.16 *et seq.*

". . . he makes himself available for the purpose of enabling inquiries or a report to be made to assist the court in dealing with him for the offence."

Refusal to co-operate with the making of a report is not an aggravating feature but may well diminish the effect of a guilty plea or any mitigation such as remorse offered on the defendant's behalf.[26]

Disclosure of report to the offender and defence

12.27 PCC(S)A 2000, s156(2)(a), replacing PCCA 1973, s.46(1) and the Crime (Sentences) Act 1997, s.50(2)(a), requires a court to give a copy of the PSR "to the offender or his counsel or solicitor". This provision is supplemented by s.156(3) which specifies that if the offender is aged under 17 and is not legally represented, "a copy of the report need not be given to him but shall be given to his parent or guardian if present in court". Good practice will normally ensure that copies of reports are supplied both to advocates and to young offenders and/or their families. On occasion, the PSR writer may have concerns about supplying parents with a copy of a report which reflects perhaps negative feelings held by a young defendant about their parents or family which have not been discussed with them but shared in confidence with the writer.

12.28 Though pre-dating and to a considerable extent overtaken by the provisions of s.156, the Magistrates' Courts (Children and Young Persons) Rules 1992, rule 10 specify as follows in respect of youth court proceedings, though rule 10 has wider application beyond pre-sentence reports—

   (3) The court shall arrange for copies of any written report before the court to be made available to—

   (a) the legal representative, if any, of the relevant minor,
   (b) any parent or guardian of the relevant minor who is present at the hearing, and
   (c) the relevant minor, except where the court otherwise directs on the ground that it appears to it impracticable to disclose the report having regard to his age and understanding or undesirable to do so having regard to potential serious harm which might thereby be suffered by him.

   (4) In any case in which the relevant minor is not legally represented and where a report which has not been made available to him in accordance with a direction under paragraph (3)(c) has been considered without being read aloud in pursuance of paragraph (2)(d) or where he or his parent or guardian has been required to withdraw from the court in pursuance of paragraph (2)(e), then—

   (a) the relevant minor shall be told the substance of any part of the information given to the court bearing on his character or conduct which the court considers to be material to the manner in which the case should be dealt with unless it appears to it impracticable so to do having regard to his age and understanding, and
   (b) the parent or guardian of the relevant minor, if present, shall be told the substance of any part of such information which the court

---

[26] *Moriarty* (1993) 14 Cr.App.R.(S.) 575).

considers to be material as aforesaid and which has reference to his character or conduct or to the character, conduct, home surroundings or health of the relevant minor, and if such a person, having been told the substance of any part of such information, desires to produce further evidence with reference thereto, the court, if it thinks the further evidence would be material, shall adjourn the proceedings for the production thereof and shall, if necessary in the case of a report, require the attendance at the adjourned hearing of the person who made the report.

Disclosure to the prosecution

12.29 PCC(S)A 2000, s.156(2)(b), replacing the Crime (Sentences) Act 1997, s.50(2)(b), requires the court to give a copy of the PSR to the prosecutor, "that is to say, the person having conduct of the proceedings in respect of the offence". Information disclosed to the prosecution in this way may be used only for the purposes set out in s.156(5)—

(a) determining whether representations as to matters contained in the report need to be made to the court; or

(b) making such representations.

The contents may not be used, for example, in connection with any other proceedings against the offender or in the investigation of other offences of which the offender is suspected.

Specific sentence reports

12.30 As a contribution to the avoidance of delay and to speeding up the provision of information to the court, practice has developed of preparing reports designed to assist the sentencing court to determine the defendant's suitability for a specific sentence envisaged by the court. SSRs have the status of pre-sentence reports, being written even if supplemented orally, but are briefer and narrower in focus. The *National Standards for the Supervision of Offenders in the Community*[27] applicable to offenders aged 18 or over envisage their most likely use where the court envisages a community punishment order of up to 100 hours or a community rehabilitation order without additional requirements. The *National Standards for Youth Justice*[28] do not indicate the kind of community sentence for which SSRs should be deployed but indicate the same format as apply to PSRs with the following minimum sources of information—

- an interview in person with the defendant;
- where appropriate, a discussion with the defendant's parents or primary carer;
- inclusion of relevant and available information from other agencies.

Use of information in reports

12.31 Pre-sentence reports are prepared for the purpose of a specific sentencing exercise and are intended to be as frank as necessary to enable the court to make an

---

[27] Home Office (2000), para. B10. See also *Probation Circular 85/99: Pre-Sentence Reports and Specific Sentence Reports* (Home Office, London, 1999).
[28] n. 16, para. 6.9.

informed decision about the appropriate sentence. The question may arise whether information contained in a report can be used for tangential purposes. This issue was posed in *Lenihan v. West Yorkshire Metropolitan Police*[29] where a mother's comments to the probation officer, as contained in the social inquiry report, were relied upon in making the mother responsible for payment of compensation in respect of £200 stolen by her 14 year old daughter. The Divisional Court stated that it was quite wrong for the report to be taken into account in deciding that issue and to do so would inhibit report preparation. Lord Donaldson commented:

> ". . . the purpose of a social inquiry report is of course to inform the court about all sorts of matters concerning the accused, usually very much for the benefit of the accused, revealing perhaps stresses and strains and difficulties which, while they do not excuse the offence or even wholly explain it, may in the interests of the accused suggest various ways of disposing of the case. Everybody knows that that is the purpose of the social inquiry report. Accordingly people are prepared to talk very frankly with probation officers, and it is in the public interest that they should do so. But if parents are faced with the possibility that, if they frankly say to a probation officer, 'Well, to some extent I was to blame for this offence, although the child was too', they are promptly going to get faced with a compensation order based on that admission made almost certainly under the cloak of confidentiality—certainly in a confidential relationship and made in the interests of the child—I think that in no time at all we shall find that parents are very much less co-operative with probation officers than they are at the moment. That would be contrary to the public interest."

12.32 The most common extraneous use of information in a report is by prison staff who can find details of an offender's needs and problems useful in planning and supervising a custodial sentence. The *National Standards for Youth Justice*[30] require PSRs, among other relevant documents to be supplied to secure or custodial centres in all instances of detention and training orders and s.91 detention sentences. Good practice suggests that this potential disclosure should be drawn to the offender's attention beforehand.

Other Reports by YOT Members etc.

12.33 Various provisions pertaining to specific non-custodial sentencing options require the court to obtain and consider reports and/or information particular to the order under consideration.

(i) *Reparation Order*: a written report under PCC(S)A 2000, s.73(5) (see para. 16.82).

(ii) *Action Plan Order*: a written report under PCC(S)A 2000, s.69(6)(a) and information about the family circumstances if the defendant is under 16 (s. 69(6)(b)) (see para. 18.05).

(iii) *Curfew Order*: information about the place proposed to be specified in the order, including information as to the attitude of any persons likely to be affected by the enforced presence of the offender, and information about

---

[29] (1981) 3 Cr. App. R.(S.) 42.
[30] n. 16, para. 8.1.3 and para 9.2.4.

the family circumstances if the defendant is under 16 (PCC(S)A 2000, s.37(8) and (9)—see para. 21.05).

Disclosure to the Offender and Defence

12.34   PCC(S)A 2000, s.157(2) specifies that where a probation officer or YOT member makes a report, other than a pre-sentence report, to any court *other than a youth court*, with a view to assisting the court in determining the most suitable method of dealing with any person in respect of an offence, the court shall give a copy of the report to the offender or his counsel or solicitor. If the offender is aged under 17 and is not legally represented, a copy need not be given to him but shall be given to his parent or guardian if present in court: s.157(3). The basis for excluding youth courts from this provision appears simply to avoid duplication of the provisions of the Magistrates' Courts (Children and Young Persons) Rules 1992, rule 10 (see para. 12.28) governing access to reports in that venue.

Information about Schooling

12.35   As noted at para. 12.10, the Magistrates' Courts (Children and Young Persons) Rules 1992, r. 10(2)(b) requires a youth court to take into consideration, among other factors, "all available information as to the general conduct, home surroundings (and) school record of the child or young person" appearing before it. Courts have long valued information from the schools attended by young offenders to assist them in these respects. The statutory duty to assist the courts arises as follows—

(a) CYPA 1969, s.9[31] places a statutory responsibility upon Local Education Authorities (LEAs) to investigate and provide information to courts dealing with children and young persons in criminal proceedings.

(b) Section 32(1) of the Education (No. 2) Act 1986 authorises LEAs to request reports for the use of the court from maintained schools within their areas.

(c) Section 103(3) of the Education Reform Act 1988 places a similar duty on grant-maintained schools to provide LEAs with the information they require to carry out their functions.

12.36   Prior to the 1991 Act a number of research studies[32] had highlighted both the importance attached by magistrates to school reports, given that teachers could be considered to have far more extended and detailed knowledge of juveniles appearing before the courts, and the wide scope of the observations and remarks contained in school reports, often of a very negative or unsubstantiated nature and based on hearsay, supposition, rumour or prediction about the juvenile's behaviour or background.

With these concerns in mind the Department for Education[33] has sought to promote greater consistency, fairness and good practice by providing guidance primarily to ensure that reports "should be comprehensive, unbiased and factual. They should have a primarily educational focus and be specific to the school experience . . . In the interests of justice, judgement and opinions should be

---

[31] See para. 12.07.
[32] *e.g.* Brown (1), n. 1
[33] *School Reports to the Courts* (Department for Education, London, 1992).

substantiated".[34] In a more detailed checklist of pointers, the guidance states that reports should: be balanced, describing strengths as well as weaknesses; avoid moral judgements and innuendo; not make unsubstantiated allegations; reflect the fact that the school's knowledge of the juvenile is not comprehensive; disclose any family or health information only on a strictly need-to-know basis; incorporate information from other agencies appropriately and sensitively. Matters relating to the school record are identified—

12.37

> *Achievement:* Performance should be related to age and potential and compared with that of other pupils in the class of similar ability. Care should be taken to identify successes as well as failures, and positive as well as negative attributes. Application motivation are equally important. Where a pupil has a statement of special educational needs which includes a direct reference to education, this should be mentioned in the report. Under the Education (Special Educational Needs) Regulations 1983 rule 11(a) a statement should not be disclosed without the consent of the child's parents, subject to certain exceptions including "on the order of any court for the purposes of any criminal proceedings".
>
> *Attendance:* This should be factual, recording the actual number of half days attended out of a total possible. A reasonable base period should be taken, *e.g.* two consecutive terms or an academic year. The pupil's record should be set in the context of the normal pattern for the year group in the school.
>
> *Behaviour:* Report writers should be able to substantiate their judgements and opinions, for example by reference to particularly serious incidents, regular occurrences of misbehaviour, any period of exclusion, temporary or permanent, or time spent in a special unit. The facts should be fairly presented and a moralistic tone avoided. Where teachers hold conflicting views, the report should attempt to provide a balanced picture by drawing attention to them. Appropriate weight should be given to strengths as well as weaknesses. Hearsay comments about behaviour out of school hours should be excluded.

12.38   As regards home surroundings, the school report should be restricted to information which the school can verify from its own knowledge of the pupil. Relevant factual information on parental attitudes to, and co-operation with the school, including attendance at parents' evenings, ensuring that homework is completed, and co-operating in disciplinary procedures, may be useful. But schools should bear in mind that a seemingly negative or indifferent attitude may not necessarily indicate an uncaring parent. Work demands, coping as a single parent or language difficulties may inhibit parental involvement.

The report writer should ideally be a teacher with current knowledge of the pupil and the guide suggests that advice should be sought from the Education Welfare Service, the School Health Service or an educational psychologist where this would throw helpful light on the pupil's attendance, behaviour or health.

Bearing in mind that the report will be disclosed to the parent and the juvenile's legal representative and, in most cases, to the juvenile, consultation and discussion

---

[34] *ibid.,* p.4.

with the parent and pupil about the report's contents before it is finalised should be regarded as good practice.

12.39 The guide offers very sensible advice which should help to avoid the submission of irrelevant or unsubstantiated material to sentencers. It is also clear that school reports should not seek to replace pre-sentence reports and that they should not contain sentencing recommendations or proposals. It is anticipated that school reports will complement pre-sentence reports. The possibility of discrepancies between school reports and those submitted by another agency is acknowledged and the advice is given that "it would be helpful to the court if discrepancies could be resolved wherever possible, whilst recognising that school reports are independent documents".

12.40 What the Department for Education guidance does not address is the crucial issue of the validity of submitting a school report to a court dealing with a criminal offence and how educational information should legitimately affect sentencing decisions. While maximum social information may be advantageous to a tribunal seeking to promote the future welfare of the juvenile, the broad requirement of CYPA 1933, s.44 upon the court to have regard to the welfare of the child or young person is now subject to the approach to sentencing introduced by the 1991 Act. This permits the court to mitigate sentence by taking into account such matters as, in the opinion of the court, are relevant in mitigation of sentence. Should juveniles be in a different position from other defendants in having their performance in an area of their lives not directly related to the offence before the court being made subject to a special and separate report simply because of their status as pupils in compulsory state education? If, say, an adult offender is serving in the Armed Forces, would it seem appropriate for the court to receive routinely a report about the individual's absentee rate, work, behaviour and disciplinary record from their commanding officer? If relevant aspects of an adult offender's life should be properly addressed in the pre-sentence report, following whatever consultation seems appropriate in the light of any views expressed by the offender, it is difficult to maintain that a young offender should be in a different position.

12.41 It should be noted that school reports can be sought and considered by the court after the young person has left school, thus making the legitimacy of such information even more questionable. The court may also receive a school report even though a pre-sentence report has not been required. As the Department for Education guidance notes, practice in this regard varies between areas, as does the availability of school reports which, a recent survey suggests, is for the most part—possibly as a result of changes in the management of schools—at a much lower level than magistrates would wish to see.[35] The case for reviewing the anomalies of CYPA 1969, s.9 and for placing juveniles on the same footing as adults, subject simply to pre-sentence report requirements, appears strong and urgent.

12.42 The *National Standard for Pre-Sentence Reports* issued in 1995[36] required the report writer, in every case where the young offender was of school age, to obtain information from the school, pupil referral unit or local education authority concerning the pupil's attendance, behaviour and performance, for use in the section of the report dealing with relevant information about the offender, adding: "In cases where the court orders additional information from the school this should be attached to the PSR." In an analysis of PSRs on 270 young offenders aged 10–15

[35] C. Ball (1995) *op. cit.*
[36] *National Standards for the Supervision of Offenders in the Community* (Home Office, 1995) Part 2, para. 37.

appearing in four youth courts, Ball and Connolly[37] found that educational information was sparsely provided, with widespread failure to comply with the 1995 guidelines, though fewer than one-third were reported to be attending school at the time when the report was written. The *National Standards for Youth Justice* make no reference to inclusion of information pertaining to the offender's education. In questionnaire returns from 265 magistrates serving the four courts studied, Ball and Connolly found that 60 per cent of justices reported feeling dissatisfied about the quality and relevance of the educational content of PSRs, while it was apparent that respondents valued school-based information, were critical of the perceived lack of concern about educational matters among youth justice workers, and considered there to be important links between educational failure and youth crime.

Medical and psychiatric reports

Youth courts

12.43 PCC(S)A 2000, s.11(1) gives magistrates the power to adjourn a case to enable a medical examination and report to be made if the following conditions are met—

(i) the defendant is charged with an offence punishable, in the case of an adult, with imprisonment on summary conviction;

(ii) the court is satisfied that the accused "did the act or made the omission charged" (in other words, the remand may in certain instances be ordered prior to conviction);

(iii) the court is of the opinion that inquiry ought to be made into the defendant's physical or mental condition.

12.44 The defendant may be remanded in custody or to secure accommodation for not more than three weeks at a time, or on bail for not more than four weeks at a time: s.11(2). Where bail is granted, s.11(3) requires the court to impose conditions under the Bail Act 1976 s.3(6)(d) that the defendant—

(a) undergoes medical examination by a registered medical practitioner or, where the inquiry is into his mental condition and the court so directs, two such practitioners;

(b) for that purpose, attend such an institution or place, or on such practitioner, as the court directs and, where the inquiry is into his mental condition, comply with any other directions which may be given to him for that purpose by any person specified by the court or by a person of any class so specified.

12.45 The Mental Health Act 1983, s.35 makes separate provision for the court to remand a defendant to hospital for a report on his or her mental condition where the following conditions are met—

(a) Either—

---

[37] C. Ball and J. Connolly, "Requiring School Attendance: A Little Used Power" [1999] Crim. L.R. 183–194. See also 20.36.

> (i) the defendant has been convicted of an offence punishable, in the case of an adult, with imprisonment on summary conviction, or
> (ii) the court is satisfied that the offender "did the act or made the omission charged", or
> (iii) the defendant has consented to the exercise of this power.

(b) the court is satisfied, on the written or oral evidence of a doctor that the defendant may be suffering from mental illness, psychopathic disorder, severe mental impairment or mental impairment;

(c) the court is of the opinion that it would be impracticable for a report on the offender's mental condition to be made if the defendant were remanded on bail;

(d) the court is satisfied on the written or oral evidence of the doctor who would be responsible for making the report (or someone representing the hospital managers) that arrangements have been made for the defendant's admission to hospital within seven days of the date of remand.

12.46   Such a remand shall be for not more than 28 days at a time but the defendant may be further remanded, though for no longer than 12 weeks in total. Power of further remand may be exercised in the defendant's absence if he or she is legally represented and the legal representative is given an opportunity to be heard. The court may terminate the remand at any time if it appears appropriate to do so.[38] The defendant so remanded is entitled to obtain an independent medical report at his or her own expense from a doctor of his or her choice and may apply to the court on the basis of such a report for the remand to hospital to be terminated.[39]

The Crown Court

12.47   Though no specific provisions govern the obtaining of medical reports by the Crown Court, the Court may exercise its inherent power to adjourn following conviction on indictment or committal for sentence to enable a report to be prepared. The Court has the same powers as magistrates to remand the defendant to hospital for reports under the Mental Health Act 1983, s.35, with one difference, namely that the Crown Court can also remand an accused person awaiting trial for an offence punishable with imprisonment in the case of an adult.[40] The Crown Court may not exercise this power in respect of a convicted person if the sentence for the offence is fixed by law.[41]

Circumstances in which medical reports are necessary

12.48   Reports from medical practitioners are required as follows—

(a) Before passing a custodial sentence

PCC(S)A 2000, s.82(1) places a general duty upon a court to obtain and consider a medical report upon a defendant "who is or appears to be mentally disordered" before passing a custodial sentence. By s.82(5) "mentally disordered" means

---

[38] section 35(7).
[39] section 35(8).
[40] section 35(2)(a).
[41] section 35(3).

suffering from a mental disorder within the meaning of the 1983 Act (*i.e.* mental illness, arrested or incomplete development of mind, psychopathic disorder and any other disorder or disability of mind: MHA 1983, s.1(2)). A medical report means "a report as to the offender's mental condition made or submitted orally or in writing by a medical practitioner approved under MHA 1983, s.12".[42] It does not need to be written and may be an oral report, for example by the court's duty psychiatrist, if such a scheme is in operation. This duty to obtain a report is subject to the caveat in s.82(2) that a court is not bound by s.82(1) if, in all the circumstances, the court is of the opinion that it is unnecessary to obtain a report.

Before passing a custodial sentence on a mentally disordered offender for any offence the court must consider.[43]—

(a) any information which is before it which relates to the offender's mental condition, whether given in a medical report, a PSR or otherwise; and

(b) the likely effect of such a sentence on that condition and on any treatment which may be available for it.

A medical report is almost certainly the most appropriate way for such issues to be addressed, though it may be that a pre-sentence report can convey the conclusions of any psychiatric assessment that has been undertaken.

If the court fails to obtain a medical report where required to do so, the Act provides the familiar safety net that sentence will not thereby be invalidated but, in any appeal against sentence, the court must obtain and consider a medical report.[44]

(b) Before making a hospital order, interim hospital order or guardianship order

12.49 Under the Mental Health Act 1983, ss. 37 and 38, the court must be satisfied on the oral or written evidence of two medical practitioners that the offender is suffering from mental disorder within the meaning of the Act such as to warrant the making of an order. One of the doctors must be a psychiatrist approved by the Home Office[45] and, in the case of an interim hospital order, one of the doctors must be employed at the hospital where the offender is to be detained. If a medical report is submitted in evidence, a copy must be given to the defence solicitor.[46] In the unlikely event that the defendant is unrepresented, he or she is not entitled to receive a copy but the gist of the report should be disclosed to the defendant.

The detailed provisions relating to the requirements, duration, enforcement and discharge of hospital and guardianship orders appropriate in rare instances for mentally disordered juveniles under the Mental Health Act, and supervision and treatment orders under the Criminal Procedure (Insanity) Act 1964 are not outlined in this volume and reference should be made to Stone.[46a]

(c) Before making a supervision order or a community rehabilitation order including a requirement of mental treatment

12.50 Under PCC(S)A 2000, Sched. 6 para. 6 before including a requirement of treatment for mental condition in a supervision order, the court must have evidence

---

[42] s.82(6).
[43] s.82(3).
[44] s.82(4)
[45] MHA 1983, s.54(1)
[46] section 54(3)(a)
[46a] N. Stone (forthcoming) *A Companion Guide to Mentally Disordered Offenders* (2nd ed., Shaw & Sons, Crayford).

from a medical practitioner approved for the purpose of MHA 1983, s.12, that the offender's mental condition is such as requires and may be susceptible to treatment. Similar pre-conditions apply before such a requirement may be included in a community rehabilitation order under PCC(S)A 2000, Sched. 2, para.5 (see 22.50).

The provisions of PCC(S)A 2000, ss.156 and 157 requiring disclosure of pre-sentence and other reports by YOT members and probation officers do not apply to medical or psychiatric reports prepared by other professionals.

PROCEDURAL CONSIDERATIONS

Time Limit and Expedited Cases

12.51   Section 22A of the Prosecution of Offences Act 1985, inserted by CDA 1998, s.44, empowers the Secretary of State to make regulations governing the maximum period which may elapse in the passage of prosecution of a young offender aged under 18, including (s.22A(1)(b)—

> "with respect to a person convicted of an offence who was under (the age of 18) at the time of his arrest for the offence or (where he was not arrested for it) the laying of the information charging him with it, as to the period within which the stage between his conviction and his being sentenced for the offence should be complete."

Such limits will apply whether the young offender is remanded on bail or in custody. This provision does not permit a court to allow any extension of the time limit. The aim is to seek to expedite the prosecution of "persistent young offenders", defined by the Home Office[47] as—

> "a person aged 10 to 17 who has been sentenced by any criminal court in the United Kingdom on three or more separate occasions for one or more recordable offences and, within three years of the last sentencing occasion is subsequently arrested or has an information laid against him for a further recordable offence."

This priority entails a demand for speedier preparation of pre-sentence reports (see 12.22). The *National Standards for Youth Justice*[48] specify that reports concerning persistent young offenders must be produced within 10 working days of request.

Remittal to another youth court

12.52   Instead of sentencing a juvenile following conviction, a youth court has discretion instead to remit the case to a youth court acting "for the place where the offender habitually resides": PCC(S)A 2000, s.8(2)(b), see 13.01. The court must inform the juvenile and their parent(s) and explain its decision in pursuance of the Magistrates Courts (Children and Young Persons) Rules, r. 11 (see 12.55). The court receiving the remittal may deal with the offender in any way in which it might have dealt with him if he had been tried and convicted by that court.

12.53   Once seized of the case, the court has all the powers which it would have had if it had dealt with the matter in the first place. This includes power to allow a

---

[47] *Delays in the Youth Justice System* (Home Office, 1997) Annex C.
[48] n. 16, para. 6.8.2.

change of plea and to conduct a trial of the allegation to which the defendant pleaded guilty before the remitting court: *Stratford Youth Court ex p. C.*[49] In the event that the court to which the case is remitted is a long distance from the remitting court, this could create no little inconvenience for witnesses. The remitting court presumably would also have power to remit to a further youth court if the young person has changed his area of habitual residence.

Age and jurisdiction

CYPA 1963, s.29

Where proceedings in respect to a young person are begun . . . for an offence and he attains the age of 18 before the conclusion of the proceedings, the court may deal with the case and make any order which it could have made if he had not attained that age.

12.54 The scope of section 29 appears extremely broad but has been qualified by the decision of the House of Lords in *Islington North Juvenile Court, ex p. Daley*[50] in regard to mode of trial. However, it appears to have clear application where a juvenile pleads guilty or is found guilty while aged under 18 but attains the age of 18 prior to sentence. This interpretation was accepted by the Divisional Court in *St. Albans Juvenile Court, ex p. Godman*[51] and approved in *Lewes Juvenile Court, ex p. Turner.*[52]

Explanation of Proposed Sentence or Order

12.55 A youth court has a duty to explain the manner in which it proposes to deal with the case and the effect of any order to be made and, in regard to the former, must allow opportunity for representations or comment to be made.

Magistrates' Courts (C & YP) Rules 1992, r. 11

(1) Before finally disposing of the case or before remitting the case to another court in pursuance of PCC(S)A 2000, s.8 the court shall inform the relevant minor and his parent or guardian, if present, or any person assisting him in his case, of the manner in which it proposes to deal with the case and allow any of those persons so informed to make representations; but the relevant minor shall not be informed as aforesaid if the court considers it undesirable so to do.

(2) On making any order, the court shall explain to the relevant minor the general nature and effect of the order unless, in the case of an order requiring his parent or guardian to enter into a recognisance, it appears to it undesirable so to do."

Deferment of Sentence

Power to Defer Sentence

12.56 Power to defer the passing of sentence following a finding of guilt, under PCC(S)A 2000, s.1, is intended to enable the court which eventually passes sentence to have regard to:

---

[49] [1997] Crim. L.R. 212.
[50] [1983] 1 AC 347.
[51] [1981] Q.B. 964.
[52] [1984] 149 J.P. 186.

(a) the offender's conduct after conviction (including where appropriate, the making by him of reparation for his offence); or

(b) any change in the offender's circumstances.

The court must be satisfied that, having regard to the nature of the offence and the offender's character and circumstances, deferment would be in the interests of justice.

Where a court has a duty to make a referral order under PCC(S)A 2000, s.17(1), the court has no discretion to defer sentence (s. 19(7)—see 16.19.

Length. The date to which sentence is deferred is fixed at the time of deferment at the discretion of the court but shall not be more than six months after the date on which deferment is announced.

Remand. In deferring sentence, the court shall be regarded as exercising power of adjourning the trial under MCA 1980, s.10(1). The offender is released without being subject to remand on bail. Additionally, s.1(4) states—

"Notwithstanding any enactment, a court which under this section defers passing sentence on an offender shall not on the same occasion remand him."

Consent. The offender must consent to deferment and this should be sought in open court. The statute does not require the consent of the parent or guardian in respect of a child defendant aged under 14 though deferment is probably an unlikely option for this age group.

Appropriate Use of Deferment

12.57 Given the strong value now accorded to avoidance of delay in dealing with young offenders and maximising their taking active responsibility for their criminal actions and the consequences, and in the light too of the increased range of measures intended to engage young offenders in programmes to reduce the likelihood of reconviction, the use of deferment may be considered a less valuable feature of youth justice.[52a] The following observations have been made of the worth of deferment without specific reference to defendants aged under 18.

"(Deferment) may be summarised as an agreement between the court and the defendant that if the defendant does what is expected of him during the deferment, he will not receive the severe sentence—normally one of custody— which the offence might otherwise warrant."[53]

Power to defer sentence was recommended by the Advisory Council on the Penal System[54] which felt that it would sometimes be advantageous for the court to

"see how in fact the offender does behave. If the offender has shown by his conduct that he genuinely intends to try to make a fresh start, the court can

---

[52a] In a speech to the Magistrates' Association, October 28, 2000, the Lord Chancellor, observing that he had heard that "relatively few" youth courts were still deferring sentence, stated: "Given the range of sentencing options now available to the court, I urge you to consider most critically whether it is ever in the interests of the young person to defer final disposal."

[53] *Sentence of the Court* (1990), para. 3.24.

[54] *Non-Custodial and Semi-Custodial Penalties* (HMSO, London, 1970) Chap. 4, para. 72.

then more readily gauge the right penalty for his offence. Thus the deferment of sentence has the merit of involving sentencers in the reformative effect of the criminal process."

12.58 The Council anticipated two distinct categories of cases where power of deferment would be helpful—

"(a) to ensure future good conduct or to enable the court to await the happening of an event, *e.g.* the obtaining of specific employment or the return of the offender to his family home; and

(b) to await the outcome of the offender's undertaking to make reparation to his victim."

"We are firmly of the opinion that there is a definite place in the penal code for the deferment of sentence to provide an opportunity for the offender to show good behaviour, to repay money which he has acquired dishonestly, to pay compensation for damage which he has caused maliciously, or to perform some other act which would indicate ability to stay out of trouble."

Deferment is thus a means of allowing the offender additional time to earn specific post-offence mitigation (now under PCC(S)A 2000, s.158(1), knowing that the court will give due credit if that time is put to good use and expectations are fulfilled. The principal concerns arising from deferment designed to promote "good conduct" have been, firstly, whether the defendant is clear what conduct is expected of him or her and, secondly, whether the desired conduct could be better promoted by other means, for example by a probation order, perhaps containing specific additional requirements. The 2000 Act includes specific mention of reparation as a possible consideration in identifying the court's expectations of the offender's conduct, thus reflecting the new prominence of reparative justice principles.

12.59 Following a number of appeals by dissatisfied defendants, coupled with research evidence that deferment was being used in some cases simply as a compromise where a court was reluctant to follow the advice given in a probation report[55] or even as a device to side-step difficult cases, the Lord Chief Justice gave a guideline judgement in *George*[56] Lord Lane C.J. made clear that the expectations of the sentencer should be clearly spelt out at the time of deferment and that deferment should be reserved for cases which cannot be dealt with in any other way.

"In many cases a short probation order may be preferable to a deferment of sentence. Such an order enables the defendant's behaviour to be monitored by the probation officer; it ensures that formal notice of the requirements of the court are given to the defendant.

On the other hand a deferment of sentence will be more appropriate where the conduct required of the defendant is not sufficiently specific to be made the subject of a condition imposed as part of a probation order without creating

---

[55] J. Corden and D. Nott (1980) "The Power to Defer Sentence," B. J. Crim, 20 at 358.
[56] [1984] 1 W.L.R. 1082.

uncertainty in the mind of the probation officer and the defendant as to whether there has been a breach of the order; for example, where the defendant is to make a real effort to find work, or where the sentencer wishes to see whether a change in the defendant's attitude and circumstances, which appears to be a possibility at the time of deferment, does in fact come about. Again, deferment may be the appropriate course where the steps to be taken by the defendant could not of their nature be the subject of a condition, for example where he is to make reparation, or at least demonstrate a real intention and capacity to do so.

These are only examples. It is unnecessary and undesirable to attempt an exhaustive definition of the circumstances in which the procedure should be employed. It is sufficient to say that it should not be adopted without careful consideration of whether the sentencer's intentions could not best be achieved by other means, and that if deferment is decided upon, care must be taken to avoid the risk of misunderstanding and a sense of injustice when the defendant returns before the court."

12.60   *Skelton*[57] presents an example of circumstances where a short probation order would have been more appropriate. The basis of the deferment was that the offender should fulfil his undertaking to receive voluntary in-patient treatment at a psychiatric hospital. The Court of Appeal said that the purpose of deferment is to see if the offender is capable of behaving himself, not to impose some form of discipline, residence or treatment. There is not, however, a neat dividing line between legitimate and improper expectations during deferment. Take, for example, an offender who is repeatedly offending because of alcohol dependency and who is now indicating the intention to seek the assistance of a specialist clinic and advisory centre. Though a condition of attendance at such a project could be a requirement of a community rehabilitation order,[58] deferment has the advantage of giving the offender the responsibility and incentive to seek help on a flexible and voluntary basis, without involving the project in any formal supervisory responsibilities.

Within the framework of sentencing since CJA 1991, deferment will probably be most appropriate where the offence is of sufficient seriousness to be at least at the threshold of custody but the court is minded to pass a non-custodial sentence if the offender takes advantage of an opportunity which holds real promise of diversion from further offending. Deferment may also give important clues about the suitability of the offender for alternative community sentences.

Procedure When Deferring Sentence

12.61   To avoid lack of clarity and subsequent understandable sense of grievance for the defendant, Lord Lane proposed the following guidelines in *George*[59]—

1.   The court should make it clear to the defendant what particular purposes of deferment it has in mind and what conduct is expected of him or her and what steps, if any, he or she is expected to take during deferment.

2.   It is essential that the deferring court should make a careful note of what has been said to the defendant.

---

[57] [1983] Crim. L.R. 686 CA.
[58] Under PCC(S)A 2000, Sched. 2, para. 6.
[59] [1984] 1 W.L.R. 1082.

3. Ideally, the defendant should be given notice in writing of what he or she is expected to do or refrain from doing, so that there can be no doubt in his or her mind.

Sentencing at the End of the Deferment Period

12.62 Section 1(5)(a) specifies that in passing sentence following the deferment period, the court has "power to deal with him, in respect of the offence for which passing sentence has been deferred, in any way in which it could have dealt with him if it had not deferred passing sentence". (Section 1(5)(b) clarifies that this power includes scope for a magistrates' court to commit the offender to the Crown Court but this is no longer an option for offenders aged under 18.) The wording of s.1(5)(a) indicates that an offender who has attained the age of 18 in the interim is dealt with by use of the powers that were available to the court at time of deferment, so that the court utilises disposals available in respect of a young person. If the court thus makes a detention and training order, s.106(6) applies to treat that sentence as a term of YOI detention (now imprisonment) (see 28.10).

Court composition: Where possible, the court should have the same composition as the deferring court. If this is not possible, it should be fully appraised of the reasoning of the deferring court.[60] Counsel who appeared for the defendant at the time of deferment should regard themselves as bound to appear when the defendant returns for sentence.[61]

Task: As outlined by Lord Lane C.J. in *George*[62]—

> "The task of the court which comes to deal with the offender at the expiration of the period of deferment is as follows. First the purpose of the deferment and any requirement imposed by the deferring court must be ascertained. Secondly the court must determine if the defendant has substantially conformed or attempted to conform with the proper expectations of the deferring court, whether with regard to finding a job or as the case may be. If he has, then the defendant may legitimately expect that an immediate custodial sentence will not be imposed. If he has not, then the court should be careful to state with precision in what respects he has failed.
>
> If the court does not set out its reasons in this way, there is a danger, particularly where the sentencing court is differently constituted from the deferring court, that it may appear that the former is disregarding the deferment and is saying that the defendant should have been sentenced to immediate imprisonment by the latter: see *Glossop* [1981] 3 Cr. App. R.(S.) 347."

12.63 As Lane C.J. indicates, the offender who conforms to stated expectations can legitimately expect a non-custodial sentence. Mere avoidance of further offending will not, however, suffice. In *Smith*,[63] a defendant convicted of burglary was expected to work regularly and reduce his alcohol consumption during deferment. The Court of Appeal upheld his eventual custodial sentence because he had failed to achieve either objective. If the offender has substantially conformed but has failed to meet expectations in some minor respect, a custodial sentence would not be justified.

---

[60] *Gurney* [1974] Crim. L.R. 472.
[61] *Ryan* [1976] Crim. L.R. 508.
[62] [1984] 1 W.L.R. 1082.
[63] (1976) 64 Cr. App. R. 116.

In *Smith*[64] the defendant convicted of social security fraud had been expected to stay in work, behave sensibly, see a probation officer and try to repay the dishonestly obtained sum. He had failed only in the latter respect and had a good excuse for the default. His eventual custodial sentence was quashed.

12.64 *Reports:* In deciding whether and to what extent an offender has conformed or complied, a pre-sentence report (or an update on any such report available at the time of deferment) will very probably be sought. To avoid unnecessary delay, this should be requested at the time of deferment.

Delay of date: A defendant under a deferred sentence should be dealt with as nearly as possible on the due date to which the sentence was deferred[65] but if sentencing takes place on a later date for some exceptional reason the court is not deprived of jurisdiction.[66] If delay does occur, this can be reflected in the sentence eventually passed. If the delay is really excessive in any particular case, it is always possible for a judge to grant an absolute discharge.[67]

Unresolved criminal charges: Offences allegedly committed during the deferment period which are not resolved by the end of that period should not influence the eventual sentence.[68] Power to postpone sentence until pending proceedings have been completed should not be exercised "save where there are strong reasons which make it necessary for the judge, before deciding what he is going to do, to know the result of the trial of the other outstanding charges" *per* Roskill L.J. in *Ingle.*[69]

No power to re-defer: The court dealing with the offender following a period of deferment does not have the option to defer sentence further.[70]

Non-appearance: If the offender does not appear on the date fixed, the court may either issue a summons requiring appearance or a warrant for the offender's arrest.[71]

Sentencing Before the End of Period of Deferment

12.65 Though an offender subject to deferment will not ordinarily be dealt with before the end of the deferment period, s.2(1) gives power to deal with him ahead of that point if during that period the offender is convicted in Great Britain of any offence ("the later offence"), even if that offence was committed prior to deferment and whether or not the offender is sentenced for the later offence during the deferment period. In essence—

    (i) Any court in England and Wales sentencing the offender for the later offence may also sentence for the deferment offence, but a magistrates' court may not sentence for a deferment offence where sentence was deferred by the Crown Court.[72]

---

[64] (1979) 1 Cr. App. R.(S.) 339.
[65] *per* Lord Lane C.J. in *Anderson* (1983) 78 Cr. App. R. 251.
[66] see *Ingle* (1974) 59 Cr. App. R. 306 and *Anderson* (1983) 78 Cr. App. R. 251.
[67] Lane C.J. in *Anderson.*
[68] *Aquilina* [1990] Crim. L.R. 134.
[69] (1974) 59 Cr.App.R. 306.
[70] section 1(3)).
[71] s.2(4).
[72] s.2(3)(a).

(ii) Where the court dealing with the later offence is the Crown Court and the deferring court was a magistrates' court, the Crown Court exercises the same powers as a magistrates' court.[73]

(iii) Where the court that deferred sentence proposes to deal with the offender ahead of the deferment date in the light of his conviction for the later offence and where he has not already been dealt with elsewhere for the deferment offence, it may issue a summons or a warrant to secure his appearance before it.[74]

(iv) Where a court deals with the deferment offence under the provisions of s.2, it has power to act in any way in which the deferring court could have dealt with him.[75] In this respect, s.1(5)(a) (see 12.62) applies.

Notice of Conviction Before Expiry of Deferment Period

12.66 Where a magistrates' court convicts an offender of a subsequent offence during the currency of a period of deferment, the clerk of the court shall give notice of the conviction to the clerk of the magistrates' court which deferred sentence or to the appropriate officer of the Crown Court, as the case may be.[76]

---

[73] s.2(3)(b).
[74] s.2(4).
[75] s.2(6)(a).
[76] Magistrates' Courts Rules 1981, r. 27.

CHAPTER 13

Sentencing other than in the Youth Court

13.01   The provisions governing powers of "adult" magistrates' courts and the Crown Court to deal with young offenders have been significantly rationalised by the consolidating provisions of PCC(S)A 2000, s.8. "Where a child or young person . . . is convicted by or before *any* court of an offence (other than homicide)" (s. 8(1)), the starting point is the statutory presumption, formerly contained in CYPA 1933, s.56 and now specified by s.8(2), that that the case should be remitted to a youth court as the appropriate venue for sentencing young offenders.

PCC(S)A 2000, s.8

(2)   The court may and, if it is not a youth court, shall unless satisfied that it would be undesirable to do so, remit the case—

  (a)   if the offender was committed for trial or sent to the Crown Court for trial under section 51 of the Crime and Disorder Act 1998, to a youth court acting for the place where he was committed for trial or sent to the Crown Court for trial;

  (b)   in any other case, to a youth court acting either for the same place as the remitting court or for the place where the offender habitually resides;

  but in relation to a magistrates' court other than a youth court this subsection has effect subject to subsection (6) below.

13.02   From this foundation principle it is possible to trace the provisions particular to magistrates' courts and the Crown Court. However, the same consolidating section covers also the scope for a youth court to remit to another youth court, in order to allow the court sitting in the location where the young offender lives to deal with the case beyond the point of conviction. For convenience, remitting in such circumstances is dealt with in Chapter 12 at 12.52.

THE CROWN COURT

13.03   Following repeal of the power under MCA 1980, s.37 to commit a young offender for sentence (CDA 1998, Sched. 8), the Crown Court usually deals with young offenders only at trial on indictment. The powers in respect of defendants aged under 18 available only to the Crown Court are as follows—

  (a)   detention under PCC(S)A 2000, s.91;

  (b)   restriction order under the Mental Health Act 1983, s.41;

(c) fine or compensation order without statutory limit;

(d) confiscation order under the Drug Trafficking Act 1994.

13.04 In all other significant respects the power of the Crown Court in dealing with a young offender committed for trial or sent to the Crown Court without need of committal under CDA 1998 s.51(5) (where charged jointly with an adult) is identical to that of a youth court and unless the higher court proposes to use one or more of its unique powers the presumption in s.8(2) applies. Upon remittal to a youth court, that court "may deal with him in any way which it might have dealt with him if he had been tried and convicted by that court": s.8(3). The offender has no right of appeal against the decision to remit (s. 8(5) or, by implication, a decision not to remit) but a right to appeal against any order of the court to which the case is remitted remains unaffected. The remitting court sends a certificate to the justices' chief executive for the relevant youth court setting out the nature of the offence and confirming the offender's conviction: s.8(4)(b). Under s.8(2)(a) the case is remitted to a youth court acting not for the place where the young offender resides but for the place where he was committed for trial or was sent for trial. If the defendant lives elsewhere, it would appear not to be open to the youth court receiving the case from the Crown Court to further remit the matter under s.8(2)(b) since it is not the court by which the defendant was convicted (s. 8(1)) and is thus not empowered to remit under s.8(2).

13.05 Interpretation of the discretion given to the Crown Court under the predecessor to s.8(2)[1] to retain sentencing responsibility for a young offender where it would be "undesirable" to remit the case has varied. In *Holden*,[2] the Court of Appeal held that the Crown Court should remit a juvenile for sentence unless of the opinion that a more severe sentence should be imposed than the lower court had power to impose or, at the opposite extreme, felt that a very lenient disposal such as conditional discharge was appropriate, in which case remittal would unnecessarily prolong the offender's predicament. However, following the changes in the sentencing powers of the juvenile court arising from CJA 1982 which aligned the sentencing powers of the Crown Court and juvenile courts to a much greater extent, the Court of Appeal gave further guidance in *Lewis*[3] remarking that "the concept of the juvenile court being the sole proper forum in which to deal with juveniles now seems . . . to be out of place". Lord Lane C.J. suggested possible reasons where it would be undesirable to remit, a list which he said should not be viewed as comprehensive:

(a) Where there has been a trial and the presiding judge is better informed as to the facts and circumstance.

(b) Where there are adult and juvenile co-defendants and there would be a risk of unacceptable disparity if the co-defendants are sentenced in different courts on different occasions.

(c) Where remission will cause delay, duplication of proceedings and fruitless expense.

(d) If the case is remitted, appeal against conviction would be to the Court of Appeal, whilst appeal against sentence would be to the Crown Court.

---

[1] CYPA 1933, s.56.
[2] (1981) 3 Cr.App.R.(S.) 78.
[3] (1984) 79 Cr.App.R. 94.

13.06 Lord Lane added that "it may become desirable to remit the case where a report has to be obtained and the judge will be unable to sit when the report becomes available" but thought that this situation should be avoided wherever possible. The effect of this guidance gave the Crown Court almost complete scope to justify retention of sentencing responsibility, particularly on ground (c). Thus the apparent presumption of remittal has become, in effect, a working presumption that the Crown Court will retain jurisdiction.

Remand following remittal

13.07 On remitting a case under s.8(2), s.8(4)(a) specifies that a court may: "subject to CJPOA 1994 s.25 (restrictions on granting bail—see 9.02) give such directions as appear to be necessary with respect to the custody of the offender or for his release on bail until he can be brought before the youth court."

Return to prison: committal to Crown Court

13.08 Where a young offender commits a further imprisonable offence following release from a sentence of s.91 detention but before the expiry of the full term of sentence, a youth court convicting him of the fresh offence may commit him to the Crown Court under PCC(S)A 2000, s.116(3)(b) either if the time for which he can be returned to custody exceeds six months or the court feels that the matter is better dealt with by the Crown Court as that court passed the original sentence. The provisions of s.116 are detailed at 29.72.

"Adult" Magistrates' Courts

13.09 The provisions of s.8(2) have effect in a magistrates' court other than a youth court, subject to s.8(6). This specifies that where an adult magistrates' court convicts a child or young person of an offence it must exercise its power to remit under s.8(2), unless the case falls within the exceptions provided by s.8(7) and (8). In effect, the adult court retains the power to deal with the case itself if—

    (i) referral to a youth offender panel under PCC(S)A 2000, s.16(2) is a mandatory requirement. If the youth court to which the case is referred would have no choice but to make a referral order, it may seem sensible for the referral to be made direct without the delay caused by remittal. This does not affect the jurisdiction of a youth court to deal with any referral back under the provisions of PCC(S)A 2000, Sched. 1 because the court which made the referral order would not be the "appropriate court" for the purposes of that Schedule;

    (ii) the court is of the opinion that the case is one which can be properly dealt with by means of—

        (a) an absolute or conditional discharge;
        (b) a fine (subject to the maximum sum permissible for the offender's age);
        (c) a parental bind over under PCC(S)A 2000, s.150 (see 14.02).

13.10 When ordering (a), (b) or (c), the court may exercise any other order that the court has power to make when discharging an offender, absolutely or conditionally.

Whereas s.8(7) explicitly states that in respect of situation (i) above "the court may, but need not, so remit the case," these words do not appear in s.8(8) in respect of situation (ii). This appears to mean that the adult court does not have discretion to remit the case if it determines that it can properly deal with the matter by means of disposals (a), (b) or (c). If the adult court has convicted a young offender of an offence committed during the "at risk" period, *i.e.* following release from a sentence of detention under PCC(S)A 2000, s.91 but before the expiry of the full term of sentence, exposing the offender to "return to prison" under PCC(S)A 2000, s.116, it appears that the court may not commit direct to the Crown Court under s.116(3)(b) but must remit to a youth court which may then decide to exercise that discretion.

Remand following remittal

13.11 The provisions of s.8(4)(a) apply, as stated above at 13.07.

CHAPTER 14

Orders against Parents

14.01 Attempts to use sanctions to oblige parents to share greater responsibility for their children's wrongdoing have a long history. In 1890 a Bill was introduced unsuccessfully seeking to make general negligence in the care and control of a child a statutory offence. In 1989 a Minister of State at the Home Office suggested that a new offence of "failure to prevent child crime" might be introduced but this idea was soon abandoned. Instead, the Criminal Justice Act 1991 sought to reinvigorate the existing scope to hold parents to account through bind over powers by imposing a duty upon courts to bind over the parents of young offenders aged under 16 if satisfied that this would assist to prevent their child's further offending. This form of prospective sanction left parents to cope as best they could. More recently, the Crime and Disorder Act 1998 introduced a new form of proactive intervention, the parenting order, making demands upon parents to co-operate in efforts intended to assist them in their task. These two measures continue in tandem under the Powers of Criminal Courts (Sentencing) Act 2000, as described in this chapter. The responsibility of parents for financial orders is addressed in Chapter 15.

BINDING OVER TO EXERCISE PROPER CONTROL

14.02 Formerly governed by CJA 1991, s.58, this power is now provided by PCC(S)A 2000, s.150, where any person aged under 18 is convicted of an offence, imprisonable or otherwise. The power is encapsulated in s.150(2)(a).

PCC(S)A 2000, s.150

(2) The powers conferred by this section are as follows—

    (a) with the consent of the offender's parent or guardian, to order the parent or guardian to enter into a recognisance to take proper care of him and exercise proper control over him;

(3) An order under this section shall not require the parent or guardian to enter into a recognisance for an amount exceeding £1,000.

(11) For the purposes of this section, taking "care" of a person includes giving him protection and guidance and "control" includes discipline.

Duty to Bind Over

14.03 Where the offender is aged under 16 when sentenced (not at point of conviction), s.150(1) specifies that it shall be the duty of the court—

    (a) to exercise those powers if it is satisfied, having regard to the circumstances of the case, that their exercise would be desirable in the interests of preventing the commission by him of further offences; and

(b) if it does not exercise them, to state in open court that it is not satisfied as mentioned in paragraph (a) above and why it is not so satisfied;

However, this duty is qualified in the light of the provisions pertaining to referral orders and the subsection has effect subject to s.19(5) which prohibits binding over under s.150 where a referral order is made (see 16.16). The same limitation applies where a court extends a referral order following further conviction during the referral period.

The rationale for imposing this duty upon sentencers was expressed in the White Paper *Crime, Justice and Protecting the Public*,[1] to encourage more routine use of a previously little used power—

> "in ensuring that parents do all they can to stop their children reoffending. The knowledge that they may forfeit up to £1,000 if they fail to meet the terms of their recognisance would be a strong incentive to improve their supervision of their children . . . The courts will be required to consider binding over the parents . . . in every case unless it would be unreasonable in the circumstances to expect the parents to be able to exercise the required degree of supervision and control".

14.04 There is little evidence that sentencers have believed that greater use of the parental bind over is an effective way of promoting parental responsibility. A commonly held view maintains that bind over powers are either superfluous and unnecessary because responsible parents will seek to exert greater control without the need for sanctions or will prove ineffective with families experiencing high levels of disharmony, poor communication and strained relationships, together with the pressures of unemployment, bad housing and poor recreational amenities. At worst, such sanctions can be counter-productive so that instead of providing an incentive to parents to stand by their adolescents, they may encourage parents to cut off links with their children for fear of being punished on their behalf. As Allen,[2] then a Home Office adviser, has remarked—

> ". . . although it is clear that the influence of the home is important in the genesis of delinquent behaviour, and many would agree that policies which encourage the development of improved parenting skills might be useful in helping to prevent it, the idea that the criminal justice system should be used to further such policies is curiously outmoded, showing a naive faith in the power of the court to influence behaviour."

14.05 In a small-scale study of youth courts in a Welsh county between July and December 1993, soon after the 1991 Act was implemented, Drakeford[3] found that a parental bind over was used on 12 (16 per cent) of 77 sentencing occasions. In the light of interviews with parents subject to bind over, Drakeford suggested that that, far from reinforcing and enhancing parental authority, "embitterment and the erosion of productive family functioning appear to have been the result". Instead of assisting parents in controlling their children, binding over appeared to

---

[1] Cm. 965, (Home Office, London, 1990), para. 8.10.
[2] Allen R. (1990) "Juvenile Offender left out of the Act" *Childright* 70, 11–12.
[3] Drakeford M. (1996) "Parents of Young people in Trouble", *Howard Journal of Criminal Justice, 35,* 242–55.

have shifted power in the young person's favour. As one parent expressed her dilemma: "She thinks she can do what she likes now and that I'll be the one in trouble. It teaches them to be less responsible, not more." Noon,[4] a practising solicitor, has speculated that orders of this nature do not strengthen families but serve "to drive a further wedge into a family structure already cracking under various stresses and strains". He suggests that courts are justified in taking the stance that "unless there are specific facts which show that an order is called for, it cannot be satisfied that an order is desirable".

Procedural Requirements

Consent

14.06 A parent or guardian cannot be bound over unless their consent is obtained, but this is not a completely open choice because, if they refuse consent and the court considers that this refusal is unreasonable, they can be fined up to £1,000 (section 150(2)(g)).

Noon[5] has identified the problems that can face the defence advocate, firstly pointing to the conflict of interest between the young offender and his parents—

> "since any mitigation which suggests the defendant is other than utterly beyond control or redemption is quite deliberately an argument in favour of an order against the hapless parents."

He suggests that though magistrates will look to the child's advocate to address them as to a binding over order and to advise the parents, the section creates such potential for parent/child conflict that "it would be quite improper to attempt to represent both". If a parent refuses to enter into a recognisance, who should then address the court as to the reasonableness of that refusal? Noon concludes that those who drafted this legislation gave no thought to how the parental voice is to be heard.

Duration

The period of the order shall not exceed three years or until the offender's 18th birthday, whichever is the shorter (section 150(4)). In the case of a bind over to ensure compliance with a community order it is implicit that liability extends for the period of the order's duration unless the offender attains the age of 18 before the order terminates.

Amount

In fixing the amount of the recognisance, the court shall take into account, among other things, the means of the parent or guardian, so far as they appear or are known to the court.[6]

Appeal

The parent or guardian may appeal against the order (section 150(8) and (9)).

---

[4] Noon R. (1992) "Binding Over Parents under Section 58 CJA 1991: Some Practical Problems", *Justice of the Peace, 156*, 803–04.
[5] n. 4.
[6] s.105(7).

Role of pre-sentence report

14.07 Though the *National Standards for Youth Justice*[7] make no explicit reference to the possibility of a parental bind over, it is worth noting the preceding version of the *National Standard for Pre-Sentence Reports*[8] in advising reporters of their role in helping sentencers to decide on the desirability of binding over a parent. The following factors were identified as of likely relevance—

- whether the juvenile is likely to benefit from increased supervision and intervention by parents;

- whether the parents' authority and control over the juvenile would be strengthened;

- whether the parents are physically in a position to exercise the necessary degree of care and control (*e.g.* the juvenile may be living away from the parents);

- the circumstances of the offence.

Ensuring Compliance with a Community Sentence

14.08 When a court exercises its power to bind over a parent and has passed a community sentence on the offender, "it may include in the recognisance a provision that the offender's parent or guardian ensure that the offender complies with the requirements of that sentence": s.150(2). This discretion applies whether the offender is aged under 16 or is older. It does not apply where the young offender is made subject to a reparation order.

Forfeiture of Recognisance

14.09 MCA 1980, s.120 applies to this kind of recognisance when made by a magistrates' court as it does to recognisances to keep the peace (section 150(5)). Under section 120(2) a recognisance can only be forfeited by an order on complaint and only the magistrates' court which imposed the bind over can order the forfeiture. The whole or part of the recognisance can be forfeited and costs can also be ordered. Forfeiture proceedings are civil in character, requiring only the civil standard of proof. The parent or guardian shall be told the nature of the alleged breach and be given the opportunity to present evidence, call witnesses or give an explanation. The complaint would normally be that their son or daughter has been convicted of a further offence committed during the period of recognisance. It is doubtful whether other behaviour indicating a lack of proper care or control would be sufficient basis of complaint. The juvenile's conviction of a further offence does not by itself amount to a breach of the order. Parents are frequently advised to deny their liability because in practice it can be very difficult to establish that they have failed to exercise proper care or control, *e.g.* if the further offence occurred while the juvenile was attending school.

The procedure to be adopted to bring the parents before the court and to enforce the recognisance, and responsibility for conduct of the case against the parents is far from clearcut. Procedure is by way of complaint[9] but the Crown Prosecution

---

[7] Youth Justice Board (2000).
[8] *National Standards for the Supervision of Offenders in the Community* (Home Office, London, 1995).
[9] MCA 1980, s.120(2)

Service is under no duty to act and it would not be good practice for the justices' clerk to make a complaint, since this would entangle the separate roles of complainant and legal adviser to the court. It is also unclear whether parents should be proceeded against in the adult court or the youth court, bearing in mind that the latter normally has jurisdiction over matters specifically assigned to it.

The Home Office, Lord Chancellor's Department and Crown Prosecution Service expressed a joint view in a letter of May 1994 to the clerk to the Leeds Justices[10] that venue should be determined locally but encouraging choice of the youth court where magistrates are "probably better able to judge whether the parent has tried to control the child or whether the child is out of parental control". The letter also favoured the court itself instigating proceedings by way of complaint, issuing a summons to the parent to attend if need be, adding that "there seems to be no reason why the prosecutor should not point out the possible breach to the court if . . . aware of it". Whether liability arising upon a juvenile's non-compliance with a community sentence is any easier to enforce remains to be established. The liability is couched in strict terms but parents may seek to establish that they have taken all reasonable steps to ensure the juvenile's compliance and should thus not be held responsible for default. The parent or guardian does not have a right of appeal against a forfeiture order.[11]

Variation or Revocation

14.10   Under section 150(10) the court which imposed the bind over may vary or revoke the order, on the application of the parent or guardian, where in the light of any change of circumstances since the order was made, this would be in the interests of justice, either to the Crown Court or, if the order was made by the Crown Court, to the Court of Appeal.

Noon[12] has speculated that this provision may be an attractive escape route for aggrieved parents who may resort to engineering their child's departure from home to achieve a change of circumstances, thus affording them the chance to be free of liability.

PARENTING ORDERS

14.11   Introduced by CDA 1998, s.8, the parenting order reflects a wish to help parents of young offenders to develop better communication skills in handling their children, exerting more consistent discipline and exercising closer supervision. Summarising the relevant body of research, the Home Office's guidance[13] accompanying implementation of the measure nationally states:

> "Research suggests that inadequate parental supervision is strongly associated with offending. For example, a Home Office study showed that 42 per cent of juveniles who had low or medium levels of parental supervision had offended, whereas for those juveniles who had experienced high levels of supervision the figure was only 20 per cent. The same research showed that the quality of relationship between parent and child is crucial. Research also suggests that the children of parents whose behaviour towards their children is harsh or erratic are twice as likely to offend."

---

[10] cited in B. Gibson, *et al.*, *The Youth Court One Year Onwards* (Waterside Press, Windwater, 1994).
[11] *Durham Justices, ex p. Laurent* [1945].
[12] n. 4.
[13] *Parenting Order: Guidance Document* (Home Office, London, 2000) para. 2.4.

The guidance notes the evidence from the United States that training parents in negotiation skills, in sticking to clear rules and rewarding good behaviour can halve offending rates. The parenting order is thus intended to raise parental standards by offering something more constructive than the simple threat to impose a financial penalty if the child re-offends. Compulsory attendance for such training, imposed on doubtless often reluctant participants, may cause parents to feel discriminated against or stigmatised as failing or inadequate in their family responsibilities.

14.12   The order was subject of pilot trials in 11 areas, from September 30, 1998 to March 31, 2000, and became available throughout England and Wales on June 1, 2000 (see 14.32). Critics[14] remain sceptical about the merits of this initiative to promote parental responsibility, suggesting that this form of intervention in parenting, though based on notions of help and support, is in reality potentially stigmatising and criminalising, and ignores wider issues of social and economic disadvantage limiting parenting capacities. An additional basis for scepticism or wariness as to the utility of this intervention arises from the modest scope provided to tackle the substantial problems faced by many parents of young offenders. If, for example, a parent is struggling with drug dependency problems inhibiting their parenting potential and absorbing family resources, a parenting order is unlikely to make any difference to their predicamant. The theory behind this kind of initiative may not translate readily into positive outcomes.

Power to Make a Parenting Order

14.13   The parenting order is not exclusively a power of criminal courts, albeit that it is in that setting that orders will primarily be made. In addition to proceedings in which a child or young person is convicted of an offence, s.8(1) specifies that an order may also be made in any court proceedings where—

- a child safety order is made in respect of a child;

- an anti-social behaviour order or sex offender order is made in respect of a child or young person;

- a person is convicted of failure to comply with a school attendance order or of failure to secure regular attendance at school of a registered pupil (Education Act 1996, ss.443 and 444).

Parent or guardian

14.14   An order may be imposed on "a person who is a parent or guardian of the child or young person": s.8(2). While a "guardian" is defined by CDA 1998, s.117(1) by reference to CYPA 1933 (s.107), the Act does not offer a definition of "parent". Home Office guidance[15] states that for this purpose "parent"—

> "has the same meaning as that contained in the Family Law Reform Act 1987, s.1, *i.e.* either of the child or young person's natural parents whether or not they were married to each other at the time of the child or young person's birth."

Though this is not coincident with holding "parental responsibility" under the Children Act 1989, the guidance[16] seeks to identify who falls within the spirit of the intention underpinning the parenting order concept—

---

[14] *e.g.* Drakeford M. and McCarthy K. "Parents, Responsibility and the New Youth Justice" in Goldson B. (ed.) *The New Youth Justice* (Russell House Publishing, Lyme Regis, 2000). For a more positive view, see C. Henricson, J. Coleman and D. Roker (2000) "Parenting in the Youth Justice Context" *Howard Journal of Criminal Justice* 39(4), 325–38.

[15] n. 13, para. 4.8.

[16] n. 13, para. 4.10.

"A parent or guardian . . . should be involved in promoting the child or young person's welfare and fulfilling their parental responsibilities towards them. The order may be made in respect of one or both parents or guardians; it will be a matter for the court to decide based on the circumstances of the case."

14.15 Though there is no statutory requirement that a parenting order should be made only if the young offender is residing at the parental home, the clear implication of ministerial comment when the measure was under debate was that the order is intended primarily for use in circumstances where the parents exercise day-to-day responsibility. A small survey of defendants aged 11 to 16 appearing in a South Wales youth court in 1998–99 showed that only 50 percent of the sample were living with their parents.[17]

Implementation arrangements

14.16 A court may not make an order unless it has been notified by the Secretary of State that arrangements for implementing the order are available in the area in which it appears to the court that the parent resides or will reside: s.8(3).

"Relevant condition"

14.17 Before making a parenting order, the court must be satisfied that "the relevant condition" is satisfied[18] which, in respect of a young offender convicted of an offence, is as specified by s.8(6)(b): "that the parenting order would be desirable in the interests of preventing the commission of any further offence by the child or young person".

Under 16s—duty to make a parenting order

14.18 Where the defendant is aged under 16 at date of conviction and the court is satisfied that the relevant condition is fulfilled, a parenting order is mandatory: s.9(1)(a). If the court is not so satisfied, the court must "state in open court that it is not and why not": s.9(1)(b). This obligation is akin to the requirement to bind over a parent or guardian under PCC(S)A 2000, s.150 (see 14.03). In any case where the obligation to bind over applies, the duty to impose a parenting order will also apply. Where the defendant is aged 16 or over, the court has discretion whether to make a parenting order.

Parental attendance and explanation of order

14.19 Though sections 8–9 do not specify that the parent or guardian shall be present in court when an order is made, s.9(3) requires that "before making a parenting order, a court shall explain to the parent in ordinary language the effect of the order" and its requirements, the possible consequences of failure to comply and the court's power to review the order under s.9(5). Home Office guidance[18a] points to the important role parents play in supporting their children in court proceedings and implies that courts will exercise their powers to enforce parental attendance where appropriate under CYPA 1933, s.34A (see 10.03). Quite apart from the provision of s.9(3), it would appear contrary to the aim of a parenting

---

[17] n. 14.
[18] s.8(2).
[18a] n. 1, para. 4.11.

order to proceed to make an order in the absence of the person concerned. The Act makes no provision for parental representation and the same problems may arise as identified in respect of parental binding over (see 14.06).

Information to the court

14.20 Sections 8–9 do not require the court to obtain or consider a report or other information about family circumstances before making a parenting order. However, the court may well have the benefit of such report or information as part of the procedural requirements that need to be satisfied before the court can make the order which it imposes on the young offender, *e.g.* an action plan order. Home Office guidance[19] suggests that the court will wish to gain some appreciation of family circumstances, either through an oral report by a YOT member or by questioning the parent or guardian. YOTs are thus advised to pursue inter-agency liaison to ensure that information is available should it be required, so that unnecessary delays are avoided. Courts are at liberty to adjourn a case for a report as to the suitability of a parenting order and the *National Standards for Youth Justice*[20] indicate the need for agreed local guidance on circumstances in which this may be appropriate and the length of adjournments. In a small survey of pre-sentence reports on young defendants aged 11–16 appearing before a South Wales youth court[21] 21 per cent of reports offered no assessment of parents and only 15 per cent suggested a central role for parents post-sentence. This analysis of recent practice suggests that provision of information in PSRs will need to develop if courts are to make informed decisions whether to make parenting orders.

Requirements of a Parenting Order

CDA 1998, s.8

(4) A parenting order is an order which requires the parent—

  (a) to comply, for a period not exceeding 12 months, with such require-ments as are specified in the order; and

  (b) subject to subsection (5) below, to attend, for a concurrent period not exceeding three months and not more than once in any week, such counselling or guidance sessions as may be specified in directions given by the responsible officer; and in this subsection 'week' means a period of seven days beginning with a Sunday.

(5) A parenting order may, but need not, include such a requirement as is mentioned in subsection (4)(b) above in any case where such an order has been made in respect of the parent on a previous occasion.

(7) The requirements that may be specified under subsection (4)(a) above are those which the court considers desirable in the interests of preventing . . . the commission of any further offence.

14.21 Requirements specified in, and directions given under, a parenting order, shall, so far as practicable, be such as to avoid (a) any conflict with the parent's religious beliefs; and (b) any interference with the times, if any, at which he normally works or attends an educational establishment: s.9(4).

---

[19] n. 13, para. 4.19.
[20] n. 7, para. 7.5.1.
[21] n. 14.

Home Office guidance[22] describes a requirement of counselling or guidance sessions under s.8(4)(b) as "the core of the order", enabling the parent "to learn, for example, how to set and enforce consistent standards of behaviour and to respond more effectively to challenging adolescent demands". Though at the heart of a parenting order, this is not a mandatory requirement if the parent has been subject previously to such an order. It is uncertain as yet whether courts and their professional advisers will be inclined to view counselling and guidance as a one-off opportunity or as an input that can usefully be included on a repeated basis.

14.22 The second element, under s.8(4)(a) and (7), which is discretionary in that a court need not specify any such requirements, consists of "requirements on the parent or guardian to exercise control over their child's behaviour".[23] Examples are offered[24]—

- seeing that the child gets to school every day;
- ensuring that that the young person is home by a certain time each night;
- ensuring that the young offender avoids visiting certain areas, such as shopping areas, unsupervised, or avoids contact with disruptive and possibly older children;
- ensuring that the young offender attends a programme or course to address relevant problems, such as anger management or substance misuse.

The court thus has complete creative discretion in designing requirements, provided that any chosen relate to the child's offending, at least indirectly. The court may also wish to assess the enforceability of any requirement which it is considering for inclusion. Thus a requirement that relates to the private life of the family could be of doubtful value if compliance cannot be monitored. While it is relatively easy to check with an external source whether a child is attending school on time or is coming to police notice after a certain time at night, it would not be possible to check whether, say, a parent is undertaking some beneficial activity with the child in private.

14.23 Length of order. Because a requirement under s.8(4)(a) may last for as long as 12 months, a parenting order may extend beyond the period during which the young offender is subject to the measure imposed on them, for example an action plan order of three months duration. Home Office guidance[25] suggests that "the length of the parenting order could be linked to" any such order.

Responsible officer

14.24 The role of "responsible officer" in giving directions under s.8(4)(b) is undertaken by one of the following, as specified in the order (*i.e.* as determined by the court)—

  (a) a probation officer;

  (b) a social worker of a local authority social services department;

 (bb) a person nominated by the Chief Education Officer of a local authority; or

  (c) a member of a youth offending team (s.8(8) as amended by CJCSA 2000, s.73).

---

[22] n. 1, para. 3.1.
[23] n. 1, para. 3.2.
[24] n. 1, para. 5.7.
[25] n. 1, para. 3.2.

CDA 1998, s.18(3) clarifies—

"(3) Where directions under a parenting order are to be given by a probation officer, the probation officer shall be an officer appointed for or assigned to the petty sessions area within which it appears to the court that the child, or, the case may be, the parent resides or will reside."

14.25 Similarly, s.18(4) provides that where the directions are to be given by a social worker or YOT member, "the social worker or member shall be a social worker of, or a member of a YOT established by, the local authority within whose area it appears to the court that the child or, as the case may be, the parent resides or will reside". In practice, the task in respect of a parent of a young offender following conviction will invariably be undertaken by a YOT member, it being one of the statutory duties of a YOT to undertake this role.[26] Where a YOT is responsible for supervision of the young offender concerned, parallel responsibility for any parenting order will "help to ensure a coherent approach to the family situation as a whole".[27]

Though the role of "responsible officer" is identified in respect only of a s.8(4)(b) requirement and it is the responsibility of the parent appears to ensure that they comply with a s.8(4)(a) requirement Home Office guidance[28] assumes that "all elements of the parenting order will be supervised by the responsible officer" who "will be responsible for . . . ensuring that the parent complies with any other requirements which the court may impose". This assumption of authority appears to be grounded in the statutory role of the responsible officer under s.9(5) to make application for variation or discharge of the order (see 14.29). There is no statutory requirement in support of a s.8(4)(a) element that the parent shall keep in touch with the responsible officer as instructed by that officer, to allow discussion of the parent's compliance, yet such meetings are intended to be standard practice under *National Standards* expectations (see 14.28). Home Office guidance[29] indicates that the responsible officer should maintain good contact with the parent or guardian". Nor is there a specific requirement that the parent shall notify the responsible officer of any change of address. The parent may well reside at the same address as the young offender but this is not invariably the case. However, it appears open to the court to utilise s.8(4)(a) to specify requirements in respect of 'keeping in touch' and notifying change of address. It is arguable that it will be a valid exercise of the responsible officer's power to give directions under s.8(4)(b) to direct that the parent gives notice of any change of address, but this is contentious because the directions that may be given appear limited to the issue of attendance.

Offenders in care or local authority accommodation

14.26 Though there is nothing to prevent the use of a parenting order where the defendant is in the care of a local authority or living in local authority accommodation, the exercise of this power in such circumstances will need to be considered carefully. The measure may, for example, be considered appropriate where a young offender subject to a care order is living at their parental home. Home Office guidance[30] advises that a court should make a parenting order in these

---

[26] CDA 1998, s.38(4)(f).
[27] n. 13, para. 6.2.
[28] n. 13, para. 3.3.
[29] n. 13, para. 6.4.
[30] n. 13, para. 4.25.

circumstances only "where it believes that the child or young person would benefit from the help and support which could be offered by a parenting order". Participation in counselling or guidance under s.8(4)(b) (see below) could help in achieving the young offender's return to their parents.

The guidance notes that in "exceptional circumstances" "there could be a need to impose specific requirements under s.8(4)(a) on the local authority, or those acting on its behalf, to help address, for example, the child or young person's offending behaviour or any other reason why the child or young person was before the court". However, there is no provision equivalent to that in PCC(S)A 2000, s.137(8), extending power to order a parent or guardian to pay financial penalties to a local authority having parental responsibility for a child or young person and, in the light of the House of Lords judgement in *Leeds City Council v. West Yorkshire Metropolitan Police*,[31] it is open to considerable doubt whether a local authority can be made subject to a parenting order.

Appeal Against a Parenting Order

14.27 CDA 1998 s.10 provides a mechanism for appeal against a parenting order. In respect of an order made following the conviction of a child or young person of an offence,[32] s.10(4) applies.

CDA 1998, s.10

(4) A person in respect of whom a parenting order is made by virtue of s.8(1)(c) above shall have the same right of appeal against the making of the order as if—

    (a) the offence that led to the making of the order were an offence committed by him; and

    (b) the order were a sentence passed on him for the offence.

In summary, where the order is made on the conviction of the young offender by a magistrates' court, appeal is made to the Crown Court, or on case stated to the Divisional Court. If the order was made by the Crown Court, on a conviction on indictment, appeal will lie to the Court of Appeal, Criminal Division.

Management of a Parenting Order

14.28 The *National Standards for Youth Justice*[33] provide the following set of provisions and timetable for implementing and managing a parenting order.

- The YOT should be informed of the order on the same day that it is made.

- First contact between the responsible officer and the parent(s) must occur "before the end of the next working day after the order is made: (para. 7.5.2). This meeting serves the purpose of explaining the requirements of the order and agreeing a draft plan for meeting those requirements. "If the parents have contact with social work agencies, they must be invited to the meeting and their views sought."

- If the requirements involve attending sessions with someone other than the responsible officer, a pre-meeting must take place no more than two weeks before sessions are due to commence: para. 7.5.3.

---

[31] [1983] 1 A.C. 29 (see 15.34).
[32] s.8(1)(c).
[33] n. 8, Part 7.5.

- Group work sessions must take place at least fortnightly (but no more than weekly): para.7.5.4.

- When the requirements have been met, the responsible officer must meet with the parent(s) to evaluate the order: para.7.5.5.

- If the parent(s) fail(s) to comply with a requirement, including meeting an appointment, the responsible officer must make contact within one working day by visit, telephone or letter. If there is no acceptable reason for the failure, a formal warning must be issued: para.7.5.6.

- In the event of more than one unacceptable failure in a period of three months, the responsible officer must meet with the parent(s) and any other involved agency to review the order. The review must explore whether there are ways the order can be made to work, whether it should be returned to court to request variation or discharge, or whether the failure to comply should be reported to the police: para.7.5.7.

Counselling or guidance

14.29 Sessions ordered to be undertaken under s.8(4)(b) may be provided by the responsible officer or by another provider, such as a social services department or a suitable voluntary sector organisation. Sessions may be group-based or may involve individual counselling or training, depending on circumstances, including consideration of cultural and social factors. Home Office guidance[34] reports that experience during the piloting trials "suggests that this should be for no less than six or seven two-hour sessions". The responsible officer and the sessions organiser should assess progress in the light of attendance and it may be appropriate for the parent to be offered "some voluntary follow-up work when the order has been completed", such as attending a parent support group.[35]

Variation and Discharge

CDA 1998, s.9

(5) If while a parenting order is in force it appears to the court which made it, on the application of the responsible officer or the parent, that it is appropriate to make an order under this subsection, the court may make an order discharging the parenting order or varying it—

(a) by cancelling any provision included in it; or

(b) by inserting in it (either in addition to or in substitution for any of its provisions) any provision that could have been included in the order if the court had then had power to make it and were exercising that power.

14.30 Jurisdiction lies with the court which made the order, irrespective of the area where the parent resides or the local authority area served by the YOT member specified as responsible officer. Application is made by way of complaint,[36] a civil procedure governed by MCA 1980, ss.51–57 and MCR 1981, r.4 and r.98,

---

[34] n. 13, para. 5.3.
[35] n. 13, para. 5.5.
[36] M.C.R. 1981, r.114, inserted by the Magistrates' Courts (Miscellaneous Amendments) Rules 1998, r.4(4).

enabling summons to be issued to gain the attendance of a parent who is not the applicant, and for a warrant to be issued if the parent does not answer to summons. If during the period of an order a parent moves to an address located in an area different from that served by the YOT member acting as responsible officer, the order will require variation to specify a YOT member for the new area.

If an application for discharge is dismissed by the court, no further application may be made under s.9(5) by any person, except with the consent of the court which made the order: s.9(6).

Failure to Comply

14.31   The sanction for non-compliance with a parenting order is supplied by CDA 1998, s.9(7).

CDA 1998, s.9

(7) If while a parenting order is in force the parent without reasonable excuse fails to comply with any requirement included in the order, or specified in directions given by the responsible officer, he shall be liable on summary conviction to a fine not exceeding level 3 on the standard scale.

Non-compliance is a non-arrestable and non-imprisonable summary offence, punishable by fine not exceeding £1,000 (current level 3 maximum) or any other measure available for a non-imprisonable offence. It is not intended that prosecution will be initiated straightforwardly by the responsible officer as prosecutor. Rather, *National Standards for Youth Justice*[37] indicate that failure to comply should be reported to the police. Home Office guidance[38] states that the police will "give the results of their investigation to the Crown Prosecution Service who will determine whether or not a prosecution should be brought". Prosecution proceeds in an adult magistrates' court, not the youth court, and before a court with jurisdiction to deal with summary offences allegedly committed in its area, which is not necessarily the area served by the court that made the order. In addition to a defence based on denial of the alleged non-compliance, the parent may raise a defence of "reasonable excuse" for non-compliance. It may be anticipated that parents will seek to defend themselves on the basis that they have done their best to assert authority and influence over their child but to limited avail.

Parenting Orders in Action

14.32   Parenting orders were piloted in 12 areas from September 1998, resulting in 179 orders in the 13 months to October 31, 1999. One area (Sunderland) generated 73 orders while others produced very few. An evaluation of this trial period[39] found some limited evidence that "courts and possibly workers see a division of parents into the 'willing' and the 'not bothered', with the latter group being unlikely to respond and the former best treated via voluntary means". Among other reasons for the slow development of orders, the researchers identified difficulties in providing a suitably wide mix of services appropriate for the varying range of experiences and problems presented by parents.

---

[37] n. 7, para. 7.5.7.
[38] n. 13, para. 9.5.
[39] Universities of Sheffield and Hull (1999) *Youth Justice Pilots Evaluation Second Interim Report: Youth Offending Teams After One Year*, 47–48.

In a final report on the pilot trials, Holdaway *et al.*[40] report that the take-up rate had been lower than expected, 284 orders being made compared with the predicted minimum of 400, though this was attributed to the hectic phase of early YOT development and competing demands on time and energy. Whereas many YOT staff had initially anticipated that voluntary attendance would be the norm, the numbers so referred had proved low and the drop-out rate considerable. Of the orders made between October 1998 and March 2000, 62 per cent of orders originated in criminal proceedings in a youth court, two-thirds of the young offenders involved receiving either a community order or a reparation order. There was little evidence of a link between work with the parent and work with the child. About half the children were living with their mother only and women were far more numerous as recipients of orders, in a ratio of three to one. Three-month orders were made more frequently in criminal proceedings and were likely to be delivered by a group programme alone. Negligible use was made of additional requirements in orders, though one YOT had a policy of including a catch-all requirement that the parent "will comply with any reasonable request of the responsible officer". Compliance rates were relatively high, though weak communication links between course facilitators and responsible officers could occasionally make it difficult to identify attendance problems. Over a half of orders had at least one failure to attend during the order, with just over a quarter having three or more failures. Group programmes had a lower failure rate than individual work, though this may reflect the fact that this form of intervention was used with parents with highest needs. Breach proceedings were initiated in 10 per cent of orders but referral to the CPS for prosecution was regarded by YOTs as cumbersome and impractical; the CPS in one area had indicated that they regarded this task as a very low priority indeed.

Whereas many YOT staff began with a negative view of the value of parenting orders, many changed their views and now felt that compulsion was an important if regrettable necessity. Overall, parents who attended parenting programmes thought that they were left with greater influence on their children's offending and truancy, and young people to some degree echoed this view.

---

[40] S. Holdaway *et al. New Strategies to Address Youth Offending: the national evaluation of the pilot youth offending teams* Occasional Paper 69 (Home Office, London, 2001) pp.99–108.

CHAPTER 15

Discharges and Financial Penalties

DISCHARGES

Power to Discharge

15.01   PCC(S)A 2000, s.12

(1) Where a court by or before which a person is convicted of an offence (not being an offence the sentence for which is fixed by law or falls to be imposed under section 109(2), 110(2) or 111(2) below) is of the opinion, having regard to the circumstances including the nature of the offence and the character of the offender, that it is inexpedient to inflict punishment, the court may make an order either—

(a) discharging him absolutely; or
(b) if the court thinks fit, discharging him subject to the condition that he commits no offence during such period, not exceeding three years from the date of the order, as may be specified in the order.

(4) Before making an order for conditional discharge, the court shall explain to the offender in ordinary language that if he commits another offence during the period of conditional discharge he will be liable to be sentenced for the original offence.

15.02   Previously governed by PCCA 1973, s.1A to 1C, power to discharge, absolutely or conditionally, may be combined with the following orders in respect of a single offence (s.12(7)): costs, compensation or deprivation under PCC(S)A 2000, s.130 and s.143; disqualification from driving under PCC(S)A 2000, s.146; restitution under PCC(S)A 2000, s.148. If an offender is convicted of more than one offence, the imposition of a discharge does not affect the court's discretion to exercise its powers of sentence in dealing with the other offences, with the exception that where a court makes a referral order in respect of an offence, it may not deal with the offender for an associated offence by means of a conditional discharge.[1]

15.03   In 1999 the percentage of children and young persons being dealt with for indictable offences who received an absolute or conditional discharge was as follows (approximate numbers in brackets):

---

[1] PCC(S)A 2000, s.19(4)(d) (see para. 16–16).

	Males	Females
10–11	54 (298)	60 (28)
12–14	39 (3,200)	51 (700)
15–17	24 (8,500)	39 (2,100)

Source: Criminal Statistics for England and Wales, 1999

Absolute Discharge

15.04   This is the lightest measure which can be ordered following conviction and implies that the process of prosecution and the finding of guilt is sufficient response to the offence for which it is made.
Wasik[2] has suggested three main justifications for granting an absolute discharge: where the offence is venial; where the offender had low culpability or high motivation but the law does not provide a defence; where the offender has suffered collateral losses or indirect, non-judicial punishment as a result of the offence.

Conditional Discharge

15.05   There is no statutory minimum period of conditional discharge. It is sound practice for the court to explain the effect of a conditional discharge personally and directly to the offender to ensure that the juvenile understands its effect but in exceptional circumstances this may be delegated to the offender's advocate, provided that the court is satisfied that explanation has been given and understood before the order is made.[3] On making a conditional discharge, a court may, if it thinks it expedient for the purpose of the reformation of the offender, allow any person who consents to do so to give security for the good behaviour of the offender.[5]

Restriction of use following police warning

15.06   Power to make an order for conditional discharge under s.12(1)((b) is subject to the provisions of CDA 1998, s.66 governing the effect of a warning issued by a constable under s.65 of that Act. Section 66(4)(a) specifies that where a person who has been warned under CDA 1998, s.65 is convicted of an offence committed within two years of the warning, the convicting court shall not make an order for conditional discharge "unless it is of the opinion that there are exceptional circumstances relating to the offence or the offender which justify its doing so". Where it concludes that exceptional circumstances apply, the court must state in open court "that it is of that opinion and why it is": s.66(4)(b). The rationale for this curtailment is that if a young offender has gone on to re-offend within a relatively short period of the opportunity afforded by a warning, he is likely to persist in offending unless required to face responsibility for his mis-behaviour and the response of the court should be to make more active demands upon the offender, such as by means of a referral order, unless there are good reasons justifying non-intervention. This restriction on the use of conditional discharge since implementation of that aspect of the 1998 Act from April 1, 2000 is likely to curtail use of this measure significantly. Discretion to impose an absolute discharge is unaffected.

---

[2] Wasik M., (1985) "The Grant of an Absolute Discharge", *Oxford Journal of Legal Studies*, 5, 211.
[3-4] *Wehner* [1977] 1 W.L.R. 1143.
[5] PCC(S)A 2000, s.12(6).

PCC(S)A 2000, Sched. 3 para. 12 provides in respect of a community rehabilitation order or a community punishment and rehabilitation order that application may be made for the order to be revoked in the interests of justice and for a conditional discharge to be substituted. However, para. 12(9) specifies that CDA 1998, s.66(4) (above) shall have effect as if reference therein to being convicted of an offence includes reference also to an application of this nature. In other words, an application for revocation and substitution may not be granted if the offender has received a warning in the two years preceding application.

Conditional discharge made on appeal

15.07   Where an order for conditional discharge is made on appeal, it shall be deemed to have been made by the court from which the appeal was brought: s.15(2). This is of relevance in determining jurisdiction to deal afresh with the offender for the offence in the event of a further offence committed during the period of discharge.

Commission of further offences

15.08   The commission of a further offence during a period of conditional discharge is commonly referred to as a breach of conditional discharge, though the term "breach" is not used in the relevant statutory provision and may cause confusion with breach of a requirement of a community order. The provisions for dealing with the original offence for which the discharge was ordered are now contained in PCC(S)A 2000, s.13. These provisions are somewhat complex, depending upon which court granted the discharge and the court before which the offender is subsequently convicted of a fresh offence. For youth justice purposes the provisions can be conveniently summarised as follows—

15.09
   (a) If, as is likely to be the most common instance of "breach", the offender was conditionally discharged by a youth court and is subsequently convicted of a further offence by a youth court acting for the same petty sessions area, the latter court may deal with the offender for the original offence as if it has just convicted the offender of that offence.[6]

   (b) If the offender was conditionally discharged by a youth court and is subsequently convicted of a further offence by a youth court acting for a different petty sessions area, then the latter court may deal with the offender for the original offence, provided that it obtains the consent of the court which made the order.[6a]

   (c) If the offender was conditionally discharged by a youth court and is subsequently convicted of a further offence by the Crown Court, the Crown Court may deal with the offender for the original offence in any manner in which the lower court could deal with the offender, if it had just convicted the offender of that offence.[7]

   (d) If the offender was conditionally discharged by the Crown Court and is subsequently convicted of a fresh offence by a magistrates' court, including

---

[6] s.13(6).
[6a] s.13(8).
[7] s.13(7).

a youth court, the lower court may commit the offender, either on bail or in custody/local authority accommodation (depending on eligibility), to be dealt with at the Crown Court.[8]

(e) If the offender was conditionally discharged by the Crown Court and is subsequently convicted of a further offence by the Crown Court, the Crown Court may deal with the offender for the original offence as if it has just convicted the offender of that offence.[9]

(f) If a juvenile offender was conditionally discharged by a youth court or adult magistrates' court for an offence which, in the case of an adult, is triable only on indictment, any court which subsequently deals afresh with the offender for the original offence after the offender has attained the age of 18 may exercise only such powers as would be available for an "either way" offence being dealt with summarily.[10]

(g) If the offender subject to a conditional discharge is convicted of a fresh offence by a court in any part of Great Britain but is not dealt with at the same time for the original offence, then the offender may be summoned back to the court which made the conditional discharge and, if the terms of the discharge and subsequent conviction are formally proved, the court may deal with the original offence as if the offender has just been convicted of that offence by that court.[11]

In dealing afresh with the original offence, a court exercising its powers under section 13(6), (7) or (8) may make a fresh conditional discharge, though this is perhaps an unlikely prospect. If a conditional discharge is made in respect of the further offence, the court can still deal afresh with the original offence in any manner it sees fit.

Limited Effect of Conviction

15.10   PCC(S)A 2000, s.14

(1) Subject to subsection (2) below . . . a conviction of an offence for which an order is made . . . discharging the offender absolutely or conditionally shall be deemed not to be a conviction for any purpose other than the purposes of the proceedings in which the order is made and of any subsequent proceedings which may be taken against the offender under s.13.

(2) Where the offender was of or over 18 years of age at the time of his conviction of the offence in question and is subsequently sentenced under this Part of this Act for that offence, subsection (1) above shall cease to apply to the conviction.

15.11   Subsection (1) thus affords the discharged offender a degree of protection from the consequences of having a conviction, such is disqualification or disability limiting its impact primarily to subsequent criminal proceedings and the resulting exposure to being sentenced for the original offence. This protection is

---

[8] s.13(5).
[9] s.13(6)).
[10] s.13(9).
[11] s.13(1).

normally lost if the offender is convicted of a further offence and is sentenced for the original offence. As a special dispensation for youth, this loss of protection is not incurred if the offender was a juvenile at the time of the original conviction and CJA 1991 extended this advantage to 17-year-olds.

For the purpose of determining whether a defendant is eligible for a referral order, PCC(S)A 2000, s.17(5) specifies that a conditional discharge counts as a previous conviction, notwithstanding the normal consequence of s.14 (see 16.10).

Financial Penalties

15.12   Offenders aged under 18 can be ordered to pay fines, compensation and costs in the same way as adults, with some minor differences in regard to the maximum sum that may be levied, in the scope for the court to order that the parent or guardian shall be responsible for payment and in powers of enforcement.

Powers of Magistrates' Courts to Fine

15.13   The power in MCA 1980, s.32(1) to fine upon summary conviction of an offence is restricted in respect of juveniles by PCC(S)A 2000, s.135. If the adult court would have power to impose a fine exceeding £1,000 for that offence, the amount that may be imposed in respect of a young person under 18 shall not exceed £1,000.[12] If the young offender is aged under 14 and the court could otherwise have imposed a fine exceeding £250, the amount of fine shall not exceed £250.[13] Though the same limitations apply to fines imposed for summary offences, the maximum that may be imposed upon an adult offender for a summary offence under the general power of MCA 1980, s.34(3) is the level 3 maximum of £1,000, and thus within the maximum for 14 to 17 year olds.

15.14   When making a referral order, a court may not order the offender to pay a fine, either for the offence for which the order is made or in respect of any connected offence: PCC(S)A 2000, s.19(4)(b). (see 16.16).

Petty persistent offenders

15.15   In respect of offenders aged 16 or over whom the court considers a fine to be the appropriate sentence but who have an unpaid fine or fines still outstanding, a curfew or community punishment order may be made as an alternative, under PCC(S)A 2000, s.59, outlined at 16.95.

Powers of the Crown Court to Fine

15.16   PCC(S)A 2000, s.127

> Where a person is convicted on indictment of any offence other than an offence for which the sentence is fixed by law, the court, if not precluded from sentencing the offender by the exercise of some other power . . ., may impose a fine instead of or in addition to dealing with him in any other way in which the court has power to deal with him, subject however to any enactment requiring the offender to be dealt with in a particular way.

There is no statutory limit to the amount of fine which may be imposed by the Crown Court either upon an adult or a juvenile. The only exceptions arise where

---

[12] s.135(1).
[13] s.135(2).

the Crown Court is dealing with an appeal from the lower court or a breach of a conditional discharge imposed by the lower court. In both cases the lower court's maximum powers apply. The Crown Court's normal duty under PCC(S)A 2000, s.139 when imposing a fine, to make an order fixing the term of detention to be served in default under PCC(S)A 2000, s.108, is not exercisable where the offender is under 18.

Fixing the Amount of a Fine

15.17   Within the maximum stated, the statutory principles to be applied by a court in fixing the amount of any fine are specified by PCC(S)A 2000, s.128—

1. The court shall inquire into the financial circumstances of the offender[14];

2. the amount shall be such as, in the opinion of the court, reflects the seriousness of the offence[15];

3. the court shall take into account the circumstances of the case including, among other things, the financial circumstances of the offender so far as they are known, or appear, to the court.[16] Consideration of the offender's financial circumstances can have the effect of both increasing or reducing the amount of the fine.[17]

While the fine should be adjusted to take account of the offender's limited means, the Court of Appeal has indicated that a fine should nevertheless represent a "hardship", since "one of the objects of the fine is to remind the offender that what he has done is wrong".[18]

Seriousness of offence

15.18   The court's assessment of the gravity of the offence will take account of aggravating and mitigating features of the offence, including the financial gain if any to the offender. When imposing fines for a number of offences, the sentencer should consider the total proposed aggregate sentence and ensure that this is proportionate to the totality of offending (as well as being within the offender's capacity to pay): PCC(S)A 2000, s.158(2)(b). PCC(S)A 2000, s.158(2)(a) specifies that any penalty, including a fine, may be mitigated by taking into account any other penalty included in the sentence. Under PCC(S)A 2000, s.158(1)(c), the court can mitigate the amount of fine imposed by taking into account any such matters as in its opinion are relevant in mitigation of sentence.

Financial circumstances order

15.19   Where a defendant has been convicted of an offence, the court may make a financial circumstances order as a preliminary initiative before sentencing: PCC(S)A 2000, s.126(1). This order requires the offender to give the court a statement of his finances as the court specifies: s.126(3). Failure to comply without reasonable excuse is a summary offence punishable by fine not exceeding level 3:

---

[14] s.128(1).
[15] s.128(2).
[16] s.128(3).
[17] s.128(4).
[18] *Olliver* (1989) 11 Cr. App. R.(S.) 10.

s.126(4). Knowingly or recklessly making a false statement or knowingly failing to disclose any material fact is also a summary offence, punishable in the case of an adult by a maximum of three months imprisonment or a fine not exceeding level 4: s.126(5).

Recent use of fine

15.20 In 1999 the percentage of young offenders sentenced for indictable offences who received a fine was as follows (approximate actual figures in brackets)—

	Males	Females
10–11	4 (22)	4 (21)
12–14	6 (400)	6 (100)
15–17	14 (4,900)	11 (600)

Use of the fine is likely to reduce in the light of the new orders now available to or required of sentencers.

Compensation Orders

15.21   PCC(S)A 2000, s.130

(1) A court by or before which a person is convicted of an offence, instead of or in addition to dealing with him in any other way, may, on application or otherwise, make an order (in this Act referred to as a "compensation order") requiring him—

   (a) to pay compensation for any personal injury, loss or damage resulting from that offence or any other offence which is taken into consideration by the court in determining sentence; or
   (b) to make payments for funeral expenses or bereavement in respect of a death resulting from any such offence, other than a death due to an accident arising out of the presence of a motor vehicle on a road;

   but this is subject to the following provisions of this section and to section 131 below.

(4) Compensation under subsection (1) above shall be of such amount as the court considers appropriate, having regard to any evidence and to any representations that are made by or on behalf of the accused or the prosecutor.

(5) In the case of an offence under the Theft Act 1968, where the property in question is recovered, any damage to the property occurring while it was out of the owner's possession shall be treated for the purposes of subsection (1) above as having resulted from the offence, however and by whomsoever the damage was caused."

15.22 There is a statutory presumption in favour of ordering compensation and "a court shall give reasons, on passing sentence, if it does not make a compensation order in a case where" it is empowered to do so: s.130(3). Compensation may be regarded as having particular significance in youth justice, given the current emphasis on reparative justice. A court may combine a compensation order with a

referral order, reparation order or an action plan order, despite th
each to include reparative action.

An order may be made even though the injured party has not so
tion and even if there would not be a civil liability to the injured party. PCC(S)A
2000, s.131(1) limits the amount of compensation that may be ordered by a
magistrates' court to £5,000 for each offence. Young offenders are subject to the
same maximum liability. If the offender asks for other offences to be taken into
consideration, the amount ordered by way of compensation for those offences shall
not exceed the statutory maximum minus the amount of compensation ordered to
be paid in respect of the substantive offence(s): s.131(2). Thus if an offender is
convicted of an offence for which compensation of £500 is ordered, the court may
only award a maximum of £4,500 in respect of the matters taken into
consideration.

15.23 A compensation order may be made "instead of or in addition to dealing
with" the offender in any other way. Where a court considers it appropriate both
to impose a fine and to make a compensation order but the offender has insufficient
means to pay both, the court "shall give preference to compensation (though it may
impose a fine as well)": s.130(12). This implies that a fine as the punishment of the
court should be reduced or even disposed with to enable compensation to be paid.

15.24 The broad principles to be followed in making compensation orders can
be summarised thus—

(i) Compensation orders are only appropriate where the case is straightforward and clear, and the amount can be readily and easily ascertained.

(ii) In the event of a failure to agree the amount of the victim's loss, the court
should not make an order unless it has received evidence; merely hearing
representations is not enough.[19] However, complex inquiries into the scale
of loss are not appropriate. The standard of proof required is not specified
but it would seem necessary that the court should be satisfied at least on
the balance of probabilities that the particular sum is appropriate.

15.25
(iii) Where there has been no loss or damage, *e.g.* property is recovered and
there is no evidence of damage, a compensation order should not be
made.[20]

(iv) A compensation order is not precluded by the fact that the offender has
made no profit or gain from the offence.

(v) Personal injury or damage includes terror or distress directly occasioned
by the offence.

(vi) The order must be precise, making clear which amounts of compensation
relate to which offences. The fixing of a "global" figure is inappropriate,[21]
unless the offences were committed against the same victim.[22] Where there
are co-defendants, separate orders should be made against each of them.[23]

---

[19] *Horsham Justices, ex p. Richards* [1985] 1 W.L.R. 986.
[20] *Sharkey* [1976] Crim. L.R. 388.
[21] *Oddy* [1974] 1 W.L.R. 1212.
[22] *Warton* [1976] Crim. L.R. 520.
[23] *Grundy* [1974] 1 W.L.R. 139.

15.26

(vii) While there may be good grounds in principle for requiring an offender to make good the harm done, a compensation order must be realistic and should not be oppressive in effect. While an order may be appropriately combined with a custodial sentence where the offender is clearly able to pay or has good prospects on release from custody, it is often inappropriate to combine a compensation order with a custodial sentence and it may be wrong in principle for the order to be hanging over the offender's head on release, inhibiting their resettlement and possibly increasing their likelihood of re-offending.[24]

The offender's means

15.27 In determining whether a compensation order should be made and the amount to be paid, the court must have regard to the means of the offender, "so far as they appear or are known to the court".[25] The prosecution is not under a duty to establish the offender's means.[26] If the defence mitigates on the basis that the offender will be able to pay substantial compensation, the advocate is obliged to check to ensure that the necessary means exist.[27] Co-defendants can properly be required to pay different sums towards compensation if their capacity to pay is different.[28]

Costs

15.28 Young offenders are liable to be ordered to pay such prosecution costs as the court considers "just and reasonable".[29] This liability is subject to the usual limitation that where any fine imposed is for £5 or less, no order for costs should be made "unless, in the particular circumstances of the case, the court considers it right to do so".[30] In addition, where a young offender "is convicted of an offence before a magistrates' court, the amount of any costs ordered to be paid by the accused . . . shall not exceed the amount of any fine imposed on him".[31]

An order should be made under section 18 where the court is satisfied that the offender has the means and ability to pay.[32] The decision on costs must be viewed in the light of the overall financial orders made by the court.[33] The order for costs should not be out of proportion to the overall penalty. Where the offender receives a custodial sentence, an order for costs should not normally be made, given that the offender has no immediate income, but this is a matter for the court's discretion.

Responsibility for Financial Penalties Imposed on Young Offenders

Parents or guardians

15.29 Because juveniles may be without means to meet financial penalties, the parent or guardian may be ordered to pay fines, costs and compensation.

---

[24] see *Parker* [1982] Crim. L.R. 130.
[25] s.130(11).
[26] *Johnstone* (1982) 4 Cr. App. R.(S.) 141.
[27] *Coughlin* (1984) 6 Cr. App. R.(S.) 102.
[28] *Beddow* (1987) 9 Cr. App. R.(S.) 235.
[29] Prosecution of Offences Act. 1985, s.18(1).
[30] section 18(4).
[31] section 18(5).
[32] *Practice Direction (Crime: Costs)* [1989] 1 W.L.R. 625.
[33] *Nottingham Justices, ex p. Fohmann* (1986) 84 Cr. App. R. 316.

PCC(S)A 2000, s.137

(1) Where—

    (a) a child or young person (that is to say, any person aged under 18) is convicted or found guilty of any offence for the commission of which a fine or costs may be imposed or a compensation order may be made; and

    (b) the court is of the opinion that the case would best be met by the imposition of a fine or costs or the making of such an order, whether with or without any other punishment,

the court shall order that the fine, compensation or costs awarded be paid by the parent or guardian of the child or young person instead of by the child or young person himself, unless the court is satisfied—

    (i) that the parent or guardian cannot be found; or

    (ii) that it would be unreasonable to make an order for payment, having regard to the circumstances of the case."

15.30 Section 137(2) makes the same provision in regard to a fine imposed on a young offender in proceedings brought under various provisions of the 2000 Act for breach of a community order, a reparation order or the supervision element of a detention and training order (or a secure training order that pre-dates the introduction of the latter order).

In the case of a young person who has attained the age of 16, s.137(3) gives the court the power to make an order under s.137(1) and (2), rather than a duty, reflecting the view that young people of 16 or 17 should, in appropriate cases, be considered to be independent and responsible for themselves.[34]

15.31 When the duty rather than the option to order parents to pay the fines of their children aged under 16 was introduced in CJA 1991, the use of the discretion to make such an order had been used somewhat sparingly. In 1988, for example, parents had been ordered to pay in only 13 per cent of cases where fines were imposed and in 21 per cent of cases where juveniles received compensation orders. A decade later the equivalent figures (for 10- to 17-year-olds) were: 10 per cent (fines) and 23 per cent (compensation). In 1999 the detailed percentage figures for orders requiring parents to pay as a percentage of fines or compensation orders imposed on young offenders for indictable offences were as follows—

	Males		*Females*	
	Fine	*Compensation*	*Fine*	*Compensation*
10–14	34	43	26	47
15–17	8	17	8	20
10–17	10	23	10	26

15.32 *Right to be heard*: No order should be made requiring a parent or guardian to pay the sum in question without giving that parent or guardian an opportunity of being heard,[35] but an order may be made against a parent or guardian who has been required to attend and be heard and fails to do so.[36]

---

[34] *Crime, Justice and Protecting the Public*, Cm. 9651, Home Office, 1990.
[35] s.137(4).
[36] s.137(5).

Unreasonable to make an order: A parent or guardian may satisfy the court that it would be unreasonable to hold them responsible for the financial penalty, for example because they did not have charge or control of the young offender at the time that the offence was committed or because the offence did not arise out of a failure to exercise due care or control of their child.

Means and circumstances: Where the parent or guardian is required to pay, the amount is determined with reference to the financial circumstances of the parent or guardian, not the juvenile.[37] The lower maximum in respect of juveniles applies, however, whether the juvenile or the parent is required to pay. The provision of s.130(12) requiring preference to be given to compensation if there is insufficient means to pay both compensation and a fine, shall apply as if reference to the offender were a reference to the parent: s.138(1)(c).

15.33   *Financial circumstances order*:   Before ordering a parent or guardian to be responsible for a financial penalty, the court may make a financial circumstances order with respect to that person, requiring a statement of their financial circumstances to be given to the court.[38] If the parent or guardian fails to comply or otherwise fails to co-operate with the court's inquiry, the court may make such determination of their circumstances as it thinks fit.[39] Failure to comply can also render the parent or guardian liable on summary conviction to a fine not exceeding level 3 on the standard scale.[40] Making a false statement may render the parent or guardian liable to the penalties specified in s.126(5), *i.e.* imprisonment not exceeding three months or a level 4 fine.

Appeal: A parent or guardian made subject to a s.137 order by a magistrates' court may appeal to the Crown Court against the order.[41] If the order is imposed by the Crown Court, appeal lies to the Court of Appeal as if the parent or guardian had been convicted on indictment and the order were a sentence passed on conviction.[42]

15.34   *Local Authorities*   Prior to CJA 1991 and following extensive litigation involving local authorities anxious to avoid financial responsibility for young offenders in their care, the House of Lords in *Leeds City Council v. West Yorkshire Metropolitan Police*[43] had ruled that no liability lay with a local authority to pay any financial penalties imposed on juveniles in their care. Local authority responsibility was reinstated by CJA 1991 s.55(5), now superseded by PCC(S)A 2000, s.137.

PCC(S)A 2000, s.137

(8) In relation to a child or young person for whom a local authority have parental responsibility and who—

    (a) is in their care; or

    (b) is provided with accommodation by them in the exercise of any functions (in particular those under the Children Act (1989) which

---

[37] PCC(S)A 2000, s.138(1)(a).
[38] s.136(1).
[39] s.138(3).
[40] s.136(2).
[41] s.137(6).
[42] s.137(7).
[43] [1983] 1 A.C. 29.

stand referred to their social services committee under the Local Authority Social Services Act 1970,

references in this section to his parent or guardian shall be construed as references to that authority.

(9) In subsection (8) "local authority" and "parental responsibility" have the same meanings as in the Children Act 1989.

15.35 The power to order a local authority to pay any financial penalties as a parent arises only where the local authority holds "parental responsibility", as defined by the 1989 Act ("all the rights, duties, powers, responsibilities and authority which by law a parent of a child has in relation to the child and his property".[44] Parental responsibility is expressly devolved on a local authority in two instances—

(i) While a care order is in force with respect to the juvenile[45];

(ii) while an emergency protection order is in force with respect to the juvenile.[46]

15.36 The Divisional Court has ruled that PCCA 1973, s.55(5), the predecessor of s.137(8), must be interpreted narrowly and that a youth court was in error in determining that a local authority had parental responsibility for a juvenile remanded to local authority accommodation under CYPA 1969, s.23 and was thus liable to meet a compensation order.[47] Laws J. found it "difficult to conceive that this bundle of legal functions could be transferred to a local authority unless statute expressly so provided".

Local authorities may seek to avoid liability by reference to the caselaw developed prior to the House of Lords ruling in *Leeds City Council v. West Yorkshire Metropolitan Police*[48] that no liability lay with local authorities. An authority may thus argue that liability does not arise where the juvenile has been placed in a community home belonging to another local authority (or with an agency in the voluntary sector) and therefore not under its control[49] or has been returned to live at the parental home[50] or where, in the individual circumstances of the case, the authority had exercised a proper degree of care and control[51] where the authority was absolved from liability because it was not guilty of neglect or breach of its duty to the public in its management of a community home. The Divisional Court acknowledged that a community home is not a secure penal institution and staff could not keep residents under perpetual supervision). The Divisional Court has acknowledged that a local authority is in a different position from a natural parent or a guardian and may be entrusted with the care of a young person who is already an offender or of a criminal propensity. The steps the authority can take to restrain such a young person may thus be limited. It is therefore inappropriate to impose an obligation upon the authority to bear financial

---

[44] Children Act 1989, s.3(11).
[45] CA 1989, s.33(3).
[46] CA 1989, s.44(4).
[47] *North Yorkshire County Council v. Selby Youth Court Justices* [1994] 1 All E.R. 991.
[48] [1983] 1 A.C. 29.
[49] *Somerset County Council v. Brice* [1973] 1 W.L.R. 1169.
[50] *Lincoln Corporation v. Parker* [1974] 1 W.L.R. 713.
[51] *Somerset County Council v. Kingscott* [1975] 1 W.L.R. 283.

responsibility for compensation to victims of crime perpetrated by young persons in its care where the authority had done everything that it reasonably and properly could to exercise its powers over the young person and protect the public from that person's offending.[52]

15.37 *Procedure:* In *Bedfordshire County Council v. DPP,*[53] the Court of Appeal set out the procedures to be followed where a court is considering the exercise of its powers against local authorities under what is now s.137.

- In any hearing of this nature, the prosecution must be strictly neutral and should not seek to promote or advance any view, confining themselves to presenting the facts and elucidating any matters affecting the reasonableness of making a compensation order.

- If minded to make an order, the court should first notify the local authority in writing, informing the authority of its right to make representations, produce evidence and be legally represented.

- The authority should be provided with copies of any documents supplied to the court by the prosecution in support of the application for compensation.

- The authority should notify the court in writing whether there is likely to be any dispute about either the amount of compensation or as to whether such an order should be made.

- If there is any dispute as to liability or the amount, a hearing must be arranged with reasonable notice to the authority.

- In advance of such a hearing, the authority should supply the court and prosecution with copies of any documents, reports or statements on which it will rely.

- In all cases the hearing should be kept as simple as possible.

15.38 Where the local authority is required to pay a fine or compensation order, the usual requirement under PCC(S)A 2000, s.128(1) or s.130(11) that the court must have regard to the offender's means shall not apply.[54]

Where a court has determined that it is unreasonable to order a local authority to pay compensation in respect of an offence committed by a young offender in its care it is wrong to order the authority to pay the costs of the prosecution.[55]

Paying within a Reasonable Time

15.39 Fines and compensation orders should be capable of being paid off within a reasonable time. What is "reasonable" will clearly depend on the circumstances. Since *Olliver*[56] it is no longer correct to consider that the sum should be payable within 12 months, as was suggested in a number of earlier cases. Lord Lane C.J. stated in *Olliver*:

---

[52] *D. v. Director of Public Prosecutions* (1995) 16 Cr.App.R.(S.) 1040.
[53] [1996] Cr.App.R.(S.) 322.
[54] s.138(2).
[55] *Leeds City Council* (1995) 16 Cr. App. R. (S.)362.
[56] (1989) 11 Cr. App. R.(S.) 10.

"there is nothing wrong in principle in the period of payment being longer, indeed much longer than one year, providing it is not an undue burden and so too severe a punishment having regard to the nature of the offence and the nature of the offender. Certainly . . . a two-year period will seldom be too long, and in an appropriate case three years will be unassailable."

15.40   Whether fines and compensation orders should be regarded on an equal footing in this respect is difficult to say. Lord Widgery C.J. in *Bradburn*[57] said that compensation orders "should be sharp in their effect rather than protracted" and that an order which would take four years to complete was "unreasonably long".

Enforcement of Financial Penalties and Orders

15.41   If a parent or guardian is required to pay any financial penalty or order and fails to do so, enforcement proceedings take place in the adult court as if the sum had been ordered upon that parent or guardian's own conviction. If the sum was imposed upon the juvenile, the order is enforced, at least initially, against the juvenile.

At the time of making the order

15.42   When the order is initially made, the youth court may:

(i)   require the money to be paid straightaway, or

(ii) require payment within a specified period of time, or

(iii) accept payment by stated instalments.

Additionally, the court may stipulate a date upon which the offender must return to court for a means inquiry if at that time any part of the financial penalty remains unpaid. The court may also make a supervision order under MCA 1980, s.88, placing the offender under the supervision of such person as the court may appoint. This order does not require the consent of the defendant. The supervisor may be a probation officer, YOT member, social worker, or a fine enforcement officer attached to the court staff. The supervisor's duty is to "advise and befriend the offender with a view to inducing him to pay the sum".[58] The supervisor is not required to collect the fine or to decide the rate of payment but simply to encourage the offender to meet their liability. This power is not normally exercised until the offender has been given the opportunity to pay and has defaulted. If a young offender aged under 21 is liable to be committed to detention in default of payment, under PCC(S)A 2000, s.108 (*i.e.* is aged 18 or over), committal may not be ordered unless the offender has first been placed under supervision, or unless the court is satisfied that supervision is "undesirable or impracticable".[59] While subject to supervision, an offender cannot be committed to custody in default of payment unless the court has "taken such steps as may be reasonably practicable" to obtain from the supervisor "an oral or written report on the offender's conduct and means".[60] The supervision order ceases to have effect on payment of the outstanding sum, or on the making of a transfer of fines order, so that enforcement

---

[57] (1973) 57 Cr. App. R. 948.
[58] Magistrates Court Rules 1981, r.56.
[59] s.88(4).
[60] s.88(6).

responsibility is transferred to another petty sessions area, or when discharged by the court that made the order.[61]

Following a means inquiry

15.43   If the juvenile defaults on payment, the magistrates' court may issue a summons requiring the juvenile to appear before the court, or issue a warrant for his or her arrest, backed or not backed for bail.[62] If the offender does not answer to summons, a warrant may be issued.[63] The purpose of the inquiry is to determine why payment has not been made, to consider the offender's current means and to determine what measures are necessary to deal effectively with the outstanding sum. The powers of the court at this stage are as follows—

1. *Further Time to Pay*: The court may allow further time for payment, either within a fixed period or, more usually, by instalment, varying where necessary the original instalment order.[64]

2. *Remission of Fine*: The court may remit part or the whole of any outstanding fine, though if the fine was imposed by the Crown Court the consent of that Court is required. MCA 1980, s.85(1) gives power to remit, "but only if (the court) thinks it just to do so having regard to a change of circumstances which has occurred . . . since the date of the conviction". In addition, PCC(S)A 2000, s.129 empowers the court to remit a fine fixed under s.128(5) of that Act on failure to co-operate with inquiries into his financial circumstances where, in retrospect, it becomes clear that the offender's financial circumstances were not as great as originally determined.

15.44   PCC(S)A 2000, s.129

(2) If, on subsequently inquiring into the offender's financial circumstances, the court is satisfied that had it had the results of that inquiry when sentencing the offender it would

(a) have fixed a smaller amount, or

(b) not have fined him,

it may remit the whole or any part of the fine.

If the fine was imposed on the parent and a term of imprisonment has been fixed in default of payment, any exercise of power to remit under s.129(2) shall reduce the term to be served by the proportion of the fine so remitted: s.129(3).

3. *Reduction or discharge of compensation order*: At any time before a compensation order has been fully complied with, the court may discharge or reduce the order under PCC(S)A 2000, s. 133 in any of the following circumstances:

(a) if a civil court has determined an amount of damage or loss less than that stated in the order, or

[61] s.88(3).
[62] MCA 1980, s.83(1).
[63] section 83(2).
[64] MCA 1980, s.85A.

(b) if the property (or part of it) has now been recovered, or

(c) where the offender's means are insufficient to satisfy in full both the compensation order and a confiscation order made in the same proceedings, or

(d) where the offender has suffered a substantial reduction in means which was unexpected at the time that the order was made, and those means seem unlikely to increase for a considerable period.

If the order was made by the Crown Court, the consent of that Court is required if the magistrates propose to act on grounds (c) or (d).

15.45

4. *Supervision order*: The court may make a supervision order under MCA 1980, s.88 (see para. 15.42).

5. *Parental responsibility*: Where the court is satisfied that the defaulter has, or has had since the date on which the sum was ordered, the means to pay the sum or any instalment of it on which he or she has defaulted, or has refused or neglected to pay it,[65] the court may either—

(a) order the defaulter's parent or guardian to enter into a recognizance to ensure that the defaulter pays the outstanding sum[70] provided that the parent or guardian consents[71] or

(b) order that the defaulter's parent or guardian shall pay the outstanding sum,[72] provided that the court is satisfied in all the circumstances that it is reasonable to make such an order.[73]

The parent or guardian must be given the opportunity to attend and be heard before an order transferring responsibility for payment is made but, if required to attend and they fail to do so, the order can be made in their absence.[74]

15.46

6. *Attendance centre order*: In circumstances where, in the case of an adult, the court could order a term of imprisonment or detention in default, it may make an attendance centre order in default. Thus, under the provisions of MCA 1980, s.82(4)(b), the court must be satisfied that the default "is due to the offender's wilful refusal or culpable neglect". All other methods of enforcing payment must have been considered or tried and it must appear to the court that they are inappropriate or unsuccessful. The normal provisions for the making of an attendance centre order must be satisfied, including the number of hours which may be imposed for the offender's age group, the availability of a suitable centre and the avoidance of interference with school or work hours.[75] Where an offender who has been ordered to attend a centre in default pays the outstanding sum, the order ceases to have effect. Part payment reduces the liability to attend on a proportionate basis. Time spent at the centre reduces the amount outstanding proportionately.

---

[65] MCA 1980, s.81(4).
[70] s.81(1)(a).
[71] s.81(2)(a).
[72] s.81(1)(b).
[73] s.81(2)(b).
[74] s.81(5).
[75] PCC(S)A 2000, s.60 (see 19.21).

15.47

7. *Attachment of earnings order*: If in employment, the juvenile defaulter is in the same position as an adult and an order may be made requiring the employer to take an amount (the "normal deduction rate") out of the defaulter's pay to forward to the court. The order must take account of the defaulter's outgoings and the court will fix a "protected earnings rate", the level below which the defaulter's earnings must not fall. Clearly, the majority of juveniles appearing before the court will either not be in work or, if employed, their employment will be insufficiently stable or their earnings will not be substantial enough to make this option feasible.

8. *Distress warrants*: MCA 1980, s.76 empowers the court to issue a distress warrant authorising bailiffs to seize goods to be sold, so that the proceeds can be applied towards the outstanding sum and to the bailiff's costs. In practice it is unlikely that the juvenile will have sufficient goods to make this power worthwhile. Magistrates are not likely to issue such a warrant unless satisfied that there would be sufficient goods to satisfy the sum owed.[76]

9. *Deduction from Income Support*: CJA 1991, s.24 and the Fines (Deductions from Income Support) Regulations 1992[77] provide for deductions to be made from Income Support Benefit where a fine or compensation order has been imposed and the offender is in default. However, no deductions may be made unless the offender is aged 18 or over at the time of the application. An application should not be made in respect of a parent or guardian who has been made liable for the financial penalty of a juvenile.[78]

---

[76] *German* (1891) 56 J.P. 358.
[77] S.I. 2182.
[78] see HOC 74/1992, para. 12.

CHAPTER 16

Non-Custodial, Non-Community Orders

16.01 This inelegantly titled chapter, defining its contents by what they are not, seeks to bring together conveniently those sentencing measures which make active demand upon a young offender but which do not have the status of community orders and are thus not subject to the statutory restrictions that apply to such orders.

REFERRAL ORDERS

16.02 Introduced by the Youth Justice and Criminal Evidence Act 1999 Part I ss.1–5 and governed now in essentially unchanged terms by PCC(S)A 2000, ss.16–32, the referral order is designed to serve as the predominant disposal where a young offender acquires their first conviction. First proposed in the 1997 White Paper[1] as a fundamental "step change" in the culture of the youth court, it is intended to ensure at this relatively early stage in an offender's criminal career that there is proper inquiry into the reasons for their offending and action taken in accord with principles of "restorative justice", *i.e.* combining elements of making restoration to the victim, promoting reintegration into the law-abiding community and taking responsibility for the consequences of one's anti-social behaviour. This measure is unusual in two main respects: first, it is a mandatory sentence if certain criteria are satisfied; secondly, the court does not determine the nature of the defendant's undertakings but delegates this responsibility to a less formal non-judicial arena, a "young offender panel", where the young person will be required to participate and negotiate an agreed programme of activities, somewhat akin to the demands of an action plan order.

16.03 This sentence is founded on the belief that the youth court is an unsatisfactory arena in which to engage properly with young people about the causes and consequences of their offending. Young defendants can readily become merely passive spectators. As the Home Secretary[2] has put it: "at worst, the young offender is wholly detached and contemptuous of what is going on . . . never asked to engage his brain as to what he has done or why he hurt the victim." "First time" young offenders are felt to be particularly open to dialogue, understanding advice and assistance (though they may have already been referred to a YOT for participation in a rehabilitation programme as a consequence of receiving a warning under CDA 1998 s.66).

In common with other recent new sentences, this measure is initially being tested in a number of pilot areas from June 1, 2000 until December 31, 2001 (see para.

---

[1] Home Office (1997) *No More Excuses: A New Approach to Tackling Youth Crime in England and Wales*, Cm. 3809, para. 9.2.
[2] *Hansard*, H.C. Vol. 334, col. 1224.

16.76) to establish its effectiveness in practice and the resource implications. The aim is to make the referral order available in all areas of England and Wales in April 2002. A court proposing to exercise this power must first be notified that arrangements are in place for implementation of referral orders in the offender's current or intended home area.[3]

Power to make a Referral Order

16.04   PCC(S)A 2000, s.16

(1) This section applies where a youth court or other magistrates' court is dealing with a person aged under 18 for an offence and—

    (a) neither the offence nor any connected offence is one for which the sentence is fixed by law;

    (b) the court is not, in respect of the offence or any connected offence, proposing to impose a custodial sentence on the offender or make a hospital order (within the meaning of the Mental Health Act 1983) in his case; and

    (c) the court is not proposing to discharge him absolutely in respect of the offence.

(4) For the purposes of this Part an offence is connected with another if the offender falls to be dealt with for it at the same time as he is dealt with for the other offence (whether or not he is convicted of the offences at the same time or by or before the same court).

16.05   The power is available to and primarily is exercised by a youth court but is also exercisable where a young offender is convicted by an adult magistrates' court which may make a referral order instead of remitting the case to a youth court under PCC(S)A 2000, s.8. Whereas many statutory provisions governing powers of sentence specify the offender's eligibility according to their age at time of conviction, s.16(1) instead specifies that the offender should be aged under 18 at the time at which the court "is dealing with" them. This appears to mean that if the offender attains their 18th birthday between conviction and sentence, a referral order ceases to be a lawful disposal. No referral order may be made in respect of any offence committed before the commencement of the Youth Justice and Criminal Evidence Act 1999, s.1[4].

16.06   The power is not available to or required of the Crown Court except where that court is exercising its appellate jurisdiction and in consequence has power under the Supreme Court Act 1981 s.48(4) to deal with a young offender in any way available to the lower court. In other instances where the Crown Court is dealing with a young offender considered suitable for a referral order, the Court is able to remit the case to a youth court for sentence, under PCC(S)A 2000, s.8(2) (see para. 13.01).

The originating legislation referred to an "associated" offence, defined in the same terms as now contained in s.16(4), but the terminology is now changed to "connected offence" to avoid confusion with "associated offence" as used in respect of generic sentencing powers and now defined in PCC(S)A 2000, s.161. An offence which the defendant asks to be taken into consideration does not appear to fall within the definition of s.16(4).

---

[3] s.16(5).
[4] s.16(7).

16.07 Exercise of this power is either mandatory or discretionary, depending on whether one of the criteria set by s.16(2) and (3) is met, but if neither set of conditions is met, a referral order may not be made. The order is firmly aimed at the window of first conviction and is not an option on second or subsequent conviction. The crucial difference between compulsory and discretionary referral conditions is whether the defendant has pleaded guilty to all connected offences (duty to refer) or has pleaded not guilty to at least one (but not all) such offence(s) (discretion to refer). The aim of the sentence is to achieve purposeful work with a young offender who has admitted criminal responsibility for at least one offence of which he is accused.

16.08 Neither the mandatory nor the discretionary power applies where: (a) the sentence is fixed by law; (b) the court proposes to impose a custodial sentence, where the provisions of PCC(S)A 2000, s.79 are satisfied, or to order detention of a mentally disordered young offender in hospital under the Mental Health Act 1983, s.37; or (c) the offence and its surrounding circumstances are such that an absolute discharge under PCC(S)A 2000, s.12(1)(a) is considered appropriate. Ball[5] has speculated that magistrates may either make inappropriate use of absolute discharges or, at the other end of the scale, may too readily conclude that only a custodial sentence can be justified, to avoid the mandatory nature of the referral order.

Duty to make a Referral Order

16.09   **PCC(S)A 2000, s.16(2)**

   (2) If—

      (a) the compulsory referral conditions are satisfied in accordance with section 17 below, and
      (b) referral is available to the court, the court shall sentence the offender for the offence by ordering him to be referred to a youth offender panel.

PCC(S)A 2000, s.17(1)

   (1) For the purposes of section 16(2) above the compulsory referral conditions are satisfied in relation to an offence if the offender—

      (a) pleaded guilty to the offence and to any connected offence;
      (b) has never been convicted by or before a court in the United Kingdom of any offence other than the offence and any connected offence; and
      (c) has never been bound over in criminal proceedings in England and Wales or Northern Ireland to keep the peace or to be of good behaviour.

16.10 The duty to make a referral order arises where the young offender satisfies two criteria—

   (a) He has admitted guilt in respect of the offence for which sentence is to be imposed and any other matter for which he stands to be dealt with on the same occasion. If the defendant has been acquitted of a denied allegation

---

[5] Ball C. 'The Youth and Criminal Evidence Act 1999 Part 1: A significant move towards restorative justice or a recipe for unintended consequences?' [2000] Crim. L.R. 211–22.

but stands to be sentenced in respect of matters which are all admitted, a referral order will be obligatory if the second criterion applies.

(b) He has neither been previously convicted of an offence in the United Kingdom nor bound over in criminal proceedings (a measure available only in England and Wales and Northern Ireland). For this purpose, s.17(5) specifies that a prior conviction leading to a conditional discharge counts as a conviction even though the consequences of such a conviction are normally limited to those specific proceedings.[6] A young person who has been absolutely discharged in a previous prosecution will be eligible for a referral order despite not being a first time convicted defendant. Similarly, a young person who has been prosecuted on any number of previous occasions but acquitted in all instances will be eligible for this measure.

16.11   The mandatory nature of the order proved the most controversial aspect of the measure in Parliament, the opposition arguing[7] that this will "produce an inflexible structure that will lead to anger and controversy", bringing what was otherwise viewed as a sensible measure into disrepute, clogging up the system and wasting the time of the panels dealing with referrals. There was much debate as to whether the elaborate exercise of referral to a panel is really necessary in the case of red traffic light violations for which a straightforward fine might seem more appropraite. The Government stood firm, convinced that all young offenders on first conviction, including red light violators (whose recklessness was seen as eminently suitable for panel attention) require to be challenged about their behaviour rather than to be simply processed as defendants.

Discretion to make a Referral Order

16.12   **PCC(S)A 2000, s.16(3)**

(3) If—

(a) the discretionary referral conditions are satisfied in accordance with section 17 below, and
(b) referral is available to the court,

the court may sentence the offender for the offence by ordering him to be referred to a youth offender panel.

PCC(S)A 2000, s.17(2)

(2) For the purposes of section 16(3) above the discretionary referral conditions are satisfied in relation to an offence if—

(a) the offender is being dealt with by the court for the offence and one or more connected offences;
(b) although he pleaded guilty to at least one of the offences mentioned in paragraph (a) above, he also pleaded not guilty to at least one of them;
(c) he has never been convicted by or before a court in the United Kingdom of any offence other than the offences mentioned in paragraph (a) above; and

---

[6] PCC(S)A 2000, s.14.
[7] *Hansard,* H.C. Vol. 334, col. 1210.

(d) he has never been bound over in criminal proceedings in England and Wales or Northern Ireland to keep the peace or to be of good behaviour.

16.12 The discretion to make a referral order arises where the young offender satisfies two criteria—

(a) He has admitted guilt in respect of at least one offence for which sentence is to be imposed but has denied at least one of those matters. If the defendant has denied all matters or the only matter before the court, there is no power to make a referral order.

(b) He has neither been previously convicted of an offence in the United Kingdom nor bound over in criminal proceedings (a measure available only in England and Wales and Northern Ireland). The provisions relating to any prior discharge, conditional or absolute, and to prior acquittals, are as indicated above in respect of a duty to make a referral order.

Ball[8] has suggested that defendants charged with relatively minor offences may plead not guilty as a tactic simply to avoid the disproportionate demands of a referral order, given that the usual expectation of discount for a guilty plea has less relevance in this context.

Variation of the eligibility criteria

16.13 Section 17(3) and (4) allow amendment (by affirmative resolution) of the categories of young offenders eligible for a referral order, either as a mandatory or discretionary sentence, in the light of the pilot trials or any subsequent experience of its usefulness or applicability. Subsection (4) details the factors which may be varied: age; plea; nature of offence; criminal record; previous disposals; the "characteristics or behaviour" or "circumstances" of any person charged in the same proceedings. Such power of amendment does not to extend to raising the current upper age limit of eligibility.

Reports and information to the court

16.14 There is no statutory requirement for a court to consider a pre-sentence report or a report specific to this disposal, or to consider information of any other kind relating to the young offender or his family circumstances. If the court has a duty to make a referral order, a report will not serve any useful purpose though a pre-sentence report may have been considered in assisting the court in determining whether to impose a custodial sentence or, less commonly, whether to make a hospital order. If the court has discretion to make a referral order, it may seek a report or ask for more specific information to assist its consideration.

Explanation of Order

16.15 On making a referral order, the court must explain to the offender in ordinary language the effect of the order and the consequences which may follow if no contract takes effect following referral (see para. 16.45) or if the offender breaches the terms of their contract.[9]

---

[8] n. 5.
[9] s.18(3).

Effect on the court's other sentencing powers

16.16 Section 19 clarifies the effect of a referral order on the court's other sentencing powers by specifying "prohibited ways" not open to the court to adopt in respect of the offence or any connected offence. The intention is to ensure that referral constitutes the entire sentence of the court, thus giving the youth offender panel maximum discretion in determining the course of action appropriate for the offender.

PCC(S)A 2000, s.19

(2) The court may not deal with the offender for the offence in any of the prohibited ways.

(3) The court—

    (a) shall, in respect of any connected offence, either sentence the offender by making a referral order or make an order discharging him absolutely; and

    (b) may not deal with the offender for any such offence in any of the prohibited ways.

(4) For the purposes of subsections (2) and (3) above the prohibited ways are—

    (a) imposing a community sentence on the offender;

    (b) ordering him to pay a fine;

    (c) making a reparation order in respect of him; and

    (d) making an order discharging him conditionally.

(5) The court may not make, in connection with the conviction of the offender for the offence or any connected offence—

    (a) an order binding him over to keep the peace or to be of good behaviour;

    (b) an order under section 150 below (binding over of parent or guardian); or

    (c) a parenting order under section 8 of the Crime and Disorder Act 1998.

16.18 The sole option available to the court, compatible with a referral order, in dealing with a connected offence, is an absolute discharge. In addition to prohibiting the use of a conditional discharge, fine, reparation order or any community order, the court may not bind over either the young offender or their parent/guardian or impose a parenting order. However, the court retains the scope to make any other ancillary for which the offender is eligible, including: costs, a compensation order, a forfeiture order or an exclusion order. Some of these measures could be included in the programme of behaviour agreed by the panel under the provisions of s.23(2) (see para. 16.40) and it remains to be seen if courts will opt to leave such considerations to the panel. Wonnacott[10] has argued that this scope substantially undermines the aim to ground the referral order in principles of restorative justice with emphasis on active negotiation of and agreement to a course

---

[10] Wonnacott C. (1999) 'The Counerfeit Contract: reform, pretence and muddled principles in the new referral order', *CFLQ*, *11(3)*, 271–287 at p. 282.

of action. Though s.19(2) to (5) limit courts' powers at the time of initial sentencing, these restrictions do not serve to limit a court's powers if the young offender is referred back to the court by the panel or stands to be dealt with for further offending while subject to a referral order: s.19(6).

16.19   Section 19(7) specifies that a court may not opt to defer sentence in instances where a referral order is mandatory under s.16(2), a logical restriction as deferment would serve no useful purpose in assisting the court's sentencing decision. However, because s.16(2) does not apply where the court is "proposing to impose a custodial sentence"[11], the circumstances in which the option of deferring sentence properly arises (see para. 12.57), so that in such a case the court would retain this discretion. If the offender fulfilled the court's expectations of the deferment period, the court would then have to impose a referral order. However, the kind of expectations that would most probably be identified may well anticipate the kind of programme of behaviour that would feature in a youth offender contract negotiated by the panel under such an order. Exercise of the mandatory power to make a referral order, coupled with the restrictions of s.19(3), does not affect any power or duty of a court under the following provisions[12]—

(a) remission to a youth court, or another such court, for sentence, under PCC(S)A 2000, s.8 (see para. 13.01);

(b) adjournment for inquiries under MCA 1980, s.10(3) (see para. 12.20);

(c) remand for reports, interim hospital order and committal to Crown Court with a view to a restriction order, under the Mental Health Act 1983, ss.35, 38, 43 or 44.

'Associated' Orders

16.20   If the young offender stands to be sentenced for more than one offence, the court may be required to, or may exercise discretion to, make more than one referral order. As the Government explained the intention during the 1999 Act's passage through Parliament[13], this "makes plain to the offender that each offence is unacceptable and forms a different basis for the referral". The consequent effect is specified by s.18(4) to (7).

16.21   **PCC(S)A 2000, s.18**

(4) Subsections (5) to (7) below apply where, in dealing with an offender for two or more connected offences, a court makes a referral order in respect of each, or each of two or more, of the offences.

(5) The orders shall have the effect of referring the offender to a single youth offender panel; and the provision made by them under subsection (1) above shall accordingly be the same in each case, except that the periods specified under subsection (1)(c) may be different.

(6) The court may direct that the period so specified in either or any of the orders is to run concurrently with or be additional to that specified in the other or any of the others; but in exercising its power under this

---

[11] s.16(1)(b).
[12] s.19(7)(a) to (c).
[13] *Hansard*, H.L. Vol. 596, col. 407.

subsection the court must ensure that the total period for which such a contract as is mentioned in subsection (1)(c) above is to have effect does not exceed twelve months.

Each order made in tandem shall be treated as "associated" with the other or each of the others: s.18(7).

Requirements of a Referral Order

16.22　　　　　　　　　PCC(S)A 2000, s.18

(1) A referral order shall—

(a) specify the youth offending team responsible for implementing the order;

(b) require the offender to attend each of the meetings of a youth offender panel to be established by the team for the offender; and

(c) specify the period for which any youth offender contract taking effect between the offender and the panel under section 23 below is to have effect (which must not be less than three nor more than twelve months).

(2) The youth offending team specified under subsection (1)(a) above shall be the team having the function of implementing referral orders in the area in which it appears to the court that the offender resides or will reside.

16.23　The basic obligation arising from the order is for the young offender to attend each meeting of the panel established for the offender by the YOT specified in the order, as determined according to s.18(2). The court thus delegates responsibility to the panel to negotiate and determine the nature of the programme to be followed. However, the court determines not the length of the order but the period for which the youth offender contract resulting from the order (under s.23) is to have effect, with a minimum of three months and a maximum of 12 months: s.18(1)(c). Though the section makes no such provision, the Explanatory Notes that accompanied the 1999 Bill anticipated that the period "will be set by the court on the basis of the seriousness of the offence to ensure that the sentence is proportionate to the offence". The prospect remains that periods may be set that reflect the court's understanding of the problems to be addressed rather than notions of proportionality. additionally, Home Office guidance[14] suggests that as the court may have examined the circumstances of the offence in some detail, sentencers may make observations in court in respect of the offence, including "any elements the court considers appropriate to include in the contract. These comments should be passed to the youth offending team, together with any relevant reports on the young person, and details of any other orders made or already in force."

Associated Orders

16.24　Periods of different lengths may be specified for associated orders and the period specified in any order may run concurrently with, or in addition to, any other period specified in an associated order. However, the young offender must be

[14] Home Office (1999) *The Referral Order*, Draft Circular Version 3, para. 2.24.

referred to a single panel, there will only be one contract and the total contract period arising from associated orders must not exceed 12 months in aggregate.

Attendance of parents etc. at panel meetings

16.25 Section 20 specifies when a court making a referral order is required to or has discretion to order the attendance of "the appropriate person" or persons at meetings of the youth offender panel dealing with the referral.

"Appropriate person" defined

16.26 Subsection (4) provides that each person who is the offender's parent or guardian is an appropriate person for this purpose, unless the offender falls within s.20(6), *i.e.* is "a child who is looked after by a local authority", within the meaning of the Children Act 1989, s.22(6). In such instances "appropriate person" means[15]—

(a) a representative of the local authority looking after the child; and

(b) each parent or guardian with whom the offender is allowed to live.

It is anticipated[16] that where local authority representation is ordered, this may be in addition to parental attendance.

Mandatory attendance

16.27 If the offender is aged under 16 at point of making the referral order, the court is obliged to make a subsidiary order requiring "at least one appropriate person" to attend panel meetings, reflecting the view that parental participation is crucial in addressing a preventing the young person's offending. However, s.20(3) provides an exception to this obligation where it would be unreasonable to require attendance, for example where a parent suffers serious ill-health.

16.28   **PCC(S)A 2000, s.20**

(3) The court shall not under this section make an order requiring a person to attend meetings of the youth offender panel—

(a) if the court is satisfied that it would be unreasonable to do so; or
(b) to an extent which the court is satisfied would be unreasonable.

Discretion to require attendance

If the offender is aged 16 or older the court has discretionary power to order an appropriate person's attendance.

Notice of the attendance order

16.29 An appropriate person is not required to be present when a Section 20 order is made and does not have the right to be heard or to make representations prior to the making of such an order. Section 20(7) specifies that if a person made subject to an order (or a local authority representative, if s.20(5) applies) is not present in court, a copy of the order must be sent to them (or the authority) forthwith.

---

[15] s.20(5).
[16] n. 14, para. 2.13.

Sanction for non-attendance

16.30 Appropriate persons required to attend panel meetings who fail to do so are liable to proceedings under the Magistrates' Courts Act 1980, s.63 for non-compliance with an order other than for payment. The court may order payment of up to £50 for each day in default or may commit to custody for a period not exceeding two months.

Youth Offender Panels

16.31 Section 21 governs the establishment and composition of the youth offender panel responsible for implementing a referral order. It is the duty of the YOT specified in the order under s.18(1)(a) (see 16.22) to establish a panel for the offender and to arrange the panel's first meeting under s.23 (see 16.40) and any subsequent meeting under s.25 (see 16.45). Panel functions and proceedings proceed in accordance with guidance issued by the Home Secretary[17] but, as a minimum, a panel must comprise of three persons[18]—

(a) one member from the relevant YOT; and

(b) two other members who are not part of the YOT, appointed in accordance with regulations issued by the Secretary of State (s.21(4)).

16.32 Wonnacott[19] has criticised the scope for serving police officers to operate as panel members in their capacity as YOT members (a) because they may be privy to prejudicial information about the offender that would not be available to the court and (b) it is undesirable for a serving police officer to be involved in any form of sentencing (though this has happened without apparent difficulty in respect of attendance centre orders). Recruitment of panel members, directly from the general public, should ensure that applicants are "properly representative of the community they intend to serve".[20] Panel members will receive training for their role and are likely to be allocated to specific, cumulative panel duties from a bank of appointees rather than be appointed on a one-off basis. In anticipating the stance that panel members will be expected to take, the Home Office Minister of State[21] has indicated:

> "We are not talking about a touchy-feely, 'pat the little dears on the head' approach. These young people need order, structure and discipline to their lives and they require a capacity to respect other people and their property. I expect those to be recruited to the panels to be capable of imparting that in no uncertain terms."

16.33 The legislation does not specify that the same members will serve throughout the life of a panel convened for a particular young offender, though this would appear to be ideal in the interests of continuity and a rapport with the offender and his parents. The *National Standards for Youth Justice*[22] states that "the YOT manager must ensure that, whenever possible, the same panel members are

---

[17] s.21(2).
[18] s.21(3).
[19] n. 6, p. 283.
[20] Youth Justice Board (2000) *National Standards for Youth Justice*, para. 7.9.1.
[21] Standing Committee E, H.C., Fourth Sitting, 15 June 1999 (afternoon), col. 79.
[22] n. 20, para. 7.9.6.

present at each meeting" but this envisages that some substitution from the bank of panel membership may on occasion be necessary.

Variation on change of residence

16.34 Where an offender's place of residence has changed or is about to change and the YOT specified in the order ("the current team") does not hold responsibility for implementing referral orders in the new area, the court which made the order may vary the order so that it instead specifies the team ("the new team") which has that function in the new area: s.21(5). This provision does not specify the process by which application is made to the court but it would seem that the initiative lies with the "current" YOT. If a further application is necessary following a further change of residence, power of variation remains with the court which made the order, a fixed jurisdiction that could create some inconvenience unless courts are willing to receive written applications or application by the local YOT on behalf of the team holding responsibility.

Where the "new" team assumes responsibility when a contract has been agreed by a panel established by the "current" team, the contract "shall be treated as if it were a contract which had taken effect under s.23 (see 16.40) between the offender and the panel being established by the new team": s.21(6)(c).

Attendance at panel meetings

16.35 The YOT specified in the order has a duty under s.22(1) to notify the offender and any "appropriate person" named in a s.20 order of the time and place of each meeting of the panel established for the offender.

Offender's non-attendance

16.36 If the offender fails to attend any part of a panel meeting, the panel has the discretion under s.22(2) either (a) to adjourn the meeting to such time and place as it may specify, or (b) to end the meeting and refer the offender back to the "appropriate court", as defined by PCC(S)A 2000, Sched.1 (see 16.58), that is the youth court for the area in which the offender lives, if he will still be under 18 when returned to court (otherwise, the adult magistrates' court for that area).

Attendance by other persons

16.37 Subject to the agreement of the panel, the offender has the option to chose a person other than an appropriate person named in a s.20 order to accompany him to any panel meeting: s.22(3). That person must be aged 18 or over and acts in the capacity of 'adult supporter'. The Government has indicated[23] that it is not envisaged that a panel's right of veto "will be exercised easily or often. Whenever possible, a young offender's choice should be respected." It need not be the same person who accompanies him on each occasion when the panel meets. Additionally, the panel may allow or invite the following to attend[24]—

(a) any person who appears to be a victim of, or otherwise affected by, the offence, or any of the offences, in respect of which the offender was referred to the panel;

---

[23] Home Office Minister of State, Standing Committee E, H.C., Fourth Sitting, June 15, 1999 (afternoon), col. 84.
[24] s.22(4).

(b) any person who appears capable of having a good influence on the offender.

16.38 It is anticipated that there will be advance contact with victims in preparation for the panel meeting but that no victim should ever be placed under pressure to attend and that if they opt not to attend they may choose instead to have their views represented at the meeting. The victim may be willing to receive reparation even if they choose not to participate in a meeting.

Though there is no provision for the offender to be legally represented at panel meetings the offender could nominate a lawyer to accompany him, though a panel may decline to agree such a nomination, given the Government's firm resistance to legal representation when an attempt was made to introduce an amendment to this effect when the 1999 Act was passing through Parliament. The Minister of State indicated[25] that he—

> "could think of nothing more destructive to the objectives of the Bill than involving lawyers in youth offender panels. That would add nothing to their operation and would seriously obstruct their objectives. . . .. (They) are designed specifically to remove barriers between the young person and consideration of their offending."

16.39 He later added that "lawyers see themselves as a shield, not as a means of encouraging or engineering the involvement of a young person in a process that requires them to confront their offending"[26]. Additionally, any scope to designate a lawyer as adult supporter is largely academic if, as seems clear, free legal assistance will not be available for this purpose. The exclusion of lawyers and the absence of legal aid are open to challenge as failing to comply with Article 6(3)(c) of the European Convention on Human Rights which provides that a person who is subject of criminal proceedings is entitled to employ a lawyer of his own choice at each stage of the criminal process, with free legal assistance where justice so demands. The Government has argued that only the court hearing where the length of the compliance period is determined is part of the criminal proceedings but, given the absence of procedural or evidential rules to protect the young offender at panel hearings, the significant demands that a panel can generate and the potentially serious consequences for the young person of a return to the youth court, legal representation is arguably of significant importance to fairness and justice.[27]

Early guidance[28] specifies that panels "will be run in accordance with restorative justice principles so that all participants can have their say about the consequences of the offending behaviour and what action needs to be taken by the young person to prevent further offending". It remains to be seen to what extent panels will operate to assist young offenders and their parents to understand the purpose of the assembly, to inform them of their rights and to give them full opportunity to participate and to articulate their views.

Agreement of Contract

16.40 At its first meeting the youth offender panel—

---

[25] Standing Committee E, H.C., Second Sitting, June 8, 1999, col. 36.
[26] Standing Committee E, H.C., Fourth Sitting, June 15, 1999 (afternoon), col. 85.
[27] See Ball, op. cit. n. 3 at p.221 and Wonnacott, op. cit. n. 6 at p. 285.
[28] n. 8, para. 3.6.

"shall seek to reach agreement with the offender on a programme of behaviour the aim (or principal aim) of which is the prevention of re-offending by the offender".[29]

Section 23(2) specifies that "the terms of the programme may, in particular, include provision for any of the following"—

(a) the offender to make financial or other reparation to any person who appears to the panel to be a victim of, or otherwise affected by, the offence, or any of the offences, for which the offender was referred to the panel;

(b) the offender to attend mediation sessions with any such victim or other person;

(c) the offender to carry out unpaid work or service in or for the community;

(d) the offender to be at home at times specified in or determined under the programme;

(e) attendance by the offender at a school or other educational establishment or at a place of work;

(f) the offender to participate in specified activities (such as those designed to address offending behaviour, those offering education or training or those assisting with the rehabilitation of persons dependent on, or having a propensity to misuse, alcohol or drugs);

(g) the offender to present himself to specified persons at times and places specified in or determined under the programme;

(h) the offender to stay away from specified places or persons (or both);

(i) enabling the offender's compliance with the programme to be supervised and recorded.

16.41 Options (a) to (h) are wide-ranging, somewhat akin to the elements that may be included in an action plan order, while the final option (i), likely to be standard in all referral order programmes, allows compliance to be supervised and recorded. Section 23(3) restricts the scope to monitor or regulate the offender's actions, specifying that the programme may not provide either for—

(a) the electronic monitoring of the offender's whereabouts (for example in respect of option (d) or (h)); or

(b) for the offender to have imposed on him any physical restriction on his movements.

16.42 No term of the programme under option (a) which provides for anything to be done to or with any victim or other affected person may be included without the consent of that person: s.23(4). This restriction would appear to apply equally relevantly to option (b). Home Office guidance[30] suggests that in negotiating the contract the panel will take into account any comments made by the sentencing

---

[29] s.23(1).
[30] n. 14, para. 3.7.

court but the panel has considerable scope to bespoke the programme of its choice. Haines[31] has identified the potential for contracts to be "punitive, controlling and retributive" rather than "restorative", and urges panels to adopt the following principles—

- measures such as community service and curfew should not be used unless it can be demonstrated that these are in the best interests of the young person;

- particularly for young and minor offenders, overly intrusive measures should be avoided in favour of interventions which seek to promote positive behaviour;

- contracts should not contain demands which the young person is left to fulfil unaided or unsupported;

- young persons should not be made responsible for actions or behaviour which they have little or no ability to control.

Youth offender contract

16.43   Where a programme has been agreed with the offender, a written record of this should be produced, "in language capable of being readily understood or explained to the offender" for his signature: s.23(5). Once signed by the offender and by a panel member on the panel's behalf, the programme takes effect as a "youth offender contract" between the panel and the offender, and a copy must be given or sent to the offender: s.23(6).

Duration of contract

16.44   Where a youth offender contract has been negotiated under s.23, s.24(2) provides that the day on which it takes effect shall be the first day of the period specified by the court under s.18(1)(c) (para. 16.22) for which it has effect. Where the panel was established in pursuance of two or more associated referral orders, the period now commencing is in accordance with the court's directions under s.18(6) (see para. 16.21): s.24(4). A contract period of less than 12 months may be extended by the appropriate court under PCC(S)A 2000, Sched. 1 paras 11 and 12 (see para. 16.74). If the referral order is revoked under the provisions of Sched.1 paras 5(2) or 14(2) the contract period expires at the time of revocation if it has not already expired.

Failure to agree contract

16.45   Where the panel and the offender are unable to reach agreement at their first meeting on the programme of behaviour to be followed, s.25(1)(b) specifies that the panel may reconvene to resume consideration at a further meeting. However, if it appears to the panel, either at the conclusion of the first meeting or at any further meeting that "there is no prospect of agreement being reached with the offender within a reasonable period after the making of the referral order", the panel shall instead refer the offender back to the appropriate court: s.25(2). Similarly, if an agreement is reached but the offender does not sign the record of

---

[31] Haines K., 'Referral Orders and Youth Offender Panels: Restorative Approaches and the New Youth Justice', in Goldson B. (ed.) *The New Youth Justice* (Russell House Publishing, Lyme Regis, 2000).

the agreement and the panel consider this failure to be "unreasonable", the panel shall end the meeting and refer the offender back to court: s.25(3).

Role of Youth Offending Team

16.46 Section 29 provides that during the period for which a contract has effect, the team specified in the order shall make arrangements for supervising the offender's compliance with the terms of the contract. The YOT member serving on the panel shall ensure that records are kept of the offender's compliance or non-compliance.

Progress Meetings

16.47 Section 26 provides for progress meetings of the panel to be convened by the relevant YOT, at the request of the panel at any time between the contract taking effect and the end of the contract period. Under s.26(2) the panel has discretion to request a progress meeting to review how the offender is progressing with their programme or "any other matter arising in connection with the contract". Home Office guidance[36] anticipates that in reality "progress meetings will be a key monitoring mechanism and the first of these will always be held within one month of the start of the contract". However, in two instances the panel must request a further meeting (s.26(3))—

(a) if the offender has notified the panel that—

  (i) he wishes to seek the panel's agreement to a variation in the terms of the contract; or
  (ii) he wishes the panel to refer him back to court with a view to revocation of the order because of "a significant change in his circumstances (such as his being taken to live abroad) making compliance . . . impractical"; or

(b) it appears to the panel that the offender is in breach of the terms of the contract.

16.48 The panel's duties at a progress meeting are specified by s.26(4) as one or more of the following, depending on what is appropriate in the circumstances—

(a) to review progress;

(b) to discuss any breach of the contract terms with the offender;

(c) to consider any variation sought by the offender;

(d) to consider any request for referral back to court.

16.49 **Breach.** In this instance, the panel may agree with the offender that the contract shall continue, either in its original form or as varied by agreement at the meeting. Alternatively, the panel may refer the offender back to court: s.26(5).

16.50 **Variation.** If a variation of terms is agreed, a record of the variation has to produced and signed. The provisions detailing procedure to be followed are as

---

[36] n. 8, para. 3.14.

apply in respect of the original agreement (see para. 16.43), including the consequences that follow if the offender does not sign the record of variation.

16.51   Change of Circumstances. If the panel is satisfied that there has been a change of circumstances as mentioned in s.26(3)(a)(ii), the panel may refer the offender back to court: s.26(10).

16.52   Final Meeting. Section 27 makes mandatory provision for a final meeting of the panel, prior to expiry of the contract period. The purpose of this meeting is (a) to review the extent of compliance to date; and (b) to decide whether the offender's compliance has been such "as to justify the conclusion that, by the time the compliance period expires, he will have satisfactorily completed the contract": s.27(2). "Compliance period" means "the period for which the contract has effect": s.27(7).

16.53   Discharge of Referral Order. Where the panel decides that the offender's compliance justifies the conclusion mentioned above, this decision "shall have the effect of discharging the referral order (or orders) as from the end of the compliance period": s.27(3). The panel is empowered to make the relevant decision in the offender's absence if this appears appropriate: s.27(5). Thus if the offender fails to attend the final meeting but compliance is otherwise satisfactory, the decision can be made without the need to take action under s.22(2) (see para. 16.36).

16.54   Referral back to Court. If the panel is not able to determine that the offender's compliance justifies the conclusion mentioned above, it shall refer the offender back to court. A final meeting cannot be adjourned to a date after the expiry of the compliance period.

Timetable to be followed in administering a Referral Order

16.55   The *National Standards for Youth Justice*[37] specify the following timetable for practice—

- A panel liaison officer (PLO) to be appointed within one working day of the making of the order.

- First meeting between PLO, offender and parents/primary carer within five working days of the making of the order (the PLO should also contact the victim during this period).

- Initial meeting of panel within 15 days of the order being made.

- Panel meeting to review progress every three months during the course of the compliance period.

- Final panel meeting must take place between five and ten working days before expiry of youth offender contract period.

'National Standards' requirements on non-compliance

16.56   The *National Standards for Youth Justice* specify the following sequence of response to non-compliance with contract conditions—

---

[37] n. 20, para. 7.9.

- In the event of any failure to comply, the panel liaison member of the YOT must visit of telephone the offender and the parents/primary carer within one working day. If there is no acceptable reason for the failure a warning letter must be issued.

- If there is more than one unacceptable failure to comply with the direct reparation component of the contract, a review meeting of the panel must be arranged within 10 working days to consider whether the order can be made to work or whether the order should be referred back to court.

- If there are more than two unacceptable failures to comply with any other part of the contract during the compliance period, a review meeting must be arranged as above.

- "Any application to the court must be made within 10 working days of the review": para. 7.9.9. (This provision appears to overlook that the procedure for referral back under PCC(S)A 2000, Sched. 1 does not provide for an "application" to be made but for a report to be sent containing an "explanation" of the referral back—see below—though any explanation is likely to include the panel's view of what action by the court is appropriate.)

Referral Back to Court

16.57 PCC(S)A 2000, Sched. 1 Part I, incorporated by s.28, makes provision for what is to happen when a youth offender panel refers an offender back to the "appropriate court".

Appropriate court

16.58 The "appropriate court" with jurisdiction for the purposes of 'referral back' is identified by Sched. 1 para.1(2), according to the offender's age on appearance at court in pursuance of that referral back—

    (a) if under 18, a youth court acting for the petty sessions area in which it appears to the youth offender panel that the offender resides or will reside;

    (b) otherwise, an adult magistrates' court acting for that area.

Basis of referral back

16.59 Referral back can arise in any of the following instances—

    (i) the offender fails to attend a panel meeting: s.22(2)(b);

    (ii) it proves impossible for the panel to reach agreement with the offender about their programme of behaviour: s.25(2)(b);

    (iii) the offender fails to sign their contract record: s.22(3)(b);

    (iv) the offender is in breach of any term of their contract: s.26(5)(b);

    (v) the offender fails to sign their revised contract record: s.26(8);

    (vi) the offender's overall compliance is insufficient to allow the panel to determine satisfactory completion of the contract, thus discharging the referral order: s.27(4);

    (vii) the panel refers back at the offender's request: s.26(10).

Mode of referral back

16.60 This is achieved by the panel sending a report to the appropriate court explaining why the offender is being referred back Sched. 1 para.2. On receiving such a report the court shall cause the offender to appear before it. To achieve this a magistrate acting for the petty sessions area for which the court acts may[38] —

(a) issue a summons requiring attendance, or

(b) if the report is substantiated on oath, issue a warrant for the offender's arrest.

Detention on warrant

16.61 If an offender is arrested on warrant which is not backed for bail and it is not possible for them to be brought immediately before the appropriate court, Sched. 1 para.4 specifies that they may be detained in a place of safety (or a remand centre/prison if the offender is now 18) for no more than 72 hours and within that period the person detaining the offender must bring them before a court (either a youth court if under 18, or an adult magistrates' court if aged 18 or older). If that court is not the "appropriate court", but a more convenient court in the light of the circumstances of their arrest, that court ("the alternative court") has power to remand the offender (further to MCA 1980 s.128 governing remand in custody or on bail) or direct that the offender be released forthwith: Sched. 1 para.4(3), depending on what is deemed necessary to secure attendance at the appropriate court.

Power of appropriate court

16.62 The court has first to determine whether the referral back was justified, depending on whether the referral was prompted by a finding of fact or through exercise of discretion, or both. Thus a referral grounded in a failure to attend a meeting involves an exercise in discretion in that the panel could have adjourned to another occasion. A failure to comply with a contract term involves both. A decision to refer back at the offender's request also requires both (as to whether there has been a significant change of circumstances and as to whether referral back is the appropriate course). Wonnacott[39] has criticised these provisions for failing to provide for the young offender to submit his own written evidence if he does not agree with the panel's report or has a complaint about his treatment at the hands of the panel (and see below at para. 16.69).

16.63 Sched. 1 para.5(1) provides that if it is proved to the satisfaction of the court, either by admission by the offender or, in a contested case, by evidence led by the relevant youth offending team—

(a) that, so far as the decision relied on any finding of fact by the panel, the panel were entitled to make that finding in the circumstances, and

(b) that, so far as the decision involved any exercise of discretion by the panel, the panel reasonably exercised that discretion in the circumstances,

the court *may* exercise the power conferred by para.5(2), namely to revoke the order (or each order, if more than one is outstanding). Where an order is thus

---

[38] Sched. 1 para. 3(2).
[39] n. 6 at p. 286.

revoked, the court "may deal with the offender for the offence in respect of which the order was made", in accordance with para.5(5).

Dealing with the original offence afresh

16.64 Sched. 1 para.5(5) specifies that the appropriate court may deal with the offender "in any manner in which (assuming section 16 had not applied) he could have been dealt with for that offence by the court which made the order". However, the court must have regard to[40]—

(i) the circumstances of the referral back to the court; and

(ii) where a contract has taken effect between the offender and the panel, the extent of compliance with its terms.

16.65 Para.5(6) specifies that powers of revocation and dealing with the offender may not be exercised unless the offender is present but are not affected by the expiry of the contract, whether before or after referral back.

Where the appropriate court deals with the offender by committal to the Crown Court for sentence, which is a likely consideration though not an obligatory course if the referral order was made by the Crown Court (see 16.06) in the first instance, para.5(7) specifies that para.5(5) shall apply as if reference to the appropriate court were to the Crown Court. If the appropriate court is an adult magistrates' court faced with dealing afresh with an indictable only offence in respect of an offender now aged 18 where the referral order was made summarily by a youth court when the offender was aged under 18, committal for sentence would seem the logical way forward as Sched. 1 makes no explicit provision for such situations.

Appeal

16.66 Sched. 1 para.6 provides a right of appeal to the Crown Court in respect of a magistrates' court's decision to re-sentence the offender under para.5(4) for the original offence. However, there is no right of appeal in respect of the court's finding of fact in respect of the panel's referral back.

Decision not to revoke referral order

16.67 The appropriate court may determine that it is not satisfied that the panel's decision to refer back was justified in regard to any finding of fact or to any exercise of discretion (*i.e.* those matters mentioned in para. 5(1)—see above). Alternatively, the court may be 'satisfied' but may nevertheless decide not to exercise power of revocation, available to it under para.5(1). Paragraph 7(2) and (3) regulate the effect in such circumstances:

(2) If either—

(a) no contract has taken effect under s.23 between the offender and the panel, or

(b) a contract has taken place . . . but the period for which it has effect has not expired,

the offender shall continue to remain subject to the referral order (orders) as if he has not been referred back to the court.

---

[40] para. 5(5)(b).

(3) If—

    (a) a contract has taken effect . . . , but

    (b) the period for which it has effect has expired (otherwise than by virtue of s.24(6)),

        the court shall make an order declaring that the referral order (or each of the referral orders) is discharged.

As Wonnacott[41] notes, where the court concludes in the young offender's favour, it has no power to allow him a second chance to negotiate a contract satisfactorily by remitting the matter to a differently constituted panel.

Court satisfied of contract completion

16.68 If the court dealing with a referral back under s.27(4) (*i.e.* on the basis that the offender has not satisfactorily completed the contract) decides that, contrary to the panel's view, the offender has completed it satisfactorily, it shall make an order declaring that the referral order is discharged: Sched. 1 para. 8.

Critique of the Contractual Process

16.69 Wonnacott[42] has argued trenchantly that "notwithstanding that the imagery is overwhelmingly consensual, in substance the contractual basis of the referral order is a sham, because all the negotiating power is in the hands of the panel". She argues that the contract is "counterfeit", firstly because the offender has nothing to bargain with—"he has nothing which the panel wants that he can threaten to withhold by not entering into the contract". Though the panel has a duty to try to reach agreement, there is no consequence for it if it fails to do so. Summing up her assessment of the coercive nature of the process, she asserts—

"For an offender the choice is a stark one. He goes into the negotiations knowing that, ultimately, if he does not accept the panel's terms, he will be returned to the youth court and punished , probably not merely for his original offence but additionally for failing to reach agreement with the panel. . . . In effect, the panel is in a position to dictate whatever terms it wants to the offender. In normal contract theory, this is called a contract which is voidable for duress. In criminal law it is called a sentence."

16.70 Secondly, "the offender is unlikely to have the resources or information to enable him to exploit whatever bargaining position he might have had to enable him to negotiate effectively", because of denial of access to resources such as legal representation (see para. 16.38) that would normally be available in defending oneself in respect of a coercive criminal disposal. Thirdly, the lack of procedural safeguards in panel proceedings will make it very difficult for young offenders to challenge bad decisions by panels. Panels are not obliged to keep records of proceedings, with the consequence that "in any dispute over what occurred at a panel meeting it will be the word of the panel against the word of the young offender."

---

[41] n. 10 at p. 282.
[42] n. 10 at p. 281.

This stark view has been countered by a Government assertion[43] that there will be a genuine climate of negotiation to enhance the prospects of gaining the goodwill of young offenders—"If they cannot see the benefit, it will do them no good anyway." Irrespective of the absence of consequences in the event of failure, it may be assumed that panels will wish to be judged by their success in achieving viable and successful outcomes.

16.71 Wonnacott[44] compares the panel process unfavourably with the Scottish children's panel system, as does Ball[45] who suggests that the referral order tries to "cherry-pick" attractive "restorative justice" elements from systems in other jurisdictions (including "family group conferences" originating in New Zealand) without subscribing to the whole package, thus muddling different principles and procedures. "Children's hearings and family group conferences operate instead of a court appearance, thus inviting rather than coercing the co-operation of families." Methods predicated on gaining the co-operation of children and their families are being adopted in the very different context of a court-imposed and sanctioned sentence.

The volume of referrals

16.72 Ball[46] adds that whereas some 70–80 per cent of young offenders in Scotland are dealt with outside of the panel system, thus allowing a manageable number of cases to be passed for panel attention, youth offender panels handling referral orders are likely to be bombarded with referrals. She estimates that around 50,000 orders will be made annually , resulting in eight new referrals per week to every YOT. With a likely minimum of three panel meetings per referral, "panels could be so overwhelmed with cases that there will be a real danger of the process becoming mechanistic and meaningless."

Further Convictions During Referral

16.73 Part Two of PCC(S)A 2000, Sched. 1 deals with instances where an offender aged under 18 who is subject to a referral order appears before a youth court or other magistrates' court to be dealt with for an offence, provided: (i) that the offender's compliance period is less than 12 months and (ii) the occasion when the referral order was made was the only other occasion in which the offender has been dealt with for an offence by a court in the United Kingdom. These provisions can be summarised as follows.

16.74

(a) If the further offence (and any associated offence) was committed *before* the referral order, the court *may* sentence the offender by making an order extending the compliance period: para.11.

(b) If the offence was committed *after* the referral order, an order extending the compliance period may be made under para.12, but only if the court is satisfied on the basis of a report (by the panel or, if no contract has yet taken effect, the relevant youth offending team) that that there are

[43] Home Office Minister of State, Standing Committee E, H.C., Fourth Sitting, June 15, 1999 (afternoon), cols. 85 and 86.
[44] n. 10.
[45] n. 5 at 217.
[46] n. 5 at 218.

exceptional circumstances which indicate that despite re-offending since referral to the panel, extension of the compliance period is likely to prevent further re-offending. Home Office guidance[47] suggests that extension is "most likely to be a satisfactory outcome where the re-offending occurs close to the outset of the referral period, or where the re-offending is in respect of a very minor offence". If of that opinion, the court must state its reasons in open court: para. 12(2)(b). An order extending the offender's compliance period must not cause it to exceed 12 months in aggregate: para. 13(1). Revocation of a referral order under Sched. 1 para. 5(2) on referral back (see 16.63) has the effect of revoking any related order made under paras. 11 or 12: para. 5(3).

16.75 Irrespective of whether the further offence was committed before or after the referral order was imposed, or whether the offender has attained the age of 18, where a court decides to deal with the further offence other than by making (i) an extension order under paras.11 or 12 (if the offender is of an eligible age), or (ii) an absolute discharge, that order of the court shall have the effect of revoking the referral order: Sched.1 para. 14(2). The court may then deal with the offender for the offence for which the referral order was imposed, in any manner in which s/he could have been dealt with for that offence by the court which made the order, provided it appears in the interests of justice to do so: para. 14(3). In dealing afresh with the original offence, account shall be taken of the extent of the offender's compliance with the terms of their contract: para. 14(4).

Referral Orders in Practice

In an interim report of the operation of the referral order in 11 pilot areas from Summer 2000, Newburn *et al.*[47a] found that 83 per cent of magistrates (compared with only 53 per cent of clerks) in those areas considered the order to be a positive development, rendering offenders more accountable. Some 84 per cent (compared with 47 per cent of clerks) felt that the referral order would make offenders more accountable. Over 90 per cent (compared with 67 per cent of clerks) felt that the introduction of restorative justice is "a step in the right direction". The length set by courts for contract performance varied widely, with little sense of logic or consistency. Panel members also expressed concern about proportionality issues, both as regards length of order and contents of contracts, some observing the comparatively minor nature of some of the offending referred for panel attention. Only 44 per cent of panels were convened within the *National Standard* requirement of 15 days, though 82 per cent were held within 25 working days. Panel membership in the first wave of recruitment did not achieve an adequate representation or reflection of the local community, being "predominantly female, middle class and middle aged". The young offender failed to attend their panel in only two per cent of instances; in 70 per cent of panels, the offender attended with one other person (most commonly their mother), more ambitious gatherings involving three or more accompanying persons occurring rarely (one per cent). Victims participated very infrequently. A delicate balance prevailed in proceedings between undue informality and inhibiting formality. Relations between panel

---

[47] n. 14 at para. 4.12.
[47a] T. Newburn *et al.* The Introduction of Referral Orders into the Youth Justice System Occasional Paper 70 (Home Office, London, 2001). See also Home Office and Youth Justice Board (2001) *Report of Referral Order Conference, November 22, 2000.*

members and their sponsoring YOT varied, some YOT members taking a steering role while others played a more passive role, assisting when called upon.

The majority (64 per cent) of panel meetings lasted between 40 and 80 minutes. Contracts were formulated in 99 per cent of instances; in most cases containing three or fewer elements. Perhaps surprisingly, a reparation element was included in only 43 per cent of contracts and the most common form was 'indirect' reparation to the community. Panel members expressed disappointment at the limited range of programmes of activities available for inclusion in contracts. Frustration was expressed by members that they seldom followed a case through from initial meeting to final review, thus presenting difficulties in grasping a case in mid-stream. In a response to the interim report the Home Office and Youth Justice Board[47b] indicate that a broader range of recruitment of panel members will be sought, that comprehensive guidance on the operation of panels will be issued in the summer of 2001, including advice on proportionality issues, and that local referral order steering groups will be established to oversee the introduction of the order in court areas.

REPARATION ORDERS

16.76 Introduced by CDA 1998, s.67 and now governed by PCC(S)A 2000, s.73 in a modified set of provisions, the reparation order is designed to provide the courts "with a new disposal to help prevent further offending by bringing home to young offenders the consequences of their behaviour and, subject to the views of the victim, by enabling them to make amends to victims".[48] It thus embodies a principle of wider application in contemporary youth justice that young offenders should "realise the distress and inconvenience that his or her actions have caused",[49] accept responsibility for those actions and do something practical which will benefit the victim or, alternatively, the community as a whole. Reparation is "about confronting and challenging the young offender" but "it should not be a mechanistic process based on an "eye for an eye" approach". Rather, it should be "tailored to meet both the needs of the victim(s) if they wish to be involved, and addressing the offending behaviour of the young offender".[50]

16.77 This measure is not within the stable of community orders and is therefore somewhat anomalous as a sentence that restricts the offender's liberty but is not subject to the 'serious enough' threshold criterion specified for community sentences by PCC(S)A 2000, s.35. It is thus available to sentencers as a measure that makes active, immediate demands, other than payment of compensation, upon less serious offenders. A second distinctive feature of the order is that a court must give reasons if it does not make a reparation order where it has power to do so.

Power to make a Reparation Order

16.78 The Crown Court or a youth court may make a reparation order where a child or young person, aged under 18 at time of conviction, is convicted of any offence, imprisonable or otherwise, other than an offence for which sentence is fixed by law.

[47b] Home Office and Youth Justice Board (2001) *Commentary on First Interim Evaluation Report* (at: www.homeoffice.gov.uk/yousys/rointrep.htm).
[48] Home Office (2000) *Guidance Document: Reparation Order*, para. 2.1.
[49] n. 48, para. 2.3.
[50] n. 48, para. 2.4.

PCC(S)A 2000, s.73

(1) Where a child or young person (that is to say, any person aged under 18) is convicted of an offence other than one for which the sentence is fixed by law, the court by or before which he is convicted may make an order requiring him to make reparation specified in the order—

(a) to a person or persons so specified; or
(b) to the community at large;

and any person so specified must be a person identified by the court as a victim of the offence or a person otherwise affected by it.

(3) In this section and section 74 below "make reparation", in relation to an offender, means make reparation for the offence otherwise than by the payment of compensation; and the requirements that may be specified in a reparation order are subject to section 74(1) to (3).

Extent and duration

16.79   As in the case of the attendance centre order, the extent of a reparation order has to be expressed as a period of hours and "shall not require the offender to work for more than 24 hours in aggregate": s.74(1)(a). As in the case of an action plan order, a reparation order is of short duration. "Any reparation required by a reparation order shall be made within three months from the date of the making of the order": s.74(8)(b). The court thus needs to specify the number of hours to be completed but the three month completion period has automatic effect and the court may not vary the three month span, for example by specifying a shorter period.

Relevance of offence seriousness

16.80   Though the court is not required to heed the generic community sentence provisions of PCC(S)A ss.35–36, s.74(2) obliges the court to have regard to the seriousness of the offence(s) in determining the requirements of the order.

PCC(S)A 2000, s.74(2)

(2) Subject to subsection (1) above, requirements specified in a reparation order shall be such as in the opinion of the court are commensurate with the seriousness of the offence, or the combination of the offence and one or more offences associated with it.

Compatibility with other sentences

16.81   Under s.73(4), a court may not make a reparation order if it proposes either—

(a) to pass a custodial sentence on the offender; or

(b) to make one or more of the following community orders which offer alternative scope for reparation—

(i) a community punishment order
(ii) a community punishment and reparation order
(iii) a supervision order which includes additional requirements under PCC(S)A 2000, Sched.6

(iv) an action plan order; or

(c) to make a referral order.

This provision does not prohibit the making of a reparation order alongside a community reparation order (under which there is no scope to order reparation), an attendance centre order or a standard supervision order, or a compensation order.

Report to be considered

16.82   Though not required to obtain and consider a pre-sentence report before making a reparation order, the court must instead comply with the requirement of s.73(5) to consider a separate form of written report.

PCC(S)A 2000, s.73(5)

(5) Before making a reparation order, a court shall obtain and consider a written report by a probation officer, a social worker of a local authority social services department or a member of a youth offending team indicating—

(a) the type of work that is suitable for the offender; and

(b) the attitude of the victim or victims to the requirements proposed to be included in the order.

16.83   Home Office guidance[51] indicates that choice of writer "may depend on the nature of the individual case and local arrangements for providing court reports" and that the local YOT should take the lead in identifying responsibility. As much preparatory work as possible should be undertaken in instances "where there is a reasonable chance that a reparation order might be imposed" to minimise delay.

The report writer should indicate the type of reparative activity which could usefully be included in the order, having regard to the defendant's needs and capabilities, the nature of the offence, and the attitude and wishes of the victim. Unlike a report in respect of an action plan order (see 18.05), there is no requirement in respect of a defendant aged under 16 for the court to consider information relating to the offender's family circumstances.

Specified area

16.84   The order shall name the petty sessions area in which it appears to the court making the order that the offender resides or will reside: s.74(4).

Specified responsible officer

16.85   The court needs to identify who will act as responsible officer and supervise the order. Under s.74(5), augmented by s.74(6) and (7), that officer shall be one of the following—

(a) a probation officer assigned to the named petty sessions area;

(b) a social worker of the local authority services department for the area specified in the order;

---

[51] n. 48, para. 3.2.

(c) a member of the YOT for the relevant local authority.

Explanation

16.86 Before making the order, the court shall explain to the offender in ordinary language: (a) the effect of the order and its requirements; (b) the consequences of non-compliance; (c) the court's power to review the order on the application of either the offender or the responsible officer.[52]

Reasons for not making an order

16.87 To reflect the importance of reparation as a central feature and expectation of youth justice, a court must explain its decision not to make a reparation order in instances where it has the discretion to do so: s.73(8).

PCC(S)A 2000, s.73(8)

(8) The court shall give reasons if it does not make a reparation order in a case where it has power to do so.

Requirements in the Order

16.88 The order shall specify the reparation to be undertaken and thus the court must indicate the requirements rather than leave this to the discretion of the responsible officer. The specifics of the reparative activity will be contained in a Schedule to the written copy of the order. Two explicit sets of provisions curtail the court's discretion.

16.89 **(a) Victim's Consent.** An order shall not require the offender to make reparation to any person (*i.e.* someone who has been identified by the court as a victim of the offence or as otherwise affected by the offence: s.73(1)) without the consent of that person: s.74(1)(b). Victim liaison prior to sentence should clearly be undertaken sensitively so as to avoid pressurising the victim to participate or to cause the victim "unrealistic expectations which may not be fulfilled", thus risking subsequent disillusionment[53]. Further, "direct reparation to the victim should not be considered where there is any possibility that the victim(s) might be put at any risk by further contact with offender".[54] If it appears that the victim is unsure of what is being suggested or seems unable to understand the concept of the order, for instance because of age, stress or illness, individual reparation will not be appropriate. Similarly, "direct reparation will not be suitable in cases where the victim appears to see it as an opportunity for revenge against the offender or insists on unreasonable reparation".[55]

Though it is not a statutory requirement, the *National Standards for Youth Justice*[56] require that the consent of victims who are willing to accept reparation "must be given in writing". "If the victim is a young person, consent must be obtained from his/her parent or primary carer", an issue that is not addressed in the provisions of the 2000 Act. Home Office guidance[57] indicates that "it should be

---

[52] s.73(7).
[53] n. 48, para. 5.2.
[54] n. 48, para. 5.6.
[55] n. 48, para. 5.9.
[56] n. 20, para. 7.6.2.
[57] n. 48, para. 5.8.

made clear to the victim that their written consent is not legally binding—if they subsequently find the prospect or experience of direct reparation distressing, the reparation order can be varied or discharged". If a victim refuses reparation they should be asked if they wish to know the nature and result of any reparation to the community which the court may order.[58] If there is no individual victim or person affected, or if such a person does not or cannot give informed consent to receive reparation, the order can require reparation to "the community at large". There is no reason why a court may not order both individual reparation and reparation to the wider community within the same order.

16.90 (b) Avoiding Conflicting Commitments. Requirements in the order shall, "as far as practicable", avoid (a) conflict with the offender's religious beliefs or the requirements of any community order to which he is subject, and (b) any interference with times when he normally attends school or works: s.74(3).

Nature of reparation

16.91 As the Home Office guidance[59] notes: "Where possible, the nature of the reparation reparation should be linked to the offence or type of offence for which the reparation is to be made." The guidance suggests as an illustration of matching that an offender who has vandalised a car might be required to wash the car every week for the length of the order. The guidance[60] adds: "Reparation may take the form of a letter of apology, a meeting or restorative conference at which the nature and consequences of the offence are discussed and the offender apologises directrly to the victim or several hours per week of practical activity." Among several further hypothetical illustrations of reparation in action—

(i) A 15-year-old who has broken into a newsagent's shop and committed criminal damage by graffiti to the walls could be required to clean off the graffiti and also spend one hour every Saturday morning helping the newsagent to sort out his stock.

(ii) A 12-year-old who has terrorised an elder woman by shouting abuse and vandalising her garden could meet her (perhaps arranged and supervised by a local voluntary organisation working on mediation between victims and offenders) to hear her describe the effect on her, to explain why he has behaved in that way and to apologise.

(iii) As an illustration of reparation to "the community at large", the Guidance suggests that a 14-year-old convicted of criminal damage to the green-house of an elder man, where the victim wants no contact with the offender, could spend two hours per week assisting the gardener at an old people's home.

Reparative activities should be suitably supervised, taking account of the young person's age and maturity, to ensure the safety of the offender who may be as young as 10–12 years old.[61]

Role of responsible officer

16.92 Reparation required by a reparation order "shall be made under the supervision of the responsible officer": s.74(8)(a). The responsible officer carries

---

[58] n. 48, para. 5.7.
[59] n. 48, para. 6.2.
[60] n. 48, para. 5.7.
[61] n. 48, para. 6.5.

the responsibility for implementation of the order, as identified by Home Office guidance—[62]

"The responsible officer will need to—

(i) ensure the young offender understnds what is required by the order, and what the consequences may be of failure to comply;

(ii) give the offender instructions as to when and where to attend to carry out any reparation;

(iii) meet the offender regularly to discuss progress with the order and monitor compliance with its requirements

(iv) liaise with the offender's parent(s) or guardian, as appropriate;

(v) liaise with those running any reparation programme in which the offender is to take part and review with them the offender's progress;

(vi) bring any discharge, variation or breach proceedings."

16.93   The generic provisions of *National Standards for Youth Justice* for court-ordered interventions (see 20.37) apply, requiring an early initial meting between the responsible officer and the offender before the end of the next working day following date of sentence and a follow-up meeting within a further five working days. However, the provisions of ss.73–74 do not go further in amplifying the responsible officer's powers. Though the reparation order may be regarded as a junior form of a community punishment order, albeit that the nature of the task is determined by the court, there is no provision equivalent to PCC(S)A 2000, s.47(1) requiring the offender to keep in touch with the responsible officer as instructed or to notify that officer of any change of address. There is also no equivalent of the power to give directions with a view to implementation of the order, as is contained in PCC(S)A 2000, s.69(1)(c) in respect of action plan orders.

16.94   Liaison with Person named in Order.   Where individual reparation is a requirement of the order, the section of *National Standards for Youth Justice* specific to reparation orders requires the responsible officer to contact the victim (or person affected) "within five working days of the order being made, to agree arrangements for reparation. If the victim no longer wants reparation to continue, the responsible officer must . . . apply to the court for a variation so that any remaining reparation can be made indirectly to the community."[63]

Enforcement of the Order

16.95a   Enforcement proceedings, dealing with failure to comply, revocation and amendment, are governed by PCC(S)A 2000, Sched. 8, which provides a common enforcement regime for reparation orders and action plan orders, outlined in Chapter 26. Beyond the procedural detail, the question at the heart of enforcement of reparation orders is the nature of the order. It has obvious similarity to the community punishment order, described in Chapter 23, in that it specifies a number of hours in which work shall be undertaken, to be completed within a set time-scale. In the case of a community punishment order it is clear that "the order remains in force until the offender has worked under it for the number of hours specified in it": s. 47(3). Further, PCC(S)A 2000, Sched. 3 para. 22 makes specific provision for the extension of the order beyond the 12 month period.

[62] n. 48, para. 4.1.
[63] n. 2, para. 7.6.4.

Despite that scope for amendment, it is clear that liability to perform work and the responsible officer's power to give instructions to work and to initiate enforcement proceedings continue beyond the 12 month period, even though no extension has been sought or granted.[63a] In respect of the reparation order, however, there are no such equivalent provisions, either in s.74 or in Sched. 8. As a consequence, enforcement has been dogged with uncertainty, the final evaluation of the pilot trials reporting that "there is a feeling that many potential breaches may run out of time and that it would be helpful if the legislation were to be amended to allow breach proceedings to be brought where the information is laid during the currency of the order".[63b] This implies that if the three month period expires while hours of reparation remain unworked the order is unenforceable. It seems clear that the order cannot be amended under Sched. 8 para. 5 since para. 5(1)(b)(ii) (see 26.09) restricts power of amendment to "inserting . . . any provision which could have been included in the order if the court had then had power to make it". As ss.73–74 do not empower a court making an order to specify a period exceeding three months, it follows that the amending court may not extend that period. However, a case may nevertheless be made that, by analogy with the community punishment order, albeit without the specific provisions that apply in that context, the order continues in force while hours remain unworked, despite the three month time expiry. This possibility must await authoritative interpretation by the Divisional Court.

Reparation Orders in Practice

16.95b Reporting on reparation order practice in areas in which YOTs and the new youth orders under CDA 1998 were piloted, Holdaway et al.[63c] note that the great majority of recipients had been convicted of a single relatively minor offence, one in six having no previous cautions, warnings or convictions. Most orders (67 per cent) were imposed following a specific sentence report. Offender assessment was often rushed and inadequate for risk assessment purposes. In 64 per cent of cases reparation was the only disposal made, though 11 per cent also involved a compensation order. In 63 per cent of cases reparation was ordered to the community, though in cases involving an individual victim, reparation was ordered in 58 per cent of instances. Victims had been consulted in 66 per cent of applicable cases, a half agreeing to some form of reparation by the offender, though there was agreement to direct reparation in only 31 per cent of instances. The researchers attribute the non-consultation rate and the low consent rate to a combination of: (i) data protection difficulties; (ii) defective consultation procedures; (iii) resistance by some YOT workers to victim consultation; (iv) tension between the requirement of victim consultation and the parallel objective of speeding up youth justice (some sentencers routinely refused to adjourn to enable victims to be consulted).

Reparative interventions were delivered in three distinct ways, either 'in-house' by YOT workers, by 'out-sourced' service providers (which could lead to delays and poor communication) or a 'mixed economy' blend of the two. Four kinds of indirect reparation were identified: (i) a fairly limited range of practical work-based activities with little regard to the kind of offence or circumstances of the offender; (ii) tasks chosen to relate as closely as possible to the offence to enable the offender

---

[63a] *Tebbutt* (1988) 10 Cr.App.R.(S.) 88.
[63b] S. Holdaway et al. *New Strategies to Address Youth Offending: the national evaluation of the pilot youth offending teams* Occasional Paper 69 (Home Office, London, 2001).
[63c] See n. 63b above.

to see the connection; (iii) activities relating to the offender's skills or interests to foster a sense of achievement; (iv) confronting offenders indirectly with the impact of their behaviour on victims, using "victim awareness" sessions or letters of apology. In outcome terms, 83 per cent of orders were completed satisfactorily. Applications for variation or revocation happened in less than two per cent of cases. Offenders agreed that they should have to put right the harm they had caused and felt that they had been treated fairly by reparation workers. Those who had met their victim were less likely to view their sentence as a soft option and had much more vivid and detailed recollection of what they had experienced. Most victims felt that offenders' interests were seen as paramount but were nevertheless pleased that they had been asked to participate. Magistrates expressed mixed views; many felt that it was more appropriate for first time offenders but expressed doubts about the extent to which victims' needs could be met by this route. A number regretted the demise of the conditional discharge.

ORDERS FOR PETTY PERSISTENT OFFENDERS

16.95 Where a young offender is aged 16 or over at point of conviction for an offence for which the court would otherwise impose a fine, the court has power instead to impose a curfew order or a community punishment order, provided that the offender satisfies the specified criteria as a petty persistent offender. The purpose is to provide some demanding alternative for repeat offenders of less serious offences who have a track record of non-payment of fine. This power was first introduced by the Crime (Sentences) Act 1997, s.37 and is now governed by PCC(S)A 2000, s.59. The power may be exercised, "notwithstanding" the restrictions contained in PCC(S)A 2000, s.35(1) and (3)(b) on imposing community sentences: s.59(4). In other words, in imposing a curfew order or community punishment order in these circumstances the court does not have to be of the opinion that the offence or offences is/are serious enough to warrant such a sentence. Further, the restriction on liberty imposed does not have to be commensurate with offence seriousness. These measures, including a community punishment order, may be imposed in respect of non-imprisonable offences, notwithstanding the normal restriction contained in PCC(S)A 2000, s.46(1) (see para. 23.03). Given the likelihood that the use of fines may reduce as a result of changes in youth justice introduced by the 1998 and 1999 Acts, this provision may not be widely used by the youth courts.

The Criteria to be Satisfied

16.96 The threshold of eligibility is not particularly high, despite the label of "persistent" offending. The statutory definition can apply, at least in respect of adults, to someone who has offended only twice while, conversely, it excludes those who continually re-offend but manage to pay their fines. The two criteria to be met for this power to be available are as follows—

    (i) the court must be satisfied that the following conditions specified in s.59(22) are fulfilled—

        (a) one or more fines imposed on the offender in respect of one or more previous offences have not been paid; and

        (b) if a fine were imposed in an amount which was commensurate with the seriousness of the offence, the offender would not have sufficient means to pay it;

(ii) if the court was not so satisfied, it "would be minded to impose a fine in respect of the offence".[64]

Non-payment of other financial penalties, such as compensation orders, do not qualify under (a) above. The court is not required to state in open court that it is making the order "instead of imposing a fine"[64a] though clearly this would be advantageous in knowing that this is the basis for imposing either of the permitted orders.

Length of Order

16.97   A curfew or community punishment order imposed under this provision is subject to the same minimum and maximum lengths as apply to these orders as community orders, under s. 37(3) and s. 46(3). The provision of C(S)A 1997, s.37 preventing exercise of power to make concurrent or consecutive orders has not been incorporated in s.59. The court cannot impose both forms of order in tandem for the same offence but there appears no reason in law why this may not be ordered when sentence is imposed for more than one offence.

Procedural Requirements prior to Sentence

16.98   Section 59(5)(b) (in respect of curfew orders) and (6)(b) (in respect of community punishment orders) state that "the other provisions of this Part" of the 2000 Act apply.

Community Punishment Order

16.99   The provisions of PCC(S)A 2000, s.36 apply in respect to obtaining and considering a pre-sentence report before forming an opinion as to the suitability of an order of this kind for the offender. The court must also be satisfied that the offender is a suitable person to perform work under such an order[65] and that provision can be made for the offender to perform work under the arrangements for such orders in the area where he lives.[66]

Curfew order

16.100   The provisions of s. 37(8) apply, requiring the court to consider information about the place to be specified, including the attitude of persons likely to be affected (see para. 21.05). The requirements shall seek to avoid conflict with the offender's school, employment and religious commitments.[67]

Use of Powers in Practice

16.101   This measure was piloted in two areas, Norfolk and Greater Manchester, from January 1, 1998. Research[68] undertaken to evaluate the measures for the first 18 months of the trial period, to June 1999, found that of 508 orders made some three-quarters were imposed on petty persistent offenders aged under 30, the

---

[64] s.59(3).
[64a] s.59(1)(c).
[65] s.46(4).
[66] s.46(6).
[67] s.37(5).
[68] Elliott R. & Airs J., *New Measures for Fine Defaulters, Petty Persistent Offenders and Others: The Reports of the Crime (Sentences) Act 1997 Pilots*, Occasional Paper (Home Office, London, 2000).

youngest being aged 16. The percentage of orders imposed on young offenders aged under 18 is not reported. Community service was far and away the most commonly used order, accounting for about three-quarters of all petty persistent offender orders in each of the areas.

Length

16.102   The average community service order length was 71 hours, with 36 percent of orders being for the minimum period of 40 hours. While courts in Greater Manchester felt able in some instances to impose the maximum of 240 hours, the longest order made in Norfolk was for 140 hours. The average curfew order was 70 days.

Offences

16.103   In both areas summary motoring offences were the most common kind of offence attracting this measure, though practice differed between the two areas. While almost eight in ten orders made in Greater Manchester were in respect of summary motoring matters, about half of Norfolk orders were made in such circumstances, with greater use for theft/handling offences (20 per cent against six per cent in Greater Manchester).

Factors affecting use

16.104   The research suggests that petty persistent offender orders were being used less frequently than similar measures in respect of fine defaulters because magistrates were less familiar with their powers in this context and because of a lack of readily to hand information about outstanding fines. Additionally, magistrates were requesting pre-sentence reports rather than specific sentence inquiries that could afford more prompt use of the measure. The probation service expressed misgivings about the adequacy of such brief inquiries, fearing that these could exacerbate the risk of either domestic violence, in the case of curfew orders, or assaults on community service staff. A further possible factor behind the relatively low use of the powers was concern about the limited powers available in the event of breach of orders.

Completion rates

16.105   Of orders made in 1998, 81 per cent of curfews and 74 per cent of community service orders were completed. Subsequent figures from Norfolk for the period to the end of June 1999 suggested that 63 per cent of petty persistent offender community service orders had been completed compared with 73 per cent of orders imposed as a community sentence. Possible reasons for this disparity include: the selection process for petty persistent offenders is less discriminating; those placed on community orders perceive themselves to be at greater risk of a custodial sentence on non-compliance; the offenders in question have by definition had difficulties in complying with fine payments and may thus be individuals who are less likely to comply with more active demands.

CHAPTER 17

Community Sentences: General

17.01 A major objective of the framework introduced by the 1991 Act was to introduce an intermediate sentencing band, giving a new conceptual coherence to a number of existing orders and adding two new powers to the sentencer's repertoire. The White Paper *Crime, Justice and Protecting the Public* had signalled the Government's belief that more offenders should be punished in the community, "particularly those convicted of property crimes and less serious offences of violence".[1] The Government thus proposed that community punishment should be recognised in its own right, bringing together penalties which combined:

"(a) partial but nevertheless substantial restriction of liberty;

(b) discipline demanded of offenders, usually extending over a number of months, requiring them to take a real measure of responsibility for fulfilling the sentence requirements;

(c) consistent enforcement so that offenders would be held to account and returned to court in the event of default."

17.02 Under the current statutory provisions, applicable to community sentencing generally, PCC(S)A 2000, ss.33–36 (as amended by CJCSA 2000), the growing stable of orders incorporated in this overarching generic identity, is as follows[2]—

(a) curfew order;

(b) community rehabilitation order (formerly probation order);

(c) community punishment order (formerly community service order);

(d) community punishment & rehabilitation order (CPRO, formerly combination order);

(e) drug treatment and testing order;

(f) attendance centre order;

(g) supervision order;

(h) action plan order;

(i) exclusion order;

(j) drug abstinence order.

---

[1] Home Office (1990) Cm. 965, para. 4.3.
[2] s.33(1).

17.03 These orders can be grouped according to age availability thus—

(i) *Offenders of any age*: curfew order; exclusion order

(ii) *Offenders aged 16 or over*: community rehabilitation order, community punishment order; community punishment & rehabilitation order; drug treatment and testing order

(iii) *Offenders aged 18 or over*: drug abstinence order

(iv) *Offenders aged under 21*: attendance centre order

(v) *Offenders aged under 18*: supervision order, action plan order.

Note that a referral order and a reparation order, while restrictive of liberty, are not classed as "community orders" and are thus not subject to the statutory provisions of ss.33–36.

COMMUNITY SENTENCES

17.04 A "community sentence" means a sentence which consists of one or more community orders: s.33(2). Courts are thus empowered to combine different available orders into a sentence, thus enabling combinations of orders for a single offence. There are two explicit exceptions to this facility—

(a) "A community sentence shall not consist of or include both a community rehabilitation order and a community punishment order": s.35(2). This restriction is designed to ensure that rehabilitation and 'punishment' can only be imposed in tandem in the form of a community punishment & rehabilitation order.

(b) A court may not impose an action plan order if the court proposes to make a community punishment order, a community rehabilitation order, a CPRO, an attendance centre order or a supervision order: s.69(5)(b).

The scope for combining community orders in other ways is considered in the separate chapters detailing the provisions pertaining to individual orders.

Restrictions on Imposing a Community Sentence

17.05 Power to impose a community order is subject to the general provision that this is not exercisable in respect of an offence for which the sentence is fixed by law or falls within the provisions of PCC(S)A 2000, ss. 109, 110 and 111, requiring a custodial sentence for certain repeated offences: s.34. Since these latter provisions apply to offences committed by offenders aged over 18, they have no relevance in youth justice. The primary consideration where a court is considering a community sentence is whether the offence or offences meet the "serious enough" threshold criterion of PCC(S)A 2000, s.35(1).

PCC(S)A 2000, s.35(1)

(1) A court shall not pass a community sentence on an offender unless it is of the opinion that the offence, or the combination of the offence and one or more offences associated with it, was serious enough to warrant such a sentence.

(2) In forming its opinion, a court shall take into account all such information as is available to it about the circumstances of the offence(s), including any aggravating or mitigating features: s.36(1).

Interpreting the "serious enough" threshold

17.06   Interpretation of this threshold has received little help from Court of Appeal guidance since its introduction in CJA 1991. The Court has given far greater attention to the "so serious" threshold to custodial sentences and in dismissing two recent appeals has adopted what may be viewed as a permissive stance to use of community sentencing. In *T and Others*[3] a number of adult male defendants had engaged in group sexual activity together in a private home. On their appeal against various community sentences for gross indecency and consensual buggery, arguing that given the private and consenting nature of their conduct a financial penalty or discharge would have been more appropriate, the Court had no difficulty in determining that the offences attracted a community sentence in principle, albeit concluding that the "more punitive" character of community service was "not necessary" in the circumstances. This interesting differentiation between different kinds of orders is considered further at 17.09. In *Hughes*,[4] a man aged 22 of previous good character appealed against imposition of a community service order of 80 hours for possession of 1.3 grams of cannabis, arguing that an offence of this nature usually attracted a fine. The Court upheld the use of a community sentence, asserting that the "serious enough" test was satisfied, but reducing his sentence to 40 hours. On the basis of these two cases the threshold appears to be low to the point where it may be doubted whether it offers any distinctive discriminative meaning. Given the fact that a community sentence will generally be endured despite a sense of grievance at the outcome, few defendants are unlikely to press such appeals.

17.07   In some instances the level of seriousness of the offence(s) will be such as to satisfy the "so serious" threshold test for custody (see 11.20 and 27.03) but there is sufficient mitigation or basis for giving the defendant the opportunity to comply with and benefit from a community sentence,[5] or even a measure of lesser weight, such as a reparation order. In several instances the Attorney-General has successfully referred community sentences to the Court of Appeal on grounds of undue leniency, most commonly in instances of more serious violence. Thus in *Attorney-General's Reference No. 8 of 1992*[6] a probation order imposed on an offender aged under 21 for manslaughter by stabbing during a street argument was replaced by a custodial sentence despite various mitigating circumstances including the offender's youth, his previous good character and his intentions to train for a professional career. The offender's good response since sentence to the community order is unlikely to influence the Appeal Court's assessment but see *Attorney-General's Reference No. 15 of 1994*.[7]

Restriction of Liberty and Suitability

17.08   PCC(S)A 2000, s.35(3)

(3) Subject to subsection (2) above and to section 69(5) below (which limits the community orders that may be combined with an action plan order), where a court passes a community sentence—

---

[3] [1999] Crim. L.R. 432.
[4] [1999] 2 Cr.App.R(S) 329.
[5] *Oliver* [1993] 1 W.L.R. 177.
[6] (1993) 14 Cr.App.R.(S.) 729.
[7] (1995) 16 Cr.App.R.(S.) 619 (detailed at 22.24).

(a) the particular order or orders comprising or forming part of the sentence shall be such as in the opinion of the court is, or taken together are, the most suitable for the offender; and

(b) the restrictions on liberty imposed by the order or orders shall be such as in the opinion of the court are commensurate with the seriousness of the offence, or the combination of the offence and one or more offences associated with it.

17.09   In determining the actual community sentence, in nature and length, the court is required to reflect the seriousness of the offence(s) to achieve a commensurate sentence. The 1990 White Paper implied that there is gradation of community orders within the community sentencing band. This is not a feature of legislation which leaves it to sentencers to work out for themselves. Apart from the difficulties in ranking very diverse kinds of demand on some objective scale of time and effort, the White Paper acknowledged the subjective dimension involved, so that the same order can impact on individuals in very different ways: "a comparatively short order may make more severe demands on some offenders than more severe orders would on others".[7a] Thus a young person in full-time work with family responsibilities could experience a community punishment order of 100 hours as more restrictive than a 200 hour order imposed on an unemployed person without domestic commitments. When these factors are brought into the equation a ranking according to restrictiveness becomes even more problematic. It is noteworthy that the Court of Appeal in *T and Others*[8] retained the view that the demands of community service (as it then was) were more punitive than apply to probation supervision, a view perhaps unwittingly maintained by the new names of the two forms of order, one becoming explicitly "punishment" in contrast to "rehabilitation". Now that the menu of community-based demands has widened to include curfew with electronic monitoring, the scope for weighing competing restriction levels, notionally or otherwise, has become far more complex. At the same time the emphasis in government-driven sentencing policy has placed emphasis, particularly in youth justice, on determining the sentence that is likely to prevent reoffending and to oblige the offender to face up to the consequences of their anti-social behaviour. This points sentencers towards parallel considerations of "suitability".

17.10   Section 35(3) requires the court to achieve dual objectives, "suitability" preceding "restriction" in the order specified by the section. The orthodox view has been offered that proportionality or "deserts" should set the limit on the degree of restrictiveness that is imposed and that considerations of suitability, reflecting the problems, risk factors and criminogenic needs posed by the offender should not lead to a more onerous burden being placed on the offender than is merited by the offence. This perhaps rather "purist" interpretation does not sit easily with the contemporary thrust in youth justice towards achieving crime prevention, public protection, reparation, benefit to the offender, as most clearly posed by the action plan order with scope to create an order to meet the challenge posed by the individual before the court. If sentencing is now understood to be offender-centred rather than offence-centred, then more emphasis will be placed on "suitability". In assessing suitability, the following factors will be relevant considerations—

(a) the defendant's circumstances, needs, abilities, difficulties;

[7a] n. 1 at para. 4.9.
[8] [1999] Crim. L.R. 432.

(b) the risk of re-offending or the potential harm to others and the kind of intervention which could reduce this risk;

(c) the demands of the order and their fit with the individual's commitments, capacities and motivation;

(d) the likelihood of successful completion in the context of competing pressures;

(e) the defendant's response to previous court orders;

(f) the motivation of the defendant to make a commitment to the demands of the proposed order.

17.11 In forming an opinion as the order or orders most suitable for the offender, the court "may take into account any information about the offender which is before it"[9] and must ordinarily consider a pre-sentence report before forming an opinion as to the suitability for the offender of the following kinds of community order[10]—

(a) a community rehabilitation order which includes an additional requirement under Sched. 3;

(b) a community punishment order.

(c) a community punishment and rehabilitation order;

(d) a drug treatment and testing order;

(e) a supervision order which includes an additional requirement under Sched. 6.

This requirement is addressed further at 12.17–12.19 and in chapters dealing with specific kinds of order, where procedural requirements as to information to be considered prior to imposing orders where a pre-sentence report is not obligatory are outlined.

Consent

17.12 A court is prevented from making a community order if the offender does not "express his willingness to comply" in the following instances only, the common feature being that the measure requires the offender to undertake a form of treatment that is relates to the bodily integrity of the subject—

(a) a requirement in a supervision order in respect of a young person aged 14 or over to submit to treatment for his mental condition[11];

(b) a requirement in a community rehabilitation order to submit to treatment for his mental condition;[12]

---

[9] s.36(2).
[10] s.36(3).
[11] PCC(S)A 2000, Sched. 6, para. 6(3)(b).
[12] PCC(S)A 2000, Sched. 2, para. 5(4)(b).

(c) a requirement in a community rehabilitation order to submit to treatment for his drug or alcohol dependency;[13]

(d) a drug treatment and testing order.[14]

However, if the offender fails to express willingness to comply in any of these instances, PCC(S)A 2000, s.79(3) empowers the court to pass a custodial sentence, notwithstanding that the "so serious" threshold test in s.79(2) is not satisfied (see 27.122).

Electronic Monitoring of Requirements in Orders

17.12a In place of the specific provision of PCC(S)A 2000 s.38 allowing electronic monitoring of curfew orders, and in part to reflect and enhance the new power to impose an exclusion order (see 21.17) and curfew and exclusion requirements in a community rehabilitation order (see 22.63 *et seq.*), CJCSA 2000 s.52 amended PCC(S)A 2000 by repealing s.38 and introducing the generic provisions of s.36B. This specifies that any community order "may include requirements for securing the electronic monitoring of the offender's compliance with any other requirements imposed by the order": s.36B(1). An order which includes such requirements "shall include provision for making a person responsible for the monitoring": s.36B(5). This broader power may nevertheless be regarded as of primary significance in respect of curfew and exclusion orders and requirements. Because this form of requirement may not be viable without the co-operation of third parties, s.36B(3)–(4) provide that the necessary consent should be obtained before the electronic monitoring requirement is included.

PCC(S)A 2000, s.36B

(3) Where—

(a) it is proposed to include in an exclusion order a requirement for securing electronic monitoring in accordance with this section; but

(b) there is a person (other than the offender) without whose co-operation it will not be practicable to secure the monitoring,

the requirement shall not be included in the order without that person's consent.

(4) Where—

(a) it is proposed to include in a community rehabilitation order or a community punishment and rehabilitation order a requirement for securing the electronic monitoring of the offender's compliance with a requirement such as is mentioned in paragraph 8(1) of Schedule 2 to this Act; but

(b) there is a person (other than the offender) without whose co-operation it will not be practicable to secure the monitoring,

the requirement shall not be included in the order without that person's consent.

---

[13] PCC(S)A 2000, Sched. 2, para. 6(5)(b).
[14] PCC(S)A 2000, s.52(7).

Binding over Parent or Guardian

17.13 Where a court binds over a parent or guardian under PCC(S)A 2000, s.150 (see 14.02) and also has passed a community sentence on the offender, it may include in the recognisance a provision that the parent or guardian ensures that "the offender complies with the requirements of that sentence": s.150(2).

Enforcement

The Government has made clear that community orders should be enforced rigorously, to build and sustain judicial and public confidence in community-based disposals. This is reflected in the two current sets of *National Standards* that regulate supervision in the community, to which frequent reference is made in the following chapters. It will be noted that the *National Standards for Youth Justice* are less stringent than the "adult" Standards but the supervision of youths who are subject to so-called "adult" orders has to be conducted by the same rubrics as those aged 18 or over. The commitment to stricter enforcement has been reflected in two recent instances of legislative change: first by amendment of PCC(S)A 2000, Sched. 3 and, secondly, by introducing benefit sanctions, both as outlined at 22.70. These measures are aimed primarily at offenders aged 18 years or older but will impact on those who attain adulthood in the course of their order.

CHAPTER 18

Action Plan Orders

18.01 Introduced by CDA 1998, s.69 as a new form of community order for young offenders and now governed by PCC(S)A 2000, s.69 in a modified set of provisions, this measure, with its purposeful-sounding contemporary title, is "designed to provide a short but intensive and individually tailored response to offending behaviour, so that factors associated with the offending can be addressed as well as the offending itself".[1] It is distinguishable from a supervision order by its brief length of three months and by the court's discretion to choose and combine requirements of a quite specific nature from a menu set out in s.70(1). It is thus intended to be the first option for young defendants whose offending is serious enough to warrant a community sentence. Because reparation can feature in an action plan order, considerations addressed in Chapter 16 in the context of reparation orders will be pertinent in this context also.

POWER TO MAKE AN ACTION PLAN ORDER

18.02   PCC(S)A 2000, s.69

(1) Where a child or young person (that is to say, any person aged under 18) is convicted of an offence and the court by or before which he is convicted is of the opinion mentioned in subsection (3) below, the court may (subject to sections 34 to 36 above) make an order which—

    (a) requires the offender, for a period of three months beginning with the date of the order, to comply with an action plan, that is to say, a series of requirements with respect to his actions and whereabouts during that period;

    (b) places the offender for that period under the supervision of the responsible officer; and

    (c) requires the offender to comply with any directions given by the responsible officer with a view to the implementation of that plan;

and the requirements included in the order, and any directions given by the responsible officer, may include requirements authorised by section 70 below.

(3) The opinion referred to in subsection (1) above is that the making of an action plan order is desirable in the interests of—

    (a) securing the rehabilitation of the offender; or

    (b) preventing the commission by him of further offences.

18.03 The order is available to a youth court or the Crown Court where an offender aged under 18 at point of conviction is convicted of any offence,

---

[1] Home Office (2000) *Guidance Document: Action Plan Order*, para. 2.1.

imprisonable or not (though see the special provision of s.70(2) (at 18.12) in respect of an order that includes a requirement of attendance centre). The court has to be satisfied that one or other of the criteria specified in s.69(3) apply, a requirement akin to the provisions of s.41(1) governing community rehabilitation orders but not required in deciding to impose a supervision order under s.63. Because the order is a community order (s.33(1)(f)), the court must also follow the generic provisions of ss.35–36 specifying restrictions on imposing community sentences, with allied procedural requirements. The court must thus be of the opinion: (i) that the offence is serious enough to warrant such a sentence; (ii) that an action plan order is the most suitable for the offender; (iii) that the restrictions imposed by the order are commensurate with the seriousness of the offence.

Incompatibility with other Sentences

18.04 **PCC(S)A 2000, s.69(5)**

(5) The court shall not make an action plan order in respect of the offender if—

(a) he is already the subject of such an order; or

(b) the court proposes to pass on him a custodial sentence or to make in respect of him a community rehabilitation order, a community punishment order, a community punishment and rehabilitation order, an attendance centre order, a supervision order or a referral order.

It is thus not possible for action plan orders imposed on separate occasions to overlap, though a defendant may be made subject to a further order if he has already completed an earlier order. The court may also not construct a community sentence combining an action plan order with another kind of community order that makes active demands on the offender, or with a referral order. The court is not precluded from combining an action plan order with either a curfew order or an exclusion order, though exclusion may feature as an action plan requirement and so is not likely to be imposed as a free-standing requirement unless, in the case of an offender aged 16 or older the court wishes to impose a restriction for a longer period than the shorter timespan of an action plan allows. There is also no restriction on combining an action plan order with a compensation order, even where the former includes a requirement to make reparation. Reparation through an action plan order is defined by s.70(3) to exclude payment by compensation and is intended to facilitate only "reparation in kind".[2] There is thus scope for financial recompense to be ordered in tandem via a compensation order.

Report to be considered

18.05 Though the court is required to take account of "all such information as is available to it about the circumstances of the offence" (s.36(1)—see 17.08) and "may take into account any information about the offender which is before it" (s.36(2)—see 17.11) in considering the suitability of an action plan order for the offender, it is not required to obtain and consider a pre-sentence report under s.36(3) and (4). Instead, the special provisions of s.69(6) for a written report apply.

PCC(S)A 2000, s.69(6)

(6) Before making an action plan order, the court shall obtain and consider—

---

[2] n. 1, para. 7.1.

(a) a written report by a probation officer, a social worker of a local authority social services department or a member of a youth offending team indicating—

(i) the requirements proposed by that person to be included in the order;

(ii) the benefits to the offender that the proposed requirements are designed to achieve; and

(iii) the attitude of a parent or guardian of the offender to the proposed requirements; and

(b) where the offender is aged under 16, information about the offender's family circumstances and the likely effect of the order on those circumstances.

18.06   The relevant youth offending team has responsibility in practice for co-ordinating arrangements for the provision of reports, identifying the appropriate report writer and ensuring the timely delivery of reports to the court. Home Office guidance[3] suggests that as the report is less extensive than a pre-sentence report, "courts might generally expect it to be completed within 10 working days of request". Accordingly, early contact with the victim is suggested to allow the victim more time to consider reparation issues. To pave the way for this kind of inquiry, investigating police officers are being encouraged to ask victims whether, should the offender be a juvenile, they are prepared to be contacted by a YOT. Where this has not been encouraged, the guidance suggests that initial contact with the victim should be undertaken by a police member of the YOT.[4]

The guidance emphasises that a report should concentrate on issues (i)-(iii) identified in s.69(6)(a) and, where the offender is aged under 16, on the information specified in s.69(6)(b) (see below). It should also indicate:(a) the hours likely to be involved in undertaking requirements and how these will fit with school or work commitments, or religious observance; (b) where reparation to the victim is intended, that the victim's consent has been obtained; (c) the officer who will be responsible for supervising the order.[5]

18.07   Offenders aged under 16.   In regard to the young offender's family circumstances, Home Office guidance indicates that "the type of information which it may be appropriate to include may relate to the parent or guardian's occupation and hours of work (if appropriate), the ages and normal daily timetables of any people (particularly siblings) living in the home, and any problems in the family situation which might make particular requirements unreasonably difficult to complete".[6]

Other statutory specifications

18.08   Specified Area.   The order shall name the petty sessions area in which it appears to the court making the order that the offender resides or will reside: s.69(8).

18.09   Specified Responsible Officer.   The court needs to identify who will act as responsible officer, supervising the order and giving directions in implementing

[3] n. 1, para. 3.3.
[4] n. 1, para. 3.4.
[5] n. 1, para. 3.7.
[6] n. 1, para. 3.6.

the order. Under s.69(4), augmented by s.69(9) and (10), that officer shall be one of the following—

(a) a probation officer assigned to the named petty sessions area;

(b) a social worker of the local authority services department for the area specified in the order;

(c) a member of the YOT for the relevant local authority.

In practice, the task will invariably be undertaken by a YOT member.

18.10 **Explanation.** Before making the order, the court shall explain to the offender in ordinary language: (a) the effect of the order and its requirements; (b) the consequences of non-compliance; (c) the court's power to review the order on the application of either the offender or the responsible officer.[7]

Requirements in the Order

18.11 The order shall require the offender to comply with one or more of seven kinds of requirement specified in s.70(1), intended to address the causes of his or her offending and/or to prevent further offending. The requirement or combination of requirements must, of course, remain commensurate with the seriousness of the offence(s) for which sentence is imposed. It is possible that the court will seek to combine the elements that appear desirable to meet the young offender's criminogenic needs and thus lose sight of commensurability. One specific limitation on the court's power, however, set by s.70(2) in respect of an attendance centre requirement. As an attendance centre order may be imposed only for an imprisonable offence, the same restriction applies to such a requirement in an action plan.

18.12   **PCC(S)A 2000, s.70**

(1) Requirements included in an action plan order, or directions given by a responsible officer, may require the offender to do all or any of the following things, namely—

(a) to participate in activities specified in the requirements or directions at a time or times so specified;

(b) to present himself to a person or persons specified in the requirements or directions at a place or places and at a time or times so specified;

(c) subject to subsection (2) below, to attend at an attendance centre specified in the requirements or directions for a number of hours so specified;

(d) to stay away from a place or places specified in the requirements or directions;

(e) to comply with any arrangements for his education specified in the requirements or directions;

(f) to make reparation specified in the requirements or directions to a person or persons so specified or to the community at large; and

(g) to attend any hearing fixed by the court under section 71 below.

---

[7] s.69(11).

(2) Subsection (1)(c) above applies only where the offence committed by the offender is an offence punishable with imprisonment.

18.13 Requirements in the order (and directions given by the responsible officer shall, "as far as practicable", avoid (a) conflict with the offender's religious beliefs or the requirements of any other community order to which he is subject, and (b) any interference with times when he normally attends school or works: s.70(5).

Power to impose a *reparation* requirement is subject to two additional constraints. No reparation should be ordered to be made to a specific person, whether victim or someone otherwise affected by the offence, without that person's consent: s.70(4). Additionally, a court may not use its power to require reparation to order payment of compensation: s.70(3).

18.14   **PCC(S)A 2000, s.70**

(3) In subsection (1)(f) above "make reparation", in relation to an offender, means make reparation for the offence otherwise than by the payment of compensation.

(4) A person shall not be specified in requirements or directions under subsection (1)(f) above unless—

(a) he is identified by the court or (as the case may be) the responsible officer as a victim of the offence or a person otherwise affected by it; and

(b) he consents to the reparation being made.

Though it is not a statutory requirement, the *National Standards for Youth Justice*[8] require that the consent of the victim who is willing to receive direct reparation is obtained in writing and, if the victim is a young person, the written consent of their parent(s) or guardian should be obtained. It should be made clear to the victim that their agreement is not legally binding upon them. "If they subsequently find the prospect or experience of direct reparation distressing", the action plan order can be varied or discharged.

18.15 Interpreting the intentions behind each of the seven specified requirements, Home Office guidance[9] comments—

(a) *Activities*: "the nature of these activities will depend on the nature of the offence, the advice of the report writer as to what kind of activities will achieve the objectives of the order, and what facilities are available in the local area." Among possible options: anger management classes, drug or alcohol misuse programmes, homework classes or mentoring in literacy or numeracy.

(b) *Specified Place and Time*: "This can help the offender to establish a routine in what may previously have been a chaotic lifestyle, and can ensure that he or she complies with any requirement to participate in specified activities." This form of requirement may be appropriate where the offender is required to attend an agency in partnership with the YOT such as a substance misuse counselling agency for assessment.

---

[8] Youth Justice Board (2000), para. 7.6.2.
[9] n. 1, para. 4.2.

(c) *Attendance Centre*: No specific guidance given, except in respect of maximum length, no ceiling being specified for action plan purposes. The guidance[10] ventures that "it is not appropriate for the number of hours to exceed" the maxima specified in PCC(S)A 2000 s.60 for attendance centre orders as a community order. This seems entirely sensible advice; an attendance centre requirement in an action plan order exceeding such length would undoubtedly be open to challenge as unlawful. Further, the three months duration of the order may place practical limits upon the number of hours that can be ordered or reduce the scope to achieve something worthwhile with the offender, depending on the frequency of sessions at the relevant attendance centre. Thus if the centre concerned operates only fortnightly for a period of two hours, it may be possible to attend for a maximum of only 12 hours within the lifespan of the order. In such instances a requirement to attend for 24 hours would take some six months and such a requirement would appear incompatible with the nature of an action plan order.

(d) *Avoiding Specified Place(s)*: "This will be particularly helpful where the offending has been influenced by the company which the offender has been keeping." Among suggested possible places: shopping centres, car parks, amusement arcades. It may also be appropriate to require the offender to stay away from the victim's property. A requirement of this nature raises questions about its enforceability and the guidance refers to the need for consultation with other agencies, such as the police, before being proposed to the court. It is not possible to use this form of requirement to oblige the offender to stay away from a named individual who might be regarded as an adverse influence on him or her.

(e) *Educational Arrangements*: "This may help offenders who may have been truanting, and committing offences when they should have been at school. It may also help disaffected offenders to make up some of the educational ground which they have lost through truanting or poor behaviour or attainment at school."

(f) *Reparation*: This is perhaps the most important element for inclusion as the Home Office advises[11] that "where possible, reparation to the victim or the community should be one of the requirements of an action plan order. This will help offenders better to understand and take responsibility for the consequences of their offending and make amends for it, and help the victim to come to terms with the offence and put it behind them." While reparation should challenge the young offender's attitudes and behaviour, it should not be a mechanistic process "based on an 'eye for an eye' approach" but should be tailored to meet the needs of both parties.[12] However, "it would be inappropriate for reparation to be included at the expense of other requirements"[13], given the availability of a reparation order. Victim liaison prior to sentence should clearly be undertaken sensitively so as to avoid pressurising the victim to participate or to cause the victim "unrealistic expectations which may not be fulfilled", thus

---

[10] n. 1, para. 4.5.
[11] n. 1, para. 3.13.
[12] n. 1, para. 6.2.
[13] n. 1, para. 4.3.

risking subsequent disillusionment.[14] Emphasising the importance of willing and informed consent by the victim, the guidance[15] notes that a
requirement to make reparation to a reluctant recipient "could revictimise
that person, making it even more difficult for them to recover from the
crime". In particular, "direct reparation should not be considered where
there is any possibility that the victim might be put at any risk by further
contact with young offender". Reparation will also be unsuitable where
the victim sees it as an opportunity for revenge or is insisting on
unreasonable reparation.

18.18

The form of reparation can vary: "a letter of apology, a meeting or
restorative or family group conference at which the nature and consequences of the offence are discussed and the offender apologises directly
to the victim, or several hours per week of practical activity which benefits
the victim or the community at large. Where possible, the nature of the
reparation should be linked to the offence or type of offence for which the
reparation is to be made".[16] The guidance[17] provides several hypothetical
illustrations of reparation in action, e.g. a 14-year-old convicted of theft
from a newsagent's shop could be required to spend one hour every
Saturday morning helping the newsagent to sort out his stock. Another
reparation option could entail victim/offender mediation, usually supervised by a mediation service working with the youth offending team. For
example: a 12-year-old who has assaulted an elder woman meets her to
hear her describe the effect on her, to explain why she has behaved in that
way and to apologise. If there is no individual victim or person affected or
if such a person does not or cannot give informed consent to receive
reparation, the order can require reparation to "the community at large",
thus involving the equivalent of community service under a community
punishment order. For example: a 14-year-old who has knocked over an
elder man and stolen his wallet, where the victim wants no contact with
the offender, could spend two hours per week assisting the gardener at an
old people's home. Reparative activities should be suitably supervised,
taking account of the young person's age and maturity, to ensure the
safety of the offender who may be as young as 10–12 years old.

(g) *Attending a Review Hearing*: This requirement is more a means to
achieving the other aims of the order rather than an end in itself, and is
outlined further below.

18.19 Unlike community rehabilitation orders or supervision orders, there is no
intrinsic or invariable explicit requirement in an action plan order for the offender
to notify the responsible officer of any change of address. Yet it is vital for the
supervisor to retain knowledge of the offender's residence in order to implement
and pursue their plan. If the newly sentenced offender changed address immediately after leaving court, the purpose of the order would be clearly frustrated. This
would not in itself provide grounds for breach proceedings since the offender is not

---

[14] n. 1, para. 6.3.
[15] n. 1, para. 6.6.
[16] n. 1, para. 7.2.
[17] n. 1, para. 7.3. Hypothetical examples of action plan orders for offences of ram-raiding in a car taken
without the owner's consent and arson by setting fire to a youth centre, suggested in draft guidance by
the Home Office (1998), are omitted in the final version.

obligated to inform their supervising officer. Of course, *National Standards for Youth Justice*[18] require that the offender should be given notice of their first meeting with the supervisor before leaving court so that if the offender disappears immediately, their whereabouts unknown, their failure to keep their appointment would provide clear grounds for breach. Supervisors may nevertheless wish to keep a clear and enforceable grip on the supervised person's home address. A solution lies with s.69(1)(c) which empowers the responsible officer to give directions "with a view to the implementation of the plan". This gives scope for an early instruction to be given that the offender must notify their supervisor of any change of address. This direction could be given immediately after sentence, by a courts officer on the supervising officer's behalf if need be, in tandem with details of the offender's first appointment. Any failure to comply could then provide the basis for breach in its own right.

Review Hearings

18.20 Action plan orders are unusual in that they permit the court to retain oversight of the offender's progress under the order. Unlike the drug treatment and testing order where review is mandatory, a further hearing, within 21 days of sentence, is an optional requirement at the court's discretion under s.70(1)(g), supplemented by the provisions of s.71.

PCC(S)A 2000, s.71

(1) Immediately after making an action plan order, a court may—

    (a) fix a further hearing for a date not more than 21 days after the making of the order; and

    (b) direct the responsible officer to make, at that hearing, a report as to the effectiveness of the order and the extent to which it has been implemented.

(2) At a hearing fixed under subsection (1) above, the court—

    (a) shall consider the responsible officer's report; and

    (b) may, on the application of the responsible officer or the offender, amend the order—

        (i) by cancelling any provision included in it; or

        (ii) by inserting in it (either in addition to or in substitution for any of its provisions) any provision that the court could originally have included in it.

18.21 Home Office guidance[19] identifies: "Such a hearing can review the offender's progress and make any necessary adjustments to the action plan, particularly where the court was unclear at the time of sentencing that a requirement could be delivered." It may also impress upon the offender the court's interest in him or her, and the importance of completing the order successfully. The guidance[20] adds that "it is not expected that courts will feel generally it to be necessary in every case". The attitude of the young person or their parents may prompt the view that particular encouragement or oversight will be worthwhile.

---

[18] n. 7, para. 7.1.1.
[19] n. 1, para. 4.2(g).
[20] n. 1, para. 9.2.

If the young offender does not attend the hearing, this would provide grounds for breach proceedings. The court has no power under s.71(2) to order a further hearing after the initial review. Though it does not appear to be a legal requirement that the offender's parent(s) or guardian attend, the guidance[21] suggests that "this should be encouraged if appropriate".

IMPLEMENTATION OF THE ACTION PLAN

18.22   In implementing the action plan the responsible officer supervising the order is required to follow the generic provisions of *National Standards for Youth Justice*[22] applicable to all court-ordered intervention, as outlined in Chapter 20 at 20.37. In addition, the Standards specific to reparation orders (see 16.94) apply to action plans that include a requirement to make reparation. Standards specific to action plan orders also apply,[23] requiring—

- A first contact between supervising officer and offender within one working day of sentence. Where practicable and appropriate, this meeting must involve the parents or primary carer. The aim is to agree how the action plan will be implemented and the time-scale within which it must take place.

- The YOT manager must ensure that the court is advised of the outcome of each action plan it makes.

Length of the Order

18.23   On the face of it, s.69(1)(a) (see 18.02) appears to anticipate straightforwardly that the order will be of three months duration. The court has no discretion to specify either a shorter or longer period. However, the expectations of an individual action plan may be fulfilled prior to the expiry of that period. Does the order continue in force, at least notionally, until the conclusion of that period or does the order terminate when requirements have been fulfilled? In this respect the order is neither like a supervision order with a clear time duration nor a community punishment order or reparation order, boundaried by task fulfilment. Irrespective of the particular elements of the offender's plan, the order places all offenders under the supervision of the responsible officer for that period, with the consequence that the offender could be directed to keep appointments with their supervisor throughout the period, even if all specified activities or reparation initiatives have been fulfilled. Certainly, the *National Standards for Youth Justice*[24] expect a minimum level of contact throughout the order, twice-weekly during the first 12 weeks and thereafter once-weekly. Responsible officers may find this continuing responsibility a somewhat hollow exercise, perceived by offenders as less than meaningful and thus increasing the possibility of non-compliance and ensuing enforcement action. Is revocation of the order a way out of this demand on offenders and their supervisors?

18.24   The relevant revocation provisions of PCC(S)A 2000, Sched. 8 contain no equivalent of the parallel provisions in Sched. 3 para. 10(4) pertaining to

---

[21] n. 1, para. 9.3.
[22] n. 7.
[23] n. 7, para. 7.7.
[24] n. 7, paras. 7.2.1–7.2.3.

community rehabilitation orders permitting revocation in circumstances where the offender has made good progress or has responded satisfactorily. It could be argued that a revocation application could be made under Sched. 8 para. 5 (see 26.39) in such circumstances, on the basis that "it is appropriate" to make a revocation order if the action plan order is to all intents and purposes completed, but the court may consider that in the absence of a specific provision as contained in Sched. 3, it has no authority to revoke the order in such circumstances. The court may also consider that three months is such a relatively short period that it is unnecessary and perhaps even wrong in principle to circumvent the intention of Parliament that the offender should be subject to statutory oversight for that period.

Enforcement of the Order

18.25 Enforcement proceedings, dealing with failure to comply, revocation and amendment, are governed by PCC(S)A 2000, Sched.8, which provides a common enforcement regime for action plan and reparation orders, detailed in Chapter 26.

ACTION PLAN ORDERS IN ACTION

18.26 This sentence was piloted in six areas from September 1998, producing a total of 553 orders by October 31, 1999. Evaluation of the first 12 months[25] reported that the order had been well received by courts and youth justice workers alike. It found favour with courts because it offers a form of early intervention that appears positive and proactive, appears to occupy a clear tariff position (though some sentencers favoured resort to the measure on first conviction with insufficient regard to offence seriusness) and can reflect both the offence and the circumstances of the offender. Practitioners apprciated the scope it offers to work constructively with offenders over a range of opportunities. It was noted that offenders and their parents like the order "because of the structure it brings to their lives, even in the short-term". It appeared to occupy the same sentencing niche as the attendance centre order, as a consequence of which the latter had fallen into disuse in some areas.

18.27 Sentencing Stage. The tension betwen the pressures of speed and the demands of justice posed widespread difficulty. Reporters were sometimes expected to devise a package "on the spot" and thus found it helpful to use "off-the-peg" programmes.

18.28 Specified Activities. Commonly, courts would be offered a core pro-gramme, typically consisting of six sessions of two/three hours each, either one-to-one or in groups, covering choices at time of offending, victim issues, peer pressure and family relationships, supplemented by other requirements according to the type and seriousness of the offence and the needs of the offender. Most YOTs offered reparative activity, similar in kind to that offered in final warning programmes, reparation orders and supervision orders. Reparation was sometimes contracted out to external agencies to deliver, though this could lead to fragmentation and militate against coherence of approach. YOTs typically contributed around 25 hours per order.

---

[25] Universities of Sheffield and Hull (1999) *Youth Justice Plots Evaluation Second Interim Report: Youth Offending Teams After One Year.*

18.29 Parental Involvement. Beyond the formal inclusion of parents by consultation prior to the making of an order, involvement was largely ad hoc and patchy, despite acknowledgement in principle that parental partcipation is beneficial. Best practice was felt to be served by more widespread and consistent attention to parental contribution.

18.30 In a subsequent final evaluation report of the pilot area experience of this order, Holdaway *et al.*[26] report that while the implicit intention of the action plan order has been to target offenders without a significant criminal history convicted of relatively more serious offences, the vast majority of those receiving this order had known previous offending but their current offence was "less serious and deserved a low-tariff sentence". "This means that just observing the current offence might lead to the conclusion that up-tariffing is apparent in the pattern of APO disposals." The authors accept, nevertheless, that the extent of offenders' pre-convictions reduced the flexibility of sentencers.

As regards content of action plan programmes, beyond the in-house core programme provided by all the pilot area YOTs the requirements were very variable. Overall, 35 per cent of offenders were required to "present themselves at a specified time and place". Attendance centre was much less often required and staying away from specified places was very rarely specified. Educational requirements were included in an average of one-third of cases but this masks considerable variation between areas, two making use of this power in two-thirds of cases and another in only one-sixth. Direct reparation was also highly variable, with one YOT requiring this in three-quarters of cases and another in three per cent only. Review hearings were used rarely in one area but in over 50 per cent of cases in another. Only four per cent of orders were varied after sentence. About two-thirds of orders were completed satisfactorily.

---

[26] S. Holdaway *et al.*, *New Strategies to Address Youth Offending: the national evaluation of the pilot youth offending teams,* Occasional Paper 69 (Home Office, London, 2001).

CHAPTER 19

Attendance Centre Orders

19.01   First introduced by the Criminal Justice Act 1948 and designated as one of the stable of community orders which can feature in a community sentence by CJA 1991, the attendance centre order is now governed by PCC(S)A 2000, s.60, succeeding CJA 1982 s.17. It remains a community order under the generic provisions of PCC(S)A 2000 Part IV Chapter I: s.33(1)(f). Attendance centre orders may also be imposed as a secondary penalty for non-payment of financial orders and as measure following breach of reparation, action plan, supervision and community rehabilitation orders. An additional complication is that attendance centre attendance can be a requirement of an action plan order under PCC(S)A 2000, s.70(1)(c) (see 18.12). Though the Home Office has asserted that "attendance centres will continue to have an important role to play within the evolving youth justice system",[1] there is some early evidence to suggest that this order has been eclipsed by the action plan order which is perceived by sentencers to occupy the same tariff niche but with greater flexibility in responding to offence and offender.[2]

19.02   An attendance centre is statutorily defined as "a place at which offenders aged under 21 may be required to attend and be given under supervision appropriate occupation or instruction in pursuance of attendance centre orders": s.62(2). The Attendance Centre Rules 1995[3] provide more detailed regulations covering staffing, attendance and discipline at centres, reinforced by a *National Standard for Attendance Centres*.[4] The Secretary of State is empowered to "make arrangements with any local authority or police authority for the use of premises of that authority": s.62(4).

AS A COMMUNITY ORDER

Power to Make an Attendance Centre Order

19.03   PCC(S)A 2000, s.60

(1) Where—

  (a) (subject to sections 34 to 36 above) a person aged under 21 is convicted by or before a court of an offence punishable with imprisonment

  (b) & (c) (*not relevant*)
      the court may, if it has been notified by the Secretary of State that an attendance centre is available for the reception of persons of his

---

[1] "Attendance Centres into the 21st Century", *Attendance Centre News*, Spring 1999.
[2] Universities of Sheffield and Hull (1999) *Youth Justice Pilots Evaluation Second Interim Report: Youth Offending Teams After One Year*, p. 43.
[3] S.I. 1995/3281.
[4] Home Office (1995).

description, order him to attend at such a centre, to be specified in the order, for such number of hours as may be so specified.

19.04 A youth court or the Crown Court can make an attendance centre order where the offender has been found guilty of an offence punishable with imprisonment, provided that the court is of the opinion that the offence, or the combination of the offence and one or more offences associated with it, is serious enough to warrant such a sentence.[5]. An order can only be made if the court has been notified by the Secretary of State that a centre is available for the reception of persons of the offender's description. The court has to be satisfied that the centre to be specified in the order is reasonably accessible to the offender, having regard to the offender's age, means of access to the centre and any other circumstances.[6] The restriction formerly contained in CJA 1982, s.17(3) that orders should not normally be imposed on offenders who had previously received a custodial sentence was repealed by CJA 1991, section 67(1). This reflects the emphasis in the 1991 Act on sentencing on the basis of seriousness of the current offence, though some sentencers may continue to feel that a young offender who has experienced custodial detention is not a likely candidate for the gentler demands of an attendance centre.

19.05 Though a court imposing an attendance centre order is able to take account of any information before it about the offender and is subject to the generic provisions of PCC(S)A 2000 ss. 34–36, outlined in chapter 17 it is not required to consider a pre-sentence report. One unusual feature of the attendance centre order is that those who run centres have no say in who comes their way, while YOT members who make proposals in pre-sentence reports may know little about attendance centres. An obvious aspect worth considering at the time of writing the pre-sentence report is whether the young offender will be able to cope with the demands. Experience suggests that youngsters who are quite withdrawn and reluctant to tackle either new or existing commitments in their life may well find the demands of the centre very difficult to sustain and may then find themselves at risk of a custodial sentence upon revocation following breach proceedings.

Availability and accessibility of centres

19.06 PCC(S)A 2000, s.60(6)

(6) An attendance centre order shall not be made unless the court is satisfied that the attendance centre to be specified in it is reasonably accessible to the person concerned, having regard to his age, the means of access available to him and any other circumstances.

Young persons are allocated to centres according to age, sex and category of centre. Centres are categorised as "junior" and "senior". Some "junior" centres take males and females under 17 but the majority take only males. There are no junior centres for females only. "Senior" centres at present take males only, primarily those aged 17–20, but with some flexibility in regard to 16 year olds. Thus the attendance centre order is not an available sentencing option for young women aged 18–20 anywhere in England and Wales and the availability for younger girls is limited. The Table summarises the arrangements for attention.

---

[5] PCC(S)(A) 2000, s.35(1) (see 17.05).
[6] s.17(7).

19.07 Before making an order the court must be satisfied that the centre is reasonably accessible to the offender in all the circumstances. The *National Standard*[7] specifies that offenders should not normally be expected to travel for

MALES

Age	Type of Centre
10–15	Junior Centre
16–17	
(a) where no senior centre	Junior Centre
(b) where a choice of centre:	
(i) orders up to 24 hours	Junior or Senior Centre according to the individual's suitability
(ii) orders 25–36 hours	Senior Centre

FEMALES

Age	Type of Centre
10–17	Junior Mixed Centre (where available)
18–20	Not available

more than one hour or ten miles each way, whichever is the greater, though "courts may consider that less demanding travelling requirements are appropriate to younger attenders". Travelling time does not count towards completion of the order.

Combining the order with other sentences or orders

19.08 The general rule applies that "courts should avoid mixing sentences which fall into well established and different categories".[8] Thus an attendance centre order should not be combined with a custodial sentence. Clearly an attendance centre order and a discharge cannot be combined for a single offence, but a fine can be imposed alongside an attendance centre order for a single offence. The 1991 Act permitted the combination of attendance centre orders with any other community orders for which the offender is eligible by age, either for a single offence or for separate offences dealt with on the same sentencing occasion. This scope is now qualified by PCC(S)A 2000, s.69(5)(b) (see 18.04) which specifies that a court may not impose both an action plan order and an attendance centre order on an offender within the same sentencing exercise. The court does, however, have the option to impose a requirement of attendance centre attendance as part of an action plan.

Length of the order

19.09   **PCC(S)A 2000, s.60 (3) & (4)**

(3) The aggregate number of hours for which an attendance centre order may require a person to attend at an attendance centre shall not be less than 12 except where—

(a) he is aged under 14; and

(b) the court is of the opinion that 12 hours would be excessive, having regard to his age or any other circumstances.

---

[7] n. 4, para. 10.
[8] *McElhorne* (1983) 5 Cr.App.R.(S.) 53.

(4) The aggregate number of hours shall not exceed 12 except where the court is of the opinion, having regard to all the circumstances, that 12 hours would be inadequate, and in that case—

(a) shall not exceed 24 where the person is aged under 16; and
(b) shall not exceed 36 where the person is aged 16 or over but under 21 or (where subsection (1)(c) above applies—*not relevant to juveniles*) under 25.

19.10 The court shall specify the number of hours of attendance, subject to the following limits:

(a) The aggregate number of hours shall not be less than 12, except where the offender is under 14 and, in the opinion of the court, 12 hours would be excessive, having regard to the offender's age or other circumstances.[9]

(b) The aggregate number of hours shall not exceed 12 except where the court is of the opinion, having regard to all the circumstances, that 12 hours would be inadequate[10]

(c) Where the court is of the opinion that 12 hours would be inadequate, the aggregate number of hours shall not exceed 24 where the offender is under 16, or 36 hours where the offender is aged 16 or over.[11] (CJA 1991 increased the maximum number of hours for 16 year olds to place them on the same footing as 17 year olds, in accordance with their status as "near adults").

(d) A further attendance centre order may be passed upon an offender whilst a previous order remains in effect and the number of hours to be specified shall be determined without regard to the number specified in the earlier order or to the fact that that order is still in force with hours outstanding.[12]

Age	Minimum Hours	Maximum Hours
10–11	12 (unless 12 is excessive)	24 (if 12 is inadequate)
12–15	12	24 (if 12 is inadequate)
16–20	12	36 (if 12 is inadequate)

Times of attendance

19.11   PCC(S)A 2000, s.60

(7) The times at which a person is required to attend at an attendance centre shall, as far as practicable, be such as to avoid—

(a) any conflict with his religious beliefs or with the requirements of any other community order to which he may be subject; and
(b) any interference with the times, if any, at which he normally works or attends school or any other educational establishment.

(8) The first time at which the person is required to attend at an attendance centre shall be a time at which the centre is available for his attendance in

[9] s.60(3).
[10] s.60(4).
[11] s.60(4).
[12] s.60(5).

accordance with the notification of the Secretary of State, and shall be specified in the order.

(9) The subsequent times shall be fixed by the officer in charge of the centre, having regard to the person's circumstances.

(10) A person shall not be required under this section to attend at an attendance centre on more than one occasion on any day, or for more than three hours on any occasion.

19.12 The times of attendance shall be such as to avoid interference as far as practicable with the offender's school hours or working hours. The order should specify the time at which the offender must first attend the centre. Subsequent times shall be fixed by the officer in charge of the centre, having regard to the offender's circumstances. An offender shall not be required to attend the centre on more than one occasion on any day or for more than three hours on any occasion. Sessions normally last two hours at junior centres and three hours at senior centres. Most centres normally open on alternate Saturdays. The expectation is that even the longest orders should be completed within six months, if offenders attend regularly.[13] (*National Standard*, 1995, para. 9). Latecomers may be refused admission.[13a]

Staffing of centres

19.13 Nearly all centres are administered by police officers (with civilian support) but this is a matter of policy and convenience rather than a statutory responsibility of the police. Each centre must have an officer in charge to whom offenders must report. A survey in February 1999 yielding replies from 93 of the total of 110 centres found that 92 per cent of officers in charge are serving or former police officers.[14] The officer in charge has responsibilities which include:

(a) maintaining a register of attendance, failure to attend and any breaches of the rules;

(b) informing each offender orally and in writing, before they leave the centre, of the date and time of their next attendance, unless this is impracticable;

(c) determining whether an attender is unfit for attendance by reason of illness, infection, or a condition likely to be detrimental to others;

(d) exercising discipline;

(e) making application to the relevant court for variation or discharge of the order or initiating breach proceedings.

Save in exceptional circumstances, a female member of staff should be present at a centre at which girls and young women attend and should, "so far as practicable", supervise their physical training.[15]

Occupation and discipline

19.14 The occupation and instruction given at a centre shall include a programme of group activities designed to assist offenders to acquire or develop

---

[13] n. 4, para. 9.
[13a] n. 3, r.6(3).
[14] n. 1.
[15] n. 3, r.4(2).

personal responsibility, self-discipline, skills and interests.[16] A survey of 93 centres in February 1999[17] showed that football was the most popular physical activity, followed by circuit training and basket ball. The most common craft activity was woodwork, being offered in nearly a half of centres. The most common subjects for lectures or discussion groups were drug and alcohol abuse and first aid, other less well covered topics ranging from offending behaviour and prison life to career choices.

The basic requirement to attend the specified centre is supplemented by ACR 1995, r. 10:

> "Persons shall while attending at a centre behave in an orderly manner and shall obey any instruction given by the officer in charge or any other member of the staff".

19.15 Though the discipline of a centre is to be maintained primarily by the personal influence of the staff,[18] the Rules specify a number of sanctions which can be exercised in the event of a breach of the rules—

(a) separation from other persons attending[19];

(b) being given an alternative form of occupation[20];

(c) being required to leave the centre for the remainder of the session[21];

(d) where misconduct is sufficiently serious, suspension from further attendance pending court appearance for breach[22];

Where the breach is serious, the officer in charge should interview the offender and caution him or her as to their future conduct at the centre before imposing the sanction.[23]

In the event of unauthorised non-attendance, a telephone call should be made, if possible, to the offender's home to find out the reason for absence. A warning letter should be sent to the offender explaining the consequences of non-attendance and giving notice of the date and time of the next session. If the offender is aged under 16, a letter should also be sent to the offender's parents advising them of the non-attendance and asking them to do all they can to ensure future attendance.

19.16 If the offender misses the next session, a final warning letter should be sent.[24] Breach action must be instituted no later than the third consecutive unauthorised absence, though proceedings may be commenced earlier than this if the officer in charge is satisfied that the offender has no intention of obeying the sentence of the court. Where unauthorised absences are not consecutive, greater flexibility is allowed but "generally no more than four non-consecutive unauthorised absences should be tolerated".[25]

---

[16] n. 3, r.4(1).
[17] n. 1.
[18] n. 3, r.9.
[19] (rule 13(a))
[20] (rule 13(b))
[21] (rule 11(1) and (2)(a))
[22] (rule 11(2)(b)).
[23] n. 4, para. 42.
[24] n. 4, para. 43.
[25] n. 4, para. 44.

Rationale of the order

19.17

"The aims of the order are to impose, in loss of leisure over a considerable period, a punishment that is generally understood by young people and to encourage them, in a disciplined environment, to make more constructive use of their leisure time. The sentence will not normally be suitable for those who have a long record of offences or who need removal from bad home surroundings, nor can it, of itself, meet a requirement for sustained supervision.[26]

19.18 The White Paper *Crime, Justice and Protecting the Public*.[27] stated that the order is useful as a punishment "when the offender does not need supervision for a long time". Nevertheless, as the quotation above suggests, it is natural for centre staff to wish to make the experience more constructive than just a "restriction on liberty". A Home Office survey of officers.[28] in charge of senior attendance centres found that:

"Most officers either stated that they agreed with the aims of a senior attendance centre as laid down by the Home Office or simply repeated these aims by mentioning such ideas as instilling discipline, punishing through loss of leisure and providing a constructive programme of activities. Some, however, mentioned aims which seemed to have a stronger welfare orientation and more than a hint of social work: to educate offenders in topics of social concern such as applying for a job; to allow them to discuss any difficulties they might have with the staff at the centre. At times an almost Victorian notion of self-improvement with the help of a paternalistic teacher came through: a centre could give a sense of achievement and a need to strive; it would whet appetites for a better way of life; it might induce higher personal standards. The aims mentioned by respondents thus covered a wide area from, on the one hand, punishment and discipline to, on the other, constructive social work help. There was no mention of any possible tension between such aims; perhaps officers were not aware of any such tension, or perhaps they considered that in the practice of a centre such contradictions were resolved and posed no problems."

19.19 The capacity of the attendance centre to be "all things to all people", with perceived advantages ranging from idealistic rehabilitation to economic pragmatism, has often been remarked on and this spread of perceptions will probably continue.

Use of the order

19.20 In 1998 the percentage of children and young persons sentenced for indictable offences who received attendance centre orders was as follows, the actual (approximate) numbers being given in brackets—

---

[26] Home Office, *The Sentence of the Court* (HMSO, London, 1990), para. 8.2.
[27] Home Office (1990), Cm. 965, para. 4.19.
[28] G. Mair, *Part-Time Punishment?* (HMSO, London, 1991), p. 152.

	Males	*Females*
10–11	11 (42)	7 (2)
12–14	18 (1400)	9 (100)
15–17	9 (300)	5 (300)

Use of this measure has remained relatively stable during the period since the 1991 Act was implemented.

IN DEFAULT OF PAYMENT

19.21   Though use of what is primarily a community sentence as a penalty for non-payment of financial orders which may have been imposed for an offence not serious enough to warrant a community sentence may seem somewhat anomalous, an attendance centre order remains an obvious sanction for young defaulters.

19.22   PCC(S)A 2000, s.60(1)(b) permits an attendance centre order to be imposed in circumstances where the court would have power in the case of an adult to commit to prison in default of payment of any sum of money "or for failing to do or abstain from doing anything required to be done or left undone". Thus the court should be satisfied that the default arises because of the offender's wilful refusal or culpable neglect.[29] The court must have regard to the provisions of PCC(S)A 2000, s.60 as regards the accessibility of centres, age and the length of the order. Payment of the full outstanding sum causes the order to cease to have effect.[30] Part payment reduces the number of hours of attendance proportionately, "that is to say by such number of complete hours as bears to the total number the proportion most nearly approximating to, without exceeding, the proportion which the part bears to the said sum".[31] This complex calculation formula can best be illustrated by an example—

> A defaulter has been made subject to a 12 hours attendance centre order for the non-payment of a fine of £90. This gives each hour a financial value of £7.50. He attends for three hours. This reduces the amount outstanding by £22.50, leaving £67.50. If he then pays £50, leaving £17.50 outstanding, he would be required to attend for a further two hours ("worth" £15 only but the hours outstanding are rounded down to the nearest complete hour).

ON BREACH OF A COMMUNITY ORDER

19.23   Courts with jurisdiction in breach proceedings may make an attendance centre order under the following provisions—

(a)   on breach of a supervision order, whether or not it also makes an order revoking or amending the breached order: PCC(S)A 2000, Sched. 7, para. 2(2)(a)(iii);

(b)   on breach of a reparation order or action plan order, whether or not it also makes an order revoking or amending the breached order: PCC(S)A 2000, Sched. 8, para. 2(2)(a)(iii).

---

[29] MCA 1980, s.82(4)(b), see 15.46.
[30] section 60(12)(a).
[31] section 60(12)(b).

(c) on breach of (i) a community rehabilitation order or a community
     punishment and rehabilitation order, where the offender is aged under 21,
     or (ii) a curfew order, where the offender is aged under 16, in each
     instance where the order is permitted to continue in force: PCC(S)A 2000,
     Sched. 3, para. 4(1)(c)(i) and (ii), and para. 5(1)(c)(i) and (ii). Exercise of
     this power is regulated by Sched. 3, para. 8. CJCSA 2000 amends Sched. 3
     paras. 4 and 5 by rewording subpara. (1) in each instance and adding
     subparas. (1A)-(1C). The purpose of the amendments is to provide courts
     with more stringent, quasi-mandatory power to impose imprisonment
     following breach by adult offenders (see 22.70) but serving also to make
     these provisions more complex. Subparas. (1C) in each instance are stated
     to apply "in a case within sub-paragraph (1A)" (which in each instance is
     stated to apply "in a case where the offender where the offender is aged
     18 or over") where the court does not impose a sentence of imprisonment
     but also in cases "not within that sub-paragraph". This thus requires
     application of subparas. (1C) in all instances where the offender remains a
     youth (see 22.70). Sub-paragraphs (1C)(c) in each instance state that an
     attendance centre order may be made where an offender aged under 21 is
     in breach of *any* community order requlated by Sched. 3, in circumstances
     where the order is allowed to continue, *i.e.* as a penalty power to punish
     the breach.

In these instances PCC(S)A 2000, s.60 is deemed to apply as if it were amended
to incorporate orders made under these provisions. The usual restrictions and
procedural requirements governing community sentences do not apply but in other
respects the court must have regard to the provisions of s.60, such as in respect of
accessibility of centres, age and length of order.

Enforcement of an Attendance Centre Order

Provisions dealing with the amendment, breach and revocation of attendance
centre orders are contained in a specific set of provisions, in PCC(S)A 2000, Sched.
5, as detailed in Chapter 26. These provisions also apply to orders made other than
as a community order, *i.e.* for default or breach, in a modified form. In respect of
attendance centre orders imposed under Sched. 3, para. 8 of Sched. 5 applies.

CHAPTER 20

Supervision Orders

20.01 The power to make a supervision order was introduced in the CYPA 1969 to offer a distinctive form of statutory supervision for juveniles. This order, together with additional requirements broadly identified as "intermedidate treat-ment", was originally intended to replace the punishments of attendance centre and detention centre with a new, constructive flexible range of local authority pro-vision. This undiluted vision of the 1969 Act was not implemented but the supervision order has nevertheless been the cornerstone of developments in modern juvenile justice.

The relevant provisions of the 1969 Act, encumbered by a welter of amendments and repeals, have now been superseded by the consolidating provisions of PCC(S)A 2000 ss.63–68, and this order must now find its place alongside the new measures introduced into youth justice by CDA 1998, notably the action plan order. The supervision order would seem more appropriate where the factors associated with the defendant's offending are complex and need longer assessment, and there are several welfare issues at stake requiring significant input over time, in collaboration with other agencies. Lasting change is thus unlikely to be achieved within three months intervention. Additionally, a supervision order allows use of resources and controls available under an intensive supervision and surveillance programme (see 11. 65), not available via an action plan order. The new legal framework essentially reproduces the 1969 foundation and, in consequence, the nature of the order in its standard format remains a somewhat imprecise or permissive entity. The core expectation of a supervision order is that the young offender is placed under the supervision of a designated agency[1] and while the order is in force, "the supervisor shall advise, assist and befriend the offender": s.64(4). For a clearer sense of the reality of supervision order practice, reference has to be made to the *National Standards for Youth Justice*[2] detailing clear expectations for the process and content of supervision.

20.02 The following Table shows the percentage of children and young persons sentenced for indictable offences in 1998 who received supervision orders, by age and sex, with actual (approximate) numbers in brackets—

	Males	*Females*
10–11	24 (93)	17 (5)
12–14	31 (2,400)	28 (100)
15–17	16 (5,600)	22 (1,100)

General Provisions

Power to make a supervision order

20.03 Where a child or young person, aged under 18, is convicted of any

---

[1] s.63(1)
[2] Youth Justice Board (2000).

offence, the court by or before which he or she is convicted may make an order placing the offender under supervision: s.63(1). The court must have regard to the generic provisions of PCC(S)A 2000, s.35 (see chapter 17) and be of the opinion that the offence, or the combination of the offence and one or more offences associated with it, is serious enough to warrant such a sentence, that the order is the most suitable for the offender and that the restrictions on liberty thus imposed are commensurate with offence seriousness.

Length of the order

20.04 There is no statutory minimum length and it is not strictly necessary for the court to specify any length. If the court simply makes a supervision order without specifying its length, s.63(7) specifies—

(7) A supervision order shall, unless it has previously been revoked, cease to have effect at the end of the period of three years, or such shorter period as may be specified in the order, beginning with the date on which the order was originally made.

In practice, courts indicate the length deemed appropriate. Length as an element of "restriction of liberty" and weighed with other factors pertaining to restrictiveness should be such as in the opinion of the court is commensurate with the seriousness of the offence(s): PCC(S)A 2000 s.35(3)(b) (see 17.08).

This assessment cannot be made on the basis simply of the time and effort which the order will demand but must also take account of the likely impact upon the offender in the light of their formal circumstances and characteristics. As the White Paper observed, ". . . a comparatively short order may make more severe demands on some offenders than more severe orders would on others" (paragraph 4.9). These are somewhat nebulous considerations which are not easily explained in distinguishing one offender from another and may cause offenders who are considered able to cope with "more severe" orders to feel an understandable grievance if their equally culpable but less resilient co-defendant receives a shorter order. In 1998 of 12, 594 supervision orders imposed supervised by the probation service, 78 per cent of orders were for one year or less, a further 21 per cent being for two years or less. The number for terms exceeding two years was thus less than two per cent.[3]

Procedural Issues

Pre-sentence report

20.05 A court is not required to consider a pre-sentence report before deciding whether an offender is suitable for a supervision order, unless the order includes requirements imposed under PCC(S)A 2000, Sched. 6 (*i.e.* any additional requirement except one imposed under the general power of section 63(6)(b) to add requirements—see 20.13). The Judicial Studies Board has nevertheless advised magistrates to obtain a PSR before making any supervision order, even where this is not a statutory requirement. Failure to obtain and consider a report where this is a mandatory requirement does not render the order invalid PCC(S)A 2000, s.36(7) but such a failure could provide basis for appeal and the court considering the

---

[3] Home Office (2000) *Probation Statistics, England and Wales, 1998*, London: Government Statistical Service.

appeal is required to obtain and consider a report. The requirement to consider a pre-sentence report does not mean that the report has to address the possibility of a supervision order with or without additional requirements, but some paragraphs of Sched. 6 authorising such requirements specify that the court must consult the supervisor or must be satisfied that the requirement is viable.

Consent

20.06 The consent of the offender is not required before a supervision order can be made but a court may not impose an additional requirement of treatment for mental condition under Sched. 6, para. 6(3)(b) in respect of an offender aged 14 or older unless he expresses his willingness to comply.

Supervising agency and area of residence

20.07 The court has discretion under s.63(1) to place the offender under the supervision of—

(a) a local authority designated in the order;

(b) a probation officer; or

(c) a member of a YOT.

In practice, supervisory responsibility will normally be exercised by a youth offending team, though responsibility may be passed to the Probation Service by local agreement if an offender attains age 18 and the order has significant time still to run. Section 63(5) and (6)(a) adds—

20.08
(5) A court shall not make a supervision order unless it is satisfied that the offender resides or will reside in the area of a local authority; and a court shall be entitled to be satisfied that the offender will so reside if he is to be required so to reside by a provision to be included in the order in pursuance of paragraph 1 of Schedule 6 to this Act.

(6) A supervision order—

(a) shall name the area of the local authority and the petty sessions area in which it appears to the court making the order (or to the court amending under Schedule 7 to this Act any provision included in the order in pursuance of this paragraph) that the offender resides or will reside.

Schedule 6 para. 1 deals with requirements to reside with a named individual. The definitions provisions of s.67(1) indicate as follows:

"reside" means habitually reside, and cognate expressions shall be construed accordingly except in paragraph 6(2) and (3) of Schedule 6.

Revocation of any Existing Order

20.09   PCC(S)A 2000, s.63(9)

(9) If a court makes a supervision order while another such order made by any court is in force in respect of the offender, the court making the new

order may revoke the earlier order (and paragraph 10 of Schedule 7 to this Act (supplementary provision) shall apply to the revocation).

Power of revocation for this specific purpose is thus extended to a sentencing court even though it is not a "relevant court" for the purposes of Schedule 7 (see 26.03). The purpose appears to be to allow a rationalisation of supervision so as to avoid the overlap of cumulative orders without the need to make special application to the relevant court. This power does not enable the court to re-sentence the offender for the original offences for which the earlier order was imposed. In the past offenders have sometimes been subject to several orders simultaneously with consequent complications for enforcement purposes. Sched. 7 para. 10 governs the supply of copies of orders revoking or amending supervision orders (see 26.13).

Copies of the order

20.10   **PCC(S)A 2000, s.63(8)**

(8) A court which makes a supervision order shall forthwith send a copy of its order—

(a) to the offender and, if the offender is aged under 14, to his parent or guardian;

(b) to the supervisor;

(c) to any local authority who are not entitled by virtue of paragraph (b) above to such a copy and whose area is named in the supervision order in pursuance of subsection (6) above;

(d) where the offender is required by the order to reside with an individual or to undergo treatment by or under the direction of an individual or at any place, to the individual or the person in charge of that place; and

(e) where a petty sessions area named in the order in pursuance of subsection (6) above is not that for which the court acts, to the justices' chief executive for the petty sessions area so named;

and, in a case falling within paragraph (e) above, shall also send to the justices' chief executive in question such documents and information relating to the case as the court considers likely to be of assistance to them.

In respect of a child or young person whose father and mother were not married to each other at time of his birth and with respect to whom a residence order is in force in the father's favour, reference to "parents", as in s.63(8)(a) (above) includes a reference to the father: s.67(2).

Combining a supervision order with other sentences or orders

20.11 The general rule broadly applies that "courts should avoid mixing sentences which fall into well-established and different categories".[4]

The general scope to combine sentences is now qualified by PCC(S)A 2000, s.69(5)(b) (see 18.04) which specifies that a court may not impose both an action plan order and a supervision order upon an offender within the same sentencing exercise.

---

[4] *McElhorne* (1983) 5 Cr.App.R.(S.) 53.

20.12   Though the 2000 Act does not prohibit combining a supervision order with a community rehabilitation order (or a CPRO) in respect of offenders aged 16 to 17, this appears completely contrary to the principle that an offender should be assessed as suitable for either the juvenile or adult form of community supervision but not both. The rationalisation of resources under the auspices of youth offending teams should render this possibility obsolete in practice. A mix of supervision order with a community punishment order for the same offence is not prohibited but appears contrary to the spirit and intentions of legislation, particularly now that reparation can be included in a supervision order under Sched. 7 para. 3 (see 20.19).

REQUIREMENTS IN A SUPERVISION ORDER

20.13   As indicated, the core requirement under a "standard" supervision order is to be supervised by the designated supervisor. The basic provision is augmented by s.63(6)(b)—

PCC(S)A 2000, s.63(6)(b)

A supervision order—

(b)   may contain such prescribed provisions as the court making the order (or amending it under Schedule 7) considers appropriate for facilitating the performance by the supervisor of his functions under section 64(4) below, including any prescribed provisions for requiring visits to be made by the offender to the supervisor;

and in paragraph (b) above "prescribed" means prescribed by rules under section 144 of the Magistrates' Courts Act 1980.

20.14   In furtherance of this provision, the following requirements are specified by MC(C&YP)R 1992, r.29(3) and in practice are included in standard orders—

(a)   That s/he shall inform the supervisor at once of any change of his/her residence or employment.

(b)   That s/he shall keep in touch with the supervisor in accordance with such instructions as may from time to time be given by the supervisor and, in particular, that s/he shall, if the supervisor so requires, receive visits from the supervisor at his/her home.

20.15   The form of a standard supervision order is prescribed by MC(C&YP)R 1992 Sched. 2 Form 38. Section 63(6)(b) thus empowers a court to include such other provisions as it considers appropriate for supervisory purposes but this general power should not be used to side-step the specific provisions of Sched.6. In practice, little use is made of this open-ended provision. By far the most important and utilised power to impose additional requirements has been in regard to participation in activities under what was formerly CYPA 1969, s.12(2) and s.12A(3)(a), *i.e.* "intermediate treatment" or "supervised activities". In 1999, of 2,192 young persons commencing supervision orders supervised by the probation service (admittedly the minority of supervision order commencements) 86 per cent were subject to no additional requirements. Some 87 per cent of additional requirements consisted of supervised activities or intermediate treatment.

Additional requirements under Schedule 6

Compliance with directions of supervisor

20.17   PCC(S)A 2000, Sched. 6, para. 2

(1) Subject to sub-paragraph (2) below, a supervision order may require the offender to comply with any directions given from time to time by the supervisor and requiring him to do all or any of the following things—

(a) to live at a place or places specified in the directions for a period or periods so specified;

(b) to present himself to a person or persons specified in the directions at a place or places and on a day or days so specified;

(c) to participate in activities specified in the directions on a day or days so specified.

(2) A supervision order shall not require compliance with directions given by virtue of sub-paragraph (1) above unless the court making it is satisfied that a scheme under section 66 of this Act (local authority schemes) is in force for the area where the offender resides or will reside; and no such directions may involve the use of facilities which are not for the time being specified in a scheme in force under that section for that area.

(3) A requirement imposed by a supervision order in pursuance of sub-paragraph (1) above shall be subject to any such requirement of the order as is authorised by paragraph 6 below (treatment for offender's mental condition).

(4) It shall be for the supervisor to decide—

(a) whether and to what extent he exercises any power to give directions conferred on him by virtue of sub-paragraph (1) above; and

(b) the form of any directions.

(5) The total number of days in respect of which an offender may be required to comply with directions given by virtue of paragraph (a), (b) or (c) of sub-paragraph (1) above shall not exceed 90 or such lesser number, if any, as the order may specify for the purposes of this sub-paragraph.

(6) For the purpose of calculating the total number of days in respect of which such directions may be given, the supervisor shall be entitled to disregard any day in respect of which directions were previously given in pursuance of the order and on which the directions were not complied with.

20.18 This constitutes the original power under the 1969 Act to impose what was known as "intermediate treatment", and reflects the breadth of potential schemes, provisions and programmes, residential and community-based, which were envisaged in the White Paper *Children in Trouble*[5] Paragraph 6(2) requires the court to be satisfied that a scheme providing appropriate facilities is available in the area where the supervised person lives or will reside. The supervisor has the discretion to decide what directions shall be given and these are not specified in the order.

"Intermediate treatment" had a somewhat erratic history; its meaning, coherence, funding and enforcement was particularly patchy and inconsistent in its

---

[5] Home Office (1968) Cmnd. 3601 (HMSO, London, 1968).

first decade of life. As a result, magistrates were not always confident that the supervised person would be required to undertake any additional demands of this nature. The Criminal Justice Act 1982 thus introduced an alternative power to impose activities requirements under CYPA 1969 s.12A, and now contained in Sched.6, para. 3(below), the crucial difference being that the court could specify the activities to be undertaken. A local authority, acting either individually or in association with other local authorities, shall "make arrangements with such persons as appear to them to be appropriate for the provision by those persons of facilities for enabling directions given by virtue of para. 2(1) to persons resident in their area": s.66(1)(a). Such arrangements shall be made in consultation with the local probation board (s.66(2)) and any such arrangements shall be specified in a "scheme" (s.66(3)), copied to the local justices' chief executive (s.66(5)).

Requirements as to activities and reparation

20.19   Originally contained in CYPA 1969 s.12A(3)(a), now PCC(S)A 2000 Sched. 6 para. 3, this provision requires the supervised person to undertake any of the requirements (a) to (c) that may be directed by the supervisor under Sched. 6 para. 2(1), and/or a requirement to "make reparation", as specified by the sentencing court. Such requirements may not be included in a supervision order which imposes paragraph 2 requirements.[6] The two forms of requirement are thus not compatible within the same supervision order. The maximum extent of para. 3 activity requirements is 90 days. The scope for requiring the offender to undertake activities is limited by para. 3(7) as regards overnight absence from home and the avoidance of interference with school attendance. Note that the paragraph does not include an equivalent provision to paragraph 2(6) allowing days when the offender does not comply to be disregarded in calculating the offender's fulfilment of obligations. Unlike parallel provisions empowering additional activity requirements in community rehabilitation orders, the role of the supervisor or person in charge of activities is not explicitly included in paragraph 3 provisions in respect of enforcing such provisions.

20.20   The 1969 Act included power under s.12D allowing a court in certain cases to impose a s.12A(3)(a) requirement as an explicit alternative to a custodial sentence but this somewhat anomalous provision was repealed by CDA 1998.

PCC(S)A 2000, Sched, 6 para. 3

(1)   This paragraph applies to a supervision order unless the order requires the offender to comply with directions given by the supervisor under paragraph 2(1) above.

(2)   Subject to the following provisions of this paragraph and paragraph 4 below, a supervision order to which this paragraph applies may require the offender—

    (a) to live at a place or places specified in the order for a period or periods so specified;

    (b) to present himself to a person or persons specified in the order at a place or places and on a day or days so specified;

    (c) to participate in activities specified in the order on a day or days so specified;

---

[6] (para. 3(1)).

(d) to make reparation specified in the order to a person or persons so specified or to the community at large;

and in this paragraph "make reparation" means make reparation for the offence otherwise than by the payment of compensation.

(6) Requirements included in a supervision order by virtue of sub-paragraph (2)(b) or (c) above shall, as far as practicable, be such as to avoid—

   (a) any conflict with the offender's religious beliefs or with the requirements of any other community order to which he may be subject; and
   (b) any interference with the times, if any, at which he normally works or attends school or any other educational establishment; and sub-paragraphs (7) and (8) below are without prejudice to this sub-paragraph.

(7) Subject to sub-paragraph (8) below, a supervision order may not by virtue of sub-paragraph (2) above include—

   (a) any requirement that would involve the offender in absence from home—

       (i) for more than two consecutive nights, or
       (ii) for more than two nights in any one week, or

   (b) if the offender is of compulsory school age, any requirement to participate in activities during normal school hours, unless the court making the order is satisfied that the facilities whose use would be involved are for the time being specified in a scheme in force under section 66 of this Act for the area in which the offender resides or will reside.

(8) Sub-paragraph (7)(b) above does not apply to activities carried out in accordance with arrangements made or approved by the local education authority in whose area the offender resides or will reside.

(9) Expressions used in sub-paragraphs (7) and (8) above and in the Education Act 1996 have the same meaning in those sub-paragraphs as in that Act.

As part of its duties under s.66(1) to "make arrangements" specified in a "scheme" (see 20.18) a local authority must also arrange facilities enabling requirements involving activities during normal school hours, as specified in para. 3(7), to be carried out effectively: s.66(1)(b).

20.21   Before imposing a paragraph 3 requirement the court must follow certain procedural steps, criteria and restrictions, as required by paragraph 3(4) and (5).

PCC(S)A 2000, Sched. 6, para. 3

(4) The court may not include requirements under sub-paragraph (2) above in a supervision order unless—

   (a) it has first consulted the supervisor as to—

       (i) the offender's circumstances, and
       (ii) the feasibility of securing compliance with the requirements, and is satisfied, having regard to the supervisor's report, that it is feasible to secure compliance with them;

(b) having regard to the circumstances of the case, it considers the requirements necessary for securing the good conduct of the offender or for preventing a repetition by him of the same offence or the commission of other offences; and

(c) if the offender is aged under 16, it has obtained and considered information about his family circumstances and the likely effect of the requirements on those circumstances.

(5) The court shall not by virtue of sub-paragraph (2) above include in a supervision order-

(a) any requirement that would involve the co-operation of a person other than the supervisor and the offender, unless that other person consents to its inclusion;

(b) any requirement to make reparation to any person unless that person—
(i) is identified by the court as a victim of the offence or a person otherwise affected by it; and
(ii) consents to the inclusion of the requirement;

(c) any requirement requiring the offender to reside with a specified individual; or

(d) any such requirement as is mentioned in paragraph 6(2) below (treatment for offender's mental condition).

Night restriction

20.22   Under Sched. 6. paragraph 3(2)(e), and subject to the overarching provisions of para. 3(1) and (5) as detailed above, the supervised person can be required: "to remain for specified periods between 6 p.m. and 6 a.m. (i) at a place specified in the order; or (ii) at one of several places so specified". This option is supplemented by para. 4 regulatory provisions.

This place or one of the specified places shall be where the supervised person lives.[7] A night restriction order shall not require the supervised person to remain at a place for longer than 10 hours on any one night[8] and shall not be imposed for more than 30 days.[9] For the purposes of calculating "days" subject to restriction, a period beginning in the evening and ending the following morning shall count as one day, namely that upon which the period begins.[10] The days subject to night restriction must not fall outside the first three months of the supervision order.[11] The supervised person is permitted to leave the place of restriction if accompanied by their parent or guardian, the supervisor or some other person specified in the order.[12]

20.23   In the years 1992–99 only 19 orders, out of a total of over 20,000 where the probation service was the supervising agency, contained this kind of requirement.

The 1990 White Paper[13] commented that it was a "valuable but under-used power":

---

[7] para. 4(1).
[8] para. 4(2).
[9] para. 4(4).
[10] para. 4(5).
[11] para. 4(3).
[12] para. 4(6).
[13] Home Office *Crime, Justice and Protecting the Public*, Cm. 965, (HMSO, London, 1990) para. 8.11.

"Young people who are free to come and go as they please at all hours are exposed to greater temptations and are at greater risk of getting into trouble. When they have already offended, that risk can be reduced by placing restrictions on their freedom of movement during the evening and night. One of the reasons for the under-use of the provision is the belief that it could be difficult to enforce. When a juvenile is living at home, his parents should know whether he is there in the evenings and at night. Most parents will exercise some control over their children's movements, especially at night. Combining the binding over of parents with a curfew imposed on the children will help ensure that curfews are enforced. The courts will be encouraged to make greater use of the power they already have."

20.24   Courts do not appear to have been persuaded by this argument and there is now statutory provision for young offenders to be made subject to curfew orders backed by electronic monitoring which is not a feature of night restriction requirements.

Requirement to refrain from activities

20.25   Under paragraph 3(2)(f), and subject to the overarching provisions of para. 3(1) and (5) as detailed above, the supervised person can be required: "to refrain from participating in activities specified in the order"—

(i) on a specified day or days during the period for which the supervision order is in force; or

(ii) during the whole of that period or a specified portion of it.

A requirement of this nature is thus not subject to the 90 day limit governing most para. 3 requirements. Very little use has been made of this power. In the years 1992–99 only six orders out of a total of over 20,000 where the probation service was the designated supervising agency contained this kind of requirement. This may suggest the enforcement problems posed by requirements of this nature. In the light of the new power to include an exclusion requirement in a community rehabilitation order, policed by electronic monitoring (see 22.64), albeit only for young offenders aged 16–17, even less use is likely to be made of this option.

Residence requirements

20.26   A requirement in respect of the offender's residence may be imposed under the following separate provisions of Schedule 6. The different powers are subject to separate limits and groundrules and it is important that those advising courts and sentencers are clear and precise as regards the provision under which a power is sought or intended. These powers have not been widely exercised to date. In the years 1992–99 only 30 orders out of a total of over 20,000 where the probation service was the designated supervising agency contained this kind of requirement.

(i) With a named individual

20.27   Under PCC(S)A 2000, Sched. 6 para. 1 a supervision order may require the offender "to reside with an individual named in the order who agrees to the requirement" being made. Such a requirement "shall be subject to any such requirement of the order as is authorised by paragraph 2 (supervisor's directions), 3 (activities etc.), 6 (mental treatment) or 7 (education)" (words in parenthesis not in original). This means that the demands of any such requirement will take precedence, even if this temporarily prevents adherence to the general requirement as to residence. This provision is not subject to any maximum time limit within the overall length of the order. It appears best suited to circumstances where it is hoped to stabilise the offender's accommodation and related circumstances by requiring him or her to live with a private individual such as a relative or a foster parent.

(ii) As directed by the supervisor

20.28   The provisions of Sched. 6 para. 2 have been outlined above but it is worth reiterating that the offender can be required under para. 2(1)(a) to live at a place or places for a period or periods as specified in the supervisor's directions. This scope to authorise the supervisor to give directions of this nature is assisted by the provisions of s.66(1) (see 20.18). This power is thus more appropriate where it is considered advantageous to allow the supervisor discretion to direct shorter periods of residence, such as to facilitate some offending behaviour programme that includes or consists of a residential component, or perhaps to remove the offender from their normal place of abode on a temporary basis in the light of certain contingencies.

(iii) As specified by the court

20.29   The provisions of Sched. 6 para. 3 have been outlined above but it is worth reiterating that the offender can be required under para. 3(1)(a) to live at a place or places for a period or periods as specified. This power is subject to the same parameters as a paragraph 2 order—a ceiling total of 90 days maximum—which may be regarded as reducing the scope to intervene effectively to stabilise an offender's living arrangements.

(iv) In local authority accommodation

20.30   Under provisions first introduced by the Children Act 1989 which repealed the power to make a care order in criminal proceedings, a court has power under Sched. 6 para. 5 to require that a supervised person shall live for a specified period in local authority accommodation, as defined by PCC(S)A 2000, s.163.

20.31   Use of this kind of requirement is an option only if a number of criteria are satisfied, as specified by para. 5(2)—

PCC(S)A 2000, Sched. 6 para. 5

(2)   The conditions are that—

    (a) a supervision order has previously been made in respect of the offender;

    (b) that order imposed—
        (i) a requirement under paragraph 1, 2, 3 or 7 of this Schedule; or

        (ii) a local authority residence requirement;

    (c) the offender fails to comply with that requirement, or is convicted of an offence committed while that order was in force; and

    (d) the court is satisfied that—

> (i) the failure to comply with the requirement, or the behaviour which constituted the offence, was due to a significant extent to the circumstances in which the offender was living; and
> (ii) the imposition of a local authority residence requirement will assist in his rehabilitation;

except that sub-paragraph (i) of paragraph (d) above does not apply where the condition in paragraph (b)(ii)above is satisfied.

In other words, this option is not available if the offender has not previously been subject to a supervision order with an additional requirement as specified. Further, he must either have failed to comply with that additional requirement (it is not enough that he failed to comply with the standard requirements of the order) or alternatively has re-offended while subject to that order. Further still, that failure or re-offending must be considered to have arisen in the context of his living arrangements (unless the previous order included a para. 5 requirement). Finally, the court must consider that a para. 5 requirement will be rehabilitive.

20.32 In addition, given the complexity of the threshold criteria and the restriction on liberty at stake, a requirement of this nature may not be imposed in respect of an offender who is not legally represented at "the relevant time" (*i.e.* the time when the court is considering whether to impose such a requirement: para. 5(8)(a)), unless he was granted a right of representation for the purposes of "the proceedings" by the Criminal Defence Service but that right was withdrawn because of his misconduct, or he refused or failed to apply for such representation despite being informed of his right to apply: para. 5(7)(a) and (b). "The proceedings" for this purpose means either "the whole proceedings" or "the part of the proceedings relating to the imposition of the requirement": para. 5(8)(b). In other words, the offender may have defaulted or misbehaved at an earlier stage before the issue of possibility of this kind of requirement arose.

The residence requirement may stipulate that the juvenile shall not live with a named person.[14] This means that the court may restrict the discretion of the local authority in placing the juvenile. Any supervision order imposing this requirement may also impose any of the requirements available under paras 2, 3, 6 and 7 of Schedule 6.

Mental treatment requirement

20.33 Under Sched. 6 para. 6 the supervised person can be required to receive treatment for his or her mental condition. The provisions are almost identical to the provisions empowering such a requirement to be imposed in a community rehabilitation order (see 22.50). In summary—

(a) the court must consider the evidence of a medical practitioner appropriately qualified under the Mental Health Act;

(b) the court must be satisfied that the mental condition of the offender is such as requires and may be susceptible to treatment but not such as to warrant detention under a hospital order;

(c) the requirement shall be that the supervised person submits to one of the following kinds of treatment—

---

[14] para. 5(5).

(i) by or under the direction of a registered medical practitioner or a chartered psychologist, specified in the order,

(ii) as a non-resident patient at a specified place,

(iii) as a resident patient in a hospital or mental nursing home;

(d) the court must be satisfied that arrangements can be or have been made for the treatment in question and, in the case of treatment as a resident patient, for the reception of the patient.

20.34 Where the offender has attained the age of 14, a treatment requirement cannot be included unless the offender *consents*.[15] Such a requirement shall not continue in force after the supervised person attains the age of 18.[16]

In the years 1992–99 only 50 orders out of a total of over 20,000 where the probation service was the designated supervising agency contained this kind of requirement, 43 being for non-residential treatment.

Education Requirement

20.35 Under PCC(S)A 2000, Sched. 6 para. 7, a supervision order, other than one which specifies a Sched. 6 para. 2 requirement, may require a supervised person of compulsory school age to comply with such arrangements for his education as may from time to time be made by his parents, being arrangements approved by the local education authority, for as long as he remains of that age. Such a requirement may not be included unless (a) the court has consulted the authority with regard to its proposal and (b) the court is "satisfied that in the view of the authority arrangements exist for the offender to receive efficient full-time education suitable to his age, ability and aptitude and to any special educational need he may have": para. 7(3). The court must also (c) consult the intended supervisor "as to the offender's circumstances" and (d) "consider the requirement necessary for securing the good conduct of the offender or for preventing a repetition by him of the same offence or the commission of other offences": para. 7(5).

20.36 In research undertaken with 265 magistrates serving four youth courts, Ball and Connolly[17] noted that though the justices valued school-based information about young defendants, were concerned about the consequences of educational disadvantage and were critical of youth justice workers' apparently cavalier attitude to the educational performance of young persons on whom they prepared PSRs, they made no use of their power to include an educational requirement in supervision orders in respect of non-school attender.[18] Hypothesising that this may reflect lack of knowledge, the authors found that only 27 per cent of lay justices and fewer than a half of stipendiaries identified the existence of such a power, some responses suggesting that magistrates do not consider education to be the business of a contemporary criminal court. Other responses suggested that even if magistrates were aware of the relevant provision, they were unclear how to apply this power or doubted if such a requirement would be enforceable or enforced. An

---

[15] para. 6(3)(b)

[16] para. 6(3).

[17] Ball C. and Connolly J., "Requiring School Attendance: A Little Used Sentencing Power", [1999] Crim. L.R., 183–194.

[18] n. 17: Ball & Connolly report that only 22 orders containing a s.12C as then applied requirement were made in 1995.

additional factor accounting for such remarkable under-use was the lack of proposals for such a requirement in PSRs. The authors conclude by speculating whether the advent of multi-agency youth offending teams will promote a sea-change making educational attainment and school attendance a far more prominent issue for youth justice workers and youth courts.

THE MANAGEMENT OF A SUPERVISION ORDER

20.37 The administration and management of a supervision order is regulated by the *National Standards for Youth Justice*[19] which provide a common code for the supervision of the following "court-ordered interventions": reparation orders, action plan orders, supervision orders, referral orders, parenting orders. The *Standards* emphasise very early and quite intensive implementation of the order with emphasis upon victim awareness and reparative opportunities.

Expectations under National Standards
Commencing supervision

20.38 The initial contact between supervising officer and offender "must be arranged to take place before the end of he next working day following the court hearing.[20] To ensure this prompt start, this meeting must be arranged before the offender leaves court. The offender's parents or primary carer should attend the initial meeting whenever possible.[21] A second follow-up meeting must take place within a further five working days[22] to complete induction, set outcomes for supervision and dates/expectations for further appointments, and to produce a draft supervision plan.

Frequency of contact

20.39 Minimum contact with the offender should occur:

- twice-weekly during the first 12 weeks; at least one of those weekly sessions must follow a programme designed to address offending and associated risk factors.
- after 12 weeks and up to the 26 week point, weekly.
- after 26 weeks, fortnightly.

This level of contact is more demanding than that specified for adult offenders (see 22.68). Contact must consist of planned appointments with a YOT member or a partner agency, or reparation activity or a groupwork programme.[23] Home visits must be offered at least monthly.[24]

Supervision plan

20.40 The Plan drafted in the light of the second meeting must be finalised within 15 days of the order being made, to include an initial assessment of the

---

[19] n. 2.
[20] n. 2, para. 7.1.1.
[21] n. 2, para. 7.1.2.
[22] n. 2, para. 7.1.3.
[23] n. 2, para. 7.2.4.
[24] n. 2, para. 7.2.5.

offender's attitude to their victim(s). "Where appropriate, action to put right the harm must be planned and undertaken within the first 12 weeks of intervention."[25] Where the offence was sexual or involved harassment or domestic violence, the victim should not be expected to have any direct contact with the offender as part of supervision. The Plan must be discussed with a YOT manager within ten working days of the order being made and collectively by the YOT within 12 weeks of sentence to ensure consistency of practice in collaboration with partner agencies. Thereafter, team reviews of the plan must occur at three monthly intervals or sooner if appropriate,[26] using the standard assessment tool (known as ASSET—see 4.20) to track progress. The offender's assessment must be updated at the end of the supervision period.

Early revocation

20.41   The supervisor must consider applying for early revocation of the order when the half-way point is reached and discuss this option with a YOT manager.[27] (In each of the years 1993–98 some seven or eight per cent of terminations of supervision orders supervised by the probation service were discharged early for good progress.[28])

Enforcement of the Order

20.42   Enforcement of supervision orders is governed by the dedicated provisions of PCC(S)A 2000, Sched. 7, reinforced by practice determined by *National Standards for Youth Justice*.[29] These provisions are detailed in Chapter 26.

THE OVERLAP OF COMMUNITY REHABILITATION AND SUPERVISION ORDERS

20.43   In proposing that courts should have the discretion to choose either the 1969 Act regime for statutory supervision (a supervision order) or that provided by the 1973 Act (a probation order), the 1990 White Paper[29a] was of the view that 16- and 17-year-olds should be dealt with as "near adults".

> "Since some 16- and 17-year-olds are more mature than others . . . there should be some flexibility in the sentencing arrangements . . . the courts should be able to select either (juvenile or adult) disposals according to the maturity of the offender and the arrangements available locally."

20.44   The Home Office Circular *Young People and the Youth Court*[30] sought to explain the concept of varying maturity, referring more helpfully to "stage of development", a less emotive term.

> "In deciding which is the most suitable community sentence for a 16- or 17-year-old, courts will need to take account both of the offender's circumstances

---

[25] n. 2, para. 7.2.6.
[26] n. 2, para. 7.2.8.
[27] n. 2, para. 7.2.10.
[28] *Probation Statistics for England & Wales, 1998*, London: Home Office.
[29] n. 2.
[29a] n. 13, para. 8.17.
[30] HOC 30/1992, para. 9.

and of the stage of his/her emotional, intellectual, social and physical development in the transition from childhood to adulthood. This decision will be a
particularly difficult one to make. Factors which are likely to be relevent
include—

- the offender's continuing dependence on or independence from his or
  her parents;

- whether he/she is leading a stable independent life, and has family
  responsibilities of his/her own;

- whether he/she is still in full-time education or in or seeking
  employment;

- the general pattern of his/her social behaviour and his/her leisure
  interests and activities;

- the nature of his/her relationship with friends and associates;

- whether he/she accepts personal responsibility for his/her actions;

- his/her attitude towards the offence and any victim; and

- whether he/she is intellectually impaired.

Information about and assessment of these factors in pre-sentence reports will
be particularly helpful to the courts in reaching their decision."

20.45 The original version of *National Standards* provided a clear[31] indication
that there should be a presumption that the supervision order is more the
appropriate form of supervision for this age group:

"While both a supervision order and a probation order are intended to assist
an offender to become more responsible and to keep out of trouble, the
clearest distinguishing feature is that the supervision order is also intended to
help a young person to develop into an adult, whereas a probation order is
more appropriate for someone who is already emotionally, intellectually,
socially and physically an adult. Since many 16- and 17-year-olds are still very
much in the stage of transition into adulthood, the supervision order may often
in practice be the more suitable form of supervision."

In addition to the list of factors identified in the Circular, *National Standards* also
mentioned the following considerations:

- How would the young person be influenced by other offenders currently
  subject to supervision orders or probation orders whom he or she may
  meet at group sessions?

- Is assistance currently being received or needed from Social Services?

The *National Standards for Youth Justice*[32] make no reference to the basis on which
such judgements should be made.

---

[31] Home Office (1992), para. 14.
[32] n. 2.

20.46 The two professional associations representing Chief Probation Officers (ACOP) and probation practitioners (NAPO) clearly favoured the view that the supervision order should be the standard order for the under 18s. ACOP[33] stated:

> "It can be argued persuasively that the criteria (in National Standards) exclude all those aged under 18. All such persons require help to develop into an adult and young persons are always at risk of being adversely influenced by more mature offenders. We do not believe that probation orders, and especially combination orders, should be used for the under 18-year-olds except in the most exceptional circumstances."

NAPO when further and stated that "if the young person needs assistance, there should be no occasion when a probation order is made rather than a supervision order". The Association has cautioned against use of the terms "maturity" and "immaturity". "Immature", it is argued, often has negative connotations and can be discriminatory, leading to judgements based on simplistic criteria or stereotypes.[34]

20.47 One question which appears not to have been raised in the debate about flexible sentencing for near-adults is whether the young person makes a once-only, irreversible step across the frontier or whether it is a reversible step, depending on the ebb and flow of circumstances in their lives, *e.g.* into and out of the family home, employment or full-time education. Might an offender who has been considered suitable for a community rehabilitation order later be viewed as more appropriate for a supervision order? As the person's suitability for different community sentences has to be considered afresh on each sentencing occasion, then it would seem proper to conclude that the step is indeed reversible. For a review of the application of the various criteria in determining the appropriate sentence for near adults, suggesting that proposals in pre-sentence reports are more likely to be influenced by considerations such as the seriousness of the offence, the young offender's previous record and assumptions about the way in which the order in question will be supervised, see Stone.[35]

20.48 The *Criminal Statistics for England and Wales*[36] revealed the comparative use of orders as a percentage of persons aged 15 to 17 sentenced in 1998 for indictable offences by sex (approximate actual numbers in brackets)—

Order	Males	Females
Supervision	16% (5,600)	22% (1,100)
Probation	5% (1,900)	7% (400)
Combination	4% (1,300)	2% (100)

20.49 It should be noted that the demands and restrictions that can be imposed as additional requirements in supervision orders can be greater than is lawful under the terms of a community rehabilitation order, *e.g.* activities requirements under Sched. 6, para 2 or 3 can extend for 90 days instead of 60 days as under Sched. 2

---

[33] ACOP (1992) *Seriousness and Proportionality in the Youth Court under the Criminal Justice Act 1991*, London: ACOP.
[34] NAPO (1992) *Limiting the Damage*, London: NAPO.
[35] N. Stone (1994) "Sentencing the Near Adult", J.P. 158, 580 and 595.
[36] Home Office (1999): London: HMSO.

para 2 or 3. The discretion given to the supervisor under Sched. 6 para 2 is significantly greater than can be exercised under a community rehabilitation order with Sched. 2 para 2 activity requirements. It would thus be wrong to regard the supervision order as intrinsically more benign. The one basic distinction between the community rehabilitation order and the supervision order lies in the name of the order. It is advantageous for the young offender who is able to grow out of crime that their record shows a distinctively juvenile penalty from which they can more readily distance themselves, rather than an adult-sounding penalty with the possible additional element of stigma attached thereto.

However, as previously noted (see 20.39), the minimum contact demands during the first 12 weeks of an order under the two respective sets of *National Standards* are different, specifying twice weekly contact in respect of a supervision order but only weekly contact in supervising a community rehabilitation order. Pragmatic self-interest exercised by hard-pressed staff anxious not to be found at fault when audits of compliance with these Standards are conducted may be the most influential factor in determining which form of order they propose to sentencing courts. Though an offender made subject to a community rehabilitation order may be spared more demanding frequency of contact, he or she may find themselves exposed to more stringent penalty powers under PCC(S)A 2000, Sched. 3 if attaining age 18 during the life of their order (see 22.70). One further considera-tion is that a supervision order attracts a shorter rehabilitation period before the conviction can be regarded as spent (see 30.48), though this disparity may change as a consequence of the current review of ROA 1974.

CHAPTER 21

Curfew Orders and Exclusion Orders

21.01 This chapter combines the two community orders that involve "negative" restriction of liberty, negative in the sense of containing the offender's freedom of movement by requiring him to remain at or to avoid a specified place, policed invariably by electronic monitoring surveillance. Though not aimed exclusively at young offenders, these orders may be regarded as part of the legal response, along with child curfew schemes, to the frequently expressed adult concern to "get young people off the streets".[1]

CURFEW ORDERS

21.02 The curfew order, somewhat akin to "night restriction" as a requirement of a supervision order (see 20.22), was introduced as a distinct community order by CJA 1991, s.12 but is now governed by PCC(S)A 2000 s.37. Though originally devised as a measure for offenders aged 16 or over, curfew order powers were extended in a modified form to all young offenders by the C(S)A 1997, s.43. The measure was subjected to extended piloting in trial areas before becoming a national sentencing option in 2000. The order is frequently referred to as "tagging" because of the scope, invariably used, to include a requirement of electronic monitoring of curfew obligations. Tagging has since become a familiar feature of the penal landscape, being available as a condition of various forms of early release from custodial sentences, as a penalty in place of a fine for persistent petty offenders (see 16.95) and, more recently, as an adjunct to the exclusion order, introduced into PCC(S)A 2000 by the Criminal Justice and Court Services Act 2000 (CJCSA 2000) (see 21.17). Curfew with electronic monitoring is also an optional penalty for breach of a requirement of a supervision order, an action plan order or reparation order under PCC(S)A 2000 Scheds 7, 8 (see 26.23). Now that a curfew requirement can be included in a community rehabilitation order (see 26.63), it remains to be seen whether curfew will be used extensively for young offenders aged 16 or 17 as an order in its own right or will be viewed by sentencers as more appropriately included alongside the other demands and benefits of community supervision.

Power to Make a Curfew Order

21.03   **PCC(S)A 2000, s.37**

    (1)   Where a person is convicted of an offence the court by or before which he is convicted may make an order requiring him to remain, for periods specified in the order, at a place so specified.

---

[1] As expressed forcefully in a study of adult perceptions of crime in Middlesborough: Brown S. (1995) "Crime and Safety in Whose Community? Age, Everyday Life and Problems of Youth Policy", *Youth and Policy*, 48, 27–48.

(2) An order under subsection (1) above is in this Act referred to as a "curfew order"

(3) A curfew order may specify different places or different periods for different days, but shall not specify—

   (a) periods which fall outside the period of six months beginning with the day on which it is made; or
   (b) periods which amount to less than two hours or more than 12 hours in any one day.

(4) In relation to an offender aged under 16 on conviction, subsection (3)(a) above shall have effect as if the reference to six months were a reference to three months.

(5) The requirements in a curfew order shall, as far as practicable, be such as to avoid—

   (a) any conflict with the offender's religious beliefs or with the requirements of any other community order to which he may be subject; and
   (b) any interference with the times, if any, at which he normally works or attends school or other educational establishment.

21.04 A youth court or the Crown Court may make a curfew order in respect of an offender aged 10 or over who has been convicted of any offence, whether imprisonable or not, other than one carrying a mandatory sentence. A curfew restriction may not extend beyond six months from the date on which the order is made or three months if the offender is aged under 16. The "place" need not be the offender's home but will probably be so. The range of restriction which can be imposed is clearly wide, ranging, in theory at least, from as little as two hours up to over 2,000 hours within the six month period. The order may specify only certain days, *e.g.* weekends.

Procedural Requirements

Information about place of confinement

21.05 Though there is no statutory requirement under PCC(S)A 2000 s.36(4) to obtain a pre-sentence report, the court is required to consider whether imposition of restrictions on liberty under a curfew order is commensurate with the seriousness of the offence(s) and whether the order is the most suitable for the offender PCC(S)A 2000, s.35(3) (a) and (b). In addition, the court must obtain particular information specified by section 37(8) and (9), best secured through a pre-sentence report.

PCC(S)A 2000, s.37

(8) Before making a curfew order, the court shall obtain and consider information about the place proposed to be specified in the order (including information as to the attitude of persons likely to be affected by the enforced presence there of the offender).

(9) Before making a curfew order in respect of an offender who on conviction is aged under 16, the court shall obtain and consider information about his family circumstances and the likely effect of such an order on those circumstances.

21.06 This requirement appears to place practical limitations upon the suitability of a curfew order. Apart from questions of the impact of the proposed confinement upon the lives of family members or others who would be affected, an offender who does not enjoy the security of tenure of an owner occupier or a tenant is not necessarily in a position to consent to remaining indoors at the specified "place" where this depends on the goodwill, hospitality or tolerance of the occupier. Though the subsection (8) does not make this explicit, the curfew would seem viable only if the occupier of the premises (if other than the defendant) gives active consent to the proposal (consent which can, of course, be withdrawn at any time, thus requiring a referral back to the relevant court). These questions arise particularly in regard to electronic monitoring (below). Subsection (8) does not specify who will be responsible for making inquiries to provide information for the court but this task is likely to fall to the relevant YOT or possibly the probation service. It is not explicit whether the consent of the defendant or their parent/ guardian should be sought before inquiries are made with third persons.

Explanation

21.07   PCC(S)A 2000, s.37

(10) Before making a curfew order, the court shall explain to the offender in ordinary language—

   (a) the effect of the order (including any additional requirements proposed to be included in the order in accordance with section 38 below (electronic monitoring));

   (b) the consequences which may follow (under Schedule 3 to this Act) if he fails to comply with any of the requirements of the order; and

   (c) that the court has power (under parts III and IV of that Schedule) to review the order on the application either of the offender or of the responsible officer.

Responsible person and monitoring arrangements

21.08   PCC(S)A 2000, s.37

(6) A curfew order shall include provision for making a person responsible for monitoring the offender's whereabouts during the curfew periods specified in the order; and a person who is made so responsible shall be of a description specified in an order made by the Secretary of State.

(7) A court shall not make a curfew order unless the court has been notified by the Secretary of State that arrangements for monitoring the offender's whereabouts are available in the area in which the place proposed to be specified in the order is situated and the notice has not been withdrawn."

(12) In this Act, "responsible officer", in relation to an offender subject to a curfew order, means the person who is responsible for monitoring the offender's whereabouts during the curfew periods specified in the order."

21.09 Responsibility for monitoring has been assigned by the Home Office to the three private sector commercial contractors providing electronic monitoring facilities nationally. Each contractor holds responsibility for a portion of England and Wales and in consequence the identity of the responsible officer will depend on the area in which the offender resides and/or the specified place is located.

Electronic monitoring

21.10 A curfew order may in addition include requirements for securing the electronic monitoring of the offender's whereabouts during the curfew periods specified in the order"[2-3] Commonly known as "tagging", this provision for electronic surveillance is not a sentence in its own right but an optional regulatory inclusion in a curfew order. In practice, a s.36B requirement is always included as standard as the hallmark of the curfew order is that it is policed exclusively by this means. The offender is required to wear a device attached to the ankle or wrist which relays a signal to monitoring equipment located at the place of confinement. Violations are relayed by telephone line to the monitoring centre.

21.11 A tagging requirement must not be included in a curfew order unless the court has been notified that monitoring arrangements are available in the area where the specified place is located. This facility became a nationally available resource from January 2000 for offenders aged 16 or older. Extension of curfew for younger offenders was delayed to await analysis of the trials that have been conducted in Greater Manchester and Norfolk from early 1998. For tagging to be viable in instances where the specified place is the offender's home address, the offender needs to reside at a settled address in a property with an existing telephone line or to which a line can be readily connected. If the offender is not the property occupier, the permission of the occupier is necessary for the telephone equipment to be installed or adapted for monitoring purposes. The offender also has to be able to offer a constant electricity supply to power the monitoring equipment.

Sentencing Principles and Practice

21.12 Though the Court of Appeal has yet to give guidance on the use of this measure, the 1990 White Paper[4] suggested that curfew orders would be:

> "helpful in reducing some forms of crime, thefts of or from cars, pub brawls and other types of disorder. A curfew order could be used to keep offenders away from particular places such as shopping centres or pubs, or to keep them at home in the evenings or at weekends".

The White Paper pointed out that "it is not the intention to keep people at home for most of the day" but to enable them to undertake constructive pursuits whether employment, training, community service or treatment for drug abuse.

21.13 Home Office research[5] of the trials of curfew orders conducted in three areas (Greater Manchester, Norfolk and Berkshire) 1995–97 was able to demonstrate the technical efficiency of electronic monitoring but also the gradual take-up of this disposal after an uncertain start. The majority of orders were imposed in adult magistrates' courts. Of 443 orders imposed between July 1995 and June 1997, only 34 and 42 were imposed by the Crown Court and youth courts respectively. The 367 orders made by adult magistrates' courts can be compared

---

[2-3] s.36(B)(1) (see 17.13).
[4] Home Office, *Crime, Justice and Protecting the Public*, Cm. 965 (HMSO, London, 1990) para. 4.20.
[5] Mair G. & Mortimer E. (1996) *Curfew Orders with Electronic Monitoring: an evaluation of the first twelve months of trials in Greater Manchester, Norfolk and Berkshire, 1995–96*, Research Study 163 (Home Office, London); Mortimer E. & May C. (1997) *Electronic Monitoring in Practice: the second year of the trials of curfew orders*, Research Study 177, London: Home Office; Mortimer E., Pereira E. & Walter I. (1999) "Making the Tag Fit: Further Analysis from the first Two Years of the Trials of Curfew Orders", *Research Findings No. 105* (Home Office, London).

with 2,900 probation orders, 2,400 CSOs and 900 combination orders made in the same courts over that period. The average length of all orders in that year was 100 days. The successful completion rate of 82 per cent compared well with CSOs (71 per cent) but the completion rate for youth court orders was less impressive at 69 per cent. Though few women were tagged (constituting only 8 per cent of orders made) their completion rate was on a par with tagged male offenders. "Stand alone" orders had a higher completion rate than those made alongside other community orders but this may be because they were often used for less serious offences. Practitioners and sentencers showed a preference for enhancing curfews by more "constructive" demands (probation staff) or the opportunity to "link punishment and help" (magistrates).

21.14 Magistrates asked to complete a sentencing choices survey indicated that they viewed curfew orders as an alternative to custodial sentences and higher end community orders. Three-quarters of sentences and probation staff interviewed suggested that tagging might be particularly appropriate—

- as a high tariff sentence for serious offenders where custody is a possibility;
- to disrupt "pattern" offending such as shoplifting, night-time burglary, weekend public disorder;
- where extra punishment is called for.

Tagging was felt to be unsuitable where:

- there is risk within the family, *e.g.* of domestic violence or because of child protection concerns, or there are contra-indicative family considerations, *e.g.* pregnancy or child care demands;
- the offender has physical or mental health problems;
- the offender is a substance misuser and/or has a chaotic lifestyle (though some magistrates felt that chaotic drug misusers might benefit from the constraints of curfew).

21.15 Sentencers also thought that "the discipline of curfew could assist in changing young people's offending behaviour but probation officers stressed the need for a stable home in such cases". The research found that families of offenders had co-operated and appeared positive in their views of tagging, as instanced by one mother who approved of this disposal since it meant that her son did not have to "mix with all those criminals".

As regards the pilot trials in Greater Manchester and Norfolk of electronically monitored curfew orders for young offenders aged under 16, the evaluation study[6] reported relatively low take-up with 155 orders being made between March 1998 and February 2000 (only two by the Crown Court), primarily in respect of boys aged 14 and 15 for lengths of two to three months and for periods of 10 to 12 hours. A quarter of defendants had some other penalty imposed at the same time, most of these being supervision orders (the new measures under the 1998 Act not being then available). Sentencers in the pilot areas had received guidance that they

---

[6] R. Elliott, J. Airs, C. Easton and R. Lewis, *Electronically Monitored Curfew for 10 to 15-Year-Olds: Report of the Pilot*, Occasional Paper (Home Office, London, 2000). It was noteworthy that several orders were imposed for longer than three months, in excess of sentencing powers, presumably through misunderstanding of this new power.

should think very carefully before curfewing children to schools. In practice, no orders specified times in term-time school hours or school as the place of curfew. Prior to the trials concern had been expressed that being tagged would either be experienced as a very visible stigma or would be seen as a prized trophy, each running the risk of young people living up to the label ascribed to them. Interviews with wearers and their families gave evidence of both kinds of reaction, though several young people appeared unaffected either way, though their tag was often a source of embarrassment or shame for their families. Schools reported no negative effect on the child's education (in two cases a positive effect was noted), though wearing a tag appeared to have hindered a child's participation in sport in four of the 13 cases where the wearer was known to be receiving education (the majority were not attending school, for example because they were excluded). In general, young offenders and their families expressed positive reaction to the sentence, most identifying as the main advantage that it had kept them out of custody (though more than half had earlier convictions only three per cent had experienced prior custody). As regards potential life-style changes, most offenders "did not develop new, socially acceptable leisure activities. Instead, many watched more television, listened to more music or slept more". In only two instances were the researchers told that the curfew had "enabled a young offender to break from a crowd of peers who had led them into trouble".

The sentence was well-regarded by magistrates who attributed the low numbers made to the small number of young offenders who were suitable for curfew. While sentencers saw the measure as a relatively high tariff penalty, the evidence suggested that "curfew was not usually used as a direct alternative to youth custody. . . . In practice, they seem to have replaced other alternatives." The researchers anticipated that there might be a higher rate of non-compliance among this age group but 73 percent of juveniles (figures for Manchester only) completed their orders, two-thirds of the total completing without breach proceedings being initiated. The completion rate was better for 15-year-olds (85 per cent) than for 14-year-olds (61 per cent).

Enforcement

21.16 Curfew orders are subject to the common enforcement code contained in PCC(S)A 2000, Sched. 3 and jurisdiction is vested primarily in the "magistrates" court acting for the petty sessions area in which "the place" specified in the order is situated.[6a] It is worth noting one aspect of these provisions, namely where the court faced with a young offender's non-compliance with his curfew order proposes to "deal with him for the offence in respect of which the order was made" (Sched. 3 para. 4(1C)(d) or 5(1C)(d) and considers that he has "wilfully and persistently" failed to comply, within the provisions of para. 4(2)(b) or para. 5(2)(b), thus enabling the court to impose a custodial sentence (for an imprisonable offence) "notwithstanding anything in PCC(S)A 2000 s.79(2)". Where the offender is aged under 15 at the point of re-sentence there is an additional criterion to be satisfied, namely that he is a "persistent offender" under the provisions of s.100(2)(a) (see 28.05) but neither para. 4 or para. 5 make reference to s.100. It appears to follow that to enable the court to exercise DTO powers in such circumstances it will need to be satisfied that they are dealing with a persistent offender. It will also need to adhere to the minimum permissible term of four months (see 28.16).

[6a] Sched. 3 para. 1(2)(a).

EXCLUSION ORDERS

21.17 A new community order introduced by CJCSA 2000, s.39 and governed by PCC(S)A 2000, s.40A, the exclusion order is intended to extend statutory control over an offender's whereabouts, not by curfew confinement to a specified place but by prohibiting the offender from entering a specified place, policed by a requirement of electronic monitoring. Though exclusion can be a stand alone order, the enabling legislation also introduces power for a court to impose exclusion as an additional requirement of a community rehabilitation order (see 22.64). It remains to be seen whether sentencers dealing with offenders aged 16 or over will opt to make s.40A orders or will prefer to incorporate such provision as a feature of community supervision.

Power to Make an Exclusion Order

21.18   PCC(S)A 2000, s.40A

(1) Where a person is convicted of an offence, the court by or before which he is convicted may (subject to sections 34 to 36 above) make an order prohibiting him from entering a place specified in the order for a period so specified of not more than one year.

(3) An exclusion order-

   (a) may provide for the prohibition to operate only during the periods specified in the order;
   (b) may specify different places for different periods or days.

(4) In relation to an offender aged under 16 on conviction, subsection (1) above shall have effect as if the reference to one year were a reference to three months.

(5) The requirements in an exclusion order shall, as far as practicable, be such as to avoid—

   (a) any conflict with the offender's religious beliefs or with the requirements of any other community order to which he may be subject; and
   (b) any interference with the times, if any, at which he normally works or attends school or any other educational establishment.

(12) In this section, "place" includes an area.

21.19 A youth court or the Crown Court may make an exclusion order in respect of an offender aged 10 or older who has been convicted of any offence, whether imprisonable or not, other than one carrying a mandatory sentence. An exclusion restriction may not extend beyond 12 months from the date on which the order is made, or three months if the offender is aged under 16 when convicted. The exclusion can apply throughout the period of the order or the court may specify that it shall apply only during specified periods. There is scope to include more than one place but it is unclear whether s.40A(3)(b) empowers exclusion from more than one place simultaneously or the offender can be excluded from different places only at separate times. The more unfettered interpretation appears to be intended. Note that "place" for exclusion purposes is defined to include "an area", thus broadening the ambit of exclusion to embrace such locations as, for example, a shopping precinct, though the more ambitious the ambit the greater the monitoring challenge.

Procedural Requirements

Monitoring arrangements

21.20 A court cannot make an exclusion order unless it has been notified that arrangements for monitoring the offender's whereabouts are available in the area in which the place to be specified in the order is located: s.40A(8). If such arrangements are in place (and it is assumed that such arrangements go in tandem with parallel curfew order monitoring arrangements), the order shall include provision for making a person responsible for monitoring the offender's whereabouts during periods of exclusion prohibition. The details of the arrangements are still awaited but it can be safely presumed that the electronic monitoring contractors will hold this responsibility. Though electronic monitoring is not an essential legal feature of exclusion orders but rather an option under s.36B, tagging will in fact be standard. The responsible person holds the powers and responsibilities of "responsible officer" for enforcement purposes under PCC(S)A 2000, Sched. 3: s.40A(13).

Information about offenders aged under 16

21.21 Though there is no statutory requirement under PCC(S)A 2000, s.36(4) to obtain a pre-sentence report, the court is required to obtain and consider information about the offender's family circumstances and the likely effect of an order on those circumstances before making an order in respect of an offender aged under 16 at time of conviction: s.40A(9).

Explanation

21.22 Before making an order, the court must explain to the offender, "in ordinary language", the effect of the order (including any requirement of electronic monitoring under s.36B), the consequences that may follow under PCC(S)A 2000, Sched. 3 if he fails to comply and the scope for the court to review the order on the application of the offender, the responsible officer or an "affected person" (see below). The court shall give a copy of the order to the offender and to the responsible officer: s.40A(11)(a).

Affected person

An "affected person" is defined by s.40A(13) as someone whose consent is required before a requirement of electronic monitoring can be included in the order under s.36B or is the beneficiary of a prohibition in the order "for the purpose (or partly for the purpose) of protecting him from being approached by the offender". On making an exclusion order the court is required to "give to any affected person any information relating to the order which the court considers it appropriate for him to have": s.40A(11)(b). An affected person is able to apply to the court exercising jurisdiction for enforcement purposes for the order to be amended under PCC(S)A 2000, Sched. 3 para. 19 but an application "must be for the cancellation of a requirement" included for the person's protection from being approached by the offender or "for the insertion of a requirement which will, if inserted, be such a requirement": para. 19(5).

Specified petty sessions area

21.23 The order shall specify the petty sessions area in which the offender resides or intends to reside: s.40A(7). The consequence is that a court acting for that PSA has jurisdiction in respect of enforcement proceedings under PCC(S)A 2000, Sched.3.

Electronic Monitoring

21.24   Where the court has been notified that electronic monitoring is available in the area where the "place" to be specified in the order is located, it may include requirements for securing the electronic monitoring of the offender's whereabouts during the periods when the prohibition operates: s.36B(1) (see 17.13). It remains to be clarified whether the monitoring focus will concentrate on tracking the offender or on establishing whether the "place" remains free of the offender's presence. The latter suggests the installation of equipment at the "place" which will detect the presence of the offender, who will be required to wear a devise that emits a signal which can be picked up by that equipment. This technique requires the co-operation and consent of the occupier of the "place", as recognised by s.36B(3).

CHAPTER 22

Community Rehabilitation Orders

22.01 The probation order was renamed the community rehabilitation order by CJCSA 2000 s.36 to further the change in this measure's status begun by CJA 1991. Governed now by PCC(S)A s.41, the legal provisions remain essentially as revised by the 1991 Act. To ease the transition required through change of name s.36 clarifies—

> (2) References in any enactment, instrument or document to a community rehabilitation order include (where the context allows) an order under any provision corresponding to that subsection (s.41(1)) which is repealed by that Act.

> (4) References in any enactment, instrument or document to a probation order—

>> (a) are to an order under any provision corresponding to s.41(1) of PCC(S)A 2000 which is repealed by that Act, and
>> (b) include (where the context allows) an order under that section.

Though primarily an adult measure, the community rehabilitation order will continue to be widely used in youth courts, despite the extended range of disposals now available for the under-18s.

Rationale of the Probation Order

With a pedigree dating back to 1907, the probation order was transformed under the 1991 Act from an expression of conditional liberty made "instead of sentencing"[1] to a "community order" within a wider framework of "punishment in the community" and restriction on liberty. The 1990 White Paper[2] justified this change of identity by claiming that the wording of section 2(1) reflected—

> "the original intention that probation should be used mainly for first, or relatively trivial offenders. Since then, probation orders have been used increasingly for persistent offenders and for those whose offences put them at risk of custody . . . In practice, the probation order can be a penalty making significant demands on the offender."

22.02 This interpretation of the origins of the probation order is of questionable accuracy and, prior to implementation of the 1991 Act, probation was being

---

[1] PCCA 1973, s.2(1), now repealed.
[2] Home Office, *Crime, Justice and Protecting the Public*, Cm.965 (HMSO, London, 1990).

used as a disposal flexibly in a wide range of cases where it was considered expedient to offer the offender the opportunity to demonstrate their capacity to conform, given supervisory oversight and support, while retaining the scope to impose punishment in the event of default. Those who proposed incorporating the probation order within a range of "intermediate sanctions"[3] acknowledged the lack of conceptual fit but suggested that offenders placed on probation have customarily experienced the disposal as punitive and thus argued that such a rationalisation had a common-sense appeal. However, the fact that a measure has a demanding impact and curtails personal freedom of choice does not make it a punishment deliberately designed to cause pain, inconvenience or erosion of autonomy. Probation, as classically conceived, aimed to enhance freedom and citizenship and was not intended to be restrictive for its own sake. Probation officers and sentencers thus experienced some difficulty in absorbing the probation order's new identity as an exercise in both restrictiveness and rehabilitation, particularly now that the "traditional" order without additional requirements is arguably the least restrictive community order.

POWER TO MAKE A COMMUNITY REHABILITATION ORDER

22.03   PCC(S)A 2000, s.41(1)

(1) Where a person aged 16 or over is convicted of an offence and the court by or before which he is convicted is of the opinion that his supervision is desirable in the interests of-

  (a) securing his rehabilitation, or
  (b) protecting the public from harm from him or preventing the commission by him of further offences,

the court may (subject to sections 34 to 36 above) make an order requiring him to be under supervision for a period specified in the order of not less than six months nor more than three years.

22.04 A youth court or the Crown Court may make a community rehabilitation order in respect of any offender aged 16 years or over who has been convicted of any offence, whether imprisonable or not, provided that the court is of the opinion that—

(a) the offence, or the combination of the offence and one or more offences associated with it, is serious enough to warrant such a sentence[4];

(b) an order is the most suitable for the offender (s.35(3)(a));

(c) the restrictions on liberty thus imposed are commensurate with offence seriousness (s.35(3)(b); and

(d) supervision is desirable in the interests of either (i) securing the offender's rehabilitation, or (ii) protecting the public from harm from the offender or preventing further offending by the offender.

---

[3] M. Wasik and A. von Hirsch "Non-Custodial Penalties and the Principles of Desert" [1988] Crim.L.R. 555; A. Bottoms "The Place of the Probation Service in the Criminal Justice System" in *The Madingley Papers II* (Central Council of Probation Committees, London, 1989).
[4] PCC(S)A 2000, s.35(1).

22.05   Though section 41(1) poses two alternative purposes of the order, rehabilitation or protection prevention, the court is not explicitly required to state which purpose it has in mind when passing sentence. *National Standards*[5] expect supervisors to pursue both aims routinely.

Length of Order

22.06   The length weighed together with the extent of requirements, in other words the extent of restriction on liberty imposed, shall be commensurate with the seriousness of the offence or that offence combined with one or more associated offences.[6] This assessment cannot be made on some objective scale of the time and effort demanded of the offender but must also encompass the anticipated impact upon the offender in the light of their personal circumstances and characteristics. Thus *Crime, Justice and Protecting the Public*[7] observed that "the lifestyle of many offenders, especially young adults, is often disorganised and impulsive . . . A comparatively short order may make more severe demands on some offenders than more severe orders would on others". However, these are somewhat elusive considerations, not easily explained in distinguishing one offender from another, and may prove difficult to articulate in open court in a way which avoids a sense of grievance for those offenders considered suitable for or more able to tackle "more severe" orders. Courts may find it easier to opt for formal equality of sentence rather than seeking individualised equality of impact.

22.07   The average imposed length of probation orders has reduced in recent years, as the following Table (for all age groups) demonstrates—

	Under 1 Year	1 Year+	2 Years+	3 Years
1983	5%	33%	58%	4%
1993	12%	49%	38%	2%
1999	11%	52%	35%	2%

Source: Probation Statistics, Home Office.

This fall reflects a changing emphasis in probation practice towards shorter, more purposeful periods of supervision, with clearer goals, rather than merely an expectation of a sustained supportive relationship. The average length of order of order in 1998 was 16.8 months.

Age of offender

22.08   The minimum age at which an offender may be placed on probation was reduced from 17 to 16 by CJA 1991. There is thus overlap in eligibility for this order and a supervision order reflecting the proposal in *Crime, Justice and Protecting the Public* that there should be some flexibility in the sentencing arrangements for 16 and 17 year olds, according to their "maturity" or stage of development and the arrangements available locally (see 20.43).

It is for the court to determine whether the offender satisfies the age requirement at date of conviction, *i.e.* the date of the finding of guilt or of plea of guilty.[8] The

---

[5] Home Office (2000) *National Standards for the Supervision of offenders in the Community*.
[6] s.35(3)(b)
[7] n. 2, para. 4.9.
[8] *T* [1979] Crim. L.R. 588; *Danga* (1992) 13 Cr.App.R.(S.) 408).

court may normally rely upon the age stated by the offender or his parents, unless there are clear indications that this is unreliable and it would be appropriate to hear evidence of date of birth.[9]

Procedural Requirements

(i) Pre-sentence Report

22.09 A court is not required to consider a pre-sentence report before deciding whether an offender is suitable for a community rehabilitation order, unless the proposed order includes an additional requirement authorised by PCC(S)A 2000, Sched. 2. but good practice usually discourages the making of standard orders (or orders which contain an additional requirement under PCC(S)A 2000, s.42(1) — see 22.20) without a PSR. Failure to obtain and consider a report where this is a mandatory requirement does not invalidate the order so made but would be an obvious basis for appeal. The court considering such appeal is required to obtain and consider a report but an appeal against a community rehabilitation order made in such circumstances is perhaps rather unlikely.

The requirement to consider a pre-sentence report does not mean that the report has to address the possibility of an order with Schedule 2 requirements but in most instances of such requirements the Schedule requires either consultation with the prospective supervising agency or the consent of any third party whose co-operation is required, or both.

(ii) Explanation and consent

22.10   **PCC(S)A 2000, s.41(7)**

(7) Before making a community rehabilitation order, the court shall explain to the offender in ordinary language—

  (a) the effect of the order (including any additional requirements proposed to be included in the order in accordance with section 42 below);

  (b) the consequences which may follow (under Part II of Schedule 3 to this Act) if he fails to comply with any of the requirements of the order; and

  (c) that the court has power (under Parts III and IV of that Schedule) to review the order on the application either of the offender or of the responsible officer.

22.11 Explanation should be given directly to the offender by the court and should not be delegated to the defence advocate or supervision officer.

The offender's consent is required only if the court proposes to impose a community rehabilitation order containing an additional requirement under PCC(S)A 2000 Sched. 2 paras. 5 or 6 (*i.e.* mental treatment or treatment for drug/alcohol dependency, detailed at 22.50 *et seq.*)

(iii) Specified area and responsible officer

22.12   **PCC(S)A 2000, s.41**

(3) A community rehabilitation order shall specify the petty sessions area in which the offender resides or will reside.

[9] *R. v. Recorder of Grimsby, ex p. Purser* [1951] 2 All E.R. 889).

(5) If the offender is aged under 18 at that time, he shall, subject to paragraph 18 of Schedule 3, be required to be under the supervision of—

(a) a probation officer appointed for or assigned to the petty sessions area specified in the order; or

(b) a member of a youth offending team established by a local authority specified in the order; and if an order specifies a local authority for the purposes of paragraph (b) above, the authority specified must be the local authority within whose area it appears to the court that the offender resides or will reside.

(6) In this Act, "responsible officer", in relation to an offender who is subject to a community rehabilitation order, means the probation officer or member of a youth offending team responsible for his supervision.

22.13 The order must specify a petty sessions area and thereafter jurisdiction in regard to the enforcement, amendment or revocation of the order will normally be exercised by a justice or magistrates' court acting for that area. Supervision of the offender will ordinarily be undertaken by a YOT member. Complications can arise if the offender lives or intends to live outside of England and Wales or is without a clear plan for their future accommodation—

(a) If the offender resides or will reside abroad, *e.g.* in the Republic of Ireland[10] a community rehabilitation order should not be imposed because the English or Welsh court cannot specify supervision and enforcement in a foreign jurisdiction.

(b) If the offender resides or will reside in Scotland or Northern Ireland, the court must be satisfied that suitable arrangements for the offender's supervision can be made by the Scottish Regional or Islands Council for the proposed home area or by the Probation Board for Northern Ireland. Transfer of orders to these two jurisdictions is regulated by PCC(S)A 2000, Sched. 4. The order must specify the offender's "locality" in Scotland together with the appropriate court of summary jurisdiction or the appropriate petty sessions district in Northern Ireland.

(c) If the offender is homeless or is an itinerant traveller, then there will clearly need to be particular consideration of the offender's suitability for a community rehabilitation order or of the viability of supervision. The youth offending team may well be able to assist the homeless young offender to obtain accommodation. If the order is considered appropriate, then the court will specify the PSA which seems most appropriate, in the anticipation that this may need to be amended as circumstances develop.

Provision for the amendment of a community rehabilitation order to substitute another petty sessions area is contained in PCC(S)A 2000, Sched. 3, para. 18.

(iv) Commencement and provision of copies of the order

22.14 A community rehabilitation order imposed by a youth court or the Crown Court comes into force on the date that the order is made. Thus an order

---

[10] *McCartan* [1958] 1 W.L.R. 933.

imposed on June 13 for 12 months expires at midnight on June 12 the following year, unless revoked in the meantime.

PCC(S)A 2000, s.41

(9) The court by which a community rehabilitation order is made shall forthwith give copies of the order to—

(a) if the offender is aged 18 or over, a probation officer assigned to the court, or

(b) if the offender is aged under 18, a probation officer or member of a youth offending team so assigned,

and he shall give a copy to the offender, to the responsible officer and to the person in charge of any institution in which the offender is required by the order to reside.

(10) The court by which such an order is made shall also, except where it itself acts for the petty sessions area specified in the order, send to the clerk to the justices for that area—

(a) a copy of the order; and

(b) such documents and information relating to the case as it considers likely to be of assistance to a court acting for that area in the exercise of its functions in relation to the order.

By analogy with *Walsh v. Barlow*[11] considered at 23.16, delivery of a copy of the order to the offender is not a pre-requisite of the coming into force of the order.

(v) Security for Good Behaviour

22.15   PCC(S)A 2000 s.41(8) specifies that, on making a community rehabilitation order, "the court may, if it thinks it expedient for the purposes of the offender's reformation, allow any person who consents to do so to give security for the good behaviour of the offender". This discretionary power is available in tandem with power under PCC(S)A 2000 s.150 to bind over the offender's parent or guardian—see 14.02

Combining with other sentences and orders

22.16   The general rule broadly applies that "courts should avoid mixing sentences which fall into well-established and different categories": *McElhorne*.[12] Thus the Court of Appeal has made clear that a probation order should never be imposed on the same occasion as a custodial sentence.[13] *Evans* has recently been reiterated, in respect of a young offender, by *Carr–Thompson*.[14] In respect of the making of a community rehabilitation order when the defendant is a serving prisoner, see *Fonteneau v. DPP*.[15]

Whereas prior to CJA 1991 a probation order was not a "punishment" and thus could not be combined with any other disposal of a punitive nature, its changed

---

[11] [1985] 1 W.L.R. 90.
[12] (1983) 5 Cr.App.R.(S.) 53.
[13] *Evans* [1959] 1 W.L.R. 26, even for different counts or separate indictments.
[14] [2000] 2 Cr.App.R.(S) 335.
[15] [2001] 1 Cr.App.R.(S) 50, noted at 24.07.

status under the Act removed such limitations with now two significant exceptions. First, a community rehabilitation order and a community punishment order may not be combined for the same offence except in the form of a community punishment and rehabilitation order (PCC(S)A 2000, s.35(2)). This provision has been interpreted to mean that the two measures may not be imposed in tandem on the same sentencing occasion, for separate offences: *Gilding v. DPP.*[16] Secondly, a court may not impose both an action plan order and a community rehabilitation order on the offender within the same sentencing exercise: PCC(S)A 2000 s.69(5)(b) (see 18.04).

22.17 Though the 2000 Act does not prohibit combining a community rehabilitation order with a supervision order, this appears to be completely contrary to the notion that an offender should be assessed as suitable for either the juvenile or the adult form of supervision but not both. A court might wish to secure the "best of both worlds" to take advantage of local resources but the consequent confusion and duplication would suggest that this would be wrong in principle. Whilst a community rehabilitation order can lawfully be combined with an attendance centre order, careful thought should be given to whether this is a realistic accumulation of demands upon a young offender. However, as an attendance centre order can be imposed as a penalty for breach of community rehabilitation order under Sched. 3, where the community rehabilitation order is allowed to continue (see 19.23), the Act clearly envisages that the two kinds of demand can be fulfilled compatibly.

REQUIREMENTS IN A COMMUNITY REHABILITATION ORDER

The standard requirements

22.18   **PCC(S)A 2000, s.41**

(11) An offender in respect of whom a community rehabilitation order is made shall keep in touch with the responsible officer in accordance with such instructions as he may from time to time be given by that officer and shall notify him of any change of address.

This specification for the standard order is reproduced intact in the form of order prescribed by the Magistrates Courts (Children and Young Persons) Rules 1992, Sched. 2, Form 47. The phrase "keep in touch" is a somewhat loose basis for supervisory authority, perhaps reflecting how much probation practice has traditionally sought to promote compliance through goodwill and negotiation. In the contemporary climate of rigorous enforcement, it is more crucial to note its legal strength. It clearly empowers the supervisor to require the offender to keep appointments with the supervisor and, it is submitted, to receive visits from the supervisor at the offender's home address. It also unambiguously requires the offender to report to a colleague nominated by the supervisor, either because the supervisor is unavailable or delegates that function to another member of the YOT team or representative of the probation service.[17] In addition to instructions regarding "when" and "where", it is submitted that s.41(11) also empowers the supervisor to give instructions regarding the manner in which the offender should

---

[16] *Gilding v. DPP The Times* May 20, 1998.
[17] *Teesside Probation Service, ex p. NAPO* (1999, unreported). See also N. Stone (2001) "The Ambit of the Standard Community Rehabilitation Order," Crim. L.R. 214.

behave when engaging in supervision or attending the premises of the supervising agency, such as an expectation that the offender will be sober, not intoxicated by alcohol or drugs, will not attend late and will not use violent, aggressive, threatening or offensive language or behaviour. Without such groundrules the business of supervision could in practice prove unworkable. It is difficult to provide instructions that will unambiguously cover all possible variations of misconduct that could frustrate supervision but the kind of instructions now routinely given as part of new supervisees' induction will cover the kind of incidents that provide the basis of most enforcement proceedings alleging breach of the order. Orders that include an additional requirement to participate in activities or to attend a community rehabilitation probation centre (under PCC(S)A 2000 Sched. 2 paras. 2 or 3) have the advantage of a specific provision that the offender shall comply with instructions given by or with the authority of the person in charge.

22.19 There is more basis for doubt whether the 'standard' requirement empowers the supervisor to instruct the offender to keep appointments with a person who is not a member of the supervising agency, such as a counsellor in a specialist field, *e.g.* addictions or sexual dysfunction. Such an initiative may be a feature of the offender's supervision plan, drawn up in compliance with *National Standards*. The adult *National Standards*[18] state that any appointment made in connection with the supervision plan is enforceable but this appears to overlook that a requirement to undertake an activity or to present oneself to a person or place can be explicitly included in the legal obligations of the order, using the specific powers available to the sentencing court under PCC(S)A 200 Sched. 2 para. 2. If Parliament has made specific provision for such additional obligations, subject to procedural safeguards and time limits, it may be argued that it is not open to the supervisor to side-step these provisions by utilising the general power of s.41(11). In the event that enforcement of instructions given under s.41(11). does not succeed through breach action, the alternative remedy may be to seek revocation on the basis that the offender's attitude makes the order unworkable in practice and its objectives unattainable.

Power to Include Additional Requirements

22.20 A court imposing a community rehabilitation order has discretion to include additional requirements, either utilising a general power to do so under PCC(S)A 2000 s.42(1) or drawing upon various specific additions provided by PCC(S)A 2000 Sched. 2. CJCSA 2000 s.42 has modified this familiar face of discretion by amending PCC(S)A 2000 s.42(2), empowering and in certain instances obliging the sentencing court to impose a "drug abstinence requirement". However, this new mandatory/discretionary power applies only where the offender is aged 18 or over on date of conviction for the offence, so does not affect the sentencing of young offenders. Accordingly, the provisions of s.42(2)(b) (given below), and also of s.42(2A)–(2F) which detail this power, need not be addressed.

General power to add requirements

PCC(S)A 2000, s.42

(1) Subject to subsection (3) below, a community rehabilitation order may in addition require the offender to comply during the whole or any part of

---

[18] n. 5.

the probation period with such requirements as the court, having regard to the circumstances of the case, considers desirable in the interests of—

(a) securing the rehabilitation of the offender; or

(b) protecting the public from harm from him or preventing the commission by him of further offences.

(2) Without prejudice to the generality of subsection (1) above,

(a) the additional requirements which may be included in a community rehabilitation order shall include the requirements which are authorised by Schedule 2 to this Act;

(b) subject to sub-sections (2D) and (2F) below, the order shall, if the first set of conditions is satisfied, include a drug abstinence requirement and may include such a requirement if the second set of conditions is satisfied.

22.21 This power appears to offer considerable scope to devise bespoke requirements to match the circumstances of the individual offender but should be read subject to the following limitations—

(a) "the payment of sums by way of damages for injury or compensation for loss shall not be included among the additional requirements of a community rehabilitation order" (s.42(3)), though compensation can be ordered as an ancillary measure or as a separate order under PCC(S)A 2000, s.130.

(b) a requirement should not be vague or unenforceable.[19] Thus a requirement not to enter amusement machine arcades (but see 22.64) or not to associate with a named person such as a co-defendant could prove very difficult to enforce;

(c) a requirement under s.42(1) should not seek to impose a form of demand for which there is alternative, precise and more appropriate statutory provision, *e.g.* to perform unpaid work akin to community punishment, to reside in a residential establishment or to take part in some form of group activity.[20]

(d) "any discretion conferred on the supervising officer pursuant to the terms of the order to regulate a probationer's activities must itself be confined within well-defined limits" (*per* Lord Bridge in *Cullen v. Rogers, note 20*);

(e) a requirement under s.42(1) should not "involve a substantial element of custodial punishment" (*per* Lord Bridge in *Cullen v. Rogers*, supra) (though stated in the context of pre-CJA 1991 law in which the probation order was made *instead of* sentence, it is submitted that this still remains a valid limitation on the use of section 42(1) powers);

(f) the restrictions on liberty imposed by any requirement under s.42(1) must be in accordance with the general rule contained in PCC(S)A 2000, s.35(3)(6) as regards commensurability with the seriousness of the offence(s) and suitability.

---

[19] *per* Lord Goddard in a *Practice Statement* (1952) 35 Cr.App.R. 207.
[20] *per* Lord Bridge in *Cullen v. Rogers* [1982] 1 W.L.R. 729.

22.22 In general, additional requirements should, if possible, be devised in accordance with those authorised and regulated by PCC(S)A 2000, Sched. 2 and ad hoc requirements should be viewed very circumspectly. A preferable option may be for the court to defer sentence, making clear its expectations of the offender. Note that a court is not required to obtain and consider a pre-sentence report before forming an opinion as to the suitability for an offender of a community rehabilitation order which includes an additional requirement under s.42(1) but is almost certainly likely to seek a report in such circumstances.

The Court of Appeal has upheld a requirement that the offender should not commit any further offence during the currency of the order.[21] Though acknowledging that the offender would not be liable to be dealt with in breach proceedings if he further offended, because of the specific exclusion now contained in PCC(S)A 2000, Sched. 3 para. 6(1), the Court nevertheless considered that the requirement was a valid use of s.42(1) powers because, if the offender committed a further offence while on probation and was brought back before the Crown Court, the order could be revoked under what is now Sched. 3 para. 11 and the offender could be dealt with afresh for the original offence. It is difficult to follow what this additional requirement added to the enforcement powers of the court. If such a requirement was added to an order imposed by a youth court, revocation could only be considered on the application of either the offender or the supervising officer as magistrates, unlike the Crown Court, have no jurisdiction to revoke on their own initiative. Further, revocation is only possible in either the Crown Court or a youth court while the order is in force. The *Peacock* decision thus seems to confuse breach and revocation proceedings. One basis for use of s.42(1) could be to require a defendant who has offended in the context of a certain kind of employment, *e.g.* work involving children or other vulnerable groups, to obtain the advance permission of the supervisor before commencing any form of employment.

Schedule 2 Requirements

22.23 PCC(S)A 2000 Sched. 2 essentially re-enacts the provisions of PCCA 1973 Sched. 1A, as amended. To that familiar list of five kinds of additional requirements, CJCSA 2000 ss. 43–45 adds two new forms of additional requirement, (a) enabling a measure that the Act introduces as a new community order in its own right—the exclusion order—to be an optional additional feature of a community rehabilitation order, and also permitting (b) curfew requirements to be included in the order. Unlike Sched. 6 governing supervision orders, Sched. 2 does not specify any power to require the offender to undertake reparation. It could be argued that such activity can be required under the broader ambit of para. 2 (see 22.41) but it would be appear preferable to make a supervision order instead to achieve this objective since Parliament has given explicit power in that context.

Requirements as to residence

PCC(S)A 2000, Sched. 2, para. 1

(1) Subject to sub-paragraphs (2) and (3) below, a community rehabilitation order may include requirements as to the residence of the offender.

(2) Before making a community rehabilitation order containing any such requirement, the court shall consider the home surroundings of the offender.

---

[21] *Peacock, The Times,* November 7, 1994.

(3) Where a community rehabilitation order requires the offender to reside in an approved hostel or any other institution, the period for which he is so required to reside shall be specified in the order.

22.24 This power is cast in very wide terms but tends to be used in two main instances: to require a period of residence at either a community rehabilitation hostel or a rehabilitation unit run by a voluntary organisation, or to provide some role for the supervising officer in determining where the offender will live beyond that of simply being informed of any change of address. Community rehabilitation hostels may be unwilling to accept residents aged under 18 because of child protection concerns for their safety, given the rising number of sex offenders in residence in establishments intended primarily for adults (see 22.29).

A residence requirement has the capacity to be both a substantial restriction of liberty and an invaluable opportunity for rehabilitative initiatives. The Court of Appeal has not given any general guidance on the appropriate use of this measure but *Attorney-General's Reference No. 15 of 1994*[22] suggested the potential of this community sentence for serious offences in some instances. The offender aged 17 had attacked a 60 year old man with a piece of wood, fracturing his skull. For causing grievous bodily harm with intent, he received a probation order with a requirement of residence at a semi-secure children's centre. Though the Court of Appeal accepted that this sentence was unduly lenient, the probation order was allowed to continue in the light of the offender's age and plea, his experience of disadvantage, his progress and increased self-discipline at the centre in the ten months on remand and six months since sentence, and the nature of the centre's "very stiff regime" (residents were not allowed out unaccompanied and had only one accompanied outing per week). It was thus not considered in the public interest to disturb this opportunity.

Residence in an approved hostel

22.25 Approved hostels may be run either directly by probation boards or by voluntary management committees. Both kinds of establishment are subject to the Approved Probation and Bail Hostel Rules 1995[23] and to the relevant provisions of the adult *National Standards*.

22.26 *Purpose of hostels: National Standards*[24] indicate that the purpose of approved hostels is "to provide an enhanced level of residential supervision with the aim of protecting the public by reducing the likelihood of offending" and thus should not be seen as simply a means of providing accommodation. Hostels enhance supervision by—

(a) imposing a supervised night-time curfew (23.00 to 06.00) which can be extended to other times of the day, as required by court order;

(b) providing 24 hour staff oversight;

(c) undertaking ongoing assessment of attitudes and behaviour;

(d) requiring compliance with clearly stated house rules which are rigorously enforced;

---

[22] [1995] 16 Cr.App.R.(S.) 619
[23] S.I. 1995/302.
[24] n. 5, paras. E1–13.

(e) providing a programme of regular supervision, support and daily monitoring that tackles offending behaviour and reduces risks.

22.27 *Admission policy: National Standards*[25] indicate that staff should deploy risk assessment procedures to identify risk of serious harm to the public, staff and other residents. Decisions should not "automatically exclude any particular category of offence" but should "reflect the ability of the hostel to manage and reduce the risks identified".

22.28 Each hostel is required to adopt an admissions policy, notified to the courts for the area in which the hostel is situated.[26] An offender who is being considered for a requirement of hostel residence is usually required to undertake a trial period of residence on "bail assessment", normally for 28 days, to gauge their suitability and attitude and to give them the opportunity to decide if they wish to make a longer term commitment. At the conclusion of that period the staff will normally provide a report to the court indicating whether a requirement of residence appears appropriate and, if so, for what duration. Paragraph 1 does not explicitly require the agreement of the hostel or institution to receive and accommodate the offender before the making of a residence requirement but the requirement would clearly be unworkable without such agreement. No hostel shall refuse to accept a person who is required by a community rehabilitation order to reside therein, except with the consent of the Secretary of State.[27]

22.29 The reduction in the minimum age for a community rehabilitation order to 16 made it necessary to re-consider the suitability of youths under 18 for a requirement of residence in approved hostels. Home Office Circular 44/1993 suggested that residence is not appropriate for many 16 and 17 year olds and indicates that all such referrals will have to be made to an Assistant Chief Probation Officer for approval, taking the following factors into consideration—

(i) Is the young person concerned still at school?

(ii) In the case of 16/17-year-old girls, does a mixed hostel have living accommodaton for the sexes which is quite distinct and separate?

(iii) Hostels do not routinely provide secure or intensively supervised accommodation, so failure of juvenile establishments to hold young offenders or control their behaviour should not be a reason to consider the adult alternative.

(iv) The risk posed to any potential resident by other residents is a factor which must be considered. Other residents could present a real risk to young offenders of injury, intimidation and contamination. This is especially true where hostels accommodate sex offenders.

(v) Hostels are required to prepare residents to move on to independent living as soon as possible. This may not be appropriate for 16 and 17 year olds who are not sufficiently mature or financially independent.

22.30 *Length of residence*: The period of residence should be specified in the order. It is questionable whether a form of wording which refers to "a period of up

---

[25] n. 5, para. E4.
[26] APHR 1995, r.10(2).
[27] APHR 1995, r.10(1).

to x months" meets the expectation of para. 1(3) with sufficient precision. It is open to the supervising officer to seek to amend the order if residence becomes unnecessary or inappropriate prior to the end of the specified period. Except with the consent of the Chief Probation Officer, no offender shall reside in a hostel for any longer than the period specified in the community rehabilitation order.[28] A resident shall not be required to cease to reside at the hostel before the expiry of the term of residence specified in the order (or of the remand period, if on bail assessment), except in case of emergency. In the event of such emergency, the hostel shall give reasonable notice to the supervising officer (if that is not the hostel manager or deputy) or to the court which granted bail (if the resident is on bail assessment).[29]

22.31 *Place of residence*: The wording of Sched. 2, para. 1 is not explicit that the requirement should specify the particular hostel or institution but a requirement which simply refers to "an approved hostel" (thus leaving it to the supervisor to allocate the offender) is both undesirable in practice and probably void for lack of certainty. The same objection would probably apply to a requirement "to reside at a hostel to be determined by the supervisor", a format which confers undue discretion upon the supervisor, contrary to the principle stated by Lord Bridge in *Cullen v. Rogers* (see 22.21). Given the careful discretion to be exercised in the placing of young persons, such imprecise requirements are highly unlikely.

22.32 *Rules of the hostel*: An approved hostel (and doubtless any residential institution) will have a set of house rules detailing the requirements and restrictions on residents. Paragraph 1 is silent as regards the residents' compliance with rules, unlike the provision in the Bail Act 1976, s.3(6A) which states that a defendant with a bail condition of residence at a hostel "may also be required to comply with the rules of the hostel". An expectation that the resident subject to a community rehabilitation order should comply with the rules of the hostel is arguably within the implicit ambit of "requirements as to residence", as a matter of commonsense but is preferable if the requirement of residence adds "and complies with the rules of the hostel". It does not follow that the hostel has total discretion as to the nature of those rules. Rules should be reasonably related to the viability of residence. For example, a rule prohibiting consumption of alcohol in the hostel addresses a legitimate issue of residence but an alternative rule prohibiting residents from drinking alcohol in public houses exceeds that ambit. If breach proceedings are initiated for non-compliance then the offender may seek to challenge the rule in question as gratuitously controlling and unrelated to the essentials of residence.

22.33 *National Standards*[40] specify that house rules shall include prohibitions on—

(a) the use of alcohol, solvents and controlled drugs, other than on prescription and following notification to hostel staff;

(b) any conduct or language that reasonably gives serious offence to hostel staff, residents or members of the public;

(c) theft of, or damage to, the property of the hostel, staff, electronic monitoring contractors or residents;

---

[28] APHR 1995, r.11(a).
[29] APHR 1995, r.12(2).
[40] n. 5, para. E3.

and shall require residents to be in the hostel for the curfew period and to make prompt payment of the weekly charge leviable upon them. Rules should be explained fully to new residents "as soon as practicable after arrival" and they should sign a copy as confirmation.[41]

22.34 A common rule requirement specifically affecting residents under 18 is that they should participate in a government scheme of youth employment training. This is necessary to ensure that they qualify for state benefit entitlement and are thus able to pay their weekly residence charge. This is thus a rule relating to viability of residence rather than an extraneous or gratuitous demand.

22.35 *Specified PSA and supervisor.* The petty sessions area specified in the order shall be the area in which the hostel or institution is situated.

22.36 *Supervision programme:* Within seven days of their arrival, a planned programme should be produced for each resident addressing their offending and the management of identified risks of harm posed, congruent with any other orders to which they may be subject and avoiding conflict with any reasonable employ-ment requirements or their religious observances.[42]

22.36 *Breach of requirement:* Absconding from the hostel constitutes a breach of supervision requirements and should be dealt with in accordance with the relevant enforcement provisions of *National Standards. National Standards*[43] requires each hostel to have a clear policy in respect of enforcement of house rules' clarifying that "minor infringements may be dealt with by informal local warnings, which must be recorded. However, serious or repeated breaches will . . . result in breach action."

Residence as directed by the supervisor

22.37 A requirement sometimes proposed or felt desirable for offenders whose living arrangements have been very unstable or otherwise a cause of concern is the very open-ended format: "to reside where directed by the responsible officer". This appears to place the onus upon the supervisor to choose where the offender should live. It would be objectionable to use this power to direct residence in an "institution" as this should properly be specified in the order and thus subject to paragraph 1(3). Nevertheless, some independent or voluntary agencies offering residential services stipulate that they will only accept a resident as a requirement of a community rehabilitation order where that requirement is drafted flexibly to reside where directed by the responsible officer. If the resident then opts to leave or is required to leave the programme, a return to court is neither the inevitable next step nor the agency's direct responsibility. It could be argued that this broad wording confers undue discretion upon the supervisor, contrary to Lord Bridge's dictum in *Cullen v. Rogers* (see 22–21). An alternative format, "to reside where approved by the responsible officer" appears to give the supervisor less power and discretion but a right to be consulted and of veto in regard to arrangements proposed by the offender.

Other residence requirements

22.38 A requirement that the offender shall reside at an establishment or institution other than an approved hostel, *e.g.* a specialist rehabilitation unit,

[41] n. 5, para. E7
[42] n. 5, para. E7.
[43] n. 4, para. E12.

operates in a similar way to residence in an approved, hostel albeit without being regulated by the APBH Rules 1995 or *National Standards*. For issues concerning the length and place of residence, rules and the relevant petty sessions area, see 22–30 *et seq.*

An order may require the offender to live with a specified person, *e.g.* a relative. Schedule 2 paragraph 1 does not explicitly require the agreement or consent of the person to accommodate the offender but the requirement would clearly be an unworkable nonsense unless such agreement was clearly forthcoming.

Requirements as to activities or attendance at a probation centre

22.39 The clear majority of additional requirements in community rehabilitation orders are of this nature. The broad purpose is to require the offender to participate in a programme of education, therapy, group activities or training intended to rehabilitate but also requiring a greater commitment of time and effort than the standard order and thus appropriate where the offence merits additional restriction on liberty. There are broadly three forms of the "programme" requirement—

(a) to report to a particular person at a specific place and comply with instructions;

(b) to participate in specified activities;

(c) to attend a probation or community rehabilitation centre.

22.40 Each of these requirements may not extend beyond 60 days of attendance (unless the offender is convicted of a sexual offence in which instance the court may direct "such greater number of days as may be specified in the direction": Sched. 2 para. 4). There is thus scope to tailor the particular requirement flexibly to suit the available facility. Thus it may be more appropriate to draft the requirement in terms of the place(s) to be attended, the person who will be responsible or the activity to be undertaken, depending on what is proposed and how it is organised. There is, however, a widespread belief that the probation centre requirement is likely to be the most sustained, intensive and demanding experience on offer within this range and that attendance at a centre is particularly appropriate for some of the most serious offenders given a community sentence.

(a) & (b) Specified place or specified activities requirement

22.41   PCC(S)A 2000, Sched. 2, para. 2

(1) Subject to the provisions of this paragraph, a community rehabilitation order may require the offender—

(a) to present himself to a person or persons specified in the order at a place or places so specified;

(b) to participate or refrain from participating in activities specified in the order—

(i) on a day or days so specified; or

(ii) during the community rehabilitation period or such portion of it as may be so specified.

(5) A place specified in an order shall have been approved by the probation board for the area in which the premises are situated as providing facilities suitable for persons subject to probation orders.

22.42   Though the two kinds of requirement are posed as alternative possibilities, they are not mutually exclusive and it would be possible to require an offender to undertake requirements of both kinds, though this would appear subject to the limitation under paragraph 2(4) and (6) that the total number of days of attendance required by an order should not exceed 60 days in aggregate (see below). Paragraph 2 is specific in regard to consultation, feasibility and the consent of other persons whose co-operation is essential for the requirement to be viable:

22.43   **PCC(S)A 2000, Sched. 2, para. 2**

(2) A court shall not include in a probation order a requirement such as is mentioned in sub-paragraph (1) above unless—

  (a) it has consulted—

    (i) in the case of an offender aged 18 or over, a probation officer; or
    (ii) in the case of an offender aged under 18, either a probation officer or a member of a youth offending team; and

  (b) it is satisfied that it is feasible to secure compliance with the requirement.

(3) A court shall not include a requirement such as is mentioned in sub-paragraph (1)(a) above or a requirement to participate in activities if it would involve the co-operation of a person other than the offender and the offender's responsible officer, unless that other person consents to its inclusion.

The maximum duration of an activities or "place" requirement and the obligations upon an offender are specified as follows, having regard to the offender's work or educational commitments:

22.44   **PCC(S)A 2000, Sched. 2, para. 2**

(4) A requirement such as is mentioned in sub-paragraph (1)(a) above shall operate to require the offender—

  (a) in accordance with instructions given by his responsible officer, to present himself at a place or places for not more than 60 days in the aggregate; and

  (b) while at any place, to comply with instructions given by, or under the authority of, the person in charge of that place.

(6) A requirement to participate in activities shall operate to require the offender—

  (a) in accordance with instructions given by his responsible officer to participate in activities for not more than 60 days in the aggregate; and

  (b) while participating, to comply with instructions given by, or under the authority of, the person in charge of the activities.

(7) Instructions given by the offender's responsible officer under sub-paragraph (4) or (6) above shall, as far as practicable, be such as to avoid—

  (a) any conflict with the offender's religious beliefs or with the requirements of any other community order to which he may be subject; and

(b) any interference with the times, if any, at which he normally works or attends school or any other educational establishment.

22.44a "As far as practicable" suggests that work or education cannot claim an absolute priority but if it is not possible to make arrangements which avoid such interference then there would clearly be doubts in the first instance as to the offender's suitability for this form of order and, if these commitments arise during the course of the order, then an application for revocation might be the most appropriate course.

There is one significant exception to the normal maximum duration of the commitment. An offender convicted of a sexual offence (as defined by PCC(S)A 2000 s.161 may be ordered to participate for "such greater number of days as may be specified" (Schedule 2, paragraph 4). This allows longer term attendance, *e.g.* at a sexual offending therapy group, up to the total length of the order.

(c) Probation centre requirement

22.45 PCC(S)A 1973, Sched. 2, para. 3

(1) Subject to the provisions of this paragraph, a community rehabilitation order may require the offender during the community rehabilitation period to attend a probation centre specified in the order.

(7) A requirement under sub-paragraph (1) above shall operate to require the offender—

(a) in accordance with instructions given by his responsible officer to attend on not more than 60 days at the centre specified in the order; and

(b) while attending there to comply with instructions given by, or under the authority of, the person in charge of the centre.

(6) References in this paragraph to attendance at a probation centre include references to attendance elsewhere than at the centre for the purpose of participating in activities in accordance with instructions given by, or under the authority of, the person in charge of the centre.

(8) In this paragraph "probation centre" means premises—

(a) at which non-residential facilities are provided for use in connection with the rehabilitation of offenders; and

(b) which are for the time being approved by the Secretary of State as providing facilities suitable for persons subject to community rehabilitation orders.

22.46 Sched. 2, para. 4 permits one exception to the normal maximum duration of attendance. An offender convicted of a sexual offence PCC(S)A 2000 s.16 may be ordered to attend for "such greater number of days as may be specified". This allows longer term attendance up to the total length of the order.

Prior consultation and the need to clarify that the proposed arrangements are feasible are specified as follows:

22.47 PCC(S)A 2000, Sched. 2, para. 3

(2) A court shall not include in a community rehabilitation order a requirement such as is mentioned in sub-paragraph (1) above unless—

(a) it has consulted—

(i) in the case of an offender aged 18 or over, a probation officer; or
(ii) in the case of an offender aged under 18, either a probation officer or a member of a youth offending team; and

(b) it is satisfied that it is feasible to secure compliance with the requirement.

(3) A court shall not include such a requirement in a community rehabilitation order unless it is satisfied—

(a) that arrangements can be made for the offender's attendance at a centre; and
(b) that the person in charge of the centre consents to the inclusion of the requirement.

22.48 As in the case of paragraph 2 requirements, instructions to attend a probation centre shall, so far as practicable, be such as to avoid conflict with the offender's religious beliefs or any other parallel community order, and any interference with the times, if any, at which the offender normally works or attends a school or other educational establishment" (paragraph 3(5)). The observations in regard to paragraph 2 (22.44) apply also here.

Requirement to refrain from activities

22.49 Under Sched. 2, para. 2(1)(b) (see 22–41) a community rehabilitation order may require the offender to "refrain from participating in activities specified in the order on a day or days specified or during the probation period or such portion of it as may be specified. This so-called "negative" requirement or "refraining order" is not subject to the usual 60 day limit and so could be ordered to run for the duration of the order. There are obvious problems in regard to such a prohibiting condition. Firstly, how feasible is it to secure compliance? A court is unlikely to favour the imposition of a requirement which the offender could ignore with impunity. Secondly, a requirement which imposes considerable restraint upon the offender's liberty might offend the dictum of Lord Bridge in *Rogers v. Cullen* opposing quasi-custodial impositions (22.21). Thirdly, a requirement which gives wide discretion to the supervising officer (*e.g.* to refrain from taking part in a specified activity without the prior permission of the supervising officer) could also be said to offend against the principles of *Rogers v. Cullen*. If, for example, the court wished to impose a requirement that the offender should keep away from football grounds following an offence of football related violence, or from licensed premises, it would probably be preferable to exercise specific powers to make a banning order (see 30.11), an exclusion order under the Licensed Premises (Exclusion of Certain Persons) Act 1980 (see 30.12). Very few orders containing an additional "negative" requirement have been made since this power became available in 1982. With the introduction under CJCSA 2000 ss. 42–44 of new powers to impose additional requirements of curfew and exclusion from entering specified places, detailed below, "refraining" requirements are likely to be used even more rarely.

(iii) Treatment of mental condition

22.50 A requirement of treatment for the offender's mental condition may be made under the provision of Sched. 2 para 5. The court must be satisfied, on the evidence of a registered medical practitioner (approved for the purpose under the Mental Health Act 1983, s.12) that the mental condition of the offender—

(a) is such as requires and may be susceptible to treatment; but

(b) is not such as to warrant the making of a hospital order or guardianship order within the meaning of the Mental Health Act.

"Mental condition" is not defined but is not restricted to the four forms of mental disorder specified by the Mental Health Act 1983, s.37 for the making of a hospital order (mental illness, psychopathic disorder, severe mental impairment or mental impairment). Treatment may be directed by a chartered psychologist, defined as a person listed on the register maintained by the British Psychological Society: para. 5.10.

22.51   **PCC(S)A 2000, Sched. 2, para. 5**

(2) The community rehabilitation order may include a requirement that the offender shall submit, during the whole of the probation period or during such part or parts of that period as may be specified in the order, to treatment by or under the direction of a registered medical practitioner or a chartered psychologist (or both, for different parts) with a view to the improvement of the offender's mental condition.

(3) The treatment required by any such order shall be such one of the following kinds of treatment as may be specified in the order, that is to say—

(a) treatment as a resident patient in a hospital or mental nursing home within the meaning of MHA 1983, but not a special hospital within the meaning of that Act;

(b) treatment as a non-resident patient at such institution or place as may be specified in the order; and

(c) treatment by or under the direction of such duly qualified medical practitioner or chartered psychologist (or both) as may be so specified;

but the nature of the treatment shall not be specified in the order except as mentioned in paragraph (a), (b) or (c) above.

(4) A court shall not by virtue of this paragraph include in a community rehabilitation order a requirement that the offender shall submit to treatment for his mental condition unless—

(a) it is satisfied that arrangements have been or can be made for the treatment intended to be specified in the order (including arrangements for the reception of the offender where he is to be required to submit to treatment as a resident patient); and

(b) the offender has expressed his willingness to comply with such a requirement.

22.52 The court must thus phrase the requirement carefully within the range of options specified in sub-paragraph (3). It would not, for instance, be lawful to stipulate "such medical treatment as may be directed by the responsible officer". Treatment "under the direction of" a medical practitioner may extend to treatment undertaken by others such as a community psychiatric nurse or a psychologist, provided that this is clearly authorised and overseen by a responsible doctor.

22.53   *Residential treatment:*   In this instance the statutory role of the responsible officer is limited by paragraph 5(5) to undertaking what "may be necessary for the purpose of the revocation or amendment of the order". As the Butler Committee on Mentally Abnormal Offenders pointed out (1975), this curtailment should not be read literally to mean an absence of involvement and good practice may well require liaison, joint work, preparation for discharge, contact with relatives, etc.

22.54   *Flexibility and discretion:*   It is clearly not possible for the court imposing the requirement to anticipate how treatment will proceed and the offender-patient's response. Scope for flexible discretion without the need for referral back to court is given by paragraph 5(6).

22.55   **PCC(S)A 2000, Sched. 2, para. 5**

(6)   Where the medical practitioner or chartered psychologist by whom or under whose direction an offender is being treated for his mental condition in pursuance of a community rehabilitation order is of the opinion that part of the treatment can be better or more conveniently given in or at an institution or place which—

   (a) is not specified in the order; and
   (b) is one in or at which the treatment of the offender will be given by or under the direction of a duly qualified medical practitioner or chartered psychologist,

   he may, with the consent of the offender, make arrangements for him to be treated accordingly.

(7)   Such arrangements as are mentioned in sub-paragraph (6) above may provide for the offender to receive part of his treatment as a resident patient in an institution or place notwithstanding that the institution or place is not one which could have been specified for that purpose in the community rehabilitation order.

(8)   Where any such arrangements as are mentioned in sub-paragraph (6) above are made for the treatment of an offender—

   (a) the medical practitioner or chartered psychologist by whom the arrangements are made shall give notice in writing to the officer responsible, specifying the institution or place in or at which the treatment is to be carried out; and
   (b) the treatment provided for by the arrangements shall be deemed to be treatment to which he is required to submit in pursuance of the community rehabilitation order.

22.56   This informal amendment without referral back to the court in the normal manner requires the consent of the offender (para. 5(6)) and, in the event of any subsequent enforcement proceedings, the issue could be raised whether the offender gave valid, informed consent to the change in treatment. This illustrates the difficulties of seeking to regulate the doctor-patient relationship by sentencing in criminal proceedings.

Sentencing guidance: A number of cases have indicated the Court of Appeal's preparedness to endorse the making of "psychiatric probation orders" where the offender has committed a serious offence and or represents a real risk to the public, e.g. Hoof[44] (arson with intent to endanger life) McDonald[45] (indecent assault) Cartwright, The Times, April 18, 1989 (reckless driving), Jones[46–47] (robbery). However, this course is likely to be adopted only where there is a reasonable prospect that such an order will have a beneficial effect upon the offender and that this outweighs the element of risk to the public.

(iv) Treatment for drug or alcohol dependency

22.57 Schedule 2, para. 6 specifies a power to require the offender to submit to treatment for their drug or alcohol dependency. This was originally proposed by the 1990 White Paper which noted a frequent "link between drug misuse and offences such as burglary and theft committed in order to gain money to buy drugs. Similarly, alcohol is implicated in a wide variety of crimes, drunken driving, offences of public disorder and domestic violence" (paragraph 4.14). The court must be satisfied as to the following pre-conditions—

(a) the offender is dependent on drugs or alcohol;

(b) the offender's dependency caused or contributed to the instant offence;

(c) the offender's dependency is such as requires and may be susceptible to treatment.

22.58 The paragraph does not specify on what basis or evidence the court must be satisfied of the above. There is no requirement that there should be evidence from a medical practitioner. "Dependency" is defined as including the offender's "propensity towards the misuse of drugs and alcohol" (paragraph 6(9)) and so is open to quite wide interpretation. The offence for which an order containing such a requirement may be imposed need not have been directly drug or alcohol related nor need the offence have been committed under the influence of drugs or alcohol. It is enough that the "dependency" contributed in some degree towards the offence.

This power has been superseded to a degree by the introduction of drug treatment and testing orders. In consequence, para. 6 (2) specifies that if the court has been notified that such orders are available in the area to be specified in the proposed community rehabilitation order, paragraph 6 shall have effect as if applicable only to offenders dependent on alcohol.

22.59   PCC(S)A 2000, Sched. 12, para. 6

(3) The community rehabilitation order may include a requirement that the offender shall submit, during the whole of the community rehabilitation period or during such part of that period as may be specified in the order, to treatment by or under the direction of a person having the necessary qualifications or experience with a view to the reduction or elimination of the offender's dependency on drugs or alcohol.

(4) The treatment required by any such order shall be such one of the following kinds of treatment as may be specified in the order, that is to say—

---

[44] (1980) 2 Cr.App.R.(S.) 299.
[45] (1983) 5 Cr.App.R.(S.) 419.
[46–47] (1992) 13 Cr.App.R.(S.) 275.

    (a) treatment as a resident in such institution or place as may be specified in the order;

    (b) treatment as a non-resident in or at such institution or place as may be so specified; and

    (c) treatment by or under the direction of such person having the necessary qualifications or experience as may be so specified; but the nature of the treatment shall not be specified in the order except as mentioned in paragraph (a), (b) or (c) above.

(4) A court shall not by virtue of this paragraph include in a community rehabilitation order a requirement that the offender shall submit to treatment for his dependency on drugs or alcohol unless (a) it is satisfied that arrangements have been or can be made for the treatment intended to be specified in the order (including arrangements for the reception of the offender where he is to be required to submit to treatment as a resident); and (b) the offender has expressed his willingness to comply with such a requirement.

22.60 The provisions of paragraph 6 closely resemble those of paragraph 5 (treatment for mental condition) but the person responsible for the treatment does not have to be medically qualified. There is no yardstick by which to determine whether the responsible person is adequately qualified or experienced. The 1990 White Paper had in mind "specialised local services, including the National Health Service".

Residential treatment: In this instance, the statutory role of the responsible officer is limited by paragraph 6(6) to carrying out what "may be necessary for the purpose of the revocation or amendment of the order", though, as in the case of psychiatric community rehabilitation orders, this may seem a highly artificial restriction in practice.

22.61 *Non-residential treatment:* Community drug or alcohol treatment agencies may prefer the least restrictive form of requirement, *e.g.* preferring to limit the length of period for which the requirement is imposed, which need not run for the full length of the order. Agencies may be very reluctant to enter into relationships with offenders on coercive-sounding terms for fear of compromising their non-controlling ethos and differentiating inappropriately between voluntary and directed clients. Some may refuse to enter into arrangements of this nature. Others may be willing to support a requirement that the offender shall attend the agency but may reserve the nature of any subsequent treatment or counselling to be negotiated privately between the agency and the client. The agency may have concerns about client confidentiality and may make clear that information to the superior will be limited to stating whether the offender has attended or not. The agency may seek to place all statutory responsible upon the superior by proposing a requirement "to receive treatment as directed by the responsible officer". This does not, however, seem to be a legal option within sub-paragraph (4) and thus no more lawful than such a requirement would be under paragraph 5.

22.62 *Flexibility and discretion:* As in the case of psychiatric treatment as a requirement of a community rehabilitation order, paragraph 6(7) and (8) give scope for flexibility and discretion in respect to treatment without having to refer the matter back to court for amendment.

(v) Curfew requirements

22.63   CJCSA 2000 s.50 introduced a new paragraph 7 into PCC(S)A 2000 Sched. 2, permitting a requirement in a community rehabilitation order that "the offender remain, for periods specified in the requirement, at a place so specified." However, if the community sentence of which the community rehabilitation order forms a part includes a curfew order in its own right, a court may not also include such a requirement: para. 7(7). The provisions governing curfew requirements are essentially the same as those governing curfew orders under PCC(S)A 2000 s.37 as regards the nature and length of the requirement and the procedures to be followed in considering and making the curfew provision. Thus the requirement has maximum duration of six months, or three months in relation to an offender aged under 16 on conviction: para. 7(3). Requirements shall, as far as practicable, avoid any conflict with the offender's religious beliefs or the requirements of any other community order to which he may be subject, and any interference with hours of work/school attendance: para. 7(4). Before making the requirement, the court shall obtain and consider information about the place proposed to be specified, including information as to the attitude of persons likely to be affected by the offender's enforced presence, and, where the offender is aged under 16 on conviction, information about his family circumstances and the likely effect of the requirement on those circumstances: para. 7(8) and (9). These provisions are detailed in Chapter 21 and thus need not be repeated here.

(vi) Exclusion requirements

22.64   CJCSA 2000 s.51 introduced a new paragraph 8 into PCC(S)A 2000 Sched. 2, permitting a requirement in a community rehabilitation order prohibiting the offender from entering a place specified in the requirement for a period so specified. However, if the community sentence of which the community rehabilitation order forms a part includes an exclusion order in its own right, a court may not also include such a requirement: para. 8(7). The provisions governing exclusion requirements are essentially the same as those governing exclusion orders under PCC(S)A 2000 s.40A (introduced by CJCSA 2000 s.39) as regards the nature and length of the requirement and the procedures to be followed in considering and making the exclusion provision. Thus the requirement has maximum duration of one year (though if the community rehabilitation order is of shorter duration then it follows that the length of the requirement is curtailed accordingly), or three months in relation to an offender aged under 16 on conviction: para. 8(4). Requirements shall, as far as practicable, avoid any conflict with the offender's religious beliefs or the requirements of any other community order to which he may be subject, and any interference with hours of work/school attendance: para. 8(5). Before making the requirement in respect of an offender aged under 16 on conviction, the court shall obtain and consider information about his family circumstances and the likely effect of the requirement on those circumstances: para. 8(8). These provisions are detailed in Chapter 21 and thus need not be repeated here.

(vii) Electronic monitoring requirements

22.65   CJCSA 2000 s.52 introduced PCC(S)A 2000, s.36B, permitting requirements in a community order "for securing the electronic monitoring of the offender's compliance with any other requirements included in the order". Though such a requirement is an inevitable complement to a curfew or exclusion requirement under Sched. 2 paras. 7 or 8, a s.36B requirement is, in theory at least, an

available option to accompany any other kind of community rehabilitation requirement. One possibility might be alongside a residence requirement under Sched. 2
para. 2. This provision is detailed at 17.13.

The Management of a Community Rehabilitation Order

22.66   The administration and management of a community rehabilitation order
is largely governed not by statute or statutory instrument but by *National Standards
for the Supervision of Offenders in the Community*. First introduced in 1992 and
first revised in 1995 as a means of achieving greater consistency and rigour in the
supervisory process, *National Standards*[48] are now in generic format, so that there
has ceased to be a specific Standard governing probation/community rehabilitation
orders. *National Standards for Youth Justice*[49] clarify that 16 and 17-year-olds
subject to community rehabilitation orders must be supervised according to the
adult *Standards*.
    Supervision[50] shall—

- address and reduce offending behaviour;

- challenge the offender to accept responsibility for the crimes committed
  and their consequences;

- contribute to the protection of the public;

- motivate and assist the offender towards a greater sense of responsibility
  and discipline;

- aid reintegration as a law-abiding member of the community;

- be arranged so as not to prevent the offender from being readily available
  to seek or take up employment if unemployed, nor conflict with an
  offender's entitlement to benefit, nor disrupt the working hours of an
  employed person, or the education of an offender in full-time education
  and to take account of religious and cultural requirements.

Commencement

22.67
- The date of the first appointment should be given to the offender, either
  by the supervising agency or by the court (acting on that agency's advice)
  before the offender leaves court, to take place within five working days of
  the order being made.[51]

- At the first meeting, the offender should be provided with written
  information setting out what is expected of them during supervision and
  what they can expect from the supervising agency. The offender should
  also receive instructions setting out the required standards of behaviour
  that apply during the period of supervision.[52] The offender should sign
  their order and indicate that they understand its requirements.

- Any additional requirements should normally commence within 12 weeks
  of the making of the order.[53] (Where the order includes a requirement of

---

[48] n. 4.
[49] Youth Justice Board (2000), Section 7.
[50] n. 4, para. C8.
[51] n. 4, para. D7.
[52] n. 4, para. D8.
[53] n. 5, para. D10.

residence in an approved probation hostel *National Standards* make separate provision for the induction of new residents in an interview with a member of the supervisory staff as soon as possible after arrival.)

Frequency of contact

22.68 "At least 12 appointments shall be made within the first 12 weeks of supervision, normally scheduled to take place weekly. There will normally be a home visit made within the first 12 weeks of the order. Six appointments shall be made within the second 12 weeks, after which appointments may reduce to monthly contacts".[54]

Supervision plan

22.69 A written supervision plan addressing risk factors, how the likelihood of re-offending is to be reduced, how offending-related needs will be addressed, the nature and frequency of contact, specifying a structured programme of supervision and setting clear targets for progress must be completed within 15 working days of the making of the order.[55] Offenders must be aware of the aims of their plan and be involved in its formulation. The plan must be reviewed at least every four months and objectives amended as necessary, depending on progress (para. C11). "At the termination of supervision there must be a final review, to be made available to the offender".[56]

Compliance and enforcement

22.70 The provisions regulating non-compliance and enforcement action are contained in PCC(S)A 2000 Sched. 3, backed by associated rubrics in *National Standards*.[57]

CJCSA 2000 amended Sched. 3, introducing the "warning provisions" of para. 2A to require the responsible officer to give a statutory warning in the event of a failure to comply, if a breach prosecution is not initiated, and to bring breach proceedings in the event of a further instance of non-compliance within 12 months. This provision is underpinned by changes to paras 4 and 5, requiring the court when dealing with an offender to whom the warning provisions apply to impose a mandatory term of imprisonment for the original offence unless of the opinion that the offender is likely to comply with the requirements of the order during the period for which it remains in force or that "exceptional circumstances" apply. These measures apply only where "the offender is aged is aged 18 or over" and hence these arguably draconian provisions will not impact upon young offenders, though they may impact on offenders who attain the age of 18 during the course of their order. However, the amended Schedule does not clarify the point at which the offender's age counts for this purpose, whether at time of their non-compliance, at the time when their non-compliance is proved or at the time when the court proposes to exercise its powers.

---

[54] n. 5, para. D13.
[55] n. 5, para. C10.
[56] n. 5, para. C12.
[57] Detailed in N. Stone, *A Companion Guide to Enforcement* (3rd edition, Ilkley, Owen Wells Publisher 1999).

Chapter 23

Community Punishment Orders

23.01 First introduced by the Criminal Justice Act 1972 and extended to 16-year-olds by CJA 1982, the community service order was renamed the community punishment order by CJCSA 2000, s.37 to give the sentence an unambiguously punitive ethos and to avoid any impression that work performed under its terms is akin to voluntary activity. To ease the transition required through change of name s.37 clarifies—.

(2) References in any enactment, instrument or document to a community punishment orderinclude (where the context allows) an order under any provision corresponding to that subsection (s.46(1)) which is repealed by that Act.

(4) References in any enactment, instrument or document to a community service order—

    (a) are to an order under any provision corresponding to s.46(1) of PCC(S)A 2000 which is repealed by that Act, and

    (b) include (where the context allows) an order under that section.

COMMUNITY PUNISHMENT ORDER AS A COMMUNITY SENTENCE

23.02 Governed now by PCC(S)A 2000 s.46, the legal provisions remain essentially as contained in PCCA 1973, as amended by CJA 1991 which designated the order as one of the "community orders" which can feature in a "community sentence". These generic provisions, now contained in PCC(S)A 2000 ss.33–36, are detailed in Chapter 17. As what is primarily an adult measure, the community punishment order is perhaps less likely to be widely applied in youth courts, given the extended range of disposals now available for the under-18s.

Power to make a Community Punishment Order

23.03   PCC(S)A 2000, s.46

(1) Where a person of or over sixteen years of age is convicted of an offence punishable with imprisonment, the court by or before which he is convicted may, (but subject to ss.34–36 above) make an order requiring him to perform unpaid work in accordance with section 47 below.

The reference in this subsection to an offence punishable with imprisonment shall be construed without regard to any prohibition or restriction imposed by or under any enactment on the imprisonment of young offenders."

(2) An order under sub-section (1) above is in this Act referred to as a "community punishment order".

23.04   A youth court or the Crown Court may make a community punishment order in respect of any offender aged 16 years or over who has been convicted of an offence punishable with imprisonment, provided that the court is of the opinion that the offence, or the combination of the offence and one or more offences associated with it, is serious enough to warrant such a sentence PCC(S)A 2000, s.35(1). The order requires the offender to perform unpaid work in accordance with the provisions of the Act. If the offence is imprisonable only upon sentence at Crown Court, it follows that a youth court cannot impose a community punishment order.

Length of order

23.05   PCC(S)A 2000, s.46

(3) The number of hours which a person may be required to work under a community punishment order shall be specified in the order and shall be in the aggregate—

(a) not less than 40; and

(b) not more than 240.

(8) Where a court makes community service orders in respect of two or more offences of which the offender has been convicted by or before the court, the court may direct that the hours of work specified in any of those orders shall be concurrent with or additional to those specified in any other of those orders, but so that the total number of hours which are not concurrent shall not exceed the maximum specified in subsection 3(b) above."

23.06   The number of hours which an offender may be required to work must be specified in the order and, in aggregate, shall be—

(a) not less than 40

(b) not more than 240.

Prior to implementation of CJA 1991 the maximum number of hours that a 16 year old could be required to work was 120 hours but this lower ceiling was removed by CJA 1991, s.10(2). This followed the proposal in the 1990 White Paper that 16 and 17 year olds should be regarded as "near adults" (see 20.43) and the Government's belief that the varied maximum "will give courts greater flexibility in using the order for 16 year olds who have been convicted of more serous offences and should encourage its use for some who might otherwise be at risk of a custodial sentence" (para. 8.18).

23.07   As the minimum length of 40 hours applies to the aggregate of hours under more than one order, this appears to suggest that consecutive orders could be made for less than 40 hours duration each. However, this is generally considered to be undesirable practice to be avoided. There would, for instance, be an obvious problem if some orders were set aside on appeal leaving one or more orders which amount in aggregate to less than 40 hours.

Where orders are imposed to run consecutively, this can create potential problems in the event of breach proceedings. Though 240 hours is the maximum that can be imposed on a single sentencing occasion, section 46(3) does not prohibit different courts on different occasions from making orders which in aggregate exceed 240 hours.[1] In *Siha* the offender was sentenced to work 180 hours community service. Six months later he received a further order for 90 hours. Though the Court of Appeal indicated that this was a valid additional order, "it is highly desirable that there should not be in existence at the same time orders which cast upon the offender a liability to perform more than a further 240 hours consecutively".[2] Because information was not available to the Court of Appeal about the number of hours already worked or outstanding under his initial order of 180 hours, the Court reduced his second order from 90 hours to 60 hours to ensure that the consecutive total still to be worked did not exceed 240 hours. There is thus a firm expectation that the court should respect the 240 hour ceiling intended by the legislature as the maximum commitment to which an offender should be subject at any time.

23.08   A further instance of the complexity of consecutive orders arose in *Meredith* (1994),[3] with the additional complication which arises where orders are imposed by courts at different levels of jurisdiction. The offender had been sentenced to an order for 80 hours by a magistrates' court and was subsequently sentenced to a further 160 hours by the Crown Court. Though the aggregate did not exceed 240 hours, the offender contended that the Crown Court subsequently had no power to deal with his non-compliance when he had failed to work as instructed after completing only 14 hours. Dismissing his claim that he was in breach of only the first of the two orders, the Court of Appeal stated that "once two community service orders are made, they are for all practical purposes one order" and he was thus in breach of both and could be dealt with by the Crown Court.

23.09   The length of a community punishment order should reflect the seriousness of the offence and the appropriate restriction on liberty commensurate with that offence, taking into account the suitability of the offender to undertake the order (s.35(3)).

Procedural requirements

Suitability and pre-sentence reports

23.10   PCC(S)A 2000, s.41(4)

> (4) A court shall not make a community punishment order in respect of an offender, after hearing (if the court thinks it necessary) an appropriate officer, is satisfied that the offender is a suitable person to perform work under such an order.

23.11   In the case of an offender aged under 18, "an appropriate officer" means "a probation officer, a social worker of a local authority social services department or a member of a youth offending team": s.46(5)(b). The requirement to consider suitability under s.46(4) should be read in conjunction with PCC(S)A s.35(3)(a) which requires the court to pass the community sentence "most suitable for the offender" (see 17.08). Before forming an opinion as to the suitability of an offender for a community punishment order, a court is ordinarily required to consider a pre-

---

[1] *Siha* (1992) 13 Cr. App. R.(S.) 588.
[2] Citing *Evans* (1977) 64 Cr. App. R. 127.
[3] 15 Cr. App. R.(S.) 528.

sentence report[4] unless of the opinion that it is unnecessary to do so.[5] However, where the offender is aged under 18 and the offence (or any associated offence) is not triable only on indictment, the court may not conclude that a report is unnecessary unless it can refer to a previous report about the offender (see 12.18). An order made without obtaining or considering a report is nevertheless a valid order[6] but such failure could be the basis for appeal. The court considering an appeal is required to obtain/consider a report[7] subject to the "get out" provisions of section 36(8) and (9) (see 12.19).

23.12 Neither the requirement to consider a report nor the scope to hear an appropriate officer means that the pre-sentence report has to address the possibility of a community punishment order or that the probation service/YOT has to be consulted on that precise prospect before an order can be made. An order can lawfully be imposed against the clear advice of the report writer or agency representative in court, albeit that frequent disregard of professional opinion is likely to lead to urgent out-of-court dialogue to resolve the obvious difficulties. In practice, the court will almost certainly wish to give the relevant agency the opportunity to assess the offender's suitability for community punishment where this is not addressed in the PSR. A court adjourning a case for a pre-sentence report may specifically indicate that it is seeking advice on the suitability of the offender for a community punishment order and has that disposal provisionally in mind.

Practice in assessing an offender's suitability for community punishment varies. In some areas the pre-sentence report writer will make the assessment, consulting a specialist community punishment officer where serious doubts arise; in other areas there may be an expectation that the offender will be separately assessed by a specialist officer before a clear proposal for community punishment can be put forward in the report.

Availability of work

23.13   PCC(S)A 2000, s.46

(6) A court shall not make a community punishment order in respect of an offender unless it is satisfied that provision for him to perform work under such an order can be made under the arrangements for persons to perform work under such orders which exist in the petty sessions area in which he resides or will reside.

(7) Subsection (6) above has effect subject to paragraphs 3 and 4 of Schedule 4 of this Act (transfer of order to Scotland and Northern Ireland).

The one inescapable requirement is for the court to be satisfied that arrangements can be made to provide work for the offender. If the relevant agency feels strongly that an individual offender could not be safely placed on any available work task or project then that would appear to block the making of an order.

---

[4] s.36(4).
[5] s.36(5).
[6] s.36(7).
[7] s.36(7).

Explanation

23.14   **PCC(S)A 2000, s.46(10)**

(10) Before making a community punishment order the court shall explain to the offender in ordinary language—

(a) the purpose and effect of the order (and in particular the requirements of the order as specified in section 47(1) to (3) belows);

(b) the consequences which may follow under Part II of Schedule 3 to this Act if he fails to comply with any of those requirements; and

(c) that the court has power (under Parts III and IV of that Schedule) to review the order on the application either of the offender or of the responsible officer.

Specified petty sessions area and responsible officer

23.15   **PCC(S)A 2000, s.46(9)**

(9) A community service order—

(a) shall specify the petty sessions area in which the offender resides or will reside; and

(b) where the offender is aged under 18 at the time the order is made, may also specify a local authority for the purposes of section 47(5)(b) below (cases where functions are to be discharged by member of a youth offending team);

and if the order specifies a local authority for those purposes, the authority specified must be the local authority within whose area it appears to the court that the offender resides or will reside.

The "responsible officer" is a pivotal figure in the administration and enforcement of the order. If the offender is aged under 18 at the time when the order is made, the functions of responsible officer are discharged either by a probation service assignee or by a member of a YOT established by a local authority as specified in the order under s.46(9): s.47(5). The choice of agency is a matter for the discretion of the court making the order and will doubtless be determined in accordance with local practice and division of responsibilities.

Provision of copies of the order

23.16   The court making an order in respect of an offender aged under 18 shall forthwith give copies of the order either to a member of the relevant YOT or to a probation officer assigned to the court, depending on the agency designated to hold responsibility for the order. That officer shall give a copy to the offender and to the responsible officer: s.46(11). If the PSA specified in the order is other than that for which the court making the order acts, the court shall also send a copy of the order to the clerk to the justices for that area, together with such documents and information relating to the case likely to be of assistance in the exercise of its functions in relation to the order: s.46(12). The order comes into force as soon as the court has pronounced sentence, irrespective of whether or when a copy of the order is given to the offender.[8]

---

[8] *Walsh v. Barlow* [1985] 1 W.L.R. 90.

Requirements of the order

23.17 The core requirements are as specified by PCC(S)A 2000, s.47(1).

PCC(S)A 2000, s.47

(1) An offender in respect of whom a community punishment order is in force shall—

    (a) keep in touch with the responsible officer in accordance with such instructions as he may from time to time be given by that officer and notify him of any change of address; and

    (b) perform for the number of hours specified in the order such work at such times as he may be instructed by the responsible officer.

(2) The instructions given by the responsible officer under this section shall, so far as practicable, be such as to avoid any conflict with the offender's religious beliefs and any interference with the times, if any, at which he normally works or attends a school or other educational establishment.

23.18 The court may not specify the dates or times when community punishment work shall be performed, nor the type of work to be undertaken, though this may be indicated in the pre-sentence report and may be a factor in assisting the court to decide whether to impose this sentence. The wording of section 47(1)(a) means that an offender can be required to report at any stage during the order when the responsible officer considers this necessary to achieve the offender's compliance with the order. This enables the offender "to be interviewed and warned of the consequences of failure to comply and helped with any difficulties which are preventing the satisfactory completion of the order".[9] The requirement to "keep in touch" can be utilised to require the offender to supply medical notes, employment details and other evidence to support a claim of "reasonable excuse" for unavailability for work.

The basic requirement to perform work is expanded by the Community Service and Combination Order Rules 1992, r. 4(1) (see 23.30) which requires the offender to comply with reasonable directions as to the manner in which the work should be undertaken and rules reasonably imposed in the interests of the health, safety and well-being of others present.

The form of a youth court community punishment order is specified by Form 43 in the Magistrates' Courts (Children and Young Persons) Rules 1992, Sched. 2.[10]

Combining community punishment with other sentences or orders

23.19 The general rule broadly applies that "courts should avoid mixing sentences which fall into well-established and different categories".[11] Thus the Court of Appeal has stated that it is wrong to make a CSO and impose a custodial sentence on the same occasion, even though (in the Crown Court) the sentences relate to different counts or separate indictments.

CJA 1991 removed the former requirement of PCCA 1973, s.14(1) that a community service order should be made "instead of dealing with (the offender) in

---

[9] Home Office (1990) *Crime, Justice and Protecting the Public*, Cm.965, London: HMSO, para. 4.15.
[10] (S.I. 1992/2071).
[11] *McElhorne* (1983) 5 Cr. App. R.(S.) 53.

any other way", thus allowing the sentencer to combine a community service order with another form of sentence or order for the same offence.

23.20   This is subject to two important restrictions:

(a)   "A community sentence shall not consist of or include both a community rehabilitation order and a community punishment order": PCC(S)A 2000 s.35(2). These two sets of requirements can be imposed for the same offence only in the form of a single community punishment and rehabilitation order, formerly known as a combination order (see Chapter 24). The Divisional Court has ruled that the two measures should not be imposed in tandem on the same serntencing occasion for separate offences: *Gilding v. DPP*.[12]

(b)   A court may not impose both an action plan order and a community punishment order on the offender within the same sentencing exercise: PCC(S)A 2000 s.69(5)(b) (see 18.04).

Though a supervision order can be equated with a community rehabilitation order in many respects, the Act is silent in regard to the mixing of supervision and community punishment orders in respect of the same offence. By analogy, however, this combination may be considered inappropriate, albeit lawful.

The court imposing a community punishment order may also make ancillary orders, including disqualification from driving, endorsement of driving licence, compensation order, costs, forfeiture.

Sentencing practice

23.21   When initially proposed, community service was recognised to offer an attractive blend of retribution, reparation and reintegration, with the additional possibility of rehabilitation.[13] The measure rapidly became established as a major sentencing option, particularly for males aged 17 to under 21, though there has been persisting concern that young women may have been discriminated against both in sentencers' perceptions of suitability for this kind of demand and in the kind of work experience offered, either relegating them to tasks that are considered "women's work" or being expected to cope in working environments with a predominantly male or sexist ethos. In 1998, 3,752 orders were imposed on boys aged 16–17, some 8.5 per cent of the total of orders made in respect of males that year.[14] For girls, the equivalent figure were 264 orders (5.4 per cent). In that year, eight per cent of boys and four per cent of girls aged 15–17 sentenced for indictable offences (excluding motoring offences) received community service orders.[15] Of orders made by the Crown Court, the offences attracting greatest numbers of C.S.O.s for boys were domestic burglary and s.20 wounding.[16]

23.22   In so far as any trends can be perceived from the Court of Appeal's view of the stature of community service, it can be said that this measure has been viewed as particularly appropriate where a young person has committed a fairly

---

[12] *The Times*, May 20, 1998.
[13] Advisory Council on the Penal System, *Non-Custodial and Semi-Custodial Penalties* (HMSO, London, 1970).
[14] Home Office, *Probation Statistics, England and Wales, 1998* (Government Statistical Service, London, 2000).
[15] Home Office (1999) *Criminal Statistics, England and Wales, 1998*.
[16] Home Office (1999) *Supplementary Criminal Statistics, England and Wales, 1998, Vol. 1*.

serious offence which seems "out of character", as the following, admittedly rather stale examples suggest—
23.23

(a) Though burglary of a dwelling house will frequently be considered "so serious", community service has sometimes been considered very appropriate for young offenders whose offence or role in the burglary was not particularly serious or culpable and whose previous record is favourable.[17]

(b) In criminal damage cases, community service has had strong appeal, *e.g. Ferreira*[18] where community service was said to be "designed" for a case of spraying graffiti on carriages at a London Underground depot: "They have done this wanton damage and therefore it behoves them to do some service to the public to put it right".

(c) Community service has on occasion been considered appropriate in cases of violence where mitigation is available such as previous good character or "out of character" loss of temper, employment or training opportunities, genuine remorse etc. For example, in *McDiarmid*[19] an offender aged 18 of previous good character threw a beer glass at a man during a public house disturbance, cutting the victim's lip. See also *Gram*.[20]

(d) Community service may be considered "tailor-made" for offences of dishonesty even if in breach of trust and involving a substantial sum, *e.g. Brown*[21] where a 19-year-old with no previous convictions had joined with another in burgling his employer's premises, taking goods worth £2,850.

23.24   The Court of Appeal has given little recent guidance on the appropriate use of this disposal or on determining how seriousness of offence should be reflected in the number of hours imposed. This reflects the comparative rarity of appeals against community service orders, either their use or their length. The Court has been reluctant to interfere in either respect. In *Cordner*,[22] the Court upheld a sentence of 100 hours imposed on a man aged 25 for theft of 50 pence from a railway ticket machine, while in *Hughes*,[23] the Court upheld a community service order for possession of cannabis imposed on a man aged 22 with no previous convictions, though reducing 80 hours to 40 hours. It is also noteworthy that in *T. and Others*,[24] where the Court upheld imposition of community sentencing in principle, it nevertheless concluded that "the more punitive element of community service was unnecessary", thus revealing a view of the comparative weight of community punishment in relation to other types of community order.

The life span of a community punishment order

23.25   The administration of "community punishment" is specified partly by statute, partly by statutory instrument, the Community Service and Combination Order Rules 1992[25] (which would carry a very cumbersome alternative title if

---

[17] *e.g. Mole* (1990) 12 Cr. App. R.(S.) 371.
[18] (1988) 10 Cr. App. R.(S.) 343.
[19] (1980) 2 Cr. App. R.(S.) 130.
[20] (1990) 12 Cr. App. R.(S.) 441.
[21] (1981) 3 Cr. App. R.(S.) 294.
[22] (1992) 13 Cr. App. R. (S.) 570.
[23] [1999] 2 Cr. App. R. (S.) 329.
[24] [1999] Crim. L.R. 432 (see 17.06).
[25] S.I. 2076/1992.

following the re-naming of the two eponymous orders), and partly by the Home Office's *National Standards.*[26] *National Standards for Youth Justice*[27] clarify that 16- and 17-year-olds subject to community punishment orders must be supervised according to the adult *Standards.*

Commencement

23.26   Whenever possible an offender newly sentenced to a community punishment order (C.P.O.) should be given the date of their first appointment before leaving court. This should take place within five working days of the order being made: *National Standards.*[28] The initial appointment counts towards completion of the hours specified in the order. The question may arise whether the offender should be required to commence work while their appeal against conviction or sentence is pending. This matter was tested before the Divisional Court in *Greater Manchester Probation Committee v. Bent*[29] The Court held that the order was in force and enforceable pending appeal and as a consequence breach proceedings could properly be brought when the offender declined to comply with work instructions. The question remains whether a court might uphold a defence of "reasonable excuse" based on pursuit of an appeal. Where an offender is already subject to community punishment hours and is given further hours under a new order, either for further offences or for breach of a community order, for the purposes of fulfilling *National Standards* "the second order shall be treated as if it were simply an extension of the first" so that no separate induction or commencement is required.[30] Any new offence may nevertheless prompt reconsideration of the possible risk posed (see below).

Assessment and induction

23.27   In common with all offenders supervised by the probation service, persons sentenced to community punishment orders must be subject to a written assessment covering: (i) the risks they present of causing serious harm to any victim of their offence, to the public, to staff or to themselves; (ii) the causes and patterns of their offending behaviour and the likelihood of their re-offending; (iii) their offence-related needs and circumstances; (iv) their motivation to change and to resolve those needs/circumstances. In addition to what may be felt to be a somewhat elaborate exercise in respect of individuals who are to fulfil work tasks, offenders subject to C.P.O.s must be assessed in respect of "their health, skills, availability for work and any placement needs such as cultural or religious considerations".[31] Offenders must not start a work placement until their risks have been assessed. It is understandably considered vital that offenders should not be allocated to a placement which might unwittingly place anyone at unacceptable or foreseeable risk or increase the likelihood of further offending. The instructions to be given to offenders at their induction meeting are detailed below.

Work arrangements and frequency

23.28   The offender's first work session should take place within 10 working days of the order being made. Offenders should be "offered a minimum of five

---

[26] Home Office (2000) *National Standards for the Supervision of Offenders in the Community.*
[27] Youth Justice Board (2000), Section 7.
[28] (1996) 160 Justice of the Peace Reports 297.
[29] n. 26, para. D7.
[30] n. 26, para. D15.
[31] n. 26, para. C9.

hours per week.[32] In consequence, an offender is expected as a minimum to keep one assessment appointment and undertake 11 work sessions, accumulating at least 55 hours, in the first 12 weeks of their order.

Work arrangements should not prevent an unemployed offender from being readily available to seek or take up employment, nor conflict with their entitlement to benefit. Echoing s.47(2), *National Standards* also specify that work instructions should not disrupt an employed person's working hours or education commitments and should take account of their religious/cultural requirements.

An innovation introduced in the revised (2000) version of *National Standards* permits responsible officers at their discretion to allow offenders to undertake "basic literacy or other work necessary to enable the offender to gain maximum benefit from the order, or to provide qualifications directly related to the work being done under the order". For example, an offender may be able to obtain a workplace Health & Safety qualification or a Food Hygiene certificate that would both enhance their present performance and enhance their future job prospects. However, such allowance in total should not exceed ten per cent of the hours prescribed in the order. Thus if an order is for the minimum 40 hours, a maximum of four hours may be used in this way.

23.29 As regards the nature of work to be undertaken, *National Standards*[33] specify that placements must—

- be assessed for the risks to individuals and property and the requirements of health and safety legislation;
- be available to meet the needs of specific individuals such as those related to their gender, race, ethnicity or ability;
- occupy offenders fully and be physically, emotionally or mentally demanding.

Work performance, non-compliance and lateness
23.30   CSSOR 1992, r.4

(1) While performing work under an order an offender shall be required to comply with any reasonable directions of the supervisor as to the manner in which the work is to be performed and with any rules reasonably imposed by the supervisor in the place of work having regard to the circumstances of that workplace, the interests of health or safety or the interests and well-being of other persons present.
(2) Where an offender—
   (a) fails to comply with any such direction or rule as is mentioned in the preceding paragraph;
   (b) in any way fails satisfactorily to perform the work he has been instructed to do;
   (c) behaves in a disorderly or disruptive manner or in a manner likely to give offence to members of the public or any person for whose benefit the work is being performed; or
   (d) reports for work later than the appointed time

---

[32] n. 26, para. D14.
[33] n. 26, para. D16.

he may (without prejudice to any proceedings for failure to comply with the requirements of the order under schedule 2 to the Criminal Justice Act 1991) be required to cease work that day and may, in addition, be required to leave the place of work forthwith; and where he is so required to cease work, the relevant officer may direct that some or all of any period of work for that day shall not be reckoned as time worked under the order.

23.31 *National Standards*[34] require that at the offender's first or induction meeting the supervising officer shall give instructions prohibiting—

(a) violent or aggressive behaviour or threats of violence;

(b) other conduct or language that might reasonably give offence to agency staff, other persons subject to supervision or members of the public;

(c) other wilful or persistent non co-operation or behaviour designed to frustrate the purpose of the offender's or other's supervision.

These are generic provisions detailing instructions to be given to all offenders. The 1995 *Standard* specific to community service also prohibited "attendance while unable to participate properly because of alcohol or non-prescribed drugs" and "work which fails to demonstrate the required level of effort or commitment". Staff may wish to expand upon the core provisions (a)–(c) by adding instructions of this kind.

Calculating time for travel, lunch breaks and bad weather

23.32   CSSOR 1992, rr. 3 and 5

3. The time spent by an offender in travelling in connection with the performance of work under an order shall not be reckoned as time worked under the order except where his relevant officer or supervisor decides that all the time so spent, or such part of it as he so decides, shall be so reckoned.

5. (1) Where bad weather prevents the performance of work, it shall be open to the supervisor to require the offender to remain in the expectation of its being possible to begin or resume work, as appropriate, or he may make arrangements for the offender to perform work at some other place or, where it is not practicable to make such arrangements, he shall dismiss the offender for the remainder of that day.

(2) Any time during which bad weather prevents the performance of work may not be reckoned as time worked under an order except where the offender remains at the place of work either in the charge of the supervisor or because he is required by him so to remain.

23.33 *National Standards*[35] amplify these rules as follows:

• Any travel time in excess of 30 minutes each way may be counted towards completion of work hours, at the discretion of the probation service, subject to an overall limit of 10 per cent of the hours specified in the order.

- Where a work session spans lunchtime and the offender is required to remain on site, up to 30 minutes may be counted towards completion of work hours, providing that the offender "remains under the supervision of the supervising officer throughout".

- Any time during which wet weather prevents work performance shall not be counted towards completion of work hours except where the supervisor requires the offender to remain. In any such instance the maximum time that may be counted towards completion of hours is 30 minutes.

Recording and reports

23.34   CSCOR, r.6

(1) The relevant officer or a person nominated by him shall make a report on an offender in respect of any week during which the offender has been instructed to perform work under the order.

(2) A report made on an offender under paragraph (1) above shall include a record of the time worked by him during the week in question, the total time worked under the order and the number of hours which remain to be worked.

(3) A copy of each report on an offender made under paragraph (1) above shall be given to him and, if it is made by another person, to the relevant officer.

This rule is reiterated by *National Standards*.[36]

Twelve months duration

23.35   PCC(S)A 2000, s.47(3)

(1) Subject to paragraph 22 of Schedule 3 to this Act, the work required to be performed under a community service order shall be performed during the period of twelve months beginning with the date of the order; but, unless revoked, the order shall remain in force until the offender has worked under it for the number of hours specified in it."

The statutory expectation is thus that the work should be completed within a year of the date of the order but the order nevertheless remains in force (and subject to enforcement proceedings) beyond that period until the offender has completed the outstanding hours. Offenders have sometimes erroneously interpreted this provision to imply that they can determine their own pace of work, provided that they fulfil the requirements within 12 months. It is clear, however, that the pace is determined by the responsible officer and that the expectation is that offenders will work steadily from the commencement of the order until completion. Even the longest order should normally be attainable within 12 months if an average minimum of five hours per week is achieved. Problems will arise, however, where

---

[36] n. 6, para. D14.

illness, injury, work commitments, suspension from CS work or a period in custody intervene.

23.36 PCC(S)A 2000, Sched. 3, para. 22 makes provision for a community punishment order to be amended on the application of either the responsible officer or the offender by extending the period. However, as section 47(3), indicates, an offender can continue to be given work instructions after the expiry of 12 months[36a] and it might be queried, in the light of this, why there is any power or necessity to seek an extension. It is nevertheless good practice to seek a time extension because this provides a helpful revised target date by which the obligation to work should be satisfied. Notwithstanding this, proceedings for revocation or breach may, however, be validly initiated after the initial 12 months have elapsed, even though an extension has not been sought, without being out of time.

Compliance and enforcement

23.37 The provisions regulating non-compliance and enforcement action under PCC(S)A 2000 Sched. 3 with associated expectations of *National Standards*.

Final review

23.38 *National Standards* specify that a final review should be "made available" to the offender at the termination of their order. This opportunity "may count as up to one hour" towards the completion of their total hours.[37]

Successful outcome

23.39 Research has sought to identify characteristics of community service work which enhance the prospects for a successful outcome. McIvor's study of CS schemes in Scotland[38] (1992) found lower levels of unacceptable absences among offenders who considered their experience on community service to have been very worthwhile. Placements which were particularly valued by offenders were characterised by work which—

    (a) maximised their contact with the beneficiaries;

    (b) enabled offenders to acquire practical or inter-personal skills;

    (c) provided offenders with a sense of benefit to recipients.

23.40 McIvor thus advocates proper attention to the potential value of community service to the offender, as well as the punitive element, by the provision of interesting, enjoyable and worthwhile tasks. She noted that though community service is not an explicitly rehabilitative sentence, offenders who had found CS to be particularly worthwhile were—

    (a) slightly less likely to be reconvicted;

    (b) reconvicted less often in the three years following sentence;

    (c) markedly less likely to be reconvicted of offences involving dishonesty.

[36a] *Tebbutt* (1988) 10 Cr.App.R.(S.) 88.
[37] n. 26, para. C12.
[38] G. McIvor, Sentenced to Service: The Operation and Impact of Community Service by Offender (Avebury, Aldershot, 1992).

In 1998 64 per cent of community service orders imposed on offenders aged 16–17 terminated upon completion of the specified hours, compared with 72 per cent for all age groups. Offenders under 18 showed a higher rate of termination because of failure to comply with requirements (20% compared with 13 per cent for all age groups or because of conviction of a futher offence (11 per cent compared with seven per cent for all age groups).

Community service as penalty for breach of a community order

23.41 A community punishment order may be imposed as a penalty where failure to comply with a community order regulated by PCC(S)A 2000, Sched. 3 is admitted or proved and the court permits the continuance of that order: Sched. 3, para 4(1C)(b) and para. 5(1C)(b).

23.42 Such an order is termed a "secondary order" (Sched. 3, para. 7(2)) and is regulated by Sched. 3 para. 7, the order that was breached being termed "the original order".[39]

Number of Hours

The number of hours which an offender may be required to work under a secondary order shall not exceed 60 in the aggregate; and, in addition, para. 7(3)(a) and (b) specify—

(a) where the relevant order is a community punishment order, the number of hours which the offender may be required to work under the secondary order shall not be such that the total number of hours under both orders exceeds the maximum specified in section 46(3) of this Act; and

(b) where the relevant order is a community punishment and rehabilitation order, the number of hours which the offender may be required to work under the secondary order shall not be such that the total number of hours under—

(i) the secondary order, and
(ii) the community service element of the combination order,

exceeds the maximum specified in section 51(1)(b) of this Act.

23.43 The Schedule is not fully clear whether the maximum aggregate allowable refers to the total number of hours ordered or remaining to be served but the former interpretation appears correct. No minimum length of order is specified and thus the Schedule allows very short orders, though responsible officers may have doubts about the appropriateness of inducting offenders into work for orders below a certain viable minimum length.

An order imposed as a breach penalty is administered and regulated in essentially the same way as a community punishment order imposed as a community sentence, subject to the special provisions of Schedule 3, para. 7(6).

---

[39] para, 7(6).

CHAPTER 24

Community Punishment and Rehabilitation Orders

24.01   First introduced by the Criminal Justice Act 1991 as a marriage of the familiar powers of probation and community service in a single community order, the combination order was renamed, somewhat laboriously, as the community punishment and rehabilitation order by CJCSA 2000, s.38 to give the sentence a more transparent identity as well as an unambiguously punitive ethos. Now regulated by PCC(S)A 2000, s.51, the legal provisions remain essentially as contained in the 1991 Act. To ease the transition required through change of name s.38 clarifies—

(2) References in any enactment, instrument or document to a community punishment and rehabilitation order include (where the context allows) an order under any provision corresponding to that subsection which is repealed by that Act.

(4) References in any enactment, instrument or document to a combination order—

   (a) are to an order under any provision corresponding to s.51(1) of PCC(S)A 2000 which is repealed by that Act, and
   (b) include (where the context allows) an order under that section.

24.02   Under section 51(1) a community punishment and rehabilitation order (CPRO) requires the offender:

(a) to be under supervision for a period specified in the order, being not less than 12 months nor more than three years; and

(b) to perform unpaid work for a number of hours no specified, being in the aggregate not less than 40 nor more than 100.

The probation or rehabilitation "element" may be regarded as the senior partner as the intention of the legislation and the clear view of the Home Office[1] has been that the community service element will normally be completed first. Though a CPRO is a single order, the statute makes little explicit provision for its enforcement treating the order essentially as two separate legal entities, thus requiring the courts to borrow as appropriate from provisions relating to community rehabilitation and community punishment orders (Sched. 3, para. 14—see 24.11). This has generated some ambiguity in enforcement proceedings.

---

[1] Home Office *National Standards for the Supervision of offenders in the Community* (HMSO, London, 1995) Chap. 6, para. 10.

Power to make a Community Punishment and Rehabilitation Order

24.03 The offender must be aged 16 or over and, as with a community punishment order, must be convicted of an offence punishable with imprisonment (other than an offence for which sentence is fixed by law). As in respect of a community rehabilitation order, the court must be of the opinion that the making of such an order is desirable in the interests of—

(a) securing the rehabilitation of the offender, or

(b) protecting the public from harm from the offender or preventing the commission by the offender of further offences.

There is no requirement that such further offences shall be of the same nature as the offence for which the offender is being sentenced. In addition, because the relevant provisions of PCC(S)A 2000 apply to CPROs as if the rehabilitation element were a community rehabilitation order and the community punishment element were a community punishment order (s. 51(4)) the court must comply with the procedural requirements of sections 41, 42, 46 and 47 of the 2000 Act specified in the making of community rehabilitation and community punishment orders.

24.04 The court is required to obtain and consider a pre-sentence report before determining the suitability of a CPRO for the offender. As with other community orders being imposed as a community sentence, the restriction on liberty imposed under a CPRO should be commensurate with the seriousness of the offence or that offence combined with other associated offences, taking into account the suitability of the order for the offender and the likely impact of the order upon the offender in the light of their personal circumstances and characteristics.

A CPRO may be imposed upon an offender who resides or intends to reside in Scotland but not if the offender resides or intends to reside in Northern Ireland.

The form of a youth court CPRO is specified by the Magistrates' Courts (Forms) Rules 1981, f. 92F (as amended by the Magistrates' Courts (CJA 1991) (Miscellaneous Amendments) Rules 1992. The standard requirements combine those which are specified in community punishment orders and standard community rehabilitation orders.

Additional Requirements

24.05 As the rehabilitation element of a CPRO is governed as if it were a community rehabilitation order, it follows that a court is empowered to include any additional requirement in the order as if it were imposing a community rehabilitation order, whether under Sched. 3 or in exercise of the general power specified by s.42(1). The court should have regard to the compatibility of such additional requirements with the offender's performance of the community punishment element, and be alert to the overall restriction upon the offender's liberty thus entailed.

Combining a CPRO with other sentences and orders

24.06 The general rule broadly applies that "courts should avoid mixing sentences which fall into well established and different categories".[2] The scope for combining a CPRO with other sentences or orders is subject to two important restrictions—

---

[2] *McElhorne* (1983) 5 Cr. App. R.(S.) 53.

(a) "A community sentence shall not consist of or include both a community rehabilitation order and a community punishment order": PCC(S)A 2000 s.35(2). These two sets of requirements can be imposed for the same offence only in the form of a single community punishment and rehabilitation order. By implication a CPRO may not be combined with either a community punishment order or a community rehabilitation order for the same offence. Further, the Divisional Court has ruled that the two measures should not be imposed in tandem on the same serntencing occasion for separate offences: *Gilding v. DPP*.[3] It appears to follow that in the same circumstances a CPRO should not be combined with a community punishment order.

(b) A court may not impose both an action plan order and a community punishment and rehabilitation order on the offender within the same sentencing exercise: PCC(S)A 2000 s.69(5)(b) (see 18.04).

24.07 A CPRO should be combined with an attendance centre order only with considerable hesitation, in view of the triple burden of responsibility which the young offender would be required to sustain. A court seeking to combine such elements in a community sentence is perhaps more likely to impose an action plan order with its greater flexibility in blending different demands upon a young offender.

A common assumption has prevailed that a community rehabilitation order or CPRO cannot be imposed where the defendant is a serving prisoner because the order commences with immediate effect at a point when supervision is clearly not a viable proposition. However, in *Fonteneau v. DPP*[4] where the offender had 17 days left to serve of his existing sentence when sentenced to a magistrates' court combination order, the Divisional Court upheld the validity of the justices' order. Lord Bingham C.J. indicated that while it is necessary to ensure that a sentence is operable in practice and any delay of this nature has to be so short as to be "minimal", in this instance the sentence was operable and, in all the circumstances, sensible and just.

Appropriate use of a community punishment and rehabilitation order

24.08 Since its introduction as a sentencing option in 1992, the combination order has not acquired the distinctive identity hoped for by many commentators. The White Paper *Crime, Justice and Protecting the Public*[5] anticipated that the order would be particularly suitable for persistent property offenders otherwise receiving custodial sentences. It was hoped that a particularly demanding non-custodial sentence combining an element of indirect reparation with an opportunity to reduce the likelihood of re-offending would have a particular appeal for sentencers in dealing with those on the borderline of custody. In this vein the Magistrates' Association, the Justices' Clerks Society and the Association of Chief Officers of Probation issued a joint discussion paper[6] suggesting that—

"Combination orders are appropriate only where a high level of restriction is required. It may be that few cases dealt with in Magistrates' Courts—and even fewer in youth courts—are likely to come within this sentencing band."

---

[3] *The Times*, May 20, 1998.
[4] [2000] Crim. L. R. 611.
[5] Home Office (1990) Cm. 965.
[6] Magistrates' Association, Association of Chief Officers of Probation and the Justices' Clerks' Society (1993) "Community Sentences and Restrictions on Liberty", *The Magistrate*, 49, 89.

24.09   The 1992 version of *National Standards* noted that "combination orders that include demanding additional requirements within the probation element are particularly onerous and are likely to be difficult to complete, especially for younger offenders".

Hopes that the use of combination orders might be restricted mainly to the Crown Court have not been realised. In the years 1994–98 around 70 per cent of all combination orders were imposed by magistrates' courts. In 1998 approximately 1,300 males aged 16–17, some nine per cent of those in the age group 15–17 receiving community sentences for indictable offences, were sentenced to combination orders. Male and female offenders aged under 18 constituted some 11 per cent of the 12,800 persons of all ages sentenced to combination orders for indictable offences in all courts in that year.

The management of a community punishment and rehabilitation order

24.10   PCC(S)A 2000, s.51 does not identify a specific "responsible officer" for CPROs, thus leaving this to be interpreted under s.41(6) for the rehabilitation element and s.47(4) for the community punishment element. The 1995 version of *National Standards* required that one officer should be identified as holding overall responsibility for the combination order so that the two elements should be administered compatibly with an appropriate overview of the totality of the sentence. Within the current version of *National Standards* the community punishment and rehabilitation order is given relatively muted distinctive attention, other than a brief indication that the two elements "should be managed together". Paragraph D17 specifies that "the standards for both . . . elements apply, *i.e.* a minimum of 12 rehabilitation appointments plus one community punishment assessment and 11 community punishment work sessions shall be arranged in the first 12 weeks". In recognition of the problems that may be posed in initiating both elements in tandem simultaneously for some offenders, paragraph D18 indicates that "exceptionally, line management may endorse a delay in the activation of either element . . . if this is desirable to achieve the overall objectives of the order". It is to be anticipated that the community punishment element may be delayed in some instances where an offender is experiencing problems that could make double compliance difficult or an unrealistic prospect. Thus the rehabilitation element may take precedence, allowing the 'punishment' element to be phased in at a suitable later point.

Enforcement of a community punishment and rehabilitation order

24.11   The generic provisions of PCC(S)A 2000, Sched. 3 designate the CPRO as a "relevant order" for its purposes but add (para. 1(4))—

(4) In this Schedule—

   (a) references to the community rehabilitation element of a community punishment and rehabilitation order are references to the order in so far as it imposes such a requirement as is mentioned in section 51(1)(a) of this Act (and in so far as it imposes any additional requirements included in the order by virtue of section 42); and

   (b) references to the community punishment element of such an order are references to the order in so far as it imposes such a requirement as is mentioned in section 51(1)(b).

Additionally, *National Standards* specify that for enforcement purposes, any unacceptable absences from either . . . element will be treated cumulatively".[7] *National Standards for Youth Justice*[8] clarify that 16- and 17-year-olds subject to CPROs must be supervised according to the adult *Standards*.

24.12   The question has arisen whether it is possible for a court to revoke one element of the order while leaving the other intact, either in breach proceedings or on hearing a revocation application or subsequent to a custodial sentence imposed for a further offence. However the logic of the CPRO suggests that the order is best regarded as an indivisible entity. Clear problems would be presented in dealing with the offender afresh for the original offence upon revocation of only one element of the order. On what basis could the court assess what sentence is appropriate for the original offence when a part of the original sentence for that offence remains in force? CPRO should be addressed and revoked as a whole, either upon a single application or by a single decision of the court. This interpretation is reinforced by the Magistrates' Court (Forms) Rules 1981, f. 92P, specifying a form for use in "revocation of a probation, community service or combination order".

---

[7] Home Office (2000) *National Standards for the Superivision of Offenders in the Community*, para. D17.
[8] Youth Justice Board (2000), Section 7.

CHAPTER 25

Drug Treatment and Testing Orders

25.01 Introduced by CDA 1998, ss.61–64 as a new form of community order, the drug treatment and testing order (DTTO) is now governed by PCC(S)A 2000, ss.52–57. The 2000 Act does not simply replicate the 1998 Act but the provisions are unchanged in effect. Akin to and statutorily modelled on the community rehabilitation order, the order is intended to enhance sentencers' powers to deal with offenders who are dependent on or who have a propensity to misuse drugs. Unusually, courts are required to take a continuing active role in the life of the order by conducting periodic reviews of the offender's progress. This measure is intended to replace the power to impose an additional requirement in a community rehabilitation order to receive treatment for drug dependency under PCC(S)A 2000, Sched. 2 para.6. Supervision of this community order has to be undertaken by a probation officer (see 25.17) and though the measure is available for offenders aged 16–17, there is no scope for a YOT member to act as responsible officer. The DTTO is thus outwith the general expectation that YOTs will undertake supervisory work with young offenders. This measure was subject to pilot trials in three areas, Croydon, Gloucestershire and Liverpool, from October 1, 1998, in anticipation of national implementation in Autumn 2000.

Power to Make a Drug Treatment and Testing Order

25.02 A DTTO may be imposed by the Crown Court or a youth court in dealing with any offence (unless, in the case of a defendant aged 18 or over, a mandatory sentencing provisions apply). As a community order, a DTTO may not be imposed unless the generic provisions of PCC(S)A 2000 ss.35–36 apply, as regards the "serious enough" threshold criterion and the requirements that the order is the "most suitable for the offender" and that the restrictions on liberty thus imposed are commensurate with the seriousness of the offence(s): see chapter 17. A pre-sentence report should be considered before the court forms an opinion as to the suitability of the offender for a DTTO: s.36(3)(d) and (4).

25.03   PCC(S)A 2000, s.52

(1) Where a person aged 16 or over is convicted of an offence, the court by or before which he is convicted may (subject to sections 34 to 36 above) make an order which—

(a) has effect for a period specified in the order of not less than six months nor more than three years ("the treatment and testing period"); and

(b) includes the requirements and provisions mentioned in sections 53 and 54 below;

but this section does not apply in relation to an offence committed
before 30th September 1998.

(3) A court shall not make a drug treatment and testing order in respect of an
offender unless it is satisfied—

(a) that he is dependent on or has a propensity to misuse drugs; and
(b) that his dependency or propensity is such as requires and may be
susceptible to treatment.

The criteria specified by s.53(3) do not require that a link must be established
between the defendant's drug misuse and the offence of which they have been
convicted.

Targeting

25.04   Type of Drug.   Home Office guidance[1] advises that as the DTTO has
been created in order to break the links between drug misuse and other types of
offending and research demonstrates that such links are strongest where the drug is
likely to cause dependency or compulsive use, the order "will most appropriately
be targeted on users of opiates, cocaine and, to some extent, amphetamines."

25.05   Type and Volume of Offence.   As regards type of offence most likely to
merit a DTTO, the guidance[2] adds—

> "It is envisaged that the vast majority of suitable candidates will be convicted
> of acquisitive crimes, committed in order to obtain money to buy drugs.
> Volume of offending is likely to be a more important consideration than the
> seriousness of individual offences."

25.06   The extent and frequency of the offender's offending may not be readily
discernible, though may be assessed on the basis of a defendant's admissions in
assessment interview. The Guidance states that "it will be important that links are
made with a variety of agencies in order that information about those committing
the greatest volume of offences can form a part of the assessment of suitability",
adding that local Drug Action Teams can assist in this process. While the Guidance
has property crime foremost in mind, it adds that offenders convicted of drug
supply who are themselves habitual users should also be considered if they are
otherwise candidates for a community sentence, though this may be unlikely under
current sentencing guidelines. Irrespective of the offence for which the offender has
been convicted, the guidance[3] advises: "If the offender discloses drug misuse as a
motivating factor in their offending, an assessment should always be made of their
suitability for a DTTO, unless it is obvious that such an order cannot or should not
be imposed".

25.07   Offender's Motivation.   It is apparent that the prospects of success in
imposing a DTTO will depend heavily on the defendant's motivation to undertake
and sustain treatment, particularly given the requirement that the defendant must
express consent to the making of the order (see 25.11). Anticipating that some

---

[1] Home Office *Guidance for Practitioners involved in Drug Treatment and Testing Order Pilots* (Home
Office, London, 'General Guidance on Targeting of the Order' 1988) para. 5.
[2] n. 1, para. 6.
[3] n. 1, para. 8.

defendants may have ulterior motives for consenting to the order without seriously wanting to change, the guidance[4] urges careful and objective assessment of motivation, advising that no pre-sentence report proposal for a DTTO should be made unless the writer and the treatment provider agree that the defendant is suitably motivated.

25.08   Offenders aged under 18.   Home Office guidance[5] notes that the targeting criterion of volume of offending—

> "should not be interpreted as ruling out offenders from the younger end of this age group who may be just at the beginning of their offending careers; indeed successful intervention at this stage could well pay major dividends in reducing subsequent offending. If a young person has drug misuse problems which are linked to a pattern of offending, they should not be excluded from consideration on the grounds that they do not yet have a long criminal record."

Pre-Sentence Testing

25.09   To enable the court to determine whether the criterion in s.52(3)(a) is met, s.52(4) authorises sampling, subject to the defendant's consent—

> (4)   For the purpose of ascertaining for the purposes of subsection (3) above whether the offender has any drug in his body, the court may by order require him to provide samples of such description as it may specify; but the court shall not make such an order unless the offender expresses his willingness to comply with its requirements.

The court may impose a DTTO only if it has been notified that arrangements for implementing such orders are available in the area to be specified in the order, *i.e.* the petty sessions area in which the offender resides or will reside (s.54(1)): s.52(5). Where such notification has been issued, the scope to impose a drug treatment requirement in a community rehabilitation order ceases: Sched. 2 para.6(2).

Treatment Arrangements

25.10   A DTTO may not be imposed unless the court is "satisfied that arrangements have or can be made for the treatment intended to be specified in the order", including arrangements for the reception of the offender where he is required to receive residential treatment: s.53(3).

Explanation and Consent

25.11   Before making a DTTO the court shall explain the effect of the order to the offender in ordinary language, covering the effect and the requirements, periodic review provisions, the consequences of non-compliance and the scope for review on application of the offender or the responsible officer: s.52(6). Because of the nature of the order, a DTTO may not be imposed "unless the offender expresses his willingness to comply with its requirements": s.52(7).

Specified PSA

25.12   A DTTO "shall include a provision specifying the petty sessions area in which it appears to the court making the order that the offender resides or will

---

[4] n. 1, para. 9.
[5] n. 1, para. 11.

reside": s.54(1). This inclusion determines who shall act as responsible officer (s.54(2)) but does not determine the court which takes responsibility for periodic review and enforcement purposes, as is explained further below at 25.21.

Copies of the Order

25.13 Where a DTTO is made (or amended at a review hearing under s.55(1)) the court "shall forthwith give copies of the order to a probation officer assigned to the court": s.57(1) and (2). Copies should then be provided to the offender, the treatment provider and the responsible officer. An exception to s.57(1) arises in less common instances where the court making the order specifies that a court acting for the petty sessions are specified in the order shall exercise jurisdiction (see 25.20), in which case, copies of the order shall be sent to the court responsible for the order which, in turn shall give copies to a probation officer assigned to it: s.57(3).

Requirements of the Order

25.14 The obligations of a DTTO are complex but can be divided into four heads—

(a) The Treatment Requirement

PCC(S)A 2000, s.53

(1) A drug treatment and testing order shall include a requirement ("the treatment requirement") that the offender shall submit, during the whole of the treatment and testing period, to treatment by or under the direction of a specified person having the necessary qualifications or experience ("the treatment provider") with a view to the reduction or elimination of the offender's dependency on or propensity to misuse drugs.

(2) The required treatment for any particular period shall be—

    (a) treatment as a resident in such institution or place as may be specified in the order; or

    (b) treatment as a non-resident in or at such institution or place, and at such intervals, as may be so specified;

but the nature of the treatment shall not be specified in the order except as mentioned in paragraph (a) or (b) above.

The nature of the treatment provider's "necessary qualifications or experience" for their role are not specified. The absence of a third treatment option, available in making a community rehabilitation order under Sched.2 para.6, permitting treatment "by or under the direction" of a specified person should serve to avoid inappropriate use of this measure.

(b) The Testing Requirement

25.15   **PCC(S)A 2000, s.53**

(4) A drug treatment and testing order shall include a requirement ("the testing requirement") that, for the purpose of ascertaining whether he has any drug in his body during the treatment and testing period, the offender shall during that period, at such times or in such circumstances as may

(subject to the provisions of the order) be determined by the treatment provider, provide samples of such description as may be so determined.

(5) The testing requirement shall specify for each month the minimum number of occasions on which samples are to be provided.

Though s.53(4) accords discretion to the treatment provider, subject to the minimum number of tests as set by the court (s.53(5)), Home Office guidance[6] indicates—

"the actual frequency of testing will also normally be as stated in the order, as that should reflect the proposals of the treatment provider; but the treatment provider should have discretion to require the offender to undergo more frequent tests than are specified in the order, for instance in response to a test failure. The maximum feasible frequency will normally be once every three days, as this should ensure that any drug consumption is detected before the traces disappear; but in some cases such frequent testing may not be necessary."

It will be noted that the requirement is to provide samples for testing and the legislation does not make any provision for action to be taken if tests prove positive. The Home Office has suggested that treatment should continue despite the occasional failed test but also states that a second failed test should always lead to formal consideration of breach action (see 25.30) and the pilot trial research (see 25.33) has reported that failed tests were one of the principal forms of non-compliance prompting breach proceedings. It could be argued that an offender has complied with his order if he has submitted to testing, even if tests indicate presence of controlled drugs.

25.16   The Act does not specify who is to carry out tests or the kind of test to be conducted. Home Office guidance[7] advises that urine testing is most practicable and cost-effective, using "immunoassay" test kits, conducted by the treatment provider "or his agent". Samples "should be supplied under controlled conditions, if not direct observation".[8] The guidance indicates[9] that the drug most closely implicated in the offender's criminal behaviour (the "index" drug) should always be tested for, but testing may extend to other drugs, including bezodiazepines. If a test is failed at this stage, revealing presence of the index drug(s), a sample should "generally be sent to a laboratory for a confirmatory Gas Chromatography/Mass Spectrometry test", except where the offender "fully admits drug misuse"[10]. Results should be returned to the treatment provider within five working days of despatch to the laboratory.[11] Test results must be communicated to the responsible officer: s.54(4)(b). Where a failed test may be used to support the initiation of breach proceedings (see 25.30) , the sample should be divided into two containers in front of the offender and one portion should be offered to the offender who may wish to undertake independent analysis. The remaining portion should be split in two, one being sent to the laboratory and the other frozen and retained for a year in case of legal challenge (para.10). If the sample tests positive for a drug other than the "index" drug, the sample should still be sent for confirmatory testing.[12]

---

[6] n. 1, 'Guidance on Drug Testing', para. 3.
[7] n. 6, para. 4.
[8] n. 6, para. 9.
[9] n. 6, para. 7.
[10] n. 6, para. 11.
[11] n. 6, para. 5.
[12] n. 1, para. 11.

(c) Supervision Requirement

25.17   PCC(S)A 2000, s.54

(2) A drug treatment and testing order shall provide that, for the treatment and testing period, the offender shall be under the supervision of a probation officer appointed for or assigned to the petty sessions area specified in the order.

(3) In this Act "responsible officer", in relation to an offender who is subject to a drug treatment and testing order, means the probation officer responsible for his supervision.

(4) A drug treatment and testing order shall—

   (a) require the offender to keep in touch with the responsible officer in accordance with such instructions as he may from time to time be given by that officer, and to notify him of any change of address; and
   (b) provide that the results of the tests carried out on the samples provided by the offender in pursuance of the testing requirement shall be communicated to the responsible officer.

(5) Supervision by the responsible officer shall be carried out to such extent only as may be necessary for the purpose of enabling him—

   (a) to report on the offender's progress to the court responsible for the order;
   (b) to report to that court any failure by the offender to comply with the requirements of the order; and
   (c) to determine whether the circumstances are such that he should apply to that court for the revocation or amendment of the order.

25.18 Supervision is thus a more limited exercise than applies in respect of a community rehabilitation order. DTTOs have not been brought within the provisions of *National Standards for the Supervision of Offenders in the Community*[13] but are the subject of separate Home Office guidance. In pursuance of the responsible officer's role in monitoring the offender's progress, interim guidance[14] states that the probation service shall "require regular reports reflecting both individual offenders' progress and treatment agencies' success in treatment", specifically a monthly report of all tests, including failures to attend, refusals to produce samples and test results.

(d) Periodic Review Requirement

25.19   PCC(S)A 2000, s.54

(6) A drug treatment and testing order shall—

   (a) provide for the order to be reviewed periodically at intervals of not less than one month;
   (b) provide for each review of the order to be made, subject to section 55(6) below, at a hearing held for the purpose by the court responsible for the order (a "review hearing");

---

[13] Home Office (2000).
[14] n. 6, para. 15.

(c) require the offender to attend each review hearing;

(d) provide for the responsible officer to make to the court responsible for the order, before each review, a report in writing on the offender's progress under the order; and

(e) provide for each such report to include the test results communicated to the responsible officer under subsection (4)(b) above and the views of the treatment provider as to the treatment and testing of the offender.

Home Office guidance[15] suggests that when making a DTTO "courts may wish to specify a schedule of review dates or intervals", thus providing a framework of goals for offenders to achieve and making listings of hearings simpler. The process of periodic review is outlined further below.

Responsible Court

25.20   PCC(S)A 2000, s.54

(7) In this section references to the court responsible for a drug treatment and testing order are references to—

(a) where a court is specified in the order in accordance with subsection (8) below, that court;

(b) in any other case, the court by which the order is made.

(8) Where the area specified in a drug treatment and testing order made by a magistrates' court is not the area for which the court acts, the court may, if it thinks fit, include in the order provision specifying for the purposes of subsection (7) above a magistrates' court which acts for the area specified in the order.

Whereas jurisdiction in respect of a community order lies with a court acting for the petty sessions area specified in the order, in the case of a DTTO jurisdiction will normally rest with the court which imposed the order, whether the Crown Court or a summary court. If a DTTO is imposed by the Court of Appeal it is treated as a Crown Court order: s.54(9). Where the order is made by a magistrates' court but the order specifies a petty sessions area other than the area for which that court acts, the court imposing the order has the discretion to order that a magistrates' court acting for that area shall be responsible for the order. Thus if an offender appears for sentence before Xtown magistrates but resides in Ytown, Xtown justices may, if they see fit, specify that Ytown justices shall exercise jurisdiction for the purposes of periodic reviews and enforcement proceedings. If the order was imposed by a youth court it appears to follow that the youth court retains jurisdiction even if the offender meantime attains the age of 18.

Periodic Reviews and Review Hearings

25.21 As specified by s.54(1), it is an integral feature of a DTTO that the order shall be reviewed periodically at intervals of not less than a month so that the court can receive a written report on the offender's progress, including the results of drug tests carried out under the provisions of the testing requirement and the views of

---

[15] n. 1, 'Guidance on Review Hearings', para. 5.

the treatment provider. The powers of the reviewing court are specified by s.55. The review may be conducted by a different Bench or judge than imposed the order and the reviewing court will then need to be acquainted with the history of the order.

25.22   This somewhat novel procedure requires the court to consider which style of hearing to adopt for reviews. Home Office guidance[16] notes that "for some offenders a more informal and non-interrogatory approach may best meet the purposes of the review. Courts will want to bear in mind the scope that hearings give for encouraging offenders who are making progress to sustain it." Courts are invited to approach the task expecting information, exploring what has taken place either since the order was made or since the last review, and being ready to question those appearing before them. "Review hearings are not breach proceedings and that should be apparent from the way in which the court conducts the hearing" (para.7). However, the court "should be firm in seeking explanations for missed appointments and decisions not to breach".[17] The guidance[18] suggests—

> "The offender who has missed appointments without reasonable excuse should be warned; the offender who has inadvertently slipped up should be encouraged to do better; the offender who is meeting the expectations of the court should be urged to maintain that progress. It is left to magistrates to deal with individual offenders as they see fit."

Legal Representation

25.23   Though review proceedings are criminal proceedings and the offender may seek legal representation, Home Office guidance[19] reminds courts that "the encounter between the sentencer and the offender is the essence of the review hearing and that they should order proceedings as far as possible to ensure that the presence of a legal representative does not allow the defendant to avoid accounting for his or her progress or the lack of it". If it emerges in the course of a hearing involving an unrepresented offender that it is in the interests of justice for the offender to be represented, for example if the court is considering revocation and re-sentence, the court should consider adjourning to enable him to obtain legal representation.

Amendment of the Order

25.24   PCC(S)A 2000, s.55

(1)   At a review hearing (within the meaning given by subsection (6) of section 54 above) the court may, after considering the responsible officer's report referred to in that subsection, amend any requirement or provision of the drug treatment and testing order.

(2)   The court—

   (a)   shall not amend the treatment or testing requirement unless the offender expresses his willingness to comply with the requirement as amended;

---

[16] n. 15, para. 6.
[17] n. 15, para. 9.
[18] n. 15, para. 10.
[19] n. 15, para. 16.

(b) shall not amend any provision of the order so as to reduce the treatment and testing period below the minimum specified in section 52(1) above, or to increase it above the maximum so specified; and

(c) except with the consent of the offender, shall not amend any requirement or provision of the order while an appeal against the order is pending.

The court thus has the discretion to adjust the requirements and provisions of the order at its own initiative without need of an application by either the responsible officer or the offender, though the court is likely to be reliant on advise from the treatment provider and/or the responsible officer. The necessity to secure the offender's consent in respect of treatment and testing means that consent must also be forthcoming for any variation to either such requirement. However, in the event that that the offender fails to express willingness, consequences arise as specified by s.55(3)—

(3) If the offender fails to express his willingness to comply with the treatment or testing requirement as proposed to be amended by the court, the court may—

(a) revoke the order; and

(b) deal with him, for the offence in respect of which the order was made, in any way in which it could deal with him if he had just been convicted by the court of the offence.

25.25 In dealing afresh with the offender under s.55(3)(b) the court shall take into account the extent of the offender's compliance with the order and may impose a custodial sentence in respect of an imprisonable offence, notwithstanding the provisions of PCC(S)A 2000, s.79(2) specifying criteria to be satisfied before such a sentence may ordinarily be imposed: s.55(4).

In respect of offenders dealt with summarily when aged under 18 for an offence which in the case of an adult is indictable-only who have now attained the age of 18, s.55(5) provides that the powers exercisable under s.55(3)(b) by the magistrates' court conducting the review "shall be powers to do either or both of the following"—

(a) to impose a fine not exceeding £5,000 for the offence in respect of which the order was made;

(b) to deal with the offender for that offence in any way in which the court could deal with him if it had just convicted him of an offence punishable with imprisonment for a term not exceeding six months.

Failure to Attend Review

25.26 Because it is a requirement of the order that the offender must attend review hearings (s.54(6)(c)), failure to attend renders the offender liable to enforcement proceedings under PCC(S)A 2000 Sched.3 for breach of their order. Action thus falls to be initiated by the responsible officer rather than by the court of its own motion though there may clearly be scope for an information to be laid immediately to initiate such proceedings if the review is being conducted by justices acting for the PSA specified in the order (see 25.12).

Further Review

25.27 Though the initial review hearing, taking place within a month of the making of the order, is obligatory, the court at that hearing (and any subsequent hearing) has a discretion provided by s.55(6) to order future reviews to occur without a hearing. Reviews without a hearing shall be conducted by a single justice or, in the Crown Court, by a judge: s.55(9). If a subsequent such review considers that the offender's progress has ceased to be satisfactory, a special hearing can be ordered: s.55(7) and (8).

PCC(S)A 2000, s.55

(6) If at a review hearing the court, after considering the responsible officer's report, is of the opinion that the offender's progress under the order is satisfactory, the court may so amend the order as to provide for each subsequent review to be made by the court without a hearing.

(7) If at a review without a hearing the court, after considering the responsible officer's report, is of the opinion that the offender's progress under the order is no longer satisfactory, the court may require the offender to attend a hearing of the court at a specified time and place.

(8) At that hearing the court, after considering that report, may—

(a) exercise the powers conferred by this section as if the hearing were a review hearing; and

(b) so amend the order as to provide for each subsequent review to be made at a review hearing.

Home Office guidance[20] suggests that courts consider requiring all offenders successfully completing a DTTO to appear for a final "graduation" hearing. This would need to be specified when the order is made under s.54(6)(b) as there is no scope to reinstate hearings once these have been suspended unless the offender's progress is unsatisfactory.

Enforcement of the Order

25.28   Breach, revocation and amendment, other than as addressed in the context of review hearings (see 25.21), are governed by PCC(S)A 2000 Sched. 3. Enforcement action is the responsibility of the probation service, in consultation with the treatment provider, "although if the treatment provider concludes that the offender is wilfully failing to co-operate with treatment, the probation service is likely to have little option other than to seek revocation or variation of the order".[21] The following deals with specialist Home Office guidance in respect of non-compliance with a testing or treatment requirement.

25.29   Refusal to provide a sample.   Such refusal "should always be interpreted as wilful failure to comply".[22] Every effort should be made to persuade the offender that a failed test is likely to have less severe consequences than refusal to provide a sample and be warned that if they persist in refusal breach proceedings will be considered following discussion with the supervising probation officer. If the offender claims that they are unable to produce a sample, they should be asked to return in 30–60 minutes. If they remain incapable of producing a sample, they should, wherever possible, be offered another appointment later the same day. If

---

[20] n. 15.
[21] n. 6, para. 14.
[22] n. 6, para. 13.

another appointment is not available or they remain incapable of producing a sample, a failure to comply should be recorded. Continued refusal should normally result in enforcement action.

25.30   Positive test result.   Where a sample supplied tests 'positive', indicating the presence of an "index" drug, "efforts should always be made to persuade the offender to disclose what drugs have been consumed, when and in what quantity, and for what reasons. A positive result "will inevitably lead to consideration whether breach action needs to be taken" but "in many cases counselling may be the right response to a first such episode".[23] A second failed test for an "index" drug should always lead to formal breach action. If such action is not taken, this decision should be confirmed by a senior probation officer.

25.31   Failure to comply with treatment.   This may be manifested in a variety of ways, such as a lack of engagement with counselling to absconding from a residential unit. "The supervising court, guided by the views of the treatment provider and the probation officer, will need to form a judgement in each case based on the extent to which it is in the best interest of achieving the objectives of the order to allow treatment to continue or to revoke and re-sentence."[24]

25.32   Other forms of non-compliance.   In the event of non-attendance, explanation should be sought promptly. The exercise of discretion whether to initiate breach proceedings after one failure to attend without satisfactory explanation or to give a warning instead will depend on the extent to which the offender is considered to pose considerable risk to the public. As regards lateness for appointments, response "needs to be proportionate to the disruption this causes to the achievement of the objectives of the order"—"the key question is 'how hard is this person trying to co-operate?'"[25]

DTTOs IN PRACTICE

25.33   An interim evaluation of experience in the pilot trial areas October 1998 to June 1999[26] reported that in two areas DTTOs have run alongside probation orders while in the third area (Liverpool) 'stand alone' orders were made. The programmes offered offenders within a multi-disciplinary environment showed marked variation in approach—

> *Croydon*: each offender has an indiviual programme comprising: stabilisation (detoxification or residential rehabilitation); groupwork programme; once weekly follow-up groups.

---

[23] n. 6, para. 12.
[24] n. 1, 'Guidance on Enforcement', para. 11.
[25] n. 24, para. 9.
[26] Turnbull P. 'Drug Treatment and Testing Orders: Interim Evaluation', *Research Findings No. 106*, London: Home Office, 1999. A final evaluation report is now available (P. Turnbull *et al. Drug Treatment Orders: Final Evaluation Report* Research Study 212 (Home Office, London, 2000)) covering experience in the pilot areas to March 2000, some 210 orders. Offenders as young as 14 were being referred to DTTO teams but the report does not indicate the extent of actual use of this disposal for young offenders. The revocation rate varied from 60 per cent in Gloucestershire to 28 per cent in Merseyside, with 40 per cent in Croydon. Court reviews were seen as a positive and potentially productive innovation, where sentencers are properly trained and continuity of participation but "sadly this has been a rare occurrence".

Gloucestershire: offenders are expected to remain drug-free after an intial period of one-to-one counselling, followed by an induction group for four weeks, moving on to a core group meeting four times weekly.

Liverpool: probation staff deal with offending issues and co-ordinate referrals to other specialist agenices whose services are puchased, while community psychiatric nurses focus on counselling and relapse prevention.

25.34   Assessment.   Some 70 per cent of referrals were accepted for assessment; 40 per cent were proposed as suitable; 33 per cent were given DTTOs. Of 78 orders made, all were in respect of offenders aged 18 or older (average age 28 years).

25.35   Frequency and Result of Testing.   The frequency of urine testing specified in the order varied between the three areas, from three times a week in Croydon, to three or four times in the first month in Liverpool. Just over a half (52 per cent) of tests for opiates proved positive and 42 per cent were positive for cocaine. However, test results do not show change in levels of drug use. Even though many offenders were still using illicit drugs they generally reported steep reductions in drug use. Practitioners felt that while testing helped to reinforce good progress in stopping drug use, "frequent testing could be both costly and damaging to the motivation of those who are considerably reducing their drug use". The average amount spent on drugs, as reported by a sample of offenders interviewed, fell from £400 a week before arrest to about £30 a week near the beginning of their order. There were commensurate reductions in acquisitive crime activity.

25.36   Expectations of Changed Pattern of Drug Use.   While one team (Gloucestershire) expected very rapid progress to drug-free status, the other two teams anticipated more gradual progress towards abstinence, accompanied by relapses. Available research indicates that reductions in drug use may take several months to achieve. "It will be difficult to achieve a balance between sentencers who may expect quick results and those who recognise that reducing drug use can be a slow and fragile process."[27]

25.37   Reviews in Court.   Due to practical difficulties only 40 per cent of hearings were conducted by the court composed as at time of making the order, thus breaking continuity. While continuity was possible in the Crown Court and with stipendiary magistrates, it was often impossible to ensure that the same lay justices followed through individual cases. Practitioners reported that courts were prepared to listen to their views and follow their recommendations.

25.38   Non-Compliance and Enforcement.   In all three areas offenders often failed to meet requirements of their order, usually by not attending appointments or failing urine tests. The consequences are not specified in detail in the research summary.

---

[27] n. 26, p. 4.

Enforcement: Community and Related Orders

26.01 "Enforcement" is used here as a generic term covering three forms of court proceedings, applications to amend or revoke community orders and breach proceedings alleging non-compliance with community orders. Four separate codes govern such proceedings, contained in various Schedules of PCC(S)A 2000—

(a) Schedule 3—relating to several 'adult' orders: community rehabilitation, community punishment, community punishment and rehabilitation, drug treatment and testing, drug abstinence, curfew and exclusion orders, previously regulated for the most part by CJA 1991 Schedule 2;

(b) Schedule 5—attendance centre orders;

(c) Schedule 7—supervision orders;

(d) Schedule 8—action plan and reparation orders (formerly CDA 1998, Sched. 5).

26.02 The provisions of Schedule 8 are closely modelled on the provisions of Schedule 7 which in turn essentially reproduce the relevant provisions of CYPA 1969. To add complexity, the provisions of Schedule 8 apply beyond community orders to reparation orders and the provisions of Schedule 3 apply to curfew and community punishment orders made not as community orders but as an alternative to a fine for petty persistent offenders. Further, there are elements of overlap between Schedules in respect of orders such as attendance centre or curfew orders made as penalties following breach of other orders. In this Chapter the focus is primarily upon provisions relating to action plan, reparation and supervision orders which are likely to be the orders most commonly made in respect of young offenders and because they are directed exclusively at young offenders. There has not been a strong tradition of breach proceedings in respect of supervision orders, in part because prior to the 1998 Act the courts' powers in dealing with non-compliance were rather limited and perhaps also because practitioner culture in youth justice had not been breach-minded. That tradition has been superseded by the clearer expectations of rigorous enforcement in the era of *No More Excuses*. In the meantime there is little or no case law to aid interpretation of the relevant enforcement provisions. Space does not permit attention to the essentially "adult" enforcement provisions of Schedule 3 which are detailed conveniently elsewhere.[1]

Courts having Jurisdiction in Enforcement Proceedings
Supervision Orders

26.03 In respect of supervision orders, jurisdiction lies with a "relevant court", depending on the age of the offender when an application is made, as specified by Sched. 7 para. 1—

---

[1] See N. Stone, *A Companion Guide to Enforcement* (3rd edition, Owen Wells, Publisher, Ilkley, 1999).

(a) under 18: a youth court acting for the petty sessions area named in the order;

(b) aged 18 or older: a magistrates' court other than a youth court acting for the named petty sessions area.

To cover instances where the offender attains age 18 during the course of proceedings, para. 1(2) specifies that if an application is made to a youth court "and while it is pending the offender . . . attains the age of 18, the youth court shall deal with the application as if he had not attained that age".

Action Plan Orders and Reparation Orders

26.04 In respect of these orders, jurisdiction lies with "the appropriate court", defined as a youth court acting for the petty sessions area named in the order: Sched. 8, para. 1. The youth court thus retains jurisdiction regardless of age considerations.

Attendance Centre Orders

26.05 Jurisdiction in respect of the enforcement of attendance centre orders varies according to the nature of the enforcement issue and the court which made the order. Generally, where an order was imposed by a youth court, jurisdiction lies with "an appropriate magistrates' court", being either—

(a) a youth court or magistrates' court acting for the petty sessions area in which the attendance centre is situated; or

(b) the court which made the order (Sched. 5 para. 4(2)).

There can thus be dual jurisdiction, giving a choice of where to initiate proceedings. The better view is probably to proceed in the court which made the order unless the offender has closer ties to the court area in which the centre is located. Though Sched. 5 specifies that enforcement applications and prosecutions are brought by "the officer in charge of the relevant centre", in practice a YOT member may act on that officer's behalf, now that the Youth Justice Board and YOTs are exercising overall responsibility for this sentence resource.

'Adult' Orders

26.06 Jurisdiction under Schedule 3 is more complex, varying according to the nature of the order and the proceedings. In the case of orders made by a youth court, jurisdiction may be summarised as follows—

(a) curfew order: a court acting for the petty sessions area in which the place specified in the order (where the person has to remain at curfew times) is situated;

(b) exclusion, community rehabilitation, community punishment, CPR, DTTO or drug abstinence order: a court acting for the petty sessions area specified in the order.

Orders Made on Appeal

26.07 In respect of orders made on appeal, each of the relevant Schedules clarify that for enforcement purposes the order shall be deemed to have been made by the court from which the appeal was brought. Thus an order made by the Crown Court on appeal from a youth court shall be deemed to be a youth court order.

Summonses for Young Offenders

26.08 As outlined below, in most instances of enforcement proceedings the young offender has to be summonsed to appear before the court. The Magistrates' Court (Children and Young Person) Rules 1992, r.26 specifies—

> Where a child or young person is charged with an offence, or is for a reason brought before a court, a summons or warrant may be issued to enforce the attendance of a parent or guardian under CYPA 1933, s.34A, in the same manner as if the information were laid upon which a summons or warrant could be issued against a defendant under the Magirstrates' Courts Act 1980 and a summons to the child or young person may include a summons to the parent or guardian to enforce his attendance for the said purpose.

Section 34A of CYPA 1933, inserted by CJA 1991, s.56, states that where a young offender is brought before a court, the court "may . . . and shall in the case of a child or young person aged under 16 require . . . a parent or guardian to attend at the court during all the stages of the proceedings" (see 10.03). This power thus applies in any enforcement proceedings initiated in respect of a person aged under 18.

AMENDMENT OF ORDERS

Supervision Orders, Action Plan Orders and Reparation Orders

26.09 In respect of a supervision order under Sched. 7 para. 5(1) and in respect of either an action plan order or a reparation order under Sched. 8 para. 5(1)—

> "if while (the order) is in force in respect of an offender it appears to (a relevant) (the appropriate) court, on the application of the (supervisor) (responsible officer) or the offender, that it is appropriate to make an order under this sub-paragraph, the court may—
>
> (a) (*not relevant to amendment*)
> (b) make an order amending it—
>
>   (i) by cancelling any (requirement) (provision) included in it; or
>   (ii) by inserting in it (either in addition to or in substitution for any of its provisions) any provision which could have been included in the order if the court had then had power to make it and were exercising that power."

Scope to amend a supervision order is subject to two restrictions specified by Sched. 7 para. 5(3)—

(a) a requirement to receive treatment for mental condition under Sched. 6 para. 6 may not be inserted after three months from the date of the order, unless it is in substitution for such a requirement already included in the order. Additionally, the court should not insert such a requirement unless satisfied on medical evidence that the criterion specified by Sched. 6 para. 6 is met (Sched. 7 para. 8(1)(c));

(b) a night restriction requirement under Sched. 6 para. 3(2)(e) may not be inserted in respect of any day which falls outside the first three months of the order.

Reference to Court on Report of Psychiatrist

26.10 Where an offender is subject to a supervision order requirement to receive treatment for mental condition under Sched. 6 para. 6 and the medical practitioner responsible for that treatment is of the opinion—

(a) that the treatment should be continued beyond the period specified in the order; or

(b) that the offender needs different treatment; or

(c) that he is not susceptible to treatment; or

(d) that he does not require further treatment,

the doctor shall make a written report to the supervisor to that effect and the supervisor shall refer it to the relevant court with a view to amendment of the order: Sched. 7, para. 6.

Procedure

26.11 The offender should normally be present before the court when it hears an amendment application (or reference under Sched. 7 para. 6). Where the supervisor makes application he may "bring the offender before the court" but the offender's presence may otherwise be achieved by summonsing him to attend. If satisfied on oath that a summons cannot be served or if the offender fails to answer to summons, a justice may issue a warrant to secure attendance. These steps are contained in Sched. 7 para 7 and Sched. 8 para. 6, as outlined at 26.19 *et seq.* and 26.41 in respect of breach and revocation proceedings.

However, the court may act in the offender's absence to amend an order in one of the following ways (para.7(9) and para. 6(9) which do not add or entail demands upon the offender—

(i) cancelling a requirement or provision; or

(ii) altering the name of any specified area; or

(iii) changing the supervisor or responsible officer; or

(iv) (in respect of a supervision order) reducing the duration of the order or any provision within it.

Supervision Orders: Criterion Justifying Amendment

26.12 When considering whether to insert, vary or cancel a requirement authorised by Sched. 6 or to exercise its powers on referral under para. 6 (above) the court must be satisfied that "the offender is unlikely to receive the care or control he needs unless the court makes the order or is likely to receive it notwithstanding the order": Sched. 7, para. 8(1).

Copies of Amending Orders

26.13 Where the court amends a supervision order, it shall send a copy of the order to the offender and, if he is aged under 14, to his parent or guardian, and to the supervisor, and to any local authority not otherwise entitled to a copy but whose area is named or has ceased to be named in the order: Sched. 7, para. 10. A copy should also be sent to any person with whom the offender is or was hitherto required to reside or to receive treatment.

Appeal

26.14 The offender may appeal to the Crown Court against any order made under amendment powers unless the amendment was of a kind that can be made in the offender's absence or, in respect of a supervision order, only consisted of provisions to which the offender consented (if of a nature requiring consent): Sched. 7 para. 12 and Sched. 8 para. 7.

Home Office Guidance

26.15 Home Office Guidance on action plan orders[2] suggests that variation may be appropriate in the following circumstances—

- where the offender's family circumstances alter, making one or more requirements impossible to comply with;
- where a particular requirement is proving completely unsuccessful in helping the offender to address his offending behaviour;
- where the victim finds involvement in the reparative element of the order distressing and does not wish to continue.

The responsible officer will need to consider whether it is appropriate to inform the victim of the application, particularly if this will result in some adjustment to the reparative element of the order, and whether to convey the victim's views to the court.

Attendance Centre Orders

26.16 Power to amend an attendance centre order is of limited scope but may be required to change the centre to be attended and/or to vary the time of the offender's first attendance. Under Sched. 5 para. 5(1), where an order is in force and on application made by the offender or by the officer in charge of the relevant centre, an appropriate magistrates' court may make an order—

(a) varying the day or hour specified in the order for the offender's first attendance at the specified centre; or

(b) substituting another centre which the court is satisfied is reasonably accessible to the offender, having regard to his age, means of access available to him and any other circumstances.

If the order was made by the Crown Court, application must be made to the court acting for the area where the centre currently specified is located. Copies of the

---

[2] Home Office (2000) *Guidance: Action Plan Orders*, para. 10.1.

amending order should be given or sent (by recorded delivery to his usual or last known place of abode) to the offender and to the officers in charge of the previously specified and the substituted centre.

BREACH OF ORDERS

Supervision Orders, Action Plan Orders and Reparation Orders

26.17 Power to deal with breach of these orders is provided by para. 2 of Schedules 7 and 8 respectively. Proceedings are brought before the relevant magistrates' court even where the order was imposed by the Crown Court.

PCC(S)A 2000, Sched. 7/8, para. 2

(1) This paragraph applies if while an action plan order or reparation order (*or supervision order*) is in force in respect of an offender it is proved to the satisfaction of the appropriate court, on the application of the responsible officer, that the offender has failed to comply with any requirement included in the order.

Prosecution is initiated not by information as in respect of Schedule 3 or Schedule 5 breach proceedings but by "application". Difficulty may be encountered in respect of the timescale governing proceedings. The wording of para. 2(1) in each Schedule appears clear, that the failure to comply must be proved to the satisfaction of the court while the order is in force. However, this may create significant difficulties for those seeking to prosecute non-compliance, particularly given the relatively brief lifespan of action plan and reparation orders (see also 16.94).

26.18 Dignan[3] refers to the uncertainties encountered by YOTs during the pilot trials of the two new orders "whether it is sufficient for the information supporting the application to be put before the court before the order expires or whether the breach procedure has to be completed before this happens". Dignan suggests that the former interpretation is preferable, being in line with breach proceedings relating to other community penalties. Convenient as this might be, avoiding the possibility that offenders may seek to delay proceedings by spurious denials of their non-compliance, he appears to confuse the two distinct routes to breach, by "information" in respect of Schedule 3 and 5 proceedings (where the significant factor is laying an information while the order is in force) and by "application", as applies in respect of these three orders. If the latter interpretation is more in accord with the provisions of the two Schedules, it is only necessary for the court to be "satisfied" of the non-compliance within the life of the order and it would be possible for the decision of the court as to what action to take under para. 2(2) to be made after the order has expired. If the former interpretation holds good, another uncertainty lies in identifying the time when an application is made, whether by contacting the court to request a breach hearing or when the application is made before the court. Schedule 7 para. 1(2), in respect of supervision orders only, refers to the possibility of an application being made and the offender attaining age 18 "while it is pending", suggesting that a formal request to the court, something akin to an information, serves to initiate the application as

---

[3] J. Dignan, *Youth Justice Pilots Evaluation: Interim Report on Reparative Work and Youth Offending Teams*, Occasional Paper, (Home Office, 2000) p. 26.

an on-going process. This in turn appears in accord with the provisions of Sched. 7 para. 7(2) and Sched. 8 para. 6(2) governing issue of a summons or warrant following an application. Home Office guidance on action plan orders[4] offers no view on this question.

Bringing the Offender before the Court

26.19 An order under para. 2(1) cannot be made unless the offender is present before the court: Sched. 7 para.7(1) and Sched. 8 para.6(1) which indicate that the supervisor/responsible officer (hereafter referred to for convenience as the prosecutor) "may bring the offender before the court" for this purpose. More usually the prosecutor will seek a summons or, less commonly, a warrant to secure the presence of the offender before the court, as authorised by para. 7(2) and para. 6(2) respectively. Herein lies a difference between supervision order enforcement and action plan/reparation order proceedings. Under Sched. 7 para. 7(2) a single justice may issue a summons or warrant, whereas under Sched. 8 para. 6(2) "the court to which an application under para. 2(1) . . . may issue a summons or warrant". The reason why a court must act in this respect in the case of an action plan/reparation order is not apparent.

Warrants

26.20 Issue of a warrant is restricted by paras. 7(3)/6(3) which incorporate in modified form the restrictions contained in MCA 1980, s.55(3) and (4) in respect of the non-appearance of defendants in civil proceedings in magistrates' courts. In effect a warrant may not be issued unless it is proved to the satisfaction of the court/justice, on oath, that the summons (a) cannot be served, or (b) was served on the offender within what appears to be a reasonable time before the hearing. Similarly, if the offender fails to appear at a subsequent hearing, a warrant may be issued if it can be shown that the offender appeared on a previous occasion in those proceedings, provided the court is satisfied that he had adequate notice of the time and place of the adjourned hearing.

26.21 Where an offender is arrested on warrant not backed for bail and cannot be brought immediately before the relevant court, paras.7(4)/6(4) specify that the person having custody of the detained person "may make arrangements for his detention in a place of safety for a period of not more than 72 hours from the time of the arrest" and, unless he is brought before the court exercising jurisdiction in the proceedings, "shall within that period bring him before" a justice (supervision orders) or a youth court (action plan/reparation orders). Where so brought before a justice/youth court, that justice or court may either direct his release forthwith or alternatively may remand him to local authority accommodation. Where the court orders remand to local authority accommodation, the court shall designate as the authority to receive him, as follows—

---

[4] Home Office (2000) *Guidance Document: Action Plan Orders*, para. 12.6. The evaluation report of the first 12 months of YOT experience by the Universities of Sheffield and Hull (1999) at p. 46 notes the commonly experienced problem of "breaching action plan orders within the time limits. If an offender misses sessions in the last four weeks or so of an order, it is extremely hard to complete the necessary paperwork and obtain a court hearing within that time. In some areas the courts have agreed to expedite breach proceedings. In others, notification of the proceedings is taken as sufficient even if the hearing itself is not within the time limit." However, in their final report (S. Holdaway *et al. New Strategies to Address Youth Offending: the national evaluation of the pilot youth offending teams* Occasional Paper 69 (Home Office, London, 2001) at p. 99) the researchers note arrangements with courts to speed up breach hearings had made this less of a problem but "it nevertheless remains difficult to breach orders for non-attendance in some courts in the latter stages of an order, simply because the order can expire before breach hearings can be arranged."

(i) supervision orders: the authority named in the order (para. 7(8));

(ii) action plan/reparation orders: the authority for the area in which he resides. If it appears that he does not reside in a local authority area, the authority in whose area the offence or an associated offence was committed, as specified by the court (para. 6(8)).

Where the offender is aged 18 or older, he shall not be remanded to local authority accommodation but may instead be remanded to a prison (provision for remand to a remand centre ceased upon implementation of CJCSA 2000).

Further Remand

26.22 When the offender appears before the court exercising jurisdiction in breach proceedings and it is necessary to adjourn the breach application, the question may arise whether the offender can be remanded in local authority accommodation (or in prison if aged 18 or older). Neither Schedule makes provision for this possibility. Schedule 7 para. 7(6) and Sched. 8 para. 6(6) empower the court to do so when the application is made under para. 5(1) but such applications are in respect of revocation and amendment proceedings (see 26.41). The power does not extend to applications made under para. 2(1). Given that in the case of a Crown Court order where the offender is sent back to that court, he may be committed in custody (see 26.23 at para 2(2)(c)), this appears to create a lacuna in the magistrates' powers. It is possible for a separate application to be made under para. 5, parallel to the breach application, thus enabling the court to side-step the absence of remand powers in para. 2 proceedings.

Power of the Court if Breach is Proved

26.23   **PCC(S)A 2000, Sched. 7/8, para. 2**

(2) Where this paragraph applies, the court—

  (a) whether or not it also makes an order under paragraph 5(1) below (revocation or amendment of order)—

    (i) may order the offender to pay a fine of an amount not exceeding £1,000; or

    (ii) subject to paragraph 3 below, may make a curfew order in respect of him; or

    (iii) subject to paragraph 4 below, may make an attendance centre order in respect of him; or

  (b) if the action plan order or reparation order was made by a magistrates' court, may revoke the order and deal with the offender, for the offence in respect of which the order was made, in any way in which he could have been dealt with for that offence by the court which made the order if the order had not been made; or

  (c) if the supervision order/action plan order or reparation order was made by the Crown Court, may commit him in custody or release him on bail until he can be brought or appear before the Crown Court.

(4) Where—

  (a) by virtue of sub-paragraph (2)(c) above the offender is brought or appears before the Crown Court, and

(b) it is proved to the satisfaction of the court that he has failed to comply with the requirement in question,

that court may deal with him, for the offence in respect of which the order was made, in any way in which it could have dealt with him for that offence if it had not made the order.

(5) Where the Crown Court deals with an offender under sub-paragraph (4) above, it shall revoke the supervision order/action plan order or reparation order if it is still in force.

(7) In dealing with an offender under this paragraph, a court shall take into account the extent to which he has complied with the requirements of the supervision order/action plan order or reparation order.

26.24 Failure to comply is proved by admission or by evidence. Home Office guidance[5] advises that "wherever possible the responsible officer should avoid involving the victim in any breach proceedings because to do so runs the risk of revictimising them". Unlike the provisions of Schedules 3 and 5, neither Schedule 7 or 8 refer to the offender's failure to comply being "without reasonable excuse", there being no clear reason for the differentiation. Home Office guidance[6] advises that "the responsible officer will need to take into account any extenuating circumstances relating to the instance(s) of breach before deciding to proceed with an application". It is submitted that it is open to the offender to raise the defence of reasonable excuse, despite the absence of explicit reference. Absolute liability cannot be intended in this context.

26.25 The provisions of para. 2(2)(a) indicate that the court may exercise one (but not more than one) of what may be referred to as the "penalty" options (fine, curfew or attendance centre) but also combine that with a revocation or amendment order. The question may be posed whether the court may thus amend or revoke the order of its own initiative. However, the reference to paragraph 5(1) appears clearly to mean that such powers can only be exercised on application, there being scope for the court to receive applications under both sets of provisions. If the order was made by the Crown Court it would appear wrong in principle for the supervising/responsible officer to make a parallel para. 5(1) application because in breach proceedings it can be argued that the intention of both Schedules is for the order to be referred back to the Crown Court under para. 2(2)(c). As indicated at 26.39, revocation in pursuance of a para. 5(1) application does not include power to deal with the offender for the offence for which the order was made. If that is in mind, the court should proceed under para. 2(2)(b). It is thus not possible for the court both to impose a penalty option and to deal with the offender afresh for the offence.

Revocation and Re-Sentence

26.26 In the case of a youth court order, para. 2(2)(b) empowers the court to "revoke and deal with the offender", whereas in respect of a Crown Court order sent back to that court under para. 2(2)(c), the Crown Court "may deal with the offender" (para. 2(4)) and "shall revoke the order if it is still in force" (para. 2(5)).

---

[5] Home Office (2000) *Guidance Document: Action Plan Order*, para, 12.6; *Guidance Document: Reparation Order*, para. 9.6.
[6] n. 5, paras 12.9 and 9.9.

Paragraph 2(5) appears properly to anticipate that in the time delay before the case is listed at Crown Court the order may expire by passage of time. However, the same may occur in the course of proceedings before the summary court. The failure to comply may be proved while the order is in force but the order may expire before the court reaches a decision as the appropriate course. It might be argued that the court should proceed to exercise its powers immediately upon determining that the offender has failed to comply. However, it may be countered that two distinct stages are involved, (i) being satisfied of the breach and (ii) determining the right response. The court may seek further information before reaching its conclusion, though YOT practitioners are likely to anticipate the court's needs and will wish to have advice ready for the court's consideration. Assistance can be gained from decided cases in respect of community service and probation orders. In *Platts*[7] the offender claimed that as his probation order had expired he should not face revocation and re-sentence (in this instance to 12 months imprisonment). The Court of Appeal dismissed this assertion, citing *Tebbutt*[8] where an offender's claim that by completing his community service hours after breach proceedings had been initiated he had rendered himself immune from revocation and re-sentence was dismissed. On the basis of these two decisions it can be argued strongly by analogy that the fact that the order has ended and that revocation has ceased to be a meaningful step does not prevent the court from proceeding under para. 2(2)(b). By the same logic, the court can exercise one of its penalty options under para. 2(2)(a) despite the demise of the order in the interim.

Crown Court Procedure and Powers

26.27   Under para. 2(4), failure to comply has to be proved to the satisfaction of the Crown Court. There is no scope for the breach application to be made direct to the Crown Court so the failure to comply has already been proved to the satisfaction of the lower court. The question may arise as to how the matter should now be proved before the higher court. The wording "it is proved to the satisfaction of the court" is different from the equivalent wording in PCC(S)A 2000, s.5(1) in respect of the power of the Crown Court on committal of an adult offender for sentence where it is specified that the Crown Court "shall inquire into the circumstances of the case and may deal with the offender . . . ". It is submitted that it is not necessary for the applicant to re-establish the breach on the basis of evidence. It cannot be correct for the offender to have the opportunity to contest the breach allegation afresh. When exercising its powers under para. 2(2)(c) the lower court is required to send a certificate, signed by a justice, giving (a) "particulars of the failure to comply with the requirement in question" and (b) "such other particulars of the case as may be desirable": para. 2(3). The findings of the lower court thus relayed should provide the basis for the Crown Court to be satisfied. This has been customary procedure in respect of breach proceedings in respect of 'adult' community orders coming before the Crown Court and PCC(S)A 2000, Sched. 3 includes identical wording to Schedules 7 and 8. Neither Schedule 7 or 8 contain a provision equivalent to Schedules 3 para. 5(4) or 5 para. 3(4) governing breach of 'adult' community orders and attendance centre orders to the effect that "any question whether there has been a failure . . . shall be determined by the court and not by verdict of a jury". It should be noted that the Crown Court has to be satisfied that the offender "has failed to comply with the requirement in

[7] [1998] 2 Cr.App.R.(S.) 34
[8] (1988) 10 Cr.App.R.(S.) 88.

question". Consequently, the Crown Court cannot be asked to adjudicate in respect of any other alleged failure to comply not proved before the lower court.

26.28 When the Crown Court is satisfied that the offender has failed to comply, para. 2(4) does not empower the court to impose any of the "penalty" measures available to the lower court under para. 2(2)(a). In this respect the provisions of Sched. 7 and 8 differ from the equivalent provisions of Schedule 3. In consequence, where the Crown Court is satisfied of non-compliance but does not consider the right course is to deal with the offender for the original offence, it appears to have little option but to take no action. It may, of course, deal with the original offence by means of a fine, curfew order or attendance centre order. It does not have power under the Schedules to return the case to the lower court with the prospect of the offender being dealt with under para. 2(2)(a) (i), (ii) or (iii).

Extent of Compliance

26.29 Paragraph 2(7) of each Schedule requires a court to take into account the extent to which the offender has complied with the requirements of the order. This obligation arises not just when the court is determining how to deal afresh with the offender for the offence for which the order was made, under para. 2(2)(b) or (4), but in any instance where it is exercising its powers under the paragraph. Home Office guidance[9] suggests that the court takes account of the extent of compliance "before the order was breached" but the statutory provisions are not so limited and embrace all compliance, including response after the breach application was initiated, though the court may consider that this phase of compliance carries less weight. Paragraph 2(7) clearly enables the court to give credit for positive efforts by the offender but the wording of the sub-paragraph does not confine itself to what might be termed mitigatory effort. Poor response may be reflected in the weight of any penalty imposed under para. 2(2)(a). However, it has been established in respect of "adult" community orders that in dealing afresh with the offender for the original offence, this provision should not be interpreted to allow poor compliance to be viewed as an aggravating feature of that offence: Clarke.[10]

Supervision Orders: Transitional Issues

26.30 Provisions governing breach powers in respect of supervision orders under CYPA 1969 were amended by CDA 1998, now incorporated into Schedule 7 of the 2000 Act. However, the 1998 Act does not specify transitional provisions, leaving in doubt when the revised penalty powers took effect. The better view is that these apply to offences committed on or after 30 September 1998, the implementation date for the relevant part of the Act. The issue came before the Court of Appeal in Miah[11] where a youth court had purported to exercise powers introduced by the 1998 Act and committed an offender to the Crown Court in breach proceedings even though the supervision order and the breach had arisen before that date. The Court quashed the custodial sentence imposed by the Crown Court following that committal and ruled that the youth court had no power to commit, on the basis that the breach had occurred before implementation date. Regrettably, the Court did not extend its judgement to consider the position that applies either where a supervision order is made before that date though non-

---

[9] n. 5, para. 12.7.
[10] [1997] 2 Cr.App.R.(S.) 163.
[11] [2000] 1 Cr.App.R.(S.) 27.

compliance arises after that date or where a supervision order is made after that date but in respect of an offence committed before that date. This ceases to be a significantly live issue by passage of time but instances may occasionally arise after implementation of the 2000 Act where the offence pre-dates implementation of the 1998 Act.

Curfew Order as Breach Penalty

26.31   Paragraph 3 of each Schedule regulates the effect of a curfew order imposed under para. 2(2)(a)(ii). An order imposed under this provision is as governed by PCC(S)A 2000, ss.37 and 38 in respect of length and duration, the factors to be considered prior making an order and arrangements for electronic monitoring (see Chapter 21). However, the generic restrictions and procedural requirements in respect of community orders contained in PCC(S)A 2000, ss.35 and 36 do not apply: para. 3(3). In respect of the special provisions for offenders aged under 16 contained in s.37(4) and (9), specifying a three month maximum length and consideration of information relating to family circumstances, the relevant date for age purposes is not "on conviction" for the offence for which the action plan/reparation/supervision order was made but "the date when his failure to comply with the order is proved to the court": para. 3(4).

26.32   In the event that the offender fails to comply with their curfew order, PCC(S)A 2000, Sched. 3 applies but as if the power conferred by Sched. 3 para. 4(1)(d) on the court before which breach is proved "to deal with the offender for the offence in respect of which the (curfew) order was made" were "a power to deal with the offender, for his failure to comply with the action plan/reparation/ supervision order, in any way in which (the appropriate) (a relevant) court could deal with him for that failure if it had just been proved to the satisfaction of that court": para. 3(5)(a). Similar provisions apply if it proves necessary to apply for the curfew order to be revoked under Sched. 3 paras. 10 or 11: para. 3(5)(b) and (c). For the purposes of these provisions, if the action plan/reparation/supervision order is no longer in force when Sched. 3 proceedings are followed, the court's powers "shall be determined on the assumption that it is still in force": para. 3(6). The curfew order is subject to amendment under Schedule 3 Part IV.

Attendance Centre Order as Breach Penalty

26.33   Paragraph 4 of each Schedule regulates the effect of an attendance centreorder imposed under para. 2(2)(a)(iii). An order made under this provision is as governed by PCC(S)A 2000, s.60 in respect of length and times of attendance and the factors to be considered prior making an order (see Chapter 19). However, the generic restrictions and procedural requirements in respect of community orders contained in PCC(S)A 2000, ss.35 and 36 do not apply: para. 4(3). Enforcement of the attendance centre order is regulated by Sched. 5 (see 26.35), as modified by para. 4(4) so that power to revoke the order and deal with the offence for which the order was made is treated as a power to deal with the offender in any way that the court which made the action plan/reparation/supervision order could deal with him in breach or revocation proceedings.

National Standards and Home Office Guidance on Breach

26.34   The generic provisions of the *National Standards for Youth Justice*[12] specify—

[12] Youth Justice Board (2000), para. 7.3.

- Unexplained missed appointments must be followed up with a visit, telephone call or, where these are not practicable, a letter within one working day.

- If there is no acceptable reason for the appointment being missed or there is other cause for concern, follow-up action with either a formal warning or breach must be taken. [Home Office guidance[13] indicates that a warning should be written and given to the offender and his parent(s) or guardian, and "should be confirmed in person, where possible".]

- Breach action must be initiated within 10 working days of the most recent failure to comply, if the offender receives more than two formal warnings during the first 12 weeks of the order. Breach action can only be stayed in exceptional circumstances with the authorisation of the YOT manager.

- Only one further formal warning can be given after the first 12 weeks of an order before breach action must be initiated.

- The police should be given all relevant information about the possible whereabouts of an offender for whom a warrant exists as a result of breach proceedings.

- In respect of orders involving reparation, victims should never be cited in any breach proceedings. Where reparation is direct to a named victim and if there is more than one unacceptable failure to undertake the agreed reparation, breach action must be initiated within 10 working days. If reparation is made to the community, breach action must be taken after no more than two unacceptable absences. Where the offender has failed to comply with direct reparation, the responsible officer must promptly inform the victim of the action being taken to enforce the order.

Attendance Centre Orders

26.35 Breach is regulated by Schedule 5, paras 1–3 which provided that proceedings may be brought on two grounds—

(a) failure to attend, or

(b) committing a breach of the rules of the centre which cannot be dealt with adequately under those rules.

Procedure

Proceedings are initiated by information to a justice acting for the relevant petty sessions area who may issue a summons requiring the offender to appear before a court acting for that area at the time specified in the summons. If the information is in writing and on oath, the justice may issue a warrant for the offender's arrest to bring them before the court. The relevant PSA is that in which the specified centre is situated or, in the case of a magistrates' court order, the PSA for the court which made the order.[14]

Powers upon Breach

If on the offender's appearance the court is satisfied that he or she has failed without reasonable excuse to attend as required or has broken a rule, the powers of

---

[13] n. 3, para. 12.6.
[14] para. 1(2).

the court depend on whether the order was made by a magistrates' court or the Crown Court.

Magistrates' Court Order

26.36   The court may—

(a)   impose a fine, not exceeding £1,000, without prejudice to the continuation of the order; or

(b)   deal with the offender, "for the offence in respect of which the order was made, in any way in which he could have been dealt with for that offence by the court which made the order if the order had not been made", at the same time revoking the order if it is still in force. On re-sentence by a magistrates' court, appeal against sentence lies to the Crown Court: para. 2(6).

Crown Court Order

26.37   The court may opt to fine the offender as under (a) above or alternatively may commit him to custody or release him on bail until he can be brought or appear before the Crown Court, sending that court particulars of the offender's non-compliance and such other particulars as may be desirable. When the offender appears before the Crown Court and it is proved to the satisfaction of that court that he has failed to attend as required or has breached the rules of he centre, the court may deal with him as in (b) above. Any question of whether the offender has failed to comply shall be determined by the court and not by jury verdict: para.3(4). The Crown Court is not given power to fine the offender as a penalty for non-compliance, as in (a) above, though it may deal with the offender afresh for the offence by means of a fine. As a consequence, if the Crown Court is satisfied of the offender's non-compliance but wishes to allow the order to continue, it appears that it will simply make no order.

Dealing with Offender for the Offence

26.38   It appears that the offender should be dealt with on the basis of the offender's age when the attendance centre order was imposed. A sentence of detention and training order thus imposed on an offender aged 18 or over shall be treated as a sentence of imprisonment by virtue of PCC(S)A 2000, s.106(6). In dealing with the offender, the court shall take into account the extent to which the offender has complied with the requirements of the attendance centre order (para. 2(5)(a)) thus allowing credit for partial performance. In the case of an offender "who has wilfully and persistently failed to comply with those requirements", the court may impose a custodial sentence, notwithstanding the usual threshold criteria specified in PCC(S)A 2000, s.79(2). Though a custodial sentence thus becomes an option, it does not follow that this is an inevitable consequence, as the offender may be suitable for another community order. The question has been raised[15] whether it is open to the court to make a fresh attendance centre order and the number of hours that could be properly specified in the new order if, say, the original order had been for 24 hours and the offender had completed eight hours. There appears nothing to restrict the court's discretion under para. 2 and a further

---

[15] 'Practical Point' (2000) *Justice of the Peace*, vol. 164, p. 768.

order would seem entirely valid. It is less clear whether the obligation to take account of the extent of compliance restricts the court to imposing, in the example posed, no more than 16 hours. "Taking account" does not mean that the offender is entitled to full credit for hours completed and to tie the court to such a mathematically derived ceiling would remove much of the point of making a further order as opposed to requiring the offender to continue with the original order. The court would appear to have greater discretion, having regard to considerations of what restriction of liberty is proportional to the offence for which the offender is being re-sentenced. Thus a further order for 24 hours would appear to be incorrect, as this would take no account of the offender's partial compliance, whereas an order of, say 18 hours, in the instant case would appear sound.

APPLICATIONS FOR REVOCATION

Supervision Orders, Action Plan Orders and Reparation Orders

26.39 *Power to Apply.* In respect of a supervision order under Sched. 7 para. 5(1) and in respect of either an action plan order or a reparation order under Sched. 8 para. 5(1)—

> "if while (the order) is in force in respect of an offender it appears to (a relevant) (the appropriate) court, on the application of the (supervisor) (responsible officer) or the offender, that it is appropriate to make an order under this sub-paragraph, the court may—
>
> (a) make an order revoking the order."

26.40 Even if the order was imposed by the Crown Court jurisdiction to hear a revocation application lies with the relevant youth or magistrates' court. There is no equivalent of PCC(S)A 2000, Sched. 3 para. 11 governing revocation of these three kinds of order following conviction of a further offence. However, if the offender receives a further sentence for a fresh offence that is not compatible with the existing order, it would be open to either the defence or the responsible officer to make an application for revocation, immediately following passing of that sentence if convenient and if the further sentence has been imposed by a court with jurisdiction over the order.

Securing the Offender's Presence in Court

26.41 The generic procedure in respect of securing the offender's presence before the court is as applies in respect of amendment applications, as detailed at 26.11 and 26.19. However, the court may make a revocation order in the offender's absence: Sched. 7 para. 7(9)(a) and Sched. 8 para. 6(9)(a). This reflects the fact that the court has no power to deal with the offender afresh for the offence in respect of which the order was made. However, as noted at 26.22, Sched. 7 para. 7(6) and Sched. 8 para. 6(6) specify that where an application is made to the court under para. 5(1) the court may remand or further remand the offender to local authority accommodation if—

(a) a warrant has been issued to secure the offender's attendance before the court; or

(b) the court considers that remanding or further remanding the offender "will enable information to be obtained which is likely to assist the court in deciding whether, and, if so, how to exercise its powers under para. 5(1)".

26.42 *Supervision Orders: Criterion Justifying Revocation.* When considering whether to revoke a supervision order the court must be satisfied that "the offender is unlikely to receive the care or control he needs unless the court makes the order or is likely to receive it notwithstanding the order": para. 8(1).

26.43 *Embargo Following Dismissal of Application.* Where the court dismisses an application to revoke an order, no further application may be made by any person except with the consent of the relevant court with jurisdiction: Sched. 8 para.5(3). This is intended to prevent spurious or vexatious applications. However, in respect of supervision orders, a further application may be made after three months has elapsed from the date of the dismissal: Sched. 7 para.5(4).

26.44 *Copies of Revocation Order.* Where the court revokes a supervision order, it shall send a copy of the order to the offender and, if he is aged under 14, to his parent or guardian, and to the supervisor, and to any local authority not otherwise entitled to a copy but whose area was named in the order: Sched. 7, para. 10. A copy should also be sent to any person with whom the offender was hitherto required to reside or to receive treatment.

26.45 *Appeal.* The offender may appeal to the Crown Court against any order made under revocation powers and also the dismissal of an application: Sched. 7 para. 12 and Sched. 8 para. 7.

26.46 *National Standards and Home Office Guidance.* The generic provisions of the *National Standards for Youth Justice*[16] specify that the responsible officer "must consider applying for early discharge (*sic*) of the order when the half-way point is reached". Where the order includes reparation, Home Office Guidance suggests that it may be appropriate to inform the victim where this may affect that reparative element. Any views of the victim may appropriately be relayed to the court considering the application.

Attendance Centre Orders

26.46 Where an order is in force and on application by either the officer in charge of the specified centre or of the offender, an appropriate court may revoke the order: Sched. 5 para. 4(1). Where the order was made by the Crown Court and that court reserved power of revocation to itself, application must be made directly to the Crown Court: para. 4(2). In the case of other, non-reserved Crown Court orders, application is made to a youth court or magistrates' court acting for the area in which the centre is located.

26.47 *Power to Re-Sentence.* Power to revoke the order "includes power to deal with the offender, for the offence in respect of which the order was made, in

---

[16] n. 612, para. 7.2.10.

any way in which he could have been dealt with for that offence by the court which made the order if the order had not been made": para. 4(3). The offender thus stands to be dealt with on the basis of powers available to the original sentencing court at the time of initial sentencing. On re-sentence by a magistrates' court, appeal against sentence lies to the Crown Court: para. 4(4).

CHAPTER 27

Custodial Sentences: General Considerations

27.01   Since the implementation of the Crime and Disorder Act 1998 and the Powers of Criminal Courts (Sentencing) Act 2000, custodial sentencing powers in respect of young offenders can be summarised as follows—

(a)   A youth court may impose only one type of custodial sentence: a detention and training order in respect of male and female offenders aged 12 to 17, for a term between four months and 24 months, under PCC(S)A 2000, s.100.

(b)   The Crown Court may impose three types of custodial sentence:

   (i)   a detention and training order, as above

   (ii)   a sentence of detention under PCC(S)A 2000, s.91 upon either juveniles aged 10 to 17 convicted on indictment of manslaughter or other grave crimes (primarily offences punishable with imprisonment for 14 years or more) or young persons convicted on indictment of certain specified road traffic offences causing death;

   (iii)   a sentence of detention during Her Majesty's pleasure under PCC(S)A 2000, s.90 as a mandatory sentence upon a juvenile convicted of murder.

27.02   With the exception of detention during Her Majesty's pleasure, which is a punishment fixed by law (PCC(S)A 2000, s. 79(1)(a)), the imposition of any of the above custodial sentences on a child or young person is subject to the same statutory restrictions and requirements as apply to the sentencing of adults. The provisions of PCC(S)A 2000, ss. 109–111 governing "required" custodial sentences for certain offences do not apply to young offenders.

RESTRICTIONS ON IMPOSING CUSTODIAL SENTENCES: THE TWO CRITERIA

27.03   PCC(S)A 2000, s.79

(2)   Subject to subsection (3) below, the court shall not pass a custodial sentence on the offender unless it is of the opinion—

(a)   that the offence, or the combination of the offence and one or more offences associated with it, was so serious that only such a sentence can be justified for the offence; or

(b)   where the offence is a violent or sexual offence, that only such a sentence would be adequate to protect the public from serious harm from him."

Subsection (3) creates an exception to the application of the criteria by permitting a court to pass a custodial sentence on an offender who refuses consent to a community sentence requiring that consent (see 17.12 and 27.122).

The seriousness criterion

27.04   The central emphasis of the sentencing framework introduced by the Criminal Justice Act 1991 was upon sentencing according to the seriousness of the offence and this is remains the predominant criterion justifying custody. The criterion specified by s.79(2)(a) is quite similar to the now superseded criterion justifying custody for a young offender aged under 21 specified by CJA 1982, s. 1(4A)(c): "the offence . . . was so serious that a non-custodial sentence for it cannot be justified". The only attempt to give general guidance as to what would bring an offence within s.1(4A)(c) was made by Lawton L.J. in *Bradbourn*[1]—

> ". . . the kind of offence which when committed by a young person would make right thinking members of the public knowing all the facts feel that justice had not been done by the passing of any sentence other than a custodial one."

27.05   Though open to criticism for being unduly sweeping, simplistic and ill-defined,[2] the Lawton test was approved by Lord Taylor C.J. in *Cox*.[3] Lord Taylor did not seek to explore whether the present phrasing of the "so serious" criterion set a different, arguably stricter test. More recently, in *Howells*,[4] Lord Bingham C.J. has described the "right-thinking member of the public test" as unhelpful and suggested that in approaching cases that are on or near the threshold, sentencers should pay attention to the following considerations—
27.06

- It will usually be helpful to begin by considering the nature and extent of the defendant's criminal intention and of any injury or damage caused to the victim.

- Other things being equal, an offence which was deliberate or premeditated will usually be more serious than one which was spontaneous and unpremeditated or which involved an excessive response to provocation.

- An offence which inflicted personal injury or mental trauma, particularly if permanent, will usually be more serious than one which inflicted financial loss only.

27.07   In forming its opinion on whether the offence is "so serious", the court must consider or take the following into account—

(i)   all such information about the circumstances of the offence (including any aggravating or mitigating factors) as is available to it PCC(S)A 2000, s.81(4)(a);

(ii)   a pre-sentence report (s.81(1)) though a court dealing with an offender aged under 18 for an offence triable only on indictment is not obliged to

---

[1] (1985) 7 Cr.App.R.(S.) 180.
[2] A. Ashworth and A. von Hirsch "Recognising Elephant Traps: The Problem of the Custody Threshold" [1997] Crim. L.R. 187–200.
[3] [1993] 1 W.L.R. 188.
[4] (1999) 1 Cr.App.R.(S.) 335.

do so if of the opinion that a report is unnecessary (s.81(2)). If the offence is triable either way or only summarily, the court can dispense with a report if a report prepared for a previous sentencing occasion is available to it and the court has had regard for it s.81(3) (see 12.12).

In *Gillette*[5] the Court of Appeal indicated that in all cases where a court is contemplating sentencing any defendant to custody for the first time, other than for a very short period indeed, it should be the invariable practice that a PSR be obtained before such sentence is passed, the only possible exception being where the defendant requests to be sentenced immediately. However, *Gillette* has been qualified by the Court in *Armsaramah*[6] where the judge had had the benefit of conducting the offender's trial and "was prepared to make every possible assumption in favour of the defendant". In such circumstances, nothing written in a PSR could have assisted the judge in dealing with the very serious offences before the court. It is submitted that the *Gillette* principle should invariably apply in the sentencing of juveniles.

Prevalence

27.08 Is the prevalence of an offence a pertinent factor in the assessment of seriousness? Lord Taylor C.J. lent support to this proposition in early cases interpreting CJA 1991. In *Cox*[7] he said "the prevalence of offences of a particular class and public concern about them are relevant to the seriousness of an instant offence, as we made clear in *Cunningham*.[8] In *Cunningham*, however, he approved of prevalence as a legitimate factor in determining the length of the custodial sentence to be passed, under section 80(2)(a) (see 27.12), once a decision in principle had been taken that the offence was "so serious". *Cox* concerned an 18 years old who had ridden a trials motorcycle recklessly without lights at night, in wet whether with poor visibility and had mounted the pavement in an attempt to avoid the police. *Cunningham* involved robbery of a small shop at knife-point. Both kinds of offence cause obvious concern, but it is unclear on what basis a court can conclude that a particular crime is increasing or is causing particular alarm. As Faulkner and Gibson[9] have remarked—

> "What will clearly not suffice is for the sentencer to rely solely on their recollections of previous cases heard in court or reports in local newspapers, or on public statements by the police, by interest groups or by local or national politicians. The court will need to be satisfied about prevalence and this implies that evidence of some sort will be needed to be considered and tested before the court has any sound basis for aggravating seriousness. Arguably the cases in which prevalence can be reliably established will be few in number, perhaps arising from local outbreaks of offences such as racial harassment, or the stealing and racing of motor vehicles."

27.09 Prevalence has been cited as a factor in the assessment of seriousness, without any apparent supporting evidence, in *Percy*,[10] a case of "ram raiding". See

---

[5] *The Times*, December 3, 1999.
[6] [2000] Crim.L.R. 1033.
[7] [1993] 1 W.L.R. 188.
[8] [1993] 1 W.L.R. 183.
[9] D. Faulkner and B Gibson (1993) "Seriousness: Right or Wrong?" J.P. 157, 195.
[10] (1993) 14 Cr.App.R.(S.) 10.

also *Pimm*[11] and *Bennett*[12] which are indicative of the Court of Appeal's wish to take a firm stand against the reckless use of vehicles by adolescents.

Scope for mitigation

If the court considers that an offence is "so serious" and the offender thus qualifies for custody, this is not conclusive in determining sentence, as Lord Taylor C.J. pointed out in *Cox* and *Oliver*[13]—

> "The court is still required to consider whether such a sentence is appropriate, having regard to the mitigating factors available and relevant to the offender, as opposed to such factors as are relevant to the offence." (*Cox*) "There may well be cases where, notwithstanding that the offence itself passes the custody threshold, there is sufficient mitigation to lead the court to impose a community sentence." (*Oliver*)

27.10   The scope for mitigation on which the court is able to draw to allow the imposition of a non-custodial sentence is very wide. It may, for instance, relate to the personal circumstances of the offender or may arise from the particular appeal of a community sentence in the circumstances of the case. Thus in *C.B.*[14] a case of repeated indecent assault by a boy aged 14 of previous good character on three young children left in his care, including oral sex and simulated intercourse, the Court of Appeal indicated that it was not wrong in principle for these offences to attract a custodial sentence. However, psychiatric and pre-sentence reports indicated that he was a good candidate for therapeutic help in the community, provided that during such intervention he could live in "a supportive environment" in which he could develop his educational opportunities and his peer relationships. Quashing a term of two years detention in favour of a supervision order, the Court of Appeal noted—

> "Sentencing a man as young as this for this type of offence will always pose problems for a court. Balanced against the interests of the offender in seeking a way to prevent further offending are, of course, the damage to the victims and public abhorrence for this type of crime."

27.11   If the offender receives a community sentence in circumstances where their offence satisfies the "so serious" criterion and subsequently re-offends while the community sentence is in force, the offender "would have deprived himself of much of the mitigation such as good character, genuine remorse, isolated lapse and similar considerations which had led the original court to pass a community rather than a custodial sentence" (*per* Taylor C.J. in *Oliver*).

Length of sentence

27.12   If an offence, either on its own or in combination with one or more associated offences, is considered to satisfy the "so serious" criterion and mitigation does not permit any sentence other than custody, the length of such sentence is determined according to PCC(S)A 2000, s.80.

---

[11] (1993) 14 Cr.App.R.(S.) 730.
[12] (1995) 16 Cr.App.R.(S.) 438.
[13] (1993) 1 W.L.R. 177 and 188.
[14] [2000] 1 Cr.App.R.(S.) 177.

PCC(S)A 2000, s.80

(2) The custodial sentence shall be—

(a) for such term (not exceeding the permitted maximum) as in the opinion of the court is commensurate with the seriousness of the offence, or the combination of the offence and one or more offences associated with it; or

(b) where the offence is a violent or sexual offence, for such longer term (not exceeding that maximum) as in the opinion of the court is necessary to protect the public from serious harm from the offender."

On the face of it, it appears possible for a violent or sexual offence to qualify for a custodial sentence not under s.79(2)(b) but under s.79(2)(a) and yet receive a longer than commensurate sentence in pursuit of section s.80(2)(b). In principle and in practice any offence which is deemed to require such longer sentence should qualify for a custodial sentence under section 79(2)(b). In reaching an opinion as to the proper length of sentence under section 80(2)(a), the court must once more take into account all such information about the circumstances of the offence, including any aggravating or mitigating features (s.81(4)(a), and must also obtain and consider a pre-sentence report before forming such opinion (subject, of course, to the familiar provision for an offence triable only on indictment and the safety net clause that no custodial sentence passed without the benefit of a PSR will thereby by invalidated).

27.13   In *Cunningham*[15] the Court of Appeal posed the question: does the provision (of s.80(2)(a)) permit the sentencing judge to take the need for deterrence into account? Lord Taylor C.J. answered in the affirmative, reiterating that the purposes of a custodial sentence "must primarily be to punish and deter . . . "commensurate with the seriousness of the offence" must mean commensurate with the punishment and deterrence which the seriousness of the offence requires." This contrasts somewhat with the cautious note of realism sounded in the 1990 White Paper[16] for that though deterrence has much immediate appeal, "it is unrealistic to construct sentencing arrangements on the basis that most offenders will weigh up the possibilities in advance and base their conduct on rational calculation". This seems particularly true of young offenders. Nevertheless, deterrence, both general and personal, remains a factor to which the Court of Appeal regularly refers (see, for example, *Chesterton*[17] noted at *Attorney-General's Reference Nos. 60 and 61 of 1997*[18]).

Given the apparently mandatory requirement of section 80(2)(a) that the custodial sentence *shall* be commensurate with the seriousness of the offence, proportionality appears on the face of it to be not merely a starting point but the finishing point in determining sentence. However, this must be qualified by the scope to mitigate sentence under PCC(S)A 2000, s.158(1) taking account of any such matters which the court considers relevant.

27.14   *Parsimony Principle for Shorter Sentences* In a significant judgement on the appropriate length of sentence in instances where a custodial sentence is right in principle but term need not be substantial, the Court of Appeal in *Ollerenshaw*[19] stated—

---

[15] [1993] 1 W.L.R. 183.
[16] Home Office *Crime, Justice and Protecting the Public*, Cm. 965 (HMSO, London, 1990), para. 2.8.
[17] [1997] 2 Cr.App.R.(S.) 297.
[18] [1998] 2 Cr.App.R.(S.) 300, noted at 27.95 and *Howe* [1998] 2 Cr.App.R.(S.) 128.
[19] [1999] 1 Cr.App.R.(S.) 65.

"Where a court is considering a comparatively short custodial sentence, of about 12 months or less, it should generally ask itself, particularly where the defendant has not been in prison, whether custody for an even shorter period might be equally effective in protecting the interests of the public and deterring criminal behaviour."

Seriousness threshold and length of sentence: case illustrations

27.15   The following survey seeks to provide some sense of the approach of the Court of Appeal to a variety of offences involving young offenders over the last five years from 1995. All cases need to be weighed with some caution in light of the changing climate of public opinion and trends in criminal behaviour within which sentencers must seek to pursue principles that reflect the public interest. Additionally, it is instructive as a general pointer to heed the Magistrates' Association *Sentencing Guidelines* (2000) with suggested "level of seriousness" points "from which discussion should properly flow", albeit that these have not been developed with youth justice specifically in mind. Reported cases inevitably reflect the more serious instances in each offence category, often with emphasis on whether a longer period of detention is appropriate under CYPA 1933 s.53(3) (now PCC(S)A 2000, s.91). The survey assumes familiarity with Appeal Court sentencing guidance applicable across the age spectrum and gives emphasis to the sentencing approach that reflects mitigation specific to young offenders. These illustrations should be located within the overall principle of 'restraint' in respect of young offenders, discussed at 11.35 *et seq.* and 29.18. Cases reported in recent years concentrate primarily on the issue of length of custodial sentence rather than whether the "so serious" threshold has been crossed. Reference may be made to older cases noted in the first edition of this text which gave more prominence to the latter consideration but these may be more of historical interest in illustrating changing sensibilities than reliably accurate reflections of current sentencing practice.

Arson

27.16   Fire-raising causes considerable anxiety for obvious reasons and is known to be attractive to many young persons as a form of experimentation or test of reckless bravado, but with the potential for unanticipated consequences significantly beyond the usual for criminal damage or vandalism, usually shocking to the perpetrator but also placing the emergency services at substantial risk. Schools can be the target for fires set by disaffected pupils as a form of deliberate, wrecking protest, with serious consequences for the education of other young people. Less commonly, the juvenile fire-setter may be revealing a deviant fascination for fire and/or the response of the emergency services of a compulsive or addictive nature. Given this range of pre-disposing factors, motive, level of culpability and likelihood of repetition, this cluster of youthful crime poses a particular challenge to sentencers. As *Leatham* (see 27.23) suggests, the sentencing climate appears to have hardened in response to juvenile arson, with greater emphasis on the consequences of this kind of delinquency.

27.16   *Horsman and Holmes*[20] Two boys aged 15 without previous convictions pleaded guilty to arson of a school from which one had been expelled, breaking in at night, bringing petrol for the purpose of fire-setting. Though noting that this was a deliberate, planned and vengeful crime, sentences of two years and three years

---

[20] (1995) 16 Cr.App.R.(S.) 130.

were reduced to 12 months and 27 months, the longer term being given to the boy who had taken the lead role.

27.17 *Bool and White*[21] Two boys aged 12 and 13 set several fires in an industrial building containing inflammable materials, one fire getting out of control causing damage to the structure of the building estimated at £350,000 to £500,000, destroying machinery worth £2m and stock worth £50,000, with additional losses of £2m. Sentences of three years detention were reduced to 18 months. The Appeal Court heeded that both boys had experienced disturbed childhoods and showed behavioural problems or learning difficulties. One had a fascination with fire but the other did not exhibit such unhealthy interest. The Court noted that if they had been aged over 15 and had been from less difficult backgrounds, three years would have been an appropriate sentence.

27.18 *Nicholls and Warden*[22] Two boys aged 12 pleaded guilty to arson of a partially built house in which they were trespassing, causing damage estimated at £50,000. Sentence of two years detention was reduced to 12 months.

27.19 *Milsom*[23] (not arson but included here as of related significance) A boy aged 15 pleaded guilty to making an explosive, having been found in possession of an explosive devise which he had made from household chemicals and two pipe guns. He was assessed as suffering conduct disorder and having an obsession with explosives. Sentence of four years was "manifestly excessive", being reduced to three years in light of evidence that he required at least 18 months in a secure unit for treatment.

27.20 *Whitbrook and Smith*[24] A youth aged 17 without previous convictions, acting with a companion aged 18, pleaded guilty to arson being reckless whether life was endangered. They had dropped a lighted firework through the letterbox of a family home at 9.15 p.m. while the occupants were asleep. The property caught fire causing the death of a boy aged 10. Sentence of three years detention was upheld. The defence has sought to argue that this was a "prank" which had gone terribly wrong and the culprits were very remorseful. The Appeal Court disagreed with the term "prank" and emphasised that "young men, even youths as young as this, must learn, if they do not know, that to engage in this kind of behaviour with fireworks is likely to have the most appalling consequences".

27.21 *Spong and Bromham*[25] Boys aged 15 and 16 pleaded guilty to arson being reckless whether life would be endangered. They had been disturbed while smoking in their school lavatories, causing them to drop their cigarettes and run away. The resulting fire had caused damage exceeding £400,000. Noting that neither had intended to create this level of havoc, the absence of any abnormal interest in fires, their good response to a bail support scheme in the year prior to their final court appearance and their exemplary behaviour since the incident, the Appeal Court reduced terms of 24 and 21 months to 15 and 12 months.

27.22 *Taylor*[26] A boy aged 14 of previous good character, one of a group of four youths who entered a paper yard, pleaded guilty to arson causing £250, 000 damage, having been egged on by the others to start a fire. Sentence of three years detention was reduced to two years. He showed little remorse or evidence of understanding the consequences of his actions and his school attendance was poor.

---

[21] [1998] 1 Cr.App.R.(S.) 32.
[22] [1998] 1 Cr.App.R.(S.) 66.
[23] [1998] 1 Cr.App.R.(S.) 306.
[24] [1998] 2 Cr.App.R.(S.) 322.
[25] [1999] 1 Cr.App.R.(S.) 417.
[26] [2000] 1 Cr.App.R.(S.) 45.

He was now making progress in a local authority secure unit which the Appeal Court felt was the right place for him to remain.

27.23   Leatham[27] A male aged 16 at time of offence, of previous good character, pleaded guilty to arson being reckless as to whether property would be destroyed. Shortly after completing his final GCSE examinations, late at night and having been drinking and smoking cannabis, he had gone to the school, smashed some windows, broken in to the art block and lit pieces of paper. When the ensuing fire got out of hand, he had panicked and run away. Damage was estimated at £400,000. The judge accepted that the offence was not pre-planned and that no accelerants were used. A psychiatric report referred to his sleep disturbance, mood swings, lack of motivation and low self-esteem in the six months leading up to his examinations, indicating that he appeared to have suffered a depressive illness for which he could be treated as part of a probation order. A pre-sentence report proposing a combination order concluded that he was motivated never to re-offend and that the risk of re-offending could be substantially reduced with treatment. Dismissing his appeal against sentence of two years detention, the Appeal Court considered that the sentencing climate had changed since cases such as *Dewberry and Stone*[28] (where a 15 year old had had sentence reduced from three years to 12 months)—

> "It may well be the case today perhaps greater emphasis is placed upon the effects of the crime, including arson, upon the victims and upon the community in general."

In this case, not only was the monetary value of the damage high but the fire had destroyed three terms of GCSE coursework, with significant consequences for those going on to further education or employment. School and community life had been considerably disrupted and public outrage was evident. "If the appellant had not been so young and of good character, a significantly longer sentence would have been justified."

27.24   Johnson[29] A youth aged 15 at the time of the arson had entered the flat of an older man who was vulnerable on account of his intoxication, subsequently attacking him and setting fires in his home, then leaving him unconscious in the burning property. Three weeks earlier, he had entered an unlocked garage of a house, stealing petrol which was set alight outside the property. While detained in a secure unit following his arrest, he joined in an attack on a member of staff and absconded. Upholding a term of nine years for arson with intent to endanger life (guilty plea) and a concurrent term of the same length for escaping from custody, the Court of Appeal indicated that though it had had regard to the *Storey* principle (see 29.18), the appellant had an appalling catalogue of offending and this was a very grave offence that could very easily have led to the victim's death. The PSR was "gloomy in the extreme" about his prospects, indicating that he had resorted to alcohol and drugs from the age of 12 and showed no remorse for his conduct. He posed substantial risk to the public and there were no obvious solutions to the risk he posed to society. Though it was reported that he had settled down in custody since sentence, this did not lead the court to take a different view of the appropriate sentence.

Domestic burglary

**27.25   The well known guideline case of *Brewster* [1998] 1 Cr. App. R.(S.) 181, though not specific to young offenders, confirmed the earlier view expressed in

---

[27] [2000] 1 Cr.App.R.(S.) 186.
[28] (1985) 7 Cr.App.R.(S.) 202.
[29] [2000] 2 Cr.App.R.(S.) 235.

Mussell and Others[30] that, although always a serious offence, dwelling house burglary is not always "so serious" and necessarily attracting a custodial sentence. The Court of Appeal noted that the decision whether a custodial sentence is required is heavily dependent on the aggravating and mitigating features of the offence, with the personal circumstances of the offender counting to a lesser extent. In indicating instances at the less serious end of the seriousness scale, Lord Bingham C.J. referred to such matters as taking a bottle of milk through an open window or a can of petrol from an outhouse, instances of the offence that fall outside the more familiar range of housebreaking. In one relatively recent instance of more substantial burglary by a young adult, *Bennett*[31] who broke in to a home at night knowing that the occupier was away on holiday and attempted to escape empty-handed when interrupted by a neighbour investigating the suspicious noise of breaking glass, the Court of Appeal concluded that the "so serious" criterion had not been satisfied and that a custodial sentence was not justified. This interpretation may not represent more contemporary judicial views, as *Winson and Poole*[32] may serve to illustrate. Boys aged 13 (first conviction) and 15 at the time of the crime pleaded guilty to daytime entry of a house through an unlocked back door, stealing a purse, keys, cash and a ring. Having regard to *Brewster*, the Appeal Court confirmed that a custodial sentence was warranted but reduced the term from 12 to nine months, in light not only of their ages and plea but their backgrounds, both boys experiencing domestic difficulties.

27.26   Several reported cases deal with instances of burglary of the homes of elder victims who may be a particular target of young offenders because of their vulnerability and who are seen as particularly deserving of the courts' protection. Within this targeting cluster, there is a clear difference between crimes deploying 'distraction' techniques to gain admittance to the home and those where the victim has faced a very frightening confrontation with an intruder, usually at night.

27.27   *Tucker*[33] A male aged 15 pleaded guilty to four burglaries of elder victims. Sentence of four years was upheld even though he had volunteered the name of his accomplice because he felt regret over the circumstances of the last offence where the victim was hit on the head by his co-offender, and he had indicated his willingness to give evidence against him. The Court indicated that the circumstances of the offences, involving deliberate targeting, must prevail over the circumstances of the offender. The term was severe but warranted.

27.28   *Attorney-General's Reference No. 24 of 1997*[34] A male aged 16 pleaded guilty to entering the home of a woman aged 78 at night, confronting her as she was asleep in bed. When she screamed, he ran off. He had been to her address before and thus knew her circumstances, and the offence was planned. The appropriate term was four years and sentence was increased from two years to 42 months.

27.29   *Simpson*[35] A male aged 16 with numerous previous convictions pleaded guilty to entering the home of a woman aged 83 at night. When she challenged him, he left but produced a knife when a neighbour sought to detain him. Sentence of 42 months for aggravated burglary was upheld, despite the defence assertion that this faced him with a "long dark tunnel". The Court asserted that it was necessary

---

[30] (1991) 12 Cr.App.R.(S.) 607.
[31] (1995) 16 Cr.App.R.(S.) 438.
[32] [1998] 1 Cr. App.(S.) 000.
[33] [1997] 1 Cr.App.(S.) 337.
[34] [1998] 1 Cr.App.(S.) 319.
[35] [1998] 1 Cr.App.(S.) 145.

to give a message of reassurance to "the housebound, aged and infirm" and of disapproval and warning to young offenders and would-be offenders.

27.30   *Carr*[36] A male aged 14 to 15 pleaded guilty to repeated burglary of the home of a woman aged 88 who was frail and had poor eyesight. He had used a variety of pretexts to gain entry so that he could steal money. Sentence of five years was upheld in light of his deliberate targeting. The offences were described as "cold-blooded and calculated in the extreme", motivated by financial greed and his level of remorse was doubtful. The need to maintain "light at the end of the tunnel" with the need to respond to "the outrage that would be felt by any right-thinking person". The appropriate term of seven years for an adult defendant had been scaled down to reflect the offender's age.

27.31   *Hanrahan*[37] (concerns a young adult) A male aged 18 without previous convictions pleaded guilty to a distraction burglary of a woman aged 90 by pretending to be a council official while his accomplice entered and stole a watch. A deterrent sentence was deemed necessary to reflect the vulnerability of such victims but sentence of four years was reduced to three as adequate to mark the gravity of the crime.

27.32   *Sleeth*[38] A girl aged 17 pleaded guilty to three counts of burglary of elder women victims who had allowed her into their homes on various deceitful pretexts. Noting that she had made a "consistent career of this kind of crime", albeit that this was her first custodial sentence, the Appeal Court reduced her term from four to three years, providing her with "an opportunity for reflection and training".

27.33   *O'Grady*[39] A boy aged 14 pleaded guilty to joint responsibility with others for three "distraction" burglaries of elder women living alone, walking uninvited into their homes on various pretexts to steal money. Sentence of six months detention (under s.53(3)) was upheld, as striking the right balance between the welfare of the applicant and considerations of punishment and deterrence. The Court was informed that he was benefiting from a structured environment, that his education had been "taken in hand" and, on release, he would be placed in a suitable foster home.

27.34   *Bruce*[40] A youth aged 16 pleaded guilty to aggravated burglary of the home of a woman aged 72 at night when she was asleep in bed. When she awoke to find him in her bedroom, he had stabbed her repeatedly to her abdomen and back. He admitted two other burglaries in the same sheltered housing complex for elder persons. He had been in a disinhibited state having consumed alcohol in combination with sleeping tablets and earlier that night had tried to self-harm by overdose of the latter. Upholding sentence of 10 years detention, the Appeal Court noted the targeting of old people and the "ruthless", intentional and terrifying nature of the attack, leading to significant injury.

27.35   The following cases illustrate recent approaches to domestic burglaries not involving vulnerable victims.

Lamb[41] Having taken a car, an offender then aged 16 broke into an unoccupied house, aided by two associates who kept watch. When police sought to stop the car afterwards, he responded by accelerating at an officer, obliging him to jump out the

---

[36] [1998] 2 Cr.App.(S.) 20.
[37] [1999] 1 Cr.App.(S.) 308.
[38] [1999] 2 Cr.App.R.(S.) 211.
[39] [2000] 1 Cr. App.(S.) 112.
[40] [2000] 2 Cr.App.R.(S.) 376.
[41] See *Mills* [1998] 2 Cr.App.R.(S.) 128 at 137.

way. He pleaded guilty to burglary and aggravated vehicle taking. The Appeal Court concluded that, in the light of the latter crime as an "associated offence" a term of 42 months for the burglary was appropriate.

27.36 *Chapple*[42] A youth aged 17 pleaded guilty to daytime burglary of the victim's flat after she had gone to work. He had previously broken into her business premises and was motivated by spite against her, telling police that it "serves the bitch right. I'll do it again", his absence of remorse being noted also in the pre-sentence report. Though a "substantial" custodial sentence was inevitable, his sentence of four years was too long and a term of 30 months was substituted.

27.37 *Mills*[43] A boy aged 13 at time of the offences pleaded guilty to three burglaries of homes while the occupants were out, asking for a similar offence to be taken into consideration. The Appeal Court considered that while sentence of 18 months detention was "at the top end of the range for one so young", it could not be considered excessive. However, in the light of "compelling mitigation" (an unhappy family life; numerous disruptions in his subsequent Care placements; a new beginning with an aunt since this episode of offending, leading to a dramatic change in his attitude and demeanour and the assessment that he would not re-offend if this arrangement continued), the Court substituted a supervision order, a course likely to offer "the better prospect that this boy will make something worthwhile of his life and that, as a result, the public are less likely to suffer at his hands in the future". (He had by then served the equivalent of an 11 month sentence.)

Commercial burglary

27.38 Few recent reported cases deal with this variation of burglary but the following is an instructive instance—

27.39 *Attorney-General's Reference Nos. 58 and 59 of 1995*[44] Youths aged 19 and 16 at time of the offence pleaded guilty to aggravated burglary of a shop at night, armed with a baseball bat and pick handle. They attacked the shopkeeper who was sleeping on the premises because he had suffered repeated break-ins. Sentence terms of 10 weeks and five months were increased to 21 months and 18 months.

Causing death by dangerous or intoxicated careless driving

27.40 Driving is adult behaviour to which adolescents understandably aspire and which poses considerable risk, particularly where the youthful driver is inexperienced, keen to impress or wanting to combine the mobility of driving with partying recreation. When this kind of crime has fatal consequences, often for a close friend of the driver and triggering considerable remorse, the courts have faced a dilemma in whether to hold the offender to account according to adult standards or to make special allowance for youth.

27.41 *Attorney-General's Reference No. 28 of 1996*[45] (a young adult) A youth aged 18 pleaded guilty to causing death by dangerous driving. He had negotiated a blind brow on the wrong side of the road at high speed, losing control so that his passenger friend was killed in the resulting crash. He had a previous conviction for dangerous driving. Sentence of six months was increased to three years.

---

[42] [2000] 1 Cr.App.(S.) 115.
[43] [2000] 2 Cr.App.R.(S.) 128.
[44] [1996] 2 Cr.App.(S.) 171.
[45] [1997] 2 Cr.App.(S.) 79.

27.42   *Branston*[46] A male aged 16 without previous convictions pleaded guilty to causing the death by dangerous driving of a cyclist, having driven at high speed after drinking alcohol, albeit for limited distance He held no licence and the car was thus uninsured. The Appeal Court observed that "in this field of sentencing the factor of youth inevitably has potentially less weight than in other areas because it is the very youth of the offender which engenders the offence". However, the Court noted his good work record and various testimonials to his worth. Reducing sentence from five years to 42 months, the Court said that it had initially had four years in mind but heeded that he had experienced hostility from other trainees because of his previous good character so that his sentence was more severe than if he were of "inherently bad character". Disqualification from driving was reduced from eight to four years in light of his age.

27.43   *Moon and Moon*[47] Two brothers aged 15 and 19 had attended a party in which the older youth was involved in a fight. To get away from the scene of trouble they drove off in their van, at slow speed through a crowd of young people on the car park, without lights, the younger brother steering from the driving seat while the older male operated the gears and clutch. They hit two 16 year old girls, one being dragged for 30 yards and suffering fatal injuries. They had continued to drive despite warnings, not realising what had happened. Noting that the 15-year-old had no previous convictions, had been overwhelmed by events and had acted in a state of panic, and was assessed as being very remorseful, the Appeal Court reduced sentence from six to three years.

27.44   *Chippendale*[48] A young adult aged 18, of previous good character, pleaded guilty to causing death by careless driving while unfit through alcohol. He had driven at 50 mph in a 30 mph zone, despite having been warned that he was not fit to drive, hitting a wall and killing a passenger. His breath reading was almost twice the legal limit. Upholding four years detention, the Appeal Court expressed grave concern about young men driving after having too much to drink and noted that "acute guilt feelings are not of great weight in such circumstances".

27.45   *Carroll*[49] A boy aged 15 at the time of the offence pleaded guilty to causing the death of his girl passenger whom he had agreed to drive to a cashpoint. While travelling at 60–70 mph in a 30 mph zone, he lost control and hit a lamp post. Sentence of four years under s.53(3) was reduced to two years YOI detention.

27.46   *Hajicosti*[50] A girl aged 17 of previous good character, who had recently passed her test and been given a car by her parents, was warned by her passenger that she was driving too fast but failed to stop at a roundabout, hitting a motorcyclist. Sentence of three years was reduced to two years detention in light of her youth, character and remorse.

27.47   *Brown*[51] A youth aged 17 of previous good character attended a party two days after passing his driving test, drinking 2½ pints of strong lager (being 10% over the limit). Three friends persuaded him to drive them home. He lost control and hit a tree, killing his best friend. The Appeal Court felt that inexperience rather than alcohol was the primary cause of the accident. Given strong personal mitigation, evidenced by excellent character references, sentence of 24 months was deemed manifestly excessive and replaced by a term of 12 months.

---

[46] [1997] 2 Cr.App.R.(S.) 184.
[47] [1997] 2 Cr.App.R.(S.) 44.
[48] [1998] 1 Cr.App.R.(S.) 192.
[49] [1998] 2 Cr.App.R.(S.) 349.
[50] [1998] 2 Cr.App.R.(S.) 396.
[51] [2000] 164 J.P. 495.

Drug offences

27.48   Drug crime causes high profile concern and talk of zero tolerance. Drug use is thought to be the strongest predictor of serious or persistent offending for boys aged 12–17. Whereas youthful drug misusers have been viewed as the targets of adult suppliers, a number of recent cases have faced the problem faced where juveniles have aspired to dealing, with the likelihood of selling to or otherwise supplying young persons of their own age and thus posing the risk of introducing child newcomers to drug dependency. Alternatively, the juvenile may seem a less risky courier for drugs because they may be less likely to attract suspicion. Should the prevalent deterrent approach of the tariff apply straightforwardly to youths? Have juvenile traffickers surrendered their youth status?

27.49   *Basid*[52] A youth aged 17 pleaded guilty to offences including possession of heroin with intent to supply. There was evidence that he had been dealing over a substantial period pre-dating his 17th birthday, amounting to over £30,000. In the light of his youth and mitigation arising from his adverse family circumstances, sentence was reduced from four to three years.

27.50   *Chesterton*[53] Four males, two aged 16 at time of offence and two aged 14, all of previous good character, pleaded guilty to supplying LSD to schoolboys. The older two had been dealing while the younger two had obtained the drug and passed it on to others. Sentence of three years s.53(3) detention was upheld for the older offenders but terms of two years were reduced to 12 months for the younger boys as the shorter sentence was considered enough to "warn them off drugs forever" and still contain an element of deterrence.

27.51   *Bristol*[54] (though the offender was a young adult, this case is of relevance because it illustrates the approach to importation couriership) A young woman aged 18 of previous good character pleaded not guilty to importation of cocaine found concealed in her shoes. She had been influenced by her boyfriend, a man in his mid-30s. Reducing sentence from 10 to eight years detention, the Appeal Court said that it was right to make some allowance for her youth, though it is in the nature of drug trafficking for the organisers to select the young, the vulnerable and those of good character—she being all three—and thus such factors must carry less weight in this context.

27.52   *Roberts*[55] (another young adult but may be indicative of the approach to small scale cannabis supply) A male student aged 20 of previous good character pleaded guilty to supplying cannabis to friends on a small scale to pay for his own use of the drug. Though reducing sentence from six to two months detention, the Appeal Court affirmed that the offence was sufficiently serious to attract a custodial sentence and indicated the aim of deterrence—it was "important that people know that if they choose to dabble in supplying drugs, even on a small scale, they lose their liberty".

27.53   *Ferrett*[56] (another young adult but pertinent) A young adult aged 18 pleaded guilty to supplying Ecstasy, amphetamine and cannabis, having been arrested following the death of a teenage girl following use of Ecstasy and amphetamine. His mother had informed the police that he had admitted to her selling drugs to other young people, though not the deceased, over a period of 12

[52] [1996] 1 Cr.App.R.(S.) 421.
[53] [1997] 2 Cr.App.R.(S.) 297.
[54] [1998] 1 Cr.App.R.(S.) 47.
[55] [1998] 1 Cr.App.R.(S.) 155.
[56] [1998] 2 Cr.App.R.(S.) 384.

months, making a profit of around £80 a week. Sentence of seven years detention was reduced to five years to reflect his age and frankness, with a further six month reduction because of parental intervention (following *Catterall*—see 11.44).

27.54   *T.*[57] Sentence of two years detention imposed on a boy aged 12 at the time of the offence and 13 at time of sentence, caught with £400 and a quantity of cocaine and heroin and convicted of possession with intent to supply, was upheld, in light of his earlier conviction for a drug offence, his mother's loss of control over him and the assessment that he required treatment being provided in a therapeutic secure unit.

Railway endangerment

27.55   As with arson, this can be an appealing way for juveniles to test their daring and to cause mischief with the adult world, but with high risks and potentially appalling consequences.

27.56   *Hawkes*[58] (involves a young adult who was treated as younger than his age) A 19-year-old with no significant record pleaded not guilty to endangering passengers on a railway with intent to injure or endanger. He had thrown a stone at an intercity train travelling at 100 mph, shattering the engine windscreen and injuring the driver. He was assessed as intellectually and socially immature, younger in his attitudes than his actual age and unlikely to instigate such dangerous behaviour. He was finding custody a daunting experience. Though the Appeal Court sought to emphasise the gravity of his crime and to deter others, sentence was reduced from five to four years.

27.57   *AH*[59] A boy aged 14 pleaded guilty to three counts of obstructing the railway in the company of an adult aged 22. They had adopted a quasi-military identity and appeared to see themselves as some kind of private army. On each occasion a train had hit the obstruction. The Court of Appeal recognised that the public danger posed by this behaviour caused very grave concern but, in the light of his "extreme youth", the fact that he had offended with someone much older and the excellent progress that he was making in a secure unit, sentence was reduced from five to three years.

Robbery

27.58   Robbery is usually a very crude form of property crime requiring little finesse but with the prospect of immediate returns. For youthful perpetrators, the most likely targets are either the old or other young persons, both vulnerable and thus prompting a reaction of outrage of which the courts are very conscious. The first set of illustrations feature what many would regard as the most heinous form of robbery, that of elder persons in their own home.

27.59   *Arrowsmith and Others*[60] Boys aged 14 and 16 pleaded guilty to robbery of a woman aged 99 in her home, her house being ransacked by a group of youths. The Appeal Court noted the dilemma posed in seeking to balance the competing interests of victims, the wider public and the offenders themselves. Elder people, whose lives are severely affected by crime of this nature, deserve the courts' protection and sentencers have to face the prevalence of this kind of predatory

---

[57] (2000) (noted in 164 J.P. 811).
[58] [1996] 2 Cr.App.R.(S.) 195.
[59] [2000] 2 Cr.App.R.(S.) 280.
[60] [1996] 1 Cr.App.R.(S.) 6.

crime against the vulnerable. On the other hand, would a long sentence "crush the offenders' spirits, thus handicapping their rehabilitation"? The dilemma was resolved by reducing terms of seven and five years by a year apiece.

27.60 *Attorney-General's Reference No. 30 of 1997*[61] A youth aged 16 at the time of the offence pleaded guilty to robbery of a woman aged 85. With an accomplice he had threatened her in her home, one of the perpetrators standing on her chest until she disclosed the whereabouts of her keys. A term of eight months detention was increased to three years, the Appeal Court indicating that four years would have been the proper term.

The following cluster of cases illustrate the approach to robbery of commercial businesses or those otherwise vulnerable through serving the public—

27.61 *Attorney-General's Reference No. 42 of 1996*[62] A youth aged 17 with a previous conviction for robbery was convicted of robbing an off-licence while on bail for another robbery allegation. He had struck the woman shopkeeper with a bottle, stealing two bottles of champagne and cash. The Appeal Court agreed that sentence of 21 months was unduly lenient. The challenge was to strike a balance between the youth of the offender, the effect of a long sentence on the perceptions of the offender and the need to deter others from committing similar offences. A term of 42 months was imposed instead.

27.62 *Courtney, Amewode and El-Whabe*[63] Boys aged 14, 13 and 15 at the time of the crime pleaded guilty to attempted robbery of a newsagent's shop, one jumping the counter and restraining and pushing the assistant while the other two tried to open the till. Sentences of two years for the first and third boy and of three years for the second boy (who also pleaded guilty to another robbery) were upheld, despite their adverse personal circumstances and histories.

27.63 *Hilden*[64] A boy aged 15 pleaded guilty to robbing a taxi driver (plus other less serious offences). Having booked a taxi, he asked to be taken to a location without housing, on arrival holding a razor blade to the driver's neck and demanding money, being handed £35. The victim suffered lacerations to his face and neck. Though this was an "appalling offence", sentence of five years was reduced to four in light of his age.

The next set of cases involve street 'mugging' robberies, some involving victims of the same age group where the robbery was a form of bullying behaviour, others being against adult vulnerable victims—

27.64 *Daley*[65] A boy aged 14 without previous convictions denied assault with intent to rob, having accosted a man aged in his 50s in the street, armed with a knife, and demanded that he hand over his wallet. When the victim indicated that he had no wallet he was pushed over. The Appeal Court considered that the use of a knife, the threats made and the prevalence of violence in Hackney, where the crime occurred, demanded a custodial sentence as an exercise in general deterrence, but noted that he had conducted himself in an exemplary manner while in custody. The balance of factors allowed reduction in sentence from five years to 30 months.

---

[61] [1998] 1 Cr.App.R.(S.) 349.
[62] [1997] 1 Cr.App.R.(S.) 388.
[63] [1997] 2 Cr.App.R.(S.) 121.
[64] [1999] 1 Cr.App.R.(S.) 386.
[65] [1996] 2 Cr.App.R.(S.) 212.

27.65   *Attorney-General's Reference No. 47 of 1996*[66] A youth aged 17 pleaded guilty to robbery of a boy aged 15 by threatening him with an air pistol, searching him and taking a ring and cash. He had committed a number of such offences though these were not before the Crown Court. Replacing a probation order with detention for nine months, though suggesting that the proper term would ordinarily be two years, the Appeal Court indicated that the courts must be—

> "conscious of the possibility of public indignation where school children or paperboys are waylaid, threatened and made to hand over money or possessions. It is important if confidence in the rule of law is to be maintained that offenders committing offences of this kind are seen to be effectively punished."

27.66   *Fenemore*[67] A boy aged 14 of previous good character pleaded guilty to robbery of a woman aged 61, pushing her over and taking her bag. Sentence of 18 months for "the act of a cowardly young thug" was upheld as "not a day too long".

27.67   *Deegan*[68] A boy aged 14 of previous good character pleaded guilty to attempted robbery of a woman aged 65, by trying to snatch her bag. She fell to the ground and was dragged along, suffering a dislocated shoulder. A term of two years detention was upheld.

27.68   *King*[69] A youth aged 17 pleaded guilty to robbery at knifepoint, with an accomplice, of a male aged 18 whom he had seen making a withdrawal from a cash-point. The victim had refused to hand over any money and had been thrown to the ground and his rucksack taken. Though the offender was only lightly convicted, having two previous appearances for shop theft resulting in conditional discharge, the Appeal Court considered three years to be "entirely the right sentence".

27.69   *Moloney*[70] A youth aged 16 at time of offence robbed a woman tourist guide by pushing her in the back, causing her to fall to the ground, then snatching her shoulder bag. When bailed for this offence, he joined with other youths in intimidating two 15-year-old boys in an amusement arcade to hand over £10. He pleaded guilty to both robberies. The Appeal Court assessed the proper sentence as 18 months detention plus 12 months consecutive, under s.53(3).

27.70   *Howe*[71] A youth aged 17 pleaded guilty to robbery of a woman aged 74, stealing her shopping bag as she walked through a quiet subway, committed with an accomplice while he was on bail. In seeking to resist the snatch she had hit her head on the tunnel wall and fell, suffering a head injury and a fractured femur, as well as psychological effects, being frightened to leave home alone. He had various previous convictions, including one for robbery. Sentence of 30 months was upheld, despite being on the borderline of undue leniency. "A sentence of general deterrence was called for."

27.71   *Whittaker*[72] A youth aged 16 broke into the home of an elder couple at night, taking a large knife from the kitchen and going upstairs where he was confronted by the male householder who had woken and got up. He threatened

---

[66] [1997] 2 Cr.App.R.(S.) 194.
[67] [1998] 1 Cr.App.R.(S.) 1767.
[68] [1998] 1 Cr.App.R.(S.) 291.
[69] See *Mills and Others* [1998] 2 Cr.App.R.(S.) 128 at 136.
[70] *ibid.*, at 138.
[71] *ibid.*, at 142.
[72] *ibid.*, at 144.

them both with a knife, demanding money and jewellery. The male victim was stabbed in the course of a struggle, suffering a punctured lung, requiring treatment in intensive care. Though the offender pleaded guilty to robbery and wounding with intent, he was assessed as showing little remorse and being concerned only for himself. He had a problem with alcohol misuse and claimed to have been very drunk at the time of offence, thus having little recall. Sentence of nine years was upheld.

27.72   *Lindsay*[73] A boy aged 13 pleaded guilty to robbery with an accomplice of a paperboy whom he pushed down a side street and threatened with a knife, so that he handed over his personal stereo set. The offence was committed while he was on bail for two daytime burglaries while occupants were out. Sentence of three years detention was reduced to two years (and two years concurrent for the burglaries being cut to 18 months). The Appeal Court noted that he had demonstrated some sympathy for the victim, unsuccessfully asking his accomplice to return the stereo at the victim's plea. At that age, terms of three years should be reserved for still more serious offending.

27.73   *Luck and Woolard*[74] Youths aged 17 and 18 pleaded guilty to robbery arising from a series of incidents in which young persons were forced to hand over money under threat of violence. Terms of 42 months were upheld in light of their serious record of offending despite being afforded every opportunity by the courts to change. These offences had occurred while they were subject to supervision orders and on bail.

27.74   *Manghan and Manghan*[75] Brothers aged 14 and 16 pleaded guilty to robbing an elder woman as she was boarding a bus, jostling her and stealing her purse. They had stolen from five other such victims in similar circumstances. Their motive was to secure the means to sustain their heroin and crack cocaine dependency. The Appeal Court noted that they had conducted a "campaign" against elder people, causing fear and distress. It was perfectly proper for the judge to include a deterrent element as this type of offence causes grave concern to the community. They had shown little on no remorse when caught, one responding "Fuck the old ladies. I don't give a fuck about them." However, terms of five years were felt to be excessive and were reduced to 42 months and four years respectively.

27.75   *McKay and Others*[76] In a group offence combining robbery and actual bodily harm, three child offenders aged 12, 12 and 13 at the time of the crime, had intimidated a boy aged 15 to hand over money and cigarettes, then inflicting an extended attack upon him lasting some 40 minutes, striking him across the head and body, including with a padlock and chain, a bicycle and a piece of wood, and singeing him with a cigarette lighter. The victim suffered extensive bruising, including haemorrhages to both eyes, requiring five days stay in hospital. Their appeal concerned the validity of a sentence of detention under s.53(3) given that the violence which caused the main concern was not the subject of an offence carrying liability to this form of sentence (see) but the Appeal Court upheld terms of two years detention for each offender for the robbery aggravated by violence inextricably bound up in that offence.

27.76   *Attorney-General's Reference No. 57 and 58 of 1999*[77] Girls aged 16 and 17 pleaded guilty to robbery of a girl aged 12 whom they approached as she was

---

[73] [1998] 2 Cr.App.R.(S.) 230.
[74] [1999] 1 Cr.App.R.(S.) 248.
[75] [2000] 1 Cr.App.R.(S.) 6.
[76] [2000] 1 Cr.App.R.(S.) 17 (see 29.12).
[77] [2000] 1 Cr.App.R.(S.) 502. See also *Smith* [2000] Crim.L.R. 613 (at 28.06).

walking home from school on separate occasions, taking first her jacket and subsequently £30. She subsequently committed suicide, though it was not suggested that this was not as a consequence of the offences. The defence suggested that she had sought the company of the two offenders, even after the offences. The Appeal Court agreed that their sentence of supervision orders was unduly lenient and that a term of "some months" would have been the right sentence. Lord Bingham C.J. observed—

> "It is easy—and often tempting—to view offences of this kind through the eyes of the offender alone and to form a judgement as to what is or may be seen to be in the best interests of the offender. That is a legitimate matter to take into account, but it is, we wish to emphasise, not the only matter. There is a public dimension to offending of this kind which the sentencing court cannot overlook. Parents are justifiably incensed when their children, on the way home from school or at school, are victimised by older children who either steal items of their property with threats as to the consequences if they do not part with it, or victimise them in any other way. . . . the offences call for a custodial sentence in order to make it plain to offenders that this is the penalty that will follow, and also to reassure those who are victims of these offences and their parents that the courts are genuinely determined to recognise their interests and their vulnerability."

27.77   However, the Court opted not to vary sentence and the case is interesting for the attention paid to the offenders' backgrounds and circumstances. One was described as "damaged" by her estrangement from her parents, so that she felt considerable self-loathing which had prompted a suicide attempt. The second girl had experienced an extremely difficult and turbulent upbringing with disrupted living arrangements and a tenuous relationship with her mother, leaving her confused and angry. She was now pregnant. It was also noted that, after a difficult start to supervision, there were signs that both were showing signs of a more positive outlook and taking advantage of opportunities open to them. Reports expressed concern that a custodial sentence would de-stabilise their lives further and could expose them to more sophisticated offenders. In consequence, the Court determined that it would be "destructive and perhaps almost cruel now to impose a custodial sentence" but "only the passage of time and the events which have occurred since sentence lead us to draw back".

27.78   *Attorney-General's Reference Nos. 7–10 of 2000*[78] Four youths aged 16, three with previous convictions, made their way through a train, robbing two passengers and attempted to rob a third, their victims being other male youths aged 16–18 who were threatened with an imitation firearm, one being assaulted. Only one offender received a custodial sentence (four months), the others receiving community orders. Emphasising the prevalence of this type of offence, the Appeal Court stated that sentence should include an element of deterrence to discourage offenders and to protect the public. Even a first time offender should expect a period of custody for such an offence in a public place and a substantial term should be the norm. In this instance the offences were aggravated by the use of a gun and the manner of their behaviour towards the travelling public. Terms of six and 12 months were substituted.

Sexual offences

27.79   The first cluster of cases involve sexual abuse committed against a much younger child victim.

---

[78] (2000) 164 J.P. 475.

27.80 *Stone*[79] A boy aged 15 pleaded guilty to rape of a girl aged six, abuse having occurred over a considerable period at the home of foster-parents with whom they were both accommodated. In the light of earlier cases such as *Reeve* (1989) 11 Cr. App. R.(S.) 178 and *Browne* (1991) 13 Cr. App. R.(S.) 92 where sentences in the range of two to three years had been imposed, sentence of four years was reduced to 30 months, but the Appeal Court said that this should not be viewed as an immutable tariff. These decisions should not be taken to reflect the current sentencing climate.

27.81 *Gascoyne*[80] A male aged 17 pleaded guilty to indecent assault on a girl aged 15 months, committed while acting as her baby-sitter. While changing her nappy he had inserted his finger in her vagina, causing bleeding. He sought help in panic, claiming she had hurt herself falling from her cot. Reducing sentence from 42 months to two years, the Court noted that he had experienced an abusive upbringing and that the victim was so young that she was unlikely to have been distressed for as long as an older child. The important consideration was how to ensure he would not commit that type of offence again. Section 44 of CJA 1991 (see 27.32) was applied to extend licence on release.

27.82 *Craig D*[81] A boy aged 15 pleaded guilty to four instances of indecent assault of a girl aged four, committed on three occasions when he had acted as her baby-sitter. He had placed his finger in her vagina and anus and had placed his penis in her mouth. He had previously been cautioned for buggery of his sister aged 5 and brother aged 10 when aged 11/12. Upholding sentence of four years, the Court noted that he presented a serious, continuing danger to children, in the light of his failure to respond to earlier intervention. Though severe, his sentence was not manifestly excessive. A pre-sentence report had suggested that no treatment would be possible within the prison system and invited the court to make a supervision order so that he could receive treatment in the community, but the Appeal Court was informed that a sex offender programme was available at an establishment to which he would now be transferred.

27.83 *LH*[82] A boy aged 12 pleaded guilty to indecent assault on a girl aged seven, committed when he delivered a newspaper to her home, going upstairs to play with her and her brother. Their father discovered him lying on top of her on a bed, both unclothed. Sentence of 12 months detention was upheld, given the seriousness of the offence, causing psychological disturbance to the victim and much stress to her parents, and the appropriateness of a deterrent sentence, even in respect of an offender of that age.

Other cases represent instances of predatory sexual violence, broadly speaking—

27.84 *Brumwell*[83] A boy aged 14 pleaded not guilty to rape of a girl aged 14. Having been her boyfriend on an on-off basis for a month in the recent past, no sexual intercourse taking place, he entered her home while she was alone, attacking her and dragging her upstairs where he raped her by force, threatening to knife her if she complained. Noting that there was no mitigation whatever, other than his age, the Appeal Court reduced sentence from six to five years.

27.85 *Attorney-General's Reference Nos. 53–55 of 1995*[84] A girl aged 17 of previous good character pleaded guilty to false imprisonment and assault but was

---

[79] (1995) 16 Cr.App.R.(S.) 407.
[80] [1996] 2 Cr.App.R.(S.) 133.
[81] [1998] 2 Cr.App.R.(S.) 292.
[82] [1997] 2 Cr.App.R.(S.) 319.
[83] [1996] 1 Cr.App.R.(S.) 213.
[84] [1997] 1 Cr.App.R.(S.) 219.

convicted at trial of aiding and abetting rape and indecent assault. The victim, a girl aged 16 who was believed to have stolen a purse, was detained and subjected to prolonged indignities, including rape and attempted rape by male co-offenders, and this offender had tried to insert a pole in her anus. Sentence was increased from 42 months to six years.

27.86 *Jonathan W*[85] A boy aged 13 without previous convictions pestered a girl acquaintance aged 12, first placing his hand inside her clothing and touching her genitals and attempting to pull her clothing down. She resisted him. He then tripped her up and lay on top of her, simulating intercourse, causing her considerable distress. Following his plea of not guilty to indecent assault, he was sentenced to eight months s.53(3) detention but this sentence was quashed in favour of a supervision order. The Appeal Court noted that this was a gratuitous, persistent assault but indicated that "when the attacker is no more than a child, the overwhelming consideration is to do the best to assist him." Though recognising a clash between two different principles, the dilemma was resolved in this instance in favour of a community sentence considered desirable in the interests of trying to achieve the offender's personal development.

27.87 *Oldfield*[86] A youth aged 16 pleaded guilty to indecent assault of a young woman whom he seized from behind as she was walking home, pushing her to the ground, placing his hand inside her trousers and touching her vulva, so that she feared rape. Sentence was reduced from four to three years because the sentencer had incorrectly approached the case as if it were in effect attempted rape.

27.88 *SM*[87] A boy aged 14 at time of offence pleaded guilty to two offences of attempted rape. He had followed a young woman aged 18 as she walked home from a party late at night and, on the pretext of offering to help her to find a telephone box, led her to a quiet area where he made sexual advances which she resisted but in which he persisted through forcible indecent assault to the point of attempted penetration of her anus and then her vagina, stopping only when police intervened. At time of offence he was subject to a recently imposed conditional discharge for offences of indecency. Reviewing sentence of five years detention, the Appeal Court recognised that these were grave offences with aggravating features but was satisfied that the judge had adopted too high a starting point or had given insufficient credit for his guilty plea. The Court observed that "where a person of such a young age is guilty of grave offences there is a special need for permanent monitoring to be paid to the prospects for change and improvement as he matures." In this instance, the offender had been placed in a regional secure unit after his arrest where he had shown a marked improvement, dissociating himself from the more disruptive element and not posing any serious threat to discipline or security. He was managing his aggression and frustrations well. After his initial denial of guilt he was engaging in work on his sexually deviant behaviour and showing willingness to tackle his sexual offending.

27.89 *Attorney-General's Reference No. 61 of 1999*[88] A boy aged 14 pleaded guilty to indecent assault of a girl aged 12 who attended the same school. While she was walking home from school, he persuaded her to accompany him into some bushes where he asked her for sex which she refused. He forced his penis into her mouth, before withdrawing and ejaculating over her leg. Reviewing sentence of a supervision order for three years, the Appeal Court noted that this kind of

[85] [1999] 1 Cr.App.R.(S.) 488.
[86] [2000] 1 Cr.App.R.(S.) 73.
[87] [2000] 1 Cr.App.R.(S.) 188.
[88] [2000] 1 Cr.App.R.(S.) 516.

behaviour "causes concern and outrage to parents, particularly parents of young girls, and calls for a punitive sentence", in this case 12 months detention under s.53(3). However, noting that the offender was undergoing treatment at a clinic specialising in this kind of sexual misconduct, showing an appropriate level of commitment, and was also making efforts to advance his education, the Court determined that it would not be in the public interest to impose a short period of custody.

27.90   G.F.[89] a youth aged 17, engaged in robbery of a number of persons walking in a wooded area, approached a woman aged 36, threatened her with what appeared to be a meat cleaver (though this was in fact made of plastic), forced her to masturbate him then raped her. In the light of his early guilty plea and indications of remorse, his youth and "sad background", sentence of six years was reduced to four years, alongside a consecutive term of two years for robbery.

Violence

27.91   Youthful violence causes particular anxiety, as noted in *Attorney-General's Reference Nos. 60 and 61 of 1997*[90] (see 27.13), where the Court of Appeal stated—

> "It is generally and increasingly recognised that serious violence, particularly among the young, is a profoundly undesirable but ever more familiar feature of society, and all too prevalent."

Young people are seen as likely to resort to violence out of proportion to the triggering factors, perhaps when disinhibited by alcohol, and to use weapons carried out of bravado or to boost self-esteem or to impress other young people, with a poorly developed sense of the dangers thus risked. The most authoritative recent general guidance from the Court of Appeal was voiced in *Attorney-General's References Nos. 59, 60 and 63*[91] (see) where Lord Bingham C.J. stated—

> "When an offender, however young, deliberately inflicts serious injury on another there is a legitimate public expectation that such an offender will be severely punished to bring home to him the gravity of the offence and to warn others of the risk of behaving in the same way. If such punishment does not follow, public confidence in the administration of the criminal law is weakened and the temptation arises to give offenders extra-judicially the punishment that the formal processes of law have not given. When we speak of the public we do not forget the victim, the party who has actually suffered the injury, and those close to him. If punishment of the offender does little to heal the victim's wounds, there is little doubt that inadequate punishment adds insult to injury."

The first cluster of cases reflect the Appeal Court's approach to what can be broadly termed peer group violence.

27.92   *Attorney-General's Reference No. 28 of 1995*[92] A male aged 17 of previous good character pleaded guilty to wounding a young man aged 18 with intent, whom he confronted in the street, goaded into a fight, punching him then

---

[89] [2000] 2 Cr.App.R.(S.) 364.
[90] [1998] 2 Cr.App.R.(S.) 330.
[91] [1999] 2 Cr.App.R.(S.) 128.
[92] [1996] 1 Cr.App.R.(S.) 410.

stabbing him in the chest. He had admitted that he habitually carried a knife. Increasing sentence from 12 months to 30 months, the Appeal Court indicated that anyone carrying a "fearful weapon" who uses it aggressively must expect a substantial period of detention.

27.93 *McNeil*[93] A boy aged 15 had had a number of aggressive encounters with the victim, in which the victim had been at least equally active in maintaining the tension or raising the stakes. A fight was arranged after the police had broken up a violent clash between them and, as the victim approached him, the boy stabbed him with fatal consequences. Upholding a term of six years for manslaughter, the Appeal Court noted that he had every opportunity to desist and to leave the scene. He had been on bail at the time on offensive weapon charges.

27.94 *Baldwin*[94] A boy aged 15 pleaded guilty to wounding with intent. He had become angry when refused admission to a party. The police had been called and he had been escorted home. He then taped a knife to his arm and went out again. He accosted a youth carrying alcohol and when the victim refused to give him a can of beer, he stabbed him in the chest, causing a collapsed lung. The Appeal Court noted that he had been intent on causing trouble that night, going out again after being already in trouble with the police. However, in the light of his efforts to change his behaviour since the attack, as well as his plea and youth, sentence was reduced from five to four years, CYPA 1933, s.44(1) being cited in support.

27.95 *Attorney-General's Reference Nos. 60 and 61 of 1997*[95] Two girls aged 12, one of previous good character and the other with convictions for robbery and actual bodily harm, pleaded guilty to wounding with intent. The first had become involved in a fight with another girl, during which the other handed her a razor blade with which she slashed the victim's face causing a permanent scar. Supervision orders were replaced by detention terms of 12 and 18 months. An adult could expect five years and the lower terms reflected their youth as well as the usual "double jeopardy" factor. The Appeal Court indicated that the public interest demanded that the use of razor blades to inflict serious injury must be met by a custodial sentence. Though they were reported to have responded well to supervision, "the public would be outraged" if custody was not imposed. "The Court has to do all it can to deter persons, even children of this age, from behaving in this way."

27.96 *Haley*[96] Two girls persuaded the victim, a girl aged 13, to accompany them to a flat where the offender, a boy aged 12 with no previous convictions, and another boy, were waiting. She was subjected to a sustained beating, involving punches, kicks and burning with cigarettes, in a bid to force her to confess to theft of a social security benefit book, so that she suffered severe bruising, abrasions and burns, and her ordeal caused longer term psychological disturbance. Sentence of three years detention for wounding with intent, amounting to "torture", was upheld.

27.97 *Attorney-General's Reference No. 18 of 1998*[97] A youth aged 16 pleaded guilty to wounding with intent, having struck the victim, another youth, in the face with a brick in the course of an unprovoked fight, causing permanent scarring and minor loss of vision. Noting that he had sustained the attack after his victim had become helpless as a result of his injuries, and that the offence was committed while

---

[93] [1997] 1 Cr.App.R.(S.) 266.
[94] [1997] 2 Cr.App.R.(S.) 260.
[95] [1998] 2 Cr.App.R.(S.) 330.
[96] [1998] 2 Cr.App.R.(S.) 226.
[97] [1999] 1 Cr.App.R.(S.) 142.

he was on licence following an earlier custodial sentence, the Appeal Court increased sentence from 12 months to three years.

27.98   *Attorney-General's Reference Nos. 30 and 31 of 1998*[98] Two youths aged 16 pleaded guilty to wounding with intent, having participated in a group attack on a male victim of the same age. The first offender had jumped on the victim's head with both feet. The victim suffered severe head injuries and post-traumatic stress, needing psychological counselling. Sentences of eight months and four months were increased to 21 and 12 months. They were noted to have convincing remorse and to have given evidence against co-offenders at trial.

27.99   *Attorney-General's Reference No. 25 of 1998*[99] A youth aged 17 at time of offence denied causing grievous bodily harm with intent. In the course of a dispute with the victim aged 16, he struck him with a golf club that the victim had been carrying, causing a fractured jaw. Though acknowledging that sentence of 18 months detention was lenient, given the seriousness of the injury, the Appeal Court determined that it was not unduly lenient and did not increase the term. The Court gave credit for the offender's efforts in the eight months following the offence when he had completed a community service order, found work and obtained accommodation for himself and his pregnant girlfriend who had since given birth. This was "positive indication of his capacity to lead a law-abiding and responsible life" and he was now "a more mature person".

27.100   *Attorney-General's Reference Nos. 59, 60 and 63 of 1998*[1] The Appeal Court, led by Lord Bingham C.J., considered three separate incidents of s.18 wounding/GBH, to develop a consistent approach to sentence, giving general guidance on the factors affecting seriousness (see 27.91).

(i)   A youth aged 18 pleaded guilty to wounding with intent committed in an intoxicated state at a party. He threw an intact beer glass into the face of a boy aged 15 who had sought to pacify a confrontation between the offender and one of the victim's friends. The glass broke causing injuries which would result in permanent scarring. The experience had profoundly affected the victim's school performance. Sentence of 18 months was unduly lenient, a proper sentence being three years on a plea of guilty or four years after contested trial.

(ii)   Following a fist fight with another youth, a youth aged 16 attacked the victim with a bottle which he had apparently broken for the purpose, stabbing him in the armpit, causing life-threatening injuries leaving lasting disabilities and scarring. Sentence of a combination order with a compensation order was unduly lenient, an appropriate sentence in a contested case being five years.

(iii)   In the course of a fight with another boy following an incident at school, a youth aged 16 produced a folding knife and stabbed the victim in the back, inflicting a deep wound which penetrated the lung and causing severe internal bleeding. A supervision order with a specified activities requirement, made partly on the basis of five months spent on remand in a secure unit, was unduly lenient. A term of 54 months would have been appropriate after contested trial, or 42 months on guilty plea.

---

[98] [1999] 1 Cr.App.R.(S.) 200.
[99] [1999] 1 Cr.App.R.(S.) 351.
[1] [1999] 2 Cr.App.R.(S.) 128.

27.101 *L*[2] A young woman aged 17 admitted s.20 wounding, having become involved in an altercation with the male victim whom she thought was harassing her sister. During an attack initiated by the offender's two male companions, she stabbed him four times with an eight-inch lock knife, twice in the thigh and twice in the stomach. Rejecting her claim that she had "poked" the victim in response to provocation to make him go away, the Crown Court imposed 10 months detention and training, a term upheld on appeal.

The next group of cases is a miscellany of violence against members of the public, other than another young person, or the police.

27.102 *Attorney-General's Reference No. 51 of 1996*[3] A youth aged 17 approached a man in the street late at night, throwing a brick at him when he ran away, striking his head. When he re-encountered the victim later that night, he chased him then stamped on his head as he lay on the ground. He pleaded guilty to wounding with intent. Sentence of 12 months for this unprovoked attack was increased to three years, the Appeal Court indicating that four years could well have been the appropriate term.

27.103 *Robinson and McManus*[4] A youth aged 16 pleaded guilty to grievous bodily harm with intent, having challenged and attacked a man in the street at night, kicking then stamping on his head. Sentence was reduced from five to four years in the light of his remorse.

27.104 *Cassidy*[5] A boy aged 14 pleaded guilty to grievous bodily harm with intent to resist arrest, having driven a car at a police motorcyclist, knocking him over so that his machine fell on him. His criminal record, including numerous offences of vehicle taking, was viewed as "appalling". Upholding sentence of five years s.53(3) detention, the Appeal Court stated that if young people "chose to indulge in an orgy of offending, particularly involving the taking and dangerous driving of motor vehicles, and if they go further and commit offences such as these, they must expect very severe punishment indeed."

27.105 *Attorney-General's Reference No. 69 of 1999*[6] A youth aged 16 pleaded guilty to wounding with intent, having stabbed a bus driver following a dispute over payment of his fare. He had aimed for the victim's ribs but inflicted a deep cut to the victim's arm which he had raised to protect himself. Overturning sentence of a two year probation order with an additional requirement of anger management training, the Court of Appeal noted that the offender was an isolated youth who had spent substantial periods of his upbringing in Pakistan, with consequent disruption to his education, and had lacked consistent parental guidance, but concluded that the judge (who had cited CYPA 1933, s.44 in opting to exercise leniency) had "allowed herself to be over-persuaded by the personal circumstances of the offender to an extent which blinded her to the requirements of the victim and the public in relation to offences of this kind". For such a serious attack on a vulnerable public servant, a term of 42 months was considered justified. He was thus given a substitute custodial term despite reports that he was maintaining "excellent" contact and achieving constructive work with the probation service.

27.106 *Attorney-General's Reference No. 75 of 1999*[7] A youth aged 17 swore at a man, a passing stranger, who had asked him to be less noisy. When the man then

---

[2] (2000) (noted in *JP* vol. 164, p. 715).
[3] [1997] 2 Cr.App.(S.) 248.
[4] [1998] 1 Cr.App.(S.) 72.
[5] [1996] 1 Cr.App.(S.) 278.
[6] [2000] 2 Cr.App.R.(S.) 53.
[7] [2000] 2 Cr.App.R.(S.) 146.

asked him not to swear in front of his young son, the offender attacked him, punching him several times in the head. The victim then found that he had also incurred a knife wound to his leg. Though noting that this s18 wounding involved a single stabbing to a comparatively less vulnerable part of the body, and that the perpetrator had no history of violent offending or of custodial sentencing, the Appeal Court determined that sentence of 15 months was inadequate and that the appropriate term would have been four years, following trial.

The last cluster of cases concern violence resulting in death and resulting sentencing for manslaughter, in four very different contexts.

27.107 *Swatson*[8] A youth aged 17 had been suspected of robbery. The victim demanded money, a share of the proceeds, threatening him with a gun. The offender subsequently shot him, having acquired a gun and a bullet-proof vest for the purpose of confronting him. He pleaded guilty. Sentence was reduced from 12 to nine years.

27.108 *Attorney-General's Reference Nos. 68 and 69 of 1996*[9] Two girls aged 12 and 13 became involved in a fight at a fairground. The victim, a girl aged 13, intervened. She was pulled off her balance then kicked as she lay on the ground, causing an unexpected but fatal haemorrhage. The Appeal Court observed that if regard were had only to the interests of the offenders, it would be recognised that they had learned their lesson and that prolonged incarceration would serve little to prevent further offending, since the risk in each case was assessed as low. However, balancing this against the need to respond to youthful violence, the Court concluded that their sentences of two years detention were lenient and that 30 months or three years would be justified. However, the Court opted not to interfere, noting that the chances of the kicks causing the victim's death were low.

27.109 *Holder*[10] A youth aged nearly 17 had been involved in a trivial dispute with another youth which was halted when police intervened. Shortly afterwards, with feelings still running high, the victim aged 15 was chased by a group including the offender, wielding sticks and bottles. When the offender caught up with the victim he stabbed him in the chest, fatally penetrating his heart. He denied the stabbing but was convicted of manslaughter. He had not previously served a custodial sentence and there were testimonials to his general good character and success on a college course. A term of nine years detention was upheld, given an adult 'tariff' of 10 to 12 years.

27.110 *Hamilton*[11] A youth aged 17 went to the home of his grandmother aged 83 to steal to gain funds to sustain his drug dependency. When she disturbed him he placed his hand over her throat to stop her screaming, causing death by strangulation. Noting that death was very quick and there had not been a sustained or repeated attack, and his subsequent efforts to overcome his drug problem, the Appeal Court reduced sentence from ten to eight years.

27.111 *Jeans*[12] Having attended a party held at a young person's parents home without their knowledge which had been terminated by police, the offender aged 16 took part in a street confrontation between two rival groups of youths, in the course of which he picked up a piece of wood. Without warning, he struck the

[8] [1997] 2 Cr.App.(S.) 140.
[9] [1997] 2 Cr.App.(S.) 280.
[10] see *Mills and Others* [1998] 2 Cr.App.R.(S.) 128 at 143.
[11] [1999] 1 Cr.App.R.(S.) 187.
[12] [1999] 2 Cr.App.R.(S.) 257.

victim in the face in the face with the wood, causing deep bruising and tearing away of his nasal septum. The victim lost consciousness through shock and he died a few days later in hospital. He pleaded guilty to manslaughter at re-trial. In the light of his youth, the "extremely unfortunate and, in medical terms, surprising consequence" of his assault, his deep shock and remorse for his conduct, his adverse background on the receiving end of violence from his step-father, a term of six years (based on a starting point of eight years) was replaced by one of four years, the starting point being considered too high.

Protection of the public criterion

27.112   The second and alternative ground justifying a custodial sentence is where the court is of the opinion.

> "where the offence is a violent or sexual offence, that only such a sentence would be adequate to protect the public from serious harm from him."[13]

It is thus the successor to the now superseded criterion justifying custody for a young offender under CJA 1982, s. 1(4A)(b), that "only a custodial sentence would be adequate to protect the public from serious harm from him". Whereas the earlier version of the criterion was non-specific in regard to the nature of the offence, the offence must now be either a violent or sexual offence within the definitions provided by PCC(S)A 2000, s.161. Use of this justification for a custodial sentence is likely to be highly exceptional in youth courts and cases raising public protection concern are much more likely to be sent the Crown Court for trial.

Violent offence

27.113   This is defined by s.161(3) as "an offence which leads, or is intended or likely to lead, to a person's death or to physical injury to a person, and includes an offence which is required to be charged as arson (whether or not it would otherwise fall within this definition)". This definition does not require that the injury caused or risked need be of a serious nature. The expansive drafting would appear to include such offences as dangerous driving, supplying dangerous drugs and more serious public order offences. On the other hand, it excludes illness or psychological harm committed by "stalking", and offences of harassment under the Harassment Act 1997, ss.2 or 4.

27.114   The ambiguity of the definition was highlighted in two decisions by differently constituted courts of the Court of Appeal considering whether robbery at knifepoint, where the victim suffers no physical injury, is a "violent" offence. In *Murray*,[14] the Court, ruled not, finding it impossible to say what the offender would have done if the victim had resisted. In *Cochranel*,[15] the, Court ruled that it was a violent offence; it is not necessary to show that injury was a necessary or probable consequence and the act could have led to physical injury if a struggle ensued. It seems difficult to distinguish the two cases on their facts and the view in *Cochrane* may seem the more persuasive. Difficulty also arises where an imitation or unloaded firearm is used.[16] As Thomas notes in his commentary on the latter case—

---

[13] PCC(S)A 2000, s.79(2)(b).
[14] [1994] Crim. L.R. 383.
[15] [1994] Crim. L.R. 382.
[16] *Touriq Khan* (1995) 16 Cr.App.R.(S.) 180 and *Palin* [1995] Crim. L.R. 435.

"An offence which is likely to cause fear or shock is not a violent offence unless it does unintentionally result in physical injury (if the victim injures himself in trying to escape, or if the intended victim injures the offender in an attempt to apprehend him, for example). In a case when no physical injury has occurred, it seems essential to establish that the offence was intended or likely to lead to physical injury, if necessary by a Newton hearing."

Sexual offence

27.115   This is defined more narrowly by reference to specific statutes and means an offence contrary to any of the following PCC(S)A 2000, s.161(2)—

    (a)   Sexual Offences Act 1956, except under ss. 30,31,33–36;

    (b)   Mental Health Act 1959, s. 128;

    (c)   Indecency with Children Act 1960;

    (d)   Theft Act 1968, s. 9 (burglary with intent to commit rape);

    (e)   Criminal Law Act 1977, s. 54;

    (f)   Protection of Children Act 1978;

    (g)   Criminal Law Act 1977, s. 1 (conspiracy to commit any of the offences in (a)–(f);

    (h)   Criminal Attempts Act 1981 (attempting to commit any of those offences);

    (i)   Inciting another to commit any of those offences.

Indecent exposure and outraging public decency are not offences within any of the specified statutes and so do not consititute a sexual offence for this purpose.

Protection from "Serious Harm"

27.116   This is defined by section 161(4) as "protecting members of the public from death or serious personal injury, whether physical or psychological, occasioned by further such offences committed by" the offender. Though s.79(2)(b) does not specify the degree of likelihood of future harm, the offender must present a substantial risk of offending that would cause such various harm.[17]

In the process of forming an opinion whether the public protection criterion is satisfied, the court must—

    (i)   obtain and consider a pre-sentence report before forming any such opinion s.81(1), though if the offence is triable only on indictment the court is not obliged to do so if of the opinion that a report is unnecessary (s.81(2);

    (ii)   take into account all such information about the circumstances of the offence (including any aggravating or mitigating factors) as is available to it s.81(4)(a)).

In addition, the court is at liberty to take into account any information about the offender which is before it (s. 81(4)(b)). There is thus no restriction on the use of

---

[17] *Crow and Pennington* (1995) 16 Cr.App.R.(S.) 409. See A. von Hirsch and A. Ashworth "Protective Sentencing under Section 2(2)(b). The criteria of dangerousness" [1996] Crim. L.R. 175–83.

information before the court. This was demonstrated in *Attorney General's Reference No. 4 of 1993 (Bingham)*[18] where the court took wide account of the offender's efforts to contact, pressurise and make sexual advances to a number of boys. Mitigating factors under s.158(1) will have less significance in circumstances where the protection of the public becomes the over-riding factor.

27.117   Clearly, the fact that an offence is "violent" or "sexual" does not preclude a non-custodial sentence. On the other hand, because the criterion is primarily based on the future risk posed by the offender, a custodial sentence may in rare instances be justified even if the instant offence is insufficiently serious to merit a custodial sentence under the "so serious" criterion. The nature and seriousness of the instant offence will clearly be a significant factor in the evaluation of risk but it is not essential to show that the offender has caused serious harm either through the present offence or in the past. In practice, cases which satisfy the public protection criterion of section 79(2)(b) will also satisfy the "so serious" criterion of section 79(2)(a) The practical impact of the public protection provision focuses upon section 80(2)(b) and the justification for imposing a longer than commensurate term of custody.

Length of sentence

27.118   Use of section 80(2)(b) (see 27.12) to impose a longer than commensurate term where this is considered necessary to protect the public from serious harm from the offender should be used with considerable caution, albeit that the exercise of this power, where the conditions set out are satisfied, is mandatory and not merely discretionary.[19] As Thomas[20] has argued, this significant power—

". . . is an extremely blunt instrument as the offender given such a longer sentence is not entitled to any special consideration under Part 2 of CJA 1991 (early release), and must serve at least half of the sentence before becoming eligible for release, even though the ceases to be dangerous during the sentence. It seems that the most sensible approach to the use of the power would be to confine it to cases where there is the clearest possible basis for inferring that the offender is dangerous, and in such cases allowing a sentence which is substantially longer than would be proportionate to the seriousness of the offence on the analogy of life imprisonment. It would be regrettable if the power were to be used rather casually, on the basis of slender evidence for inferring dangerousness, to justify sentences which are only marginally more severe than could be justified as commensurate sentences (under section 80(2)(a)). Such an approach would provide no significant degree of protection for the public in those cases where it is needed, and serve to confuse the difference in approach required by the two limbs of section 80(2)."

27.119   This power will be exercised in respect of young people only extremely rarely, in the Crown Court. Further consideration of the basis on which a longer-than-proportionate sentence should be imposed and the determination of length of such a term is thus not appropriate in this context and readers should refer to standard texts on sentencing. It is nevertheless worth noting the guidance offered by Lord Taylor C.J. in the leading case of *Crow and Pennington*[21] that in exercising

---

[18] [1993] Crim.L.R. 795.
[19] *Bowler* (1994) 15 Cr.App.R.(S.) 78.
[20] D. Thomas Commentary on *Robinson* [1993] Crim. L.R. 145.
[21] (1995) 16 Cr.App.R.(S.) 409.

this power account must be taken of the offender's age: "with younger offenders, protection of the public must be balanced against the possible added risk that may be presented on release from a crushingly long sentence".

27.120   In dealing with co-offenders, they should be assessed separately so that it may be legitimate to impose a longer than commensurate sentence on one but a commensurate sentence upon the other. In *Bestwick and Huddlestone*[22] a case of two young men involved in arson offences, the younger was assessed as a normal personality who enjoyed the excitement of fires but had no urge to light fires to experience that excitement. His co-offender was a seriously disturbed personality obsessed with lighting fires and likely to continue to set fire to property to gain excitement.

Extended sentence

27.121   PCC(S)A 2000, s85, reproducing the power originated by CDA 1998, s.58, gives a court passing sentence for a sexual or a violent offence (as defined by PCC(S)A 2000, s.161(2) and (3)—see 27.113 and 27.115) committed on or after 30 September 1998 (the date of initial implementation) to extend for the purposes of liability to early release licence any custodial sentence imposed. Power to specify extension of sentence in this respect is available irrespective of whether a longer-than-commensurate sentence is imposed under s.80(2)(b) (see 27.12) or a commensurate term is passed under s.80(2)(a). This provision can apply to young offenders only in respect of those receiving a sentence of detention under PCC(S)A 2000, s.91, and is thus outlined in that context at 29.30. By implication, this measure is available, in the case of young offenders, only to the Crown Court.

Custody on refusal to consent to community sentence

27.122   As indicated at 27.03, s.79(3) provides an exception to the threshold criteria of s.79(2), in instances where an offender refuses to express willingness to comply with the small number of disposals requiring that consent, thus frustrating the imposition of the non-custodial measure proposed by the court. Faced with this impasse, the court may resort to imposing a custodial sentence, even though the offence does not satisfy the "so serious" test. Though the court is required by s. 79(4) (see 27.124) to explain why it is imposing custody, the Act makes no reference to the basis for determining the length of sentence in circumstances where the offence does not otherwise fall within the range of custody.

This provision is allied to the scope under PCC(S)A 2000, Sched. 3, paras. 4(2)(b) and 5(2)(b) for a court to impose a custodial sentence on re-sentencing an offender who has wilfully and persistently failed to comply" with the requirements of a community order regulated by that Schedule, "notwithstanding anything in s.79(2)".

Procedural considerations

Legal representation

27.123   PCC(S)A 2000, s.83(2), superseding CJA 1982, s.3, restricts a court's power to impose a custodial sentence on an unrepresented young offender. Neither

---

[22] [1995] 16 Cr.App.R.(S.) 168.

a youth court in making a detention and training order nor the Crown Court in making a detention and training order or in passing a sentence of detention under PCC(S)A 2000, s.91 shall do so in respect of a person who is not legally represented unless he falls within the exception afforded by s.83(3). For this purpose, a defendant is legally represented if he has the assistance of counsel or a solicitor to represent him in the proceedings "at some time after he is found guilty and before he is sentenced": s.83(4).

PCC(S)A 2000, s.83

(3) This subsection applies to a person if either-

(a) he was granted a right to representation funded by the Legal Services Commission as part of the Criminal Defence Service but the right was withdrawn because of his conduct; or

(b) having been informed of his right to apply for such representation and having had the opportunity to do so, he refused or failed to apply.

Giving reasons for custody

27.124   PCC(S)A 2000, s.79

(4) Where a court passes a custodial sentence, it shall—

(a) in a case not falling within subsection (3) above, state in open court that it is of the opinion that either or both of paragraphs (a) and (b) of subsection (2) above apply and why it is of that opinion; and

(b) in any case, to explain to the offender in open court and in ordinary language why it is passing a custodial sentence on him.

(5) A magistrates' court shall cause a reason stated by it under subsection (4) above to be specified in the warrant of commitment and to be entered in the register.

The working reality of CJA 1991, s.1(4), the predecessor of s.79(4) was clarified by the Court of Appeal in *Baverstock*[23] Lord Taylor CJ indicated that (a) and (b) should not normally be a two-stage process—

". . . the judge should be able at one and the same time to explain in ordinary language the reasons for his conclusions and tell the offender why he is passing a custodial sentence. When complying with this second requirement, however, the judge will be addressing the offender directly and if, in complying with subsection 4(a), he has not used ordinary language, it will be necessary for him to go on to do so in order to comply with subsection (4)(b) . . . the precise words used by a judge are not critical. The statutory provisions are not to be treated as verbal tightropes for judges to walk. Given that the judge's approach accords with the effect of the statutory provisions, this court will not be sympathetic to appeals based on fine linguistic analysis of the sentencing remarks."

Though a magistrates' court is required to record on the warrant of commitment and in the court register its reason for passing a custodial sentence (s.79(5)), it is not required to record its reasons for determining the length of the sentence.

---

[23] [1993] 1 W.L.R. 202.

Giving reasons for longer than commensurate term

27.125   PCC(S)A 2000, s.80

(3) Where the court passes a custodial sentence for a term longer than is commensurate with the seriousness of the offence, or the combination of the offence and other offences associated with it, the court shall—

(a) state in open court that it is of the opinion that subsection (2)(b) above applies and why it is of that opinion; and

(b) explain to the offender in open court and in ordinary language why the sentence is for such a term.

Effect of time spent on remand on length of sentence

27.126   Further to the provision of CJA 1967, s. 67 that the length of any custodial sentence imposed on an offender shall be treated as reduced by any relevant period spent in police detention or prison custody, section 67(1A)(c) specifies that the following also counts for that purpose—

"any period during which, in connection with the offence for which the sentence was passed, he was remanded or committed to local authority accommodation by virtue of an order under CYPA 1969, s.23 . . . and in accommodation provided for the purpose of restricting liberty."

27.127   Thus time so spent is treated as having been served for the purpose of determining whether the offender has served a half or other portion of his or her sentence for the purposes of early release provisions, as detailed below in regard to detention under PCC(S)A 2000, s.91 see 29.34. However, in respect of a detention and training order, time spent in custody or secure remand must be taken into account in determining the length of the order and s.67 does not apply in determining the time to be served during the custodial element of sentence (see 28.17).

CHAPTER 28
Detention and Training Orders

28.01   The detention and training order, introduced by the Crime and Disorder Act 1998, ss.73 to 79 and governed now in slightly revised terms by PCC(S)A 2000, ss.100 to 107, has replaced detention in a young offender institution as the primary custodial sentence for young offenders and is the only custodial sentence available to a youth court. It is designed as a rationalised generic measure across the entire young offender age range in place of what the White Paper *No More Excuses*[1] described as a "chaotic and dysfunctional" approach to custodial sentencing in youth justice, earlier castigated as an "incoherent potpourri of custodial facilities".[2] It also supersedes the short-lived secure training order for 12- to 14-year-olds, introduced by the Criminal Justice and Public Order Act 1994, ss.1 to 4, and brought into practical effect only in April 1998. However, detention for grave crimes, long governed by CYPA 1933, s.53 and now by PCC(S)A 2000, s.91, continues unaffected. This new sentence came into operation on April 1, 2000. Sentence of YOI detention has since been abolished by CJCSA 2000 s.61, as a rationalisation of the prison estate for young adult offenders, thus making more complex the provisions governing the interplay between the two kinds of sentence that can occur when young offenders attain adulthood in the course of overlapping proceedings.

POWER TO MAKE A DETENTION AND TRAINING ORDER

28.02   This power is available to a youth court or the Crown Court, in accordance with PCC(S)A 2000, s.100(1). This provision specifies that, subject to any liability to—

(i)   detention at Her Majesty's pleasure (PCC(S)A 2000, s.90), or

(ii)   detention on conviction of "certain serious offences" (commonly known as "grave crimes") under PCC(S)A 2000, s.91, or

(iii)   custody for life on conviction of any offence that incurs a fixed sentence of life imprisonment (PCC(S)A 2000, s.93) (also repealed by CJCSA 2000),

where a child or young person is—

(a)   convicted of an offence which is punishable with imprisonment (in the case of a person aged 21 or over), and

(b)   the court is of the opinion that either or both of the threshold criteria specified by PCC(S)A 2000, s.79(2) (see 27.03) apply, or the defendant falls within the provisions of s.79(3) (failure to consent to certain community sentencing proposals—see 17.12),

---

[1] *No More Excuses: A New Approach to Tackling Youth Crime in England and Wales* (Home Office, London, 1997) Cm. 3809, para. 6.2.

[2] Labour Party, *Tackling Youth Crime: Reforming Youth Justice* (Labour Party, London, 1996).

the sentence that the court shall pass is a detention and training order: PCC(S)A 2000, s.100(1). This order is a "custodial sentence" (s.76(1)(e)) and hence the provisions of ss.79 to 82, dealing with restrictions on the imposition of, the length of and the procedural requirements for such sentences, and the additional requirements in respect of mentally disordered offenders, apply. Though a custodial sentence, the order is unique in that it combines a period in custody removing liberty with a subsequent period of supervision of equal length restricting liberty. Thus an ten month detention and training order sentence has heavier impact than a YOI detention (now, under CJCSA 2000, replaced by imprisonment) sentence of the same length, affecting liberty for the full period rather than a de facto eight months applicable to a YOI/imprisonment term subject to three months supervision after release. Authoritative judicial guidance is still awaited as to the extent to which the court should bear this in mind when determining the appropriate commensurate length of detention and training. These issues arise in respect of potential disparity between co-defendants of different ages, as discussed below at 28.27. Following *Danga*,[3] where a young offender is aged 17 at time of convcition but has attained the age of 18 by time of sentence, he falls to be sentenced as a 17 year old to a detention and training order, not to the custodial sentence that normally applies to his actual age (YOI, or imprisonment following the abolition of YOI sentencing under CJCSA 2000) (*Cassidy*[4] where the judge had mistakenly assumed that his sentence of detention and training was converted into a YOI sentence and so failed to take account of the time spent on remand in custody in determining length of sentence—see 28.17).

Definition of the Order

28.03   A detention and training order is defined by PCC(S)A 2000 s.100(3) as: "an order that the offender in respect of whom it is made shall be subject, for the term specified in the order, to a period of detention and training followed by a period of supervision." Each element comprises one-half of the total term of the order, subject to special scope in certain instances for early or delayed release (see 28.36 *et seq.*). The post-custodial phase of supervision is thus integral to the order, rather than having the appearance of an afterthought or additional liability as can be the interpretation of the provision for supervision following a sentence of detention in a young offender institution under the early release provisions of CJA 1991, s65. The integrated nature of detention and training reflects a commitment to greater continuity between the institutional and community phases of the sentence experience.

Qualifying Criteria

28.04   The sentence is subject to the same generic statutory criteria governing other custodial sentences, but with certain additional criteria for defendants aged under 15, as specified by s.100(2).

PCC(S)A 2000, s.100

(2)   A court shall not make a detention and training order—

    (a)   in the case of an offender under the age of 15 at the time of the conviction, unless it is of the opinion that he is a persistent offender;

---

[3] [1992] Q.B. 476.
[4] *Cassidy, The Times*, October 13, 2000.

(b) in the case of an offender under the age of 12 at that time, unless-

    (i) it is of the opinion that only a custodial sentence would be adequate to protect the public from further offending by him; and

    (ii) the offence was committed on or after such date as the Secretary of State may by order appoint.

(4) On making a detention and training order in a case where subsection (2) above applies, it shall be the duty of the court (in addition to the duty imposed by section 79(4) above) to state in open court that it is of the opinion mentioned in paragraph (a) or, as the case may be, paragraphs (a) and (b)(i) of that subsection.

Defendants aged under 15: 'Persistent Offender'

28.05 The statute does not provide a definition of persistence for the purpose of s.100(2)(a). There is no equivalent of s.1(5) of the Criminal Justice and Public Order Act 1994 which specified that to be eligible for a secure training order a young offender had to have been convicted of three or more imprisonable offences and either to have breached a supervision order or to have committed an imprisonable offence while subject to such an order. It is thus at the discretion of the court to determine whether the defendant meets the criterion. Home Office[5] guidance reminds courts of the definition of "persistent young offender" used to identify those to be dealt with under fast-tracking arrangements—having been convicted of a recordable offence on three or more occasions and committing another offence within three years[6]—but adds "while courts may wish to bear this in mind in approaching the sentencing of 12–14-year-old offenders, they are not bound by it in considering whether . . . they are dealing with a persistent offender".

28.06 The meaning of the term received early attention from the Court of Appeal in *Smith*[7] where a boy aged 14 without previous convictions faced sentence for three offences of robbery, two involving an offensive weapon and one false imprisonment. These had been committed in two episodes within the space of 24 hours against three other boys who were stopped in the street and bullied into handing over items, in one instance the victim being terrorised and physically abused. The Court was satisfied that this course of conduct qualified him as a "persistent offender". The Court reached the same decision in *Charlton*[8] where a boy aged 14 on bail in respect of allegations of burglary and allowing himself to be carried in a vehicle taken without consent had committed two further burglaries and an aggravated vehicle taking. He asked for seven further matters to be taken into consideration. Appealing against a 12 month detention and training order, the defence pointed out that he did not meet the definition of a "persistent offender" as provided in the "fast track" Circular.[9] The Court rejected this argument, indicating that "persistence" is a matter to be determined on the facts of the individual case, not by reference to a government circular. Here, he had burgled and then done it again, more than once. He thus satisfied the criterion specified in CDA 1998, s.73(2)(a), as then governed detention and training orders. Consideration of a defendant's persistence allows a court to have regard to any offence for

---

[5] Home Office, Lord Chancellor's Dept. & Youth Justice Board (March 30, 2000) *The Detention and Training Order* (Home Office, London, 2000), para. 6.
[6] Home Office (October 15, 1997) *Tackling Delays in the Youth Justice System*, Annex C (Home Office, London, 1997) (see 12.51).
[7] [2000] Crim. L.R. 613.
[8] *The Times*, October 11, 2000.
[9] See n. 6.

which the offender has been cautioned or, by implication, reprimanded or warned.[10] To establish persistence it is not necessary that the offender "should have been committing a string of offences either of the same or a similar character or that his failure to address his offending arose by his failure to comply with previous orders".[11]

28.07   These decisions suggest quite a wide interpretation of 'persistence' with the potential for frequent use of this form of custodial sentence for children aged under 15. The Court in *Smith* appears to have been influenced by the seriousness of the offences, especially the second episode but "seriousness" is a different dimension of offending. If an offence is very serious but is the sole instance of the defendant's offending then it is difficult to see how the offender aged under 15 could qualify for a detention and training order. This does not preclude the passing of a sentence of detention under PCC(S)A 2000, s.91, provided that the offence is a grave crime qualifying for such a sentence.[12] There is nothing to stop the court imposing a term of 24 months or less if this is considered the appropriate term, there being numerous precedents for making shorter sentences of section 53(3) detention on under 15s for whom YOI detention has not been available under pre-CDA 1998 law (see 29.15). In *Smith* the Court determined that a section 53(3) term of three years was too long and substituted 24 months detention and training. It would have been open to it to make a section 53(3) (s.91) order for that period. It happened to be in the appellant's interests in *Smith* to be regarded as a "persistent offender" as he wished to be treated as eligible for detention and training, so perhaps the issue of "persistence" was not given the attention it deserved. Thomas[13] has speculated whether it might be valid to impose a s.91 detention sentence of less than two years in circumstances where the sentencer considers that the proper term for an offence to be one other than other than one of the terms of DTO permissible under s.101(1) (see 28.12).

Defendants aged under 12

28.08   The power to pass this sentence upon defendants aged 10 to 11 has not been brought into force and no date has been set for this initiative. Extension to this age group will require an affirmative resolution by Parliament. If and when implemented, the effect will be that before a detention and training order can be passed on a defendant aged under 12, the court must be satisfied that the two criteria, under section 100(2)(a) and under section 100(2)(b)(i), apply. The latter provision does not incorporate any reference to the seriousness of the potential offending—there is no reference to protection from "serious harm", for example.

Explanations and Statements in Open Court

28.09   When passing a detention and training order, the court must comply with the following "open court" procedural requirements—

(a)   stating that it is of the opinion that either or both of the criteria in s.79(2) apply: s.79(4)(a);

---

[10] *AD* [2000] Crim. L.R. 867.

[11] *DB* [2001] Crim. L.R. 50. However, the persistence test will not necessarily be satisfied merely because the offender has committed more than one offence, particularly where the offences vary significantly in nature: *JD* (2000, unreported, 2000/5005/Z4). See N. Stone (2001) "Detention & Training Orders for Under-15 Year Olds" *Youth Justice,* 1 (forthcoming).

[12] *Jenkins-Rowe and Glover* [2000] Crim. L.R. 1022, in which a s.91 term of 15 months was imposed for a robbery on a 14-year-old boy with no criminal record.

[13] In a commentary on *Jenkins-Rowe and Glover,* n. 12.

(b) explaining to the offender why it is passing a custodial sentence: s.79(4)(b);

(c) stating that it is of the opinion that the defendant is a persistent offender: s.100(4).

Defendant subject to YOI Detention

28.09 During the period of transition following implementation of the detention and training order, the situation may arise that a defendant receiving a detention and training order is serving a sentence of YOI detention imposed under CJA 1982 s.1B before implementation. Such sentences continue in force. In such instances, section 106(2)(a) provides that if the offender has been released from YOI the new sentence takes immediate effect, whereas if the offender remains in custody the court has the discretion under section 106(2)(b) to order that detention and training takes effect immediately or at the point of release from YOI. If the offender has been released but has returned to custody under PCC(S)A 2000, s.116 following a further offence committed before expiry of the full term of sentence, their liability to complete their s.116 order takes precedence over s.106(2)(a).[14]

Re-Sentencing following Breach of Community Order

28.10 An offender sentenced to one of the following orders—

(i) reparation order

(ii) action plan order

(iii) supervision order

(iv) attendance centre order—

who returns to court in breach proceedings and is dealt with afresh for the original offence must be dealt with in any manner in which he could have been dealt with by the court which made the order if the order had not been made. In consequence, the offender may receive a detention and training order even though he has attained the age of 18. Section 106(6) (as amended by CJCSA 2000, Sched. 6 para. 166) specifies in this instance that "the person shall be treated as if he had been sentenced to imprisonment for the same term".[15] This may advantage the offender in two ways. If the term of detention and training is for nine months, the effect on "conversion" is that he is released at the halfway point and is then subject to supervision for three months under CJA 1991 s.65(3). Secondly, if the offender has spent time in custody on remand it would appear that he has this taken into account twice, once in the determination of the appropriate term of detention and

---

[14] Conversely, PCC(S)A 2000, s.106(1) specifies that where a court passes a sentence of YOI detention on an offender who is subject to a detention and training order, the sentence shall take effect as follows: if the offender has been released from detention, on the day on which it is passed; otherwise, the court has discretion whether to order that the sentence of YOI detention takes effect that day or at the time when the offender would otherwise have been released from the detention phase of his earlier sentence. Section 106(1) is repealed by CJCSA 2000 Sched. 8 as part of the abolition of sentence of YOI detention but does not appear to have been replaced by any provision relating to young adult offenders sentenced to imprisonment while still subject to a DTO.

[15] As *Cassidy* (at 28.02) demonstrates, s.106(6) applies only on re-sentence and does not serve to convert an initial sentence of detention and training passed on an 18 year old who was aged 17 at time of conviction into a prison sentence.

training under s.101(8) (see 28.17) and again in the calculation of actual time to be served in YOI or prison.

Contempt of Court and Default

28.11 Power to impose detention for default or contempt under PCC(S)A 2000, s.108 applies only to persons aged at least 18. As a community rehabilitation order may not be imposed for contempt (*Palmer*,[16] which appears also to exclude a community punishment order or any other community sentence, the only available sanction for contempt would appear to be a fine.

The Sentence Term

28.12 The detention and training order is unique as a custodial sentence in that s.101(1) specifies a number of periods for which the order may be imposed—

> (1) Subject to subsection (2) below, the term of a detention and training order made in respect of an offence (whether by a magistrates' court or otherwise) shall be 4, 6, 8, 10, 12, 18 or 24 months.

This feature of the sentence creates various complications as outlined below.

Maximum Term

28.13 Though the maximum term is one of 24 months, this power is limited by s.101(2) which specifies that the term "may not exceed the maximum term of imprisonment that the Crown Court could (in the case of an offender aged 21 or over) impose for the offence". In practice, this limitation has effect only in respect of summary only offences, for which the Crown Court can normally impose a maximum term of six months imprisonment. As a consequence, the maximum term of detention and training that may be imposed for a summary offence is six months. The offence of failing to surrender to custody (Bail Act 1976, s.6(1) and (2)) provides one exception to this rule because it carries a maximum penalty at Crown Court of 12 months imprisonment. As a consequence, a youth court could, in theory at least, impose 12 months detention and training for such an offence.

28.14 The limits on the powers of a magistrates' court to impose imprisonment or, formerly, detention in a young offender institution contained in PCC(S)A 2000, s.78(1) and the Magistrates' Courts Act 1980, s.133 (six months for a single offence or an aggregate of 12 months for more than one either way offence dealt with by consecutive terms) do not apply, because a detention and training order is neither of these kinds of sentence. The validity of this interpretation was confirmed by the Divisional Court in *Medway Youth Court, ex p. A*.[17] Though *ex p. A*. concerned the legality of a secure training order for 12 months, the Court indicated that it was "completely clear" that the justices would be able to impose a detention and training order up to the maximum of two years. This was clear because CDA 1998 abolished the power to commit a defendant aged under 18 to the Crown Court for sentence under MCA 1980 s.37 (see 13.03), thus indicating that there was no presumption that the old restrictions on magistrates' powers would continue to apply. As added reinforcement of this change in youth court powers, the 2000 Act includes the words "whether by a magistrates' court or otherwise", thus resolving

---

[16] (1992) 13 Cr.App.R.(S.) 595.
[17] [2000] 1 Cr.App.R.(S) 191.

any residual uncertainty in this regard. As a consequence, a youth court may pass a sentence entailing a custodial element of 12 months (or even longer if that element is extended for a trainee (see 28.38)) for a single indictable offence.

28.15 As Thomas[18] points out in a commentary on *ex p. A.*, this provision may conflict with the European Convention on Human Rights. Because an 18–year-old cannot be sentenced to more than six months YOI detention for a single offence without having the right of electing trial at Crown Court, a 17–year-old receiving 24 months detention from a youth court "may well consider that his rights to a fair trial (guaranteed by Article 6 of the Convention) are substantially less" than those of the young adult with whom he may well be serving sentence in the same institution. Secondly, "there seems to be an argument for saying that a juvenile who can receive the same sentence as an older defendant, but with fewer procedural safeguards ... may claim their rights under Article 6 have been subject to discrimination in contravention of Article 14".

Minimum Term

28.16 The minimum period for which a detention and training order may be made is four months, because two months' detention is considered to be the minimum period allowing constructive work to be undertaken with some prospect of reducing the likelihood of re-offending by the trainee. As a consequence, a detention and training order cannot be imposed where the maximum term for the offence, in the case of an offender aged 21 or over, is less than four months imprisonment, *e.g.* obstructing a police officer or indecent exposure. Terms less than four months cannot be imposed consecutively so as to aggregate four months or longer.[19]

Time on Remand

28.17 Whereas time spent in custody on remand normally counts towards the time to be served before release from a custodial sentence, under CJA 1967 s.67 (see 27.126), and is ignored for the purposes of sentencing, detention and training orders are unique in requiring courts to take account of custodial remand time in determining the length of the order, as specified by s.101(8). The purpose is to ensure that a young offender receiving this sentence actually undertakes a purposeful training experience and is not released quickly before any meaningful work can be completed because of the calculation of remand time. The Joint Circular *The Detention and Training Order*[20] indicates that "the YOT should be able to advise on time spent in custody on remand". Not surprisingly, this measure has generated a number of early appeals by offenders aggrieved that they have been given either insufficient or no credit for their time on remand.

PCC(S)A 2000, s.101

(8) In determining the term of a detention and training order for an offence, the court shall take account of any period for which the offender has been remanded in custody in connection with the offence, or any other offence the charge for which was founded on the same facts or evidence.

[18] [1999] Crim. L.R. 915.
[19] *Kent Youth Court, ex p. Kingwell* [1999] 1 Cr.App.R.(S.) 263.
[20] Home Office, Lord Chancellor's Department & Youth Justice Board (February 9, 2000), para. 1.10 (Home Office, London, 2000).

28.18   As Thomas[21] has identified, this creates difficulties where courts are dealing with groups of young co-defendants, some of whom may be sentenced to imprisonment because they are aged 18 or older, some to longer term detention under PCC(S)A 2000, s.91, and some to detention and training orders.

> "It will force courts . . . to make a distinction in terms of the respective sentences to reflect the fact that time on remand will be deducted automatically from the first two sentences but not from the detention and training order. This is likely to give the appearance of unwarranted disparity to those unfamiliar with these provisions."

Where a court proposes to make detention and training orders in respect of an offender for two or more offences, s.101(9) specifies that subsection (8) shall not apply but instead—

> In determining the total term of the detention and training orders it proposes to make in respect of the offender, the court shall take account of the total period (if any) for which he has been remanded in custody in connection with any of those offences, or any other offence the charge for which was founded on the same facts or evidence.

28.19   For the purposes of s.101(8) and (9), the following count as time spent on remand in custody (s.101(11) and (12))—

(a) police detention under the Police and Criminal Evidence Act 1984 or the Prevention of Terrorism (Temporary Provisions) 1989;

(b) remand or committal to custody by court order;

(c) remand or committal to local authority accommodation under CYPA 1969, s.23 and "placed and kept in secure accommodation";

(d) remand, admittance or removal to hospital under the Mental Health Act 1983, ss.35, 36, 38 or 48.

28.20   In *Haringey Youth Court, ex p. A*[22] the Divisional Court expressed concern that courts were deploying detention and training orders without inquiring what time had been spent on remand. Laws L.J. indicated that where a youth court intends to make a detention and training order it should indicate that intention in open court before retiring, so that the period spent in custody can be ascertained and properly taken into account in sentencing. However, in *Inner London Crown Court, ex. p. I*[23] decided on the same day and with the same composition, the Divisional Court interpreted CDA 1998, s.74(5) (preceding s.101(8) under the 1998 Act) to impose a duty to take account of remand time a "and not to reflect it inevitably in some specific way in the sentence passed. It does not provide for a one-to-one discount." Laws L.J. added that where the remand time had been considerable this ought to make a difference, persuading the court to pass a lower sentence, but where, as in the present case, the time had been very short (less than 24 hours) it is open to the sentencing court to determine that this should make no

---

[21] D.Thomas (1998) Annotation to Crime and Disorder Act 1998, s.74, *Current Law Statutes*, 37–81.
[22] *The Times*, May 30, 2000.
[23] *The Times*, May 12, 2000, approved in *B* [2000] Crim. L.R. 870.

difference to sentence. See also the case of *Fieldhouse and Watts*, noted below at 28.22).

As regards the fit or otherwise between the requirement to take account of remand time and the need for a detention and training order to be of a permitted length, see below at 28.25.

Permissible Terms

28.21 The requirement of s.101(1) that a court imposing a detention and training order for a single offence (or concurrent detention and training orders for more than one offence) must select one of seven permissible lengths of order has been criticised by Thomas[24] for "creating difficulties where a court has to deal with a number of defendants and wishes to distinguish between them according to their culpability, or wishes to give credit for an early plea of guilty" (in accordance with what is now PCC(S)A 2000, s.152—see 11.22). Further problems in this respect occur in the context of taking account of time spent on remand. As Thomas notes: "If the court has decided that the appropriate term of an order is 18 months but the offender has spent seven weeks in custody on remand, the court must make an order either for 12 months, giving far too much credit, or for 18 months, giving no credit at all." Home Office guidance[25] states—

> "When deciding the term of a detention and training order, the court is not required to make a precise calculation of remand time in custody and deduct that specific period from the order. The expectation is that the court will reach an overall judgement about the length of the term which it considers appropriate in all the circumstances of the case, taking account of the time spent on remand in custody."

28.22 With respect, this clarification does not appear to solve the dilemma posed above. Subsequently, in *Fieldhouse and Watts*[26] the Court of Appeal has indicated that the requirement to "take account" of any period spent in custody, that time does not have to be refelected mathematically in the term of the order. Where a period of four weeks has been spent on custodial remand, a court might properly order a non-custodial sentence in a case where it had been considering an order of four months but if the length of order considered appropriate is 18 or 24 months, the court might make no deduction. In this instance, the judge had been correct not to reflect a weekend spent in custody on remand. The Court added that the way in which a court is able to reflect longer periods spent in custody on remand will depend on all the circumstances of the particular case, including the apparent impact of any of that period in custody and the relationship between that period and the DTO period otherwise contemplated.

Consecutive Terms

28.23 The possibility of consecutive terms of detention and training arises in two ways—

> (a) the offender is convicted of more than one offence for which he is liable to a detention and training order;

---

[24] See n. 21, 37–79.
[25] n. 5, para. 13.
[26] [2000] Crim. L.R. 1020. See also *Inner London Crown Court, ex p. N and S* [2000] Crim. L.R. 871.

(b) the offender already subject to a detention and training order is convicted
of one or more further offences for which he is liable to a detention and
training order.

Section 101(3) permits consecutive sentencing in either of these circumstances,
specifying—

> A court making a detention and training order may order that its term shall
> commence on the expiry of the term of any other detention and training order
> made by that or any other court.

28.24   This provision is subject to two restrictions.

- A court may not make a detention and training order where the effect
would be that he would be subject to detention and training orders for an
aggregate term exceeding 24 months: s.101(4). Where the aggregate term
of detention and training orders exceeds 24 months, the excess shall be
treated as remitted: s.101(5).

- Where the offender is already subject to a detention and training order
under which the supervision period has already begun, a court may not
order that a further detention and training order shall commence on the
expiry of the existing order: s.101(6). If the court wishes to make a fresh
detention and training order, the new order must take effect immediately.
In this instance, the court making the new order is not subject to the 24
month maximum rule contained in s.101(4) and (5), because of the special
provision of s.101(7) allowing the previous ("old") order to be disregarded for the purposes of determining the aggregate term.

PCC(S)A 2000, s.101(7)

(7) Where a detention and training order ("the new order") is made in
respect of an offender who is subject to a detention and training order
under which the period of supervision has begun ("the old order"), the
old order shall be disregarded in determining—

(a) for the purposes of subsection (4) above whether the effect of the new
order would be that the offender would be subject to detention and
training orders for a term which exceeds 24 months; and
(b) for the purposes of subsection (5) above whether the term of the
detention and training orders to which the offender would (apart
from that subsection) be subject exceeds 24 months.

28.25   Though s.101(1) specifies the ascending permissible periods for which a
detention and training order may be imposed, the making of consecutive orders can
have the effect of creating an aggregate term outside of the permissible periods. An
offender being sentenced for two offences both of which are liable to a detention
and training order may receive ten months for one offence and four months
consecutive for the second offence, totalling 14 months in aggregate and thus
undermining the logic of the limitation on the freedom of the court to impose the
term it sees fit for a single offence. On the other hand, if the court feels confined to
the periods specified by section 101(1) the consequent inflexibility could unduly
restrict the sentencer's discretion. This problem was posed in *Norris*[27] where an

---

[27] [2001] Crim. L.R. 48.

offender aged 16 serving a term of 10 months faced further sentence for an additional offence. The judge felt constrained to impose an additional eight months in order to comply with the sub-section (the alternative would have been an additional two months). However, the Court of Appeal resolved the matter pragmatically, declaring that the unfairness this caused the offender was a greater injustice than any disruption to the modular concept of section 101(1). A term of six months was substituted, thus making an aggregate term of 16 months.

28.26 *Treated as Single Term.* Consecutive terms of detention and training (and terms of detention and training orders which are wholly or partly concurrent) are treated as a single term under s.101(13) for the purposes of calculating release eligibility and liability to supervision if—

(a) the orders were made on the same occasion, or

(b) where the orders were imposed on different occasions the trainee had not been released/transferred to the community at any point since the first order was made.

Though the Act makes no reference to the possibility that may arise where a s.91 detention order is in place but the offender stands to be sentenced for an offence committed before that sentence was imposed for which he would otherwise be eligible for a detention and training order. This question arose in *Hayward and Hayward*[28] where a youth had been involved in an affray with his older brother but subsequently received a five year s.53(3) sentence. He was then sentenced to a 10-month DTO. Quashing sentence, the Court of Appeal agreed that this was an unlawful disposal as there was a gap in the law, not rectified by PCC(S)A 2000. The only available disposal was a nominal sentence or no separate penalty, even though this would doubtless cause the co-defendant (who received a term of 18 months for the affray) a deep sense of grievance.

Age and Disparity between Defendants

28.27 The problems which can arise where the Crown Court is dealing with two or more co-defendants, one of whom is aged under 18 and the other aged 18 or over, has already been noted (28.18) in the context of the different rules relating to the effect of custodial remand time and the lack of flexibility in relation to the permitted terms of detention and training. Nevertheless, in *Ganley*[29] the Court of Appeal indicated that a court faced with two such offenders must take into account remand time to avoid creating disparity. Another aspect of parity arose in *Cooper*[30] where it was argued that unfairness arose between two co-defendants, one aged 17 and the other 19. The trial judge had sentenced them both to nine months detention for unlawful wounding on the basis that their culpability was equal. However, the older offender was eligible for release on home detention curfew 60 days earlier than the half-way point of sentence when the younger offender would be released. The Court of Appeal noted that the implementation of detention and training orders would deal with this problem because the Secretary of State could utilise the provisions of section 102(4) allowing early release (see 26.36) to achieve

---

[28] [2001] Crim. L.R. 236.
[29] *The Times,* June 7, 2000.
[30] *The Times,* April 5, 2000. See also *Elsmore,* noted at *JP* (2001) vol. 165 at 235.

broad justice between co-defendants. However, use of s.102 in this case would have allowed this offender only one month additional freedom compared with 60 days available to his older companion. Further, as pointed out below, s.102(4) is intended to reward good progress, not to achieve aims such as sentencing parity between co-offenders.

PERIOD OF DETENTION AND TRAINING

28.28   The custodial element of a detention and training order is served "in such secure accommodation as may be determined by the Secretary of State or by such other person as may be authorised by him for that purpose": s.102(1). The Youth Justice Board has been authorised to undertake such determination and acts as the commissioning and purchasing body for all forms of secure accommodation, The period spent undergoing detention and training "shall be one-half of the term of the order": s.102(2). This provision is subject to adjustment to allow early or delayed release, as permitted by s.102(3) to (5).

"Secure Accommodation"

28.29   "Secure accommodation" is defined by s.107(1) to mean the following categories—

(a)   a secure training centre, *i.e.* a centre intended for the age group previously eligible for a secure training order, 12 to 14-year-olds (though two centres receive 12–16 year olds);

(b)   a young offender institution

(c)   "accommodation provided by a local authority for the purpose of restricting the liberty of children and young persons", *i.e.* secure accommodation;

(d)   accommodation provided for the purpose of (c) above under the Children Act 1989, s.82(5) (financial support by the Secretary of State);

(e)   "such other accommodation provided for the purpose of restricting liberty as the Secretary of State may direct", a residual category that includes any Prison Service accommodation other than a YOI. Home Office guidance[31] indicates that such accommodation may be necessary when an offender needs to be held temporarily after sentence while awaiting transfer to more appropriate accommodation.[32]

The various categories in aggregate comprise "the juvenile secure estate" for which the Youth Justice Board acts as commissioning authority.[33] Thirteen male Prison Service establishments have since been designated to receive boys, normally in

---

[31] n. 20, para. 1.12.
[32] See n. 34.
[33] In April 2000 the secure estate comprised 3286 places, distributed as follows: Prison Service (2850); Local Authority (316); secure training centres (three at 40 places each = 120). The anticipated national demand for 2000–01, based on Home Office projections is 3220 places (higher rate) or 2860 (lower rate), with boys aged 15–17 comprising the greatest demand at 2670 or 2360 places, with boys aged 10–14 at 400 (360); girls aged 15–17 at 120 (110) and girls aged 10–14 at 30 places: Youth Justice Board (2000) *Juvenile Secure Estate Commissioning Strategy 2000–03*. The Board's placement policy is outlined in Youth Justice Board (2000) *Juvenile Secure Estate Placement Strategy*.

dedicated units. These are: Ashfield, Brinsford, Castington, Feltham, Hollesley Bay, Huntercombe, Lancaster Farms, Only, Portland (deselected), Stoke Heath, Thorn Cross, Werrington, Wetherby. No women's establishment serves exclusively as a YOI for females but a number of women's prisons are also designated as YOIs, having wings or units where young offenders (juvenile and young adult) being placed in Prison Service establishments should normally be allocated.[34] Present policy aims to achieve allocation of all girls subject to detention and training orders to alternative secure unit accommodation as soon as sufficient placements become available but this is not considered to be a realistic prospect before 2003/4. In consequence, the Prison Service, in collaboration with the Youth Justice Board, is in the process of rationalising provision to create detention and training facilities in five establishments: Brockhill, Bullwood Hall, Low Newton, New Hall and Styal.

28.30 The principles and key features of regimes for juveniles in Prison Service establishements is detailed in *Prison Service Order 4950*,[35] informed by criticisms made by the Chief Inspector of Prisons[36] and the Utting Report,[37] making clear that this age group must be dealt with in a distinctively different way and must do more than simply contain young offenders.[38] The Order specifies that in order to enable personal development and to prevent re-offending, establishments must provide a range of purposeful activities in which each young trainee must spoend on average at least 30 hours per week. "There must be at least 10 hours unlock each day, rising to 14 hours as resources allow, which will include six hours of education, training or work activity".[39] A Child Protection Protocol is provided to strengthen arrangements for reducing the occurrence of significant harm to children in custody and responding more effectively to incidents or allegations of significant harm. Each establishment must have a Child Protection Committee and a Child Protection Co-ordinator, acting in partnership with a Social Services Department and in accordance with Area Child Protection Committee procedures. Overarching the Order, establishments are subject to the *Young Offender Institution Rules 1988*.[40]

28.31 Inspections of all commissioned secure accommodation are to be undertaken independently of the Youth Justice Board, though not by a newly created Inspectorate. Instead, inspections are to be carried out by multi-inspectorate teams drawn from the inspectorates of prisons, probation, social services, police, education, magistrates' courts and CPS, co-ordinated by the Board, with one inspectorate taking the lead role, so that the Prisons Inspectorate will take the lead on inspection of Prison Service establishments (see note of recent reports at 11.55 *et seq.*) while

---

[34] In *R. v. Accrington Youth Court and Others, ex p. Flood* [1998] 1 W.L.R. 156 where a 16-year-old serving 8 months YOI detention challenged her detention in HMP Risley, the practice of allowing female young offenders to be held routinely in adult prisons for allocation purposes following sentence was declared illegal. In consequence, sections of five women's prisons were designated as YOI provision.
[35] *Regimes for Prisoners aged under 18* P.S.I. Ref. No. 49/1999 (July 29, 1999); *Regimes for Young Women under 18* P.S.I. Ref. No. 09/2000 (February 11, 2000).
[36] H.M. Chief Inspector of Prisons (1997) *Young Prisoners: A Thematic Review* (London, Home Office).
[37] Department of Health (1997) *People Like Us: The Report of the Review of the Safeguards for Children Living Away from Home* (London, The Stationery Office).
[38] Though policy refers to provision for the "under 18s", in reality those subject to detention and training orders remain subject to the same regime beyond their 18th birthday. In consequence, offenders aged 15 may be sharing accommodation with trainees as old as 18 or even 19. Establishments will thus need to be vigilant in face of the potential disadvantages of such a mix to ensure the protection and development of vulnerable young people.
[39] n. 35, Chapter 8, para. 8.1.2.
[40] S.I. 1422/1988, as amended by the *Young Offender Institution (Amendment) Rules 2000* (S.I. 700/2000) which amends Rule 53 to remove the punishment of cellular confinement following a disciplinary hearing for trainees aged under 18 or serving the custodial period of a detention and training order.

the Social Services Inspectorate will lead in respect of local authority secure units and secure training centres.[41]

Home Office guidance[42] declares its aim "to improve the availability and spread of accommodation so that young offenders can be held reasonably close to home in a place which reflects their individual circumstances and needs".

28.32   *Clearing House.*   The Youth Justice Board operates a central clearing house or 'Call Centre' to resolve individual placement decisions and "secure accommodation provider units" are required to notify the Clearing House daily of their bed availability to assist in locating places. When a detention and training order is in prospect, the relevant YOT should notify the Clearing House, giving an initial indication of where the young person might be most appropriately placed, including an assessment of vulnerability. Home Office guidance[43] states: "15- to 17-year-old boys will generally be placed in the nearest available Prison Service accommodation for juveniles. For other categories a secure training centre or local authority secure place may be available."[44] Boys aged 15 and 16 who are "vulnerable" should, wherever possible, be placed outside Prison Service accommodation, and "non-vulnerable" boys who require a specialist programme such as a sex offender programme not available at their nearest YOI may be allocated further afield.[45] The YOT should inform the court of the custodial facility in which the young offender is to be placed for inclusion in the warrant of commitment. While the placement is not necessary for the pronouncement of sentence, the guidance Circular suggests: "It may be helpful for the case to be stood down briefly before sentence so that the YOT can confirm the placement with the Clearing House and the warrant can then be completed immediately on sentencing."

Management of the Detention and Training Phase

28.33   The detention and training order is intended to achieve integration of both elements of sentence, the custodial ("secure facility") and supervision phases. Practice procedures expect and require the active participation of the prospective supervising officer/key worker through the custodial phase and co-ordination of effort between custodial and community staff in seeking to ensure an integrated training opportunity for the young offender. The following account seeks to summarise the relevant provisions of The Home Office Circular *The Detention and Training Order*[46] and *The National Standards for Youth Justice*.[47]

28.34

- A YOT member should be allocated as supervising officer for the trainee within one working day of sentence. A "paired" YOT member who can act in the supervising officer's absence should be identified within five working days of initial allocation.

- Secure facility staff must undertake a reception interview with the trainee within one hour of his arrival to assess his needs and level of vulnerability,

---

[41] Youth Justice Board, *A Policy for Inspection* (YJB, London, 2000).

[42] n. 20, para. 2.100.

[43] n. 20, para. 2.107.

[44] Fuller details of the Youth Justice Board's placement strategy for sentenced young people are given in Chapter 29 at 29.36.

[45] Youth Justice Board (2000) *Juvenile Secure Estate Placement Strategy*, p. 5.

[46] n. 5 and 20.

[47] Youth Justice Board, London, 2000.

having regard to the risk of self-harm and of harm both from and to other trainees. The supervising officer should send all relevant written information about the trainee within one working day of sentence.

- The supervising officer must set up a planning meeting with secure facility staff to take place within five working days following admission. The offender's parents or primary carer must be encouraged to attend and contribute. If the offender is looked after by a local authority, the social worker must be invited to attend.

- The supervising officer must visit the trainee within five working days of sentence.

- The supervising officer, in partnership with secure facility staff, must draw up an initial training plan within five working days following admission, based on the planning meeting. The plan must cover the whole period of sentence, including the period of supervision.

- The training plan must be reviewed regularly and updated in the light of progress. The first review meeting must be held within one month of the initial planning meeting, and there should be further review meetings three-monthly thereafter.

- Trainees should be encouraged to attend planning and review meetings and should be given the opportunity to submit any written representations.

- Though it is not expected that trainees will be legally represented at planning and review meetings, "if a trainee wishes to involve a legal adviser or other personal advocate in such a meeting, he may do so".[48] (Such attendance may be appropriate if there is a possibility of an application to a court for delayed release—see 28.38.)

- Offenders subject to an order of 12 months or less must be visited by a YOT member at least monthly. For offenders subject to longer terms, the frequency of visits will be agreed as part of their training plan but must not be less frequent than every two months.

Compassionate Early Release

28.35 Section 102(3) authorises the Secretary of State to release a trainee "at any time" if "satisfied that exceptional circumstances exist which justify the offender's release on compassionate grounds". Home Office guidance[49] indicates—

"This is a wholly exceptional provision, intended for use where the trainee's circumstances rather than behaviour warrant some special action. It is not possible to set out the range of circumstances in which the provision might be needed. Examples might be where the trainee has a serious illness from which he or she is not expected to recover during the custodial part of the order, or where very difficult family circumstances following a bereavement reasonably require the trainee's presence for a prolonged period. In any such case it must be clear that the exceptional step of release from the custodial part of the

---

[48] n. 20, para. 2.87.
[49] n. 20, para. 2.97.

order is the only course, and that there is no risk of danger to the public and minimal risk of further offending during the remainder of the order."

The circumstances of any case considered appropriate for this form of release by the staff of the facility in which the trainee is held should be submitted in writing to the Young Offender Group in Prison Service Headquarters. Following such release, the young offender is subject to supervision in the community for the remainder of the term of the order.

Early Release for Good Behaviour and Progress

28.36 To encourage good behaviour and progress a limited degree of flexibility in determining the trainee's date of release is provided by s.102(4) for detention and training orders of at least eight months duration. There is no scope for release subject to Home Detention Curfew under CJA 1991 s.37A as that scheme applies only to those serving sentences of imprisonment or, formerly, YOI detention.

PCC(S)A 2000, s.102(4)

(4) The Secretary of State may release the offender—

    (a) in the case of an order for a term of 8 months or more but less than 18 months, one month before the half-way point of the term of the order; and

    (b) in the case of an order for a term of 18 months or more, one month or two months before that point.

28.37 The effect is that a trainee with a term of eight months is eligible for release after serving three months in custody while at the other end of the spectrum a trainee with a term of 24 months is eligible for release after serving 10 months. Decisions are taken by governors in the case of trainees held by the Prison Service and by the Young Offender Group at Prison Service Headquarters in other instances.

Though the statute provides no criterion for the exercise of this discretion, Home Office guidance[50] identifies that the scheme is "intended to recognise particularly good progress measured against the trainee's training plan". While consideration for this opportunity is to be built into sentence planning and management of every case, it is intended to be selectively earned rather than a routine expectation. Early release should not simply reflect a good disciplinary record. To demonstrate suitability, a trainee will need to—

- have achieved demanding objectives and targets set out in their training plan, giving particular priority to those addressing offending behaviour and factors associated with offending;

- have demonstrated a positive change in attitude and behaviour, as measured against the starting point of attitude and level of achievement at point of arrival;

- present no unacceptable risk to the public; and

- confirm his willingness to comply with the training plan for the community supervision part of sentence.[51]

---

[50] n. 20, para. 2.65.
[51] n. 20, para. 2.66.

Delayed Release

28.38   The counterweight to early release is the scope for a trainee to remain in custody beyond the halfway point of their order, as permitted by s.102(5) but only by order of a youth court. This is a serious sanction, extending the trainee's loss of liberty and it is anticipated that it will be used less frequently than the reward of early release.

PCC(S)A 2000, s.102(5)

(5)   If a youth court so orders on an application made by the Secretary of State for the purpose, the Secretary of State shall release the offender—

(a) in the case of an order for a term of 8 months or more but less than 18 months, one month after the half-way point of the term of the order; and

(b) in the case of an order for a term of 18 months or more, one month or two months after that point.

28.39   *Procedure.*   If the detention and training order was made by the Crown Court jurisdiction to hear the application nevertheless rests with a youth court. The statute does not specify which youth court has jurisdiction to hear such an application. Home Office guidance[52] suggests that application "should normally be made to a youth court for the trainee's home area". This has a logical appeal and will often mean that the issue is placed before the court that made the detention and training order. It also facilitates attendance by the trainee's previous defence representative. However, it may present problems in securing the attendance of the trainee who may be accommodated some distance away. If application is made to a youth court serving the area in which the trainee is accommodated, this may make attendance by a YOT representative from the home area a problematic demand. The Circular anticipates the issue of further guidance on this innovative process, still awaited. In consequence, it is understood that no trainee has yet been made subject to a late release order. The procedure is likely to be clarified and regulated by amendment to the *Magistrates' Courts Rules*.

28.40   *Basis of Application.*   Home Office guidance[53] indicates that to warrant an application it will be necessary to consider whether the trainee has "demonstrably and wittingly failed to achieve training plan objectives and targets" that were "meaningful for and reasonably achievable by him", despite opportunity, encouragement and support. Any application should set out a "clearly and carefully balanced argument for late release"[54] which—

- demonstrates how the trainee has made particularly poor progress against the objectives and targets set in the training plan;

- records the reviews undertaken of the plan and the decisions reached, with reasons;

- sets out how the additional period in custody would be used and what it would contribute to preventing further offending by the trainee.

---

[52] n. 20, para. 2.95.
[53] n. 20, para. 2.67.
[54] n. 20, para. 2.94.

Recommendations for late release "should not be used as a disciplinary sanction".[55] Regulations governing detention and training order regimes do not allow governors to award additional days in custody for breach of rules (see 29.43 for provisions in relation to s.91 detention) or to punish by cellular confinement (see n. 38). The onus is placed on staff to deal with indiscipline by challenge, influence and special programmes, as well as lesser sanctions, but many staff experience this challenge as an unfair restriction of their powers of control. The Chief Inspector of Prisons has reported that "current evidence is that this is appreciated by the most disruptive trainees, who taunt staff with their inability to take punitive action against those who assault them or smash up their cells".[56] Power to delay release is thus of particular potential significance, despite the caveat noted above, but trainees nearing the end of their custodial period may calculate that there is insufficient time for an application to be made to delay their release and may thus feel that they can breach discipline with impunity.

SUPERVISION PERIOD

28.41   The period of supervision begins with the offender's release, whether at the half-way point of the order term or otherwise, and ends when the term of the order ends: s.103(1). Section 103(2) provides that the Secretary of State is empowered to lay an order before Parliament requiring affirmative resolution to end the supervision period at an earlier point of the order but the Government has indicated that there is no current intention to alter the present provision.

Category of Supervisor

28.42   Section 103(3) to (5) specify that supervision may be undertaken by—

(a) a probation officer assigned to the petty sessions area within which the offender resides; or

(b) a social worker of the local authority social services department within whose area the offender resides; or

(c) a member of the YOT established by the local authority within whose area the offender resides.

Supervision will usually be exercised by a YOT member except, rarely, where a probation officer or social worker is nominated as a more appropriate for the individual case. In respect of trainees who have attained age 18, practice will be determined by local agreement, though the better view is that responsibility should be exercised by YOT members to promote consistency of practice.

Notice of Supervision

28.43   A notice from the Secretary of State must be issued to each trainee before the commencement of their supervision, *i.e.* before their release from custody, specifying: (a) "the category of person for the time being responsible for his supervision"; and (b) "any requirements with which he must for the time being

---

[55] n. 20, para. 2.78.
[56] H.M. Chief Inspector of Prisons, *HMYOI Brinsford: Report of an Announced Inspection 19–23 June 2000* (H.M. Inspectorate of Prisons, Home Office, London, 2001), p. 7.

comply" (s.103(6)). This notice is not a "licence" in familiar early release parlance because the young offender is still completing an integral part of their detention and training order.

28.44 *Supervision Requirements.* The requirements specified in the notice of supervision state that whilst under supervision the trainee "must—

(a) keep in touch with your supervisor in accordance with any reasonable instructions which he/she may give you;

(b) receive visits from your supervisor in your home in accordance with any reasonable instructions which he/she may give you;

(c) reside at [. . .] and tell your supervisor if you are going to move;

(d) only take a job if your supervisor says you can and not change jobs unless your supervisor says you can;

(e) not travel outside the United Kingdom without telling your supervisor;

(f) not commit any further offences;

(g) comply with any additional requirements (as attached)."

Requirements (c) and (e) contrast with those under (d) in that these require notice to the supervisor, presumably in advance, but not the supervisor's permission.

Process of Supervision

28.45 The following account seeks to summarise the provisions of Home Office Circular guidance and *National Standards for Youth Justice*[57] for the period of supervision following transfer to the community. The supervising officer is responsible for delivering or arranging delivery of the interventions set out in the training plan.

- The supervising officer (or their deputising colleague) should see the trainee on the day of transfer.

- A YOT member must make a home visit within five working days of transfer. Home visits should thereafter be offered monthly. The purpose of home visits is to check that the trainee is living where planned and to seek to involve the trainee's family in the work of the supervision period.

- Contact must be at least twice weekly for the first 12 weeks after transfer, and thereafter at least once every ten working days.

- Following transfer, the training plan must be reviewed within ten working days and subsequently on a three monthly basis or at the end of the order, whichever is sooner. This is achieved by review meetings. The key worker or caseworker from the secure facility should be invited to attend the first review meeting. The trainee must be expected to attend each review meeting and, where appropriate, the parents or primary carer should be encouraged to attend.

- The supervising officer should monitor the trainee's accommodation, education (if below school leaving age) or links with the Gateway personal adviser (if over that age).

---

[57] n. 20 and n. 47.

Failure to Comply with Supervision Requirements

28.46 Enforcement of the requirements of the supervision notice are regulated by section 104 which specifies that breach proceedings are pursued by prosecution before a youth court, initiated on information.

PCC(S)A 2000, s.104

(1) Where a detention and training order is in force in respect of an offender and it appears on information to a justice of the peace acting for a relevant petty sessions area that the offender has failed to comply with requirements under section 103(6)(b) above, the justice—

    (a) may issue a summons requiring the offender to appear at the place and time specified in the summons before a youth court acting for the area; or

    (b) if the information is in writing and on oath, may issue a warrant for the offender's arrest requiring him to be brought before such a court.

(2) For the purposes of this section a petty sessions area is a relevant petty sessions area in relation to a detention and training order if—

    (a) the order was made by a youth court acting for it; or

    (b) the offender resides in it for the time being.

(3) If it is proved to the satisfaction of the youth court before which an offender appears or is brought under this section that he has failed to comply with requirements under section 103(6)(b) above, that court may—

    (a) order the offender to be detained, in such secure accommodation as the Secretary of State may determine, for such period, not exceeding the shorter of three months or the remainder of the term of the detention and training order, as the court may specify; or

    (b) impose on the offender a fine not exceeding level 3 on the standard scale.

Jurisdiction is shared by (a) the youth court that imposed the detention and raining order (if the order was imposed by a youth court) and (b) a youth court acting for the petty sessions area in which the trainee is currently residing, if that is a different court. The statute does not indicate which court should be chosen for the purposes of prosecution if the trainee could be prosecuted before either venue. Where the order was made by the Crown Court, (b) alone applies. The wording of s.104(1)(a) indicates that a youth court exercises jurisdiction even though the trainee has attained the age of 18. An information will normally be laid by the supervising officer.

28.47 Failure to comply is not a criminal offence in its own right. The statute does not make reference to "failure without reasonable excuse" but it is submitted that a trainee could pursue that avenue as a form of defence. If the court is satisfied that the trainee has failed to comply, its powers are limited to—

    (a) ordering detention in secure accommodation for—

        (i) a period of three months, or

(ii) the period still remaining of the detention and training term, as determined at the point when the court finds the breach proved, whichever is the shorter; or

(b) imposing a fine not exceeding £1,000. In this instance the sum shall be deemed to be a sum adjudged to be paid by a conviction (s.104(5)).

Because the length of any detention ordered under s.104(3)(a) is determined with reference to the remainder of the term of the order, this provision may encourage trainees to delay the point when their failure to comply is admitted or proved, for example by tactical denials of the allegation against them. Thus if a trainee received a detention and training order for six months, transferring to the community after three months and an allegation is brought against them after two months of their supervision period, it could seem in their interests to seek to delay proceedings by a month, thus avoiding liability to be further detained because by then the full term of the order will have expired.

28.48 The status of any detention period ordered under s.104(3)(a) is not clearly identified. Though determined in length in part by reference to the overall length of the order, it is not a continuation by extension of the custodial phase of the original detention and training order. Nor is it a fresh detention and training order. If the trainee is re-released while the term of their detention and training order remains unexpired, it would appear that their liability to supervision resumes for the remainder of that period. Thus if an offender receives a detention and training order for 18 months, transferring to the community on supervision after nine months and is proved to have failed to comply following three months subject to supervision, he is liable to be detained for three months (being a shorter period than the six months still remaining of the full term of the order). If re-released after serving that three months, a further three months of the order remain during which supervision requirements should apply. Neither Home Office guidance nor *National Standards* offer any guidance to any responsibilities to be exercised or the management of this aspect of detention and training orders. If the court orders a fine under s.104(3)(b) liability to supervision continues uninterrupted.

28.49 *Appeal.* Section 104(6) specifies that an offender may appeal to the Crown Court against any order made under s.104(3)(a) or (b), a facility not included in the 1998 Act but added as an after-thought by the Youth Justice and Criminal Evidence Act 1999, Sched.5, para.9 and now included in the consolidating Act.

FURTHER OFFENCES DURING CURRENCY OF THE ORDER

28.50 Section 105 makes provision for instances where the trainee commits an offence ("the new offence") punishable in the case of a person aged 18 or over by imprisonment after his transfer to the community and while subject to supervision before the date when the detention and training order ends. This provision is the equivalent of the power to order return to prison under PCC(S)A 2000, s.116 (see 29.72) where an offence is committed during the "at risk" period before expiry of the full term of the original sentence. Liability to return to prison under s.105 does not arise in respect of an offence committed during the detention and training phase of sentence, either within the secure accommodation or while an abscondee from custody.

(2) Subject to section 8(6) above (duty of adult magistrates' court to remit young offenders to youth court for sentence), the court by or before which a person to whom this section applies is convicted of the new offence may, whether or not it passes any other sentence on him, order him to be detained in such secure accommodation as the Secretary of State may determine for the whole or any part of the period which—

(a) begins with the date of the court's order; and
(b) is equal in length to the period between the date on which the new offence was committed and the date mentioned in subsection (1) above.

(4) Where the new offence is found to have been committed over a period of two or more days, or at some time during a period of two or more days, it shall be taken for the purposes of this section to have been committed on the last of those days.

28.52   In addition to any sentence imposed for the new offence, the court has power to order detention in secure accommodation for a period not exceeding the unexpired period of the detention and training order at the point when the new offence was committed. This liability arises irrespective of whether the trainee is convicted of the new offence before, on or after the date when the detention and training order terminates. The trainee thus gains no advantage in terms of liability by seeking to delay the date of further conviction. The period for which a person is ordered to be detained under s.105(2) shall either be served either—

(i) before and be followed by, or

(ii) concurrently with—

any sentence imposed for the new offence but, in either case, shall be disregarded in determining the appropriate length of that sentence: s.105(3). It is thus not lawful for a court to order that the period shall be served consecutive to the sentence for the new offence. Where the new offence was committed over a period of more than one day, the date on which the offence is deemed to be committed for the purpose of calculating liability to be detained is the last of those days: s.104(4).

28.53   The question may arise whether a magistrates' court convicting the offender of a further offence may order his return to secure accommodation for a period in excess of six months in instances where the remaining period of the order outstanding for the purposes of s.105(2) is longer. There is no equivalent provision to that specified in PCC(S)A 2000, s. 115(3) regulating return to custody for offenders serving other custodial sentences, which restricts magistrates' power to a maximum of six months but gives power to commit the offender to the Crown Court. It thus appears that a youth court (or magistrates' court if the offender is now of an age to be dealt with in that court) may make an order under s.105 that exceeds six months.[58]

A further question concerns whether a court dealing with an offender who remains a juvenile and intends to make an order under s.105 and also to impose a further detention and training order to be served subsequent to the s.105 period is

---

[58] This interpretation is supported by D. Thomas n. 21 at pp. 37–85.

limited in aggregate by the maximum period applicable to a detention and training order of 24 months. This issue was posed in *F. and S.*[59] in the context of two 17-year-olds who had been sentenced to further terms of 21 months YOI detention (as was then the relevant custodial sentence for their age group) and were also ordered to be returned to custody (under CJA 1991, s.40, as then applied) for periods exceeding three months to be served first, making a total term exceeding 24 months. After much technical debate, the Court of Appeal concluded that as the aggregate period had to be treated as a single term, the permissible statutory maximum had been exceeded and the s.40 return period should be reduced to three months to comply. The provisions of PCC(S)A 2000, s.101(13) (specifying that for the purpose of any reference in ss.102–105, consecutive terms shall be treated as a single term) and section 105(3) appear to mean that the same interpretation should apply with equal validity in this context.

28.54 If the court makes an order for the offender's detention under s.105 but does not impose a new detention and training order for the further offence, the question is posed as to the actual length of the period to be served. In the context of the identical provisions of CDA 1998, s.78, the forerunner of s.105, Thomas[60] considered that as the section makes no provision for the further release of an offender so detained (having no equivalent of what is now s.116(6)(a)), "it appears that (he) will be liable to be detained for the whole period ordered by the court". Though Thomas did not make the distinction, if a s.105 period is combined with a further s.100 order, it would appear to follow from the provision of s.101(13) that the aggregate shall be treated as a single term of detention and training, attracting the usual provisions governing release subject to supervision.

New Sentence of YOI Detention/Imprisonment

28.55 If an offender attains age 18 while subject to a detention and training order and is sentenced for a further offence to YOI detention (or imprisonment, following abolition of YOI detention under CJCSA 2000), the provisions of s.106(1)(a) or (b) apply. The effect depends on whether the trainee—

(a) has been transferred to the community as of "the beginning of the day" on which the YOI/prison sentence is passed; or

(b) remains in secure accommodation.

28.56 *Following Release.* In this instance the new sentence takes effect on the day on which it is passed. If (b) applies, the court has the discretion to order that the YOI/prison sentence shall take effect at the time when he would otherwise be released/transferred, thus delaying sentence until the end of the custodial phase, but may opt to require the new sentence to take effect immediately. The possibility may arise that the trainee has been released but has been ordered to be detained under section 105(3)(a) following breach of supervision. The originating statute was silent on this point but section 106(3) specifies that section 106(1)(a) "has effect subject to section 105(3)(a)", indicating that the trainee must complete their detention under section 105(3)(a) before their new YOI/prison sentence commences.

28.57 *Prior to Release.* If in circumstance (b) the court orders the YOI/prison term to take effect at the end of the custodial period of detention and training, the

[59] [2000] 1 W.L.R. 266.
[60] n. 58.

calculations of the offender's eligibility for release from the two forms of sentence will need to be made separately and independently. In theory at least, it is possible that a trainee who is liable to commence a YOI/prison sentence on completion of their custodial phase may be the subject of an application to delay their release from secure accommodation, though whether a youth court would opt to grant an application of this nature in such circumstances may be questionable.

CHAPTER 29

Detention for Grave Crimes and Murder

29.01 The distinction between the two different forms of detention previously available for young offenders, detention in a young offender institution and detention under CYPA 1933, s.53(2) and (3), was the cause of no little difficulty, so much so that some commentators, *e.g.* Thomas,[1] have argued that it would be helpful to have a single sentence with power to the Crown Court to impose longer than two years in instances where section 53(3) powers have been available. However, the 1998 Act and the 2000 Act have continued to provide two separate kinds of sentence, the powers formerly available under section 53(3) being now governed by PCC(S)A 2000, s.91, with continuing scope for complexity and controversy. This Chapter seeks to cover process and principle; cases illustrating the use and length of section 91 sentences in respect of particular kinds of offence are given in Chapter 27 in the context of the custody threshold and commensurability in sentence length.

SECTION 91 DETENTION

Power to Detain

29.02   PCC(S)A 2000, s.91

(1) Subsection (3) below applies where a person aged under 18 is convicted on indictment of—

    (a) an offence punishable in the case of a person aged 21 or over with imprisonment for 14 years or more, not being an offence the sentence for which is fixed by law; or

    (b) an offence under section 14 of the Sexual Offences Act 1956 (indecent assault on a woman); or

    (c) an offence under section 15 of that Act (indecent assault on a man) committed after 30th September 1997.

(2) Subsection (3) below also applies where a person aged at least 14 but under 18 is convicted of an offence under—

    (a) section 1 of the Road Traffic Act 1988 (causing death by dangerous driving); or

    (b) section 3A of that Act (causing death by careless driving while under influence of drink or drugs).

(3) If the court is of the opinion that none of the other methods in which the case may legally be dealt with is suitable, the court may sentence the

---

[1] D Thomas at [1999] Crim. L.R. 757 and [2001] Crim. L.R. 237.

offender to be detained for such period, not exceeding the maximum term of imprisonment with which the offence is punishable in the case of a person aged 21 or over, as may be specified in the sentence.

29.03   The maximum term of a detention and training order is 24 months. However, in the case of a juvenile convicted of a very serious crime, including young offenders aged 10 to 11 for whom detention and training orders are not available at present, a sentence of detention may be imposed under PCC(S)A 2000, s.91. Offences for which this sentence are available are restricted to those punishable with imprisonment for 14 years or longer, the only exceptions being four offences with maximum terms of ten years imprisonment—

   (i)   for all juveniles: indecent assault of a woman or a man;

   (ii)   for young persons aged 14 or older: causing death by dangerous driving; causing death by careless driving while under the influence of alcohol or drugs.

29.04   Among the more common offences which qualify for s.91 powers are—

   (i)   wounding with intent to cause grievous bodily harm or assault occasioning grievous bodily harm with intent: Offences Against the Person Act 1861, s.18 (max. term: life imprisonment);

   (ii)   rape: Sexual Offences Act 1956, s.1 (max. term: life imprisonment);

   (iii)   unlawful sexual intercourse with a girl aged under 13 years: SOA 1956, s.5 (max. term: life imprisonment);

   (iv)   arson: Criminal Damage Act 1971, s.1 (max. term: life imprisonment);

   (v)   robbery: Theft Act 1968, s.8 (max. term: life imprisonment);

   (vi)   aggravated burglary: TA 1968, s.10 (max. term: life imprisonment);

   (vii)   burglary of a dwelling: TA 1968, s.9 (max. term: 14 years).

A sentence of detention under section 91 is a "custodial sentence" (PCC(S)A 2000, s.76(1)(b) and the power to impose this sentence is subject to the restrictions and requirements of the general provisions of sections 79 to 82 governing discretionary custodial sentences (see Chapter 27). To emphasise this point, s.91(4) specifies that section 91(3) "is subject to (in particular) ss.79 and 80 above".

29.05   Detention under section 91(3) can only be imposed on conviction on indictment in the Crown Court and is thus not available either to a youth court or to the Crown Court on hearing an appeal against sentence from a youth court. A youth court retains discretion whether to commit a young offender charged with a grave crime to the Crown Court for trial, under the provisions of MCA 1980, s.24(1)(a) (see 7.37) but if an eligible offence appears to merit a greater penalty than is available under youth court powers, the youth court should take this course.[2] Responsibility for alerting the court to the possibility that s.91 applies lies with the clerk and the prosecution (*Hertfordshire Youth Court, ex p. J.*[3]).

When the alternative custodial sentence was one of detention in a young offender institution, a number of cases (for example *Venison*[4]) indicated that if the Crown

[2] *Learmonth* (1988) 10 Cr.App.R.(S.) 229.
[3] *The Times*, May 4, 1998.
[4] (1994) 15 Cr.App.R.(S.) 624.

Court intended to pass sentence under CYPA 1933, s.53(2) and (3), as then applied, care should be exercised to make the court's intention plain and explicit, without ambiguity. The authorities were helpfully reviewed and clarified in *G.F.*[5]—

29.06
- If the offender is sentenced to a term in a young offender institution, without mention of section 53(3), the ambiguity should be resolved in the defendant's favour and any time in excess of the YOI maximum should be discounted.

- If the sentencer refers to section 53(3) but indicates that the defendant will be detained in a YOI, this should stand as a section 53(3) sentence on the basis that the judge was under a misapprehension that such a sentence would be served in a YOI.

- If the sentencer had section 53(3) explicitly in mind when adjourning for reports and subsequently imposed "detention" of a length that exceeds the maximum for YOI detention without further reference to section 53(3), there was a clear intention to exercise section 53(3) powers and the sentence should be understood in that way.

- If the sentencer refers to a sentence of "detention" without reference to either YOI or section 53(3) but the context makes clear that the court had section 53(3) in mind, then commonsense should apply and the sentence should stand as a section 53(3) term. Thus in *G.F.* where the defendant was ordered "to be detained for eight years" (for rape and escape from custody) it was clear that this was intended to be a section 53(3) sentence and could not be challenged.

29.07   Following implementation of the detention and training order, the scope for ambiguity would appear significantly reduced or even eliminated, since sentence under section 100 is not simply one of "detention" but "detention and training". However, it would appear to be sound practice for a judge imposing section 91 detention to refer explicitly to the court's intention to use that provision and there may still be scope to challenge a sentence that does not clarify that intention in the hope that section 101(5) (see 28.24) will be applied to remit any excess above 24 months.

The length of section 91 detention shall not exceed the statutory maximum term of imprisonment available in respect of an adult but, if the offence carries a maximum of life imprisonment, detention for life may be appropriate if the relevant criteria governing use of a discretionary life sentence (see 29.20) are satisfied.[6]

Sentencing Principles

29.08   The use of detention for grave crimes (under CYPA 1933, s.53(3)) has been the subject of Court of Appeal interpretation and guidance in a number of leading cases, principally *Fairhurst*,[7] *Wainfur*,[8] and *Mills and Others*.[9] The following

---

[5] [2000] 2 Cr.App.R.(S.) 364.
[6] *Abbott* [1964] 1 Q.B. 489.
[7] (1986) 8 Cr.App.R.(S.) 346.
[8] [1997] 1 Cr.App.R.(S.) 43.
[9] [1998] 2 Cr.App.R.(S.) 128.

seeks to summarise and build upon these guidelines in the context of the new parallel provisions for detention and training orders.

1. Where the Offender is Eligible for a Detention and Training Order

29.09 (a) The 24 month limit on sentences of detention and training is intended to ensure that offenders of eligible age are not sentenced to lengthy periods of detention where this can be avoided. "Any sentencer must think long and hard before passing a sentence that exceeds this limit. But the co-existence of the powers contained in (section 91) recognises the fact the unwelcome but undoubted fact that some crimes committed by offenders of this age merit sentences of detention in excess of 24 months": Lord Bingham C.J. in *Mills* (at 131).

(b) To invoke section 91 powers it is not necessary that the crime committed should be of exceptional gravity, such as attempted murder, manslaughter, wounding with intent or armed robbery, but the 24 month limit should not be exceeded unless the offence is clearly one calling for a longer sentence.

29.10 (c) The *Fairhurst* judgement, updated by *Wainfur*, sought to discourage sentencers from exceeding the 24 month limit unless the case merited a significantly longer term, holding that it is generally inappropriate to pass a "grave crime" sentence of under three years. Sentencers dealing with marginal cases were encouraged to round their sentences down to bring them within the scope of the alternative form of detention (then detention in a young offender institution). This "no man's land" zone between two and three years created a dilemma for sentencers faced with a serious offence but with substantial personal mitigation who might feel that a term of 30 or 33 months was appropriate. The Court in *Mills* considered that in practice the rule had led sentencers to pass a higher sentence than they might think strictly justified rather than a lower term within *Wainfur* expectations. *Mills* thus stated that the rule should be no longer followed and indicated that if a sentencer concludes that "a longer sentence, even if not a much longer sentence, is called for, the court should impose whatever it considers the appropriate period of detention" (at p. 132). When passing a term of 24 months detention and training following guilty plea where in a contested case a longer term of "grave crime" detention would have been appropriate, this should be expressly stated, to avoid the impression that credit has not been given for plea.

(d) Where more than one "grave" offence is involved but offences vary in seriousness, provided that at least one offence is sufficiently serious to merit detention under section 91, section 91 detention sentences of under 24 months duration, whether concurrent or consecutive, may properly be imposed in respect of the other offences.

29.11 (e) In respect of cases where the offender faces sentence for more than one offence, where one or some offences are eligible for "grave crime" detention but one or some are eligible only for a detention and training order, the Appeal Court in *Mills* noted that the latter offence(s) is nevertheless an "associated" offence (under the provisions of PCC(S)A 2000 s.161) and indicated that it is "generally undesirable to impose terms concurrently under both sections". "In such a case the practice recommended by *Fairhurst* of imposing no separate penalty for the lesser offence should be adopted. If the court is minded to impose concurrent terms under the two sections, it should before doing so make quite sure that no administrative difficulty (in respect of where the offender will be detained) will result." (This latter consideration is less pertinent under new allocation arrangements.)

29.12 (f) Where the sentencer is dealing with two or more offences committed by the offender where one is eligible for a section 91(3) sentence but the other is liable only to a detention and training sentence, then if the latter offence is the more serious and the former would not justify the imposition of a term exceeding 24 months, a principle laid down in *Fairhurst* would hold that it is not proper to pass a sentence under section 91 for the former offence to compensate for the fact that 24 months detention and training would be grossly inadequate for the latter offence. However, where it can truly be said that the offender's behaviour giving rise to the latter offence is "part and parcel" of the events giving rise to the former offence, a section 91(3) sentence may be properly passed. Thus if the case involves a burglary seriously aggravated by a simultaneous indecent assault, the sexual assault can be regarded as "part and parcel" of the burglar's behaviour, thus enabling the court to impose a section 91 term for the burglary to take account of the indecent assault which is not eligible for such a sentence. However, the Appeal Court in *Mills* considered that the problem has been mitigated by the change in the law introduced by CJA 1991 allowing a court to weigh the seriousness of an offence by taking account of "associated" offences (PCC(S)A 2000, s.161). "By virtue of those provisions the court could now . . . take account of an associated offence even if it were not part and parcel of the main offence." In the subsequent case of *McKay and Others*,[10] involving a group incident of robbery followed by gratuitous violence against the victim, ultimately resulting in conviction for robbery and actual bodily harm (see 27.75) and also *Walsh*,[11] the Appeal Court cited both the "part and parcel" principle and also the "associated offence" provision, determining without further analysis that it was appropriate for the court considering the seriousness of the robbery to take account of the ABH assault. Although the robbery was technically complete before the violence continued to its worst manifestations, these offences were inextricably linked. We thus await an authoritative judgement involving two crimes which are "associated" but factually entirely distinct.

29.13 (g) Though Lord Bingham C.J. had indicated in *Mills* that the requirement that the court should be of the opinion that "none of the other methods in which the case may be legally dealt with is suitable" must be read as meaning that, in the case of 15–17 year olds, "a term longer than 24 months is called for", he modified this view in *Brown*,[12] a case involving a 15-year-old girl convicted of robbery who had been sentenced to two years YOI detention. The defence had sought to persuade the judge that she should receive a section 53(3) term of that length to enable her to be placed in local authority secure accommodation better suited to her developmental needs than a prison service facility. (She was considered very immature for her age, with a strong sense of rejection and little self-esteem. Having been excluded from school for over a year, she had urgent educational needs. A place was available for her at Aycliffe secure unit.) On appeal the Court indicated that "suitable" was not an acronym for "sufficient" and that, in exceptional cases, such as prevailed here, it is valid to impose s.53(3) detention of a length within the maximum of other detention powers, provided—

(a) there is clear and compelling evidence to show that detention in a YOI is, for demonstrable reasons, clearly unsuitable, or that detention in some

[10] [2000] 1 Cr.App.R.(S.) 17.
[11] [1997] 2 Cr.App.R.(S.) 210.
[12] [1998] Crim. L.R. 588.

other institution is so clearly more suitable as to make detention in a YOI unsuitable in comparison; and

(b) there is clear, current information that a place is available in such other institution and that that institution is willing to accept the offender.

29.14   In theory, the arrival of detention and training orders has rendered the issue at stake in *Brown* obsolete because of the flexiblity built into this sentence, so that detainees may be placed in such secure accommodation as the Secretary of State may direct. However, given the scarcity of places available in local authority secure accommodation, it seems likely that almost all young offenders aged 15 or older, especially males, will end up in YOI regimes, modified or otherwise. The imposition of a section 91 sentence in special cases might serve to give those responsible for allocations a message about the court's concern about the welfare of the young person in question. However, the procedural route to section 91 detention means that a youth court would need to be persuaded at a relatively early stage to commit the case for trial rather than being persuaded of the wisdom of the section 91 approach only point of sentence when it will be too late. Further, as Ball[13] has noted, in such instances "arguments in regard to both suitablity and the welfare of the child would need to be cogent indeed".

2. Where the Offender is Ineligible for a Detention and Training Order

29.15   Where an offender is aged between 12 and 15 but is not a "persistent" offender (see 28.05) or is aged under 12, a section 91 sentence of detention is the only form of custodial sentence for which he is eligible and if the court considers that a custodial sentence is necessary, after consideration of all factors including the offender's extreme youth, a term of less than 24 months may well be appropriate. The appropriate term of whatever length should be imposed. Among recent examples of sentences below two years: *Fenemore*[14] (see 27.66); *L.H.*[15] (see 27.83); *O'Grady*[16] (see 27.33).

3. Where the Offender is Eligible for a Detention and Training Order but not of a Required Length

29.16   This is a speculative bracket and reflects the requirement of PCC(S)A 2000, s.101 that a term of detention and training should be of a length selected from a number of permitted periods between four months and 24 months (see). As Thomas asks in his commentary on *McKay*,[17] if a sentencer considers that the proper term for an offence eligible for section 91 detention is 15 months, which is not a permitted term under section 101, will it be valid to pass a term of that length under section 91(3) on the basis that "none of the other methods in which the case may legally be dealt with is suitable", if of the view that 12 months is too short and 18 months is too long? The nature of section 91 detention is such that this route will only be an option in the youth court if the court can be persuaded to commit the young offender for trial, whereas issues such a precise length of term may arise in that jurisdiction only after conviction.

---

[13] C. Ball (1998) "*R. v. B.*: Paying due regard to the welfare of the child in criminal proceedings", *Child & Family Law Quarterly, 10(4)*, 417–424 at 423.
[14] [1998] 1 Cr.App.R.(S.) 176.
[15] [1997] 2 Cr.App.R.(S.) 319.
[16] [2000] 1 Cr.App.R.(S.) 112.
[17] D. Thomas at [1999] Crim. L.R. 757–8.

4. Deterrence

29.17 Several reported appeal cases in respect of detention under CYPA 1933, s.53(3), before and after CJA 1991, have identified that the power is wide enough to enable a court to pass on a young offender a sentence for deterrence purposes. Thus in *Ford*,[18] a case of repeated gang street robbery of women in South London, the Appeal Court upheld a term of five years detention and rejected the defence submission that the provision should not be used for general deterrence, asserting that this was a "local situation of the utmost gravity" which "can only be stopped if other youths and boys realise what is going to happen to them". The Court noted that "the welfare of the young offender (under a section 53(3) sentence) is under constant scrutiny and review. There is therefore unlikely to be any harm done to this young offender from a deterrent sentence" and added that a sentencer should weigh "most carefully in the balance deterrence on the one side against individual treatment for the rehabilitation of the young offender on the other". *Ford* was cited with approval in *O'Grady*[19] (see 27.33), a case of "distraction" burglaries of the homes of elder women. A custodial term of six months was required for the burglar aged 14 to "punish, deter and contain" him, taking account also of the promotion of his welfare. See also *Marriott and Shepherd*[20] a further case of street robbery targeting vulnerable older victims, dealt with by terms of five years, where the Appeal Court noted—

> "It is not inappropriate to impose a deterrent sentence; there may be a very real need to deter others and indeed young others from offending in like manner. But when one is passing . . . a deterrent sentence it is necessary to keep a balance between that aspect of the matter, the youth of the offender and the effect of a long sentence upon the perception of the offender, it being trite to observe that young offenders see time stretching ahead of them in a different way to that in which adults see it." (*per* Ebsworth J.)

5. Principle of Restraint

29.18 Ebworth J.'s final observation (above) links to the principle of restraint identified in *Storey*[21] that a "grave crime" sentence should not be of such length—

> "that it would seem to the young men involved, particularly if they are not outstanding intellectually, that the far end of it is out of sight . . . The sentencer should take care to select a duration on which the offender can fix his eye with a view to emerging in the foreseeable future."

This principle is sometimes expressed in terms of affording "light at the end of the tunnel" (see *Carr*[22] at 27.30). Accordingly, not only should a term of s.91 detention not be longer than would be appropriate as a sentence of imprisonment for an adult[23] but should normally be scaled down from the length of sentence appropriate for an older offender to a level that reflects the youth of the defendant and their relative grasp of the passage of time. However, this does not mean that

---

[18] (1976) 62 Cr.App.R. 303.
[19] [2000] 1 Cr.App.R.(S.) 112.
[20] (1995) 16 Cr.App.R.(S.) 428.
[21] (1984) 6 Cr.App.R.(S.) 104.
[22] [1998] 2 Cr.App.R.(S.) 20.
[23] *Burrowes* (1985) 7 Cr.App.R.(S.) 106.

courts will necessarily pass a shorter sentence where the circumstances of the case merit a substantial period of detention (see *McFarlane and Burke*[24], approving long terms for offenders aged 15 convicted of robberies of young women walking alone at night, using violence coupled with sexual threats). The survey of recent custodial sentencing at 27.15 *et seq.* further illustrates the Appeal Court's willingness to endorse long terms of detention for very serious offences, particularly for gross personal violence.

Dangerousness and Public Protection

29.19 Prior to the provisions in CJA 1991, s.1(2)(b) and s.2(2)(b) (now PCC(S)A 2000, s.79(2)(b) and s.80(2)(b)) for custodial sentences of longer than commensurate length on the criterion of public protection (see 27.112), it was acknowledged that section 53(3) powers could appropriately be used to pass a very long preventive sentence on young offenders considered to present a considerable risk to the public. The most stark instance of such a case is *Storey*[25] where a youth of 16 received a term of 20 years detention for attempted murder. The Court noted that it was an exceptional instance but felt able to fix a determinate term rather than resort to an indeterminate sentence, though the basis for that assessment is not clear from the report of the appeal. Use of section 91(3) powers to pass a longer than commensurate determinate term for public protection purposes may be deployed only in respect of a "violent" or "sexual" offence, as outlined in Chapter 27.

Discretionary Detention for Life

29.20 Detention for life will be justified in the most exceptional circumstances where the conditions to be satisfied before a discretionary life sentence may properly be imposed, as recently re-stated by the Court of Appeal in *Chapman*[26] The sentence has to be passed under the public protection provisions of what is now PCC(S)A 2000, s.80(2)(b), but also satisfying the following pre-conditions—

(a) the offender has committed an offence grave enough to merit an extremely long sentence;

(b) there are good grounds for believing that the offender may remain a serious danger to the public for a period that cannot be reliably estimated at the date of sentence. (As Widgery C.J. stated in *Bryson*[27] in upholding sentence of detention for life on a 14-year-old for arson causing £20,000 and considerable risk to life: "None of the experts give any sort of indication that a particular period of years can in this case be chosen to ensure that the public can be properly protected.")

In recent interpretations of the relevant criteria less emphasis has been given to what was previously regarded as a distinct, third pre-condition, namely that has a "continuing mental instability".

29.21 A court will be hesitant to conclude that these criteria are met in the case of a young offender except in rare instances of sexual or other violence of a very

---

[24] (1988) 10 Cr.App.R.(S.) 10.
[25] (1973) 57 Cr.App.R. 840.
[26] [2000] 1 Cr.App.R.(S.) 377.
[27] (1973) 58 Cr.App.R. 464.

worrying nature. It would clearly be wrong for the court to opt for an indeterminate sentence as a "more merciful" alternative to a long determinate term, in order to allow continual review and release as soon as it is safe to do so, as illustrated in *Hall*[28] where the 17-year-old offender, affected by glue-sniffing, had set fire to a house where he was staying, leaving the other occupants, a woman and her two young children, asleep. The Court of Appeal noted that while the offender was immature, with a disturbed childhood in local authority care and lengthy criminal record, this did not amount to "mental abnormality"). The reported cases frequently concern arson, as did *Chapman*, involving a 19-year-old resident in a rehabilitation hostel who started a fire in his room. The fire was quickly discovered and extinguished before serious damage was caused, so that the risk to life was small. No injuries were intended or sustained. He had suffered a seriously deprived childhood and had a propensity to start fires, as evidenced by two previous occasions of setting fire to his bedding, resulting in conditional discharge. Reports indicated that he presented a continuing danger to the public and it was not possible to predict when he would cease to be so. Sentence of custody for life was set aside on the basis that this offence of arson being reckless whether life was endangered, while serious, was not sufficiently grave to satisfy the first precondition, especially bearing in mind the offender's young age. The Court considered that a determinate sentence of three years was merited but, in light of the continuing risk, an additional seven years was added under what is now s.80(2)(b), making a total of ten years as a longer than commensurate determinate sentence to protect the public.

29.22 *Stanley*[29] presented closely parallel circumstances to *Chapman*, with a different outcome. The offender aged 16 pleaded guilty to arson being reckless as to whether life was endangered. On calling at a social services office to see her social worker about the withdrawal of her two year old daughter's nursery place and being informed she was not available, she sprayed petrol over the counter and doors and set light to it. This crime being committed in the direct sight of staff, quick intervention by the fire brigade limited damage to some £2,300. Her actions nevertheless showed a clear degree of premeditation and she had written a note indicating that she was going to do something serious to get back at her social worker. She had previous convictions, including one for arson, also committed against social services premises, dealt with by conditional discharge, but she had not served a custodial sentence. She had a history of friction with social services dating back to her time in Care arising from her traumatic childhood and adolescence, involving physical, sexual and emotional abuse. She was viewed as simultaneously displaying an aggressive and abusive type of grudge against authority and being a misguided, frightened teenager who through bad luck and poor judgement was struggling to cope with demands that would test persons of greater experience and maturity. (Her second child had been born in custody.) Since receiving her life sentence she had been further sentenced to 12 months detention for offences of affray and wounding committed while in secure accommodation while remanded in respect of her arson offence when she joined in an attack on a social worker.

29.23 The Court of Appeal concluded that the offence was extremely serious, enough to satisfy the first pre-condition, despite the absence of injury and the speedy extinguishment of the fire—"It needs little imagination to see how much more serious the consequences could have been." The Court also rejected the

---

[28] (1986) 8 Cr.App.R.(S.) 458.
[29] [1999] 2 Cr.App.R.(S.) 30.

second defence argument that the offender's mental instability fell short of warranting an indeterminate sentence. Though she was not suffering an identifiable mental illness, she was "a serious danger to the public and is likely, if she has her freedom, to place members of the public at risk of serious harm". Upholding the indeterminate sentence as justified and appropriate, the Court did not alter the "merciful" tariff term of 18 months set by the judge (see below), a period that is the equivalent of the three year determinate sentence viewed as appropriate in *Chapman*. With respect, it is difficult to see a clear basis for differentiating between the two cases save in respect of the anti-authority aggression that fuelled the younger offender's actions.

Determination of Tariffs

29.24 Under PCC(S)A 2000, s.82A, introduced by CJCSA 2000, s.55 and replacing provisions in C(S)A 1997, s.28(1) which in turn replaced CJA 1991, s.34, where a court passes a life sentence in circumstances where (a) the sentence is not fixed by law, or (b) the offender was aged under 18 when he committed the offence, the court shall order the "part of sentence" to be served before the provisions of C(S)A 1997, s.28 (see 29.68) governing review and release apply. Section 82A(3) specifies that the "part" (or tariff term) "shall be such as the court considers appropriate taking into account"—

(a) the seriousness of the offence or associated offences in aggregate;

(b) the effect of any direction which would otherwise have been given under PCC(S)A 2000, s.87 (credit for any period of remand in custody); and

(c) "the early release provisions as compared with CJA 1991 ss.33(2) and 35(1)" (a reference to the provisions determining that a determinate sentence long-term prisoner may be released after serving one-half of sentence and shall be released after serving two-thirds of sentence).

In respect of tariff periods fixed under the equivalent provisions of C(S)A 1997, s.28, the Court of Appeal in *Marklew and Lambert*,[30] following *ex p. Furber*,[31] determined that the sentencer should adopt one-half of the notional determinate sentence as the basis for fixing the specified period, though the court indicated that there "might be exceptional circumstances where it would be appropriate to set a longer period", up to two-thirds of the notional determinate term. In the case of Marklew, considered a highly dangerous and compulsive fire-setter, the tariff part set by the sentencer at eight years, was reduced to five years, reflecting that the proper determinate term was one of ten years.

29.25 The life sentence then falls into two parts—

(a) the period of detention imposed for punishment and deterrence, taking account of the seriousness of the offence;

(b) the residual part, the continuation of which is governed by considerations continuing risk to the public (see 29.65).

Section 82A(4) provides that the court need not specify the tariff part where of the opinion that, "because of the seriousness of the offence(s), no order should be

---

[30] [1999] 1 Cr.App.R.(S.) 6.
[31] [1998] 1 Cr.App.R.(S.) 208.

made, for reasons to be stated in open court. It is highly unlikely that this exception will be considered to apply to young offenders. Sentencing of young persons aged under 18 to life imprisonment without possibility of release is contrary to the United Nations *Convention on the Rights of the Child*, Article 37.[32] However, section 82A(5) specifies that if the offender was aged under 18 when he committed the offence, the Secretary of State "shall direct that the early release provisions shall apply as soon as he has served the part of his sentence which is specified in the direction".

Other Illustrations of Detention for Life

29.26   Recent instances where sentence of detention or custody for life has been upheld include—

Bell[33]   The offender aged 16 was convicted of assault with intent to rob and indecent assault, having approached the victim whilst she was pushing her two year old child in a pram, pointing a Stanley knife at her stomach and demanding her money. He then demanded to handle her indecently, threatening to slash the victim or her child in the throat. She had submitted and had been forced to take his penis in her mouth. The offender had previous convictions for indecent assault. Dismissing his appeal against sentence of life detention under section 53(2) for the assault with intent to rob (at that stage indecent assault was not a qualifying offence, despite being the more serious offence), the Court of Appeal held that whilst there are some cases where it is better for the sentencer to specify the number of years which the offender should serve, this was a case where no court could predict how long it would be before the appellant would be safe to be released.

29.27   *Attorney-General's Reference No. 6 of 1993 (Musgrove)*[34]   Though involving an offender aged 20, this illustrates use of life sentencing for a young adult imposed for rape. He was diagnosed to be suffering an untreatable psychopathic disorder with a propensity to commit sexual assaults.

29.28   *Carr*[35]   A girl aged 15 had committed s.18 grievous bodily harm by stabbing another schoolgirl in the back. She asked for two other offences of attempting to strangle other girls to be taken into consideration. She was assessed to be "exceptionally dangerous". Her relevant part of sentence was adjusted from 42 months to two years, in the light of psychiatric advice to the court that this was the minimum period necessary for the treatment deemed appropriate, the Appeal Court noting that "three and a half years is a very long time in the eyes and life of a child of that age".

29.29   *Sheldon*[36]   A boy aged 13 had attempted to murder a girl aged 10, his cousin, tripping her up then applying pressure to her neck so that she became unconscious. He had then committed sexual abuse, inserting an object into her

---

[32] Article 37 states that detention of a child can only be used "for the shortest appropriate time". It might also be argued that such a sentence constitutes "inhuman" punishment, contrary to international law.
[33] [1990] Crim. L.R. 206.
[34] (1994) 15 Cr.App.R.(S.) 375.
[35] [1996] 1 Cr.App.R.(S.) 191.
[36] [1996] 2 Cr.App.R.(S.) 397.

vagina. He continued to deny responsibility for the attack. Though there was no evidence of mental illness, he was assessed to represent a severe risk which could not be assessed while he maintained denial. In his appeal it was argued that the injury inflicted was not of the gravest kind; the offence was not part of a pattern of such behaviour; the risk posed was not clearly established. The defence suggested that it might help his management if he had a target such as would be provided by a determinate term. However, the Appeal Court considered that an indeterminate term, "awesome" as that was, was inevitable given that the risk was unassessable. A "ray of hope" was provided by reducing the tariff period from five to four years.

Extended Sentence

29.30 As indicated at 27.121, when passing sentence of section 91 detention for a sexual or violent offence (as defined by PCC(S)A 2000, s.161(2) and (3)) committed after 30 September 1998, the Crown Court has discretion to pass an "extended sentence" under section 85(2) in circumstances where the court considers that "the period (if any) for which the offender would, apart from this section, be subject to a licence would not be adequate for the purpose of preventing the commission by him of further offences and securing his rehabilitation": section 85(1)(b).

29.31   PCC(S)A 2000, s.85

(2) Subject to subsections (3) to (5) below, the court may pass on the offender an extended sentence, that is to say, a custodial sentence the term of which is equal to the aggregate of—

(a) the term of the custodial sentence that the court would have imposed if it had passed a custodial sentence otherwise than under this section ("the custodial term"); and

(b) a further period ("the extension period") for which the offender is to be subject to a licence and which is of such length as the court considers necessary for the purpose mentioned in subsection (1) above.

(3) Where the offence is a violent offence, the court shall not pass an extended sentence the custodial term of which is less than four years.

(4) The extension period shall not exceed—

(a) ten years in the case of a sexual offence; and
(b) five years in the case of a violent offence.

(5) The term of an extended sentence passed in respect of an offence shall not exceed the maximum term permitted for that offence.

(6) Subsection (2) of section 80 above (length of discretionary custodial sentences) shall apply as if the term of an extended sentence did not include the extension period.

An extended sentence thus comprises—

(i) a "custodial term", *i.e.* the term that the offence would otherwise have attracted, whether as commensurate with the seriousness of the offence under section 80(2)(a) or as considered necessary to protect the public as permitted by section 80(2)(b). Because of the provision of section 85(6), the court should determine the custodial term without reference to the "extension period";

(ii) an "extension period" not exceeding (a) ten years (sexual offence) or (b) five years (violent offence).

In the case of a violent offence, the custodial term must be for an minimum of four years before an extension period can be added.

29.32   Though an extended sentence is expressed as a composite term, combining both the custodial term and the extension period, together not exceeding the maximum term available for the offence, it is a device to allow the offender to be supervised on licence for a longer period than would otherwise apply. This measure is thus the more elaborate successor to CJA 1991, s.44 (now contained in PCC(S)A 2000, s.86), which allowed licence in respect of a sexual offence to extend until full sentence expiry rather than the three-quarter point of sentence. However, under section 85 the court does not have to be satisfied of the need to protect the public from serious harm from the offender, as applies under s.44/s.86. An extension period may be ordered to complement a custodial term (in respect of a sexual offence) of less than 12 months and thus not subject to licence in the absence of an extension period: *Ajaib*.[37] For the purposes of calculating liability to register under the provisions of the Sex Offenders Act 1997 (see 30.26), only the custodial term counts, not the full extent of the extended sentence: *S*.[38] Though the objective may be to ensure a longer period of statutory oversight of offenders who pose higher risk to the public, the penal consequence in the event of recall to custody is potentially substantial and early Court of Appeal guidance has indicated that use of this measure should be exercised cautiously.

29.33   Thus in *Gould*[39] a sentence comprising a five year custodial term, coupled with an extension period of five years, imposed on a young adult offender aged 20 for wounding with intent in a glassing attack, was overturned to the extent of setting aside the extension period. While affirming the correctness of the custodial period and agreeing that an extended sentence was considered correct in principle, given his previous convictions for affray and unlawful wounding, the Court of Appeal was concerned that the offender might end up serving a ten year sentence, longer than the purpose of imposing an extended sentence justified. The Court noted that he was showing "encouraging signs of wanting to change his lifestyle" and expressed hope that the experience of five years detention "will itself contribute powerfully to the ends which the judge had in mind". The extension period was therefore reduced to two years. This decision may indicate that extended sentences are likely to be used parsimoniously in respect of younger offenders.

For the effect of an extended sentence in respect of early release provisions, reference must be made to CJA 1991, s.44, revised version as inserted by CDA 1998, s.59, as outlined at 29.33.

Time in Detention

29.34   The following brings together various threads of the experience of being a section 91 detainee.

---

[37] [2000] Crim. L.R. 770.
[38] *The Times*, August 29, 2000.
[39] [2000] 2 Cr.App.R.(S.) 173.

Time Spent on Remand

Any time spent on remand in custody or the equivalent of custody in local authority secure accommodation counts towards the time to be served under a s.91 sentence (CJA 1967, s.67(5), see 27.126) and also for the purpose of determining whether a detainee has served the appropriate fraction of sentence for early release purposes (CJA 1991, s.41(1) and (2) (see 29.46a). The relevance of time spent in local authority accommodation is regulated by CJA 1967, s.67(1A)(c) which specifies that the following time shall count towards sentence—

> "any period during which, in connection with the offence for which the sentence was passed, he was remanded . . . to local authority accommodation by virutue of an order under CYPA 1969, s.23 . . . and in accommodation provided for the purpose of restricting liberty."

29.35 In *Collins*[40] the Court of Appeal ruled that this did not apply only to "secure accommodation" but that time spent in a "structured and supervised" unit also counted towards sentence. However, the House of Lords in *R. v. Secretary of State for the Home Department, ex p. A.*[41] determined that *Collins* was wrongly decided and that accommodation that is not "secure" does not satisfy section 67(1A)(c). In the case of A. the young person was not detained in his children's home and the local authority could not prevent him from absconding so that his remand was more akin to release on bail than custodial remand. It is nevertheless open to the sentencer to take account of any period spent in non-secure local authority accommodation in determining length of sentence.[42]

Placements and Outcomes

29.36 Section 91 tries to combine two objectives: secure, purposeful containment and public protection appropriate to the nature of the offence; treatment and rehabilitation appropriate to the comparative youth of the offender. Placement policy reflects this duality, coupled with pragmatic use of available resources. Responsibility for placement of section 53/section 91 detainees is the statutory responsibility of the Secretary of State but in practice is currently shared between the Home Office, through the Prison Service's "Section 53 Unit", and the Youth Justice Board. YOTs have the initial responsibility to give early warning of a possible section 91 sentence to the Section 53 Unit by completing a pre-sentence notification, thus allowing anticipation of placement.[43] When sentence is made, it a further YOT responsibility to contact the Youth Justice Board's Central Call Centre (see 28.32) for placement authorisation by the clearinghouse, within one hour of the court's decision.[44] The initial placement decision is made by the Board which is best placed to determine availability and suitability of resources. Under the terms of the Board's current placement strategy,[45] s.91 detainees are placed as follows—

- Under–12 year olds will be placed in local authority accommodation.

---

[40] (1995) 16 Cr.App.R.(S.) 156.
[41] [2000] 2 Cr.App.R.(S.) 263.
[42] In the context of an adult remanded to a bail hostel subject to a stringent 24 hour curfew, where allowance was made in sentence, see *Watson* [2000] 2 Cr.App.R.(S.) 301.
[43] Youth Justice Board (2000) *National Standards for Youth Justice*, para. 9.1.
[44] n. 43, para. 6.5.2.
[45] Youth Justice Board (2000) *Juvenile Secure Estate Placement Strategy*, para. 13.

- Detainees aged 12–14 must be placed either in a local authority unit or in a secure training centre.

- Girls aged 15–16 "should normally be given priority "for places in a local authority unit or secure training centre, but those aged 10–14 (and 15–16 year old girls on remand) take precedence.

- Boys aged 15–17 will be placed in either a YOI, a secure training centre or a local authority unit. Those aged 15–16 who are considered vulnerable should be considered for a placement outside Prison Service accommodation "if a place is available". Of the 13 YOIs contracted to accommodate juveniles (see 28.29), three operate special units for s.91 detainees.[46]

- Girls aged 17 "should normally be placed in local authority accommodation if places are available". (The implication is that otherwise this age group will be assigned to a YOI.)

- In all instances, decisions will take account of availability, individual need and closeness to home.

Once the detainee is placed, casework responsibility for decisions pertaining to his detention rests with the Section 53/91 Unit of the Prison Service, in consultation with the relevant YOT and in consultation with the Youth Justice Board.

29.37 *Outcomes Research* In a recent study of 204 young people admitted to the two specialist secure Youth Treatment Centres (as had operated until 1995), from point of entry until two years after their departure, 83 being subject to CYPA 1933, s.53 detention (of whom 18 were subject to indeterminate detention), Bullock *et al.*[47] report that "as a group, they display a higher than expected rate for almost every disadvantage and behavioural difficulty". Though no single characteristic dominated, the complexity of their needs was "mind-boggling". The study indicated five "career routes" paving the way to secure treatment: (i) "long-term child care" cases (who had experienced state care from an early age); (ii) "long-term special education" cases, presenting substantial behavioural problems requiring specialist intervention through child guidance services; (iii) "adolescent erupters" whose behaviour had deteriorated rapidly fairly late in their development; (iv) "one-off serious offenders" who had not come to agency attention until they committed a grave crime; (v) "serious and persistent offenders" who had regularly offended in their early and mid-teens, culminating in a grave crime.

29.38–29.41 The mean length of stay in YTC was just over 26 months, around a fifth being resident for over three years. Examining outcomes, the authors note that 70 per cent of leavers offended in some way and half were convicted within the two year period, a quarter in a way considered serious enough by the courts to warrant custody and 17 per cent for an offence involving some physical contact between offender and victim. Though in some instances the outcome was disastrous, the rate of offending was "less than might have been anticipated" and serious crimes were much reduced. As Bullock *et al.* remark, a secure treatment setting is not a natural place in which to spend adolescence—"the absence of ordinary role models, the anxiety of living in a small space with extremely damaged people and

---

[46] Castington, Hollesley Bay and Huntercombe YOIs.
[47] R. Bullock, M. Little & S. Millham *Secure Treatment Outcomes: The Care Careers of Very Difficult Adolescents* (Aldershot, Ashgate, 1998).

the physical and emotional distance from home all militate against the best effects of treatment." However, when comparing "like with like", the authors concluded that "specialist treatment centres appear to do better with these extremely difficult cases than do other secure units, such as those run by local authorities or YOIs". Broadly put, the study indicates that outcomes reflect: (a) the career route travelled prior to reaching the treatment centre, since this sets out within broad parameters where the young person will live and with whom; (b) the nature, quality and matching of treatment intervention with identified needs; (c) the existence of "protective factors" or individual strengths that can enable a young person to get by despite shortcomings in treatment provision. Noting too that the contrast between what young persons receive in specialist treatment centres and what help they receive after leaving is often acute, the authors conclude—

"Outcomes for very difficult young people appear to reflect the time, sophistication and effort taken by the institution selected to intervene. So, on the simple measure of conviction within two years of departure, outcomes are best from the specialist centres, next best from the medium intensive local authority settings, and worst from prison custody. These findings hold true even when young people's background characteristics, career route and protective factors are taken into account."

Community Management of the "Custodial" Phase

29.42 The *National Standards for Youth Justice*[48] specify the following practice expectations:

- A supervising officer must be allocated within one working day of sentence, together with a paired YOT colleague who can deputise for the supervisor.

- The supervising officer or his "pair" must visit the offender within five working days of sentence, and also the parents/primary carer, where appropriate.

- Where an assessment was not completed prior to sentence, this must be completed within five working days of sentence.

- Within 15 working days of sentence the supervising officer must submit information to the Section 91 Unit at the Home Office about the offender's remand to enable sentence calculation.

- The supervising officer shall attend the offender's first month's review at the secure facility and subsequent quarterly reviews.

- The supervising officer must visit the offender at least once every three months and at least monthly for the three months prior to the planned release.

- Where s.91 offenders approach the age of 18, agreement should be reached with the probation service regarding transfer of supervisory responsibility. Such change of supervisor should not occur in the final three months prior to release.

---

[48] n. 43, para. 9.2.

Disciplinary Offences in Custody

29.43 CJA 1991, s.42 provides for "additional days" to be awarded which extend the time to be served before entitlement to automatic conditional release on licence or discretionary early release on parole licence. The actual period of licence remains unchanged but commencement and completion are correspondingly delayed. The Prison Rules allow "additional days" to be remitted in certain circumstances, *e.g.* for subsequent good behaviour.

Experience of Custody

29.44 Assistance in understanding the everyday reality for young people of life in custodial establishments can be gained from Lyon *et al.*[49] who conducted focus group discussions with 84 trainees in 10 young offender institutions between December 1998 and March 1999. Thirty participants were aged under 18. They were not necessarily subject to what was then s.53 detention, nor is their particular experience separately recorded, but the general tenor of the comments seem most appropriately located here. The findings can be summarised thus—

- Many spoke of being scared, humiliated and de-personalised on first entering custody, albeit that conditions were not as bad as imagination or rumour had led them to expect. The induction process was usually of only very limited help, obliging new trainees to rely on guesswork in grasping rules and procedures that were insufficiently clear and communicated.

- Relationships with staff were often uneasy or tenuous. Trainees reported being treated in a way that exposed them to the worst of both worlds. They felt belittled because of their age while at the same time staff frequently demonstrated little understanding of the needs of young people still growing up while experiencing imprisonment. As an example of conflicting expectations, they commented that they were expected to behave like adults (which they felt they were not) but were not given the same facilities and treatment. They felt that staff should be better trained to recognise the needs of young people and their responsibility to exercise care of those in their charge. Trainees emphasised the importance of mutual respect and their wish for better guidance in surviving their sentence and making positive use of their time. Personal officer schemes were all too often notional rather than the basis of a meaningful relationship.

- Regimes were criticised for doing too little to make life safe for young people and to deal effectively with bullying, racism and the circulation of illicit drugs.

- Educational opportunities were valued and teaching staff were generally perceived in a positive light, because "they don't treat you like a prisoner; they treat you as if you were in college". Courses such as thinking skills, anger management, parenting and substance misuse were seen as relevant and helpful when available.

- Young prisoners overwhelmingly felt that they were poorly supported and neglected by outside probation staff. They reported numerous changes in

---

[49] J. Lyon, C Dennison & A Wilson *"Tell Them So They Listen": Messages from Young People in Custody*, Research Study 201 (Home Office, London, 2000).

their designated officer. Their officers appeared to demonstrate little empathy for the predicament of young prisoners.

● Time in prison was experienced as a separate world, disconnected from their lives outside. Many appreciated that imprisonment had given them "time to think" or "to get their head sorted" but they considered that their time away should be more connected to their external world of families, carers, youth justice workers, friendship circles. They felt strongly that they should be better prepared for release and be given more opportunities to adjust gradually to life outside in the community.

Recent Use of Detention for Grave Crimes

29.45   The rise in the use of this form of detention, under CYPA 1933, s.53(2), during the late 1970s and 1980s caused Harris and Timms[50] to suggest that the sentence had altered in use "from a last ditch social defence to a tariff sentence", contrary to the original intention of the 1933 Act. The significance of the sentence underwent a marked shift when it became available for 17-year-olds in late 1992. The figures for the period 1994–99 are as follows:

	1994	1995	1996	1997	1998	1999
Violence	69	67	97	104	98	111
Sexual	22	39	51	56	45	58
Burglary	51	54	101	128	133	101
Robbery	191	192	275	345	241	258
Theft/HSG	5	6	10	17	18	5
Arson	23	18	33	32	20	29
Drug	7	5	13	18	23	29
Other	19	10	29	22	15	16
All offences	387	391	609	724	593	607

Source: Criminal Statistics for England and Wales, 1999

Early Release

29.46   The provisions applicable to young offenders serving sentences under PCC(S)A 2000, s.91 (CYPA 1933, s53(2) and (3)) depend on the length of sentence—

(i)   12 months or less;

(ii)   over 12 months but less than four years;

(iii)   determinate terms of four years or longer;

(iv)   indeterminate term.

The scheme for those serving "life" (category (iv)) is outlined at 29.68 and the following deals with those serving determinate terms.

29.46a   The provisions for early release specify proportions of sentence which have to expire or be served before the detainee is either released on licence or is

[50] Harris R. & Timms N. *Secure Accommodation in Child Care* (Routledge, London, 1993) at p. 77.

entitled to unconditional release or is no longer subject to licence. The critical points of sentence are one-half, two-thirds and three-quarters. Any time on remand in custody prior to sentence which counts under CJA 1967, s.67 (see 29.34) towards the reduction of the sentence to be served also counts in the calculation of these proportions (s.41(1) and (2)).

(i) 12 Months or less

29.47 The following provisions apply to the small number of young offenders who are ineligible for a detention and training order, either because they are aged under 12 or because they do not satisfy the criterion of being a "persistent offender" applicable under section 100(2)(a) to those aged under 15 (see 28.05). As "short-term prisoners", *i.e.* serving less than four years, these detainees are entitled to be released after serving one-half of their sentence but their sentence is of insufficient length to attract liability to release on licence under CJA 1991, s.33(1). Instead, the detainee is released subject to notice of supervision under CJA 1991, s.65(1). This obligation falls within the long-standing tradition of compulsory benevolence and social defence by imposing supervision on young offenders that is not required of adults. Supervision lasts for three months from date of release (s.65(3)) and is exercised by a YOT member, a probation officer or a social worker of a local authority social services department (s.65(1)). In practice responsibility will almost certainly be undertaken by a YOT member. The requirements contained in the notice of supervision are the same as the standard conditions that apply to those released on licence after serving a term exceeding 12 months but less than four years (see 29.50).

29.48 *The Process of Supervision* The relevant provisions of the *National Standards for Youth Justice* governing work with all s.91 detainees apply and are outlined at 29.61.

29.49 *Failure to Comply* Under section 65(6), failure without reasonable excuse to comply with a requirement of supervision is punishable on summary conviction by—

(a) a fine not exceeding level 3 on the standard scale; or

(b) detention in such secure accommodation (PCC(S)A 2000, s.107) as may be specified by the Secretary of State for a period not exceeding 30 days, but the person is "not liable to be dealt with in any other way". It would thus be unlawful to discharge the young offender or, for example, to make an attendance centre order. Breach of a section 65 supervision notice is thus an imprisonable summary offence. As the offence is punishable by a further custodial sentence rather than recall to continue the original sentence, the power of the court to impose further detention is not tied to the timespan of the original sentence nor to the expiry of the notice of supervision. The fact that the person is convicted of a section 65(6) offence after the expiry of supervision does not curtail the ordering of further detention. On release from the fresh detention period, the offender is not be liable to a further period of supervision in consequence but is conviction under section 65(6) is "shall not prejudice any liability to supervision to which he was previously subject, and that liability shall accordingly continue until the end of the supervision period": section

65(8). If liability to supervision has expired meanwhile, the offender is re-released without statutory oversight.

(ii) Terms of 12 months or longer but less than four years

29.50 Detainees serving sentences of detention of this duration are treated on almost exactly the same footing as those serving terms of imprisonment of the same length, under the provisions of CJA 1991, Part II. The only difference of note affects those serving exactly 12 months, depending on their age at point of release. If aged under 18, the detainee falls to be supervised under CJA 1991, s.65, as outlined above (CJA 1991, s.43(4)(a)) whereas if released from a 12 month detention term aged 18 or older, the detainee will be released on licence, as described below. This is not likely to be an issue in practice because anyone sentenced to 12 month term of section 91 detention will invariably be aged under 18 at point of release. In consequence, the following can confidently be regarded as applying to those serving terms exceeding 12 months. The detainee has the status of short term prisoner (*i.e.* serving less than four years), being released on "automatic conditional release" (ACR) licence after serving one-half of sentence, under the terms of CJA 1991, s.33(1)(b).

29.51 *Length of Licence* Subject to the power of the sentencing court to impose an extended sentence in certain instances (see), Licence remains in force until the date on which the detainee would (but for their release) have served three-quarters of their sentence (CJA 1991, s.37(1)). This is subject to a statutory minimum period of one-quarter of the total sentence term, even if this takes the licence period beyond the three-quarters point. This minimum is designed to ensure a sufficiently useful and viable period of oversight. It has most significance when time on remand contributes to the calculation of early release (see para. 29.34). However, the licence cannot run beyond the full term 100 per cent point of sentence, even if this falls within the minimum period.

However, CJA 1991, s.65(4) provides that if licence expires in less than three months (*i.e.* because the full term of sentence is reached), the offender will remain subject to a requirement of statutory supervision under section 65(1) (see 29.47), beginning on the date of expiry and ending three months from the date of release.

29.52 *Licence Conditions* The primary licence condition is that the offender "must place himself" under the supervision of the probation officer, social services social worker or (if aged under 18 at release) YOT member nominated for the purpose, the objectives of such supervision being the protection of the public, the prevention of re-offending and the achievement of successful re-integration in the community. The specific standard conditions of supervision are as follows:

"While under supervision you must:
(i) keep in touch with your supervising officer in accordance with any reasonable instructions that you may from time to time be given;
(ii) if required, receive visits from your supervising officer at your home at reasonable hours and for reasonable periods;
(iii) live where reasonably approved by your supervising officer and notify him or her in advance of any proposed change of address;
(iv) undertake only such employment as your supervising officer reasonably approves and notify him or her in advance of any proposed change in employment or occupation;

(v) not travel outside the United Kingdom without obtaining the prior permission of your supervising officer;

(vi) be of good behavior not commit any offense and not take any action which would jeopardise the objectives of your supervision, namely to protect the public, prevent you from re-offending and secure your successful reintegration into the community."

29.53 As release on licence is automatic, short-term detainees are usually released on a "standard licence". However there is provision for the governor of the establishment from which the detainee is released to approve special additional conditions in exceptional cases, when recommended to do so by the supervising officer in the interests of devising an effective programme of supervision. Any such extra conditions must be chosen from a list of approved conditions, detailed at 29.60.

As Circular Instruction 27/1992, para. 25 pointed out:

"there is no mechanism to delay release if a prisoner declines to co-operate with supervision . . . the prisoner may have refused to give a release address. If the home area is known, the prisoner should be instructed to report to the duty officer at a probation office in the home area. If the home area is not known, it may be necessary to instruct the prisoner to report to the duty officer at a probation office in the petty sessional area where the prisoner was tried for the current offence. If agreed with the Probation Service, and as a last resort, part or all of the discharge grant may be sent to the reporting office as an incentive to turn up".

29.54 If the offenders is willing to co-operate but is genuinely homeless, the relevant reformary agency will be responsible for trying to find accommodation but it is recognised that this cannot be guaranteed, thus making licence requirements very difficult to enforce if the offender is moving around frequently between temporary bases.

29.55 *Release Direct from Court* An offender may be entitled to be released on licence direct from court if he has spent a sufficient period of time on remand in custody or following a reduction of their sentence on appeal. (Note that the former "five day rule" which operated to ensure that remission could not reduce the actual term to be served to less than five days was abolished upon introduction of early release under CJA 1991.) Such offenders are still liable to compulsory supervison and should be issued with licence or notice of supervision at the court. Court duty officers will identify the supervising officer and determine reporting instructions. Detailed guidance is provided by Circular Instruction 39/1992.

29.56 *The Process of Supervision* The relevant provisions of the *National Standards for Youth Justice* governing work with all section 91 detainees apply and are outlined at 29.61.

29.57 *Breach of Licence* Since implementation of CDA 1998 and with effect in respect of offences committed on or after January 1, 1999, the enforcement provisions of CJA 1991, s.38 requiring prosecution for a summary offence of failure to comply with licence have been repealed. Instead, "short-term" ACR licences are enforced in the same way as "long-term" licences, under the provisions of CJA 1991, s.39. These provisions are outlined below at 29.65.

29.58 *Home Detention Curfew*   Section 34A of the Criminal Justice Act 1991, inserted by CDA 1998, s.99, provides that short-term prisoners aged 18 or over serving sentences of three months or longer, save for some excepted categories, are eligible for release ahead of the half-way point of sentence subject to Home Detention Curfew, a form of licence requiring the prisoner to remain at a place or places specified for periods specified of at least nine hours in any one day (CJA 1991, s.37A). The length of curfew eligibility depends on the length of sentence, those serving eight months or more being eligible 60 days before their automatic release at the halfway point of sentence. Prisoners serving sentences that are subject to automatic conditional release licence (or to notice of supervision under CJA 1991, s.65) who are selected for home detention curfew are subject to both sets of conditions and to enforcement action in respect of non-compliance with curfew under CJA 1991, s.38A as well as to any action in respect of non-compliance with ACR licence or notice of supervision. Though power to release under section 34A applies only to "prisoners aged 18 or over", the Home Secretary may extend the opportunity to younger prisoners by repealing the words "18 or over" by statutory instrument (s.34A(5)(a)). There is no current intention to introduce this change but section 91 detainees who attain the age of 18 while serving their sentence will become eligible for consideration.

(iii) Four years or longer

29.59   Detainees serving sentence for a term of four years or longer have the status of "long-term" prisoner, being entitled to automatic conditional release only at the two-thirds point of sentence. They are, however, eligible for "discretionary conditional release" on parole after serving a half of their sentence, if this is recommended by the Parole Board. In the case of detainees serving sentence of less than 15 years, the Parole Board's recommendation for release is decisive. If the Parole Board recommends the release of a detainee serving sentence of 15 years or longer, the Home Secretary retains discretion not to release if this is considered to be contrary to the public interest. However, the Home Secretary cannot release a detainee when the Parole Board has not recommended release. If not recommended for release when first eligible (or the detainee declines to be considered) a further application may be made if at least 13 months remains to be served before the two-thirds point of sentence and automatic release on non-parole licence. In effect this benefits only those serving a term of at least 78 months.

29.60 *Criteria for Parole*   In exercising powers to give the Parole Board directions as to the matters to be taken into account in considering individuals for parole, the Home Secretary shall in particular have regard to (s. 32(6))—

(a) the need to protect the public from serious harm from offenders; and

(b) the desirability of preventing the commission by them of further offences and of securing their rehabilitation.

The Secretary of State has given Directions to the Board (1996) in respect of all determinate term prisoners that it shall consider primarily the risk to the public of a further offence being committed at a time when the prisoner would otherwise be in prison and whether such a risk is acceptable. This must be balanced against the benefit, both to the public and the offender, of early release back into the community under a degree of supervision which might help rehabilitation and so lessen the risk of re-offending in he future. Safeguarding the public may often outweigh the benefits to the offender of early release. In assessing risk to the safety of the public, the Board shall take into account—

(a) the nature and circumstances of the original offence;

(b) whether the prisoner has shown by his attitude and behaviour in custody that he is willing to address his offending behaviour by understanding its causes and its consequences for the victims concerned, and has made positive effort and progress in doing so;

(c) in the case of a violent or sexual offender, whether the prisoner has committed other offences of sex and violence, in which case the risk to the public of release on licence may be unacceptable;

(d) that a risk of violent or sexual offending is more serious than a risk of other types of offending.

29.61 The Board shall also consider whether:

- the longer period of supervision that parole would provide is likely to reduce the risk of further offences;

- the prisoner is likely to comply with licence conditions;

- the prisoner has failed to meet the requirements of licensed supervision, temporary release or bail on any previous occasion and, if so, whether this makes the risk of releasing him unacceptable;

- the resettlement plan will help secure the offender's rehabilitation;

- the supervising officer has prepared a programme of supervision and has recommended specific licence conditions.

29.62 *Length of Licence* Subject to the sentencing court's power to impose an extended sentence (see 29.30), or, in respect of a sexual offence committed on or before September 30, 1998 an extension of licence to the sentence expiry date under the original version of CJA 1991, s.44, long-term detainees remain subject to licence until the date on which, but for their release, they would have served three-quarters of their sentence (s. 37(1)), subject to a statutory minimum period of one-twelfth of the total sentence term (s. 41(3)).

29.63 *Licence Conditions* Long-term detainees released on licence are subject to such conditions as may be specified in the licence, including requirements as to supervision by a probation officer, or a YOT member if they are aged under 18 at date of release. The standard requirements are as specified for short-term detainee (see 29.52) but together with any additional conditions which may be included after consultation with the Parole Board, usually on the recommendation of the officer who will supervise the licensee. The supervising officer in respect of an adult is normally a probation officer (s.37(4)) but, in relation to a detainee released on licence under the age of 22, may be a social worker of a local authority social services department (s. 43(5)).

Extra conditions should normally be limited to appropriate choices from the following list of approved conditions—

1. Attending upon a duly qualified psychiatrist/psychologist/medical practitioner for such care, supervision or treatment as that practitioner recommends.

2. Not to engage in any work or other organised activity involving a person under a specified age.

3. To reside at a specified address and not to leave without prior approval of supervising officer; thereafter to reside as directed by supervising officer.

4. Not to reside in the same household as any child under a specified age.

5. Not to seek to approach or communicate with wife/former wife/child(ren)/ grandchildren/other named persons without prior approval of supervising officer and, where appropriate, named social services department.

6. Comply with any requirements reasonably imposed by supervising officer for purpose of ensuring that licensee address alcohol/drug/sexual/ gambling/solvent abuse/debt/offending behaviour anger problems, at specified course or centre (where appropriate).

29.64 *The Process of Supervision* The relevant provisions of the *National Standards for Youth Justice* (2000, para.9.3) governing work with all s.91 detainees specify the following—

- *Initial Contact* The supervising officer must arrange to see the offender on day of release and must make a home visit within five working days of release.

- *Subsequent Contact* Contact must be twice weekly for the first 12 weeks of licence (or notice of supervision) and then (licences only) at least once every ten working days.

- *Review of Progress* The supervising officer must arrange a review meeting to take place within the first month following release, at which the offender should attend. A member of the secure facility staff should be invited and the parents or primary carer should be encouraged to participate.

- *Non-Compliance* Unexplained missed appointments must be followed up by a YOT member (if a YOT holds supervision responsibility) by visit, telephone or, where these are not practicable, by letter, within one working day. If there is no acceptable reason for non-compliance, a formal warning must be issued or breach action commenced. If the offender receives more than two formal warnings during the first 12 weeks of supervision, breach action must be initiated within 10 working days of the most recent breach. course of the licence period. This is usually upon the application of the supervising officer to the Parole Unit of the Home Office and subject to the approval of the Parole Board. Because the original licence is issued by the Governor of the establishment from which the offender is released, any changes have to be notified to the Governor so that a fresh licence can be issued.

29.65 *Revocation and Recall* Long-term detainees (and also short-term detainees in respect of offences committed on or after January 1, 1999) are subject to revocation and recall to custody, either on the recommendation of the Parole Board under CJA 1991, s.39(1) or by order of the Home Secretary where the risk to the safety of the public appears so great as to justify urgent intervention (s.39(2)). The YOT manager is responsible for ensuring that any persistent failure to comply or any behaviour indicative of "an enhanced risk of harm to self or the community" is reported promptly to the Prison Service Sentence Enforcement Unit for action under section 39. Recall does not have to be based on specific breach of licence but my be pre-emptive in the face of increased risk causing substantial concern, particularly where further serious offences are likely to be committed.

29.66 *Rights and Procedure following Recall* An offender recalled to custody under section 39 shall be informed of the reasons for recall and may make representations in writing: s.39(3). The Secretary of State shall refer to the Parole Board any detainee who was recalled without the Board's recommendation under section 39(2) or who has opted to make representations under s.39(3): s.39(4). Where the Board recommends the release of a detainee referred to it under section 39(4), the Home Secretary shall act on that recommendation. If the Board does not recommend re-release the detainee will be further reviewed by the Board after 12 months if a minimum of 13 months remains to be served. If not released on the Board's recommendation, a detainee shall be re-released automatically at the three-quarters point of sentence, again on licence and subject to supervision until the sentence expiry date. (This liability to further licence arises if the offence was committed on or after September 30, 1998. For offences committed prior to that date, re-release at the three-quarters point is not on licence but in respect of an offender aged under 22, liability to notice of supervision under section 65 arises for three months or until 22nd birthday, whichever is the shorter.) If re-released on licence and re-recalled under section 39, the detainee remains in custody until their sentence expiry date when they shall be re-released without any licence liability.

Early Release from Extended Sentence: CJA 1991, s.44

29.67 In essence, the offender's release date is determined according to the custodial term (see 29.31). The extension period takes effect at the point when any licence to which the offender is subject by reason of the custodial term would otherwise terminate, *i.e.* at the three-quarter point of the custodial term. To illustrate, a sexual offender sentenced to an extended sentence of seven years, combining a four year custodial term and a three year extension period, will be eligible for release on parole after serving two years. If so released, he would then be on licence for 12 months followed by the extension period of three years, a total of four years subject to licence. If released at his non-parole date, after two years eight months, he would be on non-parole licence for four months followed by the further three years extension, a total of 40 months on licence.

Release from Indeterminate Detention

29.68 Where a detainee subject to a "life" sentence under section 91 (and HMP detention under section 90) has served "the relevant part" of his sentence as specified by the sentencing judge (see 29.24), he is eligible for release on licence under the Crime (Sentences) Act 1997, s.28. Release is upon the direction of the Parole Board after referral by the Home Secretary and an oral hearing before a discretionary lifer panel in accordance with the Parole Board Rules 1997. The Board must be satisfied that detention "is no longer necessary for the protection of the public": s.28(6)(b). After serving the relevant part, the detainee "may require the Secretary of State to refer his case to the Parole Board": s.28(7)(a). However, if the detainee is also serving a determinate term of detention or imprisonment, he must have served a half of that term before he may require reference to the Board:

s.28(7)(c). If a detainee is referred to the Board but his release is not directed, the detainee has the right to be referred again after a period of two years from the date of the disposal of that reference s.28(7)(b) though the Board may recommend an earlier review.

For those detainees serving an indeterminate section 53(2) term imposed prior to the implementation of CJA 1991, s.34 (see 29.24), the Home Secretary exercised transitional powers to certify a tariff term as the equivalent of the relevant part. Of 21 young offenders detained for life under section 53(2) in February 1995, seven had been given a tariff term of five years or less; eight, six to nine years; and six, ten to 14 years.

29.69 *Licence* Unless previously revoked, the licence pertaining to a released life prisoner "shall remain in force until his death": C(S)A 1997, s.31(1). The conditions of the life licence in respect of a discretionary life detainee are as recommended by the Parole Board: s.31(3)(a). The Secretary of State may not subsequently insert, vary or cancel any condition except in accordance with the recommendations of the Board.

29.70 *Recall* If recommended to do so by the Parole Board, the Secretary of State may revoke a life sentence prisoner's licence and recall him to prison: C(S)A 1997, s.32(1). Where it appears expedient in the public interest to recall the life licensee before such a recommendation is practicable, the Secretary of State may revoke the licence at his own initiative: s.32(2). An lifer recalled to custody under s.32 shall be informed of the reasons for recall and may make representations in writing: s.32(3). The Secretary of State shall refer to the Parole Board any life detainee who was recalled without the Board's recommendation under section 32(2) or who has opted to make representations under section 33(3): s.32(4). In the case of a recalled discretionary lifer, the Board conducts an oral hearing conducted as a discretionary lifer panel and if the Board directs the lifer's immediate release, the Secretary of State must give effect to that direction: s.32(5)(a).

Release on Compassionate Grounds

29.71 A s.91 detainee may be released at any time during their sentence if the Home Secretary is satisfied that "exceptional circumstances exist which justify . . . release on compassionate grounds" (CJA 1991, s.36(1)), though, in the case of a long-term or life detainee, the Home Secretary shall consult the Parole Board unless circumstances make consultation impracticable (s. 36(2)). PSO 6000 (1999) chapter 12 identifies two main categories justifying compassionate release, but only in "the most exceptional circumstances"—

(a) medical grounds, including terminal illness where death is likely to occur soon, severe incapacitation and circumstances where continued detention would endanger the prisoner's life;

(b) tragic family circumstances which could not have been foreseen at the time of sentencing.

On release, detainees are subject to licence and consequent liability to recall, depending on their status, until the expiry point of licence CJA 1991, s.42 provides for "additional days" to be awarded which extend the time to be served before entitlement to automatic conditional release on licence or discretionary early release on parole licence. The actual period of licence remains unchanged but commencement and completion are correspondingly delayed. The Prison Rules allow "additional days" to be remitted in certain circumstances, *e.g.* for subsequent good behaviour. In respect of a life licensee, power to release on compassionate grounds on the same basis as a long-term detainee under CJA 1991 s.36 is contained in C(S)A 1997, s.30.

Return to Prison

29.72 Where a person who has been released early from a determinate sentence for an "original offence" is convicted of a "new offence" punishable by imprisonment committed prior to their sentence expiry date, during what is known as the "at risk" period, he is liable to be returned to custody under the provisions of PCC(S)A 2000, s.116, formerly governed by CJA 1991, s.40. Liability arises, irrespective of the date on which he is convicted of the new offence. This provision does not apply to detention and training orders which have separate provisions under PCC(S)A 2000, s.105 governing offences during the currency of the order (see) but is specifically stated to apply to persons serving determinate sentences of detention under PCC(S)A 2000, s.91: s.116(10)(a). In the event that a young offender who has been sentenced to detention under section 91 and has re-offended after release prior to sentence expiry and remains a juvenile, if the court dealing with the further offence intends to impose a detention and training order, problems of interpretation may arise in combining the powers given under section 116 and sentencing powers under section 100. The Act makes no explicit reference to this possibility but on the face of section 116(2), the court has power to order the offender's return to detention "whether or not it passes any other sentence upon him". However, harmonisation of the two sets of provisions is far from straightforward in making sense of the practical consequences of such a combination. An answer is not provided by the provisions of section 106. As considered at 28.53, if the young offender is returned to detention in respect of re-offending during the period of a detention and training order and receives a new sentence of detention and training, the court appears to be subject to an aggregate maximum of 24 months. It is submitted that it would comply with the spirit of the detention and training order's ethos for the same ceiling to apply in this context, though the statute does not require the two periods to be treated as a single term.

Length of Return Period

29.73 Whether or not it passes any other sentence on the offender for the new offence, the court convicting him of that new offence may "order him to be returned to prison for the whole or any part of the period" which—

(a) begins with the date of the order; and

(b) is equal in length to the period between the date on which the new offence was committed and the sentence expiry date (s.116(2)).

Where the new offence was committed over two or more days, it shall be taken for the purposes of this provision to have been committed on the last of those days.

A magistrates' court may exercise the power to order return to custody even though the original sentence was necessarily imposed by the Crown Court but, in respect of an offender with an "at risk" period exceeding six months, is limited to a maximum return period of six months: s.116(3)(a). However, the justices may commit the offender in custody or on bail to the Crown Court to be dealt with: s.116(3)(b). Given that the Crown Court alone can impose detention under section 91 it will not be surprising if a youth court opted to commit in such cases. Power to commit applies to young offenders, being separate from the former power to commit for sentence under MCA 1980, s.37, repealed by the 1998 Act. In respect of the new offence, the Divisional Court in *Harrow Justices, ex p. Jordan*[51] indicated that the lower court should not deal with the latter while simultaneously committing the offender under CJA 1991, s.40 in respect of the "at risk' issue. As a matter of principle the two elements of sentencing should be dealt with by the same court. Power to refer both elements to the Crown Court has since been simplified by the provisions of PCC(S)A 2000, s.6. Power under section 6 arises in instances which include committal under section 116(3)(b): s.6(4)(d). Though section 116(5) states that section 116(3)(b)—

29.74
> "shall not be taken to confer on the magistrates' court a power to commit the person to the Crown Court for sentence for the new offence, but this is without prejudice to any such power conferred on the magistrates' court by any other provision of this Act",

section 6(2) confers that power, specifying that where the offence for which the original sentence was imposed was an indictable offence, as will certainly be the case—

> "the committing court may also commit the offender, in custody or on bail as the case may require, to the Crown Court to be dealt with in respect of any other offence whatsoever in respect of which the committing court has power to deal with him (being an offence of which he has been convicted by that or any other court)."

The period of return to custody "shall, as the court may direct, either be served before and be followed by, or be served concurrently with, the sentence imposed for the new offence": s.116(6)(b). It is thus impermissible for the court to order the section 116 period of return to be served consecutively to the sentence for the new offence.

Whether the return period precedes the new sentence or is served concurrently, it "shall be disregarded in determining the appropriate length of that sentence": s.116(6)(c). The Court of Appeal in *Taylor*[52] clarified that, in considering whether a return period should be ordered and in determining its length, the court should usually have regard to—

(a) the nature and extent of any progress made by the offender since their release;

(b) the length of interval between release and the new offence; and

(c) the nature and gravity of new offence and whether it calls for a custodial sentence;

---

[51] [1997] 1 Cr.App.R.(S.) 410.
[52] [1998] 1 Cr.App.R.(S.) 312.

(d) the totality of impact, in determining whether return should be ordered and, if so, whether it should be served before or concurrently with any new sentence.

DETENTION AT HER MAJESTY'S PLEASURE

PCC(S)A 2000, s.90

Where a person convicted of murder appears to the court to have been aged under 18 at the time the offence was committed, the court shall (notwithstanding anything in this or any other Act) sentence him to be detained during Her Majesty's pleasure.

29.75 A mandatory sentence of indefinite detention (usually known as H.M.P.) is prescribed on conviction of murder where the offender was aged 18 at the time of the offence. This power was previously long governed by CYPA 1933, s.53(1). Exercise of the power is required in a very limited number of cases, being used in the five years 1994–98 in only 88 instances, the numbers in any one year ranging from 26 (in 1997) to 10 (in 1998). Much attention has nevertheless focused on the mode of trial appropriate for the purpose (see 10.02), the length and location of detention, and the process of review to consider suitability for release on licence. Placement is addressed at 29.36 and the following concentrates on the review process in the light of recent developments in domestic and European Court of Human Rights case law.

29.76 This very special kind of "life" sentence had been administered in the same manner as an adult mandatory life sentence until the judgement of the European Court in *Hussain v. United Kingdom*[53] which prompted change introduced by the Crime (Sentences) Act 1997, s.28 which brought the review of H.M.P. cases within the provisions applying to discretionary life sentences, namely that the decision whether to release the prisoner is vested in the Parole Board. The setting of the "tariff" period, the minimum period to be served to satisfy the requirements of retribution and deterrence, remained with the Home Secretary but this residual aspect of executive control has been under severe challenge, arising from a well-publicised case of two boys aged 10 at the time of their offence, the murder of a two year old child, who had been sentenced to H.M.P. detention. The trial judge had recommended a tariff period of eight years and the Lord Chief Justice had recommended ten years. However, the Secretary of State had set a tariff term of 15 years, having considered the judicial recommendations, various petitions and media expressions of concern. The two offenders sought judicial review of the Home Secretary's decision. The House of Lords in *R. v. Secretary of State for the Home Department, ex p. Venables and Thompson*[54] while upholding the lawfulness of a tariff approach, confirmed that Parliament had intended that a sentence under section 53(1) should be different in nature to mandatory life imprisonment for murder and that in setting and operating the tariff the Home Secretary is required to take account of the welfare of the detainee in pursuance of CYPA 1933, s.44(1) and—

"to be sufficiently flexible to enable (him) to take into account the progress of the child and his development. In relation to children, the factors of

---

[53] [1996] 22 E.H.R.R. 1.
[54] [1998] A.C. 407.

retribution, deterrence and risk are not the only relevant factors: the welfare of the child is also another relevant factor." (*per* Lord Brown-Wilkinson at 499)

29.77   In this instance the Home Secretary had applied an unlawful policy by "totally excluding from consideration during the tariff period factors (*i.e.* their progress and development) necessary to determine whether release from detention would be in the interests of the welfare of the applicants". The 15 year tariff was therefore quashed.

In the light of this judgement the Home Secretary announced in November 1997 that a new approach to the fixing of H.M.P. tariffs would be adopted. An initial tariff would be set in the light of advice from the trial judge and the Lord Chief Justice, taking account of the offender's personal circumstances and representations on the offender's behalf. The Home Office would receive annual reports on the progress and development of detainees whose initial tariff had yet to expire. The attention of ministers would be drawn to any instance where there appeared to be a case for considering a reduction in tariff. When half of the initial tariff had expired the Secretary of State would consider a report on the detainee's progress and development and invite representations on the question of tariff, with a view to considering whether the tariff period originally set was still appropriate.

In subsequent proceedings before the European Court the same two detainees challenged the executive process of tariff-setting, even in the revised form, as a failure to comply with the requirements of Article 6(1) of the European Convention, entitling them to a fair and public hearing by an independent and impartial tribunal. The Court upheld that view.[55]

In consequence, the Home Secretary announced in March 2000[56] as follows:

29.78
   (i) Legislation will be introduced to provide for tariffs to be set by the trial judge in open court in the same way as for those over 18 receiving sentence of discretionary life imprisonment or custody for life. This decision would be appealable by the offender, or by the Attorney-General on grounds of undue leniency. [The promised change in law has since been brought about by CJCSA 2000, s.55, introducing PCC(S)A 2000, s.82A, outlined at 29.24, the relevant provisions being s.82A(1)(b) and (5). In the meantime, legal representatives are likely to seek an oral hearing prior to setting of tariff.]

   (ii) In respect of any new sentences imposed, pending this change in legislation, the Home Secretary has undertaken to set any tariff in line with the recommendation of the Lord Chief Justice.

   (iii) In respect of existing detainees (some 250) the Home Secretary has invited representations from those whose tariffs have not expired (around 140 cases).

      (a) Where no representations are received, the tariff will be set in accordance with the original recommendation of the Lord Chief Justice. However, if the original judicial view was higher than that set by ministers, the tariff will not be raised. If the new tariff has expired, the case will be referred immediately to the Parole Board.

---

[55] *V. and T. v. United Kingdom* [2000] 30 E.H.R.R. 121.
[56] *Hansard*, 13 March 2000, H.C. col. 21.

(b) Where detainees wish to make representations, these will be directed to the present Lord Chief Justice who will make a recommendation which the Home Secretary will treat as binding.

29.79 The Home Secretary appears to have treated the European decision as superseding rather than complementing the House of Lords judgement, with the consequence that the annual progress reports and consideration of possible tariff changes, together with a more detailed assessment at the halfway point of tariff, have been discontinued. Continuing consideration pertaining to the detainee's progress, welfare and development have thus ceased to inform tariff judgements. As Arnott and Creighton[57] suggest: "It is arguable that the reasons for introducing these reviews, reasons embedded in the nature of the sentence and the vulnerability of those who receive it, should persist irrespective of whether the sentence is fixed by the executive or the judiciary." The present process is likely to face challenge under the provisions of Article 6(1) of the European Convention of Human Rights that the offender should have the benefit of an oral hearing at the halfway point of tariff to review progress and development and to determine whether the original tariff period should be revised.

29.80 In a *Practice Statement (Juveniles: Murder Tariffs)*[58] the Lord Chief Justice has indicated the approach he will adopt in making recommendations to the Home Secretary—

- Written representations will be invited from detainees' legal advisors and also from the Director of Public Prosecutions, who can include representations on behalf of victims' families.

- The starting point will be that adopted in respect of adults sentenced to mandatory life imprisonment, namely a tariff of 14 years, increased or reduced to allow for aggravating and mitigating features.

- Aggravating features include: evidence of a planned or revenge killing; the killing of a child or a very old or otherwise vulnerable victim; evidence of sadism, gratuitous violence, or sexual maltreatment, humiliation or degradation before the killing; killing for gain in the course of burglary, robbery, blackmail, insurance fraud, etc.; multiple killings; killing a witness or potential witness to defeat the ends of justice; the killing of those doing their public duty (such as police officers, prison officers, firefighters); terrorist or politically motivated killings; use of firearms whether carried for defensive or offensive purposes; a record of serious violence; attempts to dismember or conceal the body.

- Mitigating features include: age; sub-normality or mental abnormality; provocation (in a non-technical sense) or an excessive response to a personal threat; spontaneity and the lack of pre-meditation, such as a sudden response to family pressure or to prolonged and eventually insupportable stress; mercy killing; guilty plea; hard evidence of remorse or contrition.

- Reasons for recommendations will be announced in open court.

---

[57] H. Arnott & S. Creighton (2000) *Legal Action*, June 13–16 at p. 13.
[58] [2000] 2 All E.R. 284.

Lord Woolf CJ has thus followed the lead of the Home Secretary in equating H.M.P. cases with adult life imprisonment, treating age as simply one mitigating factor in tariff setting.

Review, Release on Licence and Recall

29.81   As indicated above, H.M.P. detainees are dealt with under the same provisions as discretionary lifers, as specified by C(S)A 1997, s.28 *et seq.*, as outlined at 29.68 *et seq.*

CHAPTER 30

Ancillary Issues

ANCILLARY SENTENCING POWERS

Deprivation and forfeiture

30.01 Courts have power to deprive an offender of property used for the purposes of crime under PCC(S)A 2000, s.143 (formerly under PCCA 1973, s.43), together with other statutory powers of forfeiture provided in respect of specific offences. This power may be exercised whether or not the court also deals with the offender in any other way: s 143(4)(a). A possible use of section 143 powers against a young offender would be to ensure the confiscation of keys or implements used in the course of taking or stealing from vehicles or in burglary.

PCC(S)A 2000, s.143

(1) Where a person is convicted of an offence and the court by or before which he is convicted is satisfied that any property which has been lawfully seized from him, or which was in his possession or under his control at the time when he was apprehended for the offence or when a summons in respect of it was issued—

    (a) has been used for the purpose of committing, or facilitating the commission of, any offence, or

    (b) was intended by him to be used for that purpose, the court may (subject to subsection (5) below) make an order under this section in respect of that property.

(2) Where a person is convicted of an offence and the offence, or an offence which the court has taken into consideration in determining his sentence, consists of unlawful possession of property which—

    (a) has been lawfully seized from him, or

    (b) was in his possession or under his control at the time when he was apprehended for the offence of which he has been convicted or when a summons in respect of that offence was issued, the court may (subject to subsection (5) below) make an order under this section in respect of that property.

(5) In considering whether to make an order under this section in respect of any property, a court shall have regard—

    (a) to the value of the property; and

    (b) to the likely financial and other effects on the offender of the making of the order (taken together with any other order that the court contemplates making).

30.02 "Facilitating the commission of an offence" for this purpose includes "the taking of any steps after it has been committed for the purpose of disposing of any property to which it relates or of avoiding apprehension or detection": s.143(8). A special provision applies to a vehicle used in the course of: (a) an imprisonable offence under the Road Traffic Act 1988; (b) manslaughter; (c) wanton or furious driving.

30.03 Deprivation orders should be used only where the facts are "simple and uncomplicated" and are thus not appropriate where the property in question is subject to joint ownership.[1] However, the order should not be made without "full and proper investigation" of the prosecution's application,[2] though in most cases affecting young offender the circumstances are likely to be straightforward and obvious.

The power should not be used to forfeit property used in the commission of an offence by some person other than the offender and section 43(1)(a)(i) should be read as ". . . any offence by him", not "by anyone".[3]

30.04 Though a deprivation order may be seen primarily as a preventive measure, it almost inevitably has a punitive impact and the court should thus have regard both to the effect any order would have on the offender and to the totality of sentence. Thus if deprivation would "overdo the punishment"[4] or would have a disproportionately severe impact upon the offender,[5] an order would be inappropriate. A deprivation order may, however, be combined with an order of discharge (*i.e.* in a case where it is "inexpedient to inflict punishment") though the fact that the offender is considered to merit an absolute discharge may cause the court to feel that forfeiture is not appropriate: *Hunt*[5a], where the defendant received an absolute discharge for handling stolen goods placed in the boot of his car by friends; an order depriving him of his car was set aside on appeal.

Deprivation and Victim Compensation

30.05 Where a court makes a deprivation order in respect of an offence, whether resulting in conviction or taken into consideration, that caused a victim to suffer personal injury, loss or damage, the court may also order that any proceeds arising from the disposal of the property, not exceeding a sum specified by the court, shall be paid to that victim: s.145(1). However, the court may make an order under section 145(1) "only if it is satisfied that but for the inadequacy of the offender's means it would have made a compensation order under which the offender would have been required to pay compensation of an amount not less than the specified sum": s.145(2). It thus appears permissible to order compensation in part-satisfaction of the victim's loss and also a deprivation order with a section 145(1) order to meet the shortfall.

Where the defendant committed such an offence "by driving, attempting to drive or being in charge of a vehicle" or by failing to provide a specimen for analysis as required by the Road Traffic Act 1988, s.7, or by failing to stop and give information or to report an accident, the vehicle shall be regarded as used for the purpose of committing an offence: s.143(6).

---

[1] *Troth* (1980) 71 Cr.App.R. 1.
[2] *Pemberton* (1982) 4 Cr.App.R.(S.) 328.
[3] *Slater* [1986] 1 W.L.R. 1340, *Neville* (1987) 9 Cr.App.R.(S.) 222).
[4] *Budds* (1982) 4 Cr.App.R.(S.) 268.
[5] *Tavernor* [1976] R.T.R. 242.
[5a] [1978] Crim. L.R. 697.

Effect of Deprivation

30.06   A deprivation order operates to deprive the offender of their rights in the property which shall be taken into police possession if this has not already occurred: s.143(3). However, the order does not affect the rights of any other person. The property becomes subject to the Police (Property) Act 1897, as modified by provisions detailed in PCC(S)A 2000, s.144. No application to the court.

No application to the court can be made by a claimant after six months from the date of the forfeiture order. A claimant seeking to recover the property must satisfy the court either that he or she did not consent to the offender having possession of the property or, in the case of property seized under section 143, that he or she did not know and had no reason to suspect that the property was likely to be used for the purpose of crime. The police may dispose of the property and the proceeds of any sale are applied to public funds.

Other Statutory Powers

30.07   Statutes giving power of forfeiture and disposal or destruction which are most likely to be applied to juveniles are as follows—

Prevention of Crime Act 1953:   Section 1(2) permits an order for the forfeiture or disposal of any weapon concerned in the offence of possessing an offensive weapon in any public place without lawful authority or excuse.

A similar provision applies under the *Crossbows Act 1987* in respect of the summary offence of possession of a crossbow without adult supervision by a person under 17. No power of forfeiture is attached to the offence under CJA 1988, s.139 of having an article with a blade or point (other than a folding pocket knife) in a public place, but use may be made following conviction of the general power under section 143.

30.08   *Firearms Act 1968*:   A number of offences under the Act prohibiting the possession of firearms or ammunition by young persons are subject to forfeiture/ disposal orders under Schedule 6, Part II, paras. 7 and 8—

   (i) s.22(3): person under 15 having a shotgun without adult supervision;

   (ii) s.22(4): person under 14 having an air weapon or ammunition without lawful authority;

   (iii) s.22(5): person under 17 having an air weapon without a securely fastened cover in a public place;

   (iv) s.23(1): person under 14 making improper use of an air weapon when under supervision.

In addition, section 52 of the Act gives broad authority to the court to make such order as to forfeiture or disposal of any firearm or ammunition as it deems appropriate in the following circumstances:

   (i) where an offender is sentenced to a detention and training order or detention under PCC(S)A 2000, s.91;

   (ii) where an offender is bound over to keep the peace and the recognisance carries a condition not to possess, use or carry a firearm;

(iii) where the offender is placed on probation with an additional requirement of the order not to possess, use or carry a firearm.

This section is widely worded and does not require either that the offence should relate to the firearm or that the offender was in possession of the firearm at any particular time.

30.09 *Misuse of Drugs Act 1971*: Where a person is convicted of an offence under this statute or a drug trafficking offence under the Drug Trafficking Offences Act 1986, the court may order "anything shown to the satisfaction of the court to relate to the offence to be forfeited and either destroyed or dealt with in such other manner as the court may order" (s.27(1)). Property relating to the offence may include money[6] provided that the relationship is established but this power should be distinguished from the Crown Court's power of confiscation of the profits of dealing under the Drug Trafficking Offences Act 1986, s.1.

Exclusion and Banning Orders

30.10 Of the two powers of the court to order the offender's exclusion from specified places, licensed premises and football grounds, the latter is probably more likely to be used in respect of juveniles.

Football Grounds

30.11 Under the Public Order Act 1986, s.30, as substituted in strengthened form by the Football (Offences and Disorder) Act 1999, s.6, a person convicted of a relevant offence may be made subject to a "domestic football banning order". The order has the effect of prohibiting the offender from entering football grounds for the purpose of attending prescribed matches (*i.e.* involving a Football League team) for a minimum period of one year but for no more than three years: s.32(1). The provision applies to any offence specified in the Football Spectators Act 1989, Sched. 1. If the court is satisfied that there are reasonable grounds to believe that making the order would help to prevent violence or disorder at or in connection with prescribed football matches, "it shall be the duty of the court to impose an order: (s.30(2). Where it has power to make an order but opts not to do, "it shall state in open court that it is not satisfied that there are such reasonable grounds . . . and give reasons why it is not so satisfied": s.30(3). The order can be imposed only in addition to any sentence or discharge order made for the offence of which the offender is convicted: s.30(4).

On the application of the prosecution, the court may also order that a photograph of the defendant shall be taken and may require the offender to attend a specified police station within seven days for that purpose.

Entering a ground in breach of an order is a summary offence punishable by a fine not exceeding levels and/or six months detention (s.32(2).

A person subject to such an exclusion order may apply to the court which imposed it to terminate it, provided that at least one year has elapsed since the making of the order. Where the application is refused, a fresh application cannot be made for a further six months.

---

[6] *Beard* [1974] 1 W.L.R. 1549.

Licensed Premises

30.12 Under the Licensed Premises (Exclusion of Certain Persons) Act 1980, s.1, if a person is convicted of an offence committed on licensed premises and the court is satisfied that the offender resorted to violence or offered or threatened to resort to violence, the court may make an exclusion order prohibiting the offender from entering those premises or any other specified licensed premises for a period of not less than three months and not more than two years. Home Office Circular 51/1993 was issued to draw sentencers' attention to the availability of this power. Such an order can be made only in addition to any penalty or order imposed for the offence, including an absolute or conditional discharge. Entering licensed premises in breach of such an order is a summary offence punishable with a level 3 fine (£1,000) or one month's imprisonment or both. Because this term is below the minimum permissible period of a detention and training order it follows that this sanction is not available in respect of juveniles. At the time of such conviction, the court shall consider whether the order should continue, be terminated or varied by deleting the name of any specified premises. The order is not otherwise affected by a conviction for non-compliance.

It is unclear how wide the ambit of the order can be. In *Grady*[7] the court sought to exclude the offender from entering "licensed premises in Norfolk" for 12 months. The order was quashed on appeal because the offender was a woman of mature years of previous good character and the Court of Appeal stated that exclusion orders were designed for those who could be said to be making a nuisance of themselves in public houses. The Court did not comment on the extent of the order appealed against.

Restitution Orders

30.13 A restitution order is intended either to restore goods stolen or unlawfully removed to the person entitled to them or, if the goods are not recovered, to restore to that person the cash or goods equivalent out of money found in the offender's possession on apprehension or goods representing the proceeds of the misappropriated property.

30.14   **PCC(S)A 2000, s.148**

(1) This section applies where goods have been stolen, and either—

    (a) a person is convicted of any offence with reference to the theft (whether or not the stealing is the gist of his offence); or

    (b) a person is convicted of any other offence, but such an offence as is mentioned in paragraph (a) above is taken into consideration in determining his sentence.

(2) Where this section applies, the court by or before which the offender is convicted may on the conviction (whether or not the passing of sentence is in other respects deferred) exercise any of the following powers—

    (a) the court may order anyone having possession or control of the stolen goods to restore them to any person entitled to recover them from him; or

    (b) on the application of a person entitled to recover from the person convicted any other goods directly or indirectly representing the

---

[7] [1990] Crim. L.R. 608.

stolen goods (as being the proceeds of any disposal or realisation of the whole or part of them or of goods so representing them), the court may order those other goods to be delivered or transferred to the applicant; or

(c) the court may order that a sum not exceeding the value of the stolen goods shall be paid, out of any money of the person convicted which was taken out of his possession on his apprehension, to any person who, if those goods were in the possession of the person convicted, would be entitled to recover them from him;

and in this subsection "the stolen goods" means the goods referred to in subsection (1) above.

(4) Where the court on a person's conviction makes an order under subsection (2)(a) above for the restoration of any goods, and it appears to the court that the person convicted—

(a) has sold the goods to a person acting in good faith, or
(b) has borrowed money on the security of them from a person so acting, the court may order that there shall be paid to the purchaser or lender, out of any money of the person convicted which was taken out of his possession on his apprehension, a sum not exceeding the amount paid for the purchase by the purchaser or, as the case may be, the amount owed to the lender in respect of the loan.

30.15 Powers under section 148(2)(c) and (4) are exercisable without need for any application by any person appearing to have an interest in the property concerned: s.149(2). An order may be made under both section 148(2)(b) and (c) with reference to the stealing of the same goods, provided that the person in whose favour the orders are made does not thereby recover more than the value of those goods: s.148(3). Restitution shall only be ordered where the question of title to goods is straightforward and the evidence is clear. A criminal court is not the appropriate forum to determine complex issues of ownership.[8] Under s.148(2)(c), it is not necessary to show that money found in the offender's possession is the proceeds of the offence, merely that it belongs to the offender.[9] *Lewis* also established that a restitution order can be made for a greater sum than the offender realised from the offence, provided that it is not a sum greater than the loss occasioned by the offence. An order may be made under both section 148(2)(b) and (c), provided that the entitled person does not thereby recover more than the value of the original goods.

Disqualification and Endorsement

30.16 Juveniles are subject to the same provisions of disqualification and endorsement as adult offenders, even though they may be too young to hold a licence to drive a motor vehicle. These provisions are not detailed here but attention is drawn to considerations relating to the youth of the offender which may influence a court having discretion in regard to disqualification or the length of any period of disqualification.

[8] *Calcutt* [1985] 7 Cr.App.R.(S.) 385.
[9] *Lewis* [1975] Crim. L.R. 353.

The Persistent Driving Offender

30.17 It may be considered counter-productive to impose a long period of disqualification on an offender who has shown a tendency to drive without a licence, exposing them to greater likelihood of ignoring the licence requirements. In *Thomas*,[10] Lord Lane C.J. said—

". . . with persons like the present appellant, who seem incapable of leaving motor vehicles alone, to impose a period of disqualification which will extend for a substantial period after their release from custody may well, and in many cases certainly will, invite the offender to commit further offences in relation to motor vehicles. In other words a long period of disqualification may well be counter-productive and so contrary to the public interest."

30.18 This reasoning also appears valid in cases where a custodial sentence is not imposed at the time of disqualification. The court may feel it proper not to make the prospect of lawful driving seem so remote and unattainable as to be not worth waiting for. On the other hand, the risks arising from the defendant's bad driving may indicate that a long ban is necessary to protect the public. In considering its duty to protect the public from danger, the court may feel that a lengthy period of disqualification is justified to enable the young offender to develop in maturity.[11] The court may also consider that it is important not to inhibit unduly the young offender's employment prospects if there is a real possibility that their ability to drive will enhance their chances in the job market.[12]

Recommendations for Deportation

30.19 By the Immigration Act 1971, s.6(3) a court may, on sentencing an offender who is aged 17 or over, who is not a British citizen and who is convicted of an offence punishable for an adult with imprisonment, make a recommendation that the offender be deported. The final decision whether to deport is for the Home Secretary. The offender must be given a minimum of seven days notice in writing that a recommendation is being considered and the defence should have the opportunity to address the court on the matter. The order should be considered on the criterion whether the offender's continuing presence in the United Kingdom would be detrimental to the community, in the light of the seriousness of the offence, the offender's record and the likely impact of deportation upon third parties such as the offender's family.

It may seem unlikely that a juvenile will be considered to present sufficient likelihood of community detriment. Though no precise statistics are available, the use of this power upon 17-year-olds is extremely rare, the majority of offenders who are subject to recommendation being drug couriers. In *Ariquat* (1981) 3 Cr. App. R.(S.) 83 no evidence of community detriment was found in regard to a young offender, a 19-year-old who was convicted of indecent assault, having had sexual intercourse with a girl of 15, believing her to be aged 16. The court is entitled to consider whether the offender would suffer special hardship if deported, if for example the young person would be returned to a country which he hardly knows and which his parents have since left.

---

[10] [1983] 1 W.L.R. 1490. See also *Branston*, noted at 27.42.
[11] *Gibbons* (1987) 9 Cr.App.R.(s.) 21.
[12] See *Aspden* [1975] R.T.R. 456.

Binding Over

30.20   As a measure of "preventive justice" juveniles may be bound over to keep the peace or to be of good behaviour, either following the full hearing in an adult court of a complaint under MCA 1980, s.115 or of the court's own motion under common law powers pursuant to the Justices of the Peace Act 1361 at any time during the proceedings. A youth court does not have jurisdiction to deal with complaints under MCA 1980, s.115 so may only bind over a juvenile of its own motion. As with adult defendants, this power may be appropriate for cases of minor assault where the prosecution are prepared not to proceed, provided that the defendant agrees to be bound over. However, it is more likely that such matters will be diverted from prosecution and dealt with by a police caution.

If the charge against the juvenile proceeds to conviction, it is unclear whether the offender may be bound over without the passing of some other penalty or order. The Justices of the Peace Act 1968, s.1(7) refers to the bind over as "ancillary" to the court's jurisdiction but some courts have been prepared to bind over without additional penalty.

The bind over as a sentence has attracted a considerable degree of criticism—

> "The powers to bind an offender over at the sentencing stage are unduly wide, are productive of inconsistency and unfairness and are found unnecessary at least by some courts. They ought to be abolished at the earliest opportunity."[13]

More recently, the Law Commission[14] has proposed that the power to bind over to keep the peace and be of good behaviour, either without or upon conviction, is no longer defensible and should be abolished. The proposal has attracted considerable opposition from stipendiary and lay magistrates and justices' clerks.[15]

Procedural Requirements

30.21   *Consent*   The juvenile must consent to entering a recognisance, whether under section 115 or common law. The normal sanction for failure or refusal to enter a recognisance is imprisonment. Because a court has no power to impose imprisonment on a juvenile, a juvenile cannot be compelled to be bound over[16] but if consent is given then the bind over can properly be ordered, despite the absence of sanction.[17]

30.22   *Duration*   At the discretion of the court.

30.23   *Amount*   There is no fixed upper limit but it should be a reasonable sum, having regard to the juvenile's means and personal circumstances. This is not a financial liability which a parent or guardian may be ordered to pay under PCC(S)A 2000, s.137.

30.24   *Appeal*   There is a right of appeal to the Crown Court against an order by a magistrates' court to enter into recognisances, and to the Court of Appeal where the Crown Court orders the bind over.

---

[13] Ashworth, 1992, p. 248.
[14] Law Commision *Binding over* (Law Comm. No. 222) Cm. 2439 (HMSO, London, 1994).
[15] Justices Clerks' Society (1994) 'Response to the Law Commission's Report on Binding Over", *The Magistrate 50*, iii.
[16] *Veater v. Glennon* [1981] 1 W.L.R. 567.
[17] *Conlan v. Oxford* (1983) 5 Cr.App.R.(S.) 237.

Forfeiture of Recognisance

30.25 Procedure upon failure to comply with the requirement of the binding over follows MCA 1980, s.120, outlined above in regard to the enforcement of bind overs in respect of parents and guardians.

SEXUAL OFFENDERS

Sex Offenders: Notification Requirements

30.26 Under the provisions of the Sex Offenders Act 1997 persons who have committed certain sexual offences in the United Kingdom are required to notify the police of their current name and home address and subsequent changes of name and/or address within the United Kingdom. These provisions apply to young offenders with certain modifications in respect of qualifying offences and the period for which notification requirements apply. The following outline aims to present the provisions as they affect those dealt with under the age of 18.

Liability to notification requirements

30.27 The principal way in which a young offender becomes subject to notification requirements arises under SOA 1997, s.1(1) by—

    (a) conviction of a qualifying offence; or

    (b) receiving a reprimand or warning for such an offence (CDA 1998, s.65(9)); or

    (c) being found not guilty of such an offence by reason of insanity or being found unfit to be tried for such an offence.

Additionally, those serving sentence of detention under CYPA 1933, s.53(3) or detained in hospital under MHA 1983, s.37, such a disposal having been made in respect of a qualifying offence prior to implementation of the 1997 Act (on September 1, 1997) are within the ambit of the Act and become liable on release or discharge: s.1(3).

Qualifying Offences

30.28 These are detailed in Schedule One of the 1997 Act, including: rape, intercourse with a girl under 13, incest by a male, indecent conduct towards a child, indecent assault on a female or a male (though this is not a qualifying offence where the victim (or "the other party" to the offence) was aged 18 or over at the time of the offence *unless* the offender was sentenced to a custodial term of 30 months or longer). An attempt, conspiracy or incitement to commit any of the above offences is also a qualifying offence. Sexual intercourse with a girl aged between 13 and 16 (under SOA 1956, s.6) is not a qualifying offence where the offender was aged under 20 at the time of the offence. Indecent exposure is also not a qualifying offence.

Duration of Notification Requirements

30.29 The duration of liability to notify depends on the nature of the disposal or outcome, as stipulated by SOA 1997, s.1(4) but modified in respect of young offenders, aged under 18 on the "relevant date", by s.4(2). The modified provisions are as follows—

• Custodial term for 30 months or longer or for life	indefinite liability
• indefinite liability	
• Detention in hospital with restriction	indefinite liability
• Custodial term of more than six months but less than 30 months	five years
• Custodial term for six months or less	42 months
• Detention in hospital without restriction	42 months
• A person of any other description (including those reprimanded or warned)	30 months

30.30 A "custodial term" includes a detention and training order, a sentence of detention under CYPA 1933, s.53 or PCC(S)A 2000, ss.90 or 91: s.4(1) as amended by PCC(S)A 2000, Sched. 9 para. 189. In the case of consecutive terms of custody, the term is the aggregate of those terms. In respect of concurrent terms, the term is "equal to the aggregate of those terms after such deduction as may be necessary to ensure that no period of time is counted more than once": s.1(6).

30.31 *"Relevant Date"*   The applicable period runs in each instance from the "relevant date", as defined by section 1(8), according to the basis on which the offender becomes subject to notification requirements—

(a) Following conviction of a qualifying offence: date of conviction;

(b) Following reprimand or warning: date of reprimand or warning;

(c) Following a finding of unfitness to plead or not guilty by reason of insanity: date of finding.

Notification Requirements

30.32 *Initial Notification:*   The person is required in the first instance to notify the police of his name (and if he uses more than one name, each name used) and his home (his sole or main residence) address, specifying also his date of birth.

Updating Notification: The person must subsequently notify the police of his use of a name which has not previously been notified and of any premises in the United Kingdom where he has resided or stayed for a "qualifying period" (14 days) or two or more periods in any period of 12 months which, taken together, amount to 14 days.

Timescale: Notification must be made before the end of 14 days from the "relevant date" (see above) but any time spent in custody is disregarded for this purpose.

Means of Notification: Notification may be given in person or in writing to any police station in the offender's local police area, *i.e.* the police force serving the area in which the offender's home is located.

Informing the Offender

30.33 Though the onus lies on the offender to register, provision is made for the obligation to be drawn to the offender's attention. Those sentenced for a qualifying offence receive a certificate informing them of notification requirements from the sentencing court at point of sentence. However, there is no legal duty on the sentencer to inform the defendant as to the length of time he will required to register. This was established in *Rawlinson*[18] where an adult offender sentenced to two years imprisonment was mistakenly informed by the judge that his period was five years. While the Appeal Court noted that this was unfortunate and that it is in the interests of justice that offenders should be given accurate information, the judge had been acting in an advisory capacity and the offender had no grounds for appeal. Offenders serving custodial terms are also informed of their notification requirements by the custodial authorities.

Failure to Notify Police

30.34 If an offender fails to comply with notification requirements without reasonable excuse or provides information known to be false, he is liable on summary conviction to a fine (not exceeding level 5) or to a term of imprisonment for a term not exceeding six months: SOA 1997, s.3.

Registration in Practice

30.35 Plotnikoff and Woolfson[18a] provide an evaluation of sex offender registration in the period August 1998–April 1999, showing a national rate of compliance of 94.7 per cent, with variation between individual forces ranging from 85.4 per cent to 100 per cent. Statistics generated by the Association of Chief Police Officers according to age of registered offenders indicate that the representation of young offenders among registrants varies markedly between forces, some reporting that offenders aged under 18 account for a quarter of all registrants while others reported no registered offenders in this age group. Figures for those who failed to comply with registration requirements do not break down the total by age but the clear majority of those of all ages convicted of non-compliance were dealt with by fine or discharge.

Sex Offender Orders

30.36 Where a person aged 10 or older has been convicted of or cautioned (including being reprimanded or warned) for an offence to which the 1997 Act applies, and it appears to the police that he has subsequently given "reasonable cause to believe that an order is necessary to protect the public from serious harm from him",[19] an application may be made for a sex offender order under the provisions of CDA 1998, ss.2–4. Application is made by complaint to a magistrates' court acting for any place where it alleged that the person acted in the way that prompts concern. A sex offender order has the effect of prohibiting the person from doing anything described in the order, thus affording considerable discretion, provided that the court considers such prohibitions necessary in the interests of protecting the public from serious harm from him (s.2(4)). The order remains in force for the period specified but subject to a minimum of five years (s.2(5)), though the court may specify indefinite duration "until further order" (s.2(5)), *i.e.* until varied or discharged by the court. Appeal against the making of an order lies to the Crown Court (s.4(1)).

---

[18] *The Times*, October 27, 1999.
[18a] J. Plotnikoff and R. Woolfson *Where Are They Now?: An Evaluation of Sex Offender Registration in England and Wales,* Police Research Paper 126 (Home Office, London, 2000).
[19] CDA 1998, s.2(1)(b).

30.37 *Breach, Variation and Discharge* If the person does anything prohibited by the order, "without reasonable excuse" (s.2(8)), he is liable on summary conviction to six months imprisonment and/or fine (on indictment, five years). It is not open to the court to impose a conditional discharge for the offence (s.2(9)). Either the police applicant or the defendant may apply by complaint to the court which made the order for it to be varied or discharged, but an order may not be discharged within five years "except with the consent of both parties" (s.2(6) and (7)).

Disqualification from Working with Children

30.37a Under provisions introduced by CJCSA 2000, s.29, where an individual is convicted of an offence against a child (as specified by Schedule 4 of the Act) committed when the offender was aged under 18, and the court is satisfied that the criterion stated in s.29(4) applies, the court must make an order disqualifying him from working with children. Though not specific to sexual offenders, this sentencing provision is included here for convenience.

CJCSA 2000, s.29

(1) This section applies where either of the conditions set out below is satisfied in the case of an individual.

(2) The first condition is that—

  (a) the individual is convicted of an offence against a child committed at a time when the individual was under the age of 18, and

  (b) a qualifying sentence is imposed by a senior court in respect of the conviction.

(3) The second condition is that—

  (a) the individual is charged with an offence against a child committed at a time when the individual was under the age of 18, and

  (b) a relevant order is made by a senior court in respect of the act or omission charged against him as the offence.

(4) If the court is satisfied, having regard to all the circumstances, that it is likely that the individual will commit a further offence against a child, it must order the individual to be disqualified from working with children.

(5) If the court makes an order under this section, it must state its reasons for doing so and cause those reasons to be included in the record of the proceedings.

A "qualifying sentence" as specified by s.29(2)(b) includes (s.30(1))—

  (c) a sentence of detention during Her Majesty's pleasure,

  (d) a sentence of detention for a period of 12 months or more under section 91 of the Powers of Criminal Courts (Sentencing) Act 2000 (offenders under 18 convicted of certain serious offences),

  (e) a detention and training order for a term of 12 months or more.

30.37b A "senior court" as specified by s.29(2)(b) means, in effect, the Crown Court and a "relevant order" means an order for the offender's admission to hospital or a guardianship order under MHA 1983 s.37. An individual who is disqualified from working with children is guilty of an offence punishable by six months imprisonment (five years on indictment) if he knowingly applies for, offers to do, accepts or does any work in a "regulated position", as defined by s.36. Disqualification is of indefinite duration but a disqualified person may make apply to the relevant Tribunal (s.32) which must determine whether or not the individual should continue to be subject to the order. If the Tribunal is satisfied that the individual is now suitable to work with children, it must direct that the order is to cease to have effect; otherwise it must dismiss the application: s.32(3).

APPEALS

Appeals from a Youth Court

30.38 A decision of a youth court, like that of any Magistrates' Court, may be challenged in three ways—

(a) by an appeal by the defence to the Crown Court against conviction (if the juvenile did not plead guilty) and/or sentence, under MCA 1980, s.108;

(b) by appeal by an aggrieved person or party to the Divisional Court on a point of law by way of case stated, under MCA 1980, s.111, complaining that a decision was wrong in law or in excess of jurisdiction;

(c) by application to the High Court for judicial review of the magistrates' decision.

Because the juvenile is in essentially the same position as an adult defendant, the provisions for appeal are not detailed at length here but the following summary points may be helpful for those unfamiliar with the procedures.

Appeal to the Crown Court

30.39
- In an appeal against sentence, "sentence" means "any order made on conviction" (s.108(3)), including a conditional discharge, disqualification from driving, a recommendation for deportation, a compensation order or a hospital order. The only exceptions are an order for costs, an order for the destruction of an animal or "an order in pursuance of any enactment under which the court has no discretion as to the making of the order or its terms" (s.108(3)).

- Appeal to the Crown Court is commenced by the appellant's notice of appeal which must be lodged in writing with the justices' clerk and the prosecutor within 21 days, stating whether the appeal is against conviction or sentence or both. The 21 day time limit runs from the date of the court's order, even though conviction occurred earlier and the appeal is against conviction only. The Crown Court has discretion to extend the 21 day limit and to give leave to appeal out of time on receipt of an application in writing specifying the grounds of the application (Crown Court Rules 1982, r. 7(5) and (6)).

30.40

- The appeal at the Crown Court takes the form of a re-hearing.

- The powers of the Crown Court in considering an appeal against sentence are to make such order or sentence as the magistrates could have imposed, even if this means increasing the sentence imposed by the magistrates (Supreme Court Act 1981, s.48). On hearing an appeal against conviction, the Crown Court may confirm, reverse or vary any part of the decision appealed against or may remit the matter back to the lower court.

"Case Stated" Procedure

30.41

- Appeal by way of case stated must be made within 21 days of the justices' decision by applying in writing to the clerk of the court concerned asking the magistrates to state a case, identifying the question of law or jurisdiction on which the High Court's opinion is sought.

- If it is contended that there was no evidence on which the magistrates could reasonably have come to a particular finding of fact, the questions of fact in dispute should be stated.

- Within 21 days of receipt of the application, the clerk should prepare an initial draft of the case and supply this to the parties who then have a further 21 days in which to make representations on the draft. The magistrates then have a further 21 days in which to prepare the final version of the case stated.

- Following receipt of the final version, the applicant has ten days within which to lodge the case with the Divisional Court and within a further four days must serve notice of entry of the appeal on the respondent.

- Upon application to the magistrates for a case to be stated, the applicant loses any right of appeal to the Crown Court (MCA 1980, s.111(4)).

Bail pending Appeal against a Custodial Sentence

30.42   Where a person has given notice of appeal to the Crown Court against the decision of a youth court or has applied to a youth court to state a case for the opinion of the High Court, then if the appellant is in custody, the youth court has power under MCA 1980, s.113(1) to grant bail. This power is entirely at the court's discretion and there is no presumption in favour of bail under the Bail Act 1976, s.4. When a Crown Court judge grants a certificate that a case is fit for appeal, he or she may also bail the defendant pending determination of the appeal (Supreme Court Act 1981, s.81(1)(f)). Finally, the Court of Appeal may grant an appellant bail pending determination of the appeal (Criminal Appeal Act 1968, s.19(1)(a)).

Whether bail is appropriate in instances where the offender will otherwise be commencing a custodial sentence is a delicate question. On the one hand, it would seem unjust if the defendant is obliged to serve time in custody which is later overturned; on the other hand, the court may feel that its authority to pass sentence is undermined by releasing the defendant, whose hopes are likely to be raised by the grant of bail, only to be dashed if the appeal is unsuccessful.

30.43   In *Watton*[20] the Court of Appeal gave some guidance on its approach to granting bail pending appeal, stating that "the true question is, are there exceptional circumstances which would drive the court to the conclusion that justice can only be done by the granting of bail". The defendant in *Watton* claimed that his circumstances were "very special"—his wife's health was poor, his daughter suffered mental instability, he needed time to put his business affairs in order as he had not anticipated a prison sentence—but the Court of Appeal concluded that his case was not exceptional. A pertinent consideration may be whether there are very strong factors relating to mitigation which may not have been accorded full enough weight. The time that will elapse before appeal, coupled with the length of the custodial sentence, may also be relevant but the alternative and perhaps preferable course may be for the court to take steps to see whether the appeal can be expedited, to resolve matters as quickly as possible.[21] This preference was expressed in *Imdad Shah*[22] where a 16-year-old had received three months detention at Crown Court. Having served a month of that sentence, he was given leave to appeal by a single judge of the Court of Appeal who also released him on bail. The Court of Appeal disapproved noting that, if the appeal failed, the offender would have to return to custody for a brief period to complete his sentence and this would be unsatisfactory and disruptive for the institutional regime.

30.44
"When these short sentence cases come up on applications for leave to appeal, bail in the ordinary way should not be granted because these . . . cases can always at short notice be put in the list . . . Judges who are minded to grant leave, rather than grant bail, should take steps to see that the case is expedited."

If bail is granted but the appeal ultimately fails, the fact that there has been a long delay between release on bail and the determination of the appeal, and that the sentence would have by then been served if bail had not been sought or granted, cannot be grounds for any substantial reduction in sentence. If an appellant applies for bail, he or she should realise that if the appeal is unsuccessful then the sentence will have to be served (*Callan*[23] in which sentence of five months for possession of a firearm was reduced to four months in recognition of the substantial period spent on bail pending appeal).

Appeal by Parent

30.45   As a court sentencing a juvenile may also make orders in respect of their parent or guardian, it should be noted that the parent has a right of appeal as follows—

(a) against an order under PCC(S)A 2000 s.137 to pay a financial penalty, either to the Crown Court against a magistrates' court order (s.55(3)) or to the Court of Appeal against an order made by the Crown Court (s 137(4));

(b) against an order under MCA 1980, s.81(1)(b) directing the parent to pay a defaulting juvenile's unpaid sum, to the Crown Court (s.81(6));

---

[20] (1979) Cr.App.R. 293.
[21] See *Practice Direction (Crown Court: Bail Pending Appeal)* [1983] 1 W.L.R. 1292.
[22] (1980) 144 J.P. 618 and 637.
[23] *The Times*, July 1, 1993.

(c) against an order under PCC(S)A 2000 s.150 1991, s.58 binding over the parent to exercise proper care and control of the juvenile, either to the Crown Court against a magistrates' court order (s.150(6)) or to the Court of Appeal against an order made by the Crown Court (s.150(7))).

(d) against a parenting order under CDA 1998, s.8, as regulated by CDA 1998, s.10. If the order was imposed following the young person's conviction of an offence, appeal lies to the Crown Court from a youth court or to the Court of Appeal in respect of a Crown Court order (s.10(4)).

REHABILITATION AND SPENT CONVICTIONS

30.46   The Rehabilitation of Offenders Act 1974 provides that most convictions can become "spent" so that the convicted person is entitled to be regarded for a range of purposes as if never convicted of the offence concerned. The convicted person becomes "rehabilitated" after the "rehabilitation period" specified for the sentence or order imposed following that conviction has elapsed, provided that the offender has not been convicted of an indictable offence during that period. The primary benefits are that the ex-offender does not need to disclose a spent conviction when applying for a job, joining an organisation or taking out insurance. For certain specified occupations and purposes, for example involving work in the health service, criminal justice system or with children, a conviction can never be regarded as spent. In recognition of the fact that young offenders predominantly "grow out of crime", that their offending is a transient feature of adolescence and that changes of outlook, personality and behaviour can occur more quickly during their teen and young adult years, the Act provides that the rehabilitation period for some sentences should be shorter for young offenders than for adults.

Excluded Sentences

30.47   Sentences applicable to young offenders which are excluded from the scope of the 1974 Act by s.5(1) and in respect of which a young offender can never become rehabilitated are as follows—

(a) detention during Her Majesty's pleasure;

(b) custody for life;

(c) detention under PCC(S)A 2000, s.91 (in CYPA 1933, s.53) for a term exceeding 30 months;

(d) detention in a young offender institution for a term exceeding 30 months.

Rehabilitation Periods

30.48   The rehabilitation periods for particular sentences or disposals are set by ROA 1974, s.5(2) to (8), primarily in Table A of subsection (2) which specifies that the usual period is halved for persons under 18 at date of conviction, even where sentence was initially deferred. Where an offender receives more than one sentence or order in respect of a conviction, the pertinent rehabilitation period is that relating to the longest applicable (s.6(2)). The following summary builds in that advantageous shortening of the timescale. The specified periods run from date of conviction in each instance. Certain anomalies arise, such as the shorter periods applicable to attendance centre and supervision orders which are out of step with periods pertaining to other community orders. The length of rehabilitation periods is currently subject to government review.

(a)	detention under PCC(S)A, s 91 (or 1933, s.53) for more than 6 months but not more than 30 months	5 years
(b)	detention in a young offender institution for more than 6 months but not more than 30 months	5 years
(c)	detention in a young offender institution for 6 months or less	3½ years
(d)	secure training order	1 year after the order ceases (s.5(6)(d))
(e)	detention and training order on offender aged 15 or over at conviction (s.5(6A)(a))—	
	(i) term more than six months	5 years
	(ii) term of six months or less	3½ years
(f)	detention and training order on offender aged under 15 at conviction 1 year after order ceases	(s.5(6A)(b))
(g)	community punishment and rehabilitation order	2½ years
(h)	community punishment order	2½ years
(i)	drug treatment and testing order	2½ years
(j)	curfew order	2½ years
(k)	exclusion order	2½ years
(l)	community rehabilitation order	
	(i) conviction before 3/2/95	1 year or until order ceases, whichever is the longer
	(ii) conviction on or after 3/2/95	2½ years
(m)	supervision order	1 year or until the order ceases, whichever is the longer (s.5(5))
(n)	attendance centre order	1 year after the order ceases (s.5(6)(c))
(o)	action plan order	2½ years
(p)	reparation order	2½ years
(q)	referral order	
	(i) if young offender contract takes effect	date when contract ceases to have effect (s.5(4B)(a))

(ii)	if young offender contract does not take effect	date when such a contract would have ceased to have effect if it had taken effect (s.5(4B)(b))
(r)	fine or compensation order	2$\frac{1}{2}$ years
(s)	conditional discharge	1 year or until the order expires, whichever is the longer (s.5(4))
(t)	absolute discharge	6 months (s.5(3))
(u)	bind over to keep the peace or to be of good behaviour	1 year or until the order expires, whichever is the longer (s.5(4))
(v)	hospital order	5 years or 2 years after the order expires, whichever is the longer (s.5(7))
(w)	an order imposing disqualification, disability, prohibition or other penalty	the date the order ceases to have order ceases to have effect (s.5(8))

Cautions, Reprimands and Final Warnings

30.49 Cautions administered prior to implementation of the reprimands and warnings provisions of the Crime and Disorder Act 1998 were not within the ambit of ROA 1974, which dealt only with disposals following conviction. The 1998 Act did not address this anomaly and in consequence, warnings and reprimands could not become "spent". A recent Government Consultation Paper[24] concluded that "it is only fair that those receiving cautions, reprimands or final warnings should not be in a worse position as regards rehabilitation than those being convicted", particularly since young people who are disproportionately likely to be dealt with by such means could be adversely affected in their bid to gain a meaningful and fulfilling place in society. Arguing that such outcomes should be at the bottom end of the range of rehabilitation periods, *i.e.* below the period of six months pertaining to absolute discharge, the Paper proposes that cautions, reprimands and warnings should have no rehabilitation period and should thus become spent immediately. However, the Paper also proposes that the "exceptions order" provisions of the 1974 Act should apply to these disposals, thus limiting the protection afforded in respect of assessing a person's suitability for certain sensitive posts, occupations or professions.

Further Conviction

30.50 Section 6(4) specifies that the offender can become rehabilitated if not reconvicted of an indictable offence during the relevant rehabilitation period. If the offender is reconvicted of any offence other than a summary offence, the

---

[24] Home Office (1999) *The Rehabilitation of Offenders Act 1974 and Cautions, Reprimands and Warnings.*

rehabilitation period for the previous offence is extended to run until the expiry of the rehabilitation period pertaining to the later offence. If the offender receives an excluded sentence for the later offence, the earlier conviction is also excluded permanently from the possibility of rehabilitation. The subsequent conviction rule applies even if the later offence was committed prior to conviction or sentence for the previous offence.

Spent Convictions and Criminal Proceedings

30.51 Convictions cannot become spent for the purposes of criminal proceedings and if an offender is convicted of a further offence, the court must be provided with a statement of the defendant's previous record, whether spent or not. However a *Practice Direction (Crime: Spent Convictions)* [1975] 1 W.L.R. 1065 requires that those which are spent should, wherever practicable, be marked as such and that no one should refer in open court to a spent conviction without the authority of the judge. Such authority should be only be given where the interests of justice so require. These arrangements apply to magistrates' courts in furtherance of HOC 98/1975.

BIBLIOGRAPHY

ACOP, *Seriousness and Proportionality in the Youth Court under the Criminal Justice Act 1991* (ACOP, London, 1992)

Advisory Council on the Penal System, *Non-Custodial and Semi-Custodial Penalties* (HMSO, London, 1970)

Allen, R., "Juvenile Offenders left out of the Act" (1990) 70 *Childright* 11

Allen, R., "Out of Jail: the reduction in the use of penal custody for male juveniles 1981–1988" (1991) 30 *Howard Journal* 30.

Allen, R., *Children and Crime* (Institute for Public Policy Research, 1996)

Anderson, B., "The Criminal Justice Acts: 'Justice' by Geography" in *The Handbook of Children's Rights: Comparative Policy and Practice*, (Franklin, B., ed., Routledge, London, 1995)

Anderson, R., *Representation in the Juvenile Court* (Routledge, London, 1978)

Anderson, S., Kinsey, G. Loader, I. and Smith, C., *Cautionary Tales: Young People, Crime and Policy in Edinburgh*, (Avebury, Aldershot, 1994)

Arnott, H. and Creighton, S., (2000) *Legal Action*, June 13–16

Ashworth, A., "Abolishing the Presumption of Incapacity: *C v. DPP*" (1994) 6 *Journal of Child Law* 174

Ashworth, A., "Justifying the Grounds of Mitigation" (1994) *Criminal Justice Ethics*, 13(1)

Ashworth, A. and van Hirsch A., "Recognising Elephant Traps: The Problem of the Custody Threshold" [1997] *Crim.L.R.* 187

Audit Commission, *Misspent Youth: Young People and Crime* (Audit Commission, London, 1996)

Bailey, V., *Delinquency and Citizenship* (Clarendon Press, Oxford, 1987)

Ball, C., "Children Act 1989: origins, aims and current concerns" in *Social Work and Social Welfare Year Book No. 2* (Carter, P., Jeffs, T. and Smith, M., eds, Open University Press, Milton Keynes, 1991)

Ball, C., "Secret Justice: the Use Made of School Reports in the Juvenile Court" (1983) 13 *British Journal of Social Work*, 197

Ball, C., "Young Offenders and the Youth Court" [1992] *Crim.L.R.* 277

Ball, C., "Youth justice and the youth court—the end of a separate system?" (1995) 7 *C.F.L.Q.* 196

Ball, C., "R. v. B.: Paying Due Regard to the Welfare of the Child in Criminal Proceedings", (1998) *C.F.L.Q.* 10(4)

Ball, C., "The Youth Justice and Criminal Evidence Act 1999, Part I: a significant move towards restorative justice, or a recipe for unintended consequences?" [2000] *Crim.L.R.* 211.

Ball, C. and Connolly, J., "Requiring School Attendance: A Little Used Sentencing Power" [1999] *Crim.L.R.* 183

Ball, C. and Connolly, J., "Educationally Disaffected Young Offenders: Youth Court and Agency Responses to Truancy and School Exclusion" (2000) 40 *Brit. J. Criminol.* 594

Bevan, V. and Lidstone, K., *The Investigation of Crime: A Guide to Police Powers* (2nd ed., Butterworths, London, 1996)

Birch, D., "A Better Deal for Vulnerable Witnesses" [2000] *Crim.L.R.* 223

Bottoms, A., "On the Decriminalisation of the English Juvenile Court" in *Crime, Criminology and Public Policy*, (Hood, R., ed., Heinemann, London, 1974)

Bottoms, A., "The Place of the Probation Service in the Criminal Justice System" in *The Madingley Papers II* (Central Council of Probation Committees, London, 1989)

Bottoms, A., "The Philosophy and Politics of Punishment and Sentencing", in *The Politics of Sentencing Reform* (Clarkson, C. and Morgan, R., eds, Oxford University Press, Oxford, 1995)

Bottoms, A., *Intensive Community Supervision for Young Offenders: Outcomes, Process and Cost* (University of Cambridge, Cambridge, 1995)

Brown, D., Ellis, T. and Larcombe, K., *Changing the Code: police detention under the revised codes of practice*, Home Office Research Study No. 129 (HMSO, London, 1992)

Brown, S., *Magistrates at Work* (Open University Press, Milton Keynes, 1991)

Brown, S., "Crime and Safety in Whose Community? Age, Everyday Life and Problems of Youth Policy" (1995) *Youth and Policy 48*

Bucke, T. and Brown, D., *In police custody: police powers and suspects' rights under the revised PACE codes of practice*, Home Office Research Study No. 174 (Home Office, London, 1997)

Bullock, R., Little, M. and Millham, S., *Secure Treatment Outcomes: The Care Careers of Very Difficult Adolescents*, (Ashgate, Aldershot, 1998)

Burney, E., *JP, Magistrate, Court and Community* (Hutchinson, London, 1979)

Burney, E., *Sentencing Young People* (Gower, Aldershot, 1985)

Butler Committee on Mentally Abnormal Offenders (1975)

Cape, E., *Defending Suspects at Police Stations* (Legal Action Group, London, 1993)

Carpenter, M., *Reformatory Schools for the Children of the Perishing and Dangerous Classes and for Juvenile Offenders* (C. Gilpin, London, 1851)

Cawson, P., *Young Offenders in Care* (D.H.S.S., London, 1981)

Centre for Human Rights, Geneva, *Concluding Observations of the Committee on the Rights of the Child: United Kingdom of Great Britain and Northern Ireland, Children Act 1989, Guidance and Regulations*, Vol. 1 (Department of Health, 1990)

Children's Society, *A False Sense of Security: the case against locking up more children* (The Children's Society, London, 1993)

Colthup, N., "Child Protection in Prison" (1996) *Criminal Justice* 14

Committee on the Rights of the Child, *Concluding Observations of the Committee on the Rights of the Child: United Kingdom of Great Britain and Northern Ireland*, CRC/C/15/Add34 (Centre for Human Rights, Geneva, January 1995)

Crook. F., "A Recipe for Child Abuse", *The Guardian*, July 20, 1994

Crowley, A., *A Criminal Waste: A Study of Child Offenders Eligible for Secure Training Centres* (Children's Society, London, 1998)

Davis, G. *et al.*, *An Assessment of the Admissibility and Sufficiency of Evidence in Child Abuse Prosecution* (Home Office, London, 1999)

Department for Education, *School Reports to the Courts* (DfE, London, 1992)

Department of Health, *Children Act 1989, Guidance and Regulations*, Vol. 1, (DOH, London, 1991)

Department of Health (1997) *People Like Us: The Report of the Review of the Safeguards for Children Living Away from Home* (The Stationery Office, London, 1997)

Department of Health, *Statistical Bulletin*, 2000/15

Dignan, J., "The Crime and Disorder Act and the Prospects for Restorative Justice" [1999] *Crim.L.R.* 48–60

Dignan, J., *Youth Justice Pilots Evaluation: Interim report on Reparative Work and Youth Offending Teams*, Occasional Paper (Home Office, 2000)

Ditchfield, J.A., *Police Cautioning in England and Wales*, Home Office Research Study, No. 37 (HMSO, London, 1976)

Dixon, D., "Juvenile Suspects and the Police and Criminal Evidence Act" in *Children and the Law: Essays in Honour of Professor H.K. Bevan* (D. Freestone, ed., Hull University Press, Hull, 1990)

Downes. D., and Morgan, R., "Dumping the 'Hostages to Fortune'? The Politics of Law and Order in Post-War Britain" in *Oxford Handbook of Criminology* (Maguire, M., Morgan, R. and Reiner, R., eds, 2nd ed., Oxford University Press, Oxford, 1997)

Drakeford, M., "Parents of Young People in Trouble", (1996) *35 Howard Journal of Criminal Justice* 242

Drakeford, M. and McCarthy, K., "Parents, Responsibility and the New Youth Justice" in Goldson B., (ed.), *The New Youth Justice* (Russell House Publishing, Lyme Regis, 2000)

Elkin, W., *English Juvenile Courts* (Kegan Paul, London, 1938)

Elliott, R. and Airs, J., *New Measures for Fine Defaulters, Petty Persistent Offenders and Others: The Reports of the Crime (Sentences) Act 1997 Pilots*, Occasional Papers (Home Office, London, 2000)

Evans, R., *The Conduct of Police Interviews with Juveniles*, Research Study No. 8, Royal Commission on Criminal Justice (HMSO, London 1993)

Evans, R. "Comparing Young Adult and Juvenile Cautioning Rates in the Metropolitan Police District" [1993] *Crim.L.R.* 572

Evans, R., and Ferguson, T., *Comparing Different Juvenile Cautioning Systems in One* Home Office, *Police Force Area*, Report to the Home Office Research and Planning Unit (1991)

Evans, R. and Wilkinson, C. "Variations in Police Cautioning Policy and Practice in England and Wales" (1990) *29 Howard Journal* 155

Evidence from the Children's Department to the Committee on the Treatment of Young Offenders, Home Office 1927

Farrington, D., "Human Development and Criminal Careers" in *Oxford Handbook of Criminology* (Maguire, M., Morgan, R. and Reiner, R., eds, 2nd ed., Oxford University Press, Oxford, 1997)

Farrington, D.P. and Langan, P.A., "Changes in Crime and Punishment in England and America in the 1980s" (1992) *9 Justice Quarterly* 5

Faulkner, D. and Gibson, B., "Seriousness: Right or Wrong" (1993) *Justice of the Peace*, 157

Fionda, J., "New Labour, Old Hat: Youth Justice and the Crime and Disorder Act 1998" [1999] *Crim.L.R.* 36

Fitzgerald, M., *Ethnic Minorities and the Criminal Justice System*, Royal Commission on Criminal Justice (HMSO, London, 1993)

Fortin, J., *Children's Rights and the Developing Law* (Butterworths, London, 1998)

Foucault, M., *Discipline and Punish* (Harmondsworth, London, 1977)

Gelsthorpe, L. and Morris, A., "Juvenile Justice 1945–1992" in *Oxford Handbook of Criminology* (Maguire, M., Morgan, R. and Reiner, R., eds, Oxford University Press, Oxford, 1997)

Gelsthorpe L. and Morris, A., "Much ado about nothing — a critical comment on key provisions relating to children in the Crime and Disorder Act 1998" (1999) 11 C.F.L.Q. 209

Giller, H. and Tutt, N., "Police Cautioning of Juveniles: the Continuing Practice of Diversity" [1987] *Crim.L.R.* 367

Graham, J. and Bowling, B., *Young People and Crime*, Home Office Research Study, No. 145 (Home Office, London, 1995)

H.M. Chief Inspector of Prisons *Young Prisoners: A Thematic Review* (Home Office, London (1997))

H.M. Chief Inspector of Prisons, *HMYOI Hollesley Bay: Report of an Unannounced Full Inspection 30 November–4 December 1999* (H.M. Inspectorate of Prisons, Home Office, London, 1999)

H.M. Chief Inspector of Prisons, *HMYOI Feltham: Report of an Unannounced Full Inspection 30 November–4 December 1998* (H.M. Inspectorate of Prisons, Home Office, London, 1999)

H.M. Chief Inspector of Prisons, *HMYOI Feltham: Report on a Short Unannounced Inspection 28–30 September 1999* (H.M. Inspectorate of Prisons, Home Office, London, 2000)

H.M. Chief Inspector of Prisons, *HMYOI Hollesley Bay: Report of an Unannounced Full Inspection 30 November–4 December 1999* (H.M. Inspectorate of Prisons, Home Office, London, 1999)

H.M. Chief Inspector of Prisons, *HMYOI Onley: Report of a Full Unannounced Inspection 6–10 September 1999* (H.M. Inspectorate of Prisons, Home Office, London, 1999)

H.M. Chief Inspector of Prisons, *HMYOI Portland: Report of a Full Announced Full Inspection 24 October–3 November 1999* (H.M. Inspectorate of Prisons, Home Office, London, 2000)

H.M. Chief Inspector of Prisons, *Suicide is Everyone's Concern: Thematic Review* (H.M. Inspectorate of Prisons, Home Office, London, 1999)

H.M. Inspector of Prisons, *Young Prisoners: A Thematic Review* (H.M. Inspectorate of Prisons, Home Office, London, 1997)

Hagell, A. and Newburn, T., *Persistent Young Offenders* (Policy Studies Institute, London, 1994)

Hagell, A., Hazel, N. and Shaw, C., *Evaluation of Medway, Secure Training Centre*, Occasional Paper (Home Office, London, 2000)

Haines, K., "Referral Orders and Youth Offender Panels: Restorative approaches and the New Youth Justice" in Goldson B. (ed.), *The New Youth Justice* (Russell House Publishing, Lyme Regis, 2000)

Haines, K. & Drakeford, M., *Young People and Youth Justice* (Macmillan, Basingstoke, 1998)

Hansard, Committee E, February 14, 1984, col. 1127

Hansard (1999) H.C. vol. 334, col. 1224

Hansard, H.L. Written Answer, July 11, 2000, cols. 13–14

Harris, R. and Webb, D., *Welfare, Power and Juvenile Justice* (Tavistock, 1987)

Harwin, J., "The Battle for the Delinquent" in *Yearbook of Social Policy in Britain 1980*, 1981 (Jones, C. and Stevenson, J., eds, Routledge and Kegan Paul, London, 1981).

Hilgendorf, L., *Social Workers and Solicitors in Child Care Cases* (HMSO, London, 1981)

Hodgson, J., "Vulnerable Suspects and the Appropriate Adult" [1997] *Crim.L.R.* 785

Home Office Circular, dated April 21, 1923
Home Office, *Report of the Committee on the Treatment of Young Offenders*, Cmd. 2831, 1927.
Home Office, Cmnd. 3601, (HMSO, London, 1968)
Home Office, *Children in Trouble*, Cmnd. 3601 (HMSO, London 1968)
Home Office Circular 138/79
Home Office Circular 14/1985.
Home Office Circular 88/1985
Home Office Circular 59/1990
Home Office, *Crime, Justice and Protecting the Public*, Cm. 965 (HMSO, London, 1990)
Home Office, *The Sentence of the Court* (HMSO, London, 1990)
Home Office, *Criminal Statistics* (HMSO, London, 1991)
Home Office, *Criminal Statistics* (HMSO, London, 1992)
Home Office Circular 30/1992 *Young People and the Youth Court*
Home Office Circular 44/1993
Home Office Circular 18/1994 *National Standards for Cautioning*
Home Office, *Race and the Criminal Justice System* (Home Office, London, 1994)
Home Office, *National Standard for Attendance Centres* (1995)
Home Office, *National Standards for the Supervision of Offenders in the Community* (HMSO, London, 1995)
Home Office, *Tackling Delays in the Youth Justice System*, Annex C. (Home Office, London, 1997)
Home Office, *Review of Delay in the Criminal Justice System: a Report* (Home Office, London, 1997)
Home Office, *No More Excuses: A New Approach to Tackling Youth Crime in England and Wales*, Cm 3809 (Home Office, London, 1997)
Home Office, *Delays in the Youth Justice System* (Home Office, London, 1997)
Home Office, *Final Warning Scheme* (Home Office, London, 1998)
Home Office, *Guidance for Practitioners involved in Drug Treatment and Testing Order Pilots* (Home Office, London, 1998), "General guidance on Targeting of the Order"
Home Office, *Inter-Departmental Circular on Establishing Youth Offending Teams* (Department of Health, Welsh Office and Department for Education and Employment, 1998)
Home Office, *Measuring Performance to Reduce Delays in the Youth Justice System*, (Home Office/LCD, September 1998)
Home Office, *Interim Report on Youth Offending Teams* (Home Office, London, 1999)
Home Office, *Supplementary Criminal Statistics, England and Wales, 1998*, Vol. 1 (Home Office, London, 1999)
Home Office "Attendance Centres into the 21st Century" *Attendance Centre News*, Spring 1999
Home Office, *The Rehabilitation of Offenders Act 1974 and Cautions, Reprimands and Warnings* (Home Office, London, 1999)
Home Office, *Action for Justice*, (Home Office Justice and Victims Unit, 1999)
Home Office, *Court-ordered Secure Remands, Implementation Guidance* (Home Office, London, 1999)
Home Office, *Crime and Disorder Act 1998, Guidance Document: Child Safety Order* (Home Office: London, 1999)
Home Office, *Criminal Statistics, England and Wales, 1998* (Home Office, London, 1999)

Home Office, *Evaluation of the Youth Court Demonstration Project*, Home Office Research Study 214 (Home Office, London, 2000)

Home Office, *Crime and Disorder Act 1998, Anti-Social Behaviour Order: Guidance* (Home Office, London, 2000)

Home Office, *A Review of the Sentencing Framework*, (Home Office, London, 2000).

Home Office, *Guidance Action Plan Orders* (Home Office, London, 2000)

Home Office, *Guidance Document: Action Plan Orders* (Home Office, London, 2000)

Home Office, *Guidance Document: Reparation Order* (2000)

Home Office, *Guidance on Drug Testing* (2000)

Home Office, *Guidance on Enforcement* (2000)

Home Office, *Guidance on Review Hearings* (2000)

Home Office, *Parenting Order: Guidance Document* (Home Office, London, 2000)

Home Office, *Probation Statistics for England and Wales 1998* (Government Statistical Service, London, 2000)

Home Office, *Research & Development Statistics* (Home Office, London, 2000).

Home Office, *The Crime and Disorder Act: The Establishment and Operation of Rehabilitation (Change) Programmes under the Final Warning Scheme* (Home Office, London, 2000)

Home Office, *The Final Warning Scheme—Guidance for Police* (Home Office, London, 2000)

Home Office, *The Final Warning Scheme: Guidance for Youth Offending Teams* (Home Office, London, 2000)

Home Office, *The Referral Order*, Draft Circular Version 3 (2000)

Home Office, Lord Chancellor's Dept & Youth Justice Board, *The Detention and Training Order* (Home Office, London, 2000)

Hood, R., *Race and Sentencing* (Clarendon Press, Oxford, 1992)

Hood, R., *Sentencing the Motoring Offender* (Heinemann, London, 1972)

Howard League for Penal Reform, *Banged Up, Beaten Up, Cutting Up* (Howard League, London, 1995)

Hoyano, L., "Variations on a Theme by Pigot: Special Measures Directions for Child Witnesses" [2000] *Crim.L.R.* 250

Hoyano, L. and Keenan, C., "Innocents Betrayed? Evaluating Legal Responses to Allegations of Child Abuse" (OUP.)

Inspectorates of the Crown Prosecution Service, Magistrates' Courts and Police, *How long youth cases take* (Published in March 1999 and based on research in October and November 1998)

Justices' Clerks' Society, *The Legal Adviser Competence Framework* (January 2001)

Kidscape, *Bullying Pays! A Survey of Young Offenders* (Kidscape, London, 1994)

Labour Party, *Tackling Youth Crime: Reforming Youth Justice* (Labour Party, London, 1996)

Law Commission, *Binding over* (Law Comm. No. 222) Cm. 2439 (HMSO, London, 1994)

LCD Circular AC (92)5

Lockyer, A. and Stone, F., *Juvenile justice in Scotland: Twenty-five years of the Welfare Approach* (T. & T. Clark, Edinburgh, 1998)

Lord Chancellor's Department and Youth Justice Board, *The Detention and Training Order* (Home Office, London, February 9, 2000)

Lord Longford, *Crime—a challenge to us all* (Labour Party, London, 1964)

Lyon, J., Dennison, C. and Wilson, A., "Tell Them So They Listen": *Messages from Young People in Custody*, Research Study 201 (Home Office, London, 2000)

Magistrates' New Training Initiative (MNTI), Judicial Studies Board

Magistrates' Association, Association of Chief Officers of Probation and the Justices' Clerks' Society "Community Sentences and Restrictions on Liberty", (1993) *The Magistrate* 49

Mair, G. and May, C., *Practitioners' Views of the Criminal Justice Act: A Survey of Criminal Justice Agencies*, Research and Planning Unit Paper No. 91 (Home Office, London, 1995)

Mair, G. and Mortimer, E., *Curfew Orders with Electronic Monitoring: an evaluation of the first twelve months of trials in Greater Manchester, Norfolk and Berkshire*, 1995–96, Research Study 163 (Home Office, London, 1996)

Mair, G., *Part-Time Punishment?* (HMSO, London, 1991)

McIvor, G., *Sentenced to Service: The Operation and Impact of Community Service by Offender* (Avebury, Aldershot, 1992)

Millham, S., Bullock, R. and Hosie, K., *Locking up Children* (Saxon House, London, 1978)

Monaghan, G., "The Courts and the New Youth Justice" (2000) in Goldson, B. (ed.), *The New Youth Justice* (Russell House Publishing, Lyme Regis, 2000)

Moore, J.S., "Child Incarceration and the New Youth Justice" in Goldson, B. (ed.), *The New Youth Justice* (Russell House Publishing, Lyme Regis, 2000)

Morris, A. and Gelsthorpe, L., "Something Old, Something Borrowed, Something Blue, but Something New? A comment on the prospects for restorative justice under the Crime and Disorder Act 1998" [2000] *Crim.L.R.* 18

Morris, A. and Giller, H., *Understanding Juvenile Justice* (Croom Helm, London, 1987).

Morris, A. and Giller, H., *What Justice for Juveniles?* (Justice for Children, London, 1979)

Morris, A., Giller, H., Schwed, E. and Geach, H., *Justice for Children* (Macmillan, London, 1980)

Mortimer E., Pereira E. and Walter I., "Making the Tag Fit: Further Analysis from the first Two Years of the Trials of Curfew Orders" *Research Findings No. 105*, (Home Office, London, 1999)

Mortimer E. and May C., *Electronic Monitoring in Practice: the second year of the trials of curfew orders, Research Study 177* (Home Office, London, 1997)

Muncie, J., *Youth and Crime* (Sage, London, 1999)

NACRO, *New Approaches to Juvenile Crime, Creating More Criminals: The case against the new "secure training order" for juvenile offenders* (NACRO, London, 1994)

NACRO, Youth Crime Section Briefing, *Final Warnings — Implementation Issues* (NACRO Youth Crime Section, June 2000)

NACRO, *A New Three Rs for Young Offenders* (NACRO, London, January 1997)

NAPO *Limiting the Damage* (NAPO, London, 1992)

National Standards for Youth Justice (Youth Justice Board and Home Office, 2000)

Newburn, J., "Youth Crime and Justice", in *Oxford Handbook of Criminal Justice*, (2nd ed., Oxford University Press, Oxford, 1997)

Noon, R., "Binding Over Parents under Section 58 CJA 1991: Some Practical Problems", (1992) *Justice of the Peace 156*

Northamptonshire Diversion Unit, *Diverting People from Crime* (NACRO, London, 1998)

NSPCC, *Support for Child Witnesses in Hampshire* (NSPCC, February 1999)

Parker, H., Casburn, M. and Turnbull, D., *Receiving Juvenile Justice* (Blackwell, Oxford, 1981)

Parker, H., Sumner, M. and Jarvis, G., *Unmasking the Magistrates* (Open University Press, Milton Keynes, 1989)

Parsloe, P., *Juvenile Justice in Britain and the United States* (Routledge, Keegan Paul, London, 1978)

Penal Affairs Consortium, *The Case Against Sentencing 15–year-olds to Prison Service Custody* (Penal Affairs Consortium, London, 1992)

Pitts, J., *The Politics of Juvenile Crime* (Sage, London, 1990)

Platt, A., *The Child Savers: the Invention of Delinquency* (Chicago University Press, Chicago, 1968)

Plotnikoff, J. and Woolfson, R., *Where are They Now? An Evaluation of Sex Offender Registration in England and Wales*, Police Research Paper 126 (Home Office, London, 2000)

Pratt, J., "Corporatism: the third model of juvenile justice" (1989) 29 *Brit. J. Criminol.* 236

Preston, R.H., "Social theology and penal theory and practice: the collapse of the rehabilitative ideal and the search for an alternative", in *The Coming Penal Crisis* (Bottoms, A. and Preston, R.H., eds, Scottish Academic Press, Edinburgh, 1980)

Priestley, P., Fears, D. and Fuller, R., *Justice for Juveniles* (Routledge, Kegan Paul, London, 1977)

Prison Service Order 4950, *Regimes for Prisoners aged under 18*, P.S.I. Ref. No. 49/1999 (29 July 1999); *Regimes for Young Women under 18*, P.S.I. Ref. No. 09/2000 (11 February 2000)

Report of the Committee on the Treatment of Young Offenders, Cmd. 2831, 1927

Royal Commission on Criminal Procedure Report 1981, Cmnd. 8092, (HMSO, 1981)

Rutherford, A., *Growing Out of Crime: the New Era* (Waterside Press, Basingstoke, 1992)

Sampson, R. and Laub, J., *Crime in the Making* (Harvard University Press, Cambridge, Massachusetts, USA, 1993)

Sanders, A., "From Suspect to Trial" in *The Oxford Handbook of Criminology* (Maguire, M., Morgan, R. and Reiner, R., eds, 2nd ed., Oxford University Press, Oxford, 1997)

Save the Children, *Children aged 12–14 and the Criminal Justice System* (Save the Children Fund, London, 1994)

Smith, C.R. and Gardner, P.R., "Secure accommodation under the Children Act 1989: legislative confusion and social ambivalence" (1996) *Journal of Social Welfare and Family Law* 173–187

Smith, D., "Corporatism and the New Youth Justice" in Goldson, B., (ed.), *The New Youth Justice* (Russell House Publishing, Lyme Regis, 2000)

Smith, D.J., "Ethnic Origins, Crime and Criminal Justice" *in Oxford Handbook of Criminology* (Maguire, M., Morgan, R. and Reiner, R., eds, 2nd ed., Oxford University Press, Oxford, 1997)

Social Services Committee, House of Commons, *Children in Care*, Second Report from the Social Services Committee, 360–I (HMSO, London, 1984)

Social Services Inspectorate, *Inspection of Medway Secure Training Centre, September/October 1998* (Department of Health, London, 1999)

Standing Committee E, H.C., Fourth Sitting, June 15, 1999

Stewart, J., Smith, D. & Stewart, G., *Understanding Offending Behaviour* (Longman Harlow, 1994)

Stone, N., *A Companion Guide to Enforcement* (3rd ed., Owen Wells, Publisher, Ilkley, 1999)

Stone, N., (1994) "Sentencing the Near Adult" (1994) *Justice of the Peace 158*

Straw, Jack, and Michael, Alun, *Tackling Youth Crime: Reforming Youth Justice* (Labour Party, London, 1996)

Swindells, H. *et al.*, *Family Law and the Human Rights Act 1998* (Family Law, Bristol, 1999)

Tarling, R. and Wetherett, M., *Sentencing Practice in Magistrates' Courts*, Home Office Research Study No. 56 (HMSO, London,1980)

Tarling, R., *Analysing Offending: Data, Models and Interpretation* (HMSO, London, 1993)

Thomas, D., Commentary on Robinson [1993] *Crim.L.R.* 145

Thomas, D., *Annotation to Crime and Disorder Act 1998, s.74* (1998) *Current Law Statutes*, 37–81

Thomas, D., Commentary on Mackay [1999] *Crim.L.R.* 757

Thomas, T., *The Police and Social Workers* (2nd ed., Arena, Aldershot, 1994)

Thorpe, D., Green, C. and Smith, D., *Punishment and Welfare* (Lancaster University, 1979)

Thorpe, D., Smith, D., Green C. and Paley, J., *Out of Care* (Allen and Unwin, London, 1980)

Timms, N. and Harris, R., "Juvenile Courts and Secure Accommodation" (1993) *Journal of Social Welfare and Family Law* 40

Turnbull, P., "Drug Treatment and Testing Orders: Interim Evaluation" *Research Findings No. 106* (Home Office, London, 2000)

Tutt, N. and Giller, H., "Police Cautioning of Juveniles: the Practice of Diversity" [1983] *Crim.L.R.* 587

Universities of Sheffield and Hull (1999) *Evaluation Report of the First 12 Months of YOT Experience*

Universities of Sheffield and Hull (1999) *Youth Justice Pilots Evaluation Second Interim Report: Youth Offending Teams After one Year*

Utting, D., Bright, J. and Henricson, C., *Crime and the Family — Improving child rearing and preventing delinquency* (Family Policy Studies Centre, London, 1993)

Van Bueren, G., "Child-Oriented Justice: An International Challenge for Europe" (1992) 6 *International Journal of Law and the Family* 381

von Hirsch, A. and Ashworth, A., "Protective Sentencing under Section 2(2)(b). The criteria of dangerousness" [1996] *Crim.L.R.* 175–83

Walgrave, L. "Restorative Juvenile Justice", in *Children and Young People in Conflict with the Law* (Research Highlights in Social Work No. 30, Asquith, S.. ed., Jessica Kingsley Publishers, London, 1996)

Walker, N. and Padfield, N., *Sentencing: Theory, Law and Practice* (Butterworths, London, 1996)

Wasik, M. "The Grant of an Absolute Discharge" 3 *Oxford Journal of Legal Studies* 211

Wasik, M. and von Hirsch, A., "Non-Custodial Penalties and the Principles of Desert" [1998] *Crim.L.R.* 555

Wasik M. and von Hirsch A., "Section 29 Revised: Previous Convictions in Sentencing" [1994] *Crim. L.R.* 409

West, D. and Farrington, D., *Who Becomes Delinquent?* (Heinemann, London, 1973)

Wonnacott C., "The Couterfeit Contract: reform, pretence and muddled principles in the new referral order" (1999) *C.F.L.Q.* 11(3)

Written evidence to House of Commons Home Affairs Committee, *Juvenile Offenders* (6th Report) (HMSO, London, 1993)

Youth Court Demonstration Project, Leicestershire and Rotherham Magistrates'
    Courts (1999)
Youth Justice Board, *Juvenile Secure Estate Commissioning Strategy* 2000–03
    (2000)
Youth Justice Board, *Juvenile Secure Estate Placement Strategy* (2000)
Youth Justice Board, *Young Offender Assessment Profile — Explanatory Notes*
    (Youth Justice Board ASSET) (1999)
Youth Justice Board, *A Policy for Inspection* (YJB, London, 2000)
Youth Justice Board, *National Standards for the Supervision of Offenders in the
    Community* (1999)
Youth Justice Board, *Speeding Up Youth Justice* (May 1999)
Zander, M., *Police and Criminal Evidence Act 1984* (3rd ed., Sweet and Maxwell,
    London, 1995)
Zedner, L., (1998) "Sentencing Young Offenders", in *Fundamentals of Sentencing
    Theory* (Ashworth, A. and Wasik, M., eds, Clarendon Press, Oxford, 1998)

INDEX